D1265535

Texts and Monographs in Computer Science

Editor
David Gries

Advisory Board
F. L. Bauer
S. D. Brookes
C. E. Leiserson
M. Sipser

Helmut A. Partsch

Specification and Transformation of Programs

A Formal Approach to Software Development

Springer-Verlag Berlin Heidelberg New York
London Paris Tokyo Hong Kong

Author

Helmut A. Partsch
Department of Computer Science
Faculty for Mathematics and Informatics
Catholic University of Nijmegen
Toernooiveld 1, 6525 ED Nijmegen, The Netherlands

Series Editor

David Gries
Department of Computer Science, Cornell University
Ithaca, NY 14853, USA

ISBN 3-540-52356-1 Hardcover
Springer-Verlag Berlin Heidelberg New York
ISBN 0-387-52356-1 Hardcover
Springer-Verlag New York Berlin Heidelberg

ISBN 3-540-52589-0 Softcover (student edition)
Springer-Verlag Berlin Heidelberg New York
ISBN 0-387-52589-0 Softcover (student edition)
Springer-Verlag New York Berlin Heidelberg

Library of Congress Cataloging-in-Publication Data
Partsch, Helmut A., 1950– . – Specification and transformation of programs: a formal approach to software development/Helmut A. Partsch. p. cm. – (Texts and monographs in computer science) Includes bibliographical references.
ISBN 0-387-52356-1 (U.S.: alk. paper)
1. Computer software – Development. I. Title. II. Series. QA76.76.D47P37 1990 005.1--
dc20 90-9553

This work is subject to copyright. All rights are reserved, whether the whole or part of the material is concerned, specifically the rights of translation, reprinting, reuse of illustrations, recitation, broadcasting, reproduction on microfilms or in other ways, and storage in data banks. Duplication of this publication or parts thereof is only permitted under the provisions of the German Copyright Law of September 9, 1965, in its current version, and a copyright fee must always be paid.
Violations fall under the prosecution act of the German Copyright Law.

© Springer-Verlag Berlin Heidelberg 1990
Printed in the United States of America

The use of registered names, trademarks, etc. in this publication does not imply, even in the absence of a specific statement, that such names are exempt from the relevant protective laws and regulations and therefore free for general use.

2145/3140-5 4 3 2 1 0 – Printed on acid-free paper

Preface

"Specification and transformation of programs" is short for a methodology of software development where, from a formal specification of a problem to be solved, programs correctly solving that problem are constructed by stepwise application of formal, semantics-preserving transformation rules.

The approach considers programming as a formal activity. Consequently, it requires some mathematical maturity and, above all, the will to try something new. A somewhat experienced programmer or a third- or fourth-year student in computer science should be able to master most of this material - at least, this is the level I have aimed at.

This book is primarily intended as a general introductory textbook on transformational methodology. As with any methodology, reading and understanding is necessary but not sufficient. Therefore, most of the chapters contain a set of exercises for practising as homework. Solutions to these exercises exist and can, in principle, be obtained at nominal cost from the author upon request on appropriate letterhead.

In addition, the book also can be seen as a comprehensive account of the particular transformational methodology developed within the Munich CIP project. As such, it is to be considered as a companion and a completion of previously published books on this project, notably [Bauer Wössner 82], [Bauer et al. 85], and [Bauer et al. 87]. Links to these books are provided by cross-references whenever appropriate. This background also influenced the decision to use the language CIP-L as defined in [Bauer et al. 85] and not to experiment with new notation. Even more important was the fact that CIP-L is one of the very few languages with a formal definition of their semantics. Formal semantics is an indispensable prerequisite for transformational programming as a formally based activity. However, most of the technical information contained in this book is easily transferable to almost everyone's pet language and notation.

The Organization of the Book

The contents of the book attempt to reflect the essential steps in a sequential process of software development from the "problem" to the "machine", i.e. from an informally stated problem, via a formal problem specification, to a final, efficient program.

Chapter 1, the introduction, motivates, on the basis of traditional software engineering, the need for new, more formally based approaches in the area of software development. It outlines the basic idea of formal specification and transformational programming, explains our particular view of this new paradigm, and relates it to some other modern approaches in programming methodology. An introductory example, spanning the wide range between an informally formulated problem and an efficient program, is intended to convey a first impression of the methodology.

Chapter 2 is an excursion. It gives a brief overview of the major problems and currently used approaches in the area of requirements engineering. The need for this kind of background information to be contrasted with our approach became apparent while lecturing on the subject of this book. Someone basically familiar with the subject, or not interested in it, is advised simply to skip the chapter.

Chapters 3 to 8 form the heart of this book.

Chapter 3 deals with different aspects of formal specification. Apart from some ideas on how to convert an informally stated problem into an adequate, formal specification, it mainly introduces various language constructs for formal specification. These include algebraic types and well-known applicative concepts, but also further constructs specifically tailored to specifying problems rather than programs. The combined use of these constructs is illustrated by a collection of examples most of which reappear as starting points for transformational developments within the following chapters.

Chapter 4 introduces our basis for transformational programming. The theoretical foundation of the approach is outlined and a large collection of elementary transformation rules is given.

Chapter 5 deals with the problem of how to transform a (non-operational) formal problem description into a first (operational) solution to the problem. Within the framework of a general strategy, lots of individual techniques for mastering this important step are discussed. Particular attention is paid to the interaction between formal, mechanizable steps and human creativity.

Chapter 6 is devoted to the improvement of applicative programs. Different classes of techniques are dealt with such as merging of computations, inversion of the flow of computation, storing values rather than recomputing, or computation in advance. Simplification of recursion, as a preparatory step for a subsequent transition to an imperative program, is also discussed.

Chapter 7 elaborates on the transition from applicative to imperative programs. As this is a meanwhile well understood area, only a few, representative techniques are given. Furthermore, this chapter also contains a few transformation rules for imperative constructs, to be used mainly for "polishing" the final result of a transformational development.

Chapter 8 raises the topic of data type transformation. Various techniques for correctly implementing algebraic types are discussed as well as the important issue of joint development of control and data structure.

Chapter 9 gives a few more advanced examples. Whereas in the previous chapters the emphasis was on the transformational techniques with the examples being used for demonstration purposes, here the emphasis is on the problems themselves and how to solve them by means of our proposed methodology.

Acknowledgements

Those familiar with the Munich CIP project will find its influence throughout this book. Many of the ideas in this book originated and have been developed within the CIP group. Particular thanks are therefore due to F.L. Bauer and the late K. Samelson who have been the driving forces of the project, as well as to all colleagues from the former CIP group.

Not just by accident, the title of this book coincides with the title of our ongoing Dutch national project STOP, sponsored by NFI/NWO. It is hardly necessary to mention that research within this project also influenced the manuscript.

My previous work, which forms the basis of this manuscript, has also benefited a lot from discussions within IFIP Working Group 2.1 ("Algorithmic Languages and Calculi") over the last decade. Hence, thanks to all members of WG 2.1.

I am particularly grateful to Frank Stomp, who read nearly all previous drafts of this manuscript and gave lots of technical and stylistic suggestions for almost every paragraph.

A number of colleagues have given me substantial constructive criticism on all or parts of this manuscript. For their help I would like to thank Eerke Boiten, Dick Carpenter, Herbert Ehler, Niek van Diepen, Kees Koster, Erik Meijer, Bernhard Möller, and Norbert Völker.

Thanks are also due to the students of my course "Programmatuurkunde" at Nijmegen University who have been the "guinea pigs" over the last years. Valuable feedback was also provided by students of ESLAI at Buenos Aires when lecturing on the topic of this book, as well as by students from Technical University of Munich and University of Erlangen.

Particular thanks go to Joanna Völker who substantially improved many of the English formulations, and Greta Löw who did an excellent job in preparing the final camera-ready form.

I am also grateful to David Gries who accepted the manuscript for publication in this series and to Hans Wössner, friend and colleague in the CIP project from the beginning, and his team of Springer-Verlag for their valuable advice in preparing the book.

Finally, I thank my wife, Uschi, and son, Stefan, for their love and patience while I was writing this book.

Kleve, Spring 1990 H. Partsch

Contents

1. Introduction

LAWS OF COMPUTER PROGRAMMING

1. *Any given program, when running, is obsolete.*
2. *Any given program costs more and takes longer.*
3. *If a program is useful, it will have to be changed.*
4. *If a program is useless, it will have to be documented.*
5. *Any given program will expand to fill all available memory.*
6. *The value of a program is proportional to the weight of its output.*
7. *Program complexity grows until it exceeds the capability of the programmer who must maintain it.*

[Bloch 77]

This text is concerned with some problems of software development that are usually dealt with under the heading "software engineering". However, we entitled this text "specification and transformation of programs – a formal approach to software development" rather than just "software engineering" in order to emphasize from the very beginning that we will only be concerned with some of the technological problems of software engineering and disregard all managerial aspects.

1.1 Software Engineering

In the sixties, third-generation computing hardware was invented, and the software techniques of multiprogramming and time-sharing were developed. These capabilities provided the necessary technology for implementing new, till then unthinkable kinds of computing systems such as interactive, multi-user, on-line, and real-time systems for airline reservation, medical information and surveillance, industrial process control, and navigational guidance. As these computing systems became more numerous, more complex, and more deeply embedded in modern society, the need for systematic, engineer-like approaches to the development, operation, and maintenance of software became more and more apparent. For almost 20 years increasing attention has been paid to the technology of computer software. Software engineering, the field of study concerned with this emerging technology, has evolved into a technological discipline of considerable importance.

The term "software engineering" was created to characterize in a somewhat provocative way the topics of workshops held in Garmisch (see [Naur, Randell 68]) and Rome (see [Buxton, Randell 69]). These workshops were concerned with the technical and managerial processes used to develop and maintain computer software.

There are various definitions of the term "software engineering" all of which are essentially similar, only differing in the respective wordings. [Boehm 76] defines software engineering as

> *the practical application of scientific knowledge to the design and construction of computer programs and the associated documentation required to develop, operate, and maintain them,*

where, according to [Boehm 76], the term "design" has to be interpreted broadly in order to include activities such as software requirements analysis and redesign during software modification.

In [IEEE 83] the definition

> *the systematic approach to the development, operation, maintenance, and retirement of software*

for software engineering can be found, where "software" in turn is defined as

> *computer programs, procedures, rules, and possibly associated documentation and data pertaining to the operation of a computer system.*

[Fairley 85] uses the definition

> *software engineering is the technological and managerial discipline concerned with systematic production and maintenance of software products that are developed and modified on time and within cost estimates.*

In particular, the latter author stresses the fact that software engineering is also concerned with management problems rather than just with technological aspects. Although we generally agree with this view, in the following text we will restrict ourselves to the pure technological problems of software engineering. For the typical management aspects such as project planning, establishing an organizational environment, and cost estimation, we refer the reader to the existing literature (e.g. [Fairley 85] or [Sommerville 89]).

Thus, we will be concerned with

> *the systematic development and maintenance of certified software that correctly solves a precisely specified task.*

With respect to the meaning of the central notions "certification", "correctness", and "specification", we essentially follow the definitions given in [IEEE 83]:

certification:

(1) *A written guarantee that a system or computer program complies with its specified requirements.*

(2) *A written authorization that states that a computer system is secure and is permitted to operate in a defined environment with or producing sensitive information.*

(3) *The formal demonstration of system acceptability to obtain authorization for its operational use.*

(4) *The process of confirming that a system, software subsystem, or computer program is capable of satisfying its specified requirements in an operational environment. Certification usually takes place in the field under actual conditions, and is utilized to evaluate not only the software itself, but also the specifications to which the software was constructed. Certification extends the process of verification and validation to an actual or simulated operational environment.*

(5) *The procedure and action by a duly authorized body of determining, verifying, and attesting in writing to the qualifications of personnel, processes, procedures, or items in accordance with applicable requirements.*

correctness:

(1) *The extent to which software is free from design defects and from coding defects; that is fault free.*
(2) *The extent to which software meets its specified requirements.*
(3) *The extent to which software meets user expectations.*

specification:

(1) *A document that prescribes, in a complete, precise, verifiable manner, the requirements, design, behavior, or other characteristics of a system or system component.*
(2) *The process of developing a specification.*
(3) *A concise statement of a set of requirements to be satisfied by a product, a material, or process indicating, whenever appropriate, the procedure by means of which it may be determined whether the requirements given are satisfied.*

Although correctness will be our primary concern, we will occasionally also deal with other quality attributes for software such as (the respective definitions again follow [IEEE 83])

reliability:
The ability of a program to perform a required function under stated conditions for a stated period of time.

robustness:
The extent to which software can continue or operate correctly despite the introduction of invalid inputs.

efficiency:
The extent to which software performs its intended functions with a minimum consumption of computing resources.

portability:
The ease with which software can be transferred from one computer system or environment to another.

adaptability:
The ease with which software allows differing system constraints and user needs to be satisfied.

maintainability:

(1) *The ease with which software can be maintained.*
(2) *The ease with which maintenance of a functional unit can be performed in accordance with prescribed requirements.*
(3) *Ability of an item under stated conditions of use to be retained in, within a given period of time, a specified state in which it can perform its required functions when maintenance is performed under stated conditions and while using prescribed procedures and resources.*

modularity:
The extent to which software is composed of discrete components such that a change to one component has minimal impact on other components.

reusability:
The extent to which a module can be used in multiple applications.

Thus, summing up, the intention of this text is to contribute to the goal stated in [Bauer 72]:

> *to obtain economically software that is reliable and works efficiently on real machines.*

1.2 The Problematics of Software Development

In everyday life the problematics of software development is extensively known from the famous bank's computer that persistently produced requests to pay a debt to the amount of 0.00 dollars. It also has been the focus of many anecdotes, such as (translated from [Hach 83])

> *The automatic propulsion control in our Boeing 737 had the occasional habit during take-off at exactly 60 knots of cutting out. It was someone in our workshops – and not the manufacturers – who by chance looked at the instruction listings and found the cause. The programmer had spelled out what the propulsion control should do under 60 knots and what it sould do over 60 knots. But he had forgotten to say how it sould react at exactly 60 knots. So if at exactly 60 knots the computer asked for the appropriate instruction, it found nothing, got confused and turned itself off.*

and cartoons as in Fig. 1.1.

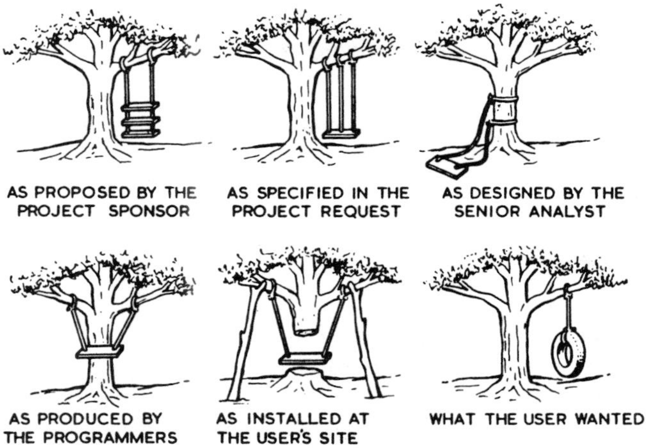

Figure 1.1. The problematics of software development [Brittan 80], © BCS 1980

These complaints about software development also can be expressed verbally as in [Bauer 72]:

What have been the complaints? Typically, they were:
- *Existing software production is done by amateurs (regardless whether at universities, software houses or manufacturers),*
- *Existing software development is done by tinkering (at the universities) or by the human wave ("million monkey") approach at the manufacturers',*
- *Existing software is unreliable and needs permanent "maintenance", the word maintenance being misused to denote fallacies which are expected from the very beginning by the producer,*
- *Existing software is messy, lacks transparency, prevents improvement or building on (or at least requires too high a price to be paid for this).*

Last, but not least, the common complaint is:
- *Existing software comes too late and at higher costs than expected, and does not fulfil the promises made for it.*

Certainly, more points could be added to this list.

Although written more than 15 years ago, these complaints are still of striking relevance today.

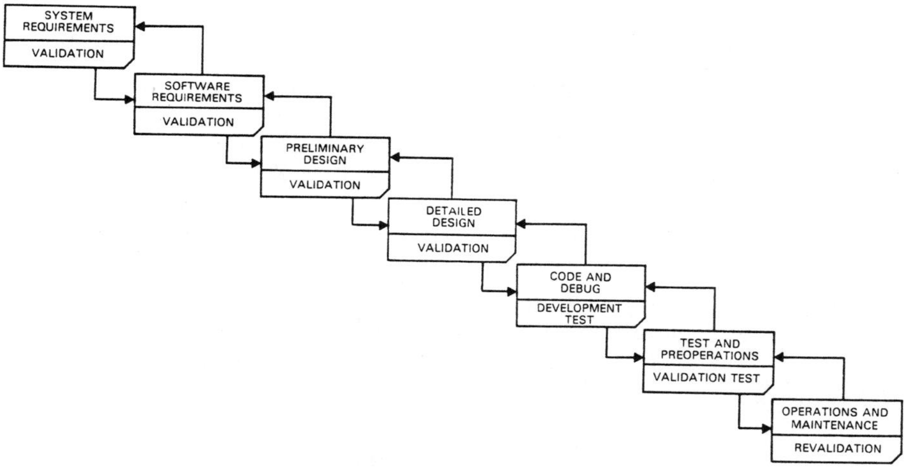

Figure 1.2. Life cycle model [Boehm 76], © IEEE 1976

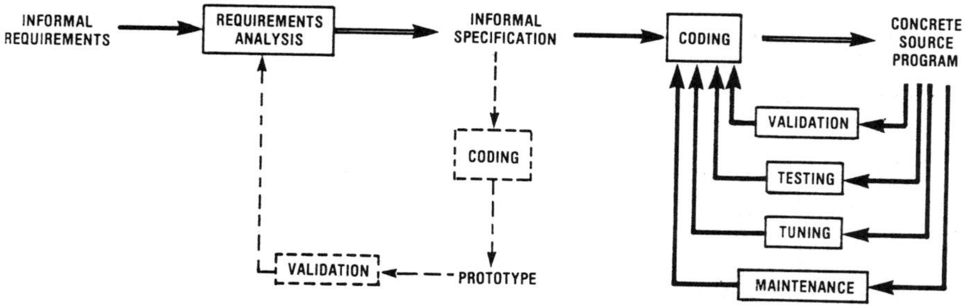

Figure 1.3. Life cycle model [Balzer et al. 83], © IEEE 1983

In order to tackle these problems, traditional software engineering attempts to utilize, for the production of software, problem-solving techniques common to all engineering disciplines. These techniques provide the basis for project planning, project management, and project organization along various 'life cycle models' (see Figs. 1.2, 1.3).

However, even professional software engineers seem to have their doubts about the usefulness of this concept, as is illustrated in Fig. 1.4.

Therefore, new concepts have been explored [Agresti 86a]. Among these, the idea of formal specification and program transformation appears to be very promising. Expressed in terms of the traditional phase-based life cycle, the basic idea of this new paradigm may be sketched as in Fig. 1.5 and Fig 1.6.

Figure 1.4. Life cycle model [Stucky 79]

In principle we share the idea of software construction expressed in these figures. Our particular view of these new paradigms will be outlined in more detail in the following sections.

1.3 Formal Specification and Program Transformation

In its widest sense, software development means

given a problem, find a program (or a set of programs) that (efficiently) solves the problem

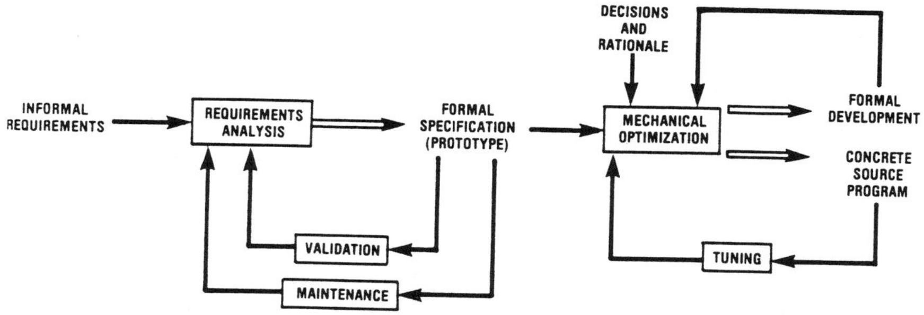

Figure 1.5. Formal specification and program transformation [Balzer et al. 83], © IEEE 1983

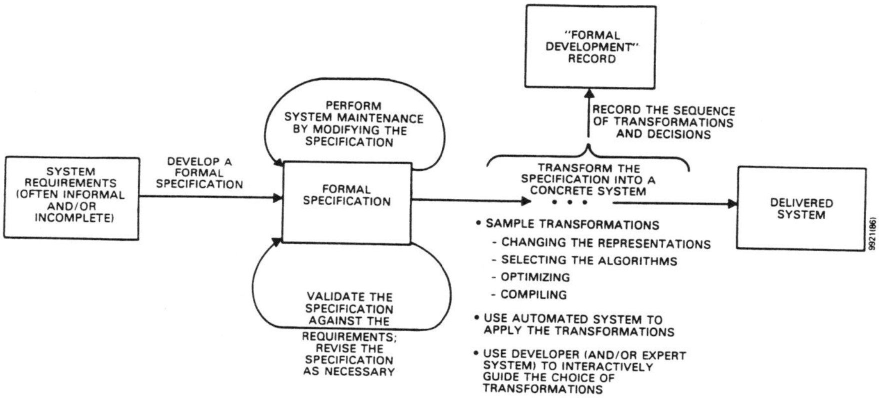

Figure 1.6. Formal specification and program transformation [Agresti 86b], © IEEE 1986

where *program* is to be taken as a synonym for *software*.

The major difficulty in solving this task is caused by the fact that the original problem description usually consists of nothing but a bunch of half-baked wishes which are neither precise, detailed, nor even complete, whereas the algorithm, by nature, has to be precisely defined and fully detailed to each single instruction. This situation is illustrated in Fig. 1.7.

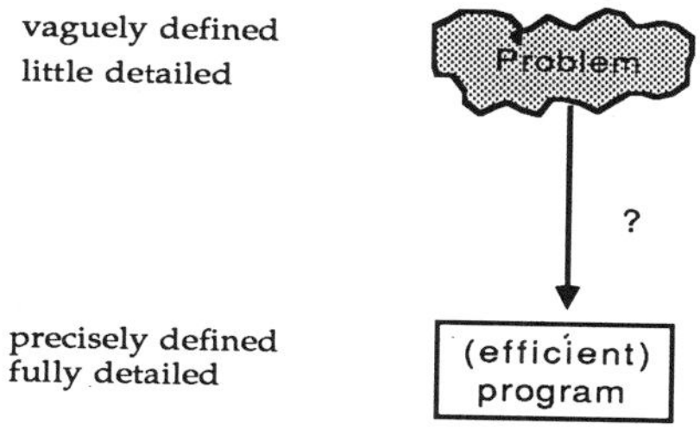

Figure 1.7. Software development

It is obvious that software development done in one large step to bridge the huge gap between these extreme positions is probably doomed to fail, that is, the resulting software will most likely not work as expected.

There are various reasons why software would not work properly. Very often, the problem given originally was simply misunderstood or misinterpreted. Therefore, it is widely accepted today that the process of software development should at least be broken into two steps (frequently called 'requirements engineering' and 'program development') with a precise, formal statement of the problem as an intermediate stage (Fig. 1.8).

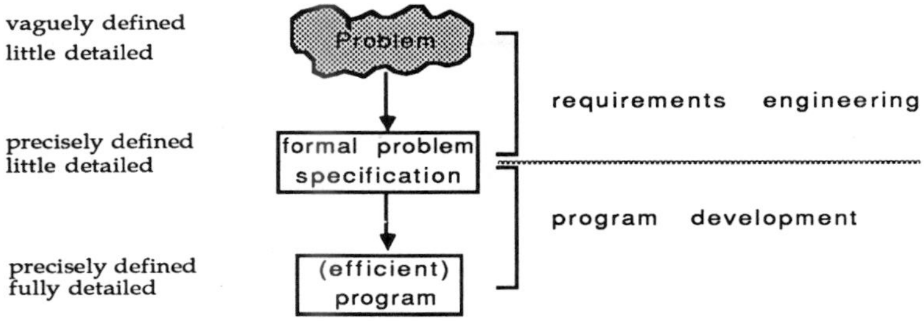

Figure 1.8. Software development in two steps

Such a **formal problem specification** states precisely and unambiguously the task to be fulfilled by the software, i.e., it describes what the problem is without giving the solution or even the details about its implementation. Such a 'separation of concerns' allows early validation (i.e., checks on whether the informal wishes are properly reflected) and thus prevents superfluous implementation work.

However, even if the problem has been properly understood, for example within a formal problem specification, it may well happen that the implemented software does not work correctly, that is, does not satisfy the given (formal) specification. The reason why such incorrect programs may appear, although one started from a formal problem specification, is simply because the step from the formal specification to the program is still too large. Therefore, it seems reasonable to introduce further intermediate stages, as illustrated in Fig. 1.9.

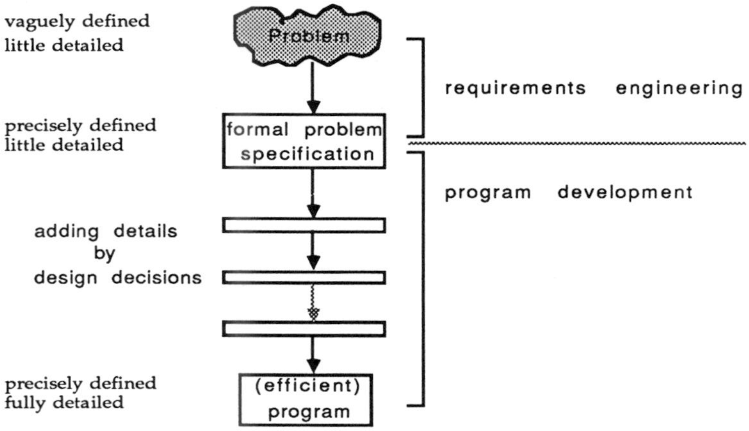

Figure 1.9. Software development in several steps

Such a refinement process should ultimately lead from a precisely defined, yet not very detailed problem specification to a fully detailed program mainly characterized by the addition of details resulting from *design decisions* during the developmental process. These additions should be chosen in such a way that the resulting program satisfies the original formal problem specification.

If the transitions from one stage to the other are done purely intellectually, that is, without any formal restrictions, the whole process follows the idea of 'stepwise refinement' [Wirth 71] that is sketched in Fig. 1.10.

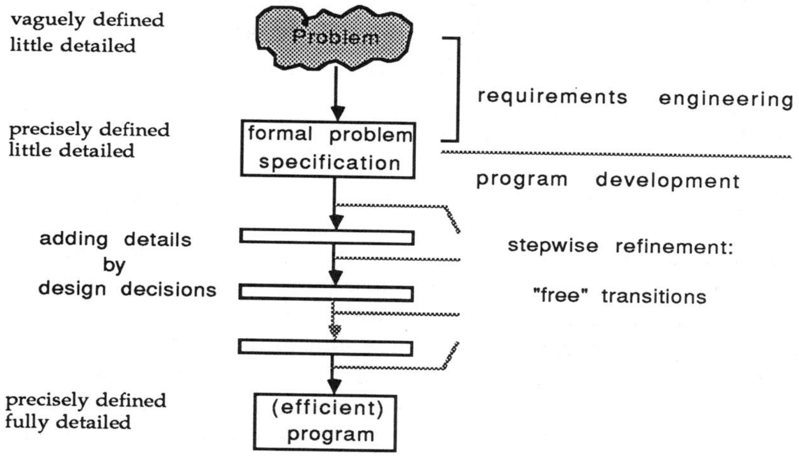

Figure 1.10. Software development by stepwise refinement

In particular with respect to the correctness of the resulting program, this approach has the essential disadvantage that the necessary verification is problem-dependent, that is, has to be done anew for any new problem.

Thus, as a next step to improving methodology, informal transitions should be forbidden and only formal, provably semantics-preserving transitions should be allowed. This is the basic idea of **transformational programming** as illustrated in Fig. 1.11.

The approach of transformational programming has quite a number of obvious benefits:

- since every transition is known to be semantics-preserving, the resulting program is *correct by construction*;
- the transitions can be expressed by schematic rules and are thus *reusable* for whole classes of problems;
- most of the transitions can be undone (by appropriate rules) which provides great *flexibility* in program development;
- formal problem specification, resulting program, and all transitions relating the one to the other provide an excellent *documentation*;
- since the entire development process works only with formal objects, one of the basic requirements for *machine support* is fulfilled.

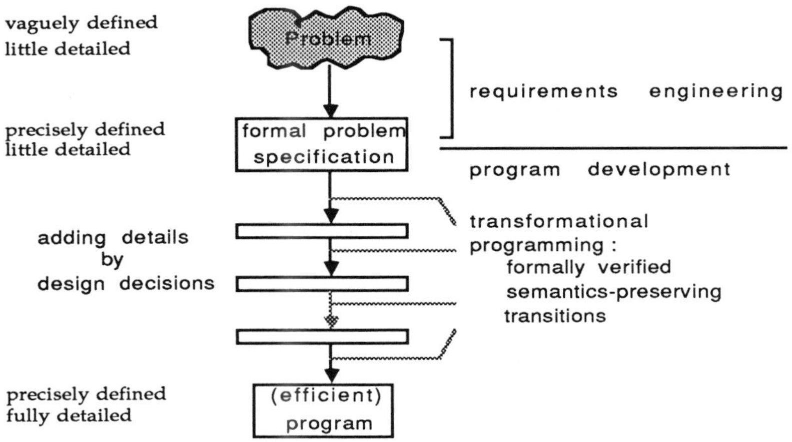

Figure 1.11. Software development by transformational programming

However, it should not be concealed that these benefits do not come free but require the investment of time, effort and discipline. Consequently, applying this methodology only pays in connection with applications where correctness is absolutely mandatory for economical, political, or ethical reasons. It certainly would be a waste to apply the methodology to all kinds of "throw-away" software.

The possibility of machine support mentioned above leads to a separation of concerns in program development between man and machine, man being responsible for creative aspects, and machine for mechanical tasks.

Typical mechanical tasks in this approach are:

- support for validating the specification,
- performing program transformations,
- support for verifying applicability conditions of transformation rules,
- keeping track of the development process.

On the other hand, typical creative aspects are:

- formalization of the problem,
- selection of suitable development strategies,
- selection of transformation rules and indication of the respective point of application,
- derivation of new rules (if necessary), including the respective proofs of their correctness.

This particular view of the software development process and the separation of work between man and machine is summarized in the acronym of the Munich transformation project called CIP (Computer-aided Intuition-guided Programming). This project dealt with various aspects of formal specification and transformational programming. For overviews of this project see [Bauer 76], [Bauer 82], [Broy 84a], [Broy, Pepper 80], [Möller 84], [Partsch, Möller 87], and [Bauer et al. 89].

1.4 Our Particular View of Transformational Programming

Due to different intentions and specific goals, there are several technically different approaches all based on the idea that software development is a stepwise, evolutionary process of applying transformation rules.

The primary goal that is most common to all efforts in the area of transformational programming is that of general support for program modification. This includes the development of operational solutions from non-operational problem descriptions, the optimization of control structures, the efficient implementation of data structures, as well as the adaptation of given programs to particular styles of programming (e.g. applicative, procedural, machine-oriented). If modification is not restricted to proper programs but is extended to include program schemes, transformation rules may also be used to formally derive new rules (which are correct by construction). Hence, to some extent, program modification also comprises rule generation.

A more specific goal of transformational programming is program synthesis, the (in most cases automatic) generation of a program from a (formal) description of the problem. Here, approaches vary with regard to the formulation of the input and the degree of automation. Program synthesis may start from specifications in (restricted) natural language, from examples in some formal language, or from mathematical assertions. Synthesis by modifying similar programs is a somewhat different approach.

Another specific goal is that of program adaptation to particular environments. This may mean that a program written in a language X is transformed (by means of transformation rules) into a program written in a language Y. This may also mean that a program for a sequential machine is transformed into one for a parallel or distributed architecture.

Other specific goals include program description and program explanation (by exhibiting the derivation history or by building up "family trees" of related algorithms) and deduction-oriented verification of programs' correctness.

Technically, the various approaches are different with respect to

- kinds of languages used for formulating problems and algorithms (new languages for formal specification, functional languages, languages specifically tailored to the paradigm of transformational programming (so-called 'wide spectrum languages'), or existing programming languages such as Pascal or Ada);
- the kind of transformation rules used (from simple purely syntactic rewrite rules up to complex transformation rules which depend on semantic properties or mathematical theorems);
- different views of the correctness of a transformation rule (from intuitively correct up to mathematically correct on the basis of a formal semantic definition);
- contents and structure of the collection of available rules (huge all-purpose catalogs of (occasionally rather specific) rules or small generative sets of powerful basic rules);
- the degree of automatization assumed for an implemented support system (exclusively user-driven, semi-automatic, fully automatic).

For further details on the different approaches to transformational programming we refer the reader to existing overviews (for example [Burstall, Feather 78], [Darlington 79], [Partsch, Steinbrüggen 83], [Feather 86], [Goldberg 86]). In [Feather 86] a short treatise on account of the state of the art in transformational programming can also be found.

In the particular view of the project CIP which we will share for our further considerations, transformational programming is considered an *evolutionary process* [Bauer 76] that usually starts from a formal problem specification (the "contract", [Bauer 81]) and ends with a program which can be efficiently executed on a given target machine.

This leads to a "life cycle of transformational program development" [Broy 84a] which is roughly characterized by the following developmental stages:

- (descriptive) formal problem specification,
- modified (descriptive) specification,
- (non-deterministic, recursive) solution,
- deterministic, tail-recursive solution,
- further modified applicative program,
- efficient procedural program.

These stages are optional, in the sense that not all of them actually must occur in a concrete program development. Furthermore, development may start at any stage and end at an arbitrary (later) stage.

The transitions between the specification and all intermediate versions of the program are done exclusively by applying transformation rules, the correctness of which is proved with respect to the semantics of the language used. In this way it is guaranteed that the final version of the program is correct, that is, meets the original specification.

The transformation rules themselves cover the entire spectrum between purely syntactic rewrites and semantics-dependent modifications.

As to the organization of the rules, CIP assumes a relatively small set of powerful basic rules which, for practical purposes, may be extended at will by rules specifically tailored to particular problem domains [Bauer et al. 79].

Basically, in CIP the development process is exclusively guided by the user, who, by choosing appropriate rules, is in particular responsible for finally coming up with a program that also satisfies further criteria such as time or space constraints. This particular view, however, excludes neither partial automatization in connection with clearly defined subtasks of the entire development process (for example, simplification of expressions) nor incorporation or implementation of tactic and strategic considerations.

1.5 Relation to Other Approaches to Programming Methodology

As illustrated above, there is an obvious relationship between transformational programming and stepwise refinement. In both approaches a development process consisting of small intellectually manageable steps is advocated in order to master complexity. However, in addition to the already mentioned differences with respect to the effort to be spent for ensuring correctness, there is a further essential difference. If in stepwise refinement a design decision leads to the introduction of a certain control structure, then this control structure is fixed from that point on. In transformational programming, however, it is possible to modify any control structure (for example, recursion into iteration). In fact, exactly those kinds of transformations (such as the finite differencing technique, Sect. 6.4.4) cause substantial improvements in efficiency during a program development. This essential difference between stepwise refinement and transformational programming has been pointed out rather early [Burstall, Feather 78]. For illustration purposes, stepwise refinement was compared with creating a sculpture out of a piece of rock, whereas transformational programming corresponds rather to modeling a sculpture using clay or plasticine.

Transformational programming is also related to the ideas of logic programming [Kowalski 83] and applicative programming (sometimes also called functional programming; see for example [Henderson 80], [Darlington et al. 82], [Darlington 87], [Bird, Wadler 88]).

The conceptual basis of logic programming is a strict separation between logical aspects of a given problem and control aspects of its solution ("algorithm = logic + control" [Kowalski 79]). In logic programming the emphasis in program development is on the logical part whereas all aspects of control are left to an interpreter that works according to a fixed, built-in, general strategy. Unfortunately, however, very often details of the evaluation strategy bias the specification. This leads to "tricky", inadequate formalizations of the problem at hand (such as the conceptually unnecessary sequentialization or the **cut** operation in PROLOG). These "dirty" effects can be avoided in transformational programming by also first focussing on the logical aspects alone and then introducing control structures that are adequate for the problem at hand in a flexible way by appropriate transformation rules. For example, 'backtracking', the central evaluation strategy used in processing logic programs, can be introduced by a single transformation rule (Sect. 5.4.2). But there also exist rules for introducing 'breadth-first search' or any other kind of evaluation strategy. Hence, the major advantage in transformational programming is the fact that for any particular program a control structure can be chosen which is optimal for the respective problem. Moreover, in logical programming, the control structure fixed by the available implementation may not only be highly inefficient, but may also cause other problems, such as non-termination.

The basic philosophy of applicative programming is similar to that of logic programming. Here too, efficiency-oriented aspects of control are left to a suitable implementation, and the focus of interest is the essence of an algorithm. Basic building blocks for formulating algorithms are here the mathematical notion of a function, of conditional, and of recursion. However, even disregarding efficiency aspects or the fact that applicative languages are not available on every machine, there are problems with applicative programs which cannot be solved by any implementation, but can be solved using the idea of program transformations. The following simple example [Bauer 85] illustrates this:

One is asked for a program which computes the floating point representation of the dual logarithm of the factorial of a given natural number.

A typical applicative solution to this problem might look as follows (where we use an

ALGOL-like notation which will be formally defined in Chap. 3):

funct *floatfac* = (**int** n: $n \geq 0$) (**real**, **int**):
  logrep(*fac*(n), 0) **where**

funct *fac* = (**int** n: $n \geq 0$) **int**:
  if $n = 0$ **then** 1 **else** $n \times fac(n-1)$ **fi**,

funct *logrep* = (**real** x, **int** i: $i \geq 0 \wedge x \geq 1/2$) (**real**, **int**):
  if $x < 1$ **then** (x, i) **else** $logrep(x \times 1/2, i + 1)$ **fi**.

floatfac is a function that computes for an integer argument n, which must be greater or equal to 0, a pair consisting of a real number (the mantissa) and an integer number (the exponent). It is defined by two auxiliary functions *fac* and *logrep*. The function *fac* computes the factorial of a non-negative integer; *logrep* computes for a real number (which is asserted to be greater than 1/2) the floating point representation of its dual logarithm.

Irrespective of how neatly the evaluation of recursive functions is implemented, almost every implementation will have problems with this solution due to the size restrictions for natural numbers which are exceeded by the factorial already for comparatively small n.

Hence, an alternative idea for a solution might be to use a factorial function that already operates on floating point representations (in order to avoid the size problems):

funct *floatfac* = (**int** n: $n \geq 0$) (**real**, **int**):
  gfac(n),

funct *gfac* = (**int** n: $n \geq 0$) (**real**, **int**):
  if $n = 0$ **then** (1, 0) **else** $logrep(n, 0) \otimes gfac(n-1)$ **fi**,

where $\otimes$, denoting the multiplication on floating point representations, is straightforwardly defined by

$$(x, i) \otimes (y, j) =_{def} (x \times y, i + j).$$

However, this solution is problematic too, as in *gfac* products of numerical-real numbers in the interval between 0 and 1 are computed, which, as is known, may lead to numerical instability.

A satisfactory, still applicative solution which circumvents both problems mentioned above can be obtained by transforming either of the specifications above into:

funct *floatfac* = (**int** n: $n \geq 0$) (**real**, **int**):
  floatfac'(n, 1, 0),

funct *floatfac'* = (**int** n, **real** x, **int** i: $n \geq 0 \wedge i \geq 0 \wedge x \geq 1/2$) (**real**, **int**):
  if $n = 0 \wedge x < 1$ **then** (x, i)
  [] $x \geq 1$ **then** $floatfac'(n, x \times 1/2, i + 1)$
  [] $n \neq 0 \wedge x < N$ **then** $floatfac'(n-1, x \times n, i)$ **fi**

(with an arbitrary natural number N), where the above-mentioned problems obviously are avoided. A formal treatment of this development can be found in Sect. 4.5.4.

It should be further mentioned at this point that applicative languages are particularly well-suited for transformational programming due to their strong algebraic properties (see for example [Backus 78], [Bird 84, 87], [Hoare et al. 87], [Meertens 86], [Roscoe, Hoare 86]). They are therefore the appropriate level for many activities in transformational programming, as can be seen in later chapters.

Finally, it should be mentioned that further, currently known approaches in the area of programming methodology, which likewise focus on program correctness as their major concern, such as program development from pre- and post-conditions ([Dijkstra 76a], [Gries 81], [Backhouse 86]), Jones's approach ([Jones 80]), or 'predicative programming' (in the sense of [Hehner et al. 86], [Morgan 86]) also can be conceptually integrated into the idea of transformational programming.

1.6 An Introductory Example

In order to illustrate the idea of problem specification and program transformation, we will deal with the 'Queens' problem'. The major purpose of this sample development is to illustrate various kinds of transformations, rather than giving a particularly "tricky" or hyper-elegant derivation. It also should be stressed explicitly that the derivation below is just one possible transformational treatment of the problem. Other treatments can be found, e.g., in [Balzer 81a] or [Smith 86].

Informally, the problem may be stated as follows:

Is it possible to place N queens ($N \in \mathbb{N}$) *on an* $N \times N$ *chessboard in such a way that they do not attack each other?*

Anyone familiar with the basic rules of chess also knows what "attack" means in this context: in order to not attack each other, two queens must not be placed in the same row (rank), the same column (file), or the same diagonal. Denoting positions on an $n \times n$ chessboard by pairs of natural numbers between 1 and n, this may be formalized by the following predicate (again in an ALGOL-like notation):

funct *nonconflict* = (**set of** ([1..*n*], [1..*n*]) *m*) **bool**:
  $\forall (i,j), (k,l) \in m$: $(i,j) \neq (k,l) \Rightarrow ((i \neq k) \wedge (j \neq l) \wedge (\mathbf{abs}(k-i) \neq \mathbf{abs}(l-j)))$.

nonconflict is a predicate, i.e., a boolean-valued function, that determines for a set m of positions (represented by pairs of natural numbers between 1 and n) whether queens on these positions do not attack each other. This predicate will be used as an auxiliary definition within a context where the implicit global parameter n (denoting the board size) will have a defined value.

Using this predicate the queens' problem can be formalized straightforwardly by

queens(*N*) **where**
funct *queens* = (**nat** *n*) **bool**:
  $\exists$ **set of** ([1..*n*], [1..*n*]) *m*: $|m| = n \wedge nonconflict(m)$.

queens is again a predicate that checks whether for a given natural number n there exists a set of positions that has exactly n elements and fulfils the predicate *nonconflict*.

The focus of interest for the subsequent development is the function *queens*. The goal we want to achieve is an efficient solution for this function. In order to reach this goal we first modify the specification, then develop a recursive solution (still disregarding efficiency), and only afterwards we apply a few optimization techniques in order to reach the intended efficiency.

As a first step, we exploit the fact that the sets asked for in the original specification are of a very particular nature: they should contain n pairs of numbers of which the respective first components should be distinct values between 1 and n (since no two queens can be on the same file). Hence, we can apply a simple data type transformation by which the set m from above is substituted by an indexed sequence s such that the property

$$(i, j) \in m \Leftrightarrow s_i = j$$

(a pair (i, j) is in the set m if and only if the i-th element of the sequence s has the value j) holds:

funct *queens* = (**nat** *n*) **bool**:
  $\exists$ **sequ of** [1..*n*] *s*: $|s| = n \wedge nconf(s)$ **where**

  funct *nconf* = (**sequ of** [1..*n*] *s*) **bool**:
    $\forall\, i, k \in [1..n]: i \neq k \Rightarrow ((s_i \neq s_k) \wedge (\mathbf{abs}(k-i) \neq \mathbf{abs}(s_k - s_i)))$.

The predicate *nconf* is an equivalent formulation of *nonconflict* for indexed sequences instead of sets. Also, the fact that *nconf* is an auxiliary predicate has been made explicit here by using the keyword **where**.

As another modification of the specification, inspired by intuition and experience, we generalize the problem by using the technique of "embedding" (Sect. 5.2):

funct *queens* = (**nat** *n*) **bool**:
  qu(<>) **where**

  funct *qu* = (**sequ of** [1..*n*] *t*: $|t| \leq n \wedge nconf(t)$) **bool**:
    $\exists$ **sequ of** [1..*n*] *s*: $|t+s| = n \wedge nconf(t+s)$.

In this generalized version of the problem it is asked whether a partial solution of the original problem can be extended to a full solution. The fact that t is a partial solution is guaranteed by the assertion $|t| \leq n \wedge nconf(t)$ in *qu*. Obviously, taking the empty sequence <> as an initial argument of *qu*, yields the original problem. The symbol "+" is used to denote the concatenation of two sequences; below, we will also use it for the addition of an element to a sequence.

Our next efforts aim at finding a recursive (operational) solution for *qu*. Introducing the case distinction

$$(|t| = n \vee |t| < n)$$

in the body of *qu* (which is straightforward from the assertion $t \leq n$) leads to

if $|t| = n$ **then** $\exists$ **sequ of** [1..*n*] *s*: $|t+s| = n \wedge nconf(t+s)$
      else $\exists$ **sequ of** [1..*n*] *s*: $|t+s| = n \wedge nconf(t+s)$ **fi**.

Obviously, both the **then** and the **else** branch can be simplified. For the **then** branch we have under the assertion $nconf(t)$ and the premise $|t| = n$:

$\exists$ **sequ of** [1..*n*] *s*: $|t+s| = n \wedge nconf(t+s)$ =	[$|t+s| = n \Leftrightarrow |s| = 0$]
$\exists$ **sequ of** [1..*n*] *s*: $|s| = 0 \wedge nconf(t+s)$ =	[$|s| = 0 \Leftrightarrow s = \langle\rangle$]
$\exists$ **sequ of** [1..*n*] s: $s = \langle\rangle \wedge nconf(t+s)$ =	[substitutivity of =]
$\exists$ **sequ of** [1..*n*] s: $nconf(t+\langle\rangle)$ =	[simplification of $\exists$]

$nconf(t+\langle\rangle)$ = [idempotency of $\langle\rangle$]
$nconf(t)$ = [validity of the assertion of qu]
true.

Similarly, for the **else** branch we have under the assertion $nconf(t)$ and the premise $|t| < n$:

$\exists$ **sequ of** $[1..n]$ s: $|t+s| = n \wedge nconf(t+s)$ =
[$|t| < n \Rightarrow ((\exists$ **sequ of** $[1..n]$ s: $|t+s| = n \wedge nconf(t+s)) \Leftrightarrow$
$(\exists$ $[1..n]$ p, **sequ of** $[1..n]$ s: $|t+(p+s)| = n \wedge nconf(t+(p+s))))$]
$\exists$ $[1..n]$ p, **sequ of** $[1..n]$ s: $|t+(p+s)| = n \wedge nconf(t+(p+s))$ =
[associativity of +]
$\exists$ $[1..n]$ p, **sequ of** $[1..n]$ s: $|(t+p)+s)| = n \wedge nconf((t+p)+s)$ =
[$nconf((t+p)+s) \Leftrightarrow (nc(t+p)$ Δ $nconf((t+p)+s))$,
where Δ denotes "sequential conjunction", cf. Sect. 3.4.1, and
$nc(t+p) =_{def} \forall$ $1 \le i \le |t|$: $(t_i \ne p) \wedge (|t|+1-i \ne$ **abs**$(p-t_i))$
is a "weaker" form of $nconf(t+p)$ which uses the fact that
$nconf(t)$ is guaranteed by the assertion of qu]
$\exists$ $[1..n]$ p, **sequ of** $[1..n]$ s: $|(t+p)+s)| = n \wedge nc(t+p)$ Δ $nconf((t+p)+s)$ =
[rearrangement of $\exists$]
$\exists$ $[1..n]$ p: $nc(t+p)$ Δ
$\exists$ **sequ of** $[1..n]$ s: $|(t+p)+s)| = n \wedge nconf((t+p)+s)$.

Consequently, from these two simplifications it follows that the body of qu can be replaced by

if $|t| = n$ **then true**
else $\exists$ $[1..n]$ p: $nc(t+p)$ Δ
$\exists$ **sequ of** $[1..n]$ s: $|(t+p)+s)| = n \wedge nconf((t+p)+s)$ **fi**.

A careful look allows to identify the last line as an instance of the original specification of qu such that by applying the technique of 'folding' (Sect. 4.3), i.e., the replacement of an expression by an equivalent function call, we obtain the recursive algorithm

funct qu = (**sequ of** $[1..n]$ t: $|t| \le n \wedge nconf(t)$) **bool**:
if $|t| = n$ **then true**
else $\exists$ $[1..n]$ p: $nc(t+p)$ Δ $qu(t+p)$ **fi**.

In order to get rid of the remaining existential quantifier, we apply a transformation rule which introduces explicit backtracking (Sect. 5.4.2):

funct qu = (**sequ of** $[1..n]$ t: $|t| \le n \wedge nconf(t)$) **bool**:
if $|t| = n$ **then true**
else $h(1, t)$ **fi where**

funct h = (**nat** i, **sequ of** $[1..n]$ t: $|t| \le n \wedge nconf(t)$) **bool**:
if $i > n$ **then false**
else if $nc(t, i)$ **then** $qu(t+i)$ ∇ $h(i+1, t)$
else $h(i+1, t)$ **fi fi**

(where the symbol ∇ denotes sequential disjunction, Sect. 3.4.1).

Next, we apply standard recursion removal techniques (Sect. 6.5) to h in order to improve efficiency. This leads to the following version (where the operation **last** yields the last element of a non-empty sequence and **lead** yields the sequence without its last element):

```
funct h = (nat i, sequ of [1..n] t: |t| ≤ n ∧ nconf(t)) bool:
  begin
    var sequ of [1..n] t := <>; var nat i := 1; var bool b;
    R: if i > n  then if |t| = 0  then b:= false; goto E
                                  else i := last t + 1; t := lead t; goto R fi
                 else if nc(t, i)  then t :=t+i;
                                        if |t| = n  then b := true; goto E
                                                    else i := 1; goto R   fi
                                   else i := i+1; goto R                  fi fi;
    E: b
  end.
```

As a last step we obtain by some final polishing, such as getting rid of superfluous definitions using the 'unfold' technique (Sect. 4.3), or representing (bounded) sequences by ordinary arrays and a counter to indicate the actually valid part of it, our final solution:

```
queens(n) where

funct queens = (nat n) bool:
  begin
    var array [1..n] a; var nat z := 0; var nat i := 1; var bool b;
    if z = n then b:= true; goto E fi;
    R: if i>n
         then if z = 0   then b:= false; goto E
                         else i := a[z] + 1; z := z – 1;  goto R fi
         else if nc(t, i) then  z := z + 1; a[z] := i;
                                if z = n  then b := true; goto E
                                          else i := 1; goto R  fi
                         else i := i+1; goto R                 fi fi;
    E: b
  end.
```

Although all steps in the above development of the final program from the formal problem specification have been motivated intuitively and carried out informally, formal transformation rules exist that allow each of these steps to be carried out formally. These transformation rules will be introduced in the following chapters.

2. Requirements Engineering

In Sect. 1.3, we introduced *requirements engineering* as that phase in the software development process where vaguely defined, little detailed user wishes are to be made into a more precise, though still little detailed specification of the problem to be solved. Moreover, we also aimed at a *formal problem specification* as the result of the requirements engineering phase. For the present chapter, however, in order to establish the relation to traditional software engineering, we will start with a somewhat broader view and consider formality as a desirable, but not mandatory objective. This means in particular that we are also going to give a short account on the state of the art in traditional requirements engineering, mainly in order to contrast it (in Chap. 3) with our approach where a precise statement of the user's wishes in terms of a formal language is aimed at.

2.1 Introduction

Requirements engineering is a field of interest in computer science. In [Kühnel et al. 87] it is defined

> *to comprise methods, languages and tools for the investigation, formulation and analysis of tasks and 'requirements' for systems.*

The notion 'system' is used there in its widest sense to include software systems, but also software/hardware systems, or even any kinds of technical or socio-economic systems that include a software system as one of their components. In the following, however, we will restrict ourselves mainly to software systems.

The importance of requirements engineering and, in particular, its enormous influence on the high cost of software [Boehm 75, 81] have long since been recognized (e.g. [Buxton, Randell 69]) – in particular as "that part of the process which leads to more failures than any other" [Schwartz 75]. However, a really satisfactory solution has not yet been found.

In a somewhat provocative way, the problematic situation in requirements engineering may be characterized by:

- lack of methods; instead
  - definition of the requirements *after* having done the implementation,
  - use of ad hoc techniques,
  - no integrated methodology for the entire development process;
- lack of suitable formalisms; rather

  - use of natural language (with all its ambiguities),
  - mixture of different formalisms (disregarding interface problems);
- lack of good tools to
  - support the production of the requirements document,
  - analyze the requirements (with respect to consistency and completeness),
  - transform the requirements definition into a design specification.

Consequently, the ultimate goal of all efforts in the area of requirements engineering is:

> a suitable formalism (for describing the requirements for a software system) properly embedded in an overall software development methodology and supported by good (maybe computer-supported) tools.

2.1.1 Basic Notions

In a more narrow sense, **requirements engineering** is also used to characterize the initial phase in the traditional life cycle model for software development. In [IEEE 83] this phase is characterized as

> *The period of time in the software life cycle during which the requirements for a software product, such as the functional and performance capabilities, are defined and documented.*

Requirements engineering comprises (at least) two important subtasks, namely **requirements specification** (or **definition**) and **requirements analysis**, where

> *Requirements specification and analysis is the translation of a user (person, business, government) need into a statement of the functions to be accomplished by an automated system, followed by an analysis of the cost and size of the projected system.* [Horowitz 75]

This is similar to the characterization given in [Zave 79] where the following activities during requirements engineering are identified:

1) ***Problem identification*** *– identify and describe the needs of a system for certain purposes.*
2) ***Problem understanding*** *– collect and analyse information about the system and its environments, as well as their interaction.*
3) ***Problem specification*** *– describe the behavior of the system.*

In the relevant literature, the term **requirements analysis** has a two-fold meaning which is clearly stated in the definition given in [IEEE 83]:

1) *The process of studying user needs to arrive at a definition of system or software requirements.*
2) *The verification of system or software requirements.*

Due to our particular view (Sect. 1.3) of the software development process where correctness is guaranteed by construction rather than established by verification, we will use the term 'requirements analysis' mainly in its first meaning.

The goal of the requirements phase is the **requirements specification** which is defined [IEEE 83] as:

> *A specification that sets forth the requirements for a system or system component; for example, a software configuration item. Typically included are functional requirements, performance requirements, interface requirements, design requirements, and development standards.*

where in turn **requirement** is defined by

1) *A condition or capability needed by a user to solve a problem or achieve an objective.*
2) *A condition or capability that must be met or possessed by a system or system component to satisfy a contract, standard, specification, or other formally imposed document. The set of all requirements forms the basis for subsequent development of the system or system component.*

A more comprehensive and detailed characterization of 'requirement' is given in [Kühnel et al. 87]. There, **requirements** for a system are defined as

> *statements on achievements to be accomplished,*

which qualitatively may be distinguished into

a) functional requirements:
   - inputs and their constraints,
   - functions the system is able to perform,
   - outputs and other reactions of the system;
b) quality attributes of the desired functions:
   - performance (time, storage),
   - maintainability,
   - reliability (failure safety, robustness, error-recognition, and error-handling),
   - portability,
   - adaptability,
   - compatibility with existing systems,
   - user comfort;
c) requirements for the implementation of the system:
   - devices to be used (e.g. existing software/hardware),
   - interfaces,
   - use of existing tools (programming language, operating system, hardware),
   - documentation;
d) requirements for test, installation and maintenance;
e) requirements for the development process:
   - global development strategies,
   - methods, languages, tools to be used,
   - available resources (manpower, budget, deadlines),
   - standards to be obeyed.

Obviously, there is an essential difference between functional and non-functional requirements: in order to be able to formulate non-functional requirements, the functionality of a system has to be known. It is particularly for this reason that nearly all approaches in requirements engineering mainly concentrate on providing formalisms to describe functional requirements.

How to proceed in order to obtain a requirements specification is characterized in [Rzepka, Ohno 85]:

> *Requirements engineering is a systematic approach to the development of requirements through an iterated process of analysing the problem, documenting the resulting requirements insights, and checking the accuracy of the understanding so gained.*

Again, a more detailed account on the individual activities that are to take place during the investigation, formulation, and analysis of requirements is given in [Kühnel et al. 87]. There, the following subtasks are identified:

a) investigation of requirements:
   - analysis of the actual state and the one aimed at (if necessary),
   - definition of the functional requirements in a dialog between specifier, customer, and user,
   - agreement on quality attributes (maybe inclusive of priorities),
   - exploration of the environment for the system itself and its development,
   - procuration of missing information;

b) formulation of requirements:
   - precise formulation of all individual requirements,
   - systematic structuring and classification of the individual requirements,
   - description of possible relationships between individual requirements;

c) analysis of requirements:
   - adequacy of the formulation (degree to which the formulation mirrors the customer's wishes),
   - investigation of the technical feasibility (Is the problem solvable at all by an algorithm? Are the requirements satisfiable with respect to the constraints on the intended environment?),
   - study on the economical feasibility (overall costs; schedule; required personnel; ratio: costs - benefits; risks),
   - checks for consistency and completeness,
   - simulations (to test user acceptance).

The main activities investigation, formulation and analysis are performed in their natural, sequential order, however, usually in several iterations. Graphically, this may be sketched as in Fig. 2.1.

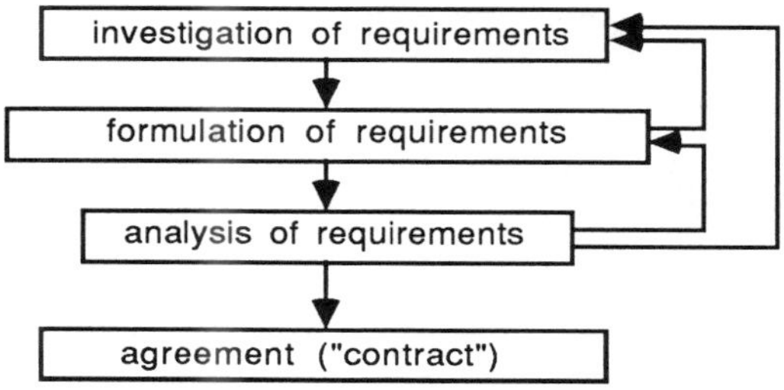

Figure 2.1. RE 'life cycle' [Kühnel et al. 87]

2.1.2 Essential Criteria for Good Requirements Definitions

As a result of analyzing various statements on requirements specification, we will present essential criteria that may serve as a yardstick to compare and evaluate specification methods and languages. Our list will contain the basic criteria from [Balzer, Goldman 79], [Balzert 81], and [Fairley 85]; however, we will come to slightly different conclusions.

The criteria result from properties necessary to cope with the problems in building the requirements definition on the one hand, and properties of good requirements definitions on the other.

Problems in building a requirements definition include:

- uncertainty in (or even impossibility of) completely predicting some system's behavior,
- complexity of a system,
- coordination and consistent integration of different sources of information (customer, user, technical expert),
- different level of detailing of the requirements,
- verification of the implemented system (with respect to the requirements).

In order to cope with these problems, the following properties of a requirements definition seem to be mandatory:

- possibility of simulation,
- means for structuring,
- suitable vehicle for communication,
- flexibility with respect to different levels of abstraction,
- formal correspondence between requirements definition and implemented system.

Hints on properties of good requirements definitions can be found in the literature. [Henderson 81] points out – in agreement with many others (e.g. [Wasserman 80]):

> *... formal specification can be used as a method of precise communication among designers, as their basis for agreement with the customer and as a way of discovering design flaws at an early stage of the design process rather than during product test. The ideal of conceptual integrity of the design is more likely to be achieved if formal methods are used. However, we must bear in mind that readability of the specification is a prime requirement.*

The similarity of this statement to statements made elsewhere is amazing. [Yeh, Zave 80], for instance, characterize the purpose of a requirements definition as follows:

> (1) *as a means of communication among users, experts, analysts, and designers*
> (2) *to support design validation*
> (3) *to control the operations and evolution of the system it specifies.*

And in [Zave 79] one can find:

... a requirement set is the common language by which all parties to the procurement communicate, and, hopefully, achieve agreement on the principal technical issues.

From these citations, we can already identify some of the main criteria for good requirements specifications:

- **abstraction** and **formality**
- **conceptual integrity**
- **readability** and **understandability**.

Some of these criteria even can be found literally in the literature, (e.g. [Zave 79]):

Solutions to requirements problems should form part of a hierarchical, top-down methodology covering the entire development cycle.

System descriptions should be formal ...

or [Yeh, Zave 80]

...the software requirements document should have the property of formality.

The latter authors also mention two further criteria:

- **modifiability**

and

- **liberality**.

Modifiability is doubtless an important criterion that is very often overlooked. According to [Lehman 80], software products are subjected to continual changes ("pressure of change is built-in") due to changing environments (and hence requirements). Thus, ease in modifiability of requirements definitions seems to be a rather important characteristic of a good specification technique.

Liberality stresses the fact that a formal specification of some program or system should not enforce a single solution, but rather allow a variety of implementations ("specification freedom" [London, Feather 82], "a family of solutions" [Yeh, Zave 80]). This, however, should not be confused with the demand for a requirements specification to be free of ambiguities.

Our list of criteria for good requirements specifications is continued by adding yet another one (that is usually – tacitly – assumed):

- **adequacy**.

Adequacy means in essence that the specification method should provide means to increase confidence – especially on the customer's side – that the formal specification really reflects his original intentions. This requires, as outlined in [Schwartz 75] that "management on both sides must ask questions, get answers, assure that all answers are clear and agreed upon" or as formulated in [Zave 79] "requirements specifications should be interpretable". Of course, this cannot work, if the specification method used does not support getting (formally justified) answers to arbitrary questions.

Finally, there are two more aspects which are particularly interesting for the practitioner:

- **range of applicability**

and

- **support by appropriate tools.**

2.1.3 The Particular Role of Formality

By nature, formality is entailed by two more basic criteria for good requirements specifications: **consistency** and **completeness**. Again, respective remarks can be found in the literature:

> ... *the SRD* (Software Requirements Document) *must be complete in that all constructs and assumptions are explicitly stated* [Yeh, Zave 80]

or

> *The single most important function of requirements analysis is to define the problem. It should provide a well-reasoned substantiation of a non-conflicting and complete set of requirements.* [Royce 75]

When asking for formality, furthermore, there seems to be a general consensus that the level of formality provided by existing programming languages is not the one really aimed at:

- *...a clear, detailed* functional *description of the total system* [Schwartz 75]
- *While the SRD specifies* what *the system is to do, it must* not *constrain* how *it is to be done* [Yeh, Zave 80]
- *A specification should state* what *a system is to do,* not how *it is to work* [Jones 80]
- *System specifications should be* non-procedural ... [Zave 79].

Hence, the aim is to have a clear and precise description of *what* a system is supposed to do, rather than a formulation of *how* it operates.

In fact, formality is a delicate issue, in particular since it cannot be seen independently of other criteria such as readability and understandability. On the one hand one would like to have the precision of mathematics, but on the other hand one would prefer to have understandability as provided by natural language:

> *However, we must realize that the primary purpose of a specification is communication among designers and between designers and implementors. Thus, the choice of a formal language in which to write a formal specification must attempt to combine the elegance and precision of mathematics and the readability of natural languages.* [Henderson 81]

These seemingly contradictory requests for the precision of mathematics and the understandability of natural language provide the framework for principle directions of research in requirements engineering.

One approach is to start from natural language and to impose some structure and precision (mainly by standardization) to an extent that is still manageable by a non-expert user.

The other principal approach starts from a rigorous formal basis (i.e. the language of the expert) and tries to provide understandability (for the user) by means of suitable methodologies or interpretation mechanisms.

The traditional approaches to requirements engineering [IEEE 77] essentially followed the first track. These approaches comprise the origins of nearly all attempts to solve the problems of requirements engineering, namely SA/SADT and PSL/PSA (Sects. 2.2.7 and 2.2.8) and all the methods that are surveyed in [Balzert 81]. The main advantage of these approaches is their user-friendliness provided by easy comprehensibility. Their major drawbacks, however, are

- *semantic imprecision*
  The range of variation for a system that conforms to the given requirements is not exactly defined. Thus, the possibility for performing the important semantic checks for consistency and completeness is substantially restricted.
- *lack of an integrated methodology*
  An integrated methodology should not only support the elaboration of the requirements definition but also allow a homogeneous development of the requirements into an implementation.
- *insufficient support for checking the adequacy of a requirements definition*
  A requirements definition should provide a good feeling about whether the problem has been properly and adequately identified or not. This implies, for example, that ambiguities are removed and questions on the system's behavior can be uniquely answered from the requirements definition.

Rather than trying to achieve a compromise between understandability and precision by partial formalization, recent approaches follow the other track by starting from a strictly formal basis and by trying to establish a connection to the original intentions of the customer by suitable methodical means. One of the possibilities to be mentioned here is the translation from formally specified requirements into (standardized) natural language [Bauer 81], [Swartout 82], [Ehler 85].

Of course, there are also approaches that fall in between these two main lines of research. These approaches work with both, with informal descriptions as well as with strict formalisms, and try to bridge the gap between them by using the computer. The feasability of these approaches, however, that are mainly based on heuristics as used in Artificial Intelligence, seems to be at least doubtful.

We are convinced that a strictly formal approach (like the one introduced in Chap. 3) is more promising. Although the remark

> *It is well known that in English (or any other natural language) it is very difficult to make a precise statement. For this reason all branches of engineering use some kind of formalized notation, be it drawing or formula. Indeed, it is the development of these formal methods which have allowed those disciplines to progress so rapidly.* [Henderson 81]

might be misinterpreted in favour of the other line of research, the importance of formal methods cannot be subjected to discussion. In addition, there are parallels to other engineering disciplines where the basis for communication between the customer and the expert always is a formalism specific to the respective discipline. Thus, for example, in house construction nobody would promote the absurd claim for a formalism that would allow an arbitrary future house owner to produce a document that is binding for the craftsmen's work. There, as in all other engineering disciplines, the production of these documents is done by the expert who then explains the facts stated in the document to his customer.

2.2 Some Formalisms Used in Requirements Engineering

In this section, we briefly survey some existing formalisms that are used within requirements engineering for describing problems. Of course, due to the overall intention of this monograph, such a synopsis can be neither complete nor comprehensive. We rather try, on the basis of a common example, to convey the respective basic ideas and to give some hints on the strengths and weaknesses of the various approaches in order to have a somewhat more profound background for our particular treatment of formal specifications within the next chapter. For more comprehensive treatments of the individual approaches, the reader is referred to the respective literature or to standard textbooks on traditional software engineering (such as [Fairley 85], [Sommerville 89]).

2.2.1 A Common Basis for Comparison

In order to ease comparisons between the different approaches we are going to deal with, we will illustrate them by means of a common, fairly simple example. Variants of this example already have been used in [Partsch, Pepper 83] and [Broy, Pepper 83] for introducing particular aspects of the algebraic specification technique (Chap. 3).

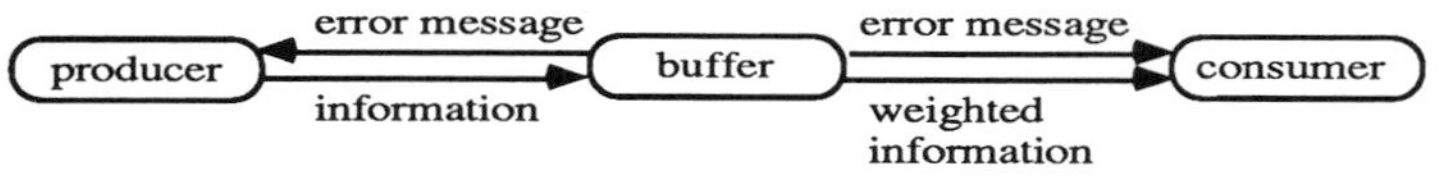

Figure 2.2. Producer-consumer system

The example deals with a bounded buffer in a simple *producer-consumer system* which may be sketched as in Fig. 2.2. The corresponding verbal requirements read:

1) *The producer sends information.*
2) *The consumer processes information according to its priority.*
3) *There is a common buffer of bounded length for storing and retrieving all information.*
4) *Storing (retrieval) result in sending an error message to the requester, if the buffer is full (empty).*
5) *All information in the buffer is tagged with priorities that determine the order of further processing.*

Like in many real-world applications, the problem described by these words and Fig. 2.2 seems to be clear at first glance. This, however, is certainly a wrong impression, since these verbal requirements are neither complete nor fully precise and hence leave ample room for specific interpretations. In the following we will even take advantage of this fact, since it allows us to take different views of the problem in order to emphasize particular aspects of a specific approach.

In addition to the use of a common example, we will further unify our survey by discussing the same aspects for all approaches to be introduced. These aspects are the basic concept of the formalism, available constructs (control structures, data structures, means for structuring, and miscellaneous additional features), methodical background, usability (expressiveness, flexibility, learnability and understandability, and range of application), and tool support for documentation, analysis, and adequacy checks.

We will start our considerations by briefly commenting on some formalisms (such as flowcharts, decision tables, grammars and regular expressions, finite state mechanisms, and Petri nets) that are frequently used in requirements engineering, although they have been introduced for rather different purposes. These formalisms have further in common that they are incorporated into more comprehensive formalisms, specifically tailored to the needs of requirements engineering, that will be discussed in later sections.

The reader not interested in details of the various approaches is advised to skip the following subsections and to resume reading with Sect. 2.2.12 or Chap. 3.

2.2.2 Flowcharts

A *flowchart* is a labeled, finite, directed graph where the arcs indicate causal relationships (the control flow) between individual operations (represented by the nodes of the graph). The operations are represented by boxes, and their meaning is

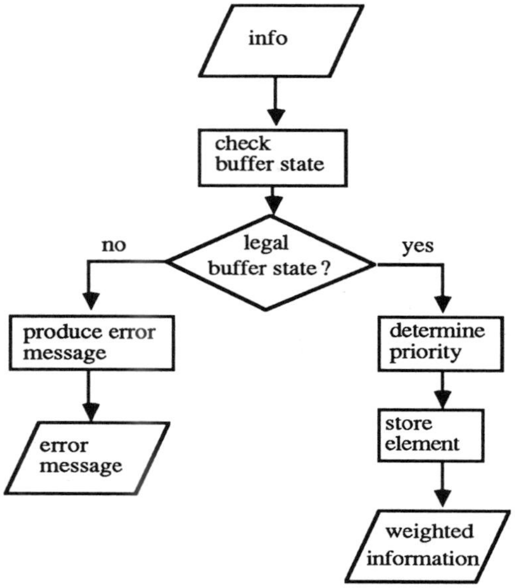

Figure 2.3. Flowchart for our sample problem

conveyed by appropriately chosen labels. In addition to denoting nodes by boxes there are also special symbols for input/output, manual activities, branching on condition, subroutine call, and parallel processing. There are no means for describing data structures.

For our buffer example, the activities in connection with storing a piece of information into the buffer could be represented by a flowchart as in Fig. 2.3.

Flowcharts can be used on arbitrary levels of abstraction, however, only for describing control-oriented aspects. The only available means for describing structural relationships is the symbol for a subroutine call. The use of flowcharts is widely considered harmful, mainly due to the lack of methodical support, particularly on how to proceed in constructing a flowchart.

Flowcharts are certainly not an appropriate formalism to be used in requirements engineering for exactly the same reasons as programming languages are not. At the best they may be used in addition to, or for the illustration of, other methods. Similar remarks hold for all variants of flowcharts, such as Nassi-Shneiderman diagrams, and also for data flow diagrams.

2.2.3 Decision Tables

Decision tables are a formalism for recording complex decision logic in a graphical way. They are widely used in data processing applications and have an extensively developed literature (see e.g. [Pooch 74]). The remarks on decision tables below carry over to all kinds of related formalisms such as event tables [Heninger 80], or transition tables (Sect. 2.2.5).

A *decision table* is a matrix that is segmented into four quadrants. The rows in the upper half of the matrix state individual conditions together with possible values (e.g. Y = yes, N = no, - = don't care; other discrete values are also allowed). The rows in the bottom half contain actions and possible decompositions into sub-actions (an X standing for the action itself). The columns provide the *decision rules*. Within each column the conjunction of all conditions having the indicated values is the precondition for a legal performance of the indicated action(s).

buffer full	N	Y	-	-	N
buffer empty	-	-	N	Y	N
storing requested	Y	Y	N	N	Y
retrieval requested	N	N	Y	Y	Y
store info	X				X
retrieve weighted info			X		X
produce error message		X		X	

Figure 2.4. Decision table for our sample problem

For our sample problem, we might have the decision table of Fig. 2.4 where, e.g., the first column indicates that information can be stored in the buffer provided the buffer is not full and there is a storing request but no (competing) retrieval request. The last column states that storage and retrieval are simultaneously allowed provided that the buffer is neither full nor empty and there are corresponding requests (but does not describe how to handle this concurrent situation).

Decision tables provide limited possibilities for checking formal completeness and ambiguity. A decision table is *formally complete*, if for all combinations of the possible values of the conditions a respective action is prescribed; it is *ambiguous* if two columns have the same condition part or if several actions occur in one column. Completeness and absence of ambiguity are usually not required.

Decision tables are a formalism for the compact representation of complex conditions to be fulfilled as a prerequisite for the performance of actions. The emphasis is on the detailed description of conditions. Actions themselves are not directly representable. The possibilities for abstraction are limited. There are intolerable limitations with respect to expressiveness mainly due to the fact that modeling a system's behavior is simply viewed as a collection of conditional rules that is provided by the columns of the decision table. Therefore, decision tables are a useful formalism mainly for representing small problems where alternative actions depend on a number of (usually interrelated) conditions.

2.2.4 Formal Languages and Grammars

Formal languages defined by Chomsky grammars (and derivatives such as two-level grammars or attribute grammars), accepting automata, or regular expressions, were originally introduced for the precise (formal) description of syntax and parts of the semantics of programming languages. Because many software systems involve processing of symbol strings or other data structures that can be defined adequately by grammars, they are used also in connection with requirements definitions.

Formal languages, in general, are sets of strings over some given character set. The language defined by a Chomsky grammar is the set of terminal strings that may be derived from a distinguished start symbol by use of the production rules of the grammar.

For our sample problem, grammars might be used to describe the structure of some of the objects involved. Thus, e.g. assuming that there are three alternative kinds of information, the data structure for weighted information could be described by the production rules

```
weighted_information ::= information priority
information ::= info 1 | info 2 | info 3
info 1 ::= ...
info 2 ::= ...
info 3 ::= ...
priority ::= ... .
```

Whereas arbitrary Chomsky grammars allow the definition of strings with certain additional structural properties, *regular expressions* are restricted to the description of strings only. They are formed from some character set by the operations alternation, composition and closure.

The data structure for weighted information could be described by the regular expression ((info 1 | info 2 | info 3) priority),

additionally assuming respective definitions for info 1, info 2, info 3, and priority.

The notion of regular expression can be extended to allow modeling of concurrency. One common definition of the effect of concurrent execution of two processes, say P1 and P2, is the interleaving of the execution histories ('traces') of P1 and P2. Interleaving of the regular expressions for P1 and P2 can be specified using an operation known as the shuffle operator. The resulting expressions are called message transfer expressions, flow expressions, and event expressions (see [Shaw 78], [Riddle 79]). *Path expressions* are another notation based on regular expressions which can be used to specify the sequencing of operations in concurrent systems.

For further details on grammars and regular expressions, see for example [Salomaa 73] or [Harrison 78]. A survey on the use of regular expressions for specifying software aspects is given in [Shaw 80].

According to their origin, formal languages are an adequate, well-known, and widely used formalism for specifying sets of strings and similar data structures. Due to their restricted range of application, however, they should be used only in addition to or as part of other concepts for formulating requirements.

2.2.5 Finite State Mechanisms

Like grammars, finite state mechanisms have been introduced originally for the description of formal languages as the set of strings accepted by some automaton. In slightly modified form they are also used for requirements definitions.

Like decision tables, *transition tables* are a graphical formalism for specifying the performance of actions as functions of the conditions that initiate those actions. Specifically, transition tables are used to specify changes in the state of a system as a function of driving forces where the *state* of a system summarizes the status of all entities in the system at a particular time.

Transition diagrams are an alternate representation for transition tables. In a transition diagram, states are represented as nodes in a finite, directed graph and transitions are represented as arcs between two nodes. Arcs are labeled with conditions that cause transitions. Transition diagrams and transition tables are also representations for finite state automata [Hopcroft, Ullman 79].

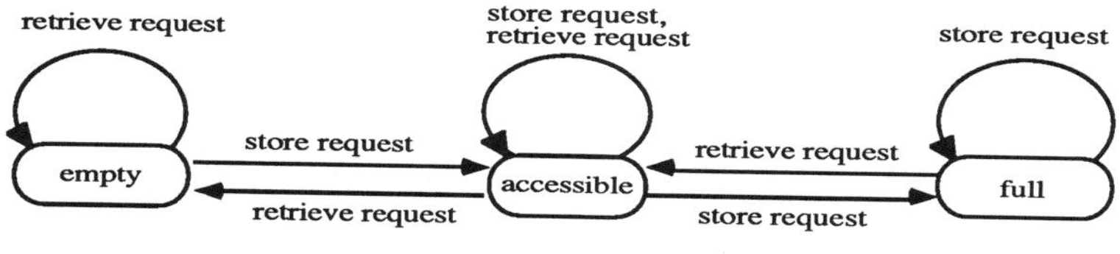

Figure 2.5. State transition diagram for our sample problem

For our sample problem a state transition diagram might be used to describe the changes in the buffer size depending on storage and retrieval requests. This is illustrated in Fig. 2.5.

Data flow diagrams, regular expressions, and transition tables (or diagrams) can be combined into *finite state mechanisms* for specification of the functional behavior of software systems [Babb, Tripp 80]. Using a finite state mechanism, a system is described by a data flow diagram consisting of a set of processes interconnected by data streams. Each of the data streams can be specified using a regular expression, and control aspects of each of the processes can be described using a transition table. An example for a data flow diagram is provided by the graphical representation of our sample system (Fig. 2.2), a definition of weighted information by means of a regular expression is given in Sect. 2.2.4, and a transition diagram for the buffer state is given in Fig. 2.5.

2.2.6 Petri Nets

Petri nets are a graphical formalism for describing dynamic aspects of system behavior which was invented in the sixties by C.A. Petri [Petri 66] in order to overcome the limitations of finite state mechanisms in specifying parallelism. They have been used to model a wide variety of situations and a vast amount of literature exists (see [Peterson 81] or [Reisig 85] for introductions and further references, or [Pless, Plünnecke 80] for a bibliography).

Conceptually, a *Petri net* is a bipartite, finite directed graph. The two types of nodes, which both also can be labeled, are called *places* (represented by circles) and *transitions* (represented by bars or boxes). Arcs only lead from one node type to a respective other one. An example of a very simple Petri net is given in Fig. 2.6.

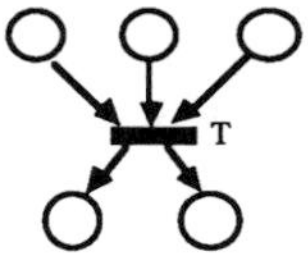

Figure 2.6. Example of a Petri net

The places in a Petri net are additionally marked by *tokens*. A transition is *enabled* if every input place has at least one token. Any enabled transition can *fire*. When a transition fires, each input place of that transition loses one token, and each output place of that transition gains one token. In the left part of Fig. 2.7 a marking of the Petri net from Fig. 2.6 is given where the transition T is enabled; the right part of Fig. 2.7 shows the marking after firing T.

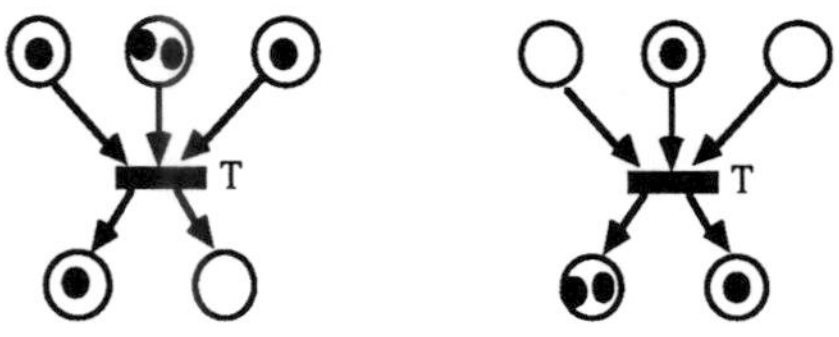

Figure 2.7. Firing of a transition

A Petri net is completely characterized by a graph, an initial marking of the places and the conditions for firing a transition. There are variants of Petri nets which mainly differ from the above description in the kinds of markings that are allowed for places and in possible further restrictions for firing a transition.

If, as above, tokens have no internal structure, the corresponding Petri nets are called *place/transition nets*. Modeling communication in our sample problem is one of the standard examples used to illustrate the idea of place/transition nets.

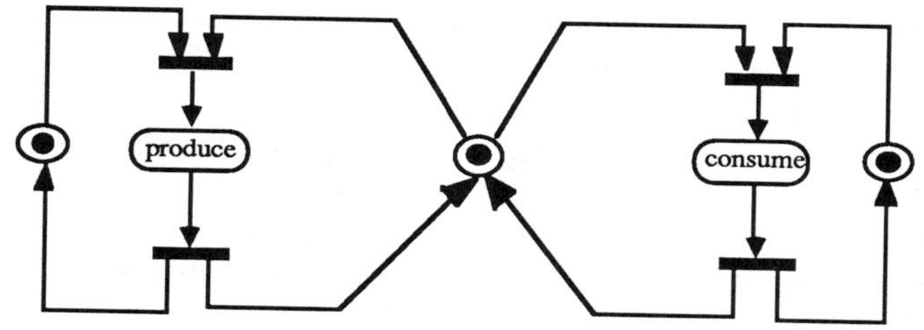

Figure 2.8. Petri net modeling "mutual exclusion" of processes (see [Bauer, Wössner 82])

In the Petri net of Fig. 2.8, by the rules for firing a transition, simultaneous access to the buffer by producer and consumer is excluded ("mutual exclusion"). However, the requirement on the restricted size of the buffer is not yet reflected. A Petri net that also deals with the restricted size of the buffer is given in Fig. 2.9 where the size of the buffer is the sum of the tokens on free space and occupied space (that are still to be supplied).

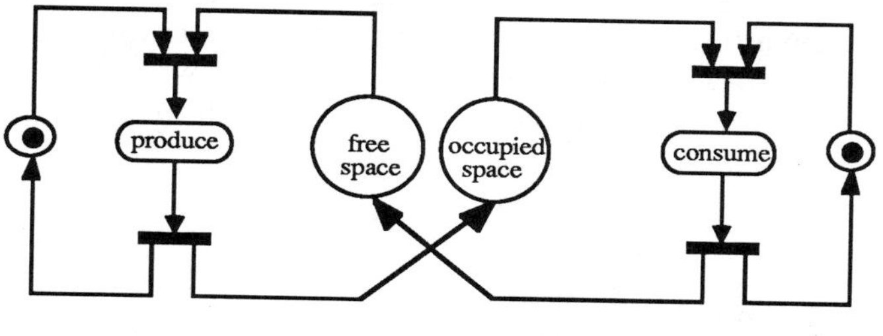

Figure 2.9. Petri net modeling a buffer with restricted size

The above examples just specify the overall behavior of the system. Like many other approaches, Petri nets may be refined by substituting transitions by subnets having exactly one input place (without incoming arcs) and one output place (without outgoing arcs).

One of the drawbacks of place/transition nets is the fact that the tokens have no structure and hence no further information is available, either for more precisely characterizing the objects that are passed between the transitions or for possibly restricting the firing of transitions depending on particular properties of the tokens.

In order to overcome the latter problem, *predicate/transition nets* have been introduced. The basic idea there is the use of two predicates (*input condition* and *output condition*) rather than one proposition for the labeling of the places. The tokens are then assumed to carry values for the free variables that occur in these predicates and in firing a transition (which is restricted by the validity of the input condition for the input tokens) new values for the output tokens are computed according to the output condition. For further details, see for example [Reisig 85].

In order to deal with the first problem, viz. more structural information about the tokens transmitted, combinations of Petri nets with algebraic specifications have been investigated (see for example [Krämer 87]).

Petri nets are a formally based approach and thus (at least in the form of predicate/transition nets) allow formal checks for consistency and completeness. Formality and a well developed theory also provide the basis for further checks, e.g. for adequacy checks by simulation. Despite their formal basis, they are comprehensible with reasonable effort, although some effort is needed to become acquainted with the formalism. They provide a sufficiently high degree of abstraction, in particular for modeling dynamic aspects of system behavior. However, their use is limited due to the lack of suitable constructs for modeling data structures. For Petri nets to be of practical use in the development of software, further development of methodology and tools is necessary.

2.2.7 SA/SADT

SA (Structured Analysis), the language of the methodology SADT (Structured Analysis and Design Technique), is a graphical formalism developed by Softech ([Ross, Schoman 77], [Ross 77], and [Ross 85]). The basic philosophy of the SADT approach is the *top-down modeling* of a system through successive refinement into levels of increased detail.

A system description in SA consists of diagrams which, in turn, are composed of labeled boxes and arrows. A box has the general form as shown in Fig. 2.10 where each of the arrows is to be seen as a representative for a whole set of arrows. The directions of the arrows as well as their meaning are standardized.

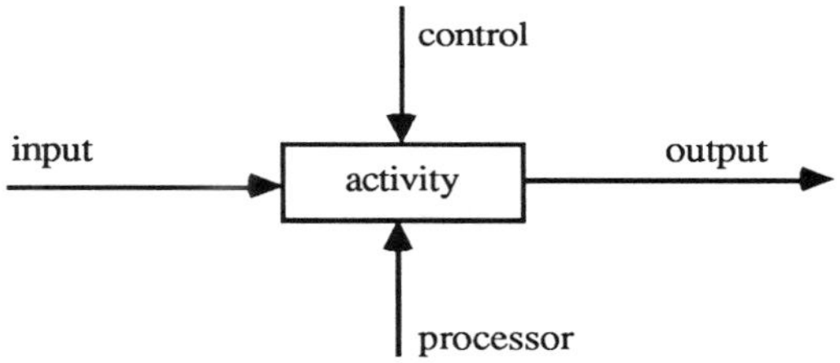

Figure 2.10. General form of an activity box

The arrows describe the interface of an *activity* (represented by the box) with its environment. An exception is provided by the processor arrows that are to be used to express any kind of support (by human expert, program, or auxiliary tools) for the activity described in the box, rather than a true interface. For our sample problem, we might have the diagram of Fig. 2.11.

SADT assumes that such a first description of a system (describing the system's behavior in a most global, very coarse way) is subjected to further refinements. An

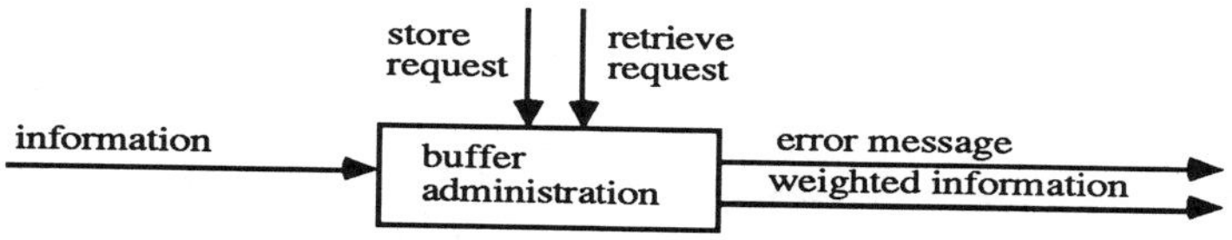

Figure 2.11. SADT diagram for our sample problem

SA description is refined by decomposing an individual box into a detailed diagram, i.e., into a new diagram exhibiting a more detailed description of the activity represented by the respective box. Each box in a detailed diagram is then further refined until a sufficient degree of detail is obtained. This process may be sketched as in Fig. 2.12.

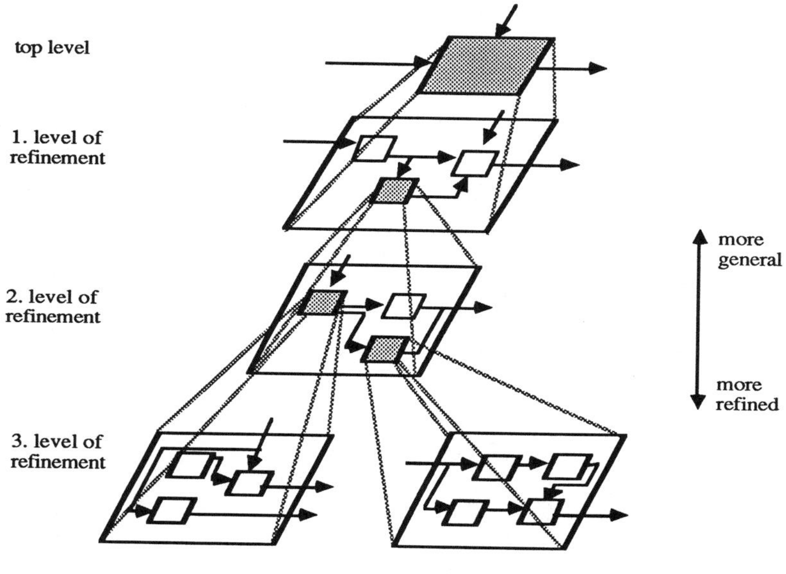

Figure 2.12. Refinement process in SADT

Applied to our buffer example a possible refinement of the activity *buffer administration* (indicated by a dotted line) is given in Fig. 2.13. A further refinement of the (new) sub-activity *store information* is shown in Fig. 2.14.

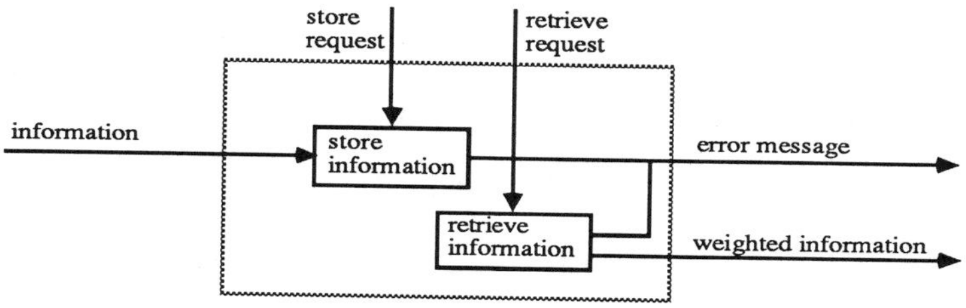

Figure 2.13. Refined diagram for our sample problem

The arrows in a diagram establish relations between the boxes. They do not reflect the flow of control, but rather describe the data communication between activities. Open-ended arrows in a detailed diagram refer to the corresponding superposed box. Although identical arrows on different levels of detail could be identified through identical labels, a special labeling convention is suggested for quick consistency checks and use of different labels on different levels.

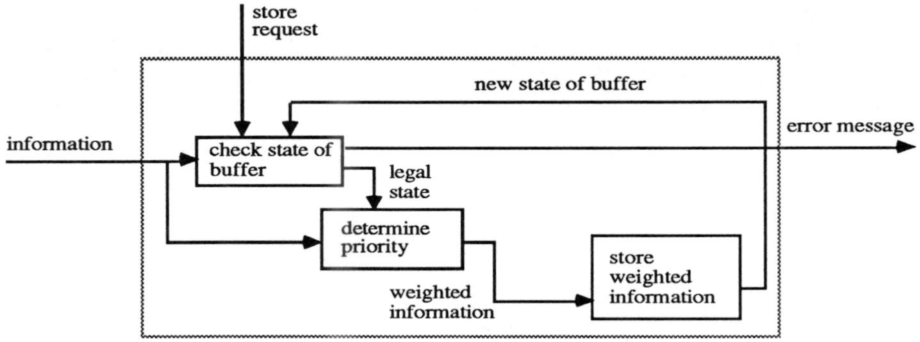

Figure 2.14. Further refined diagram for our sample problem

Dually to the activity diagrams introduced above, SA also provides, for the modeling of data, *data diagrams* where each box is of the general form given in Fig. 2.15. There too, analogous remarks on multiplicity, direction, and meaning of arrows apply. For our sample problem, we might have the data diagram of Fig. 2.16.

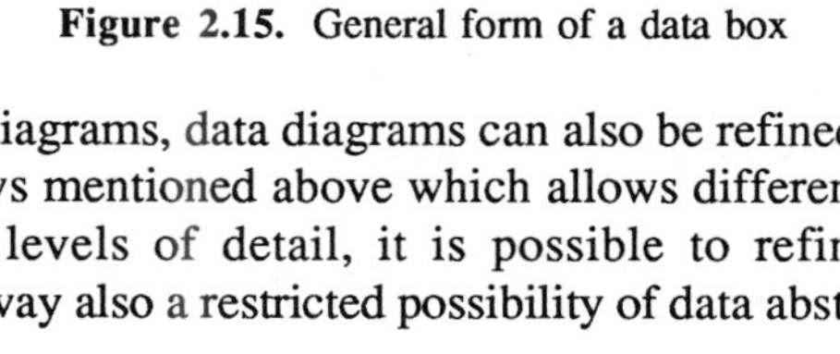

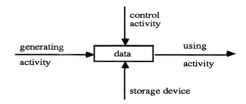

Figure 2.15. General form of a data box

As with activity diagrams, data diagrams can also be refined. Due to the labeling convention for arrows mentioned above which allows different labels for the same arrow on different levels of detail, it is possible to refine data into several components. In this way also a restricted possibility of data abstraction is provided.

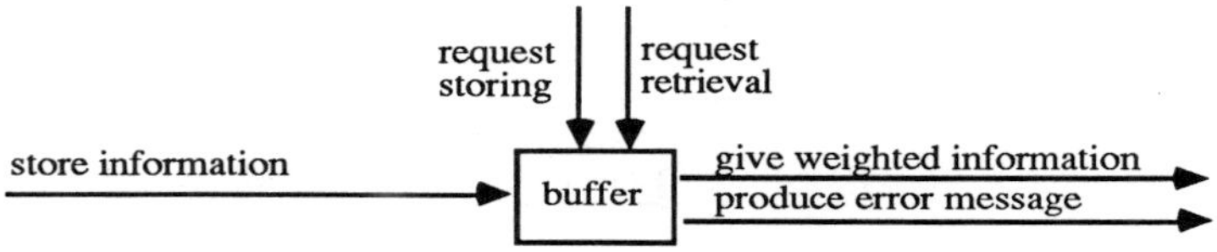

Figure 2.16. Data diagram for our sample problem

The two modeling concepts in SA, i.e. modeling of activities and data, reflect different views (with different emphasis) of the same system. Therefore, it is recommended to use both concepts simultaneously, in order to provide redundancy for (limited kinds of) consistency checks.

SA diagrams are to be drawn on particular forms that also contain further information (e.g., diagram number, creator, date, proof reader, date of last modification, etc.) relevant to the project and its organization. Apart from boxes and arrows, SA also provides further kinds of symbols [Ross, Schoman 77] which, however, are rarely used in practice [Ross 85]. Furthermore, SADT allows description of additional information by means of FEOs (For Exposition Only, extracts from SA diagrams), dictionaries for boxes, and glossaries.

SA/SADT is easily to learn and understand and thus a good vehicle for communication. It is also immediately and universally usable in its manual version which is independent of particular software. On the other hand, however, it is too general, not extensible, and, above all, too informal. This implies that important aspects such as consistency and completeness are not formally checkable.

2.2.8 PSL/PSA

PSL (Problem Statement Language) and PSA (Problem Statement Analyzer) are parts of ISDOS (Information System Design and Optimization System), the development of which started in 1968 at the University of Michigan. PSL and PSA are those parts of ISDOS that are to deal with requirements definition and analysis [Teichroew, Hershey 77].

Whereas SA/SADT follows a top-down approach by starting with a description of the entire system to be stepwisely refined, PSL takes a *bottom-up viewpoint* by providing a linguistic framework for the representation of individual requirements in the form of *objects* and *relations* which are to be collected in a relational data base.

PSL assumes that any system can be described by (typed) objects and relations between the objects and the object types. For most of the relations, the respective 'converse relation' is available, too. There is a sufficient supply of object types and relations ready-made available which allows the description of various system aspects such as flow of communication in the system, data flow, system and data hierarchy, project information, documentation, or system dynamics.

Examples for *object types* are

RWE:	Real World Entity, system component outside the software subsystem,
PROCESS:	system component that communicates with RWE,
INPUT, OUTPUT:	entity of information for the communication between system and environment,
SET:	set of collected and processed internal data.

Typical *relations* between object types are, for example GENERATES, RECEIVES, or UPDATES, with essentially the meaning provided by their natural language interpretation.

The flow of communication for our sample system might be described in PSL by

```
PROCESS buffer_administration;
   GENERATES weighted_information;
   GENERATES error_message;
   RECEIVES information;
   UPDATES buffer;
INTERFACE producer;
   GENERATES information;
   RECEIVES error_message;
INTERFACE consumer;
   RECEIVES weighted_information;
   RECEIVES error_message;
INPUT information;
OUTPUT weighted_information;
OUTPUT error_message;
SET buffer;
```

Of course, as any relational system, this linear representation also could be converted into graphical form (Fig. 2.17).

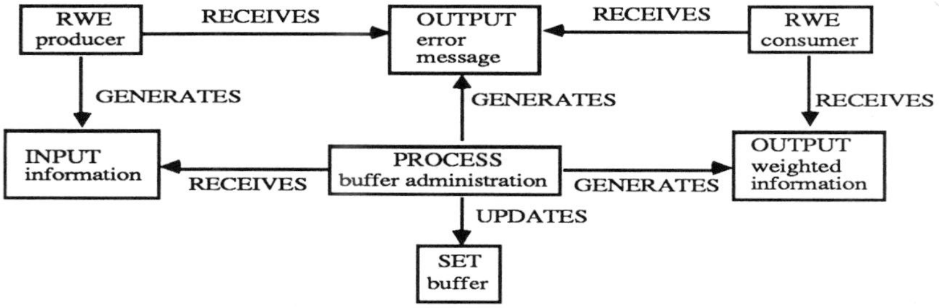

Figure 2.17. PSL description in graphical form

The only possibility for describing *control structures* in PSL is by texts within the PROCEDURE statement of a PROCESS segment. In addition to such a verbal description of an algorithm there are the UTILIZES and UTILIZED BY relations describing the calling structure of subroutines.

An example for these concepts is given by a more detailed description of the PROCESS store_information (along the same decomposition as used in the previous sections):

```
PROCESS store_information;
  PROCEDURE;
      If there is a request for storing an information into the buffer, first
      the state of the buffer is checked. If the buffer is in a legal state (i.e.
      if the buffer is not full) the priority to be attached to the information
      is determined and the weighted information is stored in the buffer.
      Otherwise a respective error message is produced;
UTILIZES check_buffer_state, determine_priority, store_information,
         produce_error_message;
```

With respect to *data structures*, PSL allows the description of hierarchical decomposition of data as well as the description of data manipulations.

An example of *hierarchical decomposition of data* is the definition of weighted information:

```
OUTPUT   weighted_information;
         CONSISTS OF priority, information;
                  GROUP priority
                        CONSISTS OF ...
                  GROUP information
                        CONSISTS OF
                            ELEMENT sub-info l
                            ELEMENT sub-info n
```

where

ELEMENT: characterizes an (atomic) object that may have a value;
GROUP: stands for a set of ELEMENTs and/or groups (GROUPS); and
CONSISTS OF: is a relation for the description of directed connections.

Again, this linear representation may be also given in a graphical form (Fig. 2.18).

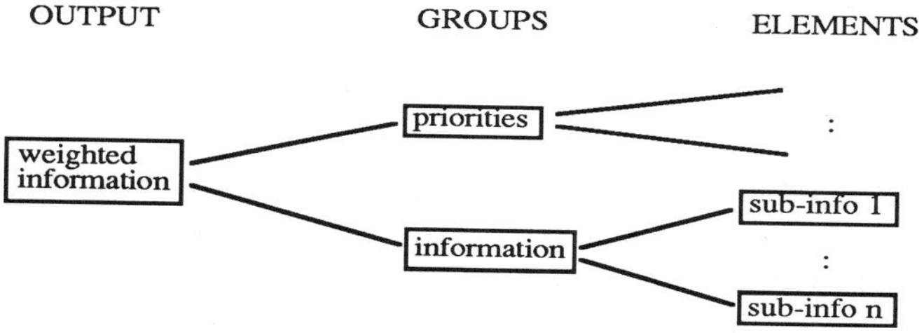

Figure 2.18. PSL data description in graphical form

Data manipulations in PSL are mainly described using the relations

USES: a process uses data,
DERIVES: a process generates data, and
UPDATES: a process administers or manipulates data.

In connection with these relations INPUT, OUTPUT, and SET are interpreted as data values (rather than system components as before).

Using these relations the data manipulation for our sample problem might be described by

```
PROCESS buffer_administration;
   USES information, priorities;
   DERIVES weighted_information, error_message;
   UPDATES buffer;
```

Analogous to the PROCEDURE statement for the description of control structures, there is a similar construct, the DESCRIPTION statement, to be used for describing, in an informal way, arbitrary aspects of data.

In addition to those concepts already mentioned, PSL allows the description of information relevant for the project, statements for documentation purposes, the description of dynamic system behavior, and quantitative statements (e.g., allowed intervals of data).

PSL descriptions are processed by the tool PSA, an interactive system working on a data base. As to the administration of information, PSA is capable of performing syntactic checks of PSL descriptions, of storing correct input in the data base, of checking consistency of the data base with PSL statements added later, and of automatically recording data base transactions in a data base modification report. For documentation and analysis purposes, PSA can generate various kinds of 'reports', each of which reflects particular aspects of the information contained in the data base.

PSL has a relatively precise definition of the syntax and parts of the semantics. It allows the description of many relevant aspects and system views in a way that is more precise and detailed as in SADT. Furthermore, it is supported by the tool PSA which provides relatively good support in documentation and analysis. However, there are also essential shortcomings, mainly with respect to expressiveness: PSL descriptions are sometimes clumsy and frequently unnatural, in particular with respect to abstraction, verbose due to a lack of compact representations, and often error-prone, since there is no possibility for data abstraction.

2.2.9 RSL/REVS

RSL (Requirements Statement Language) and REVS (Requirements Engineering and Validation System) are parts of SREM (Software Requirements Engineering Methodology) which in turn is to be considered as part of SDS (Software Development System) developed at TRW corporation [Alford 77], [Alford et al. 77], [Bell et al. 77], [Davis, Vick 77], [Dyer 77].

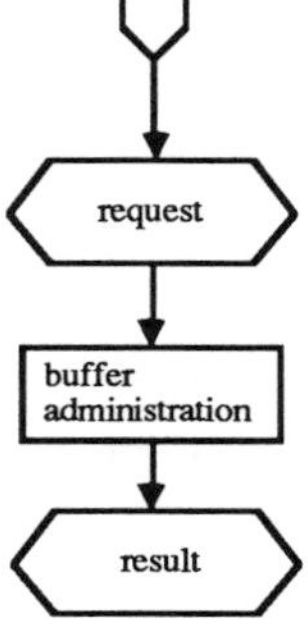

Figure 2.19. R-net for our sample problem

RSL uses the basic concept of PSL: individual requirements are described by *elements* (in PSL called objects) and (binary) *relations* between elements and element types and maintained in a data base. In addition to relations, RSL also allows *attributes* (that can be associated to element types) having values such as names, numbers, or text. As in PSL there is a predefined collection of element types, relations, and attributes.

RSL allows the description of requirements in a textual representation as well as in a graphical one in the form of R-nets (Requirements Networks). These nets are finite, directed graphs consisting of various types of nodes for describing element types and arcs between these nodes.

For our sample problem we might have the R-net of Fig. 2.19 which is the graphical counterpart of the textual description

```
R_NET: buffer.
STRUCTURE:
    INPUT_INTERFACE: request
    ALPHA: buffer_administration
    OUTPUT_INTERFACE: result
    TERMINATE
END.
```

In an R-net two classes of nodes are distinguished, primitive and complex. Primitive nodes, having one entry and one exit, serve for describing *processing units*; complex nodes, having several entries and several exits, are used for the representation of *control constructs* (such as sequencing, choice, repetition, or collaterality).

Primitive node types include:

ALPHA : indicating an action as a processing unit,
SUBNET: characterizing the macro expansion of a subnet, or
INPUT_INTERFACE, OUTPUT_INTERFACE:
for the description of the respective interfaces.

Typical complex node types are

SELECT: indicating a choice,
OR: for describing alternatives,
AND: for the representation of collateralities, and
FOR EACH: to indicate a repetition.

For each of the node types a special graphical symbol is available (such as ⊕ for an OR node, Fig. 2.20). Also for most of the node types, additional syntactic constraints are to be obeyed (e.g. in connection with an OR node, each of the outgoing edges has to be labeled by an explicit condition or OTHERWISE, Fig. 2.20).

R-nets describe the system's behavior in particular situations. In order to indicate that an R-net is activated by certain "influences" the relation ENABLES is used. Possible influences are described by INPUT_INTERFACE (where the data available at the interface implicitly define the condition which causes an activation of the net) and by EVENT (where the condition causing an activation of the net is given explicitly: if control passes the event node, the subsystem attached to this nodes is activated). Furthermore, an event may be delayed by data (expressed by the relation DELAY) such that "self-activations" (recursive calls) allow one to define operations that are performed periodically.

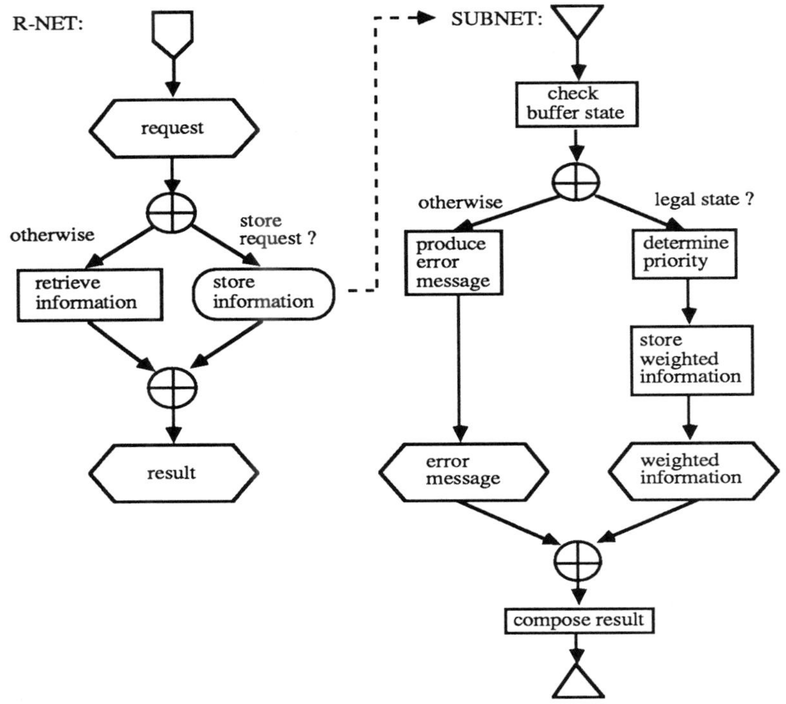

Figure 2.20. R-net with subnet

RSL also allows the description of logical relations between data structures. In particular *hierarchical relations*, use of data by different system components, or *data access* via properties of the data can be formulated.

Data structures that can be described in RSL are data composed of parts (keyword DATA, relation INCLUDES), files with sequential and associative access (keyword FILE, relation CONTAINS), messages and interfaces, and entities.

Data can be associated with a type (such as REAL, INTEGER, BOOLEAN, ENUMERATION) by the attribute TYPE. This type information can be used for simulations (cf. below).

An example of *composed data* is given by a decomposition of weighted information:

```
DATA weighted_information.
   INCLUDES
      DATA priority.
      DATA information.
DATA information.
   INCLUDES
      DATA sub-info 1.
         :
      DATA sub-info n.
DATA priority.
   TYPE INTEGER.
```

Interfaces exist in real-time systems between the software subsystem and other system components. *Messages* are comprehensions of data and files which pass interfaces as logical units. The same interface may be passed by different messages. Each message, however, can pass only one interface. An example in the context of our sample problem is

```
MESSAGE result.
    DATA weighted_information.
    DATA error_message.
```

Real-time systems have to manage informations on objects that are outside the software subsystem. These objects are described in RSL by *entities*, elements of type ENTITY. Properties of entities are reflected by associating them to particular ENTITYCLASSes.

Furthermore, RSL allows the description of *data hierarchies* (see above) as well as *hierarchies of nets*. Net hierarchies are formed by using the SUBNET symbol. Each subnet is to be considered as the refinement of some action and thus the restrictions on entries to and exits from subnets are the same as for actions (namely one entry and one exit).

Again, an example is provided by our sample problem. Here, refinement of the action store_information may lead to the R-nets given in Fig. 2.20.

Again, the same situation can be expressed by the text

```
R_NET: buffer.
STRUCTURE:
    INPUT_INTERFACE: information
    DO (store_request)
        ALPHA: store_information
    OTHERWISE
        ALPHA: retrieve_information
    END
    OUTPUT_INTERFACE: result
    TERMINATE
END.

SUBNET: store_information.
STRUCTURE:
    ALPHA: check_buffer_state;
    DO (legal state)
        ALPHA: determine_priority
        ALPHA: store_weighted_information
    OTHERWISE
        ALPHA: produce_error_message
    END
    ALPHA : compose_result
    RETURN
END.
```

In addition to the constructs discussed so far, RSL also offers concepts for documentation, for information about the project, for requirements on real-time software, and for simulations.

With respect to documentation and project organization, original requirements and design decisions, references to sources and auxiliary material, association of synonyms, and version numbers can be expressed in RSL.

In order to deal with requirements for real-time software, RSL allows the formulation of response-time requirements for certain paths in a net, and of requirements on precision and complex time relations.

For simulation purposes ALPHAs can be associated with particular attributes (called BETA and GAMMA) the values of which are executable descriptions similar to Pascal procedures.

Requirements can be expressed in RSL/REVS with a higher degree of precision than in SA/SADT and PSL/PSA. There is a real choice of external representation (text or graphics) and different system aspects can be formulated due to additional constructs. One has better possibilities for data abstraction than in PSL and requirements on time and performance constraints can be formulated, too. Due to a reasonable, well-structured, extensible set of predefined element types, relations, and attributes, requirements formulated in RSL are better readable and understandable than in PSL. The integrated methodology SREM offers acceptable methodical support for the construction of a requirements definition and there is a possibility of (automatic) simulation within the tool REVS.

However, there are also substantial weaknesses. The most important ones are the informal semantic definition of essential parts of the language, a lack of compactness in the description, difficulties with respect to modification (since fundamental principles such as "information hiding" are violated), a too strong emphasis on purely operational aspects within the R-nets, and insufficient support for adequacy checks and for the transition to later development phases.

2.2.10 EPOS

EPOS (*Entwurfsunterstützendes Projekt-Orientiertes Spezifikationssystem*, formerly *Entwurfsunterstützendes Prozeß-Orientiertes Spezifikationssystem* [IRP 80], or *Entwurfsunterstützendes Pearl-Orientiertes Spezifikationssystem* [Biewald et al. 79]) is a software design system mainly oriented towards real-time systems. It provides the languages EPOS-R for the formulation of requirements, EPOS-S for the description of the system design, and EPOS-P for formulating information concerning the project management and the administration of the product. As EPOS-S is closely related to RSL we will deal with it too, although it is intended for the description of system design rather than for the description of requirements.

EPOS-R

Relying on the view that the formulation of requirements involves people with completely different kinds of education, EPOS-R contains only "formal concepts" that are easily understandable without a particular education. In addition, EPOS-R allows an extensive use of informal, verbal descriptions, such that the degree of formalization can be determined by the user.

The formal concepts in EPOS-R are schemes for structuring, identifiable subtasks, decision tables, and a dictionary of notions.

For the formulation of requirements, EPOS-R offers uniform *schemes for structuring* which may be extended or modified in order to meet the particular needs of a certain project or application. The schemes for structuring consist of individual chapters which in turn are composed of sections. An example is given in Fig. 2.21.

Id. Nr.	chapter heading	Id. Nr.	section heading
4.	interfaces		
		4.1	...
		4.2	requirements for conceptual design
		4.2.1	strategies, methods, models to be used
		:	:
5.	functional requirements		
		5.1	....
		5.2	buffer administration
		5.2.1	processing a storing request
		5.2.1.1	...
		5.2.1.2	check buffer state
		5.2.1.3	produce error message
		5.2.1.4	determine priority
		5.2.1.5	store weighted information
		5.2.2	processing a retrieval request
		:	:

Figure 2.21. Scheme for structuring in EPOS-R

Optionally, the following chapters are recommended for a complete requirements definition:

1. system overview
2. current state and prerequisites
3. system configuration
4. interfaces
5. functional requirements
6. reactions to undesired events
7. requirements for precision
8. requirements for quality
9. requirements for reliability and safety
10. project organization
11. operation of the system
12. modifications.

Chapters and sections themselves consist of blocks which are either texts, descriptions of an identifiable subtask, references to a notion in the dictionary of notions, prompts of identifiable subtasks, or replacements of identifiable subtasks.

An EPOS-R requirements definition is usually composed of individual requirements for subtasks and individual statements on properties and abilities of the the system to be developed. These requirements can be named and are then called *identifiable subtasks*. The contents of an identifiable subtask may be given informally (by text) or formally (by decision tables). In addition, individual subtasks may be augmented with non-standardized attributes (e.g., “relevant to safety”). An example of an identifiable subtask is given in Fig. 2.22 (where (0) indicates the level of refinement).

4.2	requirements for conceptual design
4.2.1	strategies, methods, models to be used
	REQUIREMENT 3 (0): "producer and consumer communicate via a common buffer".
	REQUIREMENT 4 (0): "the buffer is of bounded length".
	REQUIREMENT 5(0): "storing and retrieval result in sending an error message, if the buffer is full, resp. empty"
	REQUIREMENT 6 (0): "retrieval is to done according to priorities". Identifier for priorities: DATA prio

Figure 2.22. Identifiable subtask in EPOS-R

Decision tables in EPOS-R are basically as introduced in Sect. 2.2.3, but with an additional declaration part and a linear representation of the decision matrix. Thus, the example from Sect. 2.2.3 is written in EPOS-R as

```
DECISIONPROCESS  buffer-administration
CONDITIONS:  buffer-full (Y, N),
             buffer-empty (Y, N),
             storing-requested (Y, N),
             retrieval-requested (Y, N).
OPERATIONS:  store-produced-info, retrieve-weighted-info, produce-error-
             message.
RULES:       (N, -, Y, N; 1),
             (Y, -, Y, N; 3),
             (-, N, N, Y; 2),
             (-, Y, N, Y; 3),
             (N, N, Y, Y; 1),
             (N, N, Y, Y; 2).
```

In the *dictionary of notions*, part of the EPOS data base, technical terms are defined and explained. It is to support the communication between all people involved in a project and to improve the legibility of the documentation.

EPOS-S

EPOS-S is very similar to RSL. It consists of *design objects*, *attributes*, and *relations* and also provides both linear and graphical representation. Again, similar to RSL, EPOS-S aims at not enforcing a particular design strategy, but rather at providing a variety of different design objects to be used for different design strategies. To this end there are design objects in EPOS-S of type:

ACTION:	functions, processes, and procedures;
MODULE:	modules and import-export relations;
DATA:	units of information;
INTERFACE:	logical interfaces;
EVENT:	events;
CONDITION:	conditions for the control flow;
DEVICE:	processing units.

Design objects are connected by data flow and/or control flow, where data flow characterizes the transmission of data between the design objects and control flow deals with the operational description of actions and operations.

For the description of the *control flow*, there are elementary operations (that operate on design objects) and control flow constructs (such as IF-THEN-ELSE). An example for a description of an action in EPOS-S is given by

```
ACTION:            processing-a-storing-request.
DESCRIPTION:
PURPOSE:           "processes a request for storing an element in the buffer".
NOTE:              "a simultaneous retrieval request must be excluded".
TEST:              "test parameters cf. document b13".
DATE:              30.7.1987
FULFILS:           REQUIREMENT 4 (0);
                   REQUIREMENT 5 (0).
DESCRIPTIONEND
DECOMPOSITION:     check-buffer-state;
                   IF legal-state
                      THEN determine-priority; store-weighted-information
                      ELSE produce-error-message.
TRIGGERED:         buffer-request.
INPUT:             information, storing-request FROM producer.
OUTPUT:            error-message TO producer.
REALIZATION:       PASCAL
PROCESSED:         micro-computer.
ACTIONEND.
```

In EPOS-S, *data structures* are mainly described using design objects of type DATA (which is used for describing all kinds of information appearing during the design process). For further characterization, either predefined data types or newly defined ones may be used. An overview of some data types is given in Fig. 2.23.

data type	meaning
FIXED	integer number with or without unit
FLOAT	floating point number with or without unit
DUR	time duration
CLOCK	actual time
CHAR	character string
BIT	bitstring
BOOLEAN	boolean expression
POINTER	pointer
<type name>	newly defined data type

Figure 2.23. Overview of some data types in EPOS-S

In a wider sense, also design objects of type INTERFACE and EVENT are to be mentioned in connection with data structures. Design objects of type INTERFACE are used to describe the exchange of data between the software system and its environment. As there is a strong coupling between data and interfaces, constructs similar to those for data are available for interfaces. Design objects of type EVENT are used to describe events influencing the processing of actions. There are three types of events: interrupts, periodic events, and events at certain absolute points in time.

Structuring in EPOS-S is provided by the design objects of type MODULE. A module allows the collection of different design objects according to some criterion. As usual, communication between modules is established by imports and exports (of actions and data).

EPOS-P

In addition to the linguistic means provided by EPOS-R for the description of requirements and by EPOS-S for system design, EPOS also allows one to formulate aspects that refer to project management and product administration. The respective constructs are provided by the language EPOS-P, which, like EPOS-S, consists of *objects* (here management objects), *attributes*, and *relations*. Typical types of management objects are activity, participant, means for realization, progress report, modification request, or error report. The latter two are tailored to the needs of product administration whereas the former object types support aspects of project management.

The transition from requirements described in EPOS-R to a system design in EPOS-S is an essential part of the EPOS philosophy. The particular way of proceeding is oriented at the design method chosen. The hints given for particular design methods are essentially the same as for SA/SADT: integral view of the system (as action, process-event structure, module, etc., according to the chosen design strategy) and successive refinement.

EPOS also provides support for the transition from an EPOS-S design to an implementation in an existing programming language. Depending on the degree of refinement and formalization, it is claimed that this transition can even be done automatically (which is not too impressive, as certain constructs in EPOS-S almost look like programming language constructs), or otherwise interactively. In addition, EPOS promises support for debugging, for automatic commenting (using information from the EPOS-S description), and for (automatic) updating of the design specification if the generated program is changed.

Similar to PSL/PSA and RSL/REVS, tool support is an integral part of the EPOS approach. All facts are stored in a common data base and are accessible by the tools

EPOS-D: generation of various kinds of texts, tables, and graphics for documentation,
EPOS-A: syntactic and "semantic" checks as well as generation of reports,
EPOS-M: support for management activities and project organization.

For the formal description of requirements, EPOS-R offers limited possibilities only, as it heavily relies on natural language, although this certainly eases readability and understandability.

More precise statements can be made in EPOS-S, the design specification language. However, here too, there are shortcomings, such as no strict separation between attributes and relations, no modern software engineering concepts (such as information hiding or abstract data types), and no really formal checks for consistency and completeness, which all have a negative impact on the understandability of an EPOS-S specification.

Unlike all the approaches discussed so far, EPOS has at least tried to provide an integral methodology for software development, although the support for this methodology certainly could be improved. Remarkable too, is the attempt to not only support the technical aspects of software development but also aspects of management and of project organization.

2.2.11 Gist

Gist is a specification language developed at the Information Sciences Institute of the University of Southern California [Balzer 81b], [London, Feather 82]. It mainly aims at providing a rich variety of expressive means for an adequate formal description of a system's behavior.

Gist is a textual language based on a relational model consisting of *objects*, *attributes*, and *relations*. A Gist specification is a formal description of valid behaviors of a system and is composed of:

- a specification of object types and relationships between them (which determines a set of possible states);
- a specification of actions (which define transitions between possible states), demons (which trigger actions), and agents (composed of demons and actions);
- a specification of constraints on states and state transitions.

Valid system behaviors are those state transition sequences which do not violate the specified constraints.

Object types are introduced by a type declaration which in its simplest form might just read

```
type buffer.
```

A type declaration may further refer to one of the predefined object types (real numbers, integers, natural numbers, characters) as in

```
type buffer_size definition natnum,
```

or it may introduce particular objects of some type, e.g. some objects as in

```
type buffer includes {empty_buffer},
```

or all objects as in

```
type buffer_state definition {empty, full, accessible}.
```

In addition, there is the possibility of forming subtypes and supertypes.

Relations between object types are introduced by their domain, e.g.

```
relation contains (buffer, weighted_information)
```

which, as it is binary, also could have equivalently been defined by an "attribute" of buffer as in

```
type buffer (contains | weighted_information).
```

It is also possible to have several attribute declarations coupled with a type definition, e.g.

```
type buffer (is_in_state | buffer_state, contains | weighted_information,
             has_size | buffer_size)
```

or

```
type weighted_information (info | information, prio | priority).
```

Any system contains a number of *actions* that are performed by the processes of the system. These actions change the state of the respective process. They may create objects, destroy objects, modify relations, or classify (or declassify) objects. The effect of an action depends on the actual state when it is called and on its parameters. For the definition of an action, Gist provides various kinds of statements, such as

- primitive statements (creation/destruction of objects by create/destroy, addition/removal of relations or classifications by insert/delete, modification of relations by update);
- call of actions;
- compound statements (conditional, sequential, alternative, preferential, or iterative behavior; grouping of statements to be considered as "atomic").

An example of a Gist action is

```
action store_information[information, buffer]
   definition
   if buffer : is_in_state = full
      then create_error_message[]
      else atomic
           create g | weighted_information || g : info = information;
           determine_priority[g, buffer];
           insert contains[buffer, g];
           update buffer_size of buffer to buffer_size + 1;
           if buffer : buffer_size = maxbuff
                      then update is_in_state of buffer to full
                      else update is_in_state of buffer to accessible
           end atomic
```

Here, an action store_information with two parameters, information and buffer, is defined. The sign ":" is used to denote the selection of an attribute associated with an object. "[]" following an action identifier indicates that the respective action has no arguments. "||" is to be read as "such that".

Demons provide Gist's mechanism for data-directed invocation of processes. A demon has a trigger and a response. A trigger is a predicate that triggers the demon's response whenever a state change induces a change in the value of the trigger's predicate from false to true. An example is

```
demon storing_request[buffer]
   trigger random[]
   response create information || a information;
   store_information[information, buffer]
```

(where "create information || a information" means "create an arbitrary object of type information" and random is to indicate that storing_request is triggered at random, rather than by a particular event).

Constraints within Gist provide a means of stating integrity conditions that must always remain satisfied. Constraints serve to restrict the set of possible states and to rule out invalid behaviors. Constraints to restrict the set of possible states may be *global* as in

```
always prohibited ∃ weighted_information ∀ buffer ||
        ¬contains(buffer, weighted_information)
```

or, equivalently,

```
always required ∀ weighted_information ∃ buffer ||
        contains(buffer, weighted_information)
```

(both stating that weighted informations only exist in some buffer) or *local*, i.e. restricted to some relation as in

```
type buffer (is_in_state | buffer_state, contains | weighted_information,
     has_size | buffer_size)
   where always prohibited buffer_size : buffer > maxbuff.
```

Constraints also may appear in connection with the definition of actions to state preconditions and postconditions to be satisfied.

Particularly for the specification of parallel and concurrent systems, Gist has the concept of *agents*. An agent is composed of a collection of actions which specify that agent's capabilities, and a collection of demons each of which specifies how the agent behaves in response to changes in the process state. An example is

```
agent buffer_administration with

demon storing_request[buffer]
   trigger random[]
   response create information || a information;
   store_information[information, buffer];

demon retrieval_request[buffer]
   trigger random[]
   response give_weighted_information[buffer];

action store_information[information, buffer]
   definition ...;

action give_weighted_information[buffer]
   definition ...
end agent
```

One of the objectives in the design of Gist was to provide a smooth transition from the formal specification to a running program. Like CIP-L [Bauer et al. 85], Gist is a wide spectrum language: it provides, in addition to the pure specification constructs, also constructs that are known from existing programming languages. In order to implement a Gist specification, the following steps are suggested [London, Feather 82]:

- eliminate high-level specification constructs by means of correctness-preserving transformations;
- choose and develop algorithms and data structures (still in Gist) that realize the system behavior given by the specification (again by using transformations);
- translate the low-level Gist specification into an existing programming language.

Although this way of proceeding is clarified in principle and also demonstrated with a number of substantial case studies, still quite a lot of non-trivial technical problems remain that range from a sound theoretical foundation for the notion of a transformation via suitable collections of transformation rules to appropriate strategies for the development of an implementation.

Although, due to the common relational basis, Gist has a lot of similarities with PSL, RSL, and EPOS, it is certainly superior to these latter approaches, since the semantics of Gist is defined formally (by state transition semantics) whereas the other approaches use a semantic definition in natural language. In this way, Gist provides the basis for the important (formal) checks of consistency and completeness, although, practically, these checks may become arbitrarily complex for particular specifications due to difficulties implied by the chosen semantic formalism.

Although Gist provides an enormous degree of expressiveness – but at the expense of clarity and comprehensibility – it lacks suitable means for clear structuring. This, in particular, creates problems with consistent modifications.

Gist specifications are abstract and liberal with respect to implementations, as details of an implementation are not given ("specification freedom", [London, Feather 82]). However, in some sense this is contradicted by the quest for Gist specifications being operational (which is a consequence of the chosen operational semantic basis).

Gist advocates an integrated methodology according to the view of software development as expressed in [Balzer et al. 83], which is basically the same as ours (Sect. 1.3). A difficulty, however, is caused by the fact that for some of the very high-level constructs of Gist a safe transition (by transformations) to an implementation is by no means obvious nor effective due to the lack of corresponding transformation rules.

In particular by the "English translator" (a tool for translating Gist specifications into restricted English [Swartout 82]) and the "behavior explainer" (a tool for the symbolic execution of Gist specifications [Swartout 83]), Gist provides assistance for checking the adequacy of a specification. Further possibilities, for example (formal) derivation of redundant properties, are not envisaged.

2.2.12 Summary

The formalisms used in requirements engineering can be split into concepts and formalisms adopted from other fields of computer science (such as flowcharts, decision tables, formal languages, finite state mechanisms, or Petri nets) and languages specifically designed for requirements engineering. Within the latter it can be further differentiated between formalisms admitting the use of natural language (such as SA, PSL, RSL, or EPOS) and purely formal languages (such as Gist). Assuming the reader to be basically familiar with the former class of formalisms, in the sequel we summarize the main aspects of the latter group according to the criteria given in Sect. 2.2.1.

Basic Concepts

SA/SADT and PSL/PSA were the first attempts to provide languages specifically tailored to the needs of requirements engineering. Moreover, they can be seen as the roots of the other approaches, as they represent the main conceptual approaches to formulate the requirements for a system.

SA favors a top-down approach that starts with an 'integral view' of the entire system and proceeds by introducing further levels of refinement where components are completely and comprehensively dealt with in more detail. For the description of the system and its components diagrams are used. These diagrams consist of labeled boxes and arrows and describe the interaction between activities and data. The meaning of these entities is conveyed via the respective labels which are formulated in natural language.

In PSL a bottom-up approach is followed which is based on a 'singular view' of particular aspects of a system. Here, rather than viewing a system (or components of a system) as a whole, particular aspects are selected and described, one after the other, using a relational approach. To this end PSL offers various object types and relations between them so that an individual requirement concerning a particular object (of some kind) can be described by its relations to other objects. The requirements for the entire system are given by the collection of all individual requirements, i.e. by all objects, object kinds, and relations between them.

RSL and EPOS try to combine both approaches, and also to extend them, e.g. with respect to the formulation of requirements for real-time systems. In RSL, (graphical) R-nets and validation paths are used to describe relationships between different system components (and thus to support an integral view). The elements of R-nets are represented by objects, attributes and relations (which reflects a singular view). EPOS provides three different languages, viz., EPOS-R, EPOS-S, and EPOS-P. EPOS-S is very much like RSL. EPOS-R provides a few constructs to formulate verbal requirements in a structured way. EPOS-P defines object kinds and relations for describing requirements concerning the project management.

All these languages rely, to a varying degree, on natural language. In contrast to this, Gist is a purely formal language. Its basic concepts are objects and relations for modeling states and (sequences of) state transitions for describing valid behaviors of a system.

Available Constructs

Whereas SA and PSL have no means to explicitly describe control structures, RSL, EPOS-S, and Gist offer quite a variety of different control constructs similar to those available in traditional programming languages. Although this is partly justified by the aim of being able to formulate requirements for communicating systems or real-time systems (where certain control constructs are necessary), the danger of misuse, i.e. writing programs instead of formulating requirements, is obvious.

All formalisms provide means for describing hierarchical compositions of data and their componentwise access. In addition, EPOS-S and Gist provide limited means for defining other kinds of data structures (arrays, stacks, or files in EPOS, and enumerations or substructures in Gist). The idea of data abstraction can only be found in SA, however, only in a limited (informal) sense. None of the languages supports the principle of "information hiding" and the combined definition of data structures and their characteristic operations, e.g. in an axiomatic way.

The possibility of describing a system in a hierarchically structured way is common to all approaches. Modular decomposition is indirectly possible in PSL and explicitly supported in EPOS and Gist. Structuring by parametrization is only possible in Gist.

Except for Gist, all formalisms allow the formulation of project relevant information. The differences are in the degree of formality and the amount of explicit constructs for this very purpose. Informations concerning documentation can be formulated in PSL, RSL, and EPOS. Constructs for formulating specific requirements for real-time systems (response-time, precision, etc.) are offered by EPOS and RSL. The latter also provides constructs for describing different kinds of simulations.

Methodical Support

For all approaches, suggestions and hints on how to proceed, in order to formulate requirements, are available. The various approaches only differ with respect to precision and the level of detail. However, except for EPOS and Gist, no methodical advice is given on how to develop a program that satisfies the requirements.

EPOS claims to provide an integral methodology – a methodology that covers the entire software development process. However, this methodology, based on an automatic transition from an EPOS-S specification to a program, only works satisfactorily for fairly low-level specifications that are already sufficiently close to a program. But this in turn then causes problems for a safe transition from the initial EPOS-R specification to this very EPOS-S specification, and thus does not really solve the problem.

Gist advocates a transformational methodology similar to ours. Major problems, however, are caused by the richness and expressiveness of the language, since for certain (sophisticated) language constructs neither rules nor strategies are available that could be used within a transformational development.

Usability

Flexibility deals with the problem of an adequate formulation of a problem. Since, except for Gist, all languages allow the use of natural language, this particular aspect of flexibility is not an issue for them. But it is not an issue for Gist either, due to the high expressiveness of the language. Flexibility also includes the question of whether different aspects of a problem can be described on appropriate levels of detail. This latter question can be answered positively only for SA, whereas for all other approaches difficulties of varying size have to be encountered.

Flexibility intersects with the problem of extensibility. Extensibility asks for the possibility of extending the formalism, if necessary. This may concern syntax, i.e. additional constructs defined in terms of existing ones, as well as semantics, i.e. concepts for new aspects. SA is not extensible at all. The other approaches are in principle (syntactically and semantically) extensible, however, not in each case in a simple and straightforward way.

For the practical use of a formalism, learnability and understandability are questions of central importance which, of course, should not be seen independently of other aspects, such as expressiveness, precision, or theoretical foundation. For the approaches dealt with in this chapter, the order of presentation reflects an increasing amount of effort for acquiring the respective formalism, but also decreasing understandability.

Some of the languages have been designed for use in particular application domains. Thus, PSL aims primarily at business applications, and RSL focuses on (embedded) real-time systems. The other languages are claimed to be universally applicable in the sense that their constructs are general enough to allow an adequate description of requirements for different application areas. Whereas this claim is vacuously true for SA, it is at least not obvious for the remaining approaches.

Tools

SA was originally designed to be applied manually. Meanwhile at least tools for documentation and consistent management of information exist. For PSL, RSL, and EPOS such tools have been integrated parts of the approach from the very beginning. For Gist they are available, too.

Likewise for all approaches tools for analysis exist, although there are significant differences with respect to the kind of analysis that is supported. As to SA, analysis is mainly restricted to syntactic aspects, whereas for PSL, RSL, and EPOS, additionally (redundant) information can be extracted from the underlying data base, which provides a basis for manual semantic checks.

A tool that allows the simulation of a requirements specification is available for RSL. Gist goes even a step further by providing a symbolic evaluator. Disregarding the possibility of extracting redundant information from the data base, none of the approaches, except for Gist, provides a particular tool for checking the adequacy of a requirements specification. For Gist, there exists an "English translator" (which translates a Gist specification into plain English) and a "behavior explainer" (which translates symbolic executions into English). Both tools are intended to provide a user with a (natural language) transcript of the formal specification in order to convince himself of its adequacy.

Summarizing Critique

Except for Gist, all approaches dealt with in the previous sections aimed at achieving a compromise between understandability and precision by partial formalization and restricted use of natural language. For all these approaches the advantage of easy understandability is compensated, if not outweighed, by severe drawbacks. These are mainly (Sect. 2.1.3) semantic imprecision, lack of an integrated methodology, and insufficient support for checking the adequacy of a requirements definition. For Gist, remarks similar to those concerning our specification method can be made.

3. Formal Problem Specification

In the previous chapter we surveyed some approaches to requirements engineering in the framework of traditional software engineering. All these approaches aim at providing a formalism for precisely describing a problem to be solved. None of them, however, except for Gist, allows the formulation of a formal problem specification in the (intuitive) sense of Sect. 1.5.

Starting with some introductory remarks about formal specifications (Sect. 3.1) and the formalization process (Sect. 3.2), this chapter introduces the essential concepts of how we deal with formal specifications of problems (Sects. 3.3 and 3.4). The individual constructs will be illustrated by means of small, fairly simple examples. In Sect. 3.6 we deal with more advanced examples in order to demonstrate the combined use of the different specification constructs. These examples will then be used in later chapters as starting points for subsequent transformational program development.

3.1 Specification and Formal Specification

This section aims at introducing, in an informal way, various notions and dictions which appear in connection with specifications. The emphasis is on giving an intuitive access to the respective dictions rather than providing definitions (in the mathematical sense). Precise definitions of those notions that are important for our further considerations will be given in later sections.

The definition of 'specification' (Sect. 1.1), specialized to requirements specification, captures all the kinds of requirements we introduced in Sect. 2.1. By analyzing these different kinds of requirements, we will find out that the functional requirements (describing the problem by stating what an intended piece of software is to do) play a distinguished role, as all remaining kinds of requirements make sense only, if the functional requirements are known. Therefore, in the following, we will concentrate on the specification of functional requirements and deal with other kinds of requirements only occasionally.

Consequently, we use the notion of a specification in a somewhat restricted sense: a *(problem) specification* is the description or definition of a *task*, i.e. a statement about some problem to be solved. Thus, problem specification in our sense is a synonym for specification of functional requirements in the sense of the previous chapter.

Typical examples of specifications are

(a) *Give a natural number which is equal to the sum of its proper divisors,*
(b) *Find all entries in the San Francisco phone-book with a two-letter family name,*
(c) *Given a natural number, find a greater or equal prime number,*
(d) *Give the greatest prime number,*
(e) *Sort an address file,*
(f) *Write an ADA compiler,*
(g) *Write a syntax-oriented text editor,*

all of which describe a certain task.

The tasks described by these specifications are obviously of a substantially different nature, due to different basic characteristics. Typical characteristics of tasks are

- *fixed* or *parametrized*
  If a task deals with one particular, specific instance of a problem, then it is *fixed*. If the task is of a schematic nature, i.e. depends on arguments, it is called *parametrized*. In practice, mainly parametrized tasks will be encountered.
- *functional* or *procedural*
  A *functional* task yields an object as a result without affecting its arguments whereas a *procedural* task changes some of its arguments (usually without producing a result).
- *solvable* or *unsolvable*
  A task is *solvable* if it can be fulfilled; otherwise, it is *unsolvable*.
- *determinate* or *indeterminate*
  A task is *determinate* if it is either unsolvable, or if it is solvable and the effect of fulfilling the task (i.e. the result in case of a functional task and the changes caused in case of a procedural task) is unique. Otherwise, it is *indeterminate*.

Among the examples above, obviously (a), (b), and (d) are fixed, whereas (c), (e), and (g) are parametrized; (f) can be both depending on whether a fixed target code is aimed at. (e) is procedural, the other ones are (more or less) functional. Except for (d), all of them are solvable. Solvability of (f) and (g), however, needs more detailed information. (a) and (c) are obviously indeterminate, (b) and (d) are determinate. (e), (f), and (g) are, strictly speaking indeterminate, too, as further information such as sorting criterion, target code, or more details on the editing process and the syntax are missing.

Each task is associated with a *set of solutions* that solve the problem given by the task. This set is empty for an unsolvable task; otherwise it is non-empty. For a determinate task the set of solutions is empty or a singleton; for an indeterminate one, it contains at least two solutions.

We characterized a specification as being the description of a task. Obviously, the same task may have several descriptions. Two specifications are considered *equivalent*, if they describe the same task. For example,

(a') *Give a perfect number*

is equivalent to specification (a) above, if we assume the usual (mathematical) meaning of the words used.

A specification is said to be *redundant*, if there exists an equivalent specification which is "simpler".

Simplicity is here to be understood in an intuitive sense, even depending on people's taste. A precise definition would require a rigorous definition of a measure for comparing specifications, which goes beyond the expositional character of these introductory remarks.

A special case of redundancy is a situation where simply omitting certain parts of a specification leads to an equivalent one. A trivial example of this kind of redundancy is

(a") *Give a perfect natural number which is equal to the sum of its proper divisors.*

A specification is said to be *descriptive*, if it describes **what** the task is (without giving a solution). If the specification describes **how** a task is to be solved, we call it *operational*. All the specifications above are descriptive. An example for an operational specification might be

(e') *Sort an address file in the following way:*
  (1) If the file is empty, nothing is to be done; otherwise:
  (2) Select the minimum element of the file and put it in front of the result of sorting the remainder of the file.

The properties of tasks carry over to specifications. Thus, for example, a specification is fixed/ parametrized or functional/procedural, if the task it describes has the respective property. For the remaining characteristics of tasks, viz. solvable/unsolvable and determinate/indeterminate, however, the dictions *satisfiable/unsatisfiable*, and *definite/ambiguous* respectively, are preferred in connection with specifications.

The various dictions introduced above are related in the following way:

task	**specification**	**set of solutions SS**
solvable	satisfiable	$\|SS\| > 0$
unsolvable	unsatisfiable	$\|SS\| = 0$
determinate	definite	$\|SS\| \leq 1$
indeterminate	ambiguous	$\|SS\| > 1$

So far we have not dealt with the language used for describing a task. Taking the specification language into account, specifications, furthermore, can be characterized to be *informal* or *formal*.

A specification is called a **formal specification**, if it is formulated in a **formal language**, i.e. a language whose syntax and semantics are explicitly established prior to its use; otherwise, we call a specification **informal**. Thus, in particular, specifications in natural language are informal.

Obviously, formal specifications entail the usual problems to be encountered in using a formal language, viz. correctness with respect to syntax and context conditions. For the semantic properties (of formal specifications) discussed below, both will be tacitly assumed.

Of course, the dictions used to characterize properties of specifications and tasks respectively, also appear in connection with formal specifications. Unfortunately however, again, further dictions are used in addition to the ones above. Thus, a formal specification is said to be *defined* or *consistent* if the task it describes is solvable, and *undefined* or *inconsistent* otherwise.

The meaning of a (formal or informal) specification is the set of possible solutions associated with the task it describes. In case of a formal specification this means that the task is defined by the meaning of the formal language. This, however, may cause problems, since the task described according to the semantic definition and the originally intended task may disagree. In fact, these problems might already occur in connection with informal specifications, in particular, if the task and its specification are given by different people.

These problems are captured by further properties that characterize the relationship between a (formal) specification and an originally intended task. These further properties are (with T denoting the original task, and T' denoting the task characterized by the meaning of the formal specification)

– *adequate* or *inadequate*

  A formal specification is called *adequate* (or *logically complete*), if T', the task described by it, is the same as the original task T; otherwise it is *inadequate*. Thus, in particular, the meaning of an adequate formal specification defines exactly the set of solutions associated with the originally given task T.

– *overspecified*

  A formal specification is *overspecified*, if its meaning (i.e., the set of solutions associated with T') is a strict subset of the set of solutions associated with the original task T. Thus, in particular, an undefined formal specification is overspecified, if the task it should describe is solvable. Likewise, a determinate formal specification is overspecified, if the original task is indeterminate.

– *underspecified*

  A formal specification is *underspecified*, if its meaning is a strict superset of the set of solutions associated with the original task T. Thus, in particular, an indeterminate formal specification is underspecified, if the original task is determinate.

Obviously, the above properties are not independent of each other, since an adequate specification is neither over- nor underspecified or, in other words, since over- and underspecification are particular kinds of inadequacy. Note, however, that the reverse direction of this implication is not true, since inadequacy captures in particular the case where the original task and the one described by the formal specification are totally different. Note also that overspecification is usually less problematic in practice than underspecification or other instances of inadequacy, in particular, if the formal specification is defined.

In the literature (e.g. [Hehner et al. 86]) further properties can be found, such as "determined" (there is only a restricted number of solutions) or "underdetermined" (any solution is possible). We will not use these properties, since in our view taking care of these properties is part of the specifier's responsibility.

It is important to be aware of the above-mentioned additional problems that could be introduced by formal specifications. Therefore, checking the respective properties of a formal specification is an essential part of the formalization process (cf. next section). However, since the latter properties characterize relationships between informal and formal notions, it also should be clear that it is impossible to (formally) verify these relationships.

Respective (formal) definitions for most of the essential properties of formal specifications will be given later in connection with the particular formalism we are going to introduce. First we discuss the problem of how to formalize an informally given task.

3.2 The Process of Formalization

Formalization is the process by which an informally given problem is turned into a formal problem specification. As mentioned earlier (Sect. 2.1), this process generally comprises at least three essential sub-activities:

- identification of the problem,
- formal description of the problem,
- analysis of the formal problem description.

3.2.1 Problem Identification

Problem identification means finding out what the problem is. The difficulties here mainly originate in the ambiguities and sources of misunderstanding inherent to the communication of different people by means of some informal language. Usually, the person who gives the problem is not the one who is to describe it formally; additionally, due to different educational and professional backgrounds, they do not speak the same language. Therefore, problem identification involves a mapping from one universe of discourse onto another one, and the essential activity concentrates on finding this mapping.

Usually a problem statement (implicitly) assumes basic knowledge about its context, the *problem domain*. For truly identifying the problem it is essential to make these implicit assumptions explicit by first identifying the relevant problem domain. Having done so, further steps in finding the above-mentioned mapping are:

- choosing a concept of the problem domain,
- representing the concept,
- defining the problem in terms of the representation of the concept.

Following [Webster 74], we will use the notion *concept* for "an idea or thought, especially a generalized idea of a class of objects; abstract notion". Hence, a concept of a (given) problem domain is an abstract view of the problem domain, free from irrelevant details, but suited to reflect its essential characteristics.

As we are concentrating on software systems, rather than on more general ones, we can further rule out arbitrary technical concepts and focus our attention onto concepts from mathematics.

In order to illustrate our notion of a (mathematical) concept, we consider the problem of building software for a traffic control system for a particular city. The problem domain here comprises, among others, the topology of the city, i.e., a street map, which has to be reflected as part of a concept of our sample problem domain. In a simplified view, a street map is a structure consisting of streets and intersections, and one straightforward concept for a street map is a finite graph.

Further examples of mathematical concepts are:

- sets, relations, mappings, functions,
- orderings and lattice structures,
- algebraic structures (e.g., groups, rings, fields, sequences, bags, trees),
- relational structures (e.g., graphs, Petri nets),
- formal systems (e.g., equational systems, grammars, automata, rewrite systems, deduction systems, systems of concurrent processes),
- differential equations,
- stochastic models,
- topological and geometric structures.

The choice of a suitable concept already entails a tremendous gain with respect to precision, as the possibilities for misunderstandings and misinterpretations are restricted. Frequently, in addition, the choice of a concept even amounts to a solution of the problem, as certain tasks for certain concepts are already generally formalized and solved.

Examples of this kind are:

- minima and maxima in orderings,
- construction and modification of particular algebraic structures,
- paths, cycles, or closures in relational structures,
- fixed points or zero valued arguments for equational systems,
- languages generated by grammars or accepted by automata,
- confluence and Church–Rosser properties of rewrite systems,
- deadlock or starvation in systems of concurrent processes,
- congruence, similarity, and translation for geometric objects.

There is a lot of freedom in *choosing a concept*. Only in rare cases is a concept obvious (even if the respective task is determinate) or straightforward, because of concrete hints that can be found in the informal problem description. Thus, for our sample problems given in Sect. 3.1, choosing a concept for (a), (c), and (d) is trivial, as it is already given in the (informal) specification. Likewise, for (b) choosing an alphabetically ordered sequence of strings as a concept is straightforward.

However, no such hints are generally available. Therefore, the choice of an adequate concept requires *decisions* with far-reaching consequences. Thus, not only the level of abstraction and the complexity of the formalization of the problem are affected, but later solutions to the problem are also enormously influenced. As a consequence, choosing an adequate concept is to be considered an art that requires great care, intuition and experience.

In general, a concept consists of:

- objects associated with certain object classes,
- operations on the object classes,
- relations between objects and/or object classes.

Since we did not assume any priorities among these constituents, this fairly general characterization of a concept comprises more restricted ones (to be found in the literature) that reflect particular views of a problem such as:

- function oriented,
- data structure oriented,

- event oriented,
- control flow oriented,
- data flow oriented.

For our further considerations, however, we will use the general characterization as given above.

Representing a concept has to deal with the refinement and the detailing of its constituents and their description on the basis of simpler notions. These may again be concepts in the above sense, or particular constructs of an available formalism. As there may be several representations of the same concept, again, a lot of freedom is provided here which involves further decisions.

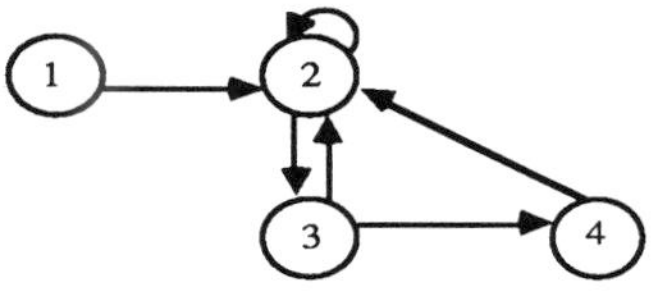

Figure 3.1. Example of a finite directed graph

The concept of a finite directed graph, which we used in connection with our sample problem admits several (equivalent) descriptions. A finite directed graph, such as the one in Fig. 3.1, can be defined at least three ways:

(a) a set of nodes and a set of edges (represented by pairs of nodes):
$(\{1, 2, 3, 4\}, \{(1, 2), (2, 2), (2, 3), (3, 2), (3, 4), (4, 2)\})$;

(b) a set of nodes and a pair of incidence functions i and o which associate to each node the set of its predecessors and successors, resp.:

$$
\begin{array}{llll}
(\{1, 2, 3, 4\}, & i: 1 \mapsto \varnothing, & o: & 1 \mapsto \{2\} \\
 & 2 \mapsto \{1, 2, 3, 4\} & & 2 \mapsto \{2, 3\} \\
 & 3 \mapsto \{2\} & & 3 \mapsto \{2, 4\} \\
 & 4 \mapsto \{3\} & & 4 \mapsto \{2\} \quad);
\end{array}
$$

(c) an adjacency matrix where component (i, j) has the value 1, if there is an edge from i to j, and 0 otherwise:

	1	2	3	4
1	0	1	0	0
2	0	1	1	0
3	0	1	0	1
4	0	1	0	0

Having decided on a concept of the problem domain and a representation of the chosen concept, it remains to define the problem in terms of the representation of the concept, which, again, entails decision making.

If, for our city map, we, for example, decided on definition (a) above, we still would have to decide on the association of streets and intersections with nodes and edges. One obvious possibility is to associate intersections with nodes, and streets with edges. However, we also might associate streets with nodes that are connected by an edge, if they intersect.

Which of several possible representations to choose depends of course on further details of the problem to be solved. For example in the first representation (intersections as nodes, streets as edges), it is easy to check how many streets are involved in an intersection, but more difficult to trace an entire street. As it may have a lot of intersections, it is represented by a path in the graph. The second representation, on the other hand, gives easy access to individual streets, but, for example, expressing that a street admits only one-way traffic is more difficult.

Other examples that illustrate the choice of possible representations of concepts and their dependence on further details of the problem are:

- concept: text;
  representations:
  - sequence of characters (e.g. for a scanner),
  - sequence of words (e.g. for a parser),
  - sequence of sentences (e.g. for a translation program),
  - sequence of lines (e.g. for a line-oriented editor),
  - tree of chapters, sections, etc. (e.g. for the retrieval of indexed terms);
- concept: mathematical formula;
  representations:
  - string (e.g. for text processing),
  - tree (e.g. for evaluation).

In Sect. 2.1 we already commented on the distinguished role of functional requirements. This distinguished role becomes even more obvious with respect to formalization: the set of potential concepts is primarily determined by the functional requirements, whereas the choice among the members of this set, the choice of a representation of the selected member, and the choice on how to formally specify the problem in terms of the representation of the concept also takes non-functional requirements into account.

3.2.2 Problem Description

If a problem has been identified properly, its (formal) description amounts to translating the result of the identification process into constructs available in the formal specification language. In particular, this means

- mapping the representation of the concept of the problem domain onto available constructs, and
- giving an expression in the formal specification language that describes the task to be fulfilled in terms of the image of the representation of the concept.

Similarly to other sub-activities of formalization, decisions are necessary here too, depending on the particular specification language. Whereas translation of the representation of the concept into available language constructs in most cases will be straightforward, the formulation of the problem proper as an expression in the specification language usually again leaves a lot of freedom. We resume this issue in later sections.

None of the decisions to be taken during the formalization process is unique, as we tried to illustrate by the simple examples above. Therefore a prime concern of any formalism for formal specification of problems is the provision of as much flexibility as possible in order to allow the adequate formulation of all possible representations of a variety of different concepts.

At least, however, any formalism for the formal specification of some task has to offer constructs that allow the representation of the constituents of a concept, i.e., objects and object classes, operations, and relations, and the formulation of expressions that reflect that task.

Conventional programming languages allow the definition of objects and object classes (called 'modes' in ALGOL and 'types' in Pascal), operations and relations (by means of function and procedure declarations), as well as arbitrary expressions. Therefore, programming languages are to be considered as specification languages, too.

However, traditional programming languages only allow the formulation of determinate, operational specifications. Likewise, new object classes can be defined only in a constructive, hence operational, way. Additionally, not all constructs offered by programming languages are really suited for problem specifications, as some of them, such as statements, procedures, loops, or pointers, are too implementation- or even machine-oriented. Hence, their use in problem specification would lead to too low a level of abstraction.

Consequently, a suitable specification language will contain only those constructs of traditional programming languages, such as function declarations or expressions, that are appropriate for formulating problem specifications on a rather high level of abstraction. Additionally, in order to overcome the above-mentioned restrictions to determinate, operational specifications, further constructs have to be provided for:

- formulating indeterminate specifications,
- expressing descriptive specifications, and
- defining object classes in a non-operational way.

In the following sections we will introduce such additional constructs. The language we are going to use is essentially a subset of the wide spectrum language CIP-L [Bauer et al. 85]. We will, however, not really be strict with respect to its syntax and also introduce notational extensions whenever appropriate.

3.2.3 Analysis of the Problem Description

The process of formalizing a problem may be considered finished, as soon as the soundness of the resulting formal specification is ensured. Most important is a check for adequacy of the formal description with respect to the originally given problem. For practical reasons, an analysis with respect to redundancy seems worthwhile, too.

Obviously, there is a causal relationship between the expressiveness of a specification language and the amount of effort that is to be spent for ensuring the adequacy of a formal specification: The fewer constructs a language offers, the longer, and thus the more "complex", expressions will be. Consequently, the relationship between the formal specification and the originally given problem will be less obvious, and thus, the more difficulties will be encountered when reasoning about adequacy.

Before dealing with adequacy itself, however, it seems worthwhile to first analyze the semantic properties of a formal specification, which we introduced in Sect. 3.1. Thus, for example, recognizing a formal specification to be undefined usually indicates a defect in the formalization process rather than unsolvability of the originally given problem. Likewise, differences between the formal specification and the originally given problem with respect to determinacy lead to a reexamination of the formalization process.

Next, an examination of the specification with respect to overspecification and underspecification is advisable. Very often, underspecification can be removed by simply adding further conditions. Similarly, overspecification frequently can be eliminated by weakening certain restrictions.

However, even if the respective semantic properties can be shown to coincide, and the absence of overspecification and underspecification is guaranteed, further considerations with respect to adequacy are necessary, which, again, may lead to redoing (parts of) the formalization process.

3.3 Definition of Object Classes and Their Basic Operations

In this section we introduce a formalism for defining object classes together with their basic operations in a non-operational way. This formalism can be used in the formulation of representations of concepts. Its theoretical basis is the notion of an algebraic type as introduced below.

In addition to introducing and discussing a general formalism for the definition of object classes, the emphasis in this section is on providing definitions of a variety of object classes as a basis for our later considerations. For more sophisticated syntactic questions we refer the reader to [Bauer et al. 85]. A detailed treatment of the theoretical background that is necessary for a fully formal semantic definition can be found in [Wirsing et al. 83].

3.3.1 Algebraic Types

Object classes can be defined by (systems of) algebraic type declarations. An algebraic type provides a rather powerful formalism for defining objects, object kinds, and their characteristic operations in an abstract, implementation-independent, and thus non-operational way. Objects are characterized implicitly by their construction, modification, and access operations, rather than explicitly by exhibiting their internal structure; operations are defined by properties describing their mutual relationship.

3.3.1.1 Types

To start with, we consider an algebraic type (see also [Bauer et al. 85]) that defines the truth values **true** and **false**, as well as the operations $\neg$ (negation), $\wedge$ (conjunction), and $\vee$ (disjunction):

type BOOL = **bool, true, false,** $\neg.$, $.\wedge.$, $.\vee.$:
  sort bool,
  bool true,
  bool false,
  funct (bool) bool $\neg.$,
  funct (bool, bool) bool $.\wedge.$,
  funct (bool, bool) bool $.\vee.$,
  laws bool x, y:
    true $\not\equiv$ **false,**
    ($\neg$ **true**) $\equiv$ **false,**
    ($\neg$ **false**) $\equiv$ **true,**
    (**true** $\wedge\, x) \equiv x$,
    (**false** $\wedge\, x$) $\equiv$ **false,**
    $(x \vee y) \equiv \neg(\neg x \wedge \neg y)$
endoftype.

The dots next to operation symbols such as $\neg$, $\wedge$, or $\vee$ indicate the number and the positions of their arguments. Thus $\neg$ is a monadic prefix operator and $\wedge$ and $\vee$ are dyadic infix operators.

Types are introduced by type declarations. A **type declaration**, as the one above, has the general form

type T = «constituents»:
  «type body»
endoftype.

A type declaration consists syntactically of

a *header* (starting with the keyword **type**) which contains:

- an identifier for the type (in the example above: BOOL); and then
- the list of **visible constituents** (defined by the type) which in turn consists (optionally; in arbitrary order) of symbols for
  - **sorts**, i.e., object kinds (in the example above: **bool**),
  - constants (in the example above: **true** and **false**), and
  - operations (in the example above: $\neg.$, $.\wedge.$, and $.\vee.$);

and a *body* which contains (optionally; in arbitrary order):

- symbols for the object kinds that are defined by the type (in the example above: **bool**);
- symbols for constants to be introduced by the type (in the example above: **true** and **false**);
- **functionalities** of the operations defined by the type
  (in the example above: **funct (bool, bool) bool** $.\wedge.$ states that $.\wedge.$ is a mapping **bool** $\times$ **bool** $\rightarrow$ **bool**);
- **axioms** (or **laws**), i.e., algebraic properties which characterize the operations semantically.

The header is part of a type's "interface": the type itself may be referred to by its name; and the list of visible constituents gives information about sorts, constants, and operations which are provided by the respective type for its environment, i.e., which can be used in other types or in programs that are built upon the respective type.

Rather than grouping the constituents of a type body according to their respective syntactic category, it is also possible to bring functionalities and corresponding axioms together. This is even advisable for larger specifications. For BOOL this would result in

type BOOL = **bool**, **true**, **false**, ¬., .∧., .∨.:
  sort **bool**,
  bool **true**,
  bool **false**,
  laws:
    true ≢ **false**,
  funct (**bool**) **bool** ¬.,
  laws:
    (¬ **true**) ≡ **false**,
    (¬ **false**) ≡ **true**,
  funct (**bool**, **bool**) **bool** .∧.,
  laws **bool** x:
    (**true** ∧ x) ≡ x,
    (**false** ∧ x) ≡ **false**,
  funct (**bool**, **bool**) **bool** .∨.,
  laws **bool** x, y:
    $(x \vee y) \equiv \neg(\neg x \wedge \neg y)$
endoftype.

The triple Σ = <S, C, F>, where S, C, and F denote the sets of all sort, constant, and operation symbols (inclusive of their respective functionalities) defined in the body of a type, is also referred to as the **signature** of that type. In case of BOOL, we have

$$\Sigma_{\mathrm{BOOL}} = (\{\mathbf{bool}\}, \{\mathbf{true}, \mathbf{false}\}, \{\neg: \mathbf{bool} \rightarrow \mathbf{bool}, \wedge: \mathbf{bool} \times \mathbf{bool} \rightarrow \mathbf{bool}, \vee: \mathbf{bool} \times \mathbf{bool} \rightarrow \mathbf{bool}\}),$$

i.e., the signature of BOOL coincides with the list of its visible constituents. In general, the signature of a type is a superset of the list of visible constituents, since the body of a type may contain additional symbols for sorts, constants, and operations that are not listed in the header. These constituents are "hidden" from outside the type and only serve for definition purposes inside the type.

The signature Σ = <S, C, F> of a type defines the **well-formed terms** of sort s, for each s∈ S, (inductively) as follows:

- every constant symbol of sort **s** and every identifier which is bound to the sort **s** by a quantification is a well-formed term of sort **s**;
- if $t_1, ..., t_n$ are well-formed terms of sorts $s_1, ..., s_n$ and f is an operation symbol with functionality **funct** $(s_1, ..., s_n)$ s, then $f(t_1, ..., t_n)$ is a well-formed term of sort s;
- there are no other well-formed terms of sort s.

According to this definition, obviously, $\neg(\neg x \wedge \neg y)$ is a well-formed term of sort **bool**.

For a type T with signature Σ, any well-formed term (of sort **s**) is called a **Σ-term** (of sort **s**). Σ-terms that do not contain free identifiers are called **closed**.

A Σ-term that is built from constant and operation symbols only, is called a **ground term**. Ground terms may be used to denote objects of some sort. An example of a ground term of sort **bool** is **true** ∧ ¬(¬**true** ∨ ¬**false**).

Conceptually, a type T is completely characterized by a pair (Σ, E) where Σ denotes a signature, and E is a collection of laws. A **law** (or **axiom**) is an arbitrary closed, well-formed first-order formula over equations and inequalities between Σ-terms.

Since we will have to deal with partialities (cf. Sect. 3.3.1.2) the symbol "≡" is defined to denote a **strong equality** which yields **true**, if both terms are undefined, or if both terms are defined and equal, and **false,** otherwise.

The simplest form of a law, as in the example BOOL, is an equation or an inequality between Σ-terms of the same sort, which is preceded by a universal quantification of its variables. In order to avoid notational overhead, a quantification (indicated by the keyword **laws**) may extend over several formulas separated by the symbol ",", which then means logical conjunction. This latter possibility was already used in the example BOOL at the beginning of this subsection.

Due to this (syntactic) definition of laws, parentheses are only necessary for formulating complex terms or for disambiguating first-order formulas over equations and inequalities. Thus in the example BOOL above, the laws could have been written simply as

true ≢ **false**,
¬ **true** ≡ **false**,
¬ **false** ≡ **true**,
true ∧ x ≡ x,
false ∧ x ≡ **false**,
$x \vee y \equiv \neg(\neg x \wedge \neg y)$.

The laws are not required to be minimal. In fact, adding properties, that are provable (cf. below) from the axioms, as additional laws, often helps in understanding a type definition. Thus, we could have added the usual properties of conjunction and disjunction, such as commutativity, associativity, and distributivity, which are provable from the given axioms. Note, however, that the law

true ≢ **false**,

which guarantees that these symbols denote different constants, is necessary here, since it cannot be proved from the other axioms.

The particular term **true** ∧ ¬(¬**true** ∨ ¬**false**) from above is also denoted by the term

¬(¬**true** ∨ ¬**false**)

since, according to the laws of BOOL

true ∧ x ≡ x

holds for arbitrary x of sort **bool**. Hence, the laws "identify" certain terms, i.e. they define a **quotient structure** on the set of well-formed terms.

In order to define the semantics of an algebraic type T = (Σ, E) with signature Σ = <S, C, F> and laws E, we first introduce the notion of a Σ-algebra:

A **Σ-algebra** A = $<(s^A)_{s\in S}, (c^A)_{c\in C}, (f^A)_{f\in F}>$ consists of

- a family $(s^A)_{s\in S}$ of carrier sets (one for each sort);
- a family $(c^A)_{c\in C}$ of objects such that $c^A \in s^A$, if the symbol c^A is of sort s;
- a family $(f^A)_{f\in F}$ of (partial) functions f^A: $s_1{}^A \times \ldots \times s_n{}^A \rightarrow s^A$, if the symbol f has the functionality **funct** (s_1, ..., s_n) s.

Furthermore, every operation f^A of an algebra A is **strict**, meaning that its application is undefined whenever one of its arguments is undefined.

As an example of a Σ-algebra we consider the algebra

$$\text{FSET} = (\mathcal{P}(\mathbb{1}), \{\mathbb{1}, \varnothing\}, \{\mathbf{C}, \cap, \cup\}),$$

where $\mathbb{1}$ denotes an arbitrary singleton set, $\mathcal{P}(\mathbb{1})$ denotes the set of all subsets of $\mathbb{1}$, and **C**, $\cap$, $\cup$ denote complement, union, and intersection, respectively. FSET is a Σ_{BOOL}-algebra with

$$\mathbf{bool}^{FSET} = \mathcal{P}(\mathbb{1}),\ \mathbf{true}^{FSET} = \mathbb{1},\ \mathbf{false}^{FSET} = \varnothing,\ \neg^{FSET} = \mathbf{C},\ \wedge^{FSET} = \cap,\ \vee^{FSET} = \cup,$$

but also with

$$\mathbf{bool}^{FSET} = \mathcal{P}(\mathbb{1}),\ \mathbf{true}^{FSET} = \varnothing,\ \mathbf{false}^{FSET} = \mathbb{1},\ \neg^{FSET} = \mathbf{C},\ \wedge^{FSET} = \cap,\ \vee^{FSET} = \cup.$$

Another Σ_{BOOL}-algebra is

$$\text{RNAT} = (\{0, 1\}, \{0, 1\}, (.+1)\ \mathbf{mod}\ 2, .\times., ((.+.)+(.\times.))\ \mathbf{mod}\ 2)$$

where 0 and 1 are supposed to be natural numbers and where +, $\times$, and **mod** denote the usual operations on natural numbers.

In order to be able to relate different Σ-algebras, we introduce the notion of Σ-homomorphisms, i.e. structure-preserving mappings between Σ-algebras:

A **weak Σ-homomorphism** Φ: A $\rightarrow$ B from a Σ-algebra A to a Σ-algebra B is a family of partial functions $(\Phi_s: s^A \rightarrow s^B)_{s\in S}$ such that for all f: $s_1 \times s_2 \times \ldots \times s_n \rightarrow s$ in F and all $a_i \in s_i{}^A$ (for i = 1, ..., n)

$$\Phi_s(f^A(a_1, \ldots, a_n)) \equiv f^B(\Phi_{s1}(a_1), \ldots, \Phi_{sn}(a_n))$$

where $\equiv$ again denotes a strong equality.

A weak Σ-homomorphism Φ where all functions Φ_s: $s^A \rightarrow s^B$ are total is called a **strong Σ-homomorphism.**

As an example we consider the Σ_{BOOL}-algebras FSET and RNAT from above. Obviously,

$$\Phi_{\mathbf{bool}}: \mathcal{P}(\mathbb{1}) \rightarrow \{0, 1\} \text{ and } \Psi_{\mathbf{bool}}: \{0, 1\} \rightarrow \mathcal{P}(\mathbb{1}),$$

defined by

$$\Phi_{\mathbf{bool}}(\varnothing) = 0,\ \Phi_{\mathbf{bool}}(\mathbb{1}) = 1, \text{ and } \Psi_{\mathbf{bool}}(0) = \varnothing,\ \Psi_{\mathbf{bool}}(1) = \mathbb{1},$$

are (strong) Σ_{BOOL}-homomorphisms.

For every signature Σ there exists a special Σ-algebra, the **term algebra** (or **word algebra**), denoted by W(Σ), which consists of all ground Σ-terms. Any other Σ-algebra A can be related to W(Σ) by a particular weak Σ-homomorphism i: W(Σ) $\rightarrow$ A. This Σ-homomorphism i, called the **interpretation** of W(Σ) in A, is defined by

$i(c) \equiv c^A$ and
$i(f(a_1, ..., a_n)) \equiv f^A(i(a_1), ..., i(a_n))$

for any constant c and term $f(a_1, ..., a_n)$ from W(Σ). The interpretation of an arbitrary term t will be abbreviated by t^A.

A Σ-algebra A is called **term-generated**, if every element of any of the carrier sets $\mathbf{s}^A$ can be obtained from the objects c^A by finitely many applications of functions f^A. Obviously, the above example FSET is term-generated. However, it would not be term-generated, if $\mathbb{1}$ was an arbitrary (non-empty) set instead of a singleton set.

An equation $t_1 \equiv t_2$ between closed Σ-terms t_1 and t_2 (of the same sort) is **valid** in a Σ-algebra A iff their interpretations $t_1{}^A$ and $t_2{}^A$ are both undefined, or both defined and equal. The validity of laws that are arbitrary first-order formulas is then defined as usual.

For our example we have, e.g.,

$$(\mathbf{false}^{FSET} \wedge^{FSET} x) = (\varnothing \cap x) \equiv \varnothing = \mathbf{false}^{FSET},$$

and, hence, $(\mathbf{false} \wedge x) \equiv \mathbf{false}$ is valid in FSET. In the same way it can be shown that the other laws of BOOL are valid in FSET, too.

A Σ-algebra A is called a **model** of a type T = (Σ, E) if it is term-generated and all laws of T are valid in A.

According to the latter definition, FSET is a model of BOOL. Another model for BOOL is provided by RNAT. Both models are obviously isomorphic.

A type T is called **consistent**, if it has at least one model; otherwise it is called **inconsistent.** Obviously, BOOL is consistent.

A type is called **monomorphic** if all its models are isomorphic. In fact, BOOL, as defined above, can be proved to be monomorphic.

The **semantics** of a type T is defined to be the family of all isomorphism classes of models of T. In the following the semantics of T will be denoted by GEN(T).

Differently from other approaches where the semantics of a type is defined as a distinguished model (e.g., an 'initial' or 'terminal' one, cf. [Wirsing et al. 83]), we prefer the above definition, as it is closer to our intuitive understanding of a formal specification: each of these models of a type definition characterizes a possible solution of the task that is formally specified by the type definition.

Because of the restriction of the semantics of a type to term-generated models, proofs by *structural induction* and *term induction* [Wirsing et al. 83] are possible.

The principle of **structural induction** allows the validity of a property

$$\forall\, \mathbf{s}\, x\colon \mathrm{P}(x)$$

to be proved for all models of a type T, if it can be shown that for all operation symbols $f \in$ F with functionality $\mathbf{s_1} \times \mathbf{s_2} \times ... \times \mathbf{s_n} \rightarrow \mathbf{s}$ (assuming without loss of generality that $\mathbf{s_1}, ..., \mathbf{s_k}$ are equal to $\mathbf{s}$ and $\mathbf{s_{k+1}}, ..., \mathbf{s_n}$ are different from $\mathbf{s}$, $0 \leq k \leq n$) the following holds:

$$\forall\, \mathbf{s_1}\, y_1, ..., \mathbf{s_n}\, y_n\colon (\mathrm{P}(y_1) \wedge ... \wedge \mathrm{P}(y_k)) \Rightarrow \mathrm{P}(f(y_1, ... y_n))$$
or $f(y_1, ... y_n)$ is not defined.

The base case for the induction is provided by all constants of sort **s** and those operations with result sort **s** that have no parameters of sort **s**.

A useful technical variant is the principle of **term induction** that allows us to prove the validity of a property

$\forall$ **s** x: P(x)

if for all terms t of sort **s** the following can be shown: if t is defined and if P(t') holds for all terms t' of sort **s** that are shorter than t, then P(t) holds, too.

Given a type T = (Σ, E), a property P is **provable** in T (denoted by T ⊢ P), if P can be deduced from the axioms E by using the first-order logical inference rules, one of the above induction principles, or the rules of partial logic [Wirsing, Broy 81].

3.3.1.2 Hierarchical Types

In order to be able to define object classes in a structured way, we extend our formalism for types and allow to build up (hierarchical) **systems of type declarations** where types may be based on other types. The hierarchical basing of a type T on a type T' is denoted by

based on T'

in the body of T; T' is then called a **primitive type** of T. If T is hierarchically based on T', all visible constituents of T' may be used in the specification of T. The **based on** relation is not transitive: if T is based on T' and T' is based on T'', the constituents of T'' may be used in T only if the body of T also contains **based on** T''. Of course, within a system of type declarations, **based on** clauses leading to a cyclic relationship make no sense and, therefore, are forbidden.

As an example of a hierarchical type we consider a simple definition of natural numbers [Bauer et al. 81]:

type NAT = **nat**, 0, *succ*, *pred*, .=0:
  based on BOOL,
  sort nat,
  nat 0,
  funct (**nat**) **nat** *succ*,
  funct (**nat**) **bool** .=0,
  funct (**nat** *x*: ¬(*x* =0)) **nat** *pred*,
  laws nat *x*:
    0 =0 ≡ **true**,
    succ(*x*) =0 ≡ **false**,
    pred(*succ*(*x*)) ≡ *x*
endoftype.

In this example, BOOL is the primitive type which is used in the definition of NAT. Rather than just referring to the respective primitive type by its name, one also could be more specific by listing explicitly those sorts, constants, and operations that are used from the primitive type. Thus, for the above example we could write

based on (**bool**, **true**, **false**, ¬) **from** BOOL;

in order to indicate that we use only the sort **bool**, the constants **true** and **false**, and the operation ¬ from the primitive type BOOL, whereas

based on BOOL

allows access to all visible constituents of BOOL.

Additionally, renaming is possible within a **based on** clause. Thus, for example, we could have written

based on (**boolean**, **T**, **F**, *not*, *and*, *or*) = BOOL

and then would have used **boolean**, **T**, **F**, *not* (instead of **bool**, **true**, **false**, $\neg$) in the definition of NAT.

Apart from hierarchical basing, the example NAT shows another peculiarity. In the example NAT, *pred* is a partial operation which can only have a defined value for arguments x for which $\neg(x = 0)$ holds. In the type definition this is formalized by means of an **assertion**, i.e. a Σ-term of sort **bool** that denotes a property which restricts the domain of an operation to those arguments for which the property is fulfilled.

Equivalently, a special (semantic) predicate **defined** could be used. In this case the functionality of *pred* had to be changed into

funct (**nat**) **nat** *pred*,

and the law

defined(*pred*(*x*)) $\Rightarrow$ $(x = 0) \equiv$ **false**

had to be added.

From this latter implication we have immediately that

$(x = 0) \equiv$ **true** $\Rightarrow$ $\neg$ **defined**(*pred*(*x*))

holds, too. But we also see that

$(x = 0) \equiv$ **true** $\Rightarrow$ **defined**(*pred*(*x*))

does not hold in general.

When using partial operations in type definitions, some care has to be taken in order not to introduce inconsistencies. For example, adding the axiom

$succ(pred(x)) \equiv x$

to the definition of NAT would result in an inconsistency. On the one hand, according to this axiom, we would have $succ(pred(0)) \equiv 0$. On the other hand, due to the assertion of *pred*, *pred*(0) is undefined and thus, due to the strictness of operations, *succ*(*pred*(0)) is undefined, too.

In order to avoid inconsistencies in connection with a partial operation f, it has to be ensured that either f is applied only to arguments that fulfil the respective assertion, as in the example NAT above, or applications of f are safe-guarded by means of conditional axioms. Thus, for example, adding

$(x = 0 \equiv$ **false**$)$ $\Rightarrow$ $(succ(pred(x)) \equiv x)$

to NAT above would do no harm, in particular, as it is a property that is provable for NAT.

Analogous to the assertions in functionalities which restrict the domain of the respective operation, domain restrictions in the quantification of the laws are allowed. Thus, for example (for t_1 and t_2 being terms of the same sort and b being a term of sort **bool**)

laws m x: b: $t_1 \equiv t_2$

is just short for

laws m x: ($b \equiv$ **true**) $\Rightarrow$ ($t_1 \equiv t_2$).

As a notational variant, we further define

laws m x: $t_1 \equiv t_2$ **provided** b

to be equivalent to the previous forms.

A (hierarchical) type T is completely characterized by a tuple (Σ, E, P_1, ..., P_n) where, for $1 \le i \le n$, the $P_i = (\Sigma_i, E_i)$ denote its primitive types with $\Sigma_i \subseteq \Sigma$. For defining the semantics of a hierarchical type further properties are needed.

For a hierarchical type T we require that a model A is **hierarchy-preserving**, i.e. that for every primitive type P_i of T the restriction of A to the signature of P_i is a model of P_i, and thus, in particular, is generated by the operations of A that correspond to the operation symbols of P_i.

Another important property for a hierarchical type T is **persistency** which means that every model of the primitive types P_i can be extended to a model of T. This guarantees that types may be implemented independent of the components which are based on them. If the primitive types are monomorphic then the type T is either persistent or inconsistent.

The **semantics** of a persistent type T then is the family of all isomorphism classes of models of T.

In a hierarchical type T = (Σ, E, P) with P = (Σ_P, E_P) terms may be distinguished with respect to their sort: A Σ-term t is **of primitive sort**, if it is of a sort from Σ_P; otherwise, it is **of non-primitive sort**. Thus, for NAT, the term *succ*(*succ*(0)) =0 is of primitive sort, whereas *succ*(*succ*(0)) is of non-primitive sort.

A hierarchical type T = (Σ, E, P) with P = (Σ_P, E_P) is called **sufficiently complete**, if for every ground term $t \in W(\Sigma)$ of primitive sort either $\neg$ **defined**(t) or $t \equiv p$ for some term $p \in W(\Sigma_P)$ is provable in T. A sufficiently complete type is hierarchy-preserving [Wirsing et al. 83]. A (syntactic) criterion that guarantees sufficient completeness is given in [Guttag, Horning 78].

Obviously, the example NAT is sufficiently complete: all ground terms t of primitive sort (here: **bool**) are of the form x =0 where x is a ground term of non-primitive sort; if x is 0 or of the form *succ*(...), t may be reduced to the term **true**, respectively **false**, according to the first two axioms of NAT; if x is of the form *pred*(...), then either x is undefined (due to the assertion of *pred*) and so is t, or x may be reduced to a term of the form 0 or *succ*(...), using the third axiom of NAT.

For a sufficiently complete type the axioms may be used for "evaluating" ground terms of primitive sort. Thus, for the type NAT from above we have

pred(*succ*(*pred*(*succ*(*succ*(0))))) =0 $\equiv$
pred(*succ*(*succ*(0))) =0 $\equiv$
succ(0) =0 $\equiv$ **false**.

3.3.1.3 Type Schemes

Types, as introduced above, can be used not only for defining elementary object kinds such as numbers, truth values, characters, but can be used also for specifying composite object kinds.

As an example we consider sequences of natural numbers. A *sequence* (sometimes also called *list*) is a sequential structure consisting of an arbitrary number of elements. A sequence containing no elements is called empty; otherwise, it is called non-empty. A sequence can be extended by adding elements to it. The elements in a sequence can be accessed sequentially: an operation **first** yields the first element of the sequence; an operation **rest** yields the sequence without the first element.

Sequences of natural numbers can be specified by the (hierarchical) type

type NATSEQU = **natsequ**, <>, .=<>, .≠<>, **first**., **rest**., .+.:
  based on BOOL,
  based on NAT,
  sort natsequ,
  natsequ <>,
  funct (**natsequ**) **bool** .=<>,
  funct (**natsequ**) **bool** .≠<>,
  funct (**natsequ** *s*: *s* ≠<>) **nat first**.,
  funct (**natsequ** *s*: *s* ≠<>) **natsequ rest**.,
  funct (**nat**, **natsequ**) **natsequ** .+.,
  laws nat *x*, **natsequ** *s*:
    <> =<> ≡ **true**,
    (*x* + *s*) =<> ≡ **false**,
    s ≠<> ≡ ¬(*s* =<>),
    first(*x* + *s*) ≡ *x*,
    rest(*x* + *s*) ≡ *s*
endoftype.

On closer inspection of this specification we see that, except for the sort symbol **nat**, the above specification does not use any other constituent defined by NAT. This means that a specification of sequences of other object kinds will follow the same pattern. Since a similar phenomenon can be observed with other composite object kinds, it seems appropriate to extend our type mechanism further and to also allow parametrized types.

Parametrized types are also called **type schemes** (or **generic types**). A declaration of a parametrized type has the general form

type T = («parameters») «constituents»:
  «type body»
endoftype.

Different to types, type schemes allow us to express certain structural principles for composite object kinds. Thus, a type scheme SEQU which gives the essential properties of the sequential composition of objects into a new (composed) object can be formally defined as follows:

type SEQU = (**sort m**) **sequ**, <>, .=<>, .≠<>, **first**., **rest**., .+.:
  based on BOOL,
  sort sequ,
  sequ <>,
  funct (**sequ**) **bool** .=<>,

```
    funct (sequ) bool .≠<>,
    funct (sequ s: s ≠<>) m first.,
    funct (sequ s: s ≠<>) sequ rest.,
    funct (m, sequ) sequ .+.,
    laws m x, sequ s:
        <> =<> ≡ true,
        (x + s) =<> ≡ false,
        s ≠<> ≡ ¬(s =<>),
        first(x + s) ≡ x,
        rest(x + s) ≡ s
endoftype.
```

The (formal) parameter **m** of SEQU is just a sort symbol. In general, arbitrary collections of constituents, i.e. sorts, constants, and operations, are allowed. Additionally, these may be restricted by assertions.

Type schemes may also be used in the definition of other types by the mechanism of instantiation. **Instantiation** is a second means (different from the **based on** clause) for structuring that may appear in a type body. It is indicated by the keyword **include** and defined by textual substitution (similar to 'macro expansion') of the body and, as the **based on** clause, coupled with the possibility of renaming. Using this mechanism, e.g., the classical example of a stack can be defined by

```
type STACK = (sort m) stack, <>, .=<>, .≠<>, top., pop., .push.:
    include SEQU(m) as (stack, <>, .=<>, .≠<>, top., pop., .push.)
endoftype
```

which, by the definition of instantiation, is equivalent to the explicit specification

```
type STACK = (sort m) stack, <>, .=<>, .≠<>, top., pop., .push.:
    based on BOOL,
    sort stack,
    stack <>,
    funct (stack) bool .=<>,
    funct (stack) bool .≠<>,
    funct (stack s: s ≠<>) m top.,
    funct (stack s: s ≠<>) stack pop.,
    funct (m, stack) stack .push.,
    laws m x, stack s:
        <> =<> ≡ true,
        (x push s) =<> ≡ false,
        s ≠<> ≡ ¬(s =<>),
        top(x push s) ≡ x,
        pop(x push s) ≡ s
endoftype.
```

In this example, <>, =<>, and ≠<> have not been renamed. Constituents that are not renamed in an instantiation simply may be left out. Thus, we also could have written

```
include SEQU(m) as (stack,,,, top., pop., .push.).
```

If only the sort is to be renamed, an instantiation can be further abbreviated to

include SEQU(**m**) **as** (**stack**, ...),

and if an instantiation is to be done without any renaming, we may simply use

include SEQU(**m**).

Of course, instantiation also may be used to define concrete instances of type schemes. Thus, for example, sequences of natural numbers also can be defined by

type NATSEQU = **natsequ**, <>, .=<>, .≠<>, **first**., **rest**., .+.:
  include SEQU(**nat**) **as** (**natsequ**, ...)
endoftype.

Type schemes do not have an independent semantics. They are only defined via instantiation.

3.3.1.4 "Degenerated" Types

In general, types (and type schemes) define new object kinds and operations. However, there are also "degenerated" forms of types which define just operations (and no new object kind). Of course, such a type has to be based on some other type T (via **based on**, instantiation, or parametrization). Therefore, it is called an **extension** of T.

A simple extension of the type NAT is

type NAT_1 = **nat**, 0, *succ*, *pred*, .=0, .=., .<.:
  include NAT,
  funct (**nat**, **nat**) **bool** .=.,
  funct (**nat**, **nat**) **bool** .<.,
  laws nat *x*, *y*:
    $x = 0 \equiv x = 0$,
    $x = y \equiv y = x$,
    $succ(x) = succ(y) \equiv x = y$,
    $x < 0 \equiv$ **false**,
    $0 < succ(x) \equiv$ **true**,
    $succ(x) < succ(y) \equiv x < y$
endoftype.

In this way, any operation over some type T can be defined via an appropriate extension of T.

Another instance of degeneration is given by types which define neither new object kinds nor new operations, but only additional properties. A typical example of such a type is the type scheme [Bauer et al. 85]

type EQUIV = (**sort m**, **funct** (**m**, **m**) **bool** *eq*):
  based on BOOL,
  laws m *x*, *y*, *z*:
    $eq(x, x) \equiv$ **true**,
    $eq(x, y) \equiv eq(y, x)$,
    ($eq(x, y) \equiv$ **true** $\wedge$ $eq(y, z) \equiv$ **true**) $\Rightarrow$ ($eq(x, z) \equiv$ **true**)
endoftype,

which states that a binary predicate *eq* on **m** is an equivalence relation. For **nat** and "=" defined by NAT_1 above, obviously EQUIV(**nat**, =) is provable.

Another example of the same kind is the type scheme

type LNSORD = (**sort m**, **funct** (**m**, **m**) **bool** *less*, **m** *c*):
  based on BOOL,
  laws m *x*, *y*, *z*:
    $(x \not\equiv c) \Rightarrow (less(c, x) \equiv \mathbf{true})$,
    $less(x, x) \equiv \mathbf{false}$,
    $(x \not\equiv y) \Rightarrow (less(x, y) \vee less(y, x)) \equiv \mathbf{true}$,
    $(less(x, y) \equiv \mathbf{true} \wedge less(y, z) \equiv \mathbf{true}) \Rightarrow (less(x, z) \equiv \mathbf{true})$
endoftype,

which states that the binary predicate *less* on **m** has the properties of a linear, Noetherian strict ordering on **m** with minimal element *c*. Again, for NAT_1 as defined above, obviously LNSORD(**nat**, <, 0) is provable.

Further examples are

type ASSOC = (**sort m**, **funct** (**m**, **m**) **m** *f*):
  laws m *x*, *y*, *z*:
    $f(f(x, y), z) \equiv f(x, f(y, z))$
endoftype

or

type NEUTRAL = (**sort m**, **funct** (**m**, **m**) **m** *f*, **m** *e*):
  laws m *x*:
    $f(x, e) \equiv f(e, x) \equiv x$,
endoftype,

stating that an operation *f* is associative, respectively that *e* is a neutral element with respect to *f*. More examples can be found in the exercises (Sect. 3.7).

Since type definitions of this degenerated kind can be viewed as abbreviations for collections of axioms, they can conveniently be used in the assertion about the parameters of some type or for a compact formulation of laws. Examples will be given in the next subsection.

3.3.2 Further Examples of Basic Algebraic Types

Like sequences, other basic structures can be defined by algebraic types. Examples that will be used later are *finite sets*, *bags*, and *finite mappings*. Further examples can be found in the literature (e.g. [Bauer et al. 81, 85]) and in the exercises (Sect. 3.7).

Finite sets can be specified by the type scheme

type SET = (**sort elem**, **funct** (**elem**, **elem**) **bool** *eq*: **include** EQUIV(**elem**, *eq*))
        set, ∅, .+., .∈ ., .∉ ., .−.:
  based on BOOL,
  sort set,
  set ∅,

funct (**set**, **elem**) **set** .+.,
funct (**elem**, **set**) **bool** .$\in$.,
funct (**elem**, **set**) **bool** .$\notin$.,
funct (**set**, **elem**) **set** .–.,
laws elem x, y, **set** s:
$y \in \varnothing \equiv$ **false**,
$y \in (s + x) \equiv$ **if** $eq(x, y)$ **then true else** $y \in s$ **fi**,
$x \notin s \equiv \neg(x \in s)$,
$(\varnothing - x) \equiv \varnothing$,
$(s + x) - y \equiv$ **if** $eq(x, y)$ **then** $s - y$ **else** $(s - y) + x$ **fi**
endoftype.

Parameters are here an object kind **elem** and a binary predicate eq on **elem**, which is asserted to have the properties of an equivalence relation on **elem**. In the assertion we have used the fact that, according to the definitions, **include** EQUIV(**m**, eq) abbreviates a boolean formula. Visible constituents of SET are

- the new object kind **set**,
- the constant $\varnothing$ (the empty set), and
- the operations
  .+. (addition of an element to a set),
  .$\in$. and .$\notin$. (test on membership or non-membership), and
  .–. (deletion of an element).

In the definition of SET an axiom such as

$y \in (s + x) \equiv$ **if** $eq(x, y)$ **then true else** $y \in s$ **fi**

is shorthand for the pair of axioms

$eq(x, y) \equiv$ **true** $\Rightarrow y \in (s + x) \equiv$ **true**,
$eq(x, y) \equiv$ **false** $\Rightarrow y \in (s + x) \equiv y \in s$.

Since there is no explicit operation for comparing objects of kind **set**, they can only be distinguished via operations of primitive result sort. Thus, for example, the terms $(s+x)+y$ and $(s+y)+x$ or the terms $s+x$ and $(s+x)+x$ are indistinguishable, i.e., addition of elements to a set is to be considered commutative and idempotent.

Using the type SET, we can define sets of natural numbers, for example by

type NATSET = **natset**, $\varnothing$, .+., .$\in$., .$\notin$., .–.:
include NAT_1,
include SET(**nat**, =) **as** (**natset**, ...),
endoftype.

Objects of sort **natset** then include

$$((((\varnothing + 0) + succ(0)) + 0) + succ(0)) - succ(0)$$

and

$$\varnothing + 0$$

which both represent the set $\{0\}$, since the first term can be reduced by the axioms of SET to the second term.

Bags, sometimes also called 'multisets', are defined by the type scheme

type BAG = (**sort m**, **funct** (**m**, **m**) **bool** *eq*: **include** EQUIV(**m**, *eq*))
  bag, $\varnothing$, .+., .$\in$., .$\notin$., .–., *#occs*:
 based on BOOL,
 based on NAT,
 sort bag,
 bag $\varnothing$,
 funct (**bag**, **m**) **bag** .+.,
 funct (**m**, **bag**) **bool** .$\in$.,
 funct (**m**, **bag**) **bool** .$\notin$.,
 funct (**bag**, **m**) **bag** .–.,
 funct (**m**, **bag**) **nat** *#occs*;
 laws m *x*, *y*, **bag** *b*:
  $y \in \varnothing \equiv$ **false**,
  $y \in (b + x) \equiv$ **if** $eq(x, y)$ **then true else** $y \in b$ **fi**,
  $x \notin b \equiv \neg(x \in b)$,
  $\varnothing - x \equiv \varnothing$,
  $(b + x) - y \equiv$ **if** $eq(x, y)$ **then** b **else** $(b - y) + x$ **fi**,
  $\#occs(x, \varnothing) \equiv 0$,
  $\#occs(y, b + x) \equiv$ **if** $eq(x, y)$ **then** $succ(\#occs(y, b))$ **else** $\#occs(y, b)$ **fi**
endoftype.

Parameters are here an object kind **m** and a binary predicate *eq* on **m**, which, again, is asserted to have the properties of an equivalence relation. Visible constituents are

- the new object kind **bag**,
- the constant $\varnothing$ (the empty bag), and
- the operations
 .+. (addition of an element to a bag),
 .$\in$. and .$\notin$. (test on membership or non-membership),
 .–. (deletion of an element), and
 #occs (number of occurrences of an element in a bag).

Apart from the additional operation *#occs*, the main difference between BAG and SET is in the definition of the operation "–". Whereas for SET we can prove

$\forall$ **set** *s*, **m** *x*: $x \in (s-x) \equiv$ **false**,

the analogous property for BAG is not true. However, for BAG we can prove

$\forall$ **bag** *b*, **m** *x*: $\#occs(x, b-x) \equiv pred(\#occs(x, b))$ **provided** $\neg\,(\#occs(x, b) = 0)$.

Analogous to the remark on SET, addition of an element to a bag is also to be considered commutative. However, addition is not idempotent, since, e.g., the terms $b+x$ and $(b+x)+x$ can be distinguished by means of the operation *#occs*.

Finite mappings associate the elements of an index set with values. They are defined by the type scheme

type MAP = (**sort index**, **sort elem**, **funct** (**index**, **index**) **bool** *eq*:
  include EQUIV(**index**, *eq*))
  map, [], .[.]←., *isdef*, .[.]:
 based on BOOL,

sort map,
map [],
funct (**map**, **index**, **elem**) **map** .[.]←.,
funct (**map**, **index**) **bool** *isdef*,
funct (**map** *m*, **index** *i*: *isdef*(*m*, *i*)) **elem** .[.],
laws index *i*, *j*, **map** *m*, **elem** *x*: ¬*eq*(*i*, *j*):
isdef([], *i*) ≡ **false**,
isdef(*m*[*i*]←*x*, *i*) ≡ **true**,
isdef(*m*[*i*]←*x*, *j*) ≡ *isdef*(*m*, *j*),
(*m*[*i*]←*x*)[*i*] ≡ *x*,
(*m*[*j*]←*x*)[*i*] ≡ *m*[*i*] **provided** *isdef*(*m*, *i*)
endoftype.

Parameters are here two object kinds **index** and **elem**, as well as a binary predicate *eq* on **index**, having the properties of an equivalence relation. The visible constituents are

- the new object kind **map**,
- the constant [] (denoting the empty map), and
- the operations
  .[.]←. (addition of a new association of an element with an index to a map),
  isdef (test, whether the map has a defined value for a given index), and
  .[.] (retrieval of the value associated with a given index).

Rather than checking definedness explicitly, as is done by the operation *isdef* in the type MAP, it is sometimes convenient to have "total maps", which are finite maps with a pre-defined value for each index:

type TMAP = (**sort index**, **sort elem**, **funct** (**index**, **index**) **bool** *eq*:
include EQUIV(**index**, *eq*))
tmap, *init*, .[.]←., .[.]:
based on BOOL,
sort tmap,
funct (**tmap**, **index**, **elem**) **tmap** .[.]←.,
funct (**tmap**, **index**) **elem** .[.],
funct (**elem**) **tmap** *init*;
laws index *i*, *j*, **tmap** *m*, **elem** *x*:
init(*x*)[*i*] ≡ *x*,
(*m*[*j*]←*x*)[*i*] ≡ **if** *eq*(*i*, *j*) **then** *x* **else** *m*[*i*] **fi**
endoftype.

The use of MAP can be illustrated, for example, with decision tables (Sect. 2.2.3). Assuming that 'conditions' are defined by respective object kinds $\mathbf{c_i}$, $1 \le i \le n$ (with equalities "$=_i$") and that 'rules' are defined by an appropriate object kind **rule**, we can first specify an object kind **condition** to be an n-tuple composed of the $\mathbf{c_i}$ and an equality "=" on **condition** as elementwise equality (Sect. 3.3.4.1). Then, decision tables can be specified by

type DEC-TABLE = **dt**, [], .[.]←., *isdef*, .[.]:
include MAP(**condition**, **rule**, =) **as** (**dt**, ...)
endoftype.

In this example, an object kind **condition** was used to characterize tuples of indices to be associated with a value by a finite mapping. Of course, rather than first defining tuples of indices by a new object kind and then using an instantiation of MAP, a direct definition of finite mappings that associate tuples of indices with values can be given. For example, for pairs of indices (of the same kind) we may use the type scheme

```
type PMAP = (sort index, sort elem, funct (index, index) bool eq:
             include EQUIV(index, eq))
             pmap, [], .[.,.]←., isdef, .[.,.]:
   based on BOOL,
   sort pmap,
   pmap [],
   funct (pmap, index, index, elem) pmap .[.,.]←.,
   funct (pmap, index index, ) bool isdef,
   funct (pmap m, index i index j: isdef(m, i, j)) elem .[.,.],
   laws index i, j, k, l, pmap m, elem x: ¬eq(i, j) ∨ ¬eq(k, l):
      isdef([], i, k) ≡ false,
      isdef(m[i, k]←x, i, k) ≡ true,
      isdef(m[i, k]←x, j, l) ≡ isdef(m, j),
      (m[i, k]←x)[i, k] ≡ x,
      (m[j, l]←x)[i, k] ≡ m[i, k] provided isdef(m, i, k)
endoftype.
```

In the same way finite mappings that associate tuples of indices of different kind with values can be defined.

3.3.3 Extensions of Basic Types

The types as defined in the examples above contain only a few operations. For practical purposes, however, a richer set of operations often allows a much more flexible and adequate formalization. Such a richer set simply may be defined as an extension (Sect. 3.3.1.4) of an existing basic type using the instantiation mechanism.

A typical example is the extension of the type SEQU with the operations

- <.> for making an element into a singleton sequence,
- .+. for the concatenation of two sequences,
- **last**. for yielding the last element,
- **lead**. for obtaining the sequence without the last element,
- .+. for attaching an element to the right of a sequence,
- |.| for determining the length of a sequence,
- .[.] for indexing, and
- .[.:.] for selecting a subsequence:

```
type ESEQU = (sort m) sequ, <>, .=<>, .≠<>, first., rest., .+.,
             .+., last., lead., .+., |.|, .[.], .[.:.]:
   based on (nat, 0, .+1, .–1) = NAT,
   include SEQU(m),
```

funct (**m**) **sequ** <.>,
funct (**sequ**, **sequ**) **sequ** .+.,
funct (**sequ** s: $s \neq$<>) **m** **last**.,
funct (**sequ** s: $s \neq$<>) **sequ** **lead**.,
funct (**sequ**, **m**) **sequ** .+.,
funct (**sequ**) **nat** |.| ,
funct (**sequ** s, **nat** i: $1 \le i \le |s|$) **m** .[.],
funct (**sequ** s, **nat** i, **nat** k: $1 \le i, k \le |s|$) **sequ** .[.:.],
laws m x, **sequ** r, s, t, **nat** i, k:
$(r+(s+t)) \equiv ((r+s)+t)$,
$s+\langle\rangle \equiv s$,
$\langle\rangle+s \equiv s$,
$x + s \equiv \langle x\rangle+s$,
$s + x \equiv s+\langle x\rangle$,
last$(s + x) \equiv x$,
lead$(s + x) \equiv s$,
$|\langle\rangle| \equiv 0$,
$|x + s| \equiv |s| +1$,
$s[1] \equiv$ **first** s **provided** $|s| \ge 1$,
$s[i] \equiv$ (**rest** s)$[i-1]$ **provided** $1 < i \le |s|$,
$s[i:k] \equiv$ **if** $i > k$ **then** <>
elsf $k < |s|$ **then** (**lead** s)$[i:k]$
elsf $i > 1$ **then** (**rest** s)$[i-1:k-1]$ **else** s **fi** **provided** $1\le i, k \le |s|$

endoftype.

The operation symbol "+" defined by ESEQU is overloaded, as it stands for three operations of different functionality:

funct (**sequ**, **sequ**) **sequ** .+.,
funct (**sequ**, **m**) **sequ** .+.,
funct (**m**, **sequ**) **sequ** .+.,

denoting concatenation of two sequences or addition of an element to a sequence at either side. The correspondence between the operation symbols in the list of visible constituents and the associated functionality is provided by the respective ordering. Which of these operations is meant in a particular context can always be disambiguated from the sorts of the respective operands. Thus, for example, in the first three axioms in the definition of ESEQU, "+" means concatenation of sequences, whereas in the remaining ones "+" denotes the addition of an element to a sequence.

Of course, ESEQU again can be extended by further operations, such as

- .$\in$. for checking whether an element occurs in a sequence,
- .$\notin$. for checking whether an element does not occur in a sequence,
- .=. for checking the equality of two sequences,
- .$\lessdot$. for checking whether a sequence is an initial segment of another sequence,
- .$\subseteq$. for checking whether a sequence is a pattern occurring in another sequence,
- *contained* for checking whether a sequence is a subsequence of another sequence.

However, this extension requires that an equality for the parameter sort is available:

type EESEQU = (**sort m**, **funct** (**m**, **m**) **bool** *eq*: **include** EQUIV(**m**, *eq*))
        sequ, <>, .=<>, .≠<>, **first**., **rest**., .+.,
        .+., **last**., **lead**., .+., |.|, .[.], .[.:.],
        .∈ ., .∉ ., .=., .≼ ., .⊆ ., *contained*:
  include ESEQU(**m**),
  funct (**m**, **sequ**) **bool** .∈ .,
  funct (**m**, **sequ**) **bool** .∉ .,
  funct (**sequ**, **sequ**) **bool** .=.,
  funct (**sequ**, **sequ**) **bool** .≼ .,
  funct (**sequ**, **sequ**) **bool** .⊆ .,
  funct (**sequ**, **sequ**) **bool** *contained*;
  laws m *x*, *y*, **sequ** *s*, *t*:
    $x \in s \equiv \exists\, \mathbf{nat}\ i{:}\ 1 \le i \le |s| \,\Delta\, eq(s[i], x)$,
    $x \notin s \equiv \neg\,(x \in s)$,
    $<> = <> \equiv \mathbf{true}$,
    $s = t \equiv eq(\mathbf{first}s, \mathbf{first}t) \wedge (\mathbf{rest}s = \mathbf{rest}t)$ **provided** $s \ne <> \wedge t \ne <>$,
    $s \preccurlyeq t \equiv (\exists\, \mathbf{sequ}\ r{:}\ s + r = t)$,
    $s \subseteq t \equiv (\exists\, \mathbf{sequ}\ r, q{:}\ q + s + r = t)$,
    $contained(<>, t) \equiv \mathbf{true}$,
    $contained(x{+}s, <>) \equiv \mathbf{false}$,
    $contained(x{+}s, y{+}t) \equiv (eq(x, y) \wedge contained(s, t)) \vee contained(x{+}s, t)$
endoftype.

If we extended our type formalism to also allow 'higher-order types' [Möller 87], we also could define an extension of SEQU that comprises the (higher-order) operations and predicates from [Bird 87].

Another example is an extension of the type SET by

- |.|, cardinality,
- .=., equality,
- .∪., set union,
- .∩., set intersection,
- .\\., set difference, and
- .⊆ ., set inclusion:

type ESET = (**sort elem**, **funct** (**elem**, **elem**) **bool** *eq*:
        include EQUIV(**elem**, *eq*))
        set, ∅, .+., .∈ ., .∉ ., .−., |.|, .=., .∪., .∩.,.\\., .⊆ .:
  based on NAT,
  include SET(**elem**, *eq*),
  funct (**set**) **nat** |.|,
  funct (**set**, **set**) **bool** .=.,
  funct (**set**, **set**) **set** .∪.,
  funct (**set**, **set**) **set** .∩.,
  funct (**set**, **set**) **set** .\\.,
  funct (**set**, **set**) **bool** .⊆ .,
  laws m *x*, **set** *a*, *b*:

$|\varnothing| \equiv 0$,
$|a + x| \equiv$ **if** $x \in a$ **then** $|a|$ **else** $succ(|a|)$ **fi**,
$\varnothing = \varnothing \equiv$ **true**,
$(a + x) = \varnothing \equiv$ **false**,
$a = b \equiv x \in b \wedge (a - x) = (b - x)$,
$a \cup \varnothing \equiv a$,
$a \cup (b + x) \equiv (a + x) \cup b$,
$a \cap \varnothing \equiv \varnothing$,
$a \cap (b + x) \equiv$ **if** $x \in a$ **then** $(a \cap b) + x$ **else** $a \cap$ b **fi**,
$a \setminus \varnothing \equiv a$,
$a \setminus (b + x) \equiv (a - x) \setminus b$,
$\varnothing \subseteq a \equiv$ **true**,
$(b + x) \subseteq a \equiv (x \in a) \wedge ((b - x) \subseteq (a - x))$
endoftype.

A last example is an extension of the type MAP by

- *dom*, the set of indices that are associated with a value by the map; and
- *ran*, the set of all elements that are associated to some index by the map:

type EMAP = (**sort index, sort elem, funct (index, index) bool** *eq*:
include EQUIV(**index**, *eq*))
map, [], .[.]←., *isdef*, .[.], *dom*, *ran*:
include MAP(**index, elem**, *eq*),
include SET(**index**, *eq*) **as** (**indexset**, ...),
include SET(**elem**, *eq*) **as** (**elemset**, ...),
funct (map) indexset *dom*,
funct (map) elemset *ran*;
laws index *i*, **map** *m*, **elem** *x*:
$dom([]) \equiv \varnothing$,
$dom(m[i] \leftarrow x) \equiv dom(m) + i$,
$ran([]) \equiv \varnothing$,
$ran(m[i] \leftarrow x) \equiv ran(m) + x$
endoftype.

Further extensions of the type EMAP, such as the addition of operations for union, intersection, difference, or composition of maps, are straightforward.

3.3.4 Formulation of Concepts as Algebraic Types

In the following we are going to exemplify how the basic types and their extensions may be used for the representation of (mathematical) concepts (Sect. 3.2.1). From the following examples the representation of other concepts as (systems of) algebraic types should be straightforward.

3.3.4.1 Tuples

Arbitrary object kinds **m** and **m'** can be combined into pairs by using the type scheme

type PAIR = (**sort m**, **sort m'**) **pair**, *mp*, *s*, *s'*:
  sort pair,
  funct (m, m') pair *mp*,
  funct (pair) m *s*,
  funct (pair) m' *s'*;
  laws m *x*, **m'** *x'*:
    $s(mp(x, x')) \equiv x$,
    $s'(mp(x, x')) \equiv x'$
endoftype.

Here, *mp* is an operation that makes two elements into a pair. Access to the elements of a pair is provided by the selectors *s* and *s'*.

If for pairs a componentwise equality is also aimed at, the above type scheme can be extended to

type EPAIR = (**sort m**, **sort m'**,
  funct (m, m) bool *eq*, **funct (m', m') bool** *eq'*:
  include EQUIV(**m**, *eq*) ∧ **include** EQUIV(**m'**, *eq'*))
  pair, *mp*, *s*, *s'*, *equ*:
  include PAIR(**m**, **m'**);
  funct (pair, pair) bool *equ*;
  laws m *x*, *y*, **m'** *x'*, *y'*:
    $equ(mp(x, x'), mp(y, y')) \equiv eq(x, y) \wedge eq'(x', y')$
endoftype.

Obviously, arbitrary tuples can be specified in an analogous way.

3.3.4.2 Relational Structures

Binary relations (without any further properties) over some object kind **m** are subsets of **m** × **m**. Thus an algebraic specification of binary relations is straightforward by appropriately instantiating the type scheme SET:

type BREL = (**sort m**, **funct (m, m) bool** .=.: **include** EQUIV(**m**, =))
  brel, *init*, *add*, *isrel*:
  based on BOOL,
  sort brel,
  brel *init*,
  funct (brel, m, m) brel *add*,
  funct (brel, m, m) bool *isrel*,
  laws brel *b*, **m** *x*, *y*, *u*, *v*:
    $isrel(init, u, v) \equiv$ **false**,
    $isrel(add(b, x, y), u, v) \equiv (x = u \wedge y = v) \vee isrel(b, u, v)$
endoftype.

The type scheme BREL specifies binary relations as objects that can be manipulated. The operation *add* allows to extend a relation by a pair of related elements. The predicate *isrel* checks whether two elements are related in a binary relation.

Arbitrary n-ary relations can be defined in an analogous way.

Based on the specification of BREL, we can define relations with various kinds of properties. One possibility here is to simply add the respective properties as further axioms on *isrel* . Another possibility is to modify the axioms for *isrel* in such a way that the respective properties are provable.

Following the second possibility a definition of partial orderings [Partsch, Broy 79] is:

```
type PORD = (sort m, funct (m, m) bool .=.: include EQUIV(m, =))
                  pord, init, add, ordered:
   based on BOOL,
   sort pord,
   pord init,
   funct (pord p, m x, m y: ¬ordered(p, y, x)) pord add,
   funct (pord, m, m) bool ordered,
   laws pord p, m x, y, u, v: ¬ordered(p, y, x):
      ordered(init, u, v)  ≡  u = v,
      ordered(add(p, x, y), u, v)  ≡ (ordered(p, u, x) ∧ ordered(p, y, v)) ∨
                                     ordered(p, u, v)
endoftype.
```

Here, *add* is an operation that extends a partial ordering by an ordered pair. The predicate *ordered* checks whether two elements are partially ordered within a given relation, either by construction or by the properties of partial orderings, viz. reflexivity, transitivity, and anti-symmetry. In fact, it can be proved that the latter properties hold for *ordered* (Ex. 3.3-9a).

Likewise, a definition of equivalences [Partsch, Broy 79] can be given by:

```
type EREL1 = (sort m, funct (m, m) bool .=.: include EQUIV(m, =))
                  erel, init, add, equiv:
   based on BOOL,
   sort erel,
   erel init,
   funct (erel, m, m) erel add,
   funct (erel, m, m) bool equiv,
   laws erel e, m x, y, u, v:
      equiv(init, u, v)  ≡  u = v,
      equiv(add(e, x, y), u, v)  ≡ (equiv(e, u, x) ∧ equiv(e, y, v)) ∨
                                   (equiv(e, u, y) ∧ equiv(e, x, v)) ∨ equiv(e, u, v)
endoftype.
```

Again, the properties for reflexivity, transitivity, and symmetry are provable for *equiv* (Ex. 3.3-9b).

A different definition for equivalences is the following one [Partsch, Broy 79] with an explicit definition of an operation *repr* for finding the representative of an equivalence class (instead of having a predicate *equiv*):

```
type EREL2 = (sort m, funct (m, m) bool .=.: include EQUIV(m, =))
                  erel, init, add, repr:
   based on BOOL,
   sort erel,
   erel init,
```

funct (**erel**, **m**, **m**) **erel** *add*,
funct (**erel**, **m**) **m** *repr*,
laws **erel** *e*, **m** *x*, *y*, *u*:
repr(*init*, *u*) ≡ *u*,
repr(*add*(*e*, *x*, *y*), *u*) ≡
if (*repr*(*e*, *x*) = *repr*(*e*, *u*)) ∨ (*repr*(*e*, *y*) = *repr*(*e*, *u*))
then *repr*(*e*, *x*) **else** *repr*(*e*, *u*) **fi**
endoftype.

3.3.4.3 Graph Structures

In this subsection we show how various kinds of graphs, such as finite directed graphs, finite directed acyclic graphs, Petri-nets, and circular lists can be specified.

Finite Directed Graphs

We assume that an object kind **node** is already defined by a type NODE. Furthermore, we assume "=" to be an equivalence relation on **node**.

For formulating the concept (a) from Sect. 3.2, we define

- *sets of nodes* by instantiation of the type scheme SET:
  type NODESET = **nodeset**, ∅, .+., .∈ ., .∉ ., .–.:
  based on NODE,
  include SET(**node**, =) **as** (**nodeset**, ...)
  endoftype;
- *edges* as pairs of nodes:
  type EDGE = **edge**, *me*, *in*, *out*, .=.:
  include EPAIR(**node**, **node**, =, =) **as** (**edge**, *me*, *in*, *out*, =)
  endoftype;
- *sets of edges* by
  type EDGESET = **edgeset**, ∅, .+., .∈ ., .∉ ., .–.:
  based on NODE,
  include SET(**edge**, =) **as** (**edgeset**, ...)
  endoftype;
- *finite directed graphs* by
  type DGRAPH$_1$ = **dgraph**, *mg*, *nodes*, *edges*:
  based on NODESET, EDGESET,
  include PAIR(**nodeset**, **edgeset**) **as** (**dgraph**, *mg*, *nodes*, *edges*),
  laws **dgraph** *g*, **edge** *e*:
  (*e*∈ *edges*(*g*)) ≡ **true** ⇒ (*in*(*e*)∈ *nodes*(*g*) ∧ *out*(*e*)∈ *nodes*(*g*)) ≡ **true**
  endoftype.

In a similar way the concepts (b) and (c) could be formulated as abstract types. Another, more constructive definition for *finite directed graphs* [Bauer et al. 89] is:

type DGRAPH$_2$ = **dgraph**, *eg*, *inc*, *isarc*:
based on NODE, BOOL,
dgraph *eg*,
funct (**dgraph**, **node**, **node**) **dgraph** *inc*,

funct (**dgraph**, **node**, **node**) **bool** *isarc*,
laws **dgraph** g, **node** x, y, x', y':
$isarc(eg, x, y) \equiv$ **false**,
$isarc(inc(g, x, y), x', y') \equiv (((x = x') \wedge (y = y')) \vee isarc(g, x', y'))$
endoftype.

Here, *eg* denotes the empty graph, *inc* is an operation that extends a graph by an edge between two nodes, and *isarc* is a predicate that checks whether two nodes are connected by a (directed) edge.

The specifications of finite directed graphs given so far are based on a fixed set of nodes (defined by NODE). A specification of finite directed graphs for different kinds of nodes is, e.g., given by the following type scheme:

type DGRAPH$_3$ = (**sort m**, **funct** (**m**, **m**) **bool** .=.: **include** EQUIV(**m**, =))
dgraph, *init*, *inc*, *nodes*, *isarc*:
based on BOOL,
include SET(**m**, =) **as** (**mset**, ...),
sort dgraph,
funct (**mset**) **dgraph** *init*,
funct (**dgraph**, **m**, **m**) **dgraph** *inc*,
funct (**dgraph**, **m**, **m**) **bool** *isarc*,
funct (**dgraph**) **mset** *nodes*,
laws **dgraph** b, **m** x, y, u, v, **mset** s:
$isarc(init(s), u, v) \equiv$ **false**,
$isarc(inc(b, x, y), u, v) \equiv (x = u \wedge y = v) \vee isarc(b, u, v)$,
$nodes(init(s)) \equiv s$,
$nodes(inc(b, x, y)) \equiv nodes(b) \cup \{x, y\}$
endoftype.

Here, *init* constructs a graph consisting of a set of isolated nodes, *inc* extends a graph by two nodes and an edge between them, *nodes* yields the set of all nodes in a graph, and *isarc* again allows us to check whether two nodes are connected by an edge.

Of course, if we are interested in further operations on graphs we may use an extension, such as:

type EDGRAPH = (**sort m**, **funct** (**m**, **m**) **bool** .=.: **include** EQUIV(**m**, =))
dgraph, *init*, *inc*, *nodes*, *isarc*, *succs*, *preds*, *rem*:
include DGRAPH$_3$(**m**, =),
funct (**m**, **dgraph**) **mset** *succs*,
funct (**m**, **dgraph**) **mset** *preds*,
funct (**m**, **dgraph**) **dgraph** *rem*,
laws **dgraph** d, **m** x, y, u, v, **mset** t:
$succs(x, init(t)) \equiv \varnothing$,
$succs(x, inc(d, u, v)) \equiv$ **if** $x = u$ **then** $succs(x, d) + v$ **else** $succs(x, d)$ **fi**,
$preds(x, init(t)) \equiv \varnothing$,
$preds(x, inc(d, u, v)) \equiv$ **if** $x = v$ **then** $preds(x, d) + u$ **else** $preds(x, d)$ **fi**,
$rem(x, init(t)) \equiv init(t - x)$,
$rem(x, inc(d, u, v)) \equiv$
if $x = u \vee x = v$ **then** $rem(x, d)$ **else** $inc(rem(x, d), u, v)$ **fi**
endoftype.

EDGRAPH is an extension of $DGRAPH_3$ that provides the following additional operations:

- *succs* (the set of all successors of a node in a graph);
- *preds* (the set of all predecessors of a node in a graph);
- *rem* (yielding the graph that results from removing a node and all edges adjacent to it).

Finite Directed Acyclic Graphs

Similarly to finite directed graphs, we can also specify directed acyclic graphs, for example by

type DAG = (**sort m**, **funct** (**m**, **m**) **bool** .=.: **include** EQUIV(**m**, =))
dag, *init*, *addp*, *adds*, *isin*, *nodes*, *isarc*:
  based on BOOL,
  include ESET(**m**, =) **as** (**mset**, ...),
  sort dag,
  funct (**mset**) **dag** *init*,
  funct (**dag**) **mset** *nodes*,
  funct (**dag** d, **m** x, **mset** s: $x \notin nodes(d) \wedge s \subseteq nodes(d)$) **dag** *addp*,
  funct (**dag** d, **mset** s, **m** x: $x \notin nodes(d) \wedge s \subseteq nodes(d)$) **dag** *adds*,
  funct (**dag**, **m**, **m**) **bool** *isarc*,
  laws dag d, **m** x, y, z, **mset** s, t: $y \notin nodes(d) \wedge s \subseteq nodes(d)$:
    $nodes(init(t)) \equiv t$,
    $nodes(addp(d, y, s)) \equiv nodes(d) + y$,
    $nodes(adds(d, s, y)) \equiv nodes(d) + y$,
    $isarc(init(t), x, y) \equiv$ **false**,
    $isarc(addp(d, z, s), x, y) \equiv (x = z \wedge y \in s) \vee isarc(d, x, y)$,
    $isarc(adds(d, s, z), x, y) \equiv (y = z \wedge x \in s) \vee isarc(d, x, y)$,
endoftype.

Here, the operations *addp* and *adds* allow to add a predecessor, resp. successor, to a set of nodes in the directed acyclic graph. In order to prevent the introduction of cycles both operations require the node to be added as predecessor, resp. successor, to be new, i.e. not yet in the graph. The operation *nodes* yields the set of all nodes in a graph, and the predicate *isarc* checks whether two nodes are connected by a (directed) edge.

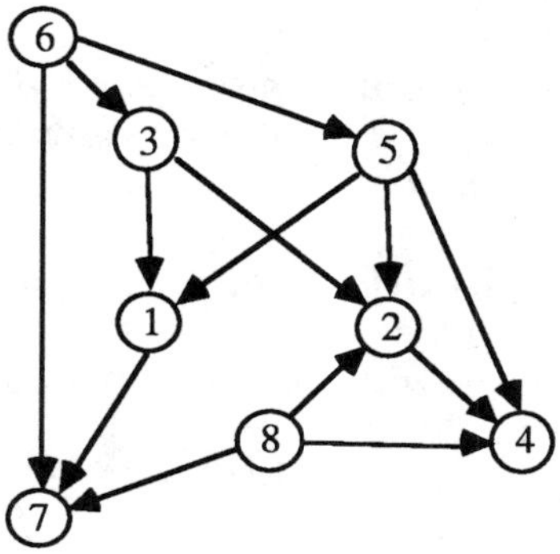

Figure 3.2. Example of a directed acyclic graph

Using the above definition, the directed acyclic graph given in Fig. 3.1 is represented, e.g. by the term

addp(*adds*(*addp*(*addp*(*adds*(*addp*(*init*({1,2}),3,{1,2}),{2},4),5,{1,2,4}),6,{3,5}),{1,6},7),8,{2,4,7}),

but also, e.g., by the term

adds(*adds*(*adds*(*adds*(*adds*(*adds*(*init*({6,8}),{6},3),{6},5),{3,5,8},2),{3,5},1),{2,5,8},4),{1,6,8},7)

or by the term

addp(*addp*(*addp*(*addp*(*addp*(*addp*(*addp*(*init*({4,7}),1,{7}),2,{4}),5,{1,2,4}),3,{1,2}),6,{3,5,7}),
8,{2,4,7}).

However, in either case, the application of *nodes* yields {1, 2, 3, 4, 5, 6, 7, 8}, as expected.

The fact that there are several terms to represent the same graph is caused by the decision of having two operations for adding new nodes, which is rather a tribute to the convenient use of the type definition than a necessity. In fact, one of the operations *addp* or *adds* would be sufficient.

Again, of course, we can define arbitrary extensions, for example,

type EDAG = (**sort m**, **funct** (**m**, **m**) **bool** .=.: EQUIV(**m**, =))
  dag, *init*, *addp*, *adds*, *isin*, *nodes*, *isarc*,
  succs, *preds*, *remove*, *sources*, *drains*:
 include DAG(**m**, =),
 funct (**m**, **dag**) **mset** *succs*,
 funct (**m**, **dag**) **mset** *preds*,
 funct (**m**, **dag**) **dag** *remove*,
 funct (**dag**) **mset** *sources*,
 funct (**dag**) **mset** *drains*,
 laws dag *d*, **m** *x*, *y*, *z*, **mset** *s*, *t*: $y \notin d \wedge s \in nodes(d)$:
  succs(*x*, *init*(*t*)) ≡ ∅,
  succs(*x*, *addp*(*d*, *y*, *s*)) ≡ **if** *x* = *y* **then** *s* **else** *succs*(*x*, *d*) **fi**,
  succs(*x*, *adds*(*d*, *s*, *y*)) ≡
   if $x \in s$ **then** *succs*(*x*, *d*) + *y* **else** *succs*(*x*, *d*) **fi**,
  preds(*x*, *init*(*t*)) ≡ ∅,
  preds(*x*, *addp*(*d*, *y*, *s*)) ≡
   if $x \in s$ **then** *preds*(*x*, *d*) + *y* **else** *preds*(*x*, *d*) **fi**,
  preds(*x*, *adds*(*d*, *s*, *y*)) ≡ **if** *x* = *y* **then** *s* **else** *preds*(*x*, *d*) **fi**
  remove(*x*, *init*(*t*)) ≡ *init*(*t*–*x*),
  remove(*x*, *addp*(*d*, *y*, *s*)) ≡
   if *x* = *y* **then** *d* **else** *addp*(*remove*(*x*, *d*), *y*, *s*–*x*) **fi**,
  remove(*x*, *adds*(*d*, *s*, *y*)) ≡
   if *x* = *y* **then** *d* **else** *adds*(*remove*(*x*, *d*), *s*–*x*, *y*) **fi**,
  sources(*init*(*t*)) ≡ *t*,
  sources(*addp*(*d*, *y*, *s*)) ≡ (*sources*(*d*)*s*)+*y*,
  sources(*adds*(*d*, *s*, *y*)) ≡ *sources*(*d*),
  drains(*init*(*t*)) ≡ *t*,
  drains(*addp*(*d*, *y*, *s*)) ≡ *drains*(*d*),
  drains(*adds*(*d*, *s*, *y*)) ≡ (*drains*(*d*)*s*)+*y*
endoftype.

Additional operations are here:
- *succs* (yielding the set of all successors of a node in a graph);
- *preds* (yielding the set of all predecessors of a node in a graph);
- *remove* (yielding the graph that results from removing a node and all edges adjacent to it);
- *sources* (yielding the set of all nodes without ingoing edges);
- *drains* (yielding the set of all nodes without outgoing edges).

Petri Nets

Following the same principle that was used in the previous specifications we can also give a specification of Petri nets (Sect. 2.2.6):

type P-NET = (**sort p**, **funct** (**p**, **p**) **bool** .=., **sort t**, **funct** (**t**, **t**) **bool** .=.:
include EQUIV(**p**, =) ∧ **include** EQUIV(**t**, =))
pnet, *init*;, *addp*, *addt*, *places*, *transitions*:
based on BOOL,
include ESET(**p**, =) **as** (**pset**, ...),
include ESET(**t**, =) **as** (**tset**, ...),
sort pnet,
pnet *init*,
funct (**pnet**) **pset** *places*,
funct (**pnet**) **tset** *transitions*,
funct (**pnet**, **t**, **p**) **pnet** *addp*,
funct (**pnet**, **p**, **t**)) **pnet** *addt*,
laws pnet *p*, **p** *x*, **t** *u*:
$places(init) \equiv \varnothing$,
$places(addp(p, u, x)) \equiv places(p) + x$,
$places(addt(p, x, u)) \equiv places(p) + x$,
$transitions(init) \equiv \varnothing$,
$transitions(addp(p, u, x)) \equiv transitions(p) + u$,
$transitions(addt(p, x, u)) \equiv transitions(p) + u$
endoftype.

This type scheme is parametrized with two object kinds **p** (places) and **t** (transitions) and equality operations on these object kinds. It defines a new object kind **pnet** (Petri net), the constant *init* (the empty Petri net) and the operations
- *addp* (for extending a Petri net by a (possibly new) transition, a (possibly new) place, and an edge leading from the one to the other);
- *addp* (for extending a Petri net by a (possibly new) place, a (possibly new) transition, and an edge leading from the one to the other);
- *places* (yielding the set of all places in a net); and
- *transitions* (yielding the set of all transitions in a net);

Using this specification, the Petri net from Fig. 3.3 for example (see also Sect. 2.2.6) can be represented by terms such as

addp(*addp*(*addp*(*addp*(*addt*(*addt*(*addp*(*addp*(*addt*(*addt*(*addt*(*addt*(*init*,a,1),c,1),c,3),e,3),1,b),3,d),b,2), d,4),2,a),2,c),4,c),4,e).

Again, however, there are other terms for representing this very same Petri net.

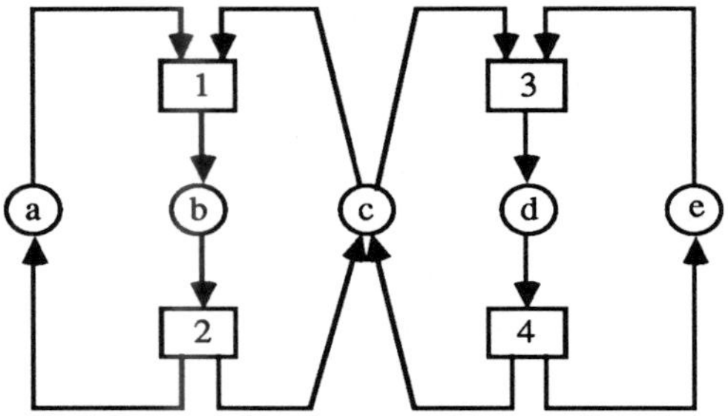

Figure 3.3. Example of a Petri net

Circular Lists

As another example we consider an algebraic specification of circular lists [Broy et al. 79a]:

type CLIST = (**sort m**) **clist**, *empty*, *isempty*, *insert*, *lmove*, *rmove*, *delete*, *read*:
  based on BOOL,
  sort clist,
  clist *empty*,
  funct (**clist**) **bool** *isempty*,
  funct (**clist**, **m**) **clist** *insert*,
  funct (**clist**) **clist** *lmove*,
  funct (**clist**) **clist** *rmove*,
  funct (**clist** c: $\neg isempty(c)$) **clist** *delete*,
  funct (**clist** c: $\neg isempty(c)$) **m** *read*,
  laws clist c, **m** x, y:
    $isempty(empty) \equiv$ **true**,
    $isempty(insert(c, x)) \equiv$ **false**,
    $lmove(empty) \equiv empty$,
    $lmove(insert(empty, x)) \equiv insert(empty, x)$,
    $lmove(insert(insert(c, x), y)) \equiv insert(lmove(insert(c, y)), x)$,
    $rmove(lmove(c)) \equiv c$,
    $delete(insert(c, x)) \equiv c$,
    $read(insert(c, x)) \equiv x$
endoftype.

This type scheme defines (for an arbitrary object kind **m**)
- the new object kind **clist**;
- the constant *empty* (the empty circular list); and
- the operations
  isempty (checking whether a circular list is empty);
  insert (for inserting an element into a circular list);
  read (yielding that element of the circular list at the current "reading position");
  lmove (for rotating the circular list by one position to the left, i.e., for moving the reading position one to the right);
  rmove (for rotating the circular list by one position to the right, i.e., for moving the reading position one to the left); and
  delete (yielding the circular list without the element at the current reading position).

The circular list represented by the term

insert(*insert*(*insert*(*empty*, 3), 2), 1)

may be sketched as

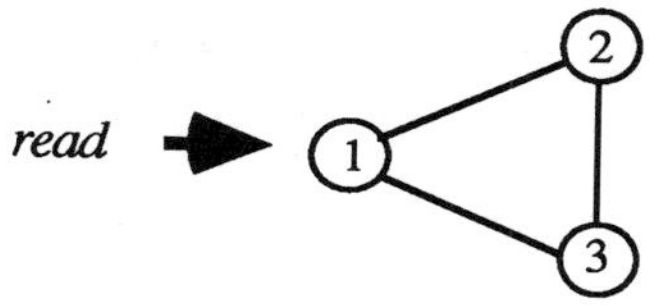

where *read* indicates the current reading position and the lines between nodes connect neighbored elements.

According to the axioms of CLIST we have

delete(*insert*(*insert*(*insert*(*empty*, 3), 2), 1)) ≡ (*insert*(*insert*(*empty*, 3), 2),

which gives a circular list to be sketched as

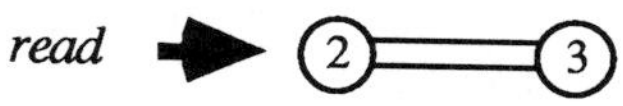

Furthermore,

lmove(*insert*(*insert*(*insert*(*empty*, 3), 2), 1)) ≡ ... ≡
insert(*insert*(*insert*(*empty*, 1), 3), 2),

or, graphically,

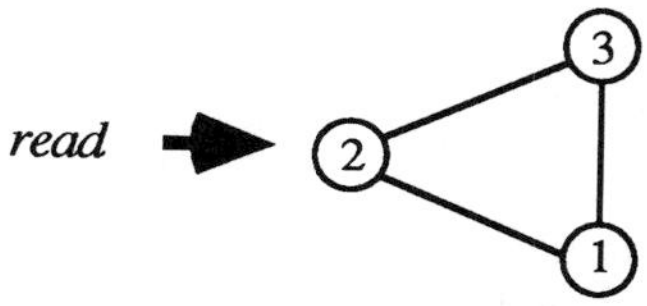

For evaluating

rmove(*insert*(*insert*(*insert*(*empty*, 3), 2), 1))

no explicit axioms are provided. However, we have, by using the axioms for *lmove* from right to left,

insert(*insert*(*insert*(*empty*, 3), 2), 1)) ≡ ... ≡
lmove(*insert*(*insert*(*insert*(*empty*, 2), 1), 3),

and hence

rmove(*insert*(*insert*(*insert*(*empty*, 3), 2), 1)) ≡ ... ≡
insert(*insert*(*insert*(*empty*, 2), 1), 3),

or, again graphically,

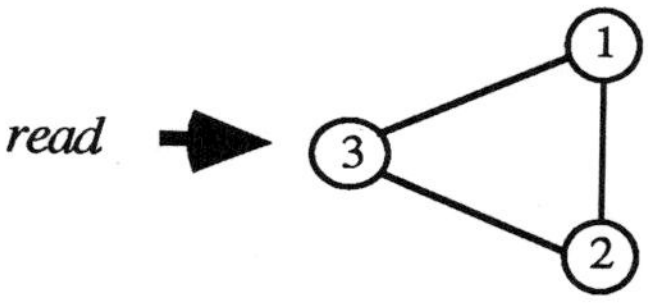

3.3.4.4 Finite State Machines

As a further example of how to specify concepts by algebraic types we consider finite state machines (a particular instance of the finite state mechanisms discussed in Sect. 2.2.5).

As in the previous examples, we assume object kinds **state, char**, and equalities "=" on these object kinds to be defined by appropriate types STATE and CHAR, respectively.

Then *sets of states* can be obtained by instantiation of SET:

type STATES = **states**, ∅, .+., .∈ ., .∉ ., .–.:
  based on STATE,
  include ESET(**state**, =) **as** (**states**, ...)
endoftype.

Again by instantiation we can define *transition tables*, for example by

type TRANSITION-TABLE =
  (**sort char**, **funct** (**char**, **char**) **bool** *eqc*, **sort state**,
  funct (**state**, **state**) **bool** *eqs*:
  include EQUIV(**char**, *eqc*) ∧ **include** EQUIV(**state**, *eqs*))
  ttable, [], .[.]←., *isdef*, .[.], .∈ ., .∉ ., *dom*, *ran*, *domstates*, **index**, *mp*:
 include EPAIR(**state**, **char**, *eqs*, *eqc*) **as** (**index**, *mp*, *s*, *c*, =),
 include EMAP(**index**, **state**, *eq*) **as** (**ttable**, ...),
 include ESET(**state**, *eqs*) **as** (**states**, ...),
 funct (**ttable**) **states** *domstates*,
 laws ttable *t*:
  domstates(*t*) ≡ {**state** *s*: ∃ **char** *c*: *mp*(*s*, *c*) ∈ *dom*(*t*)}
endoftype.

Next, we define a *finite automaton* to be a 7-tuple that satisfies additional restrictions (where **outchar**, again assumed to be defined by a suitable type, denotes a second character set):

type AUTOMATON = (**sort char**, **sort outchar**,
  funct (**state**, **char**) **outchar** *o*,
  state *init*, **states** *all*, **states** *fin*, **ttable** *tr*):
 laws state *s*, **char** *i*:
  (*init* ∈ *all*) ≡ **true**,
  (*fin* ⊆ *all*) ≡ **true**,
  (*s* ∈ *all*) ≡ **true** ⇒ **defined** *o*(*s*, *i*),
  domstates(*tr*) ≡ *all**fin*,
  (*ran*(*tr*) ⊆ *all*) ≡ **true**,
  (*s* ∈ *domstates*(*tr*)) ≡ **true** ⇒ *isdef*(*tr*, *mp*(*s*, *i*)) ≡ **true**
endoftype.

Finally, a *finite state machine* can be defined by

type FSM = (**sort char**, **sort outchar**, **funct** (**state**, **char**) **outchar** *o*,
  state *init*, **states** *all*, **states** *fin*, **ttable** *tr*:
  include AUTOMATON(**char**, **outchar**, *o*, *init*, *all*, *fin*, *tr*)) *trans*:
 include ESEQU(**char**) **as** (**instring**, ...),

include ESEQU(**outchar**) **as** (**outstring**, ...),
funct (**instring**) **outstring** *trans*,
funct (**ttable**, **state**, **instring**, **outstring**) **outstring** *transit*,
laws instring *is*, **outstring** *os*, **state** *s*, **ttable** *t*: $s \in all$:
trans(*is*) ≡ *transit*(*tr*, *init*, *is*, <>),
transit(*t*, *s*, *is*, *os*) ≡
if $s \in fin \vee is$=<> **then** *os*
else *transit*(*t*, *t*[*mp*(*s*, **first***is*)], **rest***is*, *os*+*o*(*s*, **first***is*) **fi**
endoftype.

This definition captures a particular notion of a finite state machine which stops if either a final state is reached or if the input is exhausted. Of course, other notions of a finite state machine can be described in an analogous way.

3.3.5 Modes

Certain types and type schemes occur so frequently that it is reasonable to introduce particular shorthand notations. These special types, describing Cartesian product and direct sum, are called **modes** [Bauer et al. 85]. Syntactically, modes are introduced by a **mode declaration**. Their semantics is defined via instantiations of the associated type schemes. Since modes are presupposed to be operational, i.e. to be associated with standard implementations, they provide a basis for constructing implementations of (arbitrary) types (Chap. 8).

Unlike [Bauer et al. 85], we will also use modes for abbreviating type instantiations. Thus,

mode m = T(**n**)

is defined to be an abbreviation for

include T(**n**) **as** (**m**, ...).

Thus, for example, in connection with the definition of finite directed graphs, sets of nodes could have been defined simply by

mode nodeset = SET(**node**, =).

In accordance with [Bauer et al. 85], the **product** specifies objects that are composed of a finite number k > 0 of other objects, called **components**, together with operations for construction and selection. Thus, pairs as introduced in Sect. 3.3.4.1 are a product of two components.

A product of k object kinds is introduced by

mode m = $c(\mathbf{m_1}\ s_1, \ldots, \mathbf{m_k}\ s_k)$

which is defined to be an abbreviation for

include $\mathrm{PRODUCT_k}(\mathbf{m_1}, \ldots, \mathbf{m_k})$ **as** $(\mathbf{m}, c, s_1, \ldots, s_k)$ **where**
type $\mathrm{PRODUCT_k}$ = (**sort** $\mathbf{m_1}$, ..., **sort** $\mathbf{m_k}$) **p**, *comp*, $sel_1, \ldots, sel_k$:
sort p,
funct $(\mathbf{m_1}, \ldots, \mathbf{m_k})$ **p** *comp*,
funct (**p**) $\mathbf{m_1}$ sel_1,
...,

funct (p) $\mathbf{m_k}$ sel_k;
laws $\mathbf{m_1}$ x_1, ..., $\mathbf{m_k}$ x_k:
$sel_1(comp(x_1, ..., x_k)) \equiv x_1$, ...
$sel_k(comp(x_1,, ..., x_k)) \equiv x_k$
endoftype.

The type scheme PRODUCT_k is monomorphic relative to the parameter sorts. The constructor operation *comp* – like all operations defined by types – is strict in its arguments. Also, the product as defined above is non-associative.

A typical example of the use of mode declaration is given by

mode rat = *mkrat*(**int** *numerator*, **pnat** *divisor*)

introducing rational numbers by pairs consisting of an integral number and a positive natural number.

The product as introduced above provides, except for construction and selection, no further operations for tuples. Frequently, however, at least the induced equality, i.e. componentwise equality, is needed. Therefore, we introduce, as a further abbreviation, product construction with equality (see also [Bauer et al. 87]).

Thus, e.g.

mode pair(*eq*) = *mp*($\mathbf{m_1}$(eq_1) s_1, $\mathbf{m_2}$(eq_1) s_2)

abbreviates the type EPAIR introduced in Sect. 3.3.4.1, or

mode edge(=) = *me*(**node**(=) *in*, **node**(=) *out*)

abbreviates the type EDGE (Sect. 3.3.4.3).

The (direct) **sum** specifies the disjoint union of a finite number of carrier sets, which are called **variants** of the sum. In addition to injection and (partially defined) projection operations, which are analogous to the constructor and selector operations in products, one also needs discriminating predicates. The sum of $k > 0$ carriers is introduced [Bauer et al. 85] by

mode m = $v_1(\mathbf{m_1}\ p_1)$ | ... | $v_k(\mathbf{m_k}\ p_k)$

which is defined to be an abbreviation for

include $\text{SUM}_k(\mathbf{m_1}, ..., \mathbf{m_k})$ **as** (**m**, v_1, isv_1, p_1, ..., v_k, isv_k, p_k) **where**
type SUM_k = (**sort** $\mathbf{m_1}$, ..., **sort** $\mathbf{m_k}$) **s**, mk_1, $ismk_1$, pr_1, ..., mk_k, $ismk_k$, pr_k:
sort s,
funct ($\mathbf{m_1}$) **s** mk_1,
funct (**s**) **bool** $ismk_1$,
funct (**s** x: $ismk_1(x)$) $\mathbf{m_1}$ pr_1,
...
funct ($\mathbf{m_k}$) **s** mk_k,
funct (**s**) **bool** $ismk_k$,
funct (**s** x: $ismk_k(x)$) $\mathbf{m_k}$ pr_k;
laws $\mathbf{m_1}$ x_1, ..., $\mathbf{m_k}$ x_k:
$ismk_1(mk_1(x_1)) \equiv$ **true**,
$ismk_2(mk_1(x_1)) \equiv$ **false**, ..., $ismk_k(mk_1(x_1)) \equiv$ **false**,
$pr_1(mk_1(x_1)) \equiv x_1$,
...

$ismk_k(mk_k(x_k)) \equiv$ **true**,
$ismk_1(mk_k(x_k)) \equiv$ **false**, ..., $ismk_{k-1}(mk_k(x_k)) \equiv$ **false**,
$pr_k(mk_k(x_k)) \equiv x_k$
endoftype.

As PRODUCT_k, the scheme SUM_k is monomorphic relative to the parameter sorts. A typical example for a sum mode declaration is

mode result = *error*(**string** *message*) | *correct*(**int** *res*).

The test operations isv_i do not explicitly occur in a program text. They are abbreviated by the special keyword **is**. Thus, for example, an object *r* of kind **result** can be tested to be a proper result by

r **is** *correct*,

and an improper one by

r **is** *error*.

In connection with the sum mode it is also allowed to have nullary variants (without projections), which are variants which define new constant symbols. A typical example of this kind is

mode color = *red* | *blue* | *green*

that introduces a new object kind **color** consisting of the constants *red*, *blue*, and *green*, resp.

Furthermore, sums may also be quasi-ordered such that all elements of one variant are preceded in the quasi-ordering by all elements of another variant. For details see [Bauer et al. 85].

Similar to products, sums can be formally extended by an equality in a straightforward way. Since, however, this equality simply coincides with the equality on the variants of the sum, we do not introduce a particular notation.

Frequently we will also use, as a straightforward abbreviation, sum mode declarations without explicitly naming injections and projections.

The combined use of product and sum also gives meaning to **recursive mode declarations**. Thus, by the above definitions,

mode stack = <> | *push*(**m** *first*, **stack** *rest*)

is equivalent to the definition of a stack as given in Sect. 3.3.1.3.

As a further notational device in connection with modes, **submodes** may be used as a convenient shorthand notation for expressing restrictions on objects. The meaning of submode declarations such as

mode month = (**nat** x: $1 \le x \le 12$),
mode fraction = *mkfr*(**int** *num*, **pnat** *div*: $|num| < div$),

or

mode graph = *mg*(**nodeset** *nodes*, **edgeset** *edges*:
$\forall$ **edge** e: $e \in edges \Rightarrow in(e) \in nodes \wedge out(e) \in nodes$).

is intuitively clear. For a formal definition see again [Bauer et al. 85].

3.4 Additional Language Constructs for Formal Specifications

Although algebraic types provide a powerful means for formulating formal specifications, it is convenient to have further language constructs available that build upon suitable algebraic type definitions as primitives. These language constructs will provide expressive means for formulating **expressions** of the general form

begin D_1; ...; D_n; E **end**

where the D_i denote (object or function) declarations (see below) and E is again an expression. For expressions E that are not preceded by declarations the corresponding **begin** – **end** pair may be omitted.

In the following we shall use upright uppercase characters as symbols for declarations and expressions, boldface lowercase characters for sort symbols and keywords, and italic characters for identifiers.

The **scope** of an identifier introduced by a declaration ranges from the respective declaration to the corresponding **end.** This implies, in particular, that any applied occurrence of an object identifier within an expression has to be preceded by a respective declaration. A formal specification that fulfils this requirement is said to be **formally complete**. With respect to the scope, collective declarations of (systems of) functions, which are separated by commas, are treated as a single declaration. In this way, e.g., declarations of mutually recursive functions can be handled.

In order to avoid accumulation of the bracket pairs **begin end**, right-associativity is assumed. For example,

begin D_1; **begin** D_2; E **end end**

can be abbreviated to

begin D_1; D_2; E **end**

provided no "name clashes" occur, i.e., the identifiers in D_1 and D_2 are disjoint.

As a notational variant we will also allow postponed declarations of the form

E **where** D

as an alternative for

begin D; E **end**.

The **semantics** of these expressions will be given by a family of mappings (the "breadth", [Bauer et al. 85])

$B_{\mathbf{m}}$: «syntactic expressions» → «sets of semantic values»

that associates each closed expression of kind **m**, i.e. expression without free identifiers, with a set of semantic values (of kind **m**).

To avoid the use of environments, only the semantics of closed expressions is specified. For this purpose, semantic values are considered to be expressions as well, which gives rise to "mixed expressions" containing syntactic and semantic elements (which, however, are well distinguished). The semantics is specified in such a way that any B_m is only applied to expressions whose free identifiers have been replaced by suitable semantic values.

The **semantic values** are elements of 'domains' in the sense of [Scott 70], i.e. sets with a partial order "$\leq$ " defined on them which reflects the "information contents" of its elements. The domain of **proper semantic values** is denoted by DOM⟦**m**⟧. This domain is enriched by an **error element** $\perp$ ("undefined") to

$$\text{DOM}[\![\mathbf{m}]\!]^+ =_{def} \text{DOM}[\![\mathbf{m}]\!] \cup \{\perp\}$$

with the ordering

$$x \leq^+ y \Leftrightarrow x = \perp \vee x \leq y.$$

We distinguish between semantic values of

- *object kind* characterizing objects, and semantic values of
- *function kind* characterizing correspondences.

Semantic values of object kind are associated with

- the sort symbols of algebraically defined sorts,
- tuples (of object kinds), and
- sets (of object kinds).

The domain associated with a sort symbol **s** (defined by an algebraic type T) is the carrier set s^A (of the underlying model A of T). Since every element here is only comparable with itself, the identity is taken as an ordering. In this way DOM⟦**s**⟧$^+$ becomes a **flat domain** with the ordering

$$x \leq^+ y \Leftrightarrow x = \perp \vee x = y.$$

The domain associated with tuples is defined as the "smash product" of the domains of the components of the tuples; it consists of $\perp$ and all tuples of proper semantic values. The ordering between tuples of proper semantic values is defined componentwise. Again, we have a flat ordering.

The domain associated with sets over **m** is the set of all subsets of DOM⟦**m**⟧ enriched by $\perp$. The ordering is the identity on the subsets, and hence, again, a flat ordering.

Function declarations and abstractions (Sect. 3.4.1) are associated with semantic values of function kind.

The domain associated with semantic values of function kind **funct(m)n** is defined to be a subset of DOM⟦**m**⟧ $\times$ DOM⟦**n**⟧$^+$ which contains for each $u \in$ DOM⟦**m**⟧ at least one pair of which the first component is u. The ordering on DOM⟦**funct(m)n**⟧ is the 'Egli-Milner ordering' (for further details see [Bauer et al. 85]).

For any closed expression E, the set of values obtained by B_m⟦E⟧ is never empty by definition; if an expression has no proper semantic value, e.g. in case of an undefined basic operation or in case of a non-terminating function call, then $\perp$, denoting undefined, is associated to it. Thus, the range of B_m is formally defined by

$$\mathcal{P}(\text{DOM}[\![\mathbf{m}]\!]^+) \backslash \{\varnothing\}$$

(where $\mathcal{P}$ denotes the powerset).

In the sequel we will omit the indices **m** when dealing with B_m. For semantic values u we define B⟦u⟧ = $\{u\}$. Furthermore, we will use the abbreviation

$$B^{\sim}[\![E]\!] =_{def} B[\![E]\!] \setminus \{\perp\}$$

for denoting the set of all defined values of an expression E.

The "breadth" B also enables us to make the important notions of definedness and determinacy (which were informally introduced in Sect. 3.1) more precise. As in [Bauer et al. 85], we call an expression E (of object kind)

- **defined**, iff $\bot \notin B[\![E]\!]$; and
- **determinate**, iff $|B[\![E]\!]| = 1$.

Since for all kinds of expressions E a definition of B will be given explicitly, conditions for definedness and determinacy of expressions can be computed (Ex. 3.4-1).

Furthermore, we call two expressions E_1 and E_2 (of the same object kind)

- **equivalent**, iff $B[\![E_1]\!] = B[\![E_2]\!]$ holds;

and we call

- E_1 a **descendant** of E_2, iff $B[\![E_1]\!] \subseteq B[\![E_2]\!]$ holds.

Examples that illustrate these notions will be given below.

These definitions are extended to expressions of function kind in the usual way (for details see again [Bauer et al. 85]). Thus, for example, an expression E of kind **funct(m)r** is **defined** iff $E(u)$ is defined for any $u \in \mathrm{DOM}[\![\mathbf{m}]\!]$. The other notions are extended in an analogous way.

3.4.1 Applicative Language Constructs

Basic expressions are provided by identifiers for **constants** and **operations** of the underlying basic types. Their values depend on the particular model of the basic types. For c and o being arbitrary constant and operation symbols defined by some type T, and c^A, o^A being the respective interpretations in some model A, we define

$$B[\![c]\!] =_{def} \{c^A\}$$
$$B[\![o]\!] =_{def} \{\tilde{o}^A\}$$

with $\tilde{o}^A$ being the "natural extension" of o^A which explicitly takes care of undefinedness: $\tilde{o}^A(u)$ yields $\bot$, if $o^A(u)$ is not defined.

Thus, for example, if A is the underlying model of the type NAT (Sect. 3.3.1.2) we have

$$B[\![0]\!] = \{0^A\},$$
$$B[\![succ]\!] = \{\{(0^A, succ^A(0^A))\} \cup \{((succ^A)^n(0^A), (succ^A)^{n+1}(0^A)): n \in \mathbb{N}\}\},$$
$$B[\![pred]\!] = \{\{(0^A, \bot)\} \cup \{((succ^A)^{n+1}(0^A), (succ^A)^n(0^A)): n \in \mathbb{N}\}\}$$

(where $(succ^A)^n$ is short for the n-fold application of $succ$).

Note that, by definition, constants and operations defined by algebraic types are always defined and determinate.

Further basic expressions can be built using a **conditional expression**. It has the general form

if C **then** E_1 **else** E_2 **fi**

where E_1 and E_2 are arbitrary expressions of the same kind (that also determines the kind of the conditional expression) and C is a boolean expression. The semantics of such a conditional expression is given by

$$\mathrm{B}[\![\textbf{if } C \textbf{ then } E_1 \textbf{ else } E_2 \textbf{ fi}]\!] =_{def} V_1 \cup V_2 \cup V_3$$

where

$V_1 =_{def} \{\bot\}$, if $\bot \in \mathrm{B}[\![C]\!]$, and $\varnothing$ otherwise;
$V_2 =_{def} \mathrm{B}[\![E_1]\!]$, if **true** $\in \mathrm{B}[\![C]\!]$, and $\varnothing$ otherwise;
$V_3 =_{def} \mathrm{B}[\![E_2]\!]$, if **false** $\in \mathrm{B}[\![C]\!]$, and $\varnothing$ otherwise.

Obviously, if C is a determinate expression, then this definition coincides with the usual meaning of the conditional known from existing programming languages; in this case we have

$$\mathrm{B}[\![\textbf{if } C \textbf{ then } E_1 \textbf{ else } E_2 \textbf{ fi}]\!] =_{def} \begin{cases} \{\bot\}, \text{ if } \mathrm{B}[\![C]\!] = \{\bot\} \\ \mathrm{B}[\![E_1]\!], \text{ if } \mathrm{B}[\![C]\!] = \{\textbf{true}\} \\ \mathrm{B}[\![E_2]\!], \text{ if } \mathrm{B}[\![C]\!] = \{\textbf{false}\}. \end{cases}$$

A simple example of a conditional expression is *the absolute value of an integer x*:

if $x \geq 0$ **then** x **else** $-x$ **fi**.

For frequently occurring conditional expressions of kind **bool**, we introduce particular shorthand notations. Thus, we use the sequential conjunction

$E_1 \Delta E_2$

for

if E_1 **then** E_2 **else false fi**

and the sequential disjunction

$E_1 \nabla E_2$

for

if E_1 **then true else** E_2 **fi**.

Simple examples are *a sequence s has more than one element*:

$(s \neq <>)\ \Delta\ (\textbf{rest}\, s \neq <>)$

or *a sequence s has at most one element*:

$(s = <>)\ \nabla\ (\textbf{rest}\, s = <>)$.

Nested conditionals such as

if C_1 **then** E_1 **else if** C_2 **then** E_2 **else** E_3 **fi fi**

can be abbreviated to

if C_1 **then** E_1 **elsf** C_2 **then** E_2 **else** E_3 **fi**.

Another basic construct is the **tuple** which serves for collecting values, e.g. as arguments or results of a function. A tuple (with n components) has the general form

$(E_1, ..., E_n)$

with E_i being expressions (of possibly different kinds); semantically it is defined by

$\mathrm{B}^{\sim}[\![(E_1, ..., E_n)]\!] =_{def} \mathrm{B}^{\sim}[\![E_1]\!] \times ... \times \mathrm{B}^{\sim}[\![E_n]\!]$ and
$\bot \in \mathrm{B}[\![(E_1, ..., E_n)]\!] \Leftrightarrow (\bot \in \mathrm{B}[\![E_1]\!] \vee ... \vee \bot \in \mathrm{B}[\![E_n]\!])$.

A simple example is *splitting a sequence s*:

(**first**s, **rest**s),

the breadth of which, according to the semantic definition, is $\bot$ if s is empty.

Finally, the basic construct **finite choice** allows us to choose between the values of a finite number of expressions of object kind. It has the general form

$(E_1 \,[]\, E_2 \,[]\, ...[]\, E_n)$

with E_i being expressions of the same kind.

A choice mainly will be used for the formalization of an indeterminate task. For example,

an arbitrary prime number less than 10

can be formalized by

$(2 \,[]\, 3 \,[]\, 5 \,[]\, 7)$.

A choice is semantically defined by

$B[\![(E_1 \,[]\, E_2 \,[]\, ...[]\, E_n)]\!] =_{def} \cup_{i=1..n} B[\![E_i]\!]$.

This semantic definition reflects **erratic non-determinism**, i.e. a completely arbitrary choice. This means, in particular, that e.g.

$B[\![(1 \,[]\, 2) + (1 \,[]\, 2)]\!] = \{2, 3, 4\}$,

and, hence, that

$(1 \,[]\, 2) + (1 \,[]\, 2)$

and

$2 \times (1 \,[]\, 2)$

are not equivalent, since

$B[\![2 \times (1 \,[]\, 2)]\!] = \{2, 4\} \neq B[\![(1 \,[]\, 2) + (1 \,[]\, 2)]\!]$.

However, $2 \times (1 \,[]\, 2)$ is obviously a descendant of $(1 \,[]\, 2) + (1 \,[]\, 2)$.

In the literature other possibilities of giving semantics to non-determinism can be found, such as *angelic non-determinism* (which means that whenever there is at least one defined value in the choice set, then the choice yields a defined value) and *demonic non-determinism* (which means that whenever undefined is in the choice set, the choice will yield undefined). Erratic nondeterminism has the essential advantage that it allows to model both, angelic and demonic non-determinism (for details see [Broy et al. 79b]), but not vice versa.

Differently from the other constructs introduced before, which are **deterministic**, the finite choice is a **non-deterministic construct**, as it introduces potential non-determinism. We call an expression **non-deterministic**, if it contains a non-deterministic construct. Note that a non-deterministic expression may well be determinate, as can be seen from the trivial example

$(1 \,[]\, 1)$.

However, for an arbitrary expression E only the property

E is indeterminate $\Rightarrow$ E is non-deterministic

holds.

Another non-deterministic construct is provided by the **guarded expression**. Its general form is

if C_1 **then** E_1
[] ...
[] C_n **then** E_n **else** E_{n+1} **fi**

with C_i denoting boolean expressions (called guards) and E_j denoting expressions of the same (object) kind.

For n=1 a guarded expression is equivalent to a conditional expression. For n≥2 a guarded expression as above is so defined that it is equivalent to the choice

(**if** C_1 **then** E_1 **else** G_1 **fi**
[] ...
[] **if** C_n **then** E_n **else** G_n **fi**)

where

$G_i =_{def}$ **if** C_1 **then** E_1 [] ...
[] C_{i-1} **then** E_{i-1}
[] C_{i+1} **then** E_{i+1} [] ...
[] C_n **then** E_n **else** E_{n+1} **fi**.

This means that a guarded expression may yield ⊥, if any of the guards may yield ⊥. Otherwise, if all guards yield only defined values, a guarded expression results in an arbitrary value E_i from some B⟦E_i⟧ for which the corresponding C_i evaluates to **true**.

The **else** branch in a guarded expression can be omitted. For n≥2 the meaning of the resulting construct

if C_1 **then** E_1
[] ...
[] C_n **then** E_n **fi**

is basically the same as for the guarded expression, except for the case, when all guards are defined and none of them evaluates to **true**; in this case, the result is ⊥.

A typical example of a guarded expression without **else** branch is the following expression describing the absolute value of some object *x*:

if $x \geq 0$ **then** x
[] $x \leq 0$ **then** $-x$ **fi**.

For n=1 the guarded expression (with omitted **else** branch) leads to the further borderline case

if C **then** E **fi**

which yields an arbitrary element from B⟦E⟧, if C is defined and evaluates to **true**; and ⊥, otherwise.

The central concept of any applicative language is the **application** of a function to its arguments. This application is typed: the parameter kind of the function must agree with the kind of the argument.

As usual, a function application has the general form

F(E)

where F is an expression of kind **funct(m)n** (with **m** and **n** standing for arbitrary tuples of parameter and result kinds) with B⟦F⟧ = {*f*}, and E is an expression of kind **m**. Semantically, a function application is defined by

$$B[\![F(E)]\!] =_{def} \cup_{e \in B[\![E]\!]} B[\![F(e)]\!]$$

where

$$B[\![F(e)]\!] =_{def} \begin{cases} \{v \in \mathrm{DOM}[\![\mathbf{n}]\!]+ : (e, v) \in f\}, \text{ if } e \neq \bot \text{ and } f \neq \bot \\ \{\bot\}, \text{ otherwise} \end{cases}$$

According to this definition we have, for example, with 0 denoting 0^A and 1 denoting $succ^A(0^A)$,

$$B[\![succ(0)]\!] = \{1\},$$

since (0, 1) is the only pair in B⟦*succ*⟧ with first component 0. Likewise, we have

$$B[\![pred(0)]\!] = \{\bot\},$$

and

$$B[\![succ(0) \, [] \, pred(0)]\!] = \{1, \bot\}.$$

Also according to the above definition, every argument of a function is fixed once and for all for the whole application, even if the actual argument is non-determinate ("call-time choice"). For example, for $f(x) =_{def} x+x$ we have $B[\![f(1 \, [] \, 2)]\!] = \{2, 4\}$. Note also, that the above definition implies **strictness** of the function application, i.e. if the argument is undefined then the application yields undefined, too.

Only expressions of function kind remain to be dealt with. These expressions are introduced by object and function declarations.

An **object declaration** has the general form

m *x* = E

where E is an expression of object kind that does not contain *x*.

Given a mode declaration such as

mode rat = *mkrat*(**int** *numerator*, **pnat** *divisor*)

(Sect. 3.3.5), objects of kind **rat** now can be introduced by

rat *a* = *mkrat*(–3, 4).

As a shorthand notation in connection with object declarations we also allow the omission of the constructor and write simply

rat *a* = (–3, 4),

since the constructor always can be inferred from the respective mode declaration.

Declarations have no independent meaning, i.e., if **m** *x* = E is a declaration, then B⟦**m** *x* = E⟧ is not defined as such. Meaning is only given to expressions as introduced in the beginning of this section.

The meaning of an expression containing an object declaration is reduced to the meaning of an application by

$\mathrm{B}[\![\mathbf{begin\ m}\ x = \mathrm{E}_1;\ \mathrm{E}_2\ \mathbf{end}]\!] = \mathrm{B}[\![((\mathbf{m}\ x)\mathbf{r}\colon \mathrm{E}_2)(\mathrm{E}_1)]\!]$.

Thus, for example, we have

$\mathrm{B}[\![\mathbf{begin\ nat}\ x = (1 \mathbin{[]} 2);\ x + x\ \mathbf{end}]\!] =$
$\mathrm{B}[\![((\mathbf{nat}\ x)\mathbf{nat}\colon x + x)(1 \mathbin{[]} 2)]\!] = \{2, 4\}$.

For defined and determinate E_1

$\mathrm{B}[\![\mathbf{begin\ m}\ x = \mathrm{E}_1;\ \mathrm{E}_2\ \mathbf{end}]\!]$

is furthermore equivalent to

$\mathrm{B}[\![\mathrm{E}_2[\mathrm{E}_1\ \mathbf{for}\ x]]\!]$

where $\mathrm{E}_2[\mathrm{E}_1\ \mathbf{for}\ x]$ denotes the expression E_2 with E_1 substituted for each occurrence of x.

Note that this particular definition implies that an object declaration may be used to fix a choice associated with an indeterminate expression. Thus, in contrast to the example above, for x being declared by

$\mathbf{m}\ x = (1 \mathbin{[]} 2);$

the property

$x + x = 2 \times x$

does hold.

In general,

$(\mathbf{m}\ x)\mathbf{r}\colon \mathrm{E}$

is an expression of function kind, called **abstraction**. An abstraction denotes a correspondence between arguments and results. Its semantics is defined by

$\mathrm{B}[\![(\mathbf{m}\ x)\mathbf{r}\colon \mathrm{E}]\!] =_{\mathrm{def}} \{\{(u, v) \in \mathsf{DOM}[\![\mathbf{m}]\!] \times \mathsf{DOM}[\![\mathbf{r}]\!]^{+}\colon v \in \mathrm{B}[\![\mathrm{E}[u\ \mathbf{for}\ x]]\!]\}\}$.

Note that this definition implies that an abstraction is always defined and determinate.

For the example given above we have

$\mathrm{B}[\![(\mathbf{nat}\ x)\mathbf{nat}\colon x + x]\!] =$
$\{\{(u, v) \in \mathsf{DOM}[\![\mathbf{nat}]\!] \times \mathsf{DOM}[\![\mathbf{nat}]\!]^{+}\colon v \in \mathrm{B}[\![u + u]\!]\}\} =$
$\{\{(n, n + n)\colon n \in \mathbb{N}\}\}$.

A **function declaration** has the general form

$\mathbf{funct}\ f = (\mathbf{m}\ x)\ \mathbf{r}\colon \mathrm{E}$

or equivalently

$\mathbf{funct}\ (\mathbf{m}\ x)\ \mathbf{r}\ f,\ f(x) = \mathrm{E}$

with E being an expression of kind **r** that may contain occurrences of x and f. If E contains an occurrence of f, then f is called a **recursive function**. Again, **m** and **r** stand for arbitrary argument and result kinds, respectively.

As an example of how to use function declarations in formal specifications we consider an operational specification of the problem (see also Sect. 3.1)

Sort a given sequence s of natural numbers.

A formalization is

mode natsequ = ESEQU(**nat**);
sort(*s*) **where**

funct *sort* = (**natsequ** *s*) **natsequ**:
  if *s* =<> **then** *s* **else** *min*(*s*) + *sort*(*delete*(*min*(*s*), *s*)) **fi**

where *min* determines a least element of a sequence (see below) and *delete*, removing an element from a sequence, is defined by

funct *delete* = (**nat** *x*, **natsequ** *s*) **natsequ**:
  if *s* =<> **then** *s* **elsf first***s* = x **then rest***s* **else first***s* + *delete*(*x*, **rest***s*) **fi**.

Of course, it is also possible to formulate higher-order functions, i.e., functions that have functions as arguments and/or result. An example is a function that *filters* a sequence with respect to an (arbitrary) predicate *P*:

funct *filter* = (**sequ** *s*, **funct**(**m**)**bool** *P*) **sequ**:
  if *s* =<> **then** <>
  elsf *P*(**first***s*) **then first***s* + *filter*(**rest***s*, *P*) **else** *filter*(**rest***s*, *P*) **fi**.

The semantics of an expression containing a function declaration is defined by

B⟦**begin funct** *f* = (**m** *x*) **r**: E_1; E_2 **end**⟧ $=_{def}$ B⟦E_2[*g* **for** *f*]⟧

where *g* is the least correspondence (with respect to the Egli-Milner ordering [Bauer et al. 85]) such that

B⟦(**m** *x*) **r**: E_1[*g* **for** *f*]⟧ = {*g*} holds.

This means that *g* is the least solution ('least fixed point') of the functional equation associated with the declaration of *f*. This solution always exists.

Within a function declaration a whole system of functions may be introduced which mutually refer to each other. The above definition can be straightforwardly extended to cope with this case, too. For further details we refer the reader to [Bauer et al. 85].

Within both object declarations and function declarations, restrictions of the arguments by predicates, called **assertions**, can be used.

An object declaration with assertion has the form

(**m** *x*: C) = E

where C is a boolean expression and E is an expression of object kind. Its meaning is equivalent to the meaning of

m *x* = ((**m** *y*: C) **m**: *y*)(E)

where the meaning of an abstraction (with assertion) such as

(**m** *x*: C) **r**: E

in turn is defined by

(**m** *x*) **r**: **if** C **then** E **fi**.

This means for example that

(**nat** *x*: *x* > 2) = 3

is equivalent to

nat $x = 3$,

whereas

(**nat** x: $x > 2$) = 1

is not defined.

The object declaration (**m** x: C) = E also gives meaning to an assertion restricting the parameters in a function declaration such as

funct f = (**m** x: C) **r**: E.

According to the above definitions, f is a partial function the application of which evaluates to undefined for all arguments that do not satisfy C. Note, however, that also for arguments x which fulfil C, $f(x)$ may be undefined.

Likewise, the meaning of an assertion for the result of an abstraction such as

(**m** x)(**r** y: C): E

is reduced to the meaning of

(**m** x) **r**: ((**r** y) **r**: **if** C **then** y **fi**)(E).

As an example of a function declaration with assertion we consider the problem of computing a least element of a sequence. Obviously, the problem is not defined for an empty sequence. Therefore, we define

funct *min* = (**natsequ** *s*: *s* ≠<>) **nat**:
  if rest*s* =<> **then first***s* **else min**(**first***s*, *min*(**rest***s*)) **fi**

(where **min** determines the minimum of two natural numbers).

The language constructs dealt with so far in this section allow us to formulate operational specifications. In order to be able to also formulate descriptive specifications, further constructs are introduced in the following subsections.

In the sequel we call an expression **operational**, if it is built only from those constructs that have been introduced so far. Otherwise i.e. whenever it contains one of the constructs to be introduced in the following subsections, we call it **descriptive**.

3.4.2 Quantified Expressions

Certain tasks deal with properties. Frequently one encounters informal specifications of the form

is there an x, such that ...

or specifications of the form

does ... hold for all x?.

In addition to these "explicit" occurrences of the existential and universal quantifier, there are also implicit ones. Thus, for example, an informal specification of the kind

is there a largest natural number x which equals the sum of its proper divisors allows for straightforward formalization, if it is made explicit what "largest" means:

Is there ... and there is no natural number y which is larger than x (w.r.t. the natural ordering on numbers).

In these cases it is profitable to use a respective quantifier. Thus, a formalization of the latter example might be

$\exists$ **nat** x: $x = \sigma(x) \wedge \neg(\exists$ **nat** y: $y = \sigma(y) \wedge y > x)$

or, equivalently,

$\exists$ **nat** x: $x = \sigma(x) \wedge (\forall$ **nat** y: $y = \sigma(y) \Rightarrow y \leq x)$,

where σ is assumed to be a primitive operation, available from a suitable underlying type definition, yielding the sum of the proper divisors of its argument.

For quantified expressions we have the general form

$\forall$ **m** x: P(x), resp.
$\exists$ **m** x: P(x)

where x is the **quantified variable, m** is the **domain** of the quantification, and P its **characterizing predicate**. For reasons of monotonicity (Sect. 4.1), **m** is restricted to non-functional kinds.

Here, the notation P(x) is used to indicate that the expression P may contain (free) occurrences of x. The identifier x is bound by the quantification; its scope is the quantified expression.
As in the previous subsection, **m** stands for an arbitrary object kind. If **m** is of tuple kind, the parentheses for tuple forming may be omitted. Furthermore, for components of the same kind a domain indication has to be given only once. Thus for example we may write

$\exists$ **nat** x, y, **real** z: P(x, y, z),

instead of

$\exists$ (**nat** x, **nat** y, **real** z): P(x, y, z).

The semantics of a quantified expression is given by

$$B[\![\exists\ \mathbf{m}\ x\colon P(x)]\!] \ni \begin{cases} \mathbf{false}, \text{ iff for all } u \in \mathrm{DOM}[\![\mathbf{m}]\!]\colon \mathbf{false} \in B[\![P(u)]\!] \\ \mathbf{true}, \text{ iff there exists } u \in \mathrm{DOM}[\![\mathbf{m}]\!]\colon \mathbf{true} \in B[\![P(u)]\!] \\ \quad \text{and for all } u \in \mathrm{DOM}[\![\mathbf{m}]\!]\colon B[\![P(u)]\!] \neq \{\bot\} \\ \bot, \text{ iff there exists } u \in \mathrm{DOM}[\![\mathbf{m}]\!]\colon \bot \in B[\![P(u)]\!] \end{cases}$$

and

$$B[\![\forall\ \mathbf{m}\ x\colon P(x)]\!] \ni \begin{cases} \mathbf{true}, \text{ iff for all } u \in \mathrm{DOM}[\![\mathbf{m}]\!]\colon \mathbf{true} \in B[\![P(u)]\!] \\ \mathbf{false}, \text{ iff there exists } u \in \mathrm{DOM}[\![\mathbf{m}]\!]\colon \mathbf{false} \in B[\![P(u)]\!] \\ \quad \text{and for all } u \in \mathrm{DOM}[\![\mathbf{m}]\!]\colon B[\![P(u)]\!] \neq \{\bot\} \\ \bot, \text{ iff there exists } u \in \mathrm{DOM}[\![\mathbf{m}]\!]\colon \bot \in B[\![P(u)]\!]. \end{cases}$$

These definitions simplify for a determinate predicate P in an obvious way.

According to these definitions, we have for example

$B[\![\exists\ \mathbf{nat}\ x\colon 15/x = 3]\!] = \{\bot\}$,

or

$B[\![\exists\ \mathbf{nat}\ x\colon x < (0 \,[\,]\, 1 \,[\,]\, \mathit{pred}(0))]\!] = \{\mathbf{false}, \mathbf{true}, \bot\}$.

The quantifiers ∃ and ∀ may also range over a restricted domain:

$B[\![\exists\ (\mathbf{m}\ x\colon C)\colon P]\!]$

is defined by

$B[\![\exists\ (\mathbf{m}\ x\colon C)\colon P]\!] = B[\![\exists\ \mathbf{m}\ x\colon \mathbf{if}\ C\ \mathbf{then}\ P\ \mathbf{else\ false\ fi}]\!]$;

and

$B[\![\forall\ (\mathbf{m}\ x\colon C)\colon P]\!]$

is defined by

$B[\![\forall\ (\mathbf{m}\ x\colon C)\colon P]\!] = B[\![\forall\ \mathbf{m}\ x\colon \mathbf{if}\ C\ \mathbf{then}\ P\ \mathbf{else\ true\ fi}]\!]$.

Restricted domains provide a way of getting rid of unwanted undefinednesses. Thus, for example, in the first example above, undefinedness can be avoided by restricting the domain of the quantification to natural numbers greater than 0. Then we have

$B[\![\exists\ (\mathbf{nat}\ x > 0)\colon 15/x = 3]\!] = \{\mathbf{true}\}$.

As in predicate logic, existential and universal quantification are related:

$\exists\ \mathbf{m}\ x\colon P(x)$

is equivalent to

$\neg(\forall\ \mathbf{m}\ x\colon \neg\ P(x))$.

Although the use of quantified expressions in formal specifications is obvious, it should be pointed out that it is possible to formulate even undecidable properties. Typical examples are

$\exists\ \mathbf{nat}\ x\colon x = \sigma(x) \wedge \mathbf{odd}\ x$,

'Fermat's conjecture'

$\forall\ (\mathbf{nat}\ n\colon n > 2)\colon \neg \exists\ \mathbf{nat}\ x, y, z\colon x^n + y^n = z^n$,

or 'Goldbach's conjecture'

$\forall\ (\mathbf{nat}\ n\colon n \neq 2)\colon \exists\ \mathbf{nat}\ p, q\colon n = p+q \wedge \mathit{prime}(p) \wedge \mathit{prime}(q)$

(where *prime* is assumed to be a primitive operation checking whether a natural number is prime).

As mentioned at the end of the previous subsection, formal specifications containing quantified expressions are called descriptive. In general, transforming a descriptive specification into an operational one is an important and difficult step in program development (see Chap. 5). Only if $DOM[\![\mathbf{m}]\!]$ is finite, is there an obvious (operational) implementation by exhaustive search (Sect. 5.3.2.2).

3.4.3 Choice and Description

A choice appears in most specifications that are informally given by

some ... such that ...

A typical example of this kind is (an equivalent reformulation of specification (a) from Sect. 3.1)

some natural number x such that x equals the sum of its proper divisors.

Formally, we will write for this example

some nat x: $x = \sigma(x)$,

where, as in the previous subsection, σ is assumed to yield the sum of the proper divisors of its argument.

The general form of a **choice** is

some m x: P(x)

where, again, x is the **quantified variable, m** is the **domain** of the choice, and P its **characterizing predicate**. As in quantified expressions, **m** is restricted to non-functional kinds for reasons of monotonicity.

Formally, for a determinate predicate P the semantics of a choice is defined by

$$\mathrm{B}[\![\textbf{some m } x\text{: P}(x)]\!] =_{\text{def}} \begin{cases} V, \text{ if } V \neq \varnothing \text{ and} \\ \qquad \text{for all } u \in \mathrm{DOM}[\![\mathbf{m}]\!]\text{: } \bot \notin \mathrm{B}[\![\mathrm{P}(u)]\!] \\ \{\bot\}, \text{ otherwise} \end{cases}$$

where

$V =_{\text{def}} \{u \in \mathrm{DOM}[\![\mathbf{m}]\!]\text{: } \mathrm{B}[\![\mathrm{P}(u)]\!] = \{\textbf{true}\}\}$.

This means that a choice yields an arbitrary element of DOM⟦**m**⟧, the semantic domain associated with **m**, for which P is fulfilled, provided that P is defined for all elements of DOM⟦**m**⟧; otherwise, the choice is not defined.

For an indeterminate predicate P the semantics of a choice is given by

$\mathrm{B}[\![\textbf{some m } x\text{: P}(x)]\!] =_{\text{def}} \bigcup_{p \in \mathrm{D}[\![\mathrm{P}]\!]} \mathrm{B}[\![\textbf{some m } x\text{: p}(x)]\!]$

where D⟦P⟧ denotes the set of all determinate descendants of P.

According to this definition we have, e.g.

$\mathrm{B}[\![\textbf{some nat } x\text{: } x > 1]\!] = \mathbb{N} \setminus \{0, 1\}$

and

$\mathrm{B}[\![\textbf{some nat } x\text{: } x < 0]\!] = \{\bot\}$,

since for all natural numbers x, $\mathrm{B}[\![x < 0]\!] = \{\textbf{false}\}$.

Note, that also

$\mathrm{B}[\![\textbf{some nat } x\text{: } 15/x = 3]\!] = \{\bot\}$,

since $0 \in \mathrm{DOM}[\![\textbf{nat}]\!]$ and $\mathrm{B}[\![15/0]\!] = \{\bot\}$. This in turn implies that

$\mathrm{B}[\![\textbf{some nat } x\text{: } 15/x = 3 \,[\,]\, x = 5]\!] = \{\bot, 5\}$,

since $\mathrm{B}[\![\textbf{some nat } x\text{: } x = 5]\!] = \{5\}$.

For the latter example, in order to exclude $\bot$ as a possible value, an appropriate restriction of the domain of the choice has to be added:

some (nat x: $x > 0$): $(15/x = 3 \,[\,]\, x = 5)$,

which then is equivalent to

some (**nat** x: $x > 0$): $15/x = 3$.

As in the previous subsection, the meaning of a **some** operator quantifying over a restricted domain is given by

B⟦**some** (**m** x: C): P⟧ = B⟦**some m** x: **if** C **then** P **else false fi**⟧.

Thus, for our last example we also could have written (equivalently)

some nat x: **if** $x > 0$ **then** $15/x = 3$ **else false fi**.

Note that definedness is a semantic property which is not decidable in general, as

some nat x: $x = \sigma(x) \wedge$ **odd** x

shows. Here it is simply not known whether a natural number with the required properties does exist.

Other examples exemplifying the use of the choice operator are

(a) **some int** x: $x^2 = 2$;
(b) **some real** x: $x^2 = 2$;
(c) *some decomposition of an arbitrary string s into two parts*:
(**string** s) (**string**, **string**) : **some string** u, v: $u+v = s$;
(d) *some decomposition of an arbitrary string s into two non-empty parts*:
(**string** s) (**string**, **string**) : **some string** u, v: $u+v = s \wedge u \neq$ <> $\wedge\, v \neq$ <>.

These examples illustrate the importance of the domain indication within a choice: (a) is undefined, whereas (b) is well-defined. Note that (d) is defined only for **string** s with $|s| \geq 2$.

The **some** operator is a generalization of the finite choice and thus also a non-deterministic construct. Hence, **some**-expressions are always non-deterministic – but not necessarily indeterminate.

Like the semantics of the finite choice, the semantics of the **some**-operator reflects erratic non-determinism. For our above example,

some nat x: ($15/x = 3$ [] $x = 5$),

an angelic non-deterministic semantics would yield 5, whereas a demonic non-deterministic semantics would yield $\perp$.

The **some** operator also may be used within a function declaration, thus leading to a "non-deterministic function". A typical example is provided by a descriptive specification of the problem of sorting a sequence of natural numbers (Sect. 3.4.1):

```
mode natsequ = ESEQU(nat);
sort(s) where

funct sort = (natsequ s) natsequ:
   some natsequ x: issorted(x) ∧ isperm(x, s) where

   funct issorted = (natsequ x) bool:
      x =<> ∇ rest x =<> ∇
      (∀ natsequ u, v: (u ≠<> ∧ v ≠<>) Δ (u+v = x ∧ last u ≤ first v));
```

funct *isperm* = (**natsequ** *y*, **natsequ** *t*) **bool**:
sequtobag(*y*) = *sequtobag*(*t*)

(where *sequtobag* denotes the conversion of a sequence into a bag, Ex. 3.4-3c).
Occasionally, tasks will be informally given in the form

that ... such that ....

An example of this kind is

that natural number x such that $x^2 = 4$.

This can be formalized by

that nat x: $x^2 = 4$

but also equivalently by

that int x: $x^2 = 4 \wedge x \geq 0$.

As, in contrast to the choice denoted by the **some** operator, a unique element with certain properties is to be described here, we call such an expression a **description**. The general form of a description is

that m x: $P(x)$

where, again, x is the **quantified variable**, **m** is the **domain** of the description, and P its **characterizing predicate**. Also, as before, **m** is restricted to non-functional kinds.

The semantics of a description with determinate predicate P is defined by

$$B[\![\textbf{that m } x\text{: } P(x)]\!] =_{def} \begin{cases} V, \text{ if } |V| = 1 \text{ and for all } u \in \text{DOM}[\![\textbf{m}]\!]\text{: } \bot \notin B[\![P(u)]\!] \\ \{\bot\}, \text{ otherwise} \end{cases}$$

where, again,

$$V =_{def} \{u \in \text{DOM}[\![\textbf{m}]\!]\text{: } B[\![P(u)]\!] = \{\textbf{true}\}\}.$$

This means that a description yields the unique element of $\text{DOM}[\![\textbf{m}]\!]$ for which P is fulfilled, provided P is defined for all elements of $\text{DOM}[\![\textbf{m}]\!]$ and there is a unique element that fulfils P; otherwise, the description is not defined.

Thus, for our examples above, we have

$$B[\![\textbf{that nat } x\text{: } x^2 = 4]\!] = B[\![\textbf{that int } x\text{: } x^2 = 4 \wedge x \geq 0]\!] = \{2\},$$

whereas

$$B[\![\textbf{that int } x\text{: } x^2 = 4]\!] = \{\bot\},$$

since

$$\{u \in \text{DOM}[\![\textbf{int}]\!]\text{: } B[\![u^2 = 4]\!] = \{\textbf{true}\}\} = \{-2, 2\}.$$

Of course, similar to the above, we have

$$B[\![\textbf{that nat } x\text{: } 15/x = 3]\!] = \{\bot\}.$$

As for the choice, a restriction for the domain of a description is allowed. It has the form

$B[\![$**that** (**m** x: C): P$]\!]$

and its meaning is given by

$B[\![$**that** (**m** x: C): P$]\!]$ = $B[\![$**that m** x: **if** C **then** P **else false fi**$]\!]$.

Any description can be formulated in terms of the **some** operator:

that m x: P(x)

is equivalent to

some m x: (P(x) $\wedge$ ($\forall$ **m** y: P(y) $\Rightarrow x = y$)).

In particular, this means that whenever uniqueness is doubtful for a certain task, the **some** operator should be used in the specification rather than the **that** operator.

This latter equivalence also defines the meaning of a description with indeterminate predicate P in a straightforward way.

The choice and description operators are frequently used in specifications that deal with the inverse of some function.

For example, let

funct f = (**m** x) **n**: E

be given. Then an inverse of f can be defined by

funct f^{-1} = (**n** y) **m**: **some m** x: $f(x) = y$.

If y is not among the results of f, the **some** expression in the body of f^{-1} is not defined. Hence, for ensuring definedness the assertion

$\exists$ **m** x: $f(x) = y$

has to be added to the definition of f^{-1}:

funct f^{-1} = (**n** y: $\exists$ **m** x: $f(x) = y$) **m**: **some m** x: $f(x) = y$.

If we would rather specify

funct f^{-1} = (**n** y) **m**: **that m** x: $f(x) = y$,

the above assertion had to be strengthened by additionally requiring injectivity of f:

funct f^{-1} = (**n** y: $\exists$ **m** x: $f(x) = y \wedge$ ($\forall$ **m** u, v: $f(u) = f(v) \Rightarrow u = v$)) **m**:
  that m x: $f(x) = y$.

3.4.4 Set Comprehension

Frequently a task calls for the set of all solutions rather than an arbitrary or specific one ('exhaustive non-determinism'). A typical example of this kind is

the set of all prime numbers

or, formally,

{**nat** x: *prime*(x)},

or also, using the basic property of divisibility (denoted by "|")

{**nat** x: $\forall$ (**nat** y: $1 < y < x$): $\neg$ ($y \mid x$)}.

For formalizing tasks of the above kind, we introduce **set comprehension** which, in its general form, reads

$\{\mathbf{m}\, x\colon P(x)\}$

where, as before, x is the **quantified variable**, **m** is the **domain** of the set comprehension, and P its **characterizing predicate**. Again for reasons of monotonicity, **m** is restricted to non-functional kinds.

In accordance with the semantics of quantification, the semantics of a set comprehension with determinate predicate P is defined by

$$B[\![\{\mathbf{m}\, x\colon P(x)\}]\!] =_{def} \begin{cases} \{u \in \mathrm{DOM}[\![\mathbf{m}]\!]\colon \mathbf{true} \in B[\![P(u)]\!]\}, \\ \qquad \text{iff for all } u \in \mathrm{DOM}[\![\mathbf{m}]\!]\colon B[\![P(u)]\!] \neq \{\bot\} \\ \{\bot\}, \text{otherwise} \end{cases}$$

For an indeterminate predicate P, the semantics is defined by

$$B[\![\{\mathbf{m}\, x\colon P(x)\}]\!] =_{def} \cup_{p \in D[\![P]\!]} B[\![\{\mathbf{m}\, x\colon p(x)\}]\!]$$

where, again, $D[\![P]\!]$ is the set of determinate descendants of P.

Also set comprehensions may range over a restricted domain. As before, the meaning of

$B[\![\{(\mathbf{m}\, x\colon C)\colon P\}]\!]$

is defined by

$B[\![\{(\mathbf{m}\, x\colon C)\colon P\}]\!] = B[\![\{\mathbf{m}\, x\colon \mathbf{if}\ C\ \mathbf{then}\ P\ \mathbf{else\ false\ fi}\}]\!]$.

Sets described by set comprehension should not be confused with the objects introduced by the type SET (Sect. 3.3.2): The latter ones define semantic values (of object kind) associated with the sort symbol of an algebraically defined sort (which, by definition, only covers finite sets). Sets described by a set comprehension define semantic values (of object kind) associated with sets (of object kinds) which may be infinite. In case of finite sets, however, both constructs coincide, as will be illustrated in later sections. In particular, if finiteness of the set and definedness of all its elements is guaranteed, we will use the set comprehension as an abbreviation in connection with the type SET.

There are obvious relationships between set comprehension and the other descriptive constructs. For example,

$\mathbf{some}\ \mathbf{m}\, y\colon y \in \{\mathbf{m}\, x\colon P(x)\}$

is equivalent to

$\mathbf{some}\ \mathbf{m}\, y\colon P(y)$;

or

$\{\mathbf{m}\, x\colon P(x)\} \neq \varnothing$

is equivalent to

$(\exists\, \mathbf{m}\, x\colon P(x))$.

Equivalences of this kind will be treated more comprehensively and in more detail in the next chapter.

Usually, a set comprehension ultimately aims at an algorithm enumerating its elements; this is *impossible*, if the set denoted by the set comprehension is infinite – which is allowed. Therefore, it is an important step during program development to prove finiteness of a set specified by a set comprehension.

In connection with set comprehensions, it is convenient to have further constructs at hand. We also use

- the empty set, denoted by $\varnothing$, as abbreviation for $\{\mathbf{m}\ x\colon \mathbf{false}\}$;
- the **powerset** of M, denoted by $\mathcal{P}(M)$ or 2^M, which characterizes the set of all subsets of M. (Note, that the powerset of a countably infinite set is not countable, which might cause definedness problems for program development; however, $\mathcal{P}(M)$ is finite, if M is finite.)
- the usual **set operations** such as $\in$, $\subseteq$, $\cup$, $\cap$, etc. as abbreviations (denotable by set comprehension and quantifiers)

  Thus, e.g.,

  $\{\mathbf{m}\ x\colon \mathrm{P}(x)\} \cup \{\mathbf{m}\ x\colon \mathrm{Q}(x)\}$, as usually, abbreviates to
  $\{\mathbf{m}\ x\colon \mathrm{P}(x) \vee \mathrm{Q}(x)\}$.

Further abbreviations that will be used are 'Zermelo-Fraenkel set abstraction':

$\{f(x)\colon \mathrm{P}(x)\}$ for $\{\mathbf{n}\ z\colon \exists\ \mathbf{m}\ x\colon \mathrm{P}(x) \wedge z = f(x)\}$ where $f\colon \mathbf{m} \rightarrow \mathbf{n}$,

or iterated intersections and unions such as

$\bigcup_{x \in M} F(x)$ for $\{\mathbf{n}\ z\colon \exists\ \mathbf{m}\ x\colon x \in M\ \wedge z \in F(x)\}$ where $F\colon \mathbf{m} \rightarrow 2^{\mathbf{n}}$.

3.4.5 Computation Structures

Using the mechanism of algebraic types, sorts, constants, and operations are defined "implicitly": sorts are characterized by their characteristic operations and the sets of well-formed terms; operations are given semantics by the axioms that basically describe their interactions. In order to be able to describe models of an abstract type where sorts, constants, and operations are defined explicitly and individually we introduce the concept of computation structures.

A **computation structure** is a collection of declarations for sorts, objects, and functions. Computation structures provide a means for supplying (applicative) models for types; they define components whose input/output behaviour is described by the relations between parameters and results of the functions.

The declaration of a computation structure has the form

structure CS = («parameters») «list of constituents»:
  D_1; ...; D_r
endofstructure.

Like types, structures may be parametrized. Again, arbitrary collections of sort, constant, and operation symbols are admissible as parameters which may be further restricted by assertions.

Likewise, the **list of constituents** of a computation structure corresponds to that of a type. It consists of symbols for sorts, constants, and functions, which are "visible" to the outside and, thus, usable in expressions or other structures. Since computation structures are intended as applicative implementations for types, procedure identifiers in the list of constituents are not allowed.

The **body** D_1; ...; D_r of the structure CS provides definitions at least for the symbols introduced in the list of constituents. In addition, "hidden" entities may be defined for internal use. Internally, auxiliary sorts, constants, functions, and even procedures may be explicitly defined or imported from types or other structures by instantiations. If the definition of a computation structure CS applies a type (scheme) T, CS is considered as parametrized by the constituents of T (restricted by the laws of T). The following kinds of definitions are admissible in structures:

- Instantiations of (primitive) types and type schemes. Again, unfolding of the instantiations must not lead to cycles in the primitive-relation. If the parameters of the type scheme are restricted, these restrictions must be satisfied by the arguments of the instantiation.
- Instantiations of (parametrized) structures.
- Mode declarations.
- Function declarations.
- (Collective) object declarations.
- Declarations of procedures without global variables (Chap. 7).
- Instantiations of modules (Chap. 8).

An example for a computation structure is the following one which defines the natural numbers in terms of sequences of "bits" without leading zeros [Bauer et al. 85]:

structure N = **nat**, *zero*, *succ*, *iszero*, *pred* :
  mode bit = 0 | 1;
  based on (**nat**, *empty*, *isempty*, *append*, *last*, *lead*) = SEQU(**bit**);
  nat *zero* = *empty*;

  funct *iszero* = (**nat** *n*) **bool**:
    isempty(*n*);

  funct *succ* = (**nat** *n*) **nat**:
    if *isempty*(*n*)
      then *append*(*empty*, 1)
      else **if** *last*(*n*) **is** 0 **then** *append*(*lead*(*n*), 1)
        [] *last*(*n*) **is** 1 **then** *append*(*succ*(*lead*(*n*)), 0) **fi**;

  funct *pred* = (**nat** *n*: ¬ *iszero*(*n*)) **nat**:
    if *last*(*n*) **is** 0 **then** *append*(*pred*(*lead*(*n*)), 1)
    [] *last*(*n*) **is** 1 **then**
      if *isempty*(*lead*(*n*)) **then** *empty* **else** *append*(*lead*(*n*)), 0) **fi fi**

endofstructure.

By analogy with types a (parametrized) structure CS can be instantiated by the construct

structure («constituents'») = CS(«arguments»)

which again is explained by textual replacement i.e. by replacing this construct by the body of CS (after respective renamings). If the parameters of CS are restricted by an assertion, the instantiation is admissible only if the arguments fulfil this assertion.

Again, this construct also serves for renaming. Likewise, analogous abbreviations for particular circumstances are possible.

In formal problem specifications, only the applicative constructs of computation structures should be used, whereas, for example, the use of "internal" procedures should be delayed to later stages of software development.

3.5 Structuring and Modularization

So far we have not paid any attention to the size of the problems that are to be specified. In fact, we have even assumed that the formalization process as introduced in Sect. 3.2 is not affected by problems in managing complexity mainly originating from the size of some task. In practice, however, size is a problem, and mastering the resulting complexity by introducing a suitable structure is an essential part of the formalization process.

Without explicitly mentioning it, in most of the examples in the previous sections we already used the principle of structuring to help in understanding. Thus, for example, in Sect. 3.3 almost all algebraic types were defined by suitable hierarchies of more primitive types. Likewise, in Sect. 3.4 we used either appropriate primitives, as, e.g., σ in

```
some nat x: σ(x) ∧ odd x
```

or auxiliary declarations (Sect. 3.4.3) as in

```
sort(s) where

funct sort = (natsequ t) natsequ:
   some natsequ x: issorted(x) ∧ isperm(x, t) where

   funct issorted = (natsequ x) bool:
      x =<> ∇ restx =<> ∇
      (∀ natsequ u, v: (u ≠<> ∧ v ≠<>) Δ (u+v = x ∧ lastu ≤ firstv)),

   funct isperm = (natsequ y, natsequ t) bool:
      sequtobag(y) = sequtobag(t) .
```

in order to provide structure and thus to ease understanding of the formalization.

In principle, there are two strategies for introducing structure: top-down and bottom-up proceeding.

Top-down proceeding is an iterated process that starts with the task as a whole and tries to split it up into smaller sub-tasks which in turn are subject to further decomposition. This process ends, if a suitable level of refinement is reached. A typical example for such a top-down proceeding is the methodology propagated by SA/SADT (Sect. 2.2.7).

Technically, each step in a top-down proceeding consists of two alternating activities: "decomposition" and "elaboration".

Decomposition means "to break up or separate into basic components or parts" [Webster 74]. This should include identification of the parts, a clear statement on their respective interrelation, as well as the formulation of the original task in terms of the newly introduced components.

Elaboration means "to work out carefully; develop in great detail" [Webster 74]. Elaboration aims at providing meaning for the parts introduced in decomposition. This may be done by either referring to existing basic concepts or by initiating another decomposition step.

Within our scenario for formally specifying the requirements for a system, the intertwining of decomposition and elaboration may be sketched as follows:

After having decided on an adequate concept (Sect. 3.2.1), the formalization process starts by first describing the overall behaviour of the system as a function on suitably defined abstract objects.

In a first decomposition step further, "internal" object kinds and operations are introduced in order to formalize the intuition and to give semantics to the overall system's function in terms of these newly introduced ones. In this way the complex system function is decomposed into smaller, and hopefully more easily manageable functions.

Frequently part of the semantics of the newly introduced operations over such internal object kinds follows immediately from the original, informal description (elaboration). For the remaining parts of the semantics (which often are only detected after a check for formal completeness) we proceed as above, i.e., we give meaning to functions by introducing new object kinds and new operations (further decomposition) which, in turn, are defined by elaboration and/or further decomposition. This iterated process ends as soon as we have arrived at a suitable level of pragmatics where either all object kinds and operations are completely defined or only refer to object kinds and operations that are supposed to be known.

Within the framework of algebraic specification the combination of decomposition and elaboration just described amounts to introducing a new type: decomposition roughly corresponds to introducing the signature of a type (i.e. the syntactic part) whereas elaboration aims at providing a semantics in the form of appropriate axioms for the object kinds and operations introduced by the preceding decomposition step. Particularly helpful in this context is the notion of sufficient completeness (Sect. 3.3.1.2) which supports establishing formal completeness for each level of a hierarchical specification during construction (see also [Partsch, Pepper 83]).

Bottom-up proceeding is also an iterated process that starts from the details of a problem and aims at composing them into larger units (at a higher level of abstraction). The methodology proposed by PSL/PSA (Sect. 2.2.8) is a typical bottom-up proceeding.

As with top-down proceeding, each step in bottom-up proceeding consists of two alternating sub-activities: "composition" and "specialization".

Composition means "to put together; put in proper order or form" [Webster 74]. Composition comprises the introduction of new entities, as well as a precise statement on the components of this new entity and the way how they are to be combined in order to make up a whole.

Specialization means "to make special, specific, or particular; specify," or "to direct toward or concentrate on a specific end" [Webster 74]. Usually, entities introduced by composition are too general for the particular task at hand. Specialization then tries to "adjust" these entities for the particular needs of the respective problem.

Within the framework of algebraic type specifications, bottom-up proceeding starts with a predefined collection of basic types (for example, for numbers, truth values, or characters) and basic type schemes (for example, sequences, sets, or bags, maps). Composition then means defining new types using the available basic types and type schemes, as well as the mode constructors. By specialization, all those operations that are not needed are skipped from the list of visible constituents. Additionally, specialization can also introduce further restrictions on the operations by means of assertions.

In the context of our specification formalism, proceeding top-down has the advantage that new object kinds and operations are introduced only as needed rather than by somehow combining existing operations into more complex ones without really knowing whether they are actually needed as in the strict bottom-up case. (Note that this does not imply that top-down processing forbids the use of existing types and type schemes.) In this sense, top-down processing minimizes the number of such internal object kinds and operations.

Both, top-down and bottom-up proceeding as introduced above are idealized views. In practice, both approaches will be used against the background of previous experiences which tend to push the proceedings towards each other. Thus, for example, top-down proceeding is usually influenced by the availability of predefined types and type schemes or by certain ideas on the low level representation. Likewise, in bottom-up proceeding, composition, and in particular specialization, always will be done with having the ultimate goal, namely the entire system, in mind.

Within software development the terms "structuring" and "modularization" are widely used synonymously. Structuring deals with the logical decomposition of a complex problem or task into manageable parts. *Modularization* basically aims at the same goal. Additionally it tries to achieve further goals such as modularity (Sect. 1.1) or compact formulation.

Modularity "measures" the amount of effort that is necessary for modifications. Obviously, if the modification affects only one part of the entire system, this effort is proportional to the size of the interfaces that this part shares with other parts. Therefore, modularization aims at a system structure where the respective components have minimal interfaces.

It is advantageous to have a compact problem specification using few basic concepts, as only these concepts are to be implemented. Therefore, aiming at a compact representation, in modularization one also tries to identify particular parts within a structural decomposition as instances of more general abstract principles. Parametrization and instantiation for algebraic specifications as well as abstraction and function application for applicative specifications are means offered by our specification formalism that aim at such a compact representation.

3.6 Examples

In order to demonstrate the (combined) use of the specification constructs introduced in the previous sections, we will now deal with a number of examples of varying size and complexity. These examples will be reconsidered in later sections.

3.6.1 Recognizing Palindromes

Informally, the problem to be considered in this subsection is stated as

Decide whether a given sequence of elements is a palindrome.

According to [Webster 74], a palindrome is "a word, phrase, or sentence which reads the same backward or forward".

Typical examples of palindromes are

radar, anna, madam, name no one man.

A formalization of the problem directly follows the definition in [Webster 74]:

```
mode string = ESEQU(char);

funct pal = (string s) bool:
   eq(s, rev(s)) where

   funct rev = (string s) string:
      if |s| ≤ 1 then s else last s + rev(lead rest s) + first s fi;

   funct eq = (string s1, string s2) bool:
      if s1 =<>   then s2 =<>
      [] s2 =<>   then s1 =<>
                  else (first s1 = first s2 Δ eq(rest s1, rest s2)
                       [] last s1 = last s2 Δ eq(lead s1, lead s2)) fi.
```

In order to stress the symmetry inherent to the problem we have given a "symmetric" operational definition of *eq*. Of course, we could have given also a descriptive specification of the operations *rev* and *eq*, for example,

```
funct rev = (string s) string:
   that string t: |t| = |s| Δ (∀ (nat i: 1 ≤ i ≤ |s|): t[i] = s[|s| – i + 1]),

funct eq = (string s1, string s2) bool:
   |s1| = |s2| Δ (∀ (nat i: 1 ≤ i ≤ |s1|): s1[i] = s2[i]).
```

In both cases, the definition of *eq* is based on the equality "=" on characters. An explicit definition of *eq* could have been avoided by using

```
mode string = EESEQU(char, =)
```

instead.

So far, we ignored the problem of layout characters (such as blanks or punctuation symbols) in the given string. If we also take layout characters into account, the definition of *pal* has to be changed into

```
funct pal = (string s) bool:
   eq(ignore-layouts(s), ignore-layouts(rev(s))) where

   funct ignore-layouts = (string s) string:
      if s =<> then s
      elsf islc(first s)) then ignore-layouts(rest s)
      else first s + ignore-layouts(rest s) fi;
```

funct *islc* = (**char** *s*) **bool**:
«*c* is a layout character».

To give a specification using

mode string = SEQU(**char**)

is left to the interested reader, as is an analysis of the formal specification with respect to the criteria from Sect. 3.1.

3.6.2 A Simple Number Problem

Informally, the "simple number problem" may be stated as:

Decide whether a given natural number n is of the form $2^i - 1$ *(with* $i \in \mathbb{N}$*).*

Again, a formalization is straightforward:

funct *prop* = (**nat** *n*) **bool**: ∃ **nat** *i*: $n = 2^i - 1$.

However, someone with a little experience in binary representation of numbers might have a completely different idea:

A natural number n has the desired property if the binary representation of n consists of 1's only.

This leads straightforwardly to the formalization:

mode bitsequ = ESEQU(**bit**);

funct *prop* = (**nat** *n*) **bool**:
all(*conv*(*n*)) **where**

funct *conv* = (**nat** *n*) **bitsequ**:
if *n* = 0 **then** <>
elsf odd *n* **then** *conv*(*n* **div** 2) + 1 **else** *conv*(*n* **div** 2) + 0 **fi**;

funct *all* = (**bitsequ** *b*) **bool**:
if *b* =<> **then true else last** *b* = 1 Δ *all*(**lead***b*) **fi**.

As in the palindrome example (Sect. 3.6.1), the latter formalization is already operational. To give a concise, non-operational specification using the same basic idea would require further primitives:

- **funct** *all* = (**bitsequ** *b*) **bool**:
  ∀ (**nat** *i*: $1 \le i \le |b|$): $b[i] = 1$

  which assumes indexed sequences; and

- **funct** *conv* = (**nat** *n*) **bitsequ**:
  some bitsequ *b*: $n = \sum_{i=1..|b|} b[i] \times 2^{|b|-i}$

  which assumes the usual definition for the sum operator Σ.

Analyzing the above formal specification with respect to the criteria from Sect. 3.1 is straightforward and hence left to the reader. Although obvious, proving the equivalence of both formalizations, however, is technically somewhat tedious, as theorems on the relation between divisibility and number representation are needed.

3.6.3 A Simple Bank Account System

The following problem is to be seen as a representative for a class of commercial problems. Although being rather simplified for presentation purposes, it still reflects some of the essential characteristics of this class of problems.

In the treatment below, we shall also illustrate how additional or modified requirements influence an already available specification (or parts of it).

The kernel of our simple bank account system may be informally stated as follows (see [Darlington, Feather 80] for a similar problem):

1) A bank keeps for each of its clients's accounts a transaction file that records all transactions with respect to the respective account. A transaction is supposed to be a triple consisting of a client identification (account number), the kind of transaction (credit or debit), and the amount of money involved. (It is assumed that further information about the account, such as client's name and address and special conditions, is recorded elsewhere.) Furthermore, for each transaction the bank charges a (fixed) fee. It is requested to compute the balance of a given account with respect to the previous balance and the transaction file associated with the account (e.g., in order to make sure that, in case of a transaction of kind debit, the account shows a positive balance before the transaction takes place).

A formalization on the basis of these informal requirements is straightforward and may read as follows:

```
mode ttype = C | D;
mode tr = mt(ttype kind, nat amount);
mode tfile = SEQU(tr);

funct newbal = (int oldbal, tfile t) int:
   oldbal + credits(t) – debits(t) – num(t) × fee  where

   funct credits = (tfile t) nat:
      if t =<> then 0
      elsf kind(first t) = C then amount(first t) + credits(rest t)
         else credits(rest t) fi;

   funct debits = (tfile t) nat:
      if t =<> then 0
      elsf kind(first t) = C then debits(rest t)
         else amount(first t) + debits(rest t) fi;

   funct num = (tfile t) nat:
      if t =<> then 0 else 1 + num(rest t) fi.
```

The emphasis in this specification is on clarity and structure, rather than efficiency. In Sect. 4.3 we will show how to make the above specification more efficient.

As the transaction files are modeled above by the concept of a sequence, an operational specification of the problem is straightforward. A descriptive specification could have been given as well, for example using ESEQU instead of SEQU in the definition of **tfile**:

funct *credits* = (**tfile** *t*) **nat**:
$\Sigma_{\mathbf{tr}\ tr:\ tr \in t \wedge kind(tr)=C}\ amount(tr)$;

funct *debits* = (**tfile** *t*) **nat**:
$\Sigma_{\mathbf{tr}\ tr:\ tr \in t \wedge kind(tr)=D}\ amount(tr)$;

funct *num* = (**tfile** *t*) **nat**:
$|t|$.

Returning to the original specification, we next illustrate how this formal specification has to be changed, if the initial requirements are slightly modified, say as follows:

2) *In order to attract more clients the management of the bank decides to change its charging policy: within a certain time period, a certain number of transactions is without charge (say 5 transactions a month). Checking for the time period is assumed to be achieved by the environment, and is not to be done by the program.*

Now already the effort spent in giving a well-structured formal specification pays, as only the functions *newbal* and *num* have to be modified (whereas *credits* and *debits* can be reused):

funct *newbal'* = (**int** *oldbal*, **tfile** *t*, **nat** *free*) **int**:
oldbal + *credits*(*t*) – *debits*(*t*) – *newnum*(*t*, *free*) × *fee* **where**

funct *newnum* = (**tfile** *t*, **nat** *free*) **nat**:
if *t* =<> **then** 0
elsf *free* = 0 **then** 1 + *newnum*(**rest***t*, *free*)
else *newnum*(**rest***t*, *free* –1) **fi**

The next modification of the informal requirements extends the original problem:

3) *Rather than having individual files for each account all clients's transactions are kept on a single general transaction file according to their temporal succession. Again, it is requested to compute the balance of a given account with respect to the respective previous balance of this account and the bank's general transaction file.*

An obvious possibility here is to build upon parts of our previous specification as follows:

mode acnr = (**nat** *n*: $1{,}000{,}000 \le n \le 9{,}999{,}999$);
mode gtr = *mgt*(**acnr** *acc*, **ttype** *kind*, **nat** *amount*);
mode gtfile = SEQU(**gtr**);
mode bal = *mb*(**acnr** *acc*, **int** *amount*);

funct *newgbal* = (**bal** *b*, **gtfile** *t*) **int**:
newbal(*amount*(*b*), *self*(*t*, *acc*(*b*)) **where**

funct *self* = (**gtfile** *t*, **acnr** *a*) **tfile**:
if *t* =<> **then** <>
elsf *acc*(**first***t*) = *a*
then *mt*(*kind*(**first***t*), *amount*(**first***t*)) + *self*(**rest***t*, *a*)
else *self*(**rest***t*, *a*) **fi fi**;

Frightened by the computational overhead involved in a direct execution of the above specification, one, again, might be tempted to think of a more efficient specification that computes the new balance by scanning the general transaction file only once, rather than by first selecting a subfile containing all transactions of the respective client. We will see in Sect. 4.5.3 that such a specification can be obtained from the one above in a formal way.

Whereas the previous modification caused a change of the already existing formal specification, the following one can be handled by simply adding further definitions:

4) *In addition to the general transaction file, the bank also keeps a general account file where all accounts and their respective balances are recorded. One is requested to compute for a given account file and an arbitrary transaction an update of the account file.*

A formalization here is again straightforward:

mode afile = EESEQU(**bal**, =);
mode acfile = (**afile** *af*: *isacfile*(*af*)) **where**

funct *isacfile* = (**afile** *af*) **bool**:
  |{**acnr** *a*: ∃ **int***b*: *mb*(*a*, *b*) ∈ *af*}| = |*af*|
  co an account file contains an account at most once **co**;

funct *upd* = (**acfile** *af*, **gtr** *t*: *legalacc*(*acc*(*t*), *af*)) **acfile**:
  if *acc*(**first***af*) = *acc*(*t*)
    then *mb*(*acc*(*t*), *nbal*(*amount*(**first***af*), *mt*(*kind*(*t*), *amount*(*t*)))) + **rest***af*
    else first*af* +*upd*(**rest***af*, *t*) **fi**;

funct *legalacc* = (**acnr** *a*, **acfile** *af*) **bool**:
  ∃ **bal** *b*: *b* ∈ *af* Δ *acc*(*b*) = *a*;

funct *nbal* = (**int** *oldb*, **tr** *t*) **int**:
  if *kind*(*t*) = C **then** *oldb* + *amount*(*t*) **else** *oldb* – *amount*(*t*) **fi**.

The next modification of the informal requirements asks for additional operations:

5) *Furthermore, it is necessary to be able to compute an update of the account file w.r.t. the general transaction file for a particular account, and to query the current balance of an account.*

Again, a formal specification can be built on top of our specification so far:

funct *iupdate* = (**acfile** *a*, **gtfile** *t*, **acnr** *anr*: *legalacc*(*anr*, *a*)) **acfile**:
  if *a* =<> **then** <>
  elsf *acc*(**first***a*) = *anr*
    then *mb*(*acc*(**first***a*), *newgbal*(**first***a*, *t*)) + **rest***a*
    else first*a* + *iupdate*(**rest***a*, *t*, *anr*) **fi fi**;

funct *cbal* = (**acfile** *a*, **gtfile** *t*, **acnr** *anr*) (**int** | **error**):
  if *legalacc*(*anr*, *a*) **then** *selacc*(*anr*, *iupdate*(*a*, *t*, *anr*)) **else error fi**;

funct *selacc* = (**acnr** *anr*, **acfile** *a*: *legalacc*(*anr*, *a*)) **int**:
  that bal *b*: *acc*(*b*) = *anr* ∧ *b* ∈ *a*;

The last modification we want to deal with is particularly interesting, because there are various obvious ideas leading to different formal specifications:

6) *Finally, it becomes also necessary to compute for a given account file new balances for all accounts w.r.t. to a given general transaction file.*

One idea for a formal specification is to "scan" the account file:

funct *updatef1* = (**acfile** *a*, **gtfile** *t*) **acfile**:
  if *a* =<> **then** <> **else** *mb*(*acc*(**first***a*), *newgbal*(**first***a*, *t*)) + *updatef1*(**rest***a*, *t*)) **fi**.

An alternative idea is to scan the general transaction file:

funct *updatef2* = (**acfile** *a*, **gtfile** *t*) **acfile**:
  if *t* =<> **then** *a* **else** *updatef2*(*upd*(*a*, **first***t*), **rest***t*) **fi**.

Of course, there is also a "mixed strategy" where scanning of the account file and scanning of the transaction file alternate:

funct *updatef* = (**acfile** *a*, **gtfile** *t*) **acfile**:
  if *t* =<> **then** *a*
  [] *a* =<> **then** <>
  [] *a* ≠<> **then** *mb*(*acc*(**first***a*), *newgbal*(**first***a*, *t*)) + *updatef*(**rest***a*, *t*)
  [] *t* ≠<> **then** *updatef*(*upd*(*a*, **first***t*), **rest***t*) **fi**;

Although we had to simplify the problem in order to keep the treatment of this example at a reasonable length, any realistic treatment of a similar kind of problem will essentially follow the same lines. Hence, all comments and any methodological advice will also carry over.

3.6.4 Hamming's Problem

The problem is attributed to R.W. Hamming. Its first formulation can be found in [Dijkstra 76a] where it is used to illustrate program development within the wp-calculus. For the same purpose it is also dealt with in [Gries 81] or [Dijkstra, Feijen 85]. It also has been considered in various papers on transformational techniques (see for example [Darlington 81], [WG 2.1 81]).

Deviating marginally from the original statement as given in [Dijkstra 76a], the problem may be formulated as follows:

Generate in increasing order the first N (N > 0) elements of the sequence 1, 2, 3, 4, 5, 6, 8, 9, 10, 12, ... of all natural numbers divisible by no primes other than 2, 3, or 5.

<u>Formalization</u> (first attempt)

mode natsequ = EESEQU(**nat**, =);

some natsequ *s*: $issorted(s) \wedge |s| = N \wedge (\forall$ **nat** $x: x \in s \Rightarrow H(x))$
where
  $H(x) \equiv \forall$ **nat** $y: (prime(y) \wedge y | x) \Rightarrow y \in \{2, 3, 5\}$.

Of course, there are other equivalent formulations of H, e.g.,

  $H(x) \equiv \exists$ **nat** $i, j, k: x = 2^i \cdot 3^j \cdot 5^k$.

If we analyze this formalization with respect to the criteria in Sect. 3.1, there will be no problems with

- definedness (existence of a sequence with the desired properties is obvious),
- formal completeness (a definition of the only non-primitive operation *issorted* is given in Sect. 3.4), and
- overspecification (the formalization only contains requirements that also appear in the verbal problem formulation).

The above formalization, however, is underspecified. The verbal formulation asked for

*the sequence ... of **all** natural numbers ...,*

whereas the formalization above allows arbitrary, increasingly ordered sequences, in particular also sequences having "holes" in them, such as

1, 3, 6, 8, 9, 10, ...

Underspecification means that the formalization is too "weak" and thus has to be strengthened by adding further conjuncts to capture more properties. (Note that using **that** instead of **some** would change the formalization from bad to worse because then it would be undefined.) In order to ensure that our formalization allows "dense" sequences only, we have to require that for any two numbers x and y in the sequence s, s also must contain all natural numbers between x and y that fulfil the predicate H. This leads to

<u>*Formalization*</u> (second attempt)

$$\textbf{some natsequ } s\text{: } issorted(s) \wedge |s| = N \wedge (\forall\ \textbf{nat } x\text{: } x \in s \Rightarrow H(x)) \wedge$$
$$(\forall\ \textbf{nat } x, y, z\text{: } (x \in s \wedge y \in s \wedge x \le z \le y \wedge H(z)) \Rightarrow z \in s).$$

A second attempt to analyze this formalization may lead to the observation that the formalization still is underspecified: it has been asked for

*... the **first** N (N > 0) elements ... ,*

whereas the formalization accepts any "dense" sequence with the desired properties (i.e., also sequences not starting with 1).

Probably the easiest way to establish adequacy is by simply adding the further requirement $1 \in s$. This results in

<u>*Final formalization*</u> (first version)

$$\textbf{some natsequ } s\text{: } issorted(s) \wedge |s| = N \wedge 1 \in s \wedge (\forall\ \textbf{nat } x\text{: } x \in s \Rightarrow H(x)) \wedge$$
$$(\forall\ \textbf{nat } x, y, z\text{: } (x \in s \wedge y \in s \wedge x \le z \le y \wedge H(z)) \Rightarrow z \in s).$$

Equivalent adequate formalizations may also be obtained by using different ideas:

a) *any number x in s must have the property H and all natural numbers smaller than x also fulfilling H have to be in s, too.*

   This leads to

   <u>*Final formalization*</u> (second version)

$$\textbf{some natsequ } s\text{: } issorted(s) \wedge |s| = N \wedge$$
$$(\forall\ \textbf{nat } x, y\text{: } x \in s \Rightarrow (H(x) \wedge ((y \le x \wedge H(y)) \Rightarrow y \in s)));$$

b) *s is an initial fragment of the (unlimited) ordered sequence of all natural numbers fulfilling H.*

This leads to

<u>*Final formalization*</u> (third version)

some natsequ s: $|s| = N \land s \preccurlyeq sort(settosequ\{$**nat** x: $H(x)\})$.

(Here, $s \preccurlyeq t$ holds iff s is an initial segment of t, Sect. 3.3.3, *settosequ* denotes an operator to convert a set into a sequence, and *sort* may be defined as in Sect. 3.4);

c) Rather than using an auxiliary predicate H as above, the set $m = \{$**nat** x: $H(x)\}$ also may be characterized by the following (inductive) definition [Dijkstra 76a]:

1) $1 \in m$
2) $\forall$ **nat** x: $x \in m \Rightarrow 2 \cdot x \in m \land 3 \cdot x \in m \land 5 \cdot x \in m$
3) m contains no other values than those that belong to it on account of (1) or (2).

Of course, any of the final formalizations could be taken as the starting point for a subsequent development by transformations. However, as we will see later, the form of a formal specification has a non-neglectable impact on the elegance of the subsequent transformational development.

3.6.5 Longest Ascending Subsequence ("Longest Upsequence")

As Hamming's Problem, this problem has been used in several papers, such as [Bird 81], [Broy et al. 79b], [Gram 86], [Guiho et al. 80], [Lucas, Scholl 83], [Pepper, Partsch 80], [Pritchard 81], [Sintzoff 80], in order to demonstrate various aspects of programming methodology. Informally, it may be stated as follows:

For a non-empty finite sequence s of natural numbers, find the maximum length of a subsequence of s of which the elements are in ascending order.

If we have for example

$s = < 4, 1, 3, 13, 7, 10, 8, 5, 6, 9, 11, 14, 12, 15 >$,

then

$< 4, 7, 10, 11, 14, 15 >$

would be an ascending subsequence. However, it is not one of maximum length, since for example

$s' = < 1, 3, 7, 8, 9, 11, 12, 15 >$

is obviously longer. In fact, s' can be shown to be of maximum length 8, as is

$s'' = < 1, 3, 5, 6, 9, 11, 14, 15 >$.

Hence, there may be several ascending subsequences, all having the maximum length. Therefore, the problem also may appear in different, though related forms, such as

- *Find an arbitrary longest upsequence*, or
- *Find all longest upsequences.*

Again, finding a concept of the problem domain is not a problem here, since the informal problem statement already deals with (up to isomorphism) unique mathematical terms.

The basic idea expressed in the subsequent formalization is

Determine the maximum of the set of the lengths of all ascending subsequences

and leads to

mode natsequ = EESEQU(**nat**, =);
mode natsequs = SET(**natsequ**, =);

that nat l: $l = \mathbf{max}\{|u|: u \in \mathit{upsequset}(s)\}$ **where**

funct *upsequset* = (**natsequ** s: $s \neq$<>) **natsequs**:
  {**natsequ** u: $\mathit{issorted}(u) \wedge \mathit{contained}(u, s)$}

funct *contained* = (**natsequ** u, **natsequ** s) **bool**:
  u =<> ∇
  ($\exists$ **natsequ** s_1, s_2:
    ($s_1 \neq$<> $\wedge\ s_1 + s_2 = s$) Δ (**first**u = **last**$s_1 \wedge \mathit{contained}(\mathbf{rest}u, s_2)$))

Here, again, the operational definition of *contained* is much easier than an equivalent descriptive one.

As to the soundness of this specification, formal completeness is obvious. However, definedness is not quite as obvious:

- due to the use of Δ and ∇, *contained* is defined;
- since *issorted* is defined (Sect. 3.4), so is *upsequset*; furthermore, $\mathit{upsequset}(s) \neq \emptyset$, since it contains the empty sequence, as well as all elements of s as singleton sequences, and s is known to be non-empty;
- hence, the set of all lengths of the elements from *upsequset* is non-empty and thus **max** is defined (and unique, by definition).

Here too, other formalizations are possible if different definitions of sequences are used.

3.6.6 Recognition and Parsing of Context-Free Grammars

The problems to be dealt with in this subsection are well-known in formal language theory (see, for example, [Aho, Ullman 72], [Harrison 78], [Salomaa 73]). Informally they may be stated as follows:

For a context-free grammar $G = (N, T, S, P)$ and for an arbitrary terminal word $w \in T^*$, give algorithms that
a) decide whether $w \in L(G)$, where $L(G)$ is the language generated by G;
b) under the assumption $w \in L(G)$, yield w's "structure" with respect to G.

Again, formalizing the problem domain is not a problem here, since all the notions involved are well-defined in formal language theory.

For the formalization we define the data types

mode nont = «Non-Terminals with equality "="»;
mode term = «Terminals with equality "="»;
mode nonts = ESET(**nont**, =);
mode terms = ESET(**term**, =);
mode symb = **nont** | **term**;
mode string = EESEQU(**symb**, =);
mode termstring = EESEQU(**term**, =);
mode termstrings = ESET(**termstring**, =);
mode cfprod = *pr*(**nont** *lhs*, **string** *rhs*);
mode cfprods = ESET(**cfprod**, =);
mode cfg = *cfg*(**nonts** *N*, **terms** *T*, **nont** *S*, **cfprods** *P*:
$T \neq \emptyset \wedge S \in N \wedge P \neq \emptyset$)

and the auxiliary operations

funct .→ = (**string** *u*, **string** *v*, **cfg** *G*) **bool**:
$\exists$ **cfprod** *p*, **string** *l*, *r*: $p \in P(G) \wedge u = l + lhs(p) + r \wedge v = l + rhs(p) + r$

funct *L* = (**cfg** *G*) **termstrings**:
{**termstring** *t*: $S(G) \rightarrow^* t$}

where $\rightarrow^*$ denotes the reflexive-transitive closure of $\rightarrow$ (see also Sect. 3.6.7).
Now the above problems may be formalized by

funct *rp* = (**cfg** *G*, **termstring** *w*: *isterm*(*w*, *G*)) **bool**:
$w \in L(G)$ **where**

funct *isterm* = (**termstring** *w*, **cfg** *G*) **bool**:
(w =<>) ∇ (**first***w* $\in T(G)$ Δ *isterm*(**rest***w*, *G*))

resp.

funct *pp* = (**cfg** *G*, **termstring** *w*: *isterm*(*w*, *G*)) (**parse** | **error**):
if *rp*(*G*, *w*) **then some parse** *p*: *isparse*(*p*, *w*, *G*) **else error fi**.

For the latter specification to be formally complete it is necessary to give respective definitions for

- **parse**, the data structure that describes the derivation structure of a string, and
- *isparse*(*p*, *w*, *G*), a predicate that ensures that *p* is a derivation structure of *w* with respect to *G*. (For respective formalizations, see [Partsch 86].)

3.6.7 Reachability and Cycles in Graphs

As graphs are frequently used as concepts, graph problems are involved in a lot of practical applications. From the great variety of graph problems we have chosen two representatives, viz. reachability and existence of cycles.

The *reachability problem* may be stated as follows:

Is there a path from the node $x \in N$ to the node $y \in N$ in the finite, directed graph $G = (N, E)$?

As an example, consider the graph from Fig. 3.1 (Sect. 3.2)

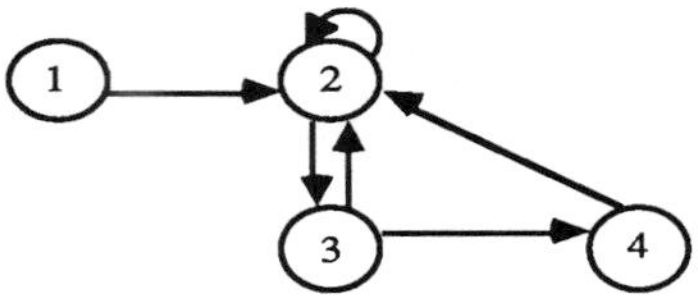

In this graph, there obviously exists a path from node 1 to node 4, but there is none, for example, from node 3 to node 1.

As discussed in Sect. 3.2, there is no unique representation for the concept "graph". Consequently, there are various possibilities for formalizing the above problem.

In the following we assume (see also Sect. 3.3.5)

mode node = «nodes»;
mode edge(=) = *e*(**node**(=) *in*, **node**(=) *out*);
mode nodes = ESET(**node**, =);
mode edges = ESET(**edge**, =);
mode nodesequ = ESEQU(**node**); and
mode graph = *g*(**nodes** *N*, **edges** *E*: ∀ **edge** $a \in E$: $in(a) \in N \wedge out(a) \in N$).

A simple formalization can be given, if $E \subseteq N \times N$ is viewed as a relation with E^* denoting the reflexive-transitive closure of E. Then the problem can be formalized by

funct *reach* = (**graph** *G*, **node** *x*, **node** *y*: $x, y \in N(G)$) **bool**:
  $e(x, y) \in (E(G))^*$.

If an operator for forming the reflexive-transitive closure of a relation is not available, still the same underlying idea can be used for a formalization where the closure needs to be defined explicitly:

funct *reach* = (**graph** *G*, **node** *x*, **node** *y*: $x, y \in N(G)$) **bool**:
  $x = y \vee e(x, y) \in close(G)$ **where**

  funct *close* = (**graph** *G*) **edges**:
    {**edge** *a*: $a \in E(G)$ ∇
    (∃ **node** *z*: $e(in(a), z) \in close(G) \wedge e(z, out(a)) \in close(G)$)}.

Alternatives for the existential formula in *close* are

- ∃ **node** *z*: $e(in(a), z) \in E(G) \,\Delta\, e(z, out(a)) \in close(G)$ or
- ∃ **node** *z*: $e(z, out(a)) \in E(G) \,\Delta\, e(in(a), z) \in close(G)$.

In either case, special care has to be taken in order to ensure definedness (Sect. 5.3.3.2).

A further formalization of the reachability problem can be based on the following idea:

There exists a non-empty sequence p of nodes in G that starts with x and ends with y, and any two neighboring nodes in p are connected by some (directed) edge.

This leads to

funct *reach* = (**graph** G, **node** x, **node** y: $x, y \in N(G)$) **bool**:
$\exists$ **nodesequ** p: $p \neq$<> Δ
(x = **first**$p \wedge y$ = **last**$p \wedge \forall$ (**nat** i: $1 \le i < |p|$): $e(p[i], p[i+1]) \in E(G)$).

Other problems directly related to the reachability problem are

- the recognition problem for formal languages (Sect. 3.6.6) and
- the problem of the shortest/longest path (if a cost function is associated with the edges of G, see for example [Berghammer 84]).

The *cycle problem* may be stated as follows:

Is there a cycle in the finite, directed graph $G = (N, E)$*?*

For the example above, there are several cycles, for example

< 2 >,
< 2, 3 >, or
< 2, 3, 4 >.

Formalizations of this problem could be based on the following characterization of the existence of a cycle:

There is a non-empty set of nodes c such that for any node n in c there is a predecessor (resp. successor) that is also in c

and yield

funct *hascycle* = (**graph** G) **bool**:
$\exists$ **nodes** c: $c \neq \emptyset \wedge (\forall$ **node** n: $n \in c \Rightarrow \exists$ **node** m: $m \in c \wedge e(m, n) \in E(G))$

resp.

funct *hascycle* = (**graph** G) **bool**:
$\exists$ **nodes** c: $c \neq \emptyset \wedge (\forall$ **node** n: $n \in c \Rightarrow \exists$ **node** m: $m \in c \wedge e(n, m) \in E(G))$

Note that the condition $c \neq \emptyset$ ensures that the specification is not underspecified.
Another idea for a formalization is

There is a sequence of nodes which forms a cycle.

This idea leads to the formalization

funct *hascycle* = (**graph** g) **bool**:
$\exists$ **nodesequ** s: *iscycle*(s) **where**

funct *iscycle* = (**nodesequ** s) **bool**:
$s \neq$<> $\Delta \forall$ (**nat** i: $1 \le i < |s|$): *isarc*(g, $s[i]$, $s[(i$ **mod** $|s|) + 1]$).

Another idea for a formalization can be based on the problem of reachability:

There is a node x in g with a path of non-zero length leading from x to x.

From the previous considerations a formalization based on the latter idea is straightforward and left as an exercise to the interested reader.

3.6.8 A Coding Problem

The problem to be considered in this subsection is taken from [Bauer 85] and may be stated in the following way:

Let the following be given
- *two finite, non-empty character sets V_1 and V_2, resp.*
- *a non-empty word N over V_1, called "message", and*
- *a "coding rule" P, a correspondence that relates non-empty words over V_1 to non-empty sets of non-empty words over V_2.*

Compute the set of all encodings of N with respect to P.

In order to illustrate the problem, consider

V_1 = {A, B, C, ...},
V_2 = {1, 2, 3, ...}
N = BARBROOM, and
P = {BAR ↦ {1, 2, 3},
  BARB ↦ {4},
  BROOM ↦ {5, 6},
  ROOM ↦ {7, 8} }.

For this particular case, there are two possible segmentations of N w.r.t. P, viz.

BAR - BROOM and
BARB - ROOM.

Hence the set of possible encodings is

{15, 16, 25, 26, 35, 36, 47, 48}.

There is no unique representation for the correspondence P. With $V1 =_{def} V_1^* \setminus \{<>\}$ and $V2 =_{def} V_2^* \setminus \{<>\}$, possible representations for P might be

$P \subseteq 2^{V1 \times V2}$ (set of pairs of non-empty words over V_1 and V_2, resp.),
$P \subseteq V1 \times 2^{V2}$ (set of pairs of words over V_1 and sets of words over V_2), or
$P \in V1 \rightarrow 2^{V2}$ (element of the set of all mappings from V1 to 2^{V2}).

Therefore, the formalization already requires making decisions, at least with respect to the data structures.

Motivated by the informal problem description we introduce the following data type definitions:

mode $\mathbf{V_1sequ}$ = EESEQU(V_1); **co** words over V_1 **co**
mode $\mathbf{V_2sequ}$ = EESEQU(V_2); **co** words over V_2 **co**
mode clear = ($\mathbf{V_1sequ}$ x: $x \neq$<>); **co** "clear words" **co**
mode code = ($\mathbf{V_2sequ}$ x: $x \neq$<>) **co** "code words" **co**
mode pair(=) = *mp*(**clear**(=) *cl*, **code**(=) *co*);
mode rule = SET(**pair**, =); **co** coding rule **co**
mode clears = SET(**clear**, =); **co** set of clear words **co**
mode codes = SET(**code**, =); **co** set of code words **co**
mode cleartext = EESEQU(**clear**, =); **co** sequence of clear words **co**
mode cleartexts = SET(**cleartext**, =); **co** set of clear texts **co**
mode codesequ = EESEQU(**code**, =); **co** set of code words **co**

Furthermore, the following auxiliary operations will turn out to be quite useful:

- **funct** *lhs* = (**rule** *P*) **clears**:
  {**clear** *l*: ∃ **code** *r*: *mp*(*l*, *r*) ∈ *P*}

  lhs(*P*) yields the set of all clear words in *P*. For our example above we have *lhs*(*P*) ={BAR, BARB, BROOM, ROOM}.

- **funct** *im* = (**clear** *l*, **rule** *P*: *l* ∈ *lhs*(*P*)) **codes**:
  {**code** *r*: *mp*(*l*, *r*) ∈ *P*}

  im(*l*, *P*) yields the set of all code words for *l* in *P*. For our example above we have, e.g. *im*(BAR, *P*) = {1, 2, 3}.

- **funct** *flat* = (**sequ** *s*) **msequ**: $\overset{|s|}{\underset{i=1}{+}}\ s[i]$ **where**

  mode sequ = EESEQU(**msequ**, =);
  mode msequ = EESEQU(**m**, =);

  flat(*s*) concatenates all elements in a sequence of sequences *s* into a sequence; for our example above we have, e.g., *flat*(<BARB, ROOM>) = BARBROOM.

- **funct** .⊕. = (**m** *x*, **msequset** *s*) **msequset**:
  {**msequ** *y*: ∃ **msequ** *z*: *z* ∈ *s* ∧ *y* = *x*+*z*} **where**
  mode msequ = EESEQU(**m**, =);
  mode msequset = SET(**msequ**, =).

  The operation .⊕. adds an element (from an object set **m** for which an equality "=" is defined) to all members of a set of sequences of these elements.

Now, the informally stated problem can be formalized as follows

funct *encodings* = (**clear** *N*, **rule** *P*) **codes**:
  $\bigcup_{a \in deco(N)}$ *encode*(*a*) **where**
  funct *deco* = (**clear** *N*) **cleartexts**:
    {**cleartext** *a*: *flat*(*a*) = *N* ∧ ∀ (**nat** *i*: 1≤*i* ≤ |*a*|): *a*[*i*] ∈ *lhs*(*P*)};

  funct *encode* = (**cleartext** *a*) **codes**:
    {**code** *c*: ∃ **codesequ** *b*: *flat*(*b*) = *c* ∧ |*b*| = |*a*| Δ
        ∀ (**nat** *i*: 1≤*i* ≤ |*a*|): *b*[*i*] ∈ *im*(*a*[*i*], *P*)}.

The idea underlying this formalization is fairly simple and straightforward:

Build the union of all possible encodings of all possible decompositions of the message with respect to the coding rule.

We leave it as an exercise to the interested reader to convince himself or herself that this formalization fulfils all the soundness criteria from Sect. 3.1.

3.6.9 Unification of Terms

The 'unification problem' may be stated as follows

Given

- $F = \{f, g, h, \dots\}$ *a finite, non-empty set of function identifiers with unique arity,*
- $K = \{a, b, c, \dots\}$ *a finite, non-empty set of constants,*
- $V = \{x, y, z, \dots\}$ *a finite, non-empty set of free variables,*
- *F, K, V pairwise disjoint,*
- *T, a set of well-formed terms over F, K, and V; and*
- $t_1, t_2 \in T$.

Are t_1 and t_2 unifiable, i.e., is there a substitution s of the free variables in t_1 and t_2 by terms such that applying s to t_1 and t_2 yields identical terms?

As an example, consider the terms

$t_1 = f(x, g(y, b))$ and
$t_2 = f(g(a, b), x)$.

Here, obviously, t_1 and t_2 are unifiable by the substitution

$x \mapsto g(a, b)$
$y \mapsto a$.

Again, related problems are

- *Give an arbitrary substitution by which t_1 and t_2 are unifiable, provided there is one.*
- *Give all substitutions by which t_1 and t_2 are unifiable.*

The unification problem plays an important role in a lot of applications in different areas, such as

- databases,
- natural language processing,
- expert systems,
- programming languages (such as PROLOG),
- automatic theorem proving.

Depending on the respective application there are also different versions of the problem (for an overview, see [Siekmann 84]):

- first-order or second-order unification;
  first-order unification allows only variables for terms whereas in second-order unification also variables for functions are admitted.
- free or unfree term structures;
  free term structures do not take into account algebraic properties of the functions considered; in unfree structures, i.e. structures with additional algebraic properties (such as commutativity, associativity, or distributivity), unification has to be done modulo these properties. (Assuming, e.g., commutativity of *f*, the substitution $y \mapsto a$ alone would suffice to unify t_1 and t_2 in the example above).

- typed or untyped terms;
  terms may additionally be decorated with types that have to be respected in unification.

In the following we restrict ourselves to first-order unification for untyped terms over free structures (see also [Manna, Waldinger 81], or [Eriksson 84]).

In order to formalize the problem, we first give an inductive definition of the notion of a term where constants are simply considered as nullary functions:

- Any $x \in K \cup V$ is a term;
- If $t_1, \ldots, t_n$ are terms and $f \in F$ is a function with arity n, then $f(t_1, \ldots, t_n)$ is a term;
- There are no other terms.

With

mode vid = «identifiers for variables with equality "="»;
mode opid = «identifiers for functions and constants»;
mode termsequ = ESEQU(**term**);
mode vidset = SET(**vid**, =);
funct *arity* = (**opid** *f*) **nat**: «arity of *f*»

terms can be defined by

mode term = *var*(**vid** *v*) |
op(**opid** *opsym*, **termsequ** *args*: *arity*(*opsym*) = |*args*|).

Furthermore, we introduce for terms an auxiliary function yielding all *variables occurring in a term*:

funct *vars* = (**term** *t*) **vidset**:
if *t* **is** *var* **then** $\{v(t)\}$
[] *t* **is** *op* **then** *vars'*(*args*(*t*)) **fi**;

funct *vars'* = (**termsequ** *ts*) **vidset**:
if *ts* =<> **then** $\varnothing$
[] *ts* ≠<> **then** *vars*(**first***t*) ∪ *vars'*(**rest***t*) **fi**,

and *equality tests* (for terms and sequences of terms)

funct $.=_t.$ = (**term** t_1, **term** t_2) **bool**:
((t_1 **is** *var* ∧ t_2 **is** *var*) Δ ($v(t_1) = v(t_2)$)) ∨
((t_1 **is** *op* ∧ t_2 **is** *op*) Δ ($opsym(t_1) = opsym(t_2)$) Δ ($args(t_1) =_{ts} args(t_2)$));

funct $. =_{ts}.$ = (**termsequ** st_1, **termsequ** st_2) **bool**:
(st_1 =<> ∧ st_2 =<>) ∇
((st_1 ≠<> ∧ st_2 ≠<>) Δ (**first**st_1 $=_t$ **first**st_2 ∧ **rest**st_1 $=_{ts}$ **rest**st_2)).

Substitutions are introduced by

mode subst = (**sub** *s*: ∀ **vid** *v*: *v* ∈ *dom*(*s*): *v* ∉ *vars*(*s*[*v*])) **where**
mode sub = EMAP(**vid**, **term**, =).

The *instantiation* of a term with a substitution is introduced by

funct .◇. = (**term** t, **subst** s) **term**:
  if t **is** *var* **then if** $v(t) \in dom(s)$ **then** $s[v(t)]\diamond s$ **else** t **fi**
  [] t **is** *op* **then** $op(opsym(t), args(t)\blacklozenge s)$ **fi**,

funct .♦. = (**termsequ** st, **subst** s) **termsequ**:
  if $st =<>$ **then** $<>$
  [] $st \neq <>$ **then** (**first**$st\diamond s$) + (**rest**$st\blacklozenge s$) **fi**.

Then the unifiability problem can be formalized by

funct *unifiable* = (**term** t_1, **term** t_2) **bool**:
  ∃ **subst** s: $t_1\diamond s =_t t_2\diamond s$.

Similarly, the problem of finding a unifier is defined by

funct *unify* = (**term** t_1, **term** t_2) (**subst** | **dummy**):
  if $unifiable(t_1, t_2)$ **then some subst** s: $t_1\diamond s =_t t_2\diamond s$ **else dummy fi**

and the problem of finding all unifiers by

funct *all-unifiers* = (**term** t_1, **term** t_2) **substset**:
  {**subst** s: $t_1\diamond s =_t t_2\diamond s$} **where**

mode substset = SET(**subst**, =).

Note that, for the latter specification being defined, a proof of the finiteness of the set comprehension in the body of *all-unifiers* is necessary, which only under additional conditions can be guaranteed.

3.6.10 The "Pack Problem"

The problem to be discussed in this subsection is essentially taken from [Goad 80] where it is used to demonstrate a programming methodology in which a program is "extracted" from a (constructive) proof of a theorem that reflects the problems to be solved. It is to be considered as a typical representative of the class of 'Knapsack-Problems' and its solution will lead to a 'backtrack program' (Sect. 5.4.2). Informally, the problem may be stated as follows:

Given

– $K = \{K_1, \ldots, K_n\}$, *a set of blocks* K_i *of different (but known) size*
– $B = \{B_1, \ldots, B_m\}$, *a set of boxes* B_i *of different (but known) size.*

Do all blocks fit into the available boxes?

Of course, as with the "upsequence problem" (Sect. 3.6.5) or the unification problem (Sect. 3.6.9), here too, interesting variants are

- *Give an (arbitrary) solution of how the blocks fit into the boxes (provided, they do),*
- *Give all solutions of how the blocks fit into the boxes.*

Practical applications of this problem are well-known (e.g. stowing all one's belongings into a limited number of boxes) as are related problems in the area of games and puzzles (all kinds of space-filling puzzles).

As an example, consider the following situation:
Let

$B = \{b_1, b_2, b_3\}$ with sizes $|b_1| = 22$, $|b_2| = 8$, $|b_3| = 13$, and
$K = \{k_1, k_2, k_3, k_4, k_5, k_6\}$ with sizes $|k_1| = 4$, $|k_2| = 13$, $|k_3| = 6$, $|k_4| = 7$, $|k_5| = 10$, $|k_6| = 2$.

If, for instance, we followed the simple-minded strategy *place the largest block into the largest box* we would associate k_2 with b_1 and then would fail. However, there is obviously a solution, e.g. by associating

k_1 with b_1
k_2 with b_3
k_3 with b_2
k_4 with b_1
k_5 with b_1
k_6 with b_2,

but this is not the only one.

The solution of the problem asks for a correspondence between blocks and boxes. Although there is no unique representation for the concept of correspondence, a formalization is straightforward. Note, however, that for purely technical reasons we prefer to use a sequence of boxes rather than a set in the formalization below.

Using

mode block = «blocks, with equality "="» and

mode box = «boxes, with equality "="»,

we assume to have available

funct $|.|$ = (**block** k) **nat:** «size of k»

funct $|.|$ = (**box** b) **nat**: «size of b»

that yield the (known) sizes of a block or a box.

Furthermore, we define

mode blockset = ESET(**block**, =) and

mode boxsequ = ESEQU(**box**)

in order to characterize (finite) sets of blocks and sequences of boxes, resp.

For representing correspondences between blocks and boxes we use

mode corr = EMAP(**block**, **box**, =)

and an auxiliary operation

funct *blocks* = (**corr** A, **box** b) **blockset:** $\{$**block** k: $A[k] = b\}$

which yields the set of all blocks associated with a box b with respect to a given correspondence A.

With these prerequisites the problem whether a correspondence between blocks and boxes exists may be formalized as follows:

funct *pack* = (**blockset** *K*, **boxsequ** *B*) **bool**:
  $\exists$ **corr** *A*: *legal*(*A*, *K*, *B*),

funct *legal* = (**corr** *A*, **blockset** *K*, **boxsequ** *B*) **bool**:
  $dom(A) = K \wedge B \supseteq ran(A) \wedge \forall$ (**nat** *i*: $1 \le i \le |B|$): $(\sum_{k \in blocks(A, B[i])} |k|) \le |B[i]|$

In checking the soundness of this formal specification, adequacy is the most interesting aspect. It can be made plausible by simply interpreting the three conjuncts within the definition of *legal*:

- $dom(A) = K$ means: all blocks are associated to boxes;
- $B \supseteq ran(A)$ means: all boxes associated to some block w.r.t. *A* are contained in *B* (also: "the number of boxes is sufficient to store all blocks");
- $(\sum_{k \in blocks(A, B[i])} |k|) \le |B[i]|$ means: the capacity of each box $B[i]$ suffices to host all blocks associated with it.

As in the previous section, we can also formalize the problem of computing an arbitrary correspondence

funct *findpack* = (**blockset** *K*, **boxsequ** *B*) (**corr** | **dummy**):
  if *pack*(*K*, *B*) **then some corr** *A*: *legal*(*A*, *K*, *B*) **else dummy fi**,

or all correspondences

funct *findallpacks* = (**blockset** *K*, **boxsequ** *B*) **corrset**:
  {**corr** *A*: *legal*(*A*, *K*, *B*)} **where**

mode corrset = SET(**corr**, =).

3.6.11 The Bounded Buffer

For specifying the bounded buffer from Sect. 2.2.1 within our formalism, we first specify *priority queues*, i.e., buffers of unlimited length (see also [Pepper et al. 82], [Partsch, Pepper 83]). As prerequisites we assume

- a type INFO which defines an object kind **info** (of informations) and
- **type** PTY-INFO = **pty-info**, *mk-pty-info*, *pty*, *info*:
  based on INFO, NAT,
  funct (**info**) **pty-info** *mk-pty-info*,
  funct (**pty-info**) **nat** *pty*,
  funct (**pty-info**) **info** *info*,
  ...
  endoftype
  which defines informations with priorities.

  Priority queues then may be specified by

  type PQUEUE = **pqueue**, *put*, *max*, *rest*, *init*, |.|:
    based on PTY-INFO, NAT,
    sort pqueue,

```
    pqueue init,
    funct (pqueue, pty-info) pqueue put,
    funct (pqueue q: |q| > 0) pty-info max,
    funct (pqueue q: |q| > 0) pqueue rest,
    funct (pqueue) nat |.|,
    laws pqueue q, r, pty-info i: |q| > 0:
       |init| ≡ 0,
       |put(r, i)| ≡ |r| + 1,
       max(put(init, i)) ≡ i,
       max(put(q, i)) ≡ if pty(i) ≥ max(q) then i else max(q) fi,
       rest(put(init, i)) ≡ init,
       rest(put(q, i)) ≡ if pty(i) ≥ max(q) then q else put(rest(q), i) fi
endoftype.
```

For specifying the buffer of limited length we use the concept of computation structures, since we have to deal with functions yielding pairs of results (which are syntactically not admitted within type declarations). Due to the applicative style of computation structures, the buffer will appear as an additional argument and result of the operations for storing and retrieving an information. If we had used a more machine-oriented concept, such as devices, these additional arguments and results could have been hidden. The transition from a computation structure to a more machine-oriented representation is considered a step in program development.

```
structure BUFFER = (nat N) buffer, sresult, rresult, init, store, retrieve:
    based on PQUEUE;
    mode buffer = (pqueue q: |q| ≤ N);
    mode sresult = (OK | error);
    mode rresult = (info | error);

    funct store = (buffer b, info i) (buffer, sresult):
       if |b| < N then (put(b, mk-pty-info(i)), OK) else (b, error) fi;

    funct retrieve = (buffer b) (buffer, rresult):
       if |b| > 0 then (rest(b), info(max(b))) else (b, error) fi

endofstructure.
```

An analysis of this specification with respect to the properties from Sect. 3.1 is straightforward and left to the reader.

3.6.12 Paraffins

This example has been inspired by [Turner 81] and is intended as another exercise in algebraic specification. Informally, the problem reads:

Design a data type for paraffins.

A *paraffin* is [Webster 74] "any hydrocarbon of the methane series", where the latter is explained as "a series of saturated hydrocarbons of the open-chain type, having the general formula $C_n H_{2n+2}$".

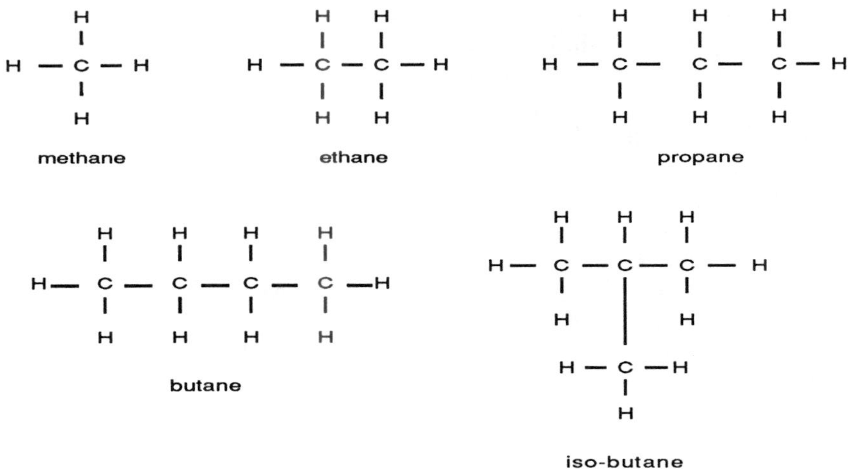

Figure 3.4. Examples for paraffins

Typical examples for paraffins are given in Fig. 3.4. There, the last two examples, butane and iso-butane, illustrate the difficulty with this problem, that is the problem of isomers which are hydrocarbons having the same formula but a different molecular structure (with different chemical properties).

In order to formalize the problem we first give an axiomatic definition of paraffins based on the auxiliary notion of (paraffin) radical:

1) *A proton is a (paraffin) radical;*
2) *3 radicals attached to 3 of the 4 free valences of a carbon atom results in a new radical;*
3) *A paraffin molecule results from attaching 4 radicals to the 4 free valences of a carbon atom;*
4) *The four valences of a carbon atom within a paraffin molecule are indistinguishable.*

Now a formalization by means of algebraic data types is straightforward:

type RADICAL = **rad**, *H*, [.,.,.]:
  sort rad,
  rad *H*,
  funct (**rad**, **rad**, **rad**) **rad** [.,.,.]
endoftype.

type PARAFFIN = **para**, <.,.,.,.>:
  based on RADICAL,
  sort para,
  funct (**rad**, **rad**, **rad**, **rad**) **para** <.,.,.,.>;
  laws rad *a*, *b*, *c*, *d*, *e*, *f*:
  (1) <[*a*, *b*, *c*], *d*, *e*, *f*> ≡ <*a*, *b*, *c*, [*d*, *e*, *f*]>,
  (2) <*a*, *b*, *c*, *d*> ≡ <*b*, *c*, *d*, *a*>,
  (3) <*a*, *b*, *c*, *d*> ≡ <*b*, *a*, *c*, *d*>
endoftype.

The axioms in PARAFFIN can be informally explained as follows:

$$
\text{(1)} \quad
\begin{array}{ccc}
a & & f \\
| & & | \\
b - \textcircled{C} - & C - e \\
| & & | \\
c & & d
\end{array}
\quad = \quad
\begin{array}{ccc}
a & & f \\
| & & | \\
b - C - & \textcircled{C} - e \\
| & & | \\
c & & d
\end{array}
$$

radical construction and paraffin construction commute

$$
\text{(2)} \quad
\begin{array}{c}
d \\
| \\
a - C - c \\
| \\
b
\end{array} \Big)
\quad = \quad
\begin{array}{c}
a \\
| \\
b - C - d \\
| \\
c
\end{array}
$$

paraffins are invariant under rotation

$$
\text{(3)} \quad
\begin{array}{c}
d \\
| \\
a - C - c \\
| \\
b
\end{array}
\quad = \quad
\begin{array}{c}
d \\
| \\
b - C - c \\
| \\
a
\end{array}
$$

paraffins are invariant under swaps.

In order to complete the formal specification, we have to analyze it with respect to the criteria discussed in Sect. 3.1. First we have to ensure definedness of the operations [.,.,.] and <.,.,.,.> by means of suitable axioms. Furthermore, as we are concerned with an algebraic specification, the discussion on adequacy has to include a reasoning about the class of models that is defined by it.

For our specification above, an 'initial model' [Wirsing et al. 83], i.e. a model where all terms are different unless their equality is deducible from the axioms, would be adequate. However, the semantics of an algebraic specification also includes a 'terminal model', i.e. a model where all terms are equal the inequality of which is not deducible from the axioms. For the above specification, therefore, the trivial model consisting of just one element is also a model – and certainly not an adequate one.

In order to achieve adequacy, we have to modify the specification such that the initial model is the only one satisfying the specification. One possibility is by giving an explicit definition of an equivalence test. As an additional exercise in formal specification we now focus on giving an explicit definition for such an equivalence test. In order to provide some generality and avoid being restricted to the paraffin problem, we consider the problem of testing equivalence with respect to an arbitrary set $\{f_1, ..., f_n\}$ of equivalence-preserving operations on the objects under consideration (see also [Turner 81]) which can be obtained from the respective axioms $\{a_1, ..., a_n\}$ of the data type. Of course, for the sake of computability, it is necessary that the equivalence classes induced by the axioms are finite.

Assuming

mode m = «object kind under consideration with equality "="», and

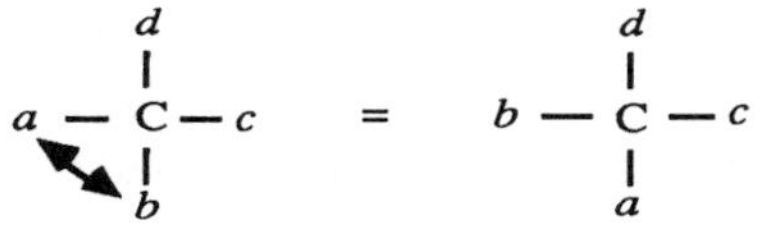

mode mset = ESET(**m**, =),

any such operation f_i has functionality **funct** (**m**) **mset** and is defined by

$f_i(x)$ = {**m** y: «y is equivalent to x w.r.t. axiom a_i»} ∪ {x}.

Of course, all these operations f_i ($1 \le i \le n$) can be combined into a single operation

funct f = (**m** x) **mset:** $\cup_{i=1..n} f_i(x)$.

They also can be extended to be applicable to sets of objects rather than individual objects:

funct F = (**mset** X) **mset:** $\cup_{x \in X} f(x)$.

Now, the equivalence test simply can be defined by

funct *equiv* = (**m** a, **m** b) **bool**: $b \in$ *equivclass*(a) **where**

funct *equivclass* = (**m** a) **mset**:
{**m** y: $\exists$ **m** $x_1, \ldots, x_k$: $x_1 = a \wedge x_k = y \wedge$
$\forall\ 1 \le j < k$: $\exists\ 1 \le i \le n$: $x_{j+1} = f_i(x_j)$}

(where the last conjunct is short for a (finite) conjunction of disjunctions).

In order to demonstrate the adequacy of this specification, we have to prove that this definition implies the usual properties of equivalences. But this is trivial, because symmetry, reflexivity, and transitivity follow immediately from the definitions.

Of course, we also could have given an operational definition for *equiv*, such as

funct *equiv* = (**m** a, **m** b) **bool**: $b \in$ *close*({a}, {a}) **where**

funct *close* = (**mset** s, **mset** t) **mset**:
if $F(t) \setminus s = \varnothing$ **then** s **else** *close*($s \cup t$, $F(t) \setminus s$) **fi**.

Proving the adequacy of this latter definition is left to the interested reader as well as applying the general definition of the equivalence test to the particular paraffin example.

3.7 Exercises

Exercise 3.3-1

Give algebraic types that define

a) the natural numbers providing only the constant 0 and the successor operation *succ*;
b) integral numbers;
c) rational numbers (as pairs of integral numbers).

Exercise 3.3-2

Give algebraic types that define

a) queues (with operations for adding an element to the end of the queue and for selecting/removing the first element);
b) double-ended queues, i.e. queues with access on both ends.

Exercise 3.3-3
Give algebraic types that define

a) binary trees where only the leaves carry information;
b) binary trees where any node carries information;
c) trees with an arbitrary number of branchings.

Exercise 3.3-4
Give algebraic types that define

a) arrays of fixed (positive) length (allowing selection and updating of elements);
b) flexible arrays with the operations [Dijkstra 76a]
   - *vac*, for generating an empty array with given bounds;
   - *put*, for assigning a value to an index;
   - *get*, for accessing the value under some index;
   - *lob*, yielding the lower bound;
   - *hib*, yielding the upper bound;
   - *hiext*, for adding an element to the array at the upper end;
   - *loext*, for adding an element to the array at the lower end.

Exercise 3.3-5
Give "degenerated" algebraic types (without constituents)

a) ORD, checking for (partial) orderings;
b) LINORD, checking for linear orderings;
c) SLINORD, checking for linear orderings with an operation *next* (that yields the next element with respect to the ordering);
d) LATTICE, checking for lattices;
e) ENUM, checking whether an operation yields an enumeration of a given basic type.

Exercise 3.3-6
Given the definitions of the types SET and BAG from Sect. 3.3.2, prove

a) $\forall$ **set** s, **m** x: $x \in (s-x) \equiv$ **false**;
b) $\forall$ **bag** b, **m** x: $\#occs(x, b-x) \equiv$
   $pred(\#occs(x, b))$ **provided** $\neg\ (\#occs(x, b) = 0)$.

Exercise 3.3-7
Give extensions of the types

a) EEMAP defining operations for the union, intersection, and difference of two maps; use suitable assertions to express the respective partialities;
b) EBAG defining the operations size, union, intersection, difference, and subbag relation;
c) ENAT defining addition and subtraction.
d) EENAT defining addition, subtraction, multiplication, and division.

Exercise 3.3-8
Give algebraic types that define

a) n-ary relations;
b) relational structures with two basic relations;
c) reflexive and transitive (binary) relations;
d) labeled (directed) graphs.

Exercise 3.3-9
Given the types PORD and EREL from Sect. 3.3.4.2, prove

a) reflexivity, transitivity, and anti-symmetry of *ordered*;
b) reflexivity, transitivity, and symmetry of *equiv*.

Exercise 3.3-10
Give a type scheme that defines associative Cartesian products.

Exercise 3.4-1
Derive, using the respective definitions, definedness and determinacy criteria for the following constructs:

a) conditional expression;
b) tuple;
c) choice;
d) function application.

Exercise 3.4-2
Derive an explicit definition of the breadth of

if C_1 **then** E_1 [] C_2 **then** E_2 **else** E_3 **fi** .

Exercise 3.4-3
Specify operations for the conversion of

a) SET into SEQU and vice versa; discuss possible problems of partiality.
b) BAG into SEQU;
c) SEQU into BAG;
d) sets of pairs into maps and vice versa; discuss possible problems of uniqueness.

Exercise 3.4-4
a) Give a formal specification of an operation *num* that converts a sequence of digits into a natural number;
b) Specify an operation for "normalizing" rational numbers represented by pairs of integral numbers.

Exercise 3.4-5
Give descriptive and operational formal specifications of operations that

a) test whether all elements in a given sequence are different;
b) delete in a sequence all multiple occurrences (but one) of elements.

Exercise 3.4-6
Give (descriptive and operational) formal specifications of the following (partial) operations on sequences:

a) *del*, that deletes from a sequence *s* an initial segment *l* of *s*;
b) *repl*, that replaces an occurrence of a pattern *p* in a sequence *s* by another sequence *q*;

c) *lmcontext*, that determines the left and right context of the leftmost occurrence of a pattern *p* in a sequence *s*;
d) *lmrepl*, that replaces the leftmost occurrence of a pattern *p* in a sequence *s* by a sequence *q*.

Exercise 3.4-7

A **Markov rule** is a pair of strings called "pattern" and "replacement". Additionally, a rule can be marked to be "terminating". A **Markov algorithm** is a rewrite system consisting of a sequence *r* of Markov rules. A Markov algorithm with rules *r*, applied to a string *s*, works as follows:

- if none of the patterns of the rules in *r* occurs in *s*, rewriting terminates and the result is *s*;
- otherwise, the first rule whose pattern *pat* occurs in *s* is used to replace the leftmost occurrence of *pat* in *s* by the corresponding replacement *rep*. If the rule applied is a terminating rule, rewriting terminates and the result is the modified string; otherwise, the Markov algorithm is applied to the modified string.

Give a formal specification of an operation that applies a Markov algorithm to a string.

Exercise 3.4-8

Give a formal specification of the following problem:
Given the sequence $s = < 1, 2, 3, 4, 5, 6, 7, 8, 9 >$ of natural numbers, it is requested to find the set of all permutations *p* of *s* which have the property that any initial segment of *p* of length i ($1 \leq i \leq 9$), considered as a decimal number, is divisible by i.

Exercise 3.4-9

Given binary trees defined by

mode bintree = *et* | *cons*(**bintree** *left*, **info** *node*, **bintree** *right*)

specify predicates that check

a) whether two binary trees are equal;
b) whether a binary tree is a subtree of another binary tree;
c) whether the nodes in a binary tree are ordered from left to right;
d) whether a binary tree *b* is balanced, i.e., iff for any non-empty subtree of *b* the heights of the respective left and right subtree differ at most by 1;
e) whether in any subtree of a given binary tree the value of the root node is the maximum of all nodes in the respective subtree;
f) whether the information *x* is contained in a binary tree *b*.

Exercise 3.4-10

Given binary trees defined by

mode bintree = *et* | *cons*(**bintree** *left*, **info** *node*, **bintree** *right*)

specify an operation that

a) merges two ordered binary trees into a single ordered binary tree;
b) converts a given sequence into a balanced binary tree;
c) converts a binary tree into a balanced one;

d) converts a binary tree into a balanced one such that the respective sequences of nodes obtained from an inorder traversal are the same;
e) converts a sequence into an ordered binary tree;
f) (non-deterministically) computes the weight w of information x with respect to b according to the following definition:

$w(x, b) =_{def}$
- 0, if $\neg isin(x, b)$
- 1, if $x = node(b)$
- $2 \times w(x, left(b))$, if $isin(x, left(b))$
- $2 \times w(x, right(b)) + 1$, if $isin(x, right(b))$.

Exercise 3.4-11

For a finite, directed graph G give formal specifications of the following problems:

a) Is G connected ?
b) Does G contain an "Eulerian path", i.e. a path containing each node of the graph exactly once ?
c) Does G contain a "Hamilton circle", i.e. a cycle containing each node of the graph exactly once ?
d) An operation that computes the "costs" of an also given path (consisting of a sequence of nodes) in G using a function w that associates to each edge a weight.

Exercise 3.5-1

Let bracketed strings be defined by

mode bstring = SEQU(**bracket**) **where**

mode bracket = [|].

Give a (descriptive or operational) formal specification for the predicate

funct *correct* = (**bstring** *b*) **bool**:

that checks whether b is correctly bracketed, i.e., conforms to the context-free grammar

S ::= <> | [S] | SS.

Exercise 3.5-2

Let BL denote a blank and NL denote the "new line" character. Given furthermore the mode declarations

mode char = «any character different from BL and NL with equality "="»;
mode word = EESEQU(**char**, =);
mode ws = **word** | NL | BL;
mode line = EESEQU(**ws**, =);
mode text = EESEQU(**line**, =),

give formal specifications for the following operations:

a) **funct** *length* = (**line** *l*) **nat**:

that computes the number of characters different from NL contained in *l*.

b) **funct** *same* = (**text** *t*, **line** *l*) **bool:**

that checks whether the sequence of all words in *t*, resp. *l* are the same.

c) **funct** *format* = (**line** *in*, **nat** *max*: $in \neq \langle\rangle \wedge$
$(\forall$ **word** w: $w \in in \Rightarrow |w| \leq max)$) **text:**

that converts a line *in* into a text *t* that consists of the same words and fulfils the following additional restrictions:

1) *t* contains no empty lines;
2) any line in *t* has a length of at most *max*;
3) any line in *t* starts and ends with a word; two consecutive words in the same line are separated by exactly one blank;
4) no line of *t* starts with a word that could have fit into the preceding line.

Exercise 3.5-3

The following algebraic data type [Broy 84a] defines binary directed graphs:

type BIG = (**sort m**, **funct(m, m) bool** .=.: **include** EQUIV(**m**, =))
  big, *ebig*, *put*, *left*, *right*:
  based on BOOL,
  sort big,
  big *ebig*,
  funct (**big**, **m**, **m**, **m**) **big** *put*,
  funct (**big**, **m**) **m** *left*,
  funct (**big**, **m**) **m** *right*;
  laws big *g*, **m** *x*, *x'*, *y*, *z*:
    $left(ebig, x) \equiv x$,
    $left(put(g, x, y, z), x) \equiv y$,
    $left(put(g, x, y, z), x') \equiv left(g, x')$ **provided** $\neg(x = x')$,
    $right(ebig, x) \equiv x$,
    $right(put(g, x, y, z), x) \equiv z$,
    $right(put(g, x, y, z), x') \equiv right(g, x')$ **provided** $\neg(x = x')$
endoftype.

Thus for example for **m** = **nat**, the term

$put(put(put(ebig, 5, 6, 5), 1, 2, 3), 2, 1, 4)$

denotes the graph

a) Specify an extension EBIG of BIG by adding an operation

funct (**m** *x*, **big** *g*) **bool** *isin*

that checks whether *x* is contained in *g*.

b) Specify a predicate

funct (**m** x, **m** y, **big** g) **bool** *ispath*

that checks whether there is a (directed) path from x to y in g.

c) Specify a predicate

funct (**big** g) **bool** *connected*

that checks whether all nodes in g are connected via (undirected) edges.

4. Basic Transformation Techniques

In this chapter we introduce the theoretical foundations of transformational programming together with a variety of simple transformation rules. In the following chapters, these will be considered as a basis for deriving and proving correct further, more advanced, compact rules. Additionally, we will also show that these basic rules together with elementary strategies are already sufficient to do transformational program development for certain specific tasks. The examples will start from formal specifications as developed in Sect. 3.6.

4.1 Semantic Foundations

The theoretical background of the transformational methodology is a formal calculus of transformations that is described in [Pepper 84]. We will just summarize its essence without dealing with all technical details. The central notions within this calculus are 'program schemes' and 'transformation rules'.

In [Pepper 84], a **program** is a well-formed term over the signature PL of an algebraic type that defines a programming language over some (exchangeable) set of primitive types (for more details on this way of defining programming languages see, e.g., [Broy et al. 82]). In this view, the abstract syntax of the expression language introduced in Sect. 3.4 is given as a signature enriching the signatures of those types that specify the basic objects and operations (using the algebraic specification formalism introduced in Sect. 3.3). As in Sect. 3.4, the **semantics** of a program is defined by the mapping B that associates a set of semantic values to each program.

A **program scheme** is a term from W(PL∪X), the term algebra (cf. Sect. 3.3.1.1) over PL∪X, i.e. a term over PL containing free variables from a countable set X of (typed) **scheme parameters**. Program schemes are a generalization of programs; programs are program schemes that do not contain free variables, i.e., terms from W(PL).

Simple examples of program schemes are

F(E, E')

or

if $x \le y$ **then** x **else** y **fi**

(where F, E, and E' are scheme parameters for expressions).

Instances are finite partial mappings Θ: X → W(PL ∪ X) from scheme parameters to program schemes. For a program scheme p and an instance Θ, the

instantiation pΘ of p with Θ is obtained by simultaneously substituting all scheme parameters in p by program schemes according to Θ. An instance Θ is called a **ground instance** if for all $x \in X$ we have $x\Theta \in$ W(PL).

Thus, e.g., the instantiation of

F(E, E')

with the instance

F $\mapsto$.≤.,
E $\mapsto$ x, and
E' $\mapsto$ y

results in

$x \leq y$.

The important semantic notions 'defined' and 'determinate' (Sect. 3.4) straightforwardly carry over to program schemes: A program scheme E containing (at most) the scheme variable x of kind **m** is called

- **defined** iff $\bot \notin$ B⟦E[u **for** x]⟧;
- **determinate** iff |B⟦E[u **for** x]⟧| = 1

for all $u \in$ DOM⟦**m**⟧. For denoting definedness and determinacy, we use the special semantic predicates DEF and DET, respectively.

As an example we consider the program scheme

if $x \leq y$ **then** x **else** y **fi**.

Assuming that, defined by a suitable environment, x and y are of kind **nat**, and .≤. is of kind **funct(nat, nat)bool**, we have, according to the semantic definition given in Sect. 3.4.1,

DET[x], DET[y], and DET[.≤.],

and hence

DET[$x \leq y$].

Thus, together, we have

DET[**if** $x \leq y$ **then** x **else** y **fi**].

Under the same assumptions, we have also DEF[.≤.], hence

DEF[$x \leq y$] iff DEF[x] and DEF[y],

and further

DEF[**if** $x \leq y$ **then** x **else** y **fi**] iff DEF[x] and DEF[y].

Note, however, that, according to the semantic definition given in Sect. 3.4.1, an analogous reasoning for an arbitrary declared function f (instead of .≤.) is only valid, if additionally termination of f is guaranteed.

The instantiation of a semantic predicate is obtained by the instantiations of the program schemes involved.

For instance the instantiation of

DEF[F(E, E')]

with the instance from above results in

DEF[$x \le y$].

The semantic predicates 'equivalent' and 'descendant' (Sect. 3.4) are also extended to program schemes: Let E_1 and E_2 be program schemes (of the same kind) containing (at most) the scheme variable x of kind **m**. We call

- E_1 **equivalent** to E_2 iff B⟦E_1[u **for** x]⟧ = B⟦E_2[u **for** x]⟧; and
- E_1 a **descendant** of E_2 iff B⟦E_1[u **for** x]⟧ $\subseteq$ B⟦E_2[u **for** x]⟧

for all $u \in$ DOM⟦**m**⟧. We use "≡" and "⊑" as special semantic predicates to denote equivalence and descendance, respectively. Note that the use of "≡" for the equality of breadths and the use of "≡" in the axioms of algebraic types (Sect. 3.3) coincide.

Thus, under the same assumptions as above and the additional assumption DET[$x \le y$],

if $x \le y$ **then** x **else** y **fi**

is equivalent to

if $x \le y$ **then** x [] $\neg(x \le y)$ **then** y **fi**,

since the respective breadths are obviously the same, provided DET[$x \le y$]. Since furthermore DET[$x \le y$] is vacuously true (see above) the equivalence holds even unconditionally.

Likewise, convincing oneself that

if $x \le y$ **then** x **else** y **fi**

is a descendant of

(x [] y)

is straightforward from the respective definitions.

The semantic predicates over program schemes are the **atomic formulas** which form the basis of the transformational calculus. An atomic formula A is **valid** if for all ground instances Θ the ground formula AΘ holds in the semantic model of PL.

Over these atomic formulas, positive implicational formulas (Horn clauses, or **clauses** for short) can be formulated. These clauses have the forms

$$A_1, \ldots, A_n \vdash B, \text{ resp. } \vdash B,$$

with A_i ($1 \le i \le n$) (called antecedents) and B (called the consequent) being atomic formulas. Free variables in A_i or B are assumed to be universally quantified. A clause is **valid** if for all ground instances Θ for which $A_1\Theta, \ldots, A_n\Theta$ hold, also BΘ holds.

Clauses are the components of **inferences**, which provide a second level of implicational formulas. Inferences are denoted by

$$\frac{C_1, \ldots, C_m}{D}$$

where C_j ($1 \le j \le m$) (called premises) and D (called the conclusion) are clauses. An inference is **valid** iff D is valid whenever the C_j ($1 \le j \le m$) are valid.

Examples of valid inferences are

$$\frac{\vdash \mathsf{DET}[E_i]\ (1 \le i \le n)}{\vdash \mathsf{DET}[F(E_1, ..., E_n)]}$$

or

$$\frac{\vdash \mathsf{DEF}[F], \mathsf{DEF}[E_i]\ (1 \le i \le n)}{\vdash \mathsf{DEF}[F(E_1, ..., E_n)]}$$

if we additionally assume that the E_i are expressions of kind $\mathbf{m_i}$ and F is an expression of kind $\mathbf{funct(m_1, ..., m_n)m}$.

Transformation rules are special inferences of the form

$$\frac{C}{\vdash \mathrm{REL}[I, O]}$$

where C is a set of applicability conditions (cf. below) and REL a binary semantic predicate (read as 'transformable') over program schemes, i.e. 'equivalent' or 'descendant'. I and O are also called **input scheme** and **output scheme** respectively.

A transformation rule is **correct**, if it constitutes a valid inference, i.e. if the programs schemes I and O are in the semantic relation indicated by REL whenever the applicability conditions are valid. All rules to be given in the sequel are correct in this sense.

A simple example of a correct transformation rule is

$$\frac{\vdash \mathsf{DEF}[B]}{\vdash \textbf{if } B \textbf{ then } E \textbf{ else } E \textbf{ fi} \equiv E\ .}$$

Applicability conditions are Horn clauses over an enrichment of PL∪X, i.e. they may contain additional syntactic and semantic predicates over program schemes. For clauses $A_1, ..., A_n \vdash B$ and $A_1, ..., A_n \vdash C$, we use the abbreviation $A_1, ..., A_n \vdash B, C$.

Applying a transformation rule

$$\frac{C}{\vdash \mathrm{REL}[I, O]}$$

to a program scheme t is defined to result in a new inference

$$\frac{C\Theta}{\vdash \mathrm{REL}[t, O\Theta]}$$

where Θ is determined by **matching** the input scheme I against t, $C\Theta$ denotes the instantiation of C with Θ, and $O\Theta$ of O with Θ.

As an example we consider the transformation rule from above and the program scheme

if $x \le y$ **then** $f(x)$ **else** $f(x)$ **fi**.

Here, matching yields the instance

$B \mapsto x \le y$,
$E \mapsto f(x)$,

and hence application of the rule yields the inference

$$\frac{\vdash \mathsf{DEF}[x \le y]}{\vdash \textbf{if } x \le y \textbf{ then } f(x) \textbf{ else } f(x) \textbf{ fi} \equiv f(x)} \; .$$

This way of defining the application of a transformation rule has the particular advantage that the verification of the respective applicability conditions may be deferred. This is important, since it allows us to avoid useless verification efforts in case of a blind alley in a development. As another consequence, the idea of program verification is captured in our approach by the trivial general rules

$$\frac{\vdash \mathrm{E} \equiv \mathrm{E'}}{\vdash \mathrm{E} \equiv \mathrm{E'}} \quad \text{resp.} \quad \frac{\vdash \mathrm{E} \subseteq \mathrm{E'}}{\vdash \mathrm{E} \subseteq \mathrm{E'}} \; .$$

These rules state that E can be *transformed* into E' by *finding* E' and *verifying* its semantic relationship with E. They also illustrate once more the difference between transformation and verification: transformation rules are instances of these general rules where, by syntactic specialization of E, the effort of finding E' and proving its semantic relationship to E is reduced.

A programming language PL is said to be **monotonic** with respect to the semantic relation REL, if for arbitrary program schemes t1 and t2, and arbitrary (syntactically legal) **contexts** cn for t1 and t2,

$$\frac{\vdash \mathrm{REL[t1, t2]\,]}}{\vdash \mathrm{REL[cn[t1], cn[t2]]}}$$

is a valid inference (where cn[t] denotes the embedding of t in the context cn).

All language constructs introduced in Chap. 3 are monotonic with respect to equivalence and the descendant relation [Bauer et al. 85].

Monotonicity allows us, in particular, to straightforwardly extend the notions 'equivalence' and 'descendance' to program schemes P and P' that are not expressions, i.e., that are not associated with values by means of the "breadth function" B. In such a case REL[P, P'] is short for REL[cn[P], cn[P']] for all contexts cn for which cn[P] (and cn[P'], resp.) are expressions.

For a monotonic programming language PL, transformation rules also can be applied locally. **Local application** of

$$\frac{\mathrm{C}}{\vdash \mathrm{REL[I, O]}}$$

to a program scheme t = cn[p] then yields

$$\frac{\mathrm{C}\Theta}{\vdash \mathrm{REL[t, cn[O\Theta]]}}$$

where Θ now is determined by matching I against p (rather than t).

Within the calculus sketched above, each step in a transformational development amounts to deriving a new inference. An additional way of deriving new inferences from available ones is provided by the mechanism of meta-inferences.

Meta-inferences provide a third level of implicational formulas. As these formulas are valid in any implicational calculus, they provide a means for reasoning about both clauses and inferences. A typical example of such a meta-inference is the 'cut rule' (a variant of 'modus ponens') which reads

From $A_1,\ldots,A_n \vdash B$ **and** $B, B_1,\ldots,B_m \vdash C$ **infer** $A_1,\ldots,A_n, B_1,\ldots,B_m \vdash C$

for clauses, and

From $\dfrac{C_1, \ldots, C_m}{D}$ **and** $\dfrac{D, D_1, \ldots, D_k}{E}$ **infer** $\dfrac{C_1, \ldots, C_m, D_1, \ldots, D_k}{E}$

for inferences.

Using this meta-inference, from

$\vdash \mathsf{DEF}[.\le.]$

and

$$\frac{\vdash \mathsf{DEF}[x], \mathsf{DEF}[y], \mathsf{DEF}[.\le.]}{\vdash \mathsf{DEF}[x \le y]}$$

we can infer

$$\frac{\vdash \mathsf{DEF}[x], \mathsf{DEF}[y]}{\vdash \mathsf{DEF}[x \le y]}$$

and further

$$\frac{\vdash \mathsf{DEF}[x], \mathsf{DEF}[y]}{\vdash \textbf{if } x \le y \textbf{ then } f(x) \textbf{ else } f(x) \textbf{ fi} \equiv f(x)}\ .$$

For further examples and further details we refer the reader to [Pepper 84]. By the meta-inference mechanism (under certain conditions), all inferences constituting a program development can be combined into a single inference

$$\frac{C}{\vdash \mathrm{REL}[s, r]}$$

where s is the initial specification of the problem, r is the result of the development, and C is the set of applicability conditions that guarantee the semantic relation REL to hold between s and r.

4.2 Notational Conventions

In order to keep our presentation at a reasonable length, we introduce a few abbreviations and conventions for the subsequent chapters.

4.2.1 Program Schemes

As in Chap. 3, we use upright uppercase characters for expressions, strings of boldface lowercase characters for sort identifiers (of object kinds) and keywords, and strings of italic characters for object and function identifiers and (primitive) operation symbols.

Expression symbols occasionally will be augmented with "arguments" in order to stress certain dependences on particular objects. In this case, the set of "arguments" is to indicate a superset of possible arguments, i.e. not all of them actually have to occur, and those not listed explicitly, do not occur at all.

Following this convention,

$E(f, x, y)$

denotes an expression (scheme) which contains at most f, x, and y as identifiers. Concrete instances of this expression scheme are

if $x \le y$ **then** $f(x)$ **else** $f(y)$ **fi**

or

if $x \le y$ **then** x **else** y **fi**

but not

if $x \le y$ **then** $f(x)$ **else** $g(y)$ **fi**

if g is a free identifier.

We also allow expressions to be augmented with "substitutions" for free identifiers. Thus,

E[E' **for** x, h **for** f]

denotes the consistent (simultaneous) replacement of x by the expression E' and the replacement of f by the identifier h. For the instances given above the indicated substitution results in

if E' $\le y$ **then** h(E') **else** $h(y)$ **fi**,

respectively

if E' $\le y$ **then** E' **else** y **fi**.

We further assume that during this substitution bound variables are renamed to resolve name clashes.

In addition to the language constructs introduced in Chap. 3 we will occasionally also use abbreviations such as

if $[]_{i=1..n}$ B_i **then** E_i **fi**

for

if B_1 **then** E_1 [] B_2 **then** E_2 ... [] B_n **then** E_n **fi**

or

$\exists_{i=1..n} (B_i \wedge E_i)$

for

$(B_1 \wedge E_1) \vee (B_2 \wedge E_2) \vee ... \vee (B_n \wedge E_n)$,

and the like.

Furthermore, in order to avoid an accumulation of **begin** - **end** pairs, subordination in systems of functions, coupled with "suppression" of arguments of the subordinated function that remain constant, will be frequently indicated just by indentation. Thus, for example we will use

funct *sort* = (**natsequ** *s*) **natsequ**:
  some natsequ *x*: *issorted*(*x*) ∧ *isperm*(*x*, *s*) **where**

  funct *issorted* = (**natsequ** *x*) **natsequ**: ...;

  funct *isperm* = (**natsequ** *y*) **natsequ**: ...

as an abbreviation for the definition of *sort* given in Sect. 3.4.3.

4.2.2 Transformation Rules

For the sake of legibility we will denote transformation rules, as in [Bauer et al. 85], by

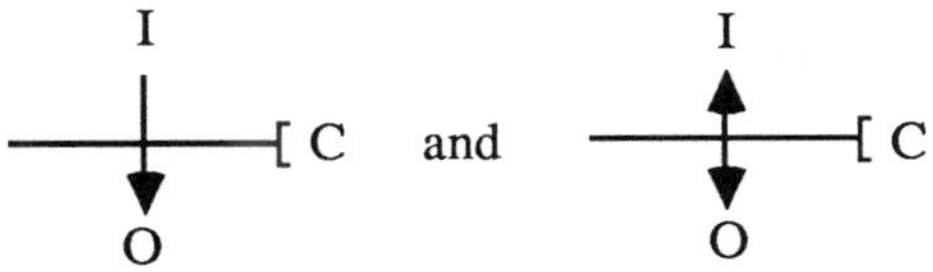

with input scheme I, output scheme O, applicability condition C, and ⇣ (resp. ⇕) denoting descendance (resp. equivalence) rather than

$$\frac{C}{\vdash O \subseteq I} \quad \text{and} \quad \frac{C}{\vdash I \equiv O}.$$

In order to shorten the formulation of transformation rules even more, all further considerations are to be seen relative to the

General assumption:

All program schemes in transformation rules are supposed to be syntactically valid and context-correct.

Within the applicability conditions, we will distinguish between syntactic and semantic ones. For their formulation we use particular predicates (see [Bauer et al. 85] for more details), such as the syntactic predicates

- KIND, yielding the kind (Sect. 3.4.1) of some syntactic entity,
- NOTOCCURS, testing the absence of some identifier in a given syntactic entity,
- DECL, yielding the declaration of some entity

or the semantic predicates introduced in Sect. 4.1.

In order to further improve readability, only semantic conditions will be formulated as *applicability conditions*. Syntactic restrictions which are not covered by our general assumption on syntactic validity and context-correctness are added to the rules as *syntactic constraints*.

Following common practice, the syntactic predicates KIND and DECL will be used in the forms

KIND[*x*] = **m**, resp.
DECL[*f*] = E

rather than in the forms

KIND[x **is m**], resp.
DECL[f **is** E].

If the absence of some identifier in a syntactic entity is already guaranteed by the convention on "expressions with arguments" (Sect. 4.2.1), a respective syntactic constraint will not be given explicitly. For example,

NOTOCCURS[y **in** E(f, x)]

is always true by convention.

For applicability conditions of the particular form $\vdash$ C we simply omit the symbol "$\vdash$" and briefly write C. Otherwise notations such as $C \vdash I \equiv O$ or $C \vdash I \supseteqq O$ (Sect. 4.1) will be used.

A typical example of this latter kind is the rule

- <u>*Modification of a conditional*</u>

if B **then** E_1 **else** E_2 **fi**

$$\Big\downarrow \quad \left[\begin{array}{l} B \equiv \mathbf{true} \vdash E_1 \supseteqq F_1, \\ B \equiv \mathbf{false} \vdash E_2 \supseteqq F_2 \end{array}\right.$$

if B **then** F_1 **else** F_2 **fi**

or its variant

- **if** B **then** E_1 **else** E_2 **fi**

$$\Big\updownarrow \quad \left[\begin{array}{l} B \equiv \mathbf{true} \vdash E_1 \equiv F_1, \\ B \equiv \mathbf{false} \vdash E_2 \equiv F_2 \end{array}\right.$$

if B **then** F_1 **else** F_2 **fi.**

Note that for defined B these rules are immediate consequences of the monotonicity of our language constructs with respect to equivalence and the descendant relation. Note also that (due to the meaning of "≡") conditions such as B ≡ **true** implicitly ensure the definedness of B.

For the particular situation of conditions

DEF[f] $\vdash$ DEF[f'],
DEF[f'] $\vdash$ DEF[f],

we use the abbreviation

DEF[f] $\Leftrightarrow$ DEF[f'].

Furthermore, we allow the abbreviation of applicability conditions by "degenerated" type schemes (Sect. 3.3.1.4). Thus an applicability condition such as

EQUIV(**m**, =)

formalizes the requirement that "=" is an equality predicate on **m**. Likewise, associativity of an operation p will be abbreviated by

ASSOC(p)

and existence of a neutral element e with respect to an operation p by

NEUTRAL(e, p),

where ASSOC and NEUTRAL are the type schemes defined in Sect. 3.3.1.4.

4.2.3 Program Developments

In the following chapters we will give sample developments. Within these, the emphasis is on demonstrating, following a certain strategy, how to technically apply an individual transformation rule to a concrete program. We do not aim at giving short and elegant derivations of particular algorithms.

For the presentation of these sample developments, we use a straightforward kind of semi-formalism in order to give additional hints to the reader and thus to ease understanding. We will clearly exhibit the logical structure of a derivation, the program part we are interested in, the motivation behind a sequence of transformation steps, and the strategy that is followed. To this end we use the keywords

- **Main development/Subdevelopment**
  to characterize the hierarchical structure of some development; subdevelopments are further subclassified using standard decimal classification if necessary;
- **Focus**
  to indicate the syntactic entity which is to be transformed;
- **Goal**
  to indicate the motivation underlying some development; here, we mainly characterize informally the program we are aiming at;
- **Strategy**
  to characterize the strategy that is used in the development;
- **Transformations**
  as a header for individual transformation steps which refer to individual transformation rules by name.

Within each level of the hierarchical structure, the individual transformation steps are simply ordered sequentially and indicate the rule that was applied and the result of its application. From the respective context, it should be straightforward to detect collateralities among the individual steps. Therefore, in contrast to [Partsch 86], we do not mention these collateralities explicitly.

This semi-formalism will be used rigorously in the first examples we are going to deal with, in order to convince the reader that every little step in a derivation, even an intuitively obvious one, can be done according to a formal rule. In later developments, however, we will use the formalism in a more liberal way, without explicitly giving obvious subdevelopments, mainly in order to focus the reader's attention on the essential steps of a derivation.

For the same reason, only non-obvious verifications of applicability conditions will be dealt with explicitly.

4.3 The Unfold/Fold System

A small, rather powerful set of basic transformation rules is the one given in [Burstall, Darlington 77] or also [Darlington 75]. It consists of the following transformation rules:

- *unfold*

  Unfold (of a function call) means the replacement of a function call by the body of the function, with replacement of the formal parameters by the respective actual ones (in compiler construction this technique is known as 'macro expansion').

  - <u>*unfold* (for functions)</u>

    f(E) resp. f(E)

    ⟶ [DEF[E], DET[E]

    E'[E **for** x] E' **where** **m** x = E

    <u>Syntactic constraints:</u> <u>Syntactic constraints:</u>

    NOTOCCURS[x **in** E], NOTOCCURS[x **in** E],

    DECL[f] = **funct** (**m** x) **n**: E', DECL[f] = **funct** (**m** x) **n**: E';

  Similarly, *unfold* (of an object) means the replacement of an object identifier by the expression denoting its value.

  - <u>*unfold* (for objects)</u>

    E'

    ⟶ [DEF[E], DET[E]

    E'[E **for** x]

    <u>Syntactic constraints:</u>

    NOTOCCURS[x **in** E],

    DECL[x] = (**m** x = E) .

In the latter case, as in the first variant of *unfold* (for a function call), the condition about definedness and determinacy is necessary in order to ensure correctness of the respective rules:

For example, for the expression

(1 [] 2) + (1 [] 2)

we have

$B[\![(1 \;[]\; 2) + (1 \;[]\; 2)]\!] = \{2, 3, 4\}$

and hence this expression is obviously not a descendant of

m x = (1 [] 2); $x + x$,

since

$B[\![\mathbf{m}\; x = (1 \;[]\; 2);\; x + x]\!] = \{2, 4\}$.

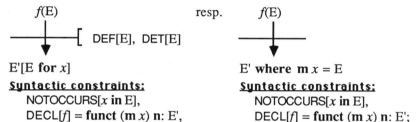

Likewise, the expression

funct f = (**nat** n) **nat**: **if** $n = 0$ **then** 0 **else** $f(n + 1)$ **fi**;
nat $y = f(x)$; **if** $x = 0$ **then** y **else** 3 **fi**

is undefined for $x \neq 0$, whereas

funct f = (**nat** n) **nat**: **if** $n = 0$ **then** 0 **else** $f(n + 1)$ **fi**;
if $x = 0$ **then** $f(x)$ **else** 3 **fi**

is always defined.

– *fold*
Fold is the inverse of *unfold*, i.e. the formation of a (recursive) call from an expression which is an instance of some function body, or the introduction of an identifier for a certain expression. Formalizations of the respective rules are essentially obtained by replacing ↓ by ↑ in the rules above:

- *fold* (for functions)

E'[E **for** x] resp. E' **where m** x = E

↓ [DEF[f(E)]

f(E)

Syntactic constraints:
NOTOCCURS[x **in** E],
DECL[f] = **funct** (**m** x) **n**: E', DECL[f] = **funct** (**m** x) **n**: E';

(resp.: E' **where m** x = E ↓ [DEF[f(E)] f(E); Syntactic constraints: NOTOCCURS[x **in** E], DECL[f] = **funct** (**m** x) **n**: E';)

- *fold* (for objects)

E'[E **for** x]

↓

E'

Syntactic constraints:
NOTOCCURS[x **in** E],
DECL[x] = (**m** x = E);

- *fold* (with assertion)

E'[E **for** x]

↓ [DEF[f(E)],
P(E) ≡ **true**

f(E)

Syntactic constraints:
NOTOCCURS[x **in** E],
DECL[f] = **funct** (**m** x: P(x)) **n**: E'.

Folding is known to preserve only partial correctness [Kott 78, 82], since it may lead to non-termination. A sufficient way to ensure total correctness of *folding* is by giving an explicit proof of termination (Sect. 4.4.5.5).

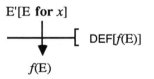

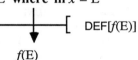

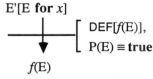

- *apply property*

  apply property means the application of some property that holds in the problem domain (usually axioms and theorems of the underlying data types) or for the particular algorithm at hand. In this way, *apply property* stands for a whole class of rules that allow to bring in additional knowledge and ideas. Technically, this rule can be seen as shorthand for converting such a property (usually an equivalence or a conditional equivalence) into a transformation rule and then applying this rule.

- *define*

  define means the introduction of a new function declaration. Here, (syntactic) correctness requires that the newly introduced identifier must not yet exist in the respective scope. Similar to *apply property*, *define* can be used to introduce new ideas into a program development. In fact, both contribute essentially to the power of the unfold/fold system.

- *instantiate*

  instantiate means the evaluation of a function call for concrete values. Again, this rule is but a shorthand for first *unfold*ing the call with the respective values and then *apply*ing *properties* in order to simplify the resulting expression.

- *abstract*

  abstract basically means the introduction of a new name for an expression. This may lead to the introduction of an auxiliary function declaration:

•   E

    ↓   [f(E") ≡ E'

    E[f(E") **for** E'] **where**
    funct f = (**m** x) **n**: F
    Syntactic constraints:
        NOTOCCURS[f **in** E]

(Note that the body F of the auxiliary function f is defined implicitly by the applicability condition f(E") ≡ E'.)

It may also lead to the introduction of a constant declaration:

•   E

    ↓

    E[x **for** E'] **where** **m** x = E'
    Syntactic constraints:
        NOTOCCURS[x **in** E].

The main difference between *abstraction* and *folding* is the fact that *abstraction* introduces a new declaration, whereas *fold* uses an existing one. Like *folding*, *abstraction* can be combined with the introduction of an assertion, too.

Trivial rules, such as the elimination of a superfluous declaration, are not explicitly mentioned, but tacitly assumed.

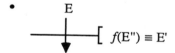

The rules introduced above are advocated to be used within the

> **Strategy** ("unfold - fold strategy")
>
> – unfold;
> – rearrange;
> – fold

where "rearrange" is further determined by the intended final folding.

To illustrate this strategy and the rules above we reconsider part (1) of the "simple bank account system" (Sect. 3.6.3). Given the formal specification

funct *newbal* = (**int** *oldbal*, **tfile** *t*) **int**:
oldbal + *credits*(*t*) – *debits*(*t*) – *num*(*t*) × *fee* **where**

funct *credits* = (**tfile** *t*) **nat**:
  if *t* =<> **then** 0
  elsf *kind*(**first***t*) = C **then** *amount*(**first***t*) + *credits*(**rest***t*)
                else *credits*(**rest***t*) **fi**;

funct *debits* = (**tfile** *t*) **nat**:
  if *t* =<> **then** 0
  elsf *kind*(**first***t*) = C **then** *debits*(**rest***t*)
                else *amount*(**first***t*) + *debits*(**rest***t*) **fi**;

funct *num* = (**tfile** *t*) **nat**:
  if *t* =<> **then** 0 **else** 1 + *num*(**rest***t*) **fi**

an equivalent (more efficient) definition for *newbal* can be derived as follows:

Main development

Focus: function *newbal*
Goal: recursive formulation of *newbal* independent of *credits*, *debits*, and *num*
Strategy: unfold - fold
Transformations:

step 1: unfold *credits*

oldbal +
if *t* =<> **then** 0
elsf *kind*(**first***t*) = C **then** *amount*(**first***t*) + *credits*(**rest***t*)
              else *credits*(**rest***t*) **fi**
– *debits*(*t*) – *num*(*t*) × *fee*

step 2: apply property: distributivity of operations over conditional (Sect. 4.4.5.2)

if *t* =<>
  then *oldbal* + 0 – *debits*(*t*) – *num*(*t*) × *fee*
  elsf *kind*(**first***t*) = C
    then *oldbal* + *amount*(**first***t*) + *credits*(**rest***t*) – *debits*(*t*) – *num*(*t*) × *fee*
    else *oldbal* + *credits*(**rest***t*) – *debits*(*t*) – *num*(*t*) × *fee* **fi**

step 3: instantiate:

– *debits*(*t*) ≡ 0   [if *t* = <> holds]
– *num*(*t*) ≡ 0   [if *t* = <> holds]

– *debits*(*t*) ≡ *debits*(**rest***t*) [if $t \neq$ <> and *kind*(**first***t*) =C hold]
– *debits*(*t*) ≡ *amount*(**first***t*) + *debits*(**rest***t*) [if $t \neq$ <> and *kind*(**first***t*) $\neq$ C hold]
– *num*(*t*) ≡ 1 + *num*(**rest***t*) [if $t \neq$ <> holds]

```
if t =<>
   then oldbal + 0 – 0 – 0 × fee
   elsf kind(first t) = C
      then oldbal + amount(first t) + credits(rest t) – debits(rest t)
           – (1 + num(rest t)) × fee
      else oldbal + credits(rest t) – (amount(first t) + debits(rest t))
           – (1 + num(rest t)) × fee  fi
```

step 4: apply properties; simplification rules from arithmetic

```
if t =<>
   then oldbal
   elsf kind(first t) = C
      then oldbal + amount(first t) – fee  + credits(rest t)
           – debits(rest t) – num(rest t) × fee
      else oldbal – amount(first t) – fee + credits(rest t)
           – debits(rest t) – num(rest t) × fee  fi
```

step 5: fold *newbal*

```
funct newbal = (int oldbal, tfile t) int:
   if t =<>
      then oldbal
      elsf kind(first t) = C
         then newbal(oldbal+ amount(first t) – fee, rest t)
         else newbal(oldbal – amount(first t) – fee, rest t) fi.
```

4.4 Further Basic Transformation Rules

Although the set of rules given in the previous section already allows us to do quite a number of interesting program developments, it is limited, since it mainly focuses on transforming applicative programs. As we aim at applying the transformational methodology also to other styles of programming, a richer set of basic transformations will be needed. These further basic rules may be classified as follows:

- the axiomatic rules of the language definition [Bauer et al. 85],
- rules about predicates [Manna 74], known from predicate calculus,
- basic set theoretic rules,
- axioms of the underlying data types, and
- derived basic transformation rules.

For each of these classes, a few representative examples are given in the sequel, mainly examples that will be used in later derivations. For a more elaborate treatment, we refer to the literature ([Bauer et al. 87] gives a rather comprehensive collection of basic transformation rules). It should be stressed again that syntactic validity and context-correctness are generally assumed for all program schemes occurring in the rules below.

The proofs for all non-axiomatic rules are straightforward from the semantic description of the language [Bauer et al. 85] and, hence, left to the interested reader.

For all the rules given below we generally assume the following

Syntactic constraints:

KIND[E, E', E_i] = **m**,

KIND[B, B_i, P, P_i, R, S, T] = **bool**.

In the rules concerning predicates, conjunction and disjunction are used as dyadic operators. Of course, all of these rules might be generalized to an arbitrary number of conjuncts and disjuncts. Similarly, most of these rules also hold for Δ and ∇, the sequential variants of $\wedge$ and $\vee$.

4.4.1 Axiomatic Rules of the Language Definition

The **axiomatic** (or **definitional**) **rules** of the language definition define new language constructs in terms of existing ones and can be found on all notational levels. Typical examples are

- *Δ-definition* ("sequential conjunction")

  $P_1 \, \Delta \, P_2$

  ⇕

  if P_1 **then** P_2 **else false fi**

- *∇-definition* ("sequential disjunction")

  $P_1 \, \nabla \, P_2$

  ⇕

  if P_1 **then true else** P_2 **fi**

- *⇨-definition* ("sequential implication")

  P_1 ⇨ P_2

  ⇕

  if P_1 **then** P_2 **else true fi**

- *Definition of guarded expression*

  if B **then** E_1 [] $\neg$B **then** E_2 **fi**

  ⇕ [DET[B]

  if B **then** E_1 **else** E_2 **fi**

- *Suppression of constant arguments*

  funct f = (**m** x, **n** y) **r**:
  E(x, y, f(x, $K_1(y)$), ..., f(x, $K_n(y)$))

  $\Updownarrow$

  funct f = (**m** x, **n** y) **r**:
  $f'(y)$ **where**
  funct f' = (**n** y) **r**:
  E(x, y, $f'(K_1(y))$, ..., $f'(K_n(y))$) .

Further examples that will be reintroduced and discussed later (Chap. 7) are

- *Variable declaration*

  var m x:= E_1; E_2

  $\Updownarrow$

  m x = E_1; E_2
  Syntactic constraints:
  NOTOCCURS[x **in** E_1]

(Note here that the language CIP-L [Bauer et al. 85] does not allow "side-effects" in expressions.)

- *Definition of the empty statement*

  skip; S

  $\Updownarrow$

  S

  S; **skip**

  $\Updownarrow$

  S

- **while** *loop and jumps*

  while B **do** S **od**

  $\Updownarrow$

  begin l: **if** B **then** S; **goto** l **else skip fi end**
  Syntactic constraints:
  NOTOCCURS[l **in** S, B] .

The latter rule relates **while** loops and jumps. How to obtain either of these constructs from recursive functions will be dealt with in Chap. 7.

There are further axiomatic rules in [Bauer et al. 85], in particular in connection with specifications. Some of these are to be seen as derived in our context, since we already introduced the respective constructs by elementary means. Examples will be given in the following sections.

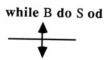

4.4.2 Rules About Predicates

A typical example for rules about predicates relates existential and universal quantification:

- *Existential and universal quantification*

  $\exists$ **m** x: P

  $\updownarrow$

  $\neg$ ($\forall$ **m** x: $\neg$ P).

Additionally, of course, there are the known algebraic properties of the logical connectives, such as commutativity, associativity, distributivity, annihilation, idempotency, de Morgan's laws, etc.

The connection between $\wedge$, $\vee$ and Δ, ∇ is established by

- P $\wedge$ R

  $\updownarrow$ [DEF[R]

  P Δ R

  P $\vee$ R

  $\updownarrow$ [DEF[R]

  P ∇ R .

These rules allow, in particular, to replace usual logical connectives by their respective sequential counterpart, and thus to speed up the evaluation of expressions.

Furthermore we have rules such as

- *Assertion-importation*

  funct f = (**m** x: R) **bool**: P

  $\downarrow$ [R $\equiv$ **true** $\vdash$ S $\equiv$ **true**

  funct f = (**m** x: R) **bool**: P $\wedge$ S

- *Conjunction of a consequence*

  P

  $\downarrow$ [P $\equiv$ **true** $\vdash$ R $\equiv$ **true**

  P Δ R

or

- *Disjunction of a consequence*

  P

  $\downarrow$ [P $\equiv$ **false** $\vdash$ R $\equiv$ **false**

  P ∇ R

where the respective inverses of the latter two rules are well-known from predicate calculus. Other useful rules [Manna 74] are for example

- *Quantifier elimination*

$\forall\ \mathbf{m}\ x$: P

$\updownarrow$

P

Syntactic constraints:
NOTOCCURS[x **in** P]

$\exists\ \mathbf{m}\ x$: P

$\updownarrow$

P

Syntactic constraints:
NOTOCCURS[x **in** P]

- *Rearrangement of quantifiers*

$\forall\ \mathbf{m}\ x\ \forall\ \mathbf{n}\ y$: P

$\updownarrow$

$\forall\ \mathbf{n}\ y\ \forall\ \mathbf{m}\ x$: P

$\exists\ \mathbf{m}\ x\ \exists\ \mathbf{n}\ y$: P

$\updownarrow$

$\exists\ \mathbf{n}\ y\ \exists\ \mathbf{m}\ x$: P

or

- *Quantification and implication*

$(\forall\ \mathbf{m}\ x$: P$) \Rightarrow (\exists\ \mathbf{m}\ x$: R$)$

$\updownarrow$

$\exists\ \mathbf{m}\ x$: $(\mathrm{P} \Rightarrow \mathrm{R})$.

4.4.3 Basic Set Theoretic Rules

Similarly to the rules from predicate calculus, basic rules about sets are provided by the well-known algebraic properties of the set operators, such as commutativity, associativity, distributivity, annihilation, and idempotence. Further examples are quite obvious rules such as

- *Reduction of a set comprehension*

$\{\mathbf{m}\ x$: P$\}$

$\updownarrow$ [P $\equiv$ **false**

$\varnothing$,

- *$\in$-simplification*

E $\in$ $\{\mathbf{m}\ x$: P$\}$

$\updownarrow$ [DEF[$\{\mathbf{m}\ x$: P$\}$], DEF[E], DET[E]

P[E **for** x]

with the special case

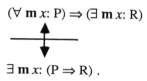

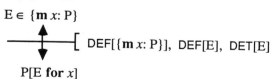

$x \in \varnothing$

$\Updownarrow$

false

or (derived) rules in connection with set abstraction in Zermelo-Fraenkel set theory ([Darlington 75] gives examples).

4.4.4 Rules from Axioms of the Underlying Data Types

In essence, the axioms of algebraic types (cf. Sect. 3.3) are transformation rules, too. However, some care is necessary with respect to definedness. Additionally, if axioms are to be considered as rules, the availability of the operations of the respective type has to be ensured by appropriate syntactic constraints.

For example, for the type STACK (Sect. 3.3.1.2) we have the rule

- *pop*(*push*(S, E))

  $\Updownarrow$ [DEF[S] ⊢ DEF[E]

  S

<u>**Syntactic constraints:**</u>
KIND[S] = **mstack**,
DECL[**mstack**] = (**mode mstack** = STACK(**m**)).

Of course, all axioms defined by algebraic types, and all properties deducible from axioms, can be converted into transformation rules in an analogous way.

4.4.5 Derived Basic Transformation Rules

A few more useful derived basic rules, especially for specifications, are given below. These rules are either

- simplification rules,
- rules for rearranging expressions,
- rules relating different specification constructs, or
- rules for conditional and guarded expressions.

4.4.5.1 Simplification Rules

Some simplification rules already have been given above, such as *quantifier elimination*, *reduction of a set comprehension*, or ∈*-simplification*.

In order to simplify **some** expressions we have rules such as

- <u>**some**-*simplification*</u>

some m x: x = E

⇕ [EQUIV(**m**, =)

E

some m x: P(x)

⇓ [DEF[P], P(y) ≡ **true**

y

or

- **some m** x: P ∧ R

⇓

(**some m** x: P) ∧ R

<u>**Syntactic constraints:**</u>

NOTOCCURS[x **in** R] .

For simplifying quantifiers we have, e.g.,

- <u>∃-*simplification*</u>

∃ **m** x: x = E

⇕ [DEF[E], DET[E], EQUIV(**m**, =)

true

or variants such as (cf. [Manna 74])

- ∃ **m** x: P(x) ∧ x = E

⇕ [DEF[P], DEF[E], DET[E], EQUIV(**m**, =)

P(E)

and

- <u>∀-*simplification*</u>

∀ **m** x: P(x) ∨ ¬(x = E)

⇕ [DEF[P], DEF[E], DET[E], EQUIV(**m**, =)

P(E) .

Very often, conditional expressions can be simplified according to the rules

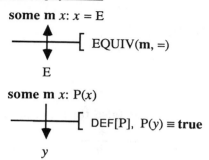

- *Elimination of a conditional*

$$\textbf{if } B \textbf{ then } E \textbf{ else } E \textbf{ fi} \quad \Updownarrow \; [\; \mathrm{DEF}[B] \quad E$$

or

- $$\textbf{if true then } E_1 \textbf{ else } E_2 \textbf{ fi} \quad \Updownarrow \quad E_1 \qquad\qquad \textbf{if false then } E_1 \textbf{ else } E_2 \textbf{ fi} \quad \Updownarrow \quad E_2 .$$

Together with the respective definitions of Δ and ∇, we get further

- *Annullation of Δ*

$$\textbf{true } \Delta\, E \quad \Updownarrow \quad E \qquad\qquad \textbf{false } \Delta\, E \quad \Updownarrow \quad \textbf{false}$$

- *Annullation of ∇*

$$\textbf{true } \nabla\, E \quad \Updownarrow \quad \textbf{true} \qquad\qquad \textbf{false } \nabla\, E \quad \Updownarrow \quad E .$$

Another example is

- *Restriction of choice*

$$E_1 \;[]\; E_2 \;[]\; \ldots \;[]\; E_n \quad \Downarrow \; [\; 1 \le i \le n \quad E_i$$

with

- $$E \;[]\; E \quad \Updownarrow \quad E$$

as a special variant.

4.4.5.2 Rearrangement Rules

Frequently, simplification of expressions requires restructuring of components. In this context, a useful rule is

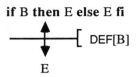

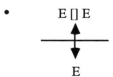

- *Distributivity of function call over conditional*

  f(**if** B **then** E_1 **else** E_2 **fi**)

  $$\updownarrow$$

  if B **then** *f*(E_1) **else** *f*(E_2) **fi** .

  Special instances of this rule are rules for operations and tuple construction:

- *Distributivity of operations over conditional*

  if B **then** E_1 **else** E_2 **fi** $\oplus$ E

  $$\updownarrow$$

  if B **then** $E_1 \oplus$ E **else** $E_2 \oplus$ E **fi**

- *Distributivity of tuple construction over conditional*

  (E, **if** B **then** E_1 **else** E_2 **fi**)

  $$\updownarrow$$

  if B **then** (E, E_1) **else** (E, E_2) **fi** .

Of course, analogous rules also hold for guarded expressions instead of conditionals.

Other rules about distributivity are

- *Distributivity of a quantifier*

  $\forall$ **m** *x*: (P $\wedge$ R)

  $$\updownarrow$$

  ($\forall$ **m** *x*: P) $\wedge$ ($\forall$ **m** *x*: R)

  $\exists$ **m** *x*: (P $\vee$ R)

  $$\updownarrow$$

  ($\exists$ **m** *x*: P) $\vee$ ($\exists$ **m** *x*: R)

- *Distributivity of* **some** *over guarded expression*

  some m *x*: **if** $[]_{i=1..n}$ B_i **then** E **fi**

  $$\updownarrow$$

  if $[]_{i=1..n}$ B_i **then some m** *x*: E **fi**

  Syntactic constraints:

  NOTOCCURS[*x* **in** B_i] ($1 \le i \le n$)

- *Distributivity of* **some** *over conditional*

  some m *x*: **if** B **then** E_1 **else** E_2 **fi**

  $$\updownarrow$$

  if B **then some m** *x*: E_1 **else some m** *x*: E_2 **fi**

  Syntactic constraints:

  NOTOCCURS[*x* **in** B]

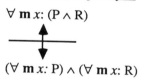

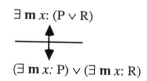

or

- *Distributivity of* **some** *over tuple construction*

some (**m** x, **n** y): P ∧ R

↕

(**some** **m** x: P, **some** **n** y: R)

Syntactic constraints:

NOTOCCUR[x **in** R, y **in** P]

Further rules for the rearrangement of expressions include

- *Rearrangement of a conditional expression*

if B **then** E_1 **else** E_2 **fi**

↕

if ¬B **then** E_2 **else** E_1 **fi**

- *Rearrangement of branches in a guarded expression*

if $[]_{i = 1..j-1}$ B_i **then** E_i
[] B_j **then** E_j
[] B_{j+1} **then** E_{j+1}
$[]_{i = j+2..n}$ B_i **then** E_i **fi**

↕

if $[]_{i = 1..j-1}$ B_i **then** E_i
[] B_{j+1} **then** E_{j+1}
[] B_j **then** E_j
$[]_{i = j+2..n}$ B_i **then** E_i **fi**

(which, applied several times, allows arbitrary rearrangements of branches) or

- *Rearrangement of quantified expressions*

∃ **m** x: ∃ **n** y: (P ∧ S)

↕

(∃ **m** x: P) ∧ (∃ **n** y: S)

Syntactic constraints:

NOTOCCURS[x **in** S, y **in** P]

∀ **m** x: ∀ **n** y: (P ∨ S)

↕

(∀ **m** x: P) ∨ (∀ **n** y: S)

Syntactic constraints:

NOTOCCURS[x**in** S, y **in** P].

A particular kind of rearrangement rules involves a fusion or a splitting of constructs, such as

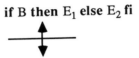

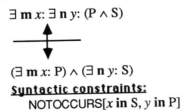

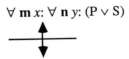

- *Fusion of a choice*

  (**some m** x: P [] **some m** x: Q)

  ↓

  some m x: (P ∨ Q)

- *Splitting of a quantifier*

  ∃ **m** x: P

  ↕ [DEF[R]

  (∃ (**m** x: R): P) ∨ (∃ (**m** x: ¬R): P)

  ∀ **m** x: P

  ↕ [DEF[R]

  (∀ (**m** x: R): P) ∧ (∀ (**m** x: ¬R): P)

- *Splitting of a set comprehension*

  {**m** x: P ∧ R}

  ↕

  {**m** x: P} ∩ {**m** x: R}

  {**m** x: P ∨ R}

  ↕

  {**m** x: P} ∪ {**m** x: R}

or

- *Skolemization*

  some m x: ∃ **n** y: P(y) ∧ Q(x, y)

  ↓ [P(y) ≡ **true** ⊢ (∃ **m** x: Q(x, y)) ≡ **true**

  n y = **some n** y': P(y');
  some m x: Q(x, y) .

For all the specification constructs finally we have [Bauer et al. 85] for Q' ∈ {∃, **some**, **that**}

- *Filter promotion*

  Q' **m** x: (P Δ R)

  ↕

  Q' (**m** x: P): R

and

- ∀ **m** x: **if** P **then** R **else true fi**

  ↕

  ∀ (**m** x: P): R .

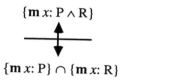

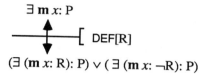

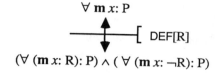

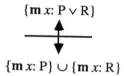

4.4.5.3 Rules Relating Different Specification Constructs

Relationships between different specification constructs are established by the rules

- <u>**some**-*expression and finite choice*</u>

  some m x: $x = E_1 \vee x = E_2$

  $\updownarrow$ [DEF[E_i], DET[E_i] (i = 1, 2), EQUIV(**m**, =)

  $(E_1 \; [] \; E_2)$

- <u>*Description and* **some**-*expression*</u>

  that m x: P

  $\updownarrow$ [EQUIV(**m**, =)

  some m x: P $\wedge$ ($\forall$ **m** y: P[y **for** x] $\Rightarrow x = y$)

  Syntactic constraints:
  NOTOCCURS[y **in** P]

- <u>*Choice and quantification*</u>

  some n x: $\exists$ **m** y: (P(y) $\wedge f(y) = x$)

  $\updownarrow$ [EQUIV(**m**, =)

  f(**some m** y: P(y))

- <u>*Quantification and set comprehension*</u>

  $\exists$ **m** x: P

  $\updownarrow$

  {**m** x: P} $\neq \varnothing$

- <u>*Set comprehension and existential quantification*</u>

  {**m** x: $\exists$ **n** y: P(y) $\wedge$ Q(x, y)}

  $\updownarrow$

  $\cup_{\mathbf{n}\ y:\ P(y)}$ {**m** x: Q(x, y)}

  Syntactic constraints:
  NOTOCCURS[x **in** P]

- <u>*Existential quantification and guarded expression*</u>

  $\exists_{i = 1..n} (B_i \wedge E)$

  $\updownarrow$ [$(\exists_{i=1..n} B_i) \equiv$ **true**

  if $[]_{i = 1..n}$ B_i **then** E **fi** .

4.4.5.4 Rules for Conditional and Guarded Expressions

Finally, there are some useful rules about guarded expressions (with obvious variants for conventional conditionals) and conditionals:

- *Unification of guards*

$$\begin{array}{l} \textbf{if } []_{i = 1..j-1}\ B_i \textbf{ then } E_i \\ []\ B_j \textbf{ then } E' \\ []\ B_{j+1} \textbf{ then } E' \\ []_{i = j+2..n}\ B_i \textbf{ then } E_i \textbf{ fi} \end{array}$$

$$\Updownarrow$$

$$\begin{array}{l} \textbf{if } []_{i = 1..j-1}\ B_i \textbf{ then } E_i \\ []\ B_j \vee B_{j+1} \textbf{ then } E' \\ []_{i = j+2..n}\ B_i \textbf{ then } E_i \textbf{ fi} \end{array}$$

which comprises the introduction/elimination of duplicated branches as a special case,

- *Refinement of guards*

$$\begin{array}{l} \textbf{if } []_{i = 1..j-1}\ B_i \textbf{ then } E_i \\ []\ B_j \textbf{ then } E_j \\ []_{i = j+1..k-1}\ B_i \textbf{ then } E_i \\ []\ B_k \textbf{ then } E_k \\ []_{i = k+1..n}\ B_i \textbf{ then } E_i \textbf{ fi} \end{array}$$

$$\Downarrow \quad \left[\begin{array}{l} B_j' \equiv \textbf{true} \vdash B_j \equiv \textbf{true}, \\ (B_j \wedge \neg B_j') \equiv \textbf{true} \vdash B_k \equiv \textbf{true}, E_j \equiv E_k \end{array}\right.$$

$$\begin{array}{l} \textbf{if } []_{i = 1..j-1}\ B_i \textbf{ then } E_i \\ []\ B_j' \textbf{ then } E_j \\ []_{i = j+1..k-1}\ B_i \textbf{ then } E_i \\ []\ B_k \textbf{ then } E_k \\ []_{i = k+1..n}\ B_i \textbf{ then } E_i \textbf{ fi} \end{array}$$

- *Refinement of branches*

$$\textbf{if } []_{i = 1..n}\ B_i \textbf{ then } E_i \textbf{ fi}$$

$$\Updownarrow \quad \left[\ \mathrm{DEF}[B_j] \vdash \mathrm{DEF}[C], \right.$$

$$\begin{array}{l} \textbf{if } []_{i = 1..j-1}\ B_i \textbf{ then } E_i \\ []\ B_j \wedge C \textbf{ then } E_j \\ []\ B_j \wedge \neg C \textbf{ then } E_j \\ []_{i = j+1..n}\ B_i \textbf{ then } E_i \textbf{ fi} \end{array}$$

- *Local refinement of a guarded expression*

$$\textbf{if } []_{i=1..n}\ B_i \ \textbf{then } E_i \ \textbf{fi}$$

$$\updownarrow \quad [\ B_j \equiv \textbf{true} \ \vdash \ E_j \equiv E_j'$$

$$\begin{array}{l}\textbf{if } []_{i=1..j-1}\ B_i \ \textbf{then } E_i \\ []\ B_j \ \textbf{then } E_j' \\ []_{i=j+1..n}\ B_i \ \textbf{then } E_i \ \textbf{fi}\end{array}$$

- *Reduction of a guarded expression*

$$\textbf{if } []_{i=1..n}\ B_i \ \textbf{then } E_i \ \textbf{fi}$$

$$\updownarrow \quad [\ B_j \equiv \textbf{false}$$

$$\begin{array}{l}\textbf{if } []_{i=1..j-1}\ B_i \ \textbf{then } E_i \\ []_{i=j+1..n}\ B_i \ \textbf{then } E_i \ \textbf{fi}\end{array}$$

or

- *Normalization of a conditional*

$$\textbf{if if } B \ \textbf{then } B_1 \ \textbf{else } B_2 \ \textbf{fi then } E_1 \ \textbf{else } E_2 \ \textbf{fi}$$

$$\updownarrow$$

$$\begin{array}{l}\textbf{if } B \ \textbf{then if } B_1 \ \textbf{then } E_1 \ \textbf{else } E_2 \ \textbf{fi} \\ \qquad \textbf{else if } B_2 \ \textbf{then } E_1 \ \textbf{else } E_2 \ \textbf{fi fi}.\end{array}$$

4.4.5.5 Reduction of Applicability Conditions

Applying transformation rules within derivations also requires a proof of the respective applicability conditions. Very often, the respective conditions are either ensured by corresponding properties of the underlying data types, or, in case of equivalence (or descendance) between program schemes, they can be proved by using transformation rules again. There are, however, also applicability conditions dealing with determinacy and definedness. For these latter cases, rules can be derived from the semantic definition of the language, for example,

$$\frac{}{\vdash \ \mathsf{DET}[x]} \quad \text{or} \quad \frac{}{\vdash \ \mathsf{DEF}[x]}$$

(where x is a constant or operation symbol from an algebraic type).

Other rules allow definedness and determinacy information to be propagated through syntactic constructs, for example,

$$\frac{\vdash \ \mathsf{DET}[B], \mathsf{DET}[E], \mathsf{DET}[E']}{\vdash \ \mathsf{DET}[\textbf{if } B \ \textbf{then } E \ \textbf{else } E' \ \textbf{fi}]} \ .$$

Further examples of this kind,

$$\mathsf{DET}[E], E \equiv E' \vdash \ \mathsf{DET}[E']$$

or

$$\frac{\vdash \mathsf{DEF}[F],\ \mathsf{DEF}[E_i]\ (1 \le i \le n)}{\vdash \mathsf{DEF}[F(E_1, \ldots, E_n)]}$$

can be found in Sect. 4.1 or in [Bauer et al. 87].

Definedness of recursive function definitions includes termination, which can be proved as follows:

Let

funct f = (**m** x) **n**: E

be a function definition where E contains n (possibly nested) recursive calls of the form $f(E_i)$.

For proving termination of f, we have to find a mapping

τ: DOM⟦**m**⟧$^+ \to$ M

for all proper semantic values of kind **m** into a Noetherian ordering (M, $\prec$) such that for all $1 \le i \le n$ and $u \in$ DOM⟦**m**⟧$^+$

$\tau(E_i[u$ **for** $x]) \prec \tau(u)$

holds. Then, if all basic operations in E are defined, $f(u)$ is defined as well.

The problem in proving termination is finding an appropriate Noetherian ordering (M, $\prec$). In many cases this is obvious, such as (Sect. 3.6.1) in

funct *rev* = (**string** *s*) **string**:
  if $|s| \le 1$ **then** *s* **else last***s* + *rev*(**lead rest***s*) + **first***s* **fi**.

Here, with

τ: DOM⟦**string**⟧$^+ \to \mathbb{N}$,
$\tau(s) =_{def} |s|$,

we have (for s with $|s| \ge 2$)

$\tau($**lead rest**$s) = |s|-2 < |s| = \tau(s)$,

and hence *rev* is defined.

If **m** is a tuple, using a lexicographic ordering on tuples or an ordering composed of orderings on the components of the tuple will do. An example (Sect. 3.6.3) is

funct *updatef* = (**acfile** *a*, **gtfile** *t*) **acfile**:
  if *t* =<> **then** *a*
  [] *a* =<> **then** <>
  [] *a* ≠<> **then** *mb*(*acc*(**first***a*), *newgbal*(**first***a*, *t*)) + *updatef*(**rest***a*, *t*)
  [] *t* ≠<> **then** *updatef*(*upd*(*a*, **first***t*), **rest***t*) **fi**.

Here, with

τ: DOM⟦(**acfile**, **gtfile**)⟧$^+ \to \mathbb{N} \times \mathbb{N}$,
$\tau(a, t) =_{def} (|a|, |t|)$,

we have (for a, t with $a \ne$<>, $t \ne$<> and $(i, k) < (m, n) =_{def} (i < m) \vee (i = m \wedge k < n)$)

$\tau($**rest**$a, t) = (|a|-1, |t|) < (|a|, |t|) = \tau(a, t)$, and
$\tau(upd(a,$ **first**$t),$ **rest**$t) = (|a|, |t|-1) < (|a|, |t|) = \tau(a, t)$,

and hence *updatef* is defined.

However, also with

τ: DOM⟦**(acfile, gtfile)**⟧$^+ \to \mathbb{N}$,
$\tau(a, t) =_{def} |a| + |t|$,

we have (for a, t with $a \neq$<>, $t \neq$<>)

τ(**rest**a, t) = $|a|+|t|-1 < |a| + |t| = \tau(a, t)$, and
τ(upd(a, **first**t), **rest**t) = $|a|+|t|-1 < |a| + |t| = \tau(a, t)$,

which also proves the definedness of *updatef*.

In other cases, however, it can be fairly difficult to find a suitable ordering. A typical example is the well-known function

funct f = (**nat** n) **nat**:
  if $n \leq 1$ **then** 1 **elsf even** n **then** $f(n$ **div** 2) **else** $f(3n + 1)$ **fi**,

the termination of which has not yet been proved.

4.5 Sample Developments with Basic Rules

In this section we illustrate how the transformation rules introduced in the previous sections are to be used for transformational program development. Since these are the first complete examples dealt with, the presentation will be much more detailed than some of those to be given later on. But we omit the verifications of the respective applicability conditions, since they are obvious.

4.5.1 Simple Number Problem

We start from the formal specification given in Sect. 3.6.2:

funct *prop* = (**nat** n) **bool** :
  all(*conv*(n)) **where**

  funct *conv* = (**nat** n) **bitsequ**:
    if $n = 0$ **then** <>
    elsf odd n **then** *conv*(n **div** 2) + 1 **else** *conv*(n **div** 2) + 0 **fi**,

  funct *all* = (**bitsequ** b) **bool** :
    if b =<> **then true else last**b = 1 Δ *all*(**lead**b) **fi**

<u>Main development</u>

Focus: function *prop*
Goal: recursive formulation of *prop* independent of *conv* and *all*
Strategy: unfold - fold
Transformations:

step 1: unfold *conv*

all(**if** $n = 0$ **then** <>
  elsf odd n **then** *conv*(n **div** 2) + 1 **else** *conv*(n **div** 2) + 0 **fi**)

step 2: distributivity of function call over conditional

if *n* = 0 **then** *all*(<>)
elsf odd *n* **then** *all*(*conv*(*n* **div** 2) + 1) **else** *all*(*conv*(*n* **div** 2) + 0) **fi**

<u>Subdevelopment 1</u>

Focus: *all*(<>)
Goal: simplification (under premise *n* = 0)
Transformations:

step 1.1: unfold *all*

if <> =<> **then true else last**<> = 1 Δ *all*(**lead**<>) **fi**

step 1.2: laws of ESEQU (<> =<> ≡ **true**)

if true then true else last<> = 1 Δ *all*(**lead**<>) **fi**

step 1.3: elimination of conditional

true

<u>Subdevelopment 2</u>

Focus: *all*(*conv*(*n* **div** 2) + 1)
Goal: simplification (under premise *n* ≠ 0 Δ **odd** *n*)
Transformations:

step 2.1: unfold *all*

if *conv*(*n* **div** 2)+1 =<>
then true
else last(*conv*(*n* **div** 2) + 1) = 1 Δ *all* (**lead**(*conv*(*n* **div** 2) + 1)) **fi**

step 2.2: laws of ESEQU and BIT

if false then true else true Δ *all*(*conv*(*n* **div** 2)) **fi**

step 2.3: elimination of conditional

true Δ *all*(*conv*(*n* **div** 2))

step 2.4: annullation of Δ

all(*conv*(*n* **div** 2))

<u>Subdevelopment 3</u>

Focus: *all*(*conv*(*n* **div** 2) + 0)
Goal: simplification (under premise *n* ≠ 0 Δ ¬(**odd** *n*))
Transformations:

steps 3.1-3.4 (as in Subdevelopment 2):

false

<u>Main Development continued</u>

if *n* = 0 **then true elsf odd** *n* **then** *all*(*conv*(*n* **div** 2)) **else false fi**

step 3: fold *prop*

funct *prop* = (**nat** *n*) **bool**:
if *n* = 0 **then true elsf odd** *n* **then** *prop*(*n* **div** 2) **else false fi**

4.5.2 Palindromes

The starting point of our development is the formal specification from Sect. 3.6.1:

funct *pal* = (**string** *s*) **bool**:
  eq(*s*, *rev*(*s*)) **where**

  funct *rev* = (**string** *s*) **string**:
    if |*s*| ≤ 1 **then** *s* **else last***s* + *rev*(**lead rest***s*) + **first***s* **fi**;

  funct *eq* = (**string** s_1, **string** s_2) **bool**:
    if $s_1 = <>$ **then** $s_2 = <>$
    [] $s_2 = <>$ **then** $s_1 = <>$
          else (**first**s_1 = **first**s_2 Δ *eq*(**rest**s_1, **rest**s_2)
            [] **last**s_1 = **last**s_2 Δ *eq*(**lead**s_1, **lead**s_2)) **fi**

<u>Main development</u>
Focus: function *pal*
Goal: recursive formulation of *pal* independent of *rev* and *eq*
Strategy: unfold - fold
Transformations:

step 1: unfold *rev*

eq(*s*, **if** |*s*| ≤ 1 **then** *s* **else last***s* + *rev*(**lead rest***s*) + **first***s* **fi**)

step 2: distributivity of function call over conditional

if |*s*| ≤ 1 **then** *eq*(*s*, *s*) **else** *eq*(*s*, **last***s* + *rev*(**lead rest***s*) + **first***s*) **fi**

step 3: instantiations:

- *eq*(*s*, *s*) ≡ **true** [if |*s*| ≤ 1 holds]
- *eq*(*s*, **last***s* + *rev*(**lead rest***s*) + **first***s*) ≡
  (**first***s*) = (**last***s*) Δ *eq*(**lead rest***s*, *rev*(**lead rest***s*)) [if |*s*| > 1 holds]

if |*s*| ≤ 1 **then true else first***s* = **last***s* Δ *eq*(**lead rest***s*, *rev*(**lead rest***s*)) **fi**

step 3: fold *pal*

funct *pal* = (**string** *s*) **bool**:
  if |*s*| ≤ 1 **then true else first***s* = **last***s* Δ *pal*(**lead rest***s*) **fi**

step 4: definition of Δ and subsequent simplification

funct *pal* = (**string** *s*) **bool**:
  if |*s*| ≤ 1 **then true**
  elsf first*s* ≠ **last***s* **then false else** *pal*(**lead rest***s*) **fi**.

Derivations for the other specifications in Sect. 3.6.1 are analogous.

4.5.3 The Simple Bank Account Problem Continued

In Sect. 4.3 we dealt with a program development for part (1) of the formal specification from Sect. 3.6.3. For part (2) we start from the specification

```
funct newbal' = (int oldbal, tfile t, nat free) int:
   oldbal + credits(t) – debits(t) – newnum(t, free) × fee  where
funct newnum = (tfile t, nat free) nat:
   if t =<> then 0
   elsf free = 0 then 1 + newnum(rest t, free) else newnum(rest t, free –1) fi
```

and the definitions of *credits* and *debits* from part (1).

<u>**Main development**</u>

Focus: function *newbal'*

Goal: recursive formulation of *newbal'* independent of *credits*, *debits*, and *newnum*

Strategy: unfold - fold

Transformations:

step 1: unfold *credits*

```
oldbal +
if t =<> then 0
elsf kind(first t) = C then amount(first t) + credits(rest t)
                else credits(rest t) fi
– debits(t) – newnum(t, free) × fee
```

step 2: distributivity of operations over conditional

```
if t =<> then oldbal + 0 – debits(t) – newnum(t, free) × fee
elsf kind(first t) = C
   then oldbal + amount(first t) + credits(rest t) – debits(t) –
          newnum(t, free) × fee
   else oldbal + credits(rest t) – debits(t) – newnum(t, free) × fee  fi
```

step 3: instantiations:

```
–  debits(t) ≡ 0                                 [ if t = <> holds ]
–  newnum(t, free) ≡ 0                           [ if t = <> holds ]
–  debits(t) ≡ debits(rest t)                    [ if t ≠ <> and kind(first t) = C hold ]
–  debits(t) ≡ amount(first t) + debits(rest t)  [ if t ≠ <> and kind(first t) ≠ C hold ]
–  newnum(t, free) ≡
      if free = 0 then 1 + newnum(rest t, free)
                  else newnum(rest t, free –1) fi [ if t ≠ <> holds ]
```

```
if t =<> then oldbal + 0 – 0 – 0 × fee
elsf kind(first t) = C
   then oldbal + amount(first t) + credits(rest t) – debits(rest t) –
      if free = 0 then 1 + newnum(rest t, free)
                  else newnum(rest t, free –1) fi × fee
   else oldbal + credits(rest t) – (amount(first t) + debits(rest t)) –
      if free = 0 then 1 + newnum(rest t, free)
                  else newnum(rest t, free –1) fi × fee fi
```

step 4: distributivity of operations over conditional

```
if t =<> then oldbal + 0 – 0 – 0 × fee
elsf kind(first t) = C
   then if free = 0
```

```
            then oldbal + amount(first t) + credits(rest t) - debits(rest t) -
                             (1 + newnum(rest t, free)) × fee
             else oldbal + amount(first t) + credits(rest t) - debits(rest t) -
                             newnum(rest t, free -1) × fee  fi
    else  if free = 0
            then oldbal + credits(rest t) - (amount(first t) + debits(rest t)) -
                             (1 + newnum(rest t, free)) × fee
            else oldbal + credits(rest t) - (amount(first t) + debits(rest t)) -
                             newnum(rest t, free -1) × fee  fi fi
```

step 5: properties and simplification rules from arithmetic

```
if t =<> then oldbal
elsf kind(first t) = C
   then if free = 0
         then oldbal + amount(first t) - fee + credits(rest t) - debits(rest t) -
                          newnum(rest t, free) × fee
         else oldbal + amount(first t) + credits(rest t) - debits(rest t) -
                          newnum(rest t, free -1) × fee  fi
   else if free = 0
         then oldbal - amount(first t) - fee + credits(rest t) - debits(rest t) -
                          newnum(rest t, free) × fee
         else oldbal - amount(first t) + credits(rest t) - debits(rest t) -
                          newnum(rest t, free -1) × fee  fi fi
```

step 6: fold *newbal'*

```
funct newbal' = (int oldbal, tfile t, nat free) int:
   if t =<> then oldbal
   elsf kind(first t) = C
      then if free = 0  then newbal'(oldbal + amount(first t) - fee , rest t, free)
                        else newbal'(oldbal + amount(first t), rest t, free-1) fi
      else if free = 0  then newbal'(oldbal - amount(first t) - fee, rest t, free)
                        else newbal'(oldbal - amount(first t), rest t, free-1) fi fi
```

In a similar way we can also develop a program for part (3):

```
funct newgbal = (bal b, gtfile t) int:
   newbal(amount(b), self(t, acc(b))) where

   funct self = (gtfile t, acnr a) tfile:
      if t =<> then  <>
      elsf acc(first t) = a then mt(kind(first t), amount(first t)) + self(rest t, a)
               else self(rest t, a) fi;
```

<u>Main development</u>

Focus: function *newgbal*
Goal: recursive formulation of *newgbal* independent of *newbal* and *self*
Strategy: unfold - fold
Transformations:

step 1: unfold *self*

```
newbal(amount(b),
   if t =<> then <>
   elsf acc(first t) = acc(b)
      then mt(kind(first t), amount(first t)) + self(rest t, acc(b))
      else self(rest t, acc(b)) fi)
```

step 2: distributivity of function call and conditional

```
if t =<> then newbal(amount(b), <>)
elsf acc(first t) = acc(b)
   then newbal(amount(b), mt(kind(first t), amount(first t)) +
                  self(rest t, acc(b)))
   else newbal(amount(b), self(rest t, acc(b))) fi
```

step 3: instantiations:

```
– newbal(amount(b), <>) ≡ amount(b)
– newbal(amount(b), mt(kind(first t), amount(first t)) + self(rest t, acc(b))) ≡
     if kind(first t) = C
        then newbal(amount(b) + amount(first t) – fee, self(rest t, acc(b)))
        else newbal(amount(b) – amount(first t) – fee, self(rest t, acc(b))) fi ≡
     if kind(first t) = C
        then newbal(amount(mb(acc(b), amount(b) + amount(first t) – fee)),
                    self(rest t, acc(b)))
        else newbal(amount(mb(acc(b), amount(b) – amount(first t) – fee)),
                    self(rest t, acc(b))) fi
```

```
if t =<> then amount(b)
elsf acc(first t) = acc(b)
   then if kind(first t) = C
      then newbal(amount(mb(acc(b), amount(b) + amount(first t) – fee)),
                  self(rest t, acc(b)))
      else newbal(amount(mb(acc(b), amount(b) – amount(first t) – fee)),
                  self(rest t, acc(b))) fi
   else newbal(amount(b), self(rest t, acc(b))) fi
```

step 4: apply properties:

```
– acc(b) = acc(mb(acc(b), amount(b) + amount(first t) – fee))  [ if kind(first t) =C holds ]
– acc(b) = acc(mb(acc(b), amount(b) – amount(first t) –fee))   [ if kind(first t) ≠C holds ]
```

```
if t =<> then amount(b)
elsf acc(first t) = acc(b)
   then if kind(first t) = C
      then newbal(amount(mb(acc(b), amount(b) + amount(first t) – fee)),
            self(rest t, acc(mb(acc(b), amount(b) + amount(first t) – fee))))
      else newbal(amount(mb(acc(b), amount(b) – amount(first t) – fee)),
            self(rest t, acc(mb(acc(b), amount(b) + amount(first t) – fee)))) fi
   else newbal(amount(b), self(rest t, acc(b))) fi
```

step 5: fold *newgbal*

funct *newgbal* = (**bal** *b*, **gtfile** *t*) **int**:
  if *t* =<> **then** *amount*(*b*)
  elsf *acc*(**first***t*) = *acc*(*b*)
    then if *kind*(**first***t*) = C
      then *newgbal*(*mb*(*acc*(*b*), *amount*(*b*) + *amount*(**first***t*) – *fee*), **rest***t*)
      else *newgbal*(*mb*(*acc*(*b*), *amount*(*b*) – *amount*(**first***t*) – *fee*), **rest***t*) **fi**
    else *newgbal*(*b*, **rest***t*) **fi**

The remaining parts of this problem will be dealt with in later chapters, as techniques are needed which have not yet been introduced.

4.5.4. Floating Point Representation of the Dual Logarithm of the Factorial

This problem was introduced in Sect. 1.5. Our development starts from the specification

funct *floatfac* = (**int** n: $n \geq 0$) (**real**, **int**):
  logrep(*fac*(n), 0) **where**

  funct *fac* = (**int** n: $n \geq 0$) **int**:
    if $n = 0$ **then** 1 **else** $n \times fac(n-1)$ **fi**;

  funct *logrep* = (**real** x, **int** i: $i \geq 0 \wedge x \geq 1/2$) (**real**, **int**):
    if $x < 1$ **then** (x, i) **else** *logrep*($x \times 1/2$, $i + 1$) **fi**.

<u>Main development</u>

Focus: function *floatfac*
Goal: recursive formulation of *floatfac* independent of *fac* and *logrep*
Strategy: unfold - fold
Transformations:

step 1: abstract

floatfac'(n, 1, 0) **where**

funct *floatfac'* = (**nat** n, **real** x, **int** i: $n \geq 0 \wedge i \geq 0 \wedge x \geq 1/2$) (**real**, **int**):
  logrep($x \times fac(n)$, i)

New focus: function *floatfac'*
step 2: unfold *fac*

logrep($x \times$ **if** $n = 0$ **then** 1 **else** $n \times fac(n-1)$ **fi**, i)

step 3: distributivity of operation over conditional

logrep(**if** $n = 0$ **then** $x \times 1$ **else** $x \times n \times fac(n-1)$ **fi**, i)

step 4: distributivity of function call over conditional

if $n = 0$ **then** *logrep*($x \times 1$, i) **else** *logrep*($x \times n \times fac(n-1)$, i) **fi**

step 5: definition of guarded expression

if $n = 0$ **then** $logrep(x \times 1, i)$
[] $n > 0$ **then** $logrep(x \times n \times fac(n-1), i)$ **fi**

step 6: refinement of guards (with arbitrary $N \geq 1$)

if $n = 0 \wedge x < 1$ **then** $logrep(x \times 1, i)$
[] $n = 0 \wedge x \geq 1$ **then** $logrep(x \times 1, i)$
[] $n > 0 \wedge x \geq N$ **then** $logrep(x \times n \times fac(n-1), i)$
[] $n > 0 \wedge x < N$ **then** $logrep(x \times n \times fac(n-1), i)$ **fi**

step 7: apply properties:

- $(n = 0) \equiv$ **true** $\vdash 1 \equiv fac(n)$
- $(n > 0) \equiv$ **true** $\vdash n \times fac(n-1) \equiv fac(n)$

if $n = 0 \wedge x < 1$ **then** $logrep(x \times 1, i)$
[] $n = 0 \wedge x \geq 1$ **then** $logrep(x \times fac(n), i)$
[] $n > 0 \wedge x \geq N$ **then** $logrep(x \times fac(n), i)$
[] $n > 0 \wedge x < N$ **then** $logrep(x \times n \times fac(n-1), i)$ **fi**

step 8: unification and refinement of guards

if $n = 0 \wedge x < 1$ **then** $logrep(x \times 1, i)$
[] $x \geq 1$ **then** $logrep(x \times fac(n), i)$
[] $n > 0 \wedge x < N$ **then** $logrep(x \times n \times fac(n-1), i)$ **fi**

step 9: instantiation of *logrep* in first and second branch:

- $logrep(x \times 1, i) \equiv (x, i)$ [if $x < 1$ holds]
- $logrep(x \times fac(n), i) \equiv logrep(x \times 1/2 \times fac(n), i + 1)$ [if $x \geq 1$ holds]

if $n = 0 \wedge x < 1$ **then** (x, i)
[] $x \geq 1$ **then** $logrep(x \times 1/2 \times fac(n), i + 1)$
[] $n > 0 \wedge x < N$ **then** $logrep(x \times n \times fac(n-1), i)$ **fi**

step 10: fold *floatfac'* (with assertion)

funct *floatfac'* = (**int** n, **real** x, **int** i: $n \geq 0 \wedge i \geq 0 \wedge x \geq 1/2$) (**real**, **int**):
  if $n = 0 \wedge x < 1$ **then** (x, i)
  [] $x \geq 1$ **then** $floatfac'(n, x \times 1/2, i + 1)$
  [] $n \neq 0 \wedge x < N$ **then** $floatfac'(n - 1, x \times n, i)$ **fi**.

A shorter derivation can be obtained if, in step 2, an appropriate case introduction (Sect. 5.3.1.1) is used instead of unfolding *fac*.

4.6 Exercises

Exercise 4.3-1

Give examples that show the necessity of the applicability conditions for *fold*.

Exercise 4.3-2

Give a transformation rule for introducing, by abstraction, an auxiliary function with an assertion for its arguments.

Exercise 4.4-1

Prove, by using transformations, the correctness of the rules

a) *$\forall$-simplification*;
b) *splitting of a quantifier*

(Take special care of the applicability conditions).

Exercise 4.4-2

Prove, or disprove the correctness of the following "equivalences":

a) $(a \mathbin{\Delta} b) \mathbin{\nabla} c \equiv (a \mathbin{\Delta} (b \mathbin{\nabla} c)) \mathbin{\nabla} (\neg a \mathbin{\Delta} c)$;
b) $(a \mathbin{\nabla} b) \mathbin{\Delta} c \equiv (a \mathbin{\nabla} (b \mathbin{\Delta} c)) \mathbin{\Delta} (\neg a \mathbin{\nabla} c)$;
c) $(a \mathbin{\Delta} b) \mathbin{\nabla} c \equiv (a \mathbin{\nabla} c) \mathbin{\Delta} (b \mathbin{\nabla} c)$;
d) $(a \mathbin{\nabla} b) \mathbin{\Delta} c \equiv (a \mathbin{\Delta} c) \mathbin{\nabla} (b \mathbin{\Delta} c)$;
e) $a \Rightarrow b \equiv \neg a \mathbin{\nabla} b$;
f) $a \vee (b \Rightarrow c) \equiv$ **true**.

Add applicability conditions, if possible, to ensure correctness.

Exercise 4.4-3

Prove, by transformations, the correctness of the rules

a) $\{\mathbf{m}\, x: x \in (S \cup T) \wedge P(x)\}$

$\Updownarrow$

$\{\mathbf{m}\, x: x \in S \wedge P(x)\} \cup \{\mathbf{m}\, x: x \in T \wedge P(x)\}$;

b) **if** B ∇ (C Δ D) **then** E_1 **else** E_2 **fi**

$\Updownarrow$

if B **then** E_1
elsf $\neg$C **then** E_2 **elsf** D **then** E_1 **else** E_2 **fi**.

Exercise 4.4-4

Prove or disprove the correctness of the following "rules". Add applicability conditions, if possible, to ensure correctness.

a) **if** B **then if** C **then** E_1 **else** E_2 **fi fi**

$\Updownarrow$ [DET[B], DET[C]

if B $\wedge$ C **then** E_1 [] B $\wedge \neg$C **then** E_2 **fi**

b) **if** B **then** E [] C **then** E **fi**

$\Updownarrow$ [DET[B], DET[C]

if B $\vee$ C **then** E **fi**

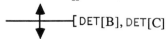

c) **if** B **then** E_1 [] ¬B **then if** C **then** E_2 [] ¬C **then** E_3 **fi fi**

$\Updownarrow$ [DET[B], DET[C]

if C **then** E_2 [] ¬C **then if** B **then** E_1 [] ¬B **then** E_3 **fi fi**

Exercise 4.4-5

Prove the termination of

a) **funct** f = (**nat** m, **nat** n) **nat**:
  if $m \neq 0 \wedge n \neq 0$ **then if odd** m **then** $f(m+1, n-1)$ **else** $f(n, m/2)$ **fi else** 1 **fi**;

b) **funct** *ack* = (**nat** x, **nat** y) **nat**:
  if $x = 0$ **then** $y+1$
  elsf $y = 0$ **then** $ack(x-1, 1)$ **else** $ack(x-1, ack(x, y-1))$ **fi**.

Exercise 4.5-1

Derive the instantiations of step 3 in Sect. 4.5.2 by means of elementary transformations.

Exercise 4.5-2

Given the formal specification

funct d = (**natsequ** s, **nat** x, **natsequ** t) **natsequ**:
  t + *delete*(s) **where**

  funct *delete* = (**natsequ** s) **natsequ**:
    if s =<> **then** s
    elsf first$s$ = x **then rest**s **else first**s + *delete*(**rest**s) **fi**

derive, by transformations, a version of d that is independent of *delete*.

Exercise 4.5-3

Given the formal specification

funct *mult* = (**nat** a, **nat** b) **nat**:
  if b=0 ∨ a=0 **then** 0 **else** $mult(a-1, b-1) + a + b - 1$ **fi**;

funct *quad* = (**nat** a) **nat**:
  $mult(a, a)$

derive, by using the unfold/fold strategy, a recursive solution for *quad* which is independent of *mult*.

Exercise 4.5-4

Given the formal specification

funct *ge* = (**nat** a, **nat** b) **bool**:
  if b=0 **then true elsf** a=0 **then false else** $ge(a-1, b-1)$ **fi**,

funct *sub* = (**nat** a, **nat** b) (**nat** | **dummy**):
  if b=0 **then** a **elsf** a=0 **then dummy else** $sub(a-1, b-1)$ **fi**

derive, by using the unfold/fold strategy, a recursive solution for

funct *gesub* = (**nat** a, **nat** b) (**bool**, (**nat** | **dummy**)):
  ($ge(a, b)$, $sub(a, b)$)

which is independent of *ge* and *sub*.

Exercise 4.5-5

Given the formal specification

> **funct** *sub* = (**nat** *a*, **nat** *b*: $b \le a$) **nat**:
> **that nat** *k*: *add*(*k*, *b*) = *a* **where**
>
> **funct** *add* = (**nat** *a*, **nat** *b*) **nat**:
> **if** *b* = 0 **then** *a* **else** *add*(*a*, *b*–1) + 1 **fi**

derive a (recursive) solution for *sub*.

Exercise 4.5-6

Given

> **mode natsequ** = SEQU(**nat**);
>
> **funct** *sumsquares* = (**natsequ** *n*) **nat**:
> *sum*(*squares*(*n*)) **where**
>
> **funct** *squares* = (**natsequ** *n*) **natsequ**:
> **if** *n* =<> **then** <> **else** (**first***n*)^2 + *squares*(**rest***n*) **fi**;
>
> **funct** *sum* = (**natsequ** *n*) **nat**:
> **if** *n* =<> **then** 0 **else** **first***n* + *sum*(**rest***n*) **fi**;

derive (by program transformations) a version of *sumsquares* that is independent of *squares* and *sum* by using the unfold/fold strategy.

5. From Descriptive Specifications to Operational Ones

This chapter deals with the problem

Given a descriptive problem specification, how may a solution be derived?.

Since solving this problem needs ideas, experience, and intuition on the developer's side, it should be clear that it cannot be solved by purely mechanical reasoning. Transformations in this context can only provide a frame indicating possible *directions of thought* because the developer usually has to find new entities which are (descriptively) characterized by their properties in the respective applicability conditions. Consequently, all the rules to be discussed in the following sections have in common that the transformations they describe are rather straightforward whereas the verification of the respective applicability conditions often requires human intuition and ingenuity.

It is, of course, always possible (and also allowed) to *find* (by inspiration) an arbitrary solution to the problem and to *prove* that it meets the specification (using such techniques as those introduced in [Dijkstra 76a] or [Gries 81]). We are, however, more interested in giving methodological advice and concrete techniques that allow us to *derive* a solution from the problem specification within a deductive framework. Note that this neither excludes intuition in finding solutions nor verification of a solution found by intuition. It rather means that verification is to be considered as a special case of program development by transformations – as is also stated in the respective transformation rule in Sect. 4.1.

For our initial descriptive specifications of some problem P, we assume the following general form (see also [Manna, Waldinger 80], [Merritt 82], [Smith 83]):

funct f = (**m** x: C(x)) **n**:
  some n y: R(x, y).

That is, given some input of sort **m** that satisfies some predicate C (the 'precondition'), the solution to the problem P is computed by a function f which produces as output some y of sort **n** such that for x and y a predicate R (describing the 'input-output relation' of the problem) holds. If it can be proved that there is a unique solution to the problem, **that** (as a stronger descriptor) will be used.

This general form uses an assertion to take care of partiality. In fact, it is sufficient to consider descriptive specifications of the general form

funct f = (**m** x) **n**:
  some n y: R(x, y),

as this form can always be obtained by transforming the above form.

Corresponding to the semantics of an assertion (Sect. 3.4.1), a given specification

funct f = (**m** x: C(x)) **n**:
  some n y: R(x, y)

can be transformed into

funct f = (**m** x) **n**:
  if C(x) **then** **some n** y: R(x, y) **else** **some n** y: **false** **fi**.

The distributivity of **some** over the conditional (Sect. 4.4.4) yields

some n y: **if** C(x) **then** R(x, y) **else** **false** **fi**.

By the definition of Δ (cf. Sect. 4.4.1) we obtain

funct f = (**m** x) **n**:
  some n y: C(x) Δ R(x, y)

and hence the postulated form without assertion.

If we want to take care of partialities explicitly, we shall introduce a dummy element (as a distinguished (possibly additional) constant of the respective domain), and the general form then reads

funct f = (**m** x) (**n** | **dummy**):
  if C(x) **then** **some n** y: R(x, y) **else** **dummy** **fi**.

In fact, what we are actually doing is defining a new mode **dummy** consisting of one object (which, deliberately, also is denoted by **dummy**) and building the sum (Sect. 3.3.5) of **n** and **dummy** to form a supermode of **n**.

In order to find an operational solution for f, this latter form requires us to find an operational definition for the predicate C. For functions that are predicates themselves, we assume the general patterns

funct p = (**m** x) **bool**:
  R(x),

resp.

funct p = (**m** x) (**bool** | **dummy**):
  if C(x) **then** R(x) **else** **dummy** **fi**.

Of course, before starting to develop a program from a given formal specification, soundness of the specification (Sect. 3.2.3) should be checked. This means, in particular, that it should be guaranteed that an algorithmic solution to the specified problem exists.

Given a descriptive problem specification, we finally aim at deriving a correct algorithm that additionally is efficient (with respect to the currently still dominant von Neumann architecture of machines). In order to achieve this goal, we will follow the

<u>Strategy</u>

Given a descriptive formal specification

- derive some solution (irrespective of efficiency considerations);
- improve this solution.

It is the first part of this strategy that the following subsections will focus on.

As in Chap. 4, the rules given below should be considered as examples or representatives of classes of rules. With respect to their formulation, and especially to the applicability conditions, we have tried to find a compromise between generality and complexity. This implies in particular that for some of the rules, less restrictive but more complicated applicability conditions might be found. Occasionally we give specific variants of rules, especially if these variants are to be used within an example.

5.1 Transforming Specifications

It seems rather obvious that the actual form of a formal specification has an enormous influence on the elegance and conciseness of a subsequent transformational development. For example, in the case of the "simple number problem" (Sect. 3.6.2), the developments starting from the descriptive and the operational specification, respectively, are essentially different (Sect. 3.6.2 and Ex. 5.1-1), although the resulting algorithms are the same.

In general, however, there is a substantial difference between an operational and a descriptive specification of the same problem, not only with respect to the development, but also with respect to the resulting algorithms: An operational specification typically entails one specific algorithm whereas a descriptive specification usually allows several different algorithms to be derived.

But even different descriptive specifications of the same problem may lead to different algorithms, as can be seen from the following (simple) examples:

a) The "reachability problem in finite graphs" (Sect. 3.6.7) can be specified via

   - a sequence of nodes, or
   - a sequence of edges.

   Program development starting with either of these specifications will result in completely different algorithms, whose relative efficiencies cannot be compared without having further knowledge of the respective input graph.

b) The problem of the "truncated dual logarithm" is informally stated as follows:

   Find the minimum number of digits of the binary representation of an arbitrary natural number $n \in \mathbb{N}\backslash\{0\}$.

   The problem is investigated in [Bauer, Wössner 83] where the following (equivalent) formalizations are used as starting points for respective transformational developments that end in *substantially different* algorithms:

   1) **that nat** a: $a \geq 1 \ \Delta\ (2^{a-1} \leq n \wedge n < 2^a)$
   2) **that nat** a: $a \geq 1 \ \Delta\ (2^{a-1} \leq n \wedge (\forall$ **nat** b: $b \geq a \Rightarrow 2^b > n))$
   3) **that nat** a: $a \geq 1 \ \Delta\ (2^a > n \wedge (\forall$ **nat** c: $c < a \Rightarrow 2^c \leq n))$.

Due to the fact that both an algorithm and its derivation are influenced by the particular form of the respective specification, it seems worthwhile to already start the transformational activities on the level of formal specifications. According to the different characteristics of formal specifications (Sect. 3.1), different kinds of transformations are to be considered here. These transformations comprise transitions to equivalent specifications, such as

- *transitions between descriptive specifications,*
- *transitions from descriptive to operational specifications,*
- *transitions between operational specifications,*
- *transitions from* (descriptive or operational) *specifications to less redundant ones,*

but also transitions leading to a descendant (Sect. 4.1) in case of an indeterminate specification.

For the transition between descriptive specifications, a large number of rules for transforming specification constructs, in particular quantified formulas and descriptions, has already been considered in Sect. 4.4. Further obvious rules for set comprehensions are e.g. $\in$*-simplification* (Sect. 4.4.3) and rules such as

- *$\cup$-flattening*

$$\bigcup_{\mathbf{m}\ x:\ x \in M} \mathrm{E}(x) \ \mathbf{where\ set\ m}\ M = \bigcup_{\mathbf{m}\ y} \mathrm{E'}(y)$$

$$\updownarrow$$

$$\bigcup_{\mathbf{m}\ y} \bigcup_{\mathbf{m}\ x:\ x \in \mathrm{E'}(y)} \mathrm{E}(x),$$

or

- $\{\mathbf{set\ m}\ X: X \subseteq \mathrm{S} \cup \mathrm{T}\}$

$$\updownarrow$$

$$\{\mathbf{set\ m}\ X: X \subseteq \mathrm{S}\} \cup \{\mathbf{set\ m}\ X: X \subseteq \mathrm{T}\}.$$

Here, **set m** denotes objects of kind set (Sect. 3.4.4), i.e., possibly infinite sets, which should not be confused with the (finite) sets introduced by the algebraic type SET. Of course, the above rules hold for the latter ones, too.

Another rule dealing with set comprehensions is the following one which is a weaker form of the idea of "filter promotion" (Sect. 4.4.5.2):

- $\{\mathbf{m}\ x: x \in M \wedge (\mathrm{P} \wedge \mathrm{Q})\}$

$$\updownarrow$$

$$\{\mathbf{m}\ x: x \in \{\mathbf{m}\ y: y \in M \wedge \mathrm{P}[y\ \mathbf{for}\ x]\} \wedge \mathrm{Q})\}$$

Syntactic constraints:
NOTOCCURS[y **in** P].

The use of this particular rule in transforming descriptive specifications may be illustrated with the following simple problem (Ex. 3.4-8):

Given the sequence s =<1, 2, 3, 4, 5, 6, 7, 8, 9> of natural numbers, one is requested to find all permutations p of s such that any initial segment of p of length i (1 ≤ i ≤ 9), considered as a decimal number, is divisible by i.

A descriptive specification of the problem is straightforward:

find(*perms*(<1, 2, 3, 4, 5, 6, 7, 8, 9>)) **where**

mode natsequ = EESEQU(**nat**, =);
mode natsequset = ESET(**natsequ**, =);

funct *perms* = (**natsequ** *s*) **natsequset**:
  {**natsequ** *t*: *sequtoset*(*t*) = *sequtoset*(*s*) ∧ |*s*| = |*t*|},

funct *sequtoset* = (**natsequ** *s*) **natsequset**:
  if *s* =<> **then** ∅ **else** **first***s* + *sequtoset*(**rest***s*) **fi**,

funct *find* = (**natsequset** *s*) **natsequset**:
  {**natsequ** *t*: $t \in s \,\Delta\, \forall$ (**nat** *i*: $1 \le i \le |t|$): (*num*(*t*[1:*i*]) **mod** *i*) = 0},

funct *num* = (**natsequ** *s*) **nat**:
  if *s* =<> **then** 0 **elsf** |*s*| = 1 **then** **first***s* **else** (*num*(**lead***s*) × 10) + **last***s* **fi**.

An operational definition of this specification can be given in a straightforward way. The resulting algorithm, however, would be intolerably inefficient. Therefore, before transforming to an operational definition, we transform the specification using the rule given above. Practically, this means conversion of the universally quantified expression in *find* into a conjunction and using the conjuncts to reduce the result of *perms* according to the above rule.

Let p denote the desired sequence and p_i denote its constituting elements. From the definition of the essential property in *find* the following facts can be derived:

- p_2, p_4, p_6, p_8 are even; p_1, p_3, p_5, p_7, p_9 are odd;
- $p_5 = 5$; p_1, p_9 are arbitrary odd digits;
- $p_4 \in \{2, 6\} \wedge p_8 \in \{2, 6\}$;
- $p_2 \in \{4, 8\} \wedge p_6 \in \{4, 8\}$;
- $p_8 = 2 \Rightarrow (p_7 \in \{3, 7\} \wedge p_4 = 6)$;
- $p_8 = 6 \Rightarrow (p_7 \in \{1, 9\} \wedge p_4 = 2)$;
- $p_4 = 2 \Rightarrow (p_8 = 6 \wedge p_6 = 8 \wedge ((p_1 + p_3) \textbf{ mod } 3) = 2)$;
- $p_4 = 6 \Rightarrow (p_8 = 2 \wedge p_6 = 4 \wedge (p_1 + p_3) \textbf{ mod } 3 = 1)$;
- $p_4 = 2 \Rightarrow ((p_1 = 1 \wedge p_3 = 7) \vee (p_1 = 7 \wedge p_3 = 1)) \wedge p_7 = 9$;
- $p_4 = 6 \Rightarrow ((p_1 = 3 \wedge p_3 = 1 \wedge p_7 = 7) \vee (p_1 = 1 \wedge p_3 = 3 \wedge p_7 = 7) \vee$
  $(p_1 = 7 \wedge p_3 = 9 \wedge p_7 = 3) \vee (p_1 = 9 \wedge p_3 = 7 \wedge p_7 = 3) \vee$
  $(p_1 = 1 \wedge p_3 = 9 \wedge p_7 \in \{3, 7\}) \vee (p_1 = 9 \wedge p_3 = 1 \wedge p_7 \in \{3, 7\}))$;

All these facts allow to transform our initial specification into:

find(*ps*) **where**

natsequset *ps* = {<1, 4, 7, 2, 5, 8, 9, 6, 3>, <7, 4, 1, 2, 5, 8, 9, 6, 3>,
  <3, 8, 1, 6, 5, 4, 7, 2, 9>, <1, 8, 3, 6, 5, 4, 7, 2, 9>,
  <7, 8, 9, 6, 5, 4, 3, 2, 1>, <9, 8, 7, 6, 5, 4, 3, 2, 1>,
  <1, 8, 9, 6, 5, 4, 3, 2, 7>, <9, 8, 1, 6, 5, 4, 3, 2, 7>,
  <1, 8, 9, 6, 5, 4, 7, 2, 3>, <9, 8, 1, 6, 5, 4, 7, 2, 3>};

funct *find* = (**natsequset** *s*) **natsequset**:
  {(**natsequ** *t*: $t \in s$): (*num*(*t*[1:7]) **mod** *i*) = 0},

from which, by simple evaluation,

{<3, 8, 1, 6, 5, 4, 7, 2, 9>}

is obtained as a result.

Rules for the transition from descriptive specifications to operational ones are the subject of the remainder of this chapter.

Rules for the transition between operational specifications, i.e. the modification of applicative programs (e.g. with respect to efficiency) is the subject of Chap. 6.

Rules for the transition from a specification to a less redundant one include

- $\mathrm{P} \wedge \mathrm{R}$

  ↓ [$\mathrm{P} \equiv$ **true** $\vdash \mathrm{R} \equiv$ **true**

  P

or

- $\mathrm{P} \vee \mathrm{R}$

  ↓ [$\mathrm{P} \equiv$ **false** $\vdash \mathrm{R} \equiv$ **false**

  P.

Other rules for removing redundancy are the simplification rules introduced in Chap. 4.

As an example of how to remove redundancy, consider the following formal specification

mode natsequ = EESEQU(**nat**, =);
funct *issorted* = (**natsequ** *s*) **bool**:
  ∀ (**nat** i, j: $1 \le i < |s| \wedge 1 < j \le |s| \wedge i < j$): $s[i] \le s[j]$.

Using the rule *conjunction of a consequence* (Sect. 4.4.2) this can be transformed into

funct *issorted* = (**natsequ** *s*) **bool**:
  ∀ (**nat** i, j: $1 \le i < |s| \wedge 1 < j \le |s| \wedge i < j$): $s[i] \le s[j]$ Δ
  ∀ (**nat** i: $1 \le i < |s|$): $s[i] \le s[i + 1]$

and, due to the definedness of the added conjunct, further into

funct *issorted* = (**natsequ** *s*) **bool**:
  ∀ (**nat** i: $1 \le i < |s|$): $s[i] \le s[i + 1] \wedge$
  ∀ (**nat** i, j: $1 \le i < |s| \wedge 1 < j \le |s| \wedge i < j$): $s[i] \le s[j]$.

Now, due to transitivity of ≤, obviously

∀ (**nat** i: $1 \le i < |s|$): $s[i] \le s[i + 1] \equiv$ **true** $\vdash$
∀ (**nat** i, j: ($1 \le i < |s| \wedge 1 < j \le |s| \wedge i < j$): $s[i] \le s[j] \equiv$ **true**,

such that using the rule above yields immediately

funct *issorted* = (**natsequ** *s*) **bool**:
  ∀ (**nat** i: $1 \le i < |s|$): $s[i] \le s[i+1]$.

In a similar way the formal specification

funct *issorted* = (**natsequ** *s*) **bool**:
  s =<> ∇ **rest**s =<> ∇
  ∀ (**natsequ** u, v: $u \ne$<> $\wedge\ v \ne$<>):
    $(u + v = s) \Rightarrow$ (*issorted*(u) ∧ *issorted*(v) ∧ **last**$u \le$ **first**v)

can be transformed into the (less redundant) equivalent specification

funct *issorted* = (**natsequ** *s*) **bool**:
  s =<> ∇ **rest**s =<> ∇
  ∀ (**natsequ** u, v: $u \neq$<> ∧ $v \neq$<>): $(u + v = s) \Rightarrow$ (**last**$u \leq$ **first**v).

Very frequently, the question whether the actual specification is the appropriate one for a smooth development can only be answered in later stages of a development, in particular in case of blind alleys. In such a situation it pays to "backtrack" and to transform the specification according to the knowledge gained in the development that failed. This is because transformations on the level of specification are much more lucid than on that of imperative programs. How this works out in concrete examples can be seen in [Pepper, Partsch 80] where the upsequence problem (Sect. 3.6.5) is used as an example.

Transforming formal specifications also includes the transformation of the data types involved. This subject will be dealt with independently in Chap. 8.

5.2 Embedding

Embedding – sometimes also called **generalization** – is a general principle known in mathematics for a long time: if the original formulation of a problem does not lead to a solution straightforwardly, one tries to solve a more general problem that includes the original problem as a special case. Although solving a problem by looking at a more general one sounds paradoxical at first glance, it really isn't: anyone who has at least a little experience in doing proofs by induction knows the "trick" of using an induction hypothesis which is a generalization of the theorem to be proved in order to smooth the proof.

Finding a suitable generalization certainly requires intuition and experience and cannot be done by purely mechanical reasoning. However, intuition can be guided by looking for appropriate embeddings in a systematic way. In this way, when analyzing the supposed general form of a problem specification (see introduction to Chap. 5)

funct f = (**m** x) **n**:
  some n y: $R(x, y)$

we can (formally) identify the following possibilities for embedding:

- embedding of the data types (**m** or **n**);
- embedding of the domain (of f);
- embedding of the range (of f).

According to the theory of (algebraic) abstract types [Wirsing et al. 83], *embedding of a data type* T means using, instead of T, a type T' that is a "correct implementation" of T (Chap. 8).

Simple examples of embedding of the data type are considering

- elements as singleton sequences or sets
- natural numbers as integral numbers, or
- natural numbers as singleton sets of integral numbers.

The effect that is intended with an *embedding of the data type* is to switch to another data type in order

- to unify different data types that occur in the same specification; or
- to make available primitive data type operations with different (algebraic) properties.

An example of the first kind is given by the "unification problem" of Sect. 3.6.9. The original problem is specified by

funct *unify* = (**term** t_1, **term** t_2) (**subst** | **dummy**):
  if *unifiable*(t_1, t_2) **then some subst** s: $t_1 \diamond s =_t t_2 \diamond s$
                else dummy fi where

  funct *unifiable* = (**term** t_1, **term** t_2) **bool**:
    $\exists$ **subst** s: $t_1 \diamond s =_t t_2 \diamond s$

where $\diamond$ denotes the instantiation of terms. In the definition of $\diamond$ (Sect. 3.6.9), however, also $\blacklozenge$, the instantiation of sequences of terms is used. Just for the sake of economy in writing, it seems appropriate here to consider the (more general) problem of unifying sequences of terms rather than individual terms, i.e. to start the transformational development from

funct *unify* = (**term** t_1, **term** t_2) (**subst** | **dummy**):
  if *s-unifiable*($<t_1>$, $<t_2>$) **then some subst** s: $<t_1> \blacklozenge s =_{ts} <t_2> \blacklozenge s$
                else dummy fi where

  funct *s-unifiable* = (**termsequ** st_1, **termsequ** st_2) **bool**:
    $\exists$ **subst** s: $st_1 \blacklozenge s =_{ts} st_2 \blacklozenge s$.

Another example of the same kind is given by the "recognition problem" of Sect. 5.5.2.

Examples of the second kind are given by extending a data type in order to circumvent partialities, for example by "adding" $+\infty$ and $-\infty$ to the natural numbers. In this way, a minimum/maximum operation on sets of natural numbers can be made total by defining $min(\emptyset) = +\infty$ and $max(\emptyset) = -\infty$.

Of course, *embedding of the data type* applies to the data types in the domain and the range of *f*.

Embedding of the domain also comprises several sub-cases. First of all, there is the usual meaning of transition to a more general domain (of *f*) such that the original one is obtained by projection (see also Sect. 6.1.2).

A typical example of this kind is the generalization of a constant of the specification to a parameter (see also [Aubin 75], [Gries 81], [Vytopil, Abdali 81], [Pettorossi 87]). More precisely, if

funct f = (**m** x) **n**:
  some n y: R(x, y)

and if c is a constant of some sort **p** occurring in the predicate R, then we have equivalently,

funct f = (**m** x) **n**:
  $f'(x, c)$ **where**

funct f = (**m** x, **p** z) **n**:
  some n y: R'(x, y, z)

provided R' fulfils

R'(x, y, c) $\equiv$ R(x, y)

for arbitrary **m** x, **n** y.

With respect to a later termination proof, it is advisable to choose for **p** a well-founded set [Schmitz 78]. Furthermore, it is also advisable to introduce, together with the embedding, suitable assertions about the "new" parameters – either for the sake of definedness or for keeping valuable context information (Sect. 5.3).

As a typical example consider the specification (Sect. 5.1)

funct *issorted* = (**natsequ** x) **bool**:
  $\forall$ (**nat** i: $1 \le i < |x|$): $x[i] \le x[i+1]$.

Here, 1 is a constant and $|x|$ behaves like a constant. Hence they can be made into parameters as discussed above. However, in order to ensure definedness of the auxiliary function *isord* independent of its context, an appropriate assertion is needed:

funct *issorted* = (**natsequ** x) **bool**:
  isord(x, 1, $|x|$) **where**

  funct *isord* = (**natsequ** x, **nat** l, **nat** r: $1 \le l \wedge r \le |x|$) **bool**:
    $\forall$ (**nat** i: $l \le i < r$): $x[i] \le x[i+1]$.

If the original specification does not contain a priori constants to be made into parameters, they can often be introduced using particular properties of the underlying data types. Well-known examples are neutral elements as 1 in

$n \equiv n \times 1$

for arbitrary natural numbers n, or <> in

(∗) $s \equiv s$+<> $\equiv$ <>+s $\equiv$ <>+s+<> $\equiv$ <>+s+<>+<> $\equiv$ ...

for arbitrary sequences s.

Similar kinds of embeddings can be found by *decomposition properties* of the respective data types. E.g., for arbitrary sequences s

$\exists$ **sequ** a, b: $s = a + b$

can be used. An example for this kind of embedding is to be found in the development of the "cycle problem" of Sect. 5.5.4.

In fact, an *embedding of the domain* was already used in Sect. 4.5.4 where

funct *floatfac* = (**int** n: $n \ge 0$) (**real**, **int**):
  logrep(*fac*(n), 0)

was transformed (by abstraction) into

funct *floatfac* = (**int** n: $n \ge 0$) (**real**, **int**):
  floatfac'(n, 1, 0) **where**

  funct *floatfac'* = (**nat** n, **real** x, **int** i: $n \ge 0 \wedge i \ge 0 \wedge x \ge 1/2$) (**real**, **int**):
    logrep($x \times fac(n)$, i).

Embedding of the range means a transition from

some n y: $\mathrm{R}(x, y)$

to

y **where** (**n** y, **p** z) = **some** (**n** y', **p** z'): $\mathrm{R}'(x, y', z')$

within f, where R' has to fulfil (for arbitrary **m** x, **n** y, **p** z)

$$\mathrm{R}(x, y) \equiv \mathrm{R}'(x, y, z).$$

Since the result of f is independent of the choice of z, any **p** c with $\mathrm{R}(x, y) \equiv \mathrm{R}'(x, y, c)$ could be used. Thus, embedding of the range can be subsumed under embedding of the domain. However, sometimes developing an operational definition for $\mathrm{R}'(x, y', z')$ is easier to handle.

Rather than using a relation R' that is equivalent to the original relation R, embedding also can be combined with 'refinement'. By **refinement** we simply mean a transition from R to a (non-empty) relation R' according to the following rule:

- <u>*Refinement*</u>

  funct f = (**m** x) **n**:
    some n y: $\mathrm{R}(x, y)$

  ↓ [$\mathrm{R}'(x, y) \equiv$ **true** $\vdash$ $\mathrm{R}(x, y) \equiv$ **true**,
      $(\exists$ **n** y: $\mathrm{R}(x, y)) \equiv$ **true** $\vdash$ $(\exists$ **n** y: $\mathrm{R}'(x, y)) \equiv$ **true**

  funct f = (**m** x) **n**:
    some n y: $\mathrm{R}'(x, y)$.

An example of how to use this rule is given by the "reachability problem" in finite directed graphs (Sect. 3.6.7):

mode nodesequ = ESEQU(**node**, =);

funct *reach* = (**graph** G, **node** x, **node** y: $x, y \in N(G)$) **bool**:
  $\exists$ **nodesequ** p: $p \neq\langle\rangle\ \Delta$
    $(x =$ **first**$p \wedge y =$ **last**$p \wedge \forall$ (**nat** i: $1 \le i < |p|$): $e(p[i], p[i+1]) \in E(G))$.

Here, the predicate symbol R from above corresponds to

$p \neq\langle\rangle\ \Delta\ (x =$ **first**$p \wedge y =$ **last**$p \wedge \forall$ (**nat** i: $1 \le i < |p|$): $e(p[i], p[i+1]) \in E(G))$.

If there exists a path from x to y in G then there also exists a path in which each node of G occurs at most once, so that for the predicate symbol R' from above we can choose $\mathrm{R}\ \Delta\ |p| \le |N(G)|$. Hence, the second condition for the refinement is fulfilled. The first condition for the refinement is trivially fulfilled here, due to the general rule [Manna 74]:

$(\mathrm{P}(x)\ \Delta\ \mathrm{Q}(x)) \equiv$ **true** $\vdash$ $\mathrm{P}(x) \equiv$ **true**.

Therefore, *refinement* is applicable and results in

funct *reach* = (**graph** G, **node** x, **node** y: $x, y \in N(G)$) **bool**:
  $\exists$ **nodesequ** p: $p \neq\langle\rangle\ \Delta$
    $(x =$ **first**$p \wedge y =$ **last**$p \wedge$
    $\forall$ (**nat** i: $1 \le i < |p|$): $e(p[i], p[i+1]) \in E(G))\ \Delta\ |p| \le |N(G)|$

where $|p| \le |N(G)|$ has been added as an additional conjunct.

All the considerations above provide useful hints on looking for embeddings but they are not exhaustive as example (*) above clearly demonstrates. Thus, finding a suitable embedding is part of the developer's ingenuity or experience. The methodology just provides the formal framework to guide the developer's thoughts. This is manifest in the fact that the rules below (and also most of the following ones) introduce "new information" (E, i_n, i_m below) in the respective output schemes that is related to the expressions in the respective input schemes by suitable applicability conditions.

By combining the possibilities for embedding discussed above with refinement we have the rule

- *Embedding*

  some n y: R(x, y)

  ↓ [R'($i_m(x)$, $i_n(y)$, E) ≡ **true** ⊢ R(x, y) ≡ **true**,
  (∃ **n** y: R(x, y)) ≡ **true** ⊢ (∃ **n** y: R'($i_m(x)$, $i_n(y)$, E)) ≡ **true**

  funct f = (**m** x) **n**:
  some n y: R'($i_m(x)$, $i_n(y)$, E)

  Syntactic constraints:
  KIND[i_m] = **funct (m) m'**,
  KIND[i_n] = **funct (n) n'**.

Of course, also a variant (with the same syntactic constraints) for embedding without refinement can be proved:

- **funct** f = (**m** x) **n**:
  some n y: R(x, y)

  ↕ [R'($i_m(x)$, $i_n(y)$, E) ≡ R(x, y)

  funct f = (**m** x) **n**:
  some n y: R'($i_m(x)$, $i_n(y)$, E).

For purely technical reasons, it is sometimes convenient to use a further variant of the rule above (again with the same syntactic constraints) that introduces an auxiliary function declaration:

- **funct** f = (**m** x) **n**:
  some n y: R(x, y)

  ↕ [R'($i_m(x)$, $i_n(y)$, E) ≡ R(x, y)

  funct f = (**m** x) **n**:
  f'($i_m(x)$, E) **where**
  funct f'= (**m** x, **p** z) **n**:
  some n y: R'(x, $i_n(y)$, z)

which immediately results from the variant above and the basic rule of abstraction (Sect. 4.3).

For embeddings introducing auxiliary operations, the simultaneous introduction of an assertion for the auxiliary operation is captured by rules such as

- **funct** f = (**m** x) **n**:
  some n y: R(x, y)

  $\Big\downarrow$ $\left[\begin{array}{l}(\exists\ \mathbf{n}\ y\text{: R}(x, y)) \equiv \mathbf{true} \vdash (\text{P}(x, \text{E})\ \Delta\ \exists\ \mathbf{n}\ y\text{: Q}(x, y, \text{E})) \equiv \mathbf{true},\\ (\text{P}(x, \text{E})\ \Delta\ \text{Q}(x, y, \text{E})) \equiv \mathbf{true} \vdash \text{R}(x, y) \equiv \mathbf{true}\end{array}\right.$

  funct f = (**m** x) **n**:
  f'(x, E) **where**
  funct f'= (**m** x, **p** z: P(x, z)) **n**:
  some n y: Q(x, y, z)

and obvious further variants thereof.

Variants of all these rules for dealing with descriptive specifications of predicates are also obvious. In the sequel either of these variants will be referred to as embedding.

5.3 Development of Recursive Solutions from Problem Descriptions

Operational specifications use the applicative language constructs introduced in Sect. 3.4.1. Transforming a descriptive specification into an operational one therefore means a transition from a problem description into an applicative program. For this transition, we will introduce basic rules together with a general strategy, but also some compact rules for particular specification constructs and specific data structures.

5.3.1 A General Strategy

One of the most frequently used tactics in transforming descriptive specifications into (recursive) algorithms is the 'unfold/fold-strategy' ([Burstall, Darlington 77] and Sect. 4.3). Although this tactics works quite well for a number of examples (as could be seen in Sects. 4.3 and 4.5), it is too narrow for arbitrary problem specifications. Therefore we suggest the more general

> <u>Strategy</u> (Generalized unfold/fold-strategy)
>
> – Decompose and detail the specification;
> – Simplify and rearrange expressions;
> – Compose a recursive routine.

Unfold is only one technique to be used in decomposition and detailing. Others are *case introduction* (Sect. 5.3.1.1), use of *decomposition lemmas* of data types, or any other theorems of the problem domain that involve decomposition.

The second step of the strategy is to comprise all simplifications resulting from "contracting" data type axioms (such as s+<> ≡ s), simplification rules for language constructs (Sect. 4.4), as well as rearrangements induced either by the *recomposition* technique (Sect. 5.3.1.2) or by commutativity or associativity properties (and variants and mixtures thereof) of the respective data types.

Fold, the "inverse" of *unfold*, is among the techniques to be used in the composition step (together with its variants that guarantee the prevention of non-terminating loops (Sect. 5.3.1.3), as well as the *introduction of invariants* (Sect. 5.3.1.4), and all the techniques mentioned for decomposition, applied in reverse order.

In an idealistic view, these three steps would be applied one after the other. However, there is neither a strict ordering among the constituent transformations of each step, nor is the segmentation into these three steps always unique. Hence, any sequential presentation is to be considered as a topological sorting of the underlying partial ordering. In this sense, any particular derivation represents a whole class of derivations.

Actually, in practical program developments, these steps very often appear mixed, since, for example whenever a possibility for simplification is detected, one is tempted to perform it – irrespective of the phase one is working in.

As mentioned earlier, our general strategy relies heavily on the use of axioms and theorems of the underlying data types. Apart from *unfold* and *fold* there are a few other, general, data type independent techniques. These will be discussed in the following subsections. For the proofs of most of the rules to be discussed we refer the reader to [Partsch 86].

5.3.1.1 Case Introduction

An important technique in connection with decomposition is the introduction of a case distinction that allows us to consider different cases individually.

For our general form of a problem description

funct f = (**m** x: P(x)) **n**:
  some n y: R(x, y),

we can prove the rule

- <u>*Case introduction*</u>

  funct f = (**m** x: P(x)) **n**:
    some n y: R(x, y)

  $\Updownarrow$ [P(x) ≡ **true** ⊢ ($\exists_{i=1..n}$ $B_i(x)$) ≡ **true**

  funct f = (**m** x: P(x)) **n**:
    if $[]_{i=1..n}$ $B_i(x)$ **then some n** y: R(x, y) **fi.**

The simplification of this rule for a problem description without assertion is obvious. Note also that "disjointedness" of the B_i is not required.

For predicates, we have the following variant

- **funct** p = (**m** x: P(x)) **bool**:
    ∃ **n** y: R(x, y)

  $\Updownarrow$ [P(x) ≡ **true** ⊢ ($\exists_{i=1..n}$ $B_i(x)$) ≡ **true**

  funct p = (**m** x: P(x)) **bool**:
    $\exists_{i=1..n}$ ($B_i(x)$ Δ ∃ **n** y: R(x, y)).

Furthermore, using the respective basic rules (Sect. 4.4), we get further (obvious) variants for the conventional **if-then-else** alternative, such as

- **funct** f = (**m** x: P(x)) **n**:
  some n y: R(x, y)

  $\Updownarrow$ [P(x) ≡ **true** ⊢ (B(x) ∨ ¬B(x)) ≡ **true**

  funct f = (**m** x: P(x)) **n**:
  if B(x) **then some n** y: R(x, y) **else some n** y: R(x, y) **fi.**

In the sequel we will refer to either of these rules simply by *case introduction*, and frequently also give the additional information on the tautology used.

The tautologies in the applicability conditions of the above rules are usually provided by the underlying data type definitions. As an example consider the "minimum element problem"

Find a minimum element of a non-empty sequence of natural numbers

which can be formalized straightforwardly as

mode natsequ = EESEQU(**nat**, =);
funct *minel* = (**natsequ** s: s ≠<>) **nat**:
  some nat x: $x \in s$ Δ (∀ **nat** y: $y \in s \Rightarrow x \leq y$).

Here we have obviously

(s ≠<>) ≡ **true** ⊢ (**rest**s =<> ∨ **rest**s ≠<>)) ≡ **true**

and, hence, using the rule *case introduction* we get immediately

funct *minel* = (**natsequ** s: s ≠<>) **nat**:
  if rest$s$ =<> **then some nat** x: $x \in s$ Δ (∀ **nat** y: $y \in s \Rightarrow x \leq y$)
  [] **rest**s ≠<> **then some nat** x: $x \in s$ Δ (∀ **nat** y: $y \in s \Rightarrow x \leq y$) **fi.**

Of course, the next efforts aim at simplifying the generated guarded expression (using the rule *modification of a conditional* from Chap. 4).

For the first branch, we have

(**rest**s =<>) ≡ **true** ⊢ **some nat** x: $x \in s$ Δ (∀ **nat** y: $y \in s \Rightarrow x \leq y$) ≡ **first**$s$.

For the second branch we use again *case introduction*

...
[] **rest**s ≠<> **then**
  if first$s$ ≤ *minel*(**rest**s) **then some nat** x: $x \in s$ Δ (∀ **nat** y: $y \in s \Rightarrow x \leq y$)
    else some nat x: $x \in s$ Δ (∀ **nat** y: $y \in s \Rightarrow x \leq y$) **fi fi**

which allows simplification to

...
[] **rest**s ≠<> **then**
  if first$s$ ≤ *minel*(**rest**s) **then first**s
    else some nat x: $x \in$ **rest**s Δ (∀ **nat** y: $y \in$ **rest**$s \Rightarrow x \leq y$) **fi fi**

and, finally, *folding*:

funct *minel* = (**natsequ** *s*: *s* ≠<>) **nat**:
  if rest*s* =<> **then first***s*
  [] **rest***s* ≠<> **then**
    if first*s* ≤ *minel*(**rest***s*) **then first***s* **else** *minel*(**rest***s*) **fi fi**.

For this particular example, the rules introduced so far sufficed to derive an operational specification. In general, apart from the simplification rules introduced in Chap. 4, further rules will be needed, such as the *recomposition* rule to be introduced next.

5.3.1.2 Recomposition

Within the strategy outlined at the beginning of this section, rearrangement of certain expressions is an important preparatory step for subsequent composition.

Apart from pure decomposition lemmas from the respective data type, such as (for sequences *s*)

(*s* ≠<>) ≡ **true** ⊢ *s* ≡ (**first***s* + **rest***s*),

this step occasionally requires us to introduce new auxiliary functions that allow the recomposition of some expression by a suitable new function (such as *c'* below). The idea is captured by the following rule:

- <u>*Recomposition*</u>

some p *y*: P(*c*(*x*), *y*)

⟶ [(Q(*x*, *z*) ⇒ P(*c*(*x*), *c'*(*z*))) ≡ **true**,
  (∃ **p** *y*: P(*c*(*x*), *y*)) ≡ **true** ⊢ (∃ **r** *z*: Q(*x*, *z*)) ≡ **true**

c'(**some r** *z*: Q(*x*, *z*))

<u>**Syntactic constraints:**</u>
KIND[*c*] = **funct** (**n**) **m**,
KIND[*c'*] = **funct** (**r**) **p**.

The operation *c* in this rule is a 'constructor operation' that constructs from an object of kind **n** an object of kind **m**. Rather than using *c*, we also could have used a 'decomposition operation' *d* of kind **funct** (**m**) **n**. Since, however, decomposition operations are usually partial operations, we have preferred the form above, thus circumventing the problems of partiality.

From a proof of the rule above it is easily seen that the converse direction of the rule *recomposition* holds, if

(Q(*x*, *z*) ⇔ P(*c*(*x*), *c'*(*z*))) ≡ **true**

and, additionally, *c'* is surjective.

The rule schema *recomposition* comprises a lot of special instances for particular forms of **n**, **r**, *c*, *c'*, and Q. For example, for **n** and **r** being pairs (**m**, **m**) and (**p**, **p**), resp., and Q being a conjunction, a frequently used instance of the rule reads:

- **some p** y: $\mathrm{P}(c(x, x'), y)$

$$\Big\downarrow \left[\begin{array}{l} ((\mathrm{P}(x, z) \wedge \mathrm{P}(x', z')) \Rightarrow \mathrm{P}(c(x, x'), c'(z, z'))) \equiv \mathbf{true}, \\ (\exists\, \mathbf{p}\, y\colon \mathrm{P}(c(x, x'), y)) \equiv \mathbf{true} \vdash (\exists\, \mathbf{r}\, z, z'\colon \mathrm{P}(x, z) \wedge \mathrm{P}(x', z')) \equiv \mathbf{true} \end{array}\right.$$

$c'(\mathbf{some}\ \mathbf{p}\ z, \mathbf{p}\ z'\colon \mathrm{P}(x, z) \wedge \mathrm{P}(x', z'))$

Syntactic constraints:

KIND[c] = **funct (m, m) m**,
KIND[c'] = **funct (p, p) p**.

Other useful instances are, e.g.,

- **some p** y: $\mathrm{R}(x, y)$

$$\Big\downarrow \left[\begin{array}{l} (\mathrm{R}(d_2(x), z) \Rightarrow \mathrm{R}(x, c'(d_1(x), z))) \equiv \mathbf{true}, \\ (\exists\, \mathbf{p}\, y\colon \mathrm{R}(x, y)) \equiv \mathbf{true} \vdash (\exists\, \mathbf{p}\, z\colon \mathrm{R}(d_2(x), z)) \equiv \mathbf{true} \end{array}\right.$$

$c'(d_1(x), \mathbf{some}\ \mathbf{p}\ z\colon \mathrm{R}(d_2(x), z))$

Syntactic constraints:

KIND[d_1] = **funct (m) n**,
KIND[d_2] = **funct (m) n**

or

- **some n** y: $\mathrm{Q}(x, x', y, z)$

$$\Big\downarrow \left[\begin{array}{l} (\forall_{i=1..n}\ \mathrm{Q}(x, d_i(x'), y_i, \mathrm{K}_i(x', z)) \Rightarrow \\ \quad \mathrm{Q}(x, x', c'(x', y_1, \ldots, y_n), z')) \equiv \mathbf{true}, \\ (\exists\, \mathbf{n}\, y\colon \mathrm{Q}(x, x', y, z)) \equiv \mathbf{true} \vdash \\ \quad (\exists\, \mathbf{n}\, y_i\colon \mathrm{Q}(x, d_i(x'), y_i, \mathrm{K}_i(x', z))) \equiv \mathbf{true} \quad (1 \le i \le n) \end{array}\right.$$

$c'(x', \mathbf{some}\ \mathbf{n}\ y_1\colon \mathrm{Q}(x, d_1(x'), y_1, \mathrm{K}_1(x', z)), \ldots,$
$\quad \mathbf{some}\ \mathbf{n}\ y_n\colon \mathrm{Q}(x, d_n(x'), y_n, \mathrm{K}_n(x', z)))$

Syntactic constraints:

KIND[x, x'] = **m**,
KIND[z] = **n**.

Of course, there are also variants for predicates, e.g.

- $\exists$ **p** y: $\mathrm{P}(c(x), y)$

$$\Big\downarrow \left[\begin{array}{l} (\mathrm{Q}(x, z) \Rightarrow \mathrm{P}(c(x), c'(z))) \equiv \mathbf{true}, \\ (\exists\, \mathbf{p}\, y\colon \mathrm{P}(c(x), y)) \equiv \mathbf{true} \vdash (\exists\, \mathbf{r}\, z\colon \mathrm{Q}(x, z)) \equiv \mathbf{true} \end{array}\right.$$

$\exists\, \mathbf{r}\, z\colon \mathrm{Q}(x, z)$

Syntactic constraints:

KIND[c] = **funct (n) m**,
KIND[c'] = **funct (r) p**.

The importance of the rules *case introduction* and *recomposition* in connection with deriving algorithms from descriptive specifications is acknowledged by many other authors. The particular role of abstract data types and *decomposition lemmas* to be used for *case introduction* is emphasized in [Guiho et al. 80], [Guiho 83], and [Gresse 83]. A combined strategy of *case introduction* and *recomposition* is dealt with in [Smith 83, 85a, b] and called *divide-and-conquer*. In contrast to the former authors the latter also recognizes the impact of suitable (new) composition operators for the divide-and-conquer idea (see also [Mehlhorn 84]). Apart from combining the two rules into one, his approach differs technically from ours in enforcing definedness by requiring the existence of a suitable well-founded ordering with respect to the decomposition. Although generally aiming at compact rules, we prefer to have separate rules for dealing with these two aspects, since they provide much greater flexibility with respect to program development.

In order to demonstrate the use of the rules above within program development, consider again the "sorting problem" (Sect. 3.4.3)

funct *sort* = (**natsequ** *a*) **natsequ**:
  some natsequ *s*: *issorted*(*s*) ∧ *isperm*(*s*, *a*)

where *issorted*(*s*) tests whether *s* is sorted (Sect. 5.1), and *isperm*(*s*, *a*) tests whether *s* is a permutation of *a* (Sect. 3.4.3).

For arbitrary sequences *t* the tautology

$(|t| \leq 1 \vee |t| > 1) \equiv$ **true**

holds such that application of *case introduction* yields

if $|a| \leq 1$ **then some natsequ** *s*: *issorted*(*s*) ∧ *isperm*(*s*, *a*)
[] $|a| > 1$ **then some natsequ** *s*: *issorted*(*s*) ∧ *isperm*(*s*, *a*) **fi**.

By simple local manipulations (provable with respect to the data type axioms, the definition of *issorted*, and the rule *local refinement of a guarded expression* from Sect. 4.4.5.4), we can derive

if $|a| \leq 1$ **then** *a*
[] $|a| > 1$ **then some natsequ** *s*: *issorted*(*s*) ∧ *isperm*(*s*, a_1+a_2) **where**
  (**natsequ** a_1, **natsequ** a_2) = **some** (**natsequ** a_1', **natsequ** a_2'):
    $|a_1'| \geq 1 \wedge |a_2'| \geq 1 \wedge a_1'+a_2' = a$ **fi**.

Now, obviously, the syntactic conditions for the (first variant of the) *recomposition* transformation are fulfilled with

natsequ	for	**p, m**
+	for	*c*, and
sort(*s*) = *t*	for	P(*s*, *t*).

If we furthermore define a function *merge* (corresponding to *c'* in the rule) with the property (prescribed by the transformation)

$((sort(a_1) = b_1 \wedge sort(a_2) = b_2) \Rightarrow (sort(a_1+a_2) = merge(b_1, b_2))) \equiv$ **true**

then the application of *recomposition* yields the final result

funct *sort* = (**natsequ** *a*) **natsequ**:
  if $|a| \leq 1$ **then** *a*
  [] $|a| > 1$ **then** *merge*(*sort*(a_1), *sort*(a_2)) **where**
    (**natsequ** a_1, **natsequ** a_2) = **some** (**natsequ** a_1', **natsequ** a_2'):
      $|a_1'| \geq 1 \wedge |a_2'| \geq 1 \wedge a_1'+a_2' = a$ **fi**,

which, depending on the particular form of the function *merge*, comprises well-known algorithms such as 'merge-sort' or 'insertion-sort'.

The derivation above contains an important design decision which for the case $|a| > 1$ led to splitting of *a* into two non-empty sequences. Of course, there are other possibilities, for example

...
[] $|a| > 1$ **then some natsequ** s: $issorted(s) \wedge isperm(s, x+l+r)$ **where**
nat x = **first**a;
(**natsequ** l, **natsequ** r) = **some** (**natsequ** l', **natsequ** r'):
$isperm$(**rest**a, $l'+r'$) $\wedge \forall$ (**nat** y: $y \in l'$): $y \leq x \wedge \forall$ (**nat** y: $y \in r'$): $y > x$ **fi**.

Here, we have (for **nat** x, **natsequ** l, r, b_1, b_2)

$$((sort(l) = b_1 \wedge sort(x) = x \wedge sort(r) = b_2) \Rightarrow (sort(x+l+r) = b_1 + x + b_2)) \equiv \textbf{true}$$

and hence, by application of the *recomposition* rule and subsequent *folding*, we get

funct $sort$ = (**natsequ** a) **natsequ**:
if $|a| \leq 1$ **then** a
[] $|a| > 1$ **then** $sort(l) + x + sort(r)$ **where**
nat x = **first**a;
(**natsequ** l, **natsequ** r) = **some** (**natsequ** l', **natsequ** r'):
$isperm$(**rest**a, $l'+r'$) $\wedge \forall$ (**nat** y: $y \in l'$): $y \leq x \wedge \forall$ (**nat** y: $y \in r'$): $y > x$ **fi**

which is the well-known 'quicksort' algorithm.

5.3.1.3 Preservation of Context Information and Introduction of Invariants

By the catchword 'preservation of context information', we try to capture a phenomenon that mainly appears when working with *embedding* and the *unfold/fold*-strategy. It can already be observed in simple examples as shown below.

Consider, for example, the usual recursive definition of the factorial

funct fac = (**nat** n) **nat**:
if $n = 0$ **then** 1 **else** $n \times fac(n-1)$ **fi**.

For deriving a tail-recursive version, *embedding* can be used:

funct fac = (**nat** n) **nat**:
$fact(n, 1)$ **where**

funct $fact$ = (**nat** n, **nat** m) **nat**:
$m \times fac(n)$.

Then *unfolding* the original definition of *fac* in *fact* and simple manipulations straightforwardly lead to

funct $fact$ = (**nat** n, **nat** m) **nat**:
if $n = 0$ **then** m **else** $m \times n \times fac(n-1)$ **fi**.

Finally, by folding one comes up with

funct $fact$ = (**nat** n, **nat** m) **nat**:
if $n = 0$ **then** m **else** $fact(n-1, m \times n)$ **fi**

which is, of course, quite satisfactory here.

Nevertheless, *folding* caused loss of information – which could be used profitably in less trivial examples – since the recursive version of *fact* no longer mirrors the information

- $m = 1$ (from the original embedding call *fact*(n, 1)) or
- $\exists$ **nat** m': $m = m' \times (n+1)$ (by analyzing the formation of the recursive call).

In other words, after *folding* the information on the "internal structure" of the additional parameter is lost. This information, however, often can be used, later in the development, for improving efficiency.

In order to maintain this information, we just have to add an appropriate assertion to *fact* such that the entire definition reads:

funct *fac* = (**nat** n) **nat**:
 fact(n, 1) **where**

 funct *fact* = (**nat** n, **nat** m: $(m = 1) \vee \exists$ **nat** m': $m = m' \times (n+1)$) **nat**:
  if $n = 0$ **then** m **else** *fact*($m \times n$, $n-1$) **fi**.

This modification exhibits also very clearly what really happened: the domain chosen for the above *embedding* was too "large" in the sense that it contains elements that never will occur as actual arguments in calls of *fact*. On the other hand, the assertion that restricts the domain strongly depends on the development leading to the recursive algorithm. One might think of combining the two steps for achieving a composition and for preserving the context information into one rule. However, we refrained from doing so in order to avoid a much more complicated applicability condition.

Now we focus on the problem of how to construct the respective assertion in the general case. This can be done in two steps:

First, we use the following transformation rule:

- <u>*Preservation of context information*</u>

funct f = (**m** x) **r**:
 $g(x, \mathrm{E})$ **where**
 funct g = (**m** z, **n** y) **r**:
  if $\mathrm{T}(z, y)$ **then** $\mathrm{H}(z, y)$
  elsf $[]_{i=1..n}$ $\mathrm{B}_i(z, y)$ **then** $\mathrm{E}_i(g(\mathrm{K}_{i,1}(z, y)), \ldots, g(\mathrm{K}_{i,ni}(z, y)), z, y)$ **fi**

$\updownarrow$ CONST[E], EQUIV(**m**, =), EQUIV(**n**, =)

funct f = (**m** x) **r**:
 $g'(x, \mathrm{E})$ **where**
 funct g' = (**m** z, **n** y: $(y = \mathrm{E}) \nabla (\exists$ **m** z', **n** y': $\neg\mathrm{T}(z', y') \Delta$
   $\exists_{i=1..n} (\mathrm{B}_i(z', y') \Delta \exists_{j=1..ni}(z, y) = \mathrm{K}_{i,j}(z', y'))))$ **r**:
  if $\mathrm{T}(z, y)$ **then** $\mathrm{H}(z, y)$
  elsf $[]_{i=1..n}$ $\mathrm{B}_i(z, y)$ **then** $\mathrm{E}_i(g'(\mathrm{K}_{i,1}(z, y)), \ldots, g'(\mathrm{K}_{i,ni}(z, y)), z, y)$ **fi**.

Here, the semantic predicate CONST[E} is used to abbreviate the requirement that E is defined and determinate and does not contain free identifiers.

Second, we have to simplify the generated assertion appropriately. For the factorial example the application of the above transformation results in the assertion

$(m = 1) \nabla \exists$ **nat** m', **nat** n': $n' \neq 0 \; \Delta \; (n, m) = (n'-1, m' \times n')$.

From $n' \neq 0 \Delta n = n'-1$ we can conclude $n' = n+1$, and, hence, yield the simplified formula as stated above.

Thus, both steps are part of the more general

> **Strategy**
>
> – Develop a recursive version of an (embedded) function *f*;
> – Apply the rule *preservation of context information* to *f*;
> – Simplify the generated assertion;
> – Use the assertion for further simplifications in the body of *f*.

With more complicated functions, simplifying the assertion may become non-trivial. As an example, we refer to the development of 'Earley's algorithm' [Partsch 84, 86]. Similarly, for certain algorithms, the assertion generated in this particular way may be too weak to allow substantial simplifications. Hence, stronger assertions should be looked for.

The above rule is an instance of an even more general rule for adding arbitrary invariants as assertions. It is easily seen that the assertion introduced by the previous rule indeed fulfils the conditions postulated for Q in the following rule:

- *Invariant-introduction*

funct $f = (\mathbf{m}\ x)\ \mathbf{r}$:
  $g(x, \mathrm{E})$ **where**
  funct $g = (\mathbf{m}\ z, \mathbf{n}\ y)\ \mathbf{r}$:
    if $\mathrm{T}(z, y)$ **then** $\mathrm{H}(z, y)$
    elsf $[]_{i=1..n}\ \mathrm{B}_i(z, y)$ **then** $\mathrm{E}_i(g(\mathrm{K}_{i,1}(z, y)), \ldots, g(\mathrm{K}_{i,ni}(z, y)), z, y)$ **fi**

$\Updownarrow$ $\quad$ $\mathrm{Q}(z, \mathrm{E}) \equiv \mathbf{true}$,
$\quad$ $(\mathrm{Q}(z, y)\ \Delta\ \neg\mathrm{T}(z, y)\ \Delta\ \mathrm{B}_i(z, y)) \equiv \mathbf{true}\ \vdash$
$\quad\quad$ $(\forall_{i=1..ni}\ \mathrm{Q}(\mathrm{K}_{i,j}(z, y))) \equiv \mathbf{true}\ \ (1 \le i \le n)$

funct $f = (\mathbf{m}\ x)\ \mathbf{r}$:
  $g(x, \mathrm{E})$ **where**
  funct $g = (\mathbf{m}\ z, \mathbf{n}\ y\text{: } \mathrm{Q}(z, y))\ \mathbf{r}$:
    if $\mathrm{T}(z, y)$ **then** $\mathrm{H}(z, y)$
    elsf $[]_{i=1..n}\ \mathrm{B}_i(z, y)$ **then** $\mathrm{E}_i(g(\mathrm{K}_{i,1}(z, y)), \ldots, g(\mathrm{K}_{i,ni}(z, y)), z, y)$ **fi**.

Note that the applicability conditions are mainly needed for the downward direction of the rule. In the upward direction, the rule is valid without applicability conditions, provided *f* is defined. This means that, in a situation as described by the output scheme of the above rule, assertions almost always can be omitted.

5.3.1.4 Looping-Preventing Folding

In addition to the fact that valuable context information might get lost in connection with *folding*, it is also known [Kott 78, 82] that *folding* only preserves partial correctness, i.e. that it may introduce non-termination. In principle, there are two possibilities for non-termination of a recursive function: *divergence* and *looping*.

Divergence usually characterizes an operational behaviour where a (recursive) call generates new arguments without ever reaching a "terminal" argument. A typical example is

$f(3)$ **where**
funct f = (**nat** x) **nat**:
  if $x = 0$ **then** 0 **else** $f(x+1)$ **fi**.

By *looping* we characterize a situation where in the course of (recursive) computations a previous (non-terminal) argument appears again and again. A typical example for *looping* is obtained by changing the recursive call $f(x+1)$ from above into $f(x)$.

Any recursive function can be safe-guarded against non-termination by adding an argument to stop the computation if the nesting depth of recursive calls exceeds a certain bound ('depth bound', [Nilsson 82]). However, in general, this way of enforcing termination is not a correct transformation in the sense of Sect. 4.1.

Apart from the way just sketched there is no other way of getting rid of *divergence*. However, there is another, brute-force approach to guarantee the absence of loops in recursive programs. This is to simply keep track of all "previously" considered arguments (using an additional parameter M of an appropriate sort) and thus enforce termination by exclusion of all recursive calls with arguments already in M. (Informally, this idea is used in [Reif, Scherlis 82] as 'coerced termination'.)

For arbitrary functions, the correctness of this latter transformation may still be a problematic issue. This is because it is not generally clear what the result of the respective function should be in case of an enforced termination, due to the large number of possibilities. In the case of predicates, however, there are just two possibilities, and choosing **true** or **false** – depending on the particular predicate – usually will lead to a correct transformation. Therefore, our further considerations will be restricted to predicates.

In transformational program development, loops are frequently introduced in connection with *folding*. Hence, it seems natural to consider *folding* and the prevention of loops simultaneously.

Semantically, *enforced termination* in general means a transition to a 'more defined' function [Manna 74], whereas *folding* implies 'less definedness'. Hence, coupling *folding* and *enforced termination* has to be done in such a way that finally equivalence with the original specification is established.

We can prove the following transformation rule:

- <u>Looping-preventing folding</u>

funct f = (**m** x) **bool**:
  $P(x)$

$$\Big\downarrow \quad \begin{bmatrix} P(x) \equiv (T(x) \vee (\exists_{y \in N} B(x, y) \wedge P(K(x, y)))), \\ \mathsf{DEF}[P(x)], \\ |R(x)| < \infty, \\ RT(x) = \varnothing \vdash P(x) \equiv \mathbf{false} \end{bmatrix}$$

funct f = (**m** x) **bool**:
  $g(x, \varnothing)$ **where**
  funct g = (**m** x, **mset** M) **bool**:
    $x \notin M \wedge (T(x) \vee (\exists_{y \in N} B(x, y) \wedge g(K(x, y), M + x)))$

Syntactic constraints:
DECL[**mset**] = SET(**m**, =),
DECL[**nset**] = SET(**n**, =),
KIND[N] = **nset**

where

$$R(x) =_{def} \begin{cases} \{x\}, & \text{if } T(x), \\ \{x\} \cup \bigcup_{z \in M(x)} R(z), & \text{otherwise} \\ \quad \text{with } M(x) =_{def} & \{K(x, y): \neg T(x) \,\Delta\, \exists_{y \in N} B(x, y)\}, \end{cases}$$

$$RT(x) =_{def} \{\mathbf{m}\ z: z \in R(x) \,\Delta\, T(z)\}.$$

The use of this latter rule can be demonstrated with the "reachability problem" in finite directed graphs (Sect. 3.6.7):

funct *reach* = (**graph** G, **node** x, **node** y: $x, y \in N(G)$) **bool**:
  $\exists$ **nodesequ** p: $p \neq\langle\rangle\ \Delta$
    $(x = \mathbf{first}p \wedge y = \mathbf{last}p \wedge \forall\ (\mathbf{nat}\ i{:}\ 1 \le i < |p|){:}\ e(p[i], p[i+1]) \in E(G))$.

By abstraction, this can be transformed into

funct *reach* = (**graph** G, **node** x, **node** y: $x, y \in N(G)$) **bool**:
  reach'(x) **where**

  funct *reach'* = (**node** z) **bool**:
    $\exists$ **nodesequ** p: $p \neq\langle\rangle\ \Delta$
      $(z = \mathbf{first}p \wedge y = \mathbf{last}p \wedge \forall\ (\mathbf{nat}\ i{:}\ 1 \le i < |p|){:}\ e(p[i], p[i+1]) \in E(G))$.

The function *reach'* obviously fits the input scheme of the above rule. With the choice

node z	for	**m** x,
$(z = y)$	for	$T(x)$,
$\exists$ **node** v: $v \in N(G) \wedge e(z, v) \in E(G)$	for	$\exists_{y \in N} B(x, y)$,
(v, y)	for	$K(x, y)$

the validity of the recursion equation in the first condition of *looping-preventing folding* can be proved. Furthermore, we have

$R(z) \equiv \{$**node** v: $v \in N(G) \wedge \exists$ **nodesequ** p: $p \neq\langle\rangle\ \Delta$
  $(z = \mathbf{first}p \wedge v = \mathbf{last}p \wedge \forall\ (\mathbf{nat}\ i{:}\ 1 \le i < |p|){:}\ e(p[i], p[i+1]) \in E(G))$

such that due to the finiteness of $N(G)$ and $E(G)$, the second and the third condition of the rule are also fulfilled.
Finally,

$RT(z) \equiv \{$**node** v: $v \in R(z) \wedge v = y\}$

and hence

$(RT(z) = \varnothing) \equiv$ **true** $\vdash$
  $(\exists$ **nodesequ** p: $p \neq\langle\rangle\ \Delta$
  $(z = \mathbf{first}p \wedge y = \mathbf{last}p \wedge \forall\ (\mathbf{nat}\ i{:}\ 1 \le i < |p|){:}\ e(p[i], p[i+1]) \in E(G))) \equiv$ **false**,

and the last condition is also fulfilled.

Thus the rule *looping-preventing folding* is applicable and its application (after unfolding *reach'*) results in

funct $reach$ = (**graph** G, **node** x, **node** y: $x, y \in N(G)$) **bool**:
  $reach''(z, \varnothing)$ **where**

  mode nodeset = SET(**node**, =);

  funct $reach''$ = (**node** z, **nodeset** M) **bool**:
    $z \notin M \; \Delta \; ((z = y) \; \nabla$
        $(\exists$ **node** v: $v \in N(G) \; \Delta \; e(z, v) \in E(G)) \; \Delta \; reach''(v, M+z)))$.

Obviously, the above transformation rule becomes considerably simpler for finite domains (where the divergence problem vanishes) as was the case in the above example.

It is furthermore obvious that the rule above also carries over to other types of recursion equations for the characterizing predicate P, such as

- $P(x) \equiv (T(x) \; \nabla \; \exists_{i=1..n} (B_i(x) \; \Delta \; P(K_i(x))))$,
- $P(x, y) \equiv (T(x, y) \; \nabla \; \exists_{i=1..n} (B_i(x) \; \Delta \; P(K_i(x), y)))$, or
- $P(x, y) \equiv (T(x, y) \; \nabla \; \exists_{z \in N} (P(x, z) \; \Delta \; P(z, y)))$.

Applications of these variants, for example to appropriate variants of the "reachability problem", are obvious and left to the interested reader.

As with most of our rules, the rule above may be considered as a representative for a whole class of rules. For the problems in this class, a recursion equation is valid of which the least fixed point is not the one aimed at (see also the discussion of the 'Bellman equations' in [Berghammer 84]).

We have characterized the above way of enforcing termination "brute-force" since it causes obvious inefficiencies due to the additional book-keeping. However, as can be seen from respective examples, this can also be done in quite an economic way: either the additional parameter vanishes anyhow during the subsequent development (as in the development of Earley's recognizer in [Partsch 84]), or one of the original parameters may be used to achieve the same effect (as in the development of the 'Schorr-Waite algorithm' in [Broy, Pepper 82] or the 'path algorithm' in [Reif, Scherlis 82]).

In some sense, *looping-preventing folding* may also be considered as a "condensed redevelopment": the first applicability condition reflects a previous development leading from an embedded specification to a stage where *folding* could be a next step; the remaining applicability conditions "correct" the embedding and thus guarantee the correctness of *folding* for the "redeveloped" version.

Of course, there may be situations where both effects, *preservation of context information* and *looping-preventing folding,* are aimed at. In this case, of course, *looping-preventing folding* has to be done first.

5.3.2 Compact Rules for Particular Specification Constructs

The strategy and the rules introduced in the previous section may be used not only in the development of concrete programs, but also for deriving new compact rules –

which, however, requires some additional information about the specification to be dealt with.

As these compact rules are but condensed forms of schematic developments, it is obvious that all applicability conditions (from these developments) will reappear in the compact rules. In addition to the large number of conditions in the compact rules, intuition and experience are required from the developer in satisfying each of these conditions. Hence, the use of these compact rules should be left to the experienced developer. Learners should use the simple rules along the lines of the strategy introduced in the previous subsection.

5.3.2.1 Operationalization of a Choice

Given a descriptive specification of the form

funct f = (**m** x) **n**:
  some n y: R(x, y),

intuitively, any solution aims at finding an object y of kind **n** that fulfils the postulated predicate.

In principle, there are two ways of finding such a y: one possibility is to search through the domain **m** (starting from the given argument x) until an object of kind **m** is found from which the result aimed at can easily be computed. The other possibility is to search through the range **n**, starting from a distinguished element of kind **n**, by "approximating" the desired result. Both ways will be dealt with in the sequel.

The two ways of "finding a solution" for a descriptive specification of the above form also can be found in Smith's work on 'algorithm design' [Smith 85a, 85b, 86, 87, 88]. In [Smith, Lowry 89], they are called 'problem reduction' and 'local search', respectively. Smith further distinguishes particular instances of the 'problem reduction' idea such as 'complementation sieves', 'divide-and-conquer', 'global search', or 'branch-and-bound'. Such a more detailed treatment, however, requires additional knowledge about properties of the data types involved or the form of the predicate R. In our setting, specific rules for these particular instances can be derived by combining the rules given below with appropriate other rules.

In either case, in order to be able to refer to the original specification by name, we start our development from a new definition

funct f' = (**m** x) **n**:
  some n y: R(x, y),

which, obviously, is equivalent to the original one.

In following the first way, we start aiming at finding a boolean expression B such that (for arbitrary **m** x)

(*) $\mathrm{B}(x) \equiv \textbf{true} \vdash \mathrm{R}(x, \mathrm{H}(x)) \equiv \textbf{true}$,

holds, i.e. in case B(x) holds, H(x) provides a possible solution.

Now, *case introduction* (with $\mathrm{B}(x) \vee \neg\mathrm{B}(x)$) leads to

if B(x) **then some n** y: R(x, y) **else some n** y: R(x, y) **fi**,

where, according to the condition on B the **then** branch immediately can be simplified to H(x).

If we have additionally (for arbitrary **m** x, **n** y)

(**) $\quad B(x) \equiv \textbf{false} \vdash R(x, y) \equiv R(K(x), y)$

also the **else** branch can be transformed to

some n y: $R(K(x), y)$.

Now, folding is possible and yields immediately

funct f' = (**m** x) **n**:
  if $B(x)$ **then** $H(x)$ **else** $f'(K(x))$ **fi**,

if also termination of f' can be proved. To this end we require, furthermore,

(***) $\quad \mathrm{DEF}[f(x)] \Leftrightarrow \mathrm{DEF}[f'(x)]$.

Hence we have established the rule

• <u>*Operationalization of a choice I*</u>

E **where**
funct f = (**m** x) **n**:
  some n y: $R(x, y)$

$$\left[\begin{array}{l} B(x) \equiv \textbf{true} \vdash R(x, H(x)) \equiv \textbf{true}, \\ B(x) \equiv \textbf{false} \vdash R(x, y) \equiv R(K(x), y), \\ \mathrm{DEF}[f(x)] \Leftrightarrow \mathrm{DEF}[f'(x)] \end{array}\right.$$

E[f' **for** f] **where**
funct f' = (**m** x) **n**:
  if $B(x)$ **then** $H(x)$ **else** $f'(K(x))$ **fi**.

Note, that the condition for *case introduction* needs not to be required explicitly, as it follows immediately from the last condition.

For an example of how to use this rule, consider again the "minimum element problem" (see also Sect. 5.3.1.1):

funct *minel* = (**natsequ** s: $s \neq$<>) **nat**:
  minel'(**first**s, **rest**s) **where**

  funct *minel'* = (**nat** z, **natsequ** s) **nat**:
    some nat m: $(m = z \vee m \in s) \,\Delta\, m \le z \,\Delta\, (\forall$ **nat** n: $n \in s \Rightarrow m \le n)$.

Matching *minel'* with the input scheme of the rule yields the instance

(**nat**, **natsequ**)	for	**m**
(z, s)	for	x
nat	for	**n**
m	for	y, and
$(m = z \vee m \in s) \,\Delta\, m \le z \,\Delta\, (\forall$ **nat** n: $n \in s \Rightarrow m \le n)$	for	$R(x, y)$.

If we additionally choose

(s =<>)	for	$B(x)$
z	for	$H(x)$
(*min*(z, **first**s), **rest**s)	for	$K(x)$

we can prove

– $(s = \langle\rangle) \equiv \mathbf{true} \vdash (z = z \vee z \in s) \,\Delta\, z \le z \,\Delta\, (\forall\, \mathbf{nat}\ n: n \in s \Rightarrow z \le n) \equiv \mathbf{true}$;

– $(s = \langle\rangle) \equiv \mathbf{false} \vdash$
$(m = z \vee m \in s) \,\Delta\, m \le z \,\Delta\, (\forall\, \mathbf{nat}\ n: n \in s \Rightarrow m \le n) \equiv$
$(m = min(z, \mathbf{first}s) \vee m \in \mathbf{rest}s) \,\Delta\, m \le min(z, \mathbf{first}s) \,\Delta$
$(\forall\, \mathbf{nat}\ n: n \in \mathbf{rest}s \Rightarrow m \le n)$.

Since, furthermore, the definedness condition is fulfilled as well, the rule *operationalization of a choice I* is applicable and yields

funct *minel''* = (**nat** *z*, **natsequ** *s*) **nat**:
  if *s* =<> **then** *z* **else** *minel''*(*min*(*z*, **first***s*), **rest***s*) **fi**.

For a lot of cases, however, (**) will be hard to establish. Therefore, we aim at weaker conditions that allow a similar kind of reasoning. The basic idea here is to use the *recomposition* technique introduced in the previous subsection. More precisely, if

$B(x) \equiv \mathbf{false} \vdash (R(d_2(x), z) \Rightarrow R(x, c'(d_1(x), z))) \equiv \mathbf{true}$

and

$(\neg B(x) \,\Delta\, \exists\, \mathbf{n}\ y: R(x, y)) \equiv \mathbf{true} \vdash (\exists\, \mathbf{n}\ z: R(d_2(x), z)) \equiv \mathbf{true}$

hold instead of (**), we get, in the **else** branch, by the (appropriate variant of the) rule *recomposition*

$c'(d_1(x), \mathbf{some}\ \mathbf{n}\ y: R(d_2(x), y))$

such that – provided (***) holds, too – folding yields

funct *f'* = (**m** *x*) **n**:
  if B(*x*) **then** H(*x*) **else** $c'(d_1(x), f'(d_2(x)))$ **fi**.

Again, we have proved a transformation rule, viz.

• <u>*Operationalization of a choice II*</u>

E **where**
funct *f* = (**m** *x*) **n**:
  some n *y*: R(*x*, *y*)

↓
$B(x) \equiv \mathbf{true} \vdash R(x, H(x)) \equiv \mathbf{true}$,
$B(x) \equiv \mathbf{false} \vdash (R(d_2(x), z) \Rightarrow R(x, c'(d_1(x), z))) \equiv \mathbf{true}$,
$(\neg B(x) \,\Delta\, \exists\, \mathbf{n}\ y: R(x, y)) \equiv \mathbf{true} \vdash (\exists\, \mathbf{n}\ z: R(d_2(x), z)) \equiv \mathbf{true}$,
DEF[*f*(*x*)] ⇔ DEF[*f'*(*x*)]

E[*f'* **for** *f*] **where**
funct *f'* = (**m** *x*) **n**:
  if B(*x*) **then** H(*x*) **else** $c'(d_1(x), f'(d_2(x)))$ **fi**.

Both rules given above reflect a linear search on **m** (where the ordering is induced by K and d_2, respectively). Further variants, for example leading to tree-like recursions (that reflect non-linear searches on **m**) can be derived using other particular variants of the *recomposition* transformation. Note that according to the remarks at the beginning of Chap. 5, initial specifications with explicit assertions are captured by these rules, too.

As an example of how to use this latter rule, consider again the "minimum element problem":

funct *minel* = (**natsequ** *s*: *s* ≠<>) **nat**:
minel'(**first***s*, **rest***s*) **where**

funct *minel'* = (**nat** *z*, **natsequ** *s*) **nat**:
some nat *m*: $(m = z \vee m \in s) \Delta m \leq z \Delta (\forall$ **nat** $n: n \in s \Rightarrow m \leq n)$.

Matching the input schema of the rule yields the same instance as above. If we additionally choose

(*s* =<>)	for	B(*x*)
z	for	H(*x*)
z	for	$d_1(x)$
(**first***s*, **rest***s*)	for	$d_2(x)$
min	for	*c'*

we can now prove (for arbitrary *z*)

- (*s* =<>) ≡ **true** ⊢ $((z = z \vee z \in s) \Delta z \leq z \Delta (\forall$ **nat** $n{:}n \in s \Rightarrow z \leq n)) \equiv$ **true**;
- (*s* =<>) ≡ **false** ⊢
  $((m =$ **first***s* $\vee m \in$ **rest***s*$) \Delta m \leq$ **first***s* $\Delta (\forall$ **nat** $n: n \in$ **rest***s* $\Rightarrow m \leq n)) \Rightarrow$
  $((min(z, m) = z \vee min(z, m) \in s) \Delta min(z, m) \leq z \Delta$
  $(\forall$ **nat** $n: n \in s \Rightarrow min(z, m) \leq n)) \equiv$ **true**.

Since the remaining conditions are also fulfilled, the rule *operationalization of a choice II* is applicable and yields

funct *minel''* = (**nat** *z*, **natsequ** *s*) **nat**:
if *s* =<> **then** *z* **else** *min*(*z*, *minel''*(**first***s*, **rest***s*)) **fi**.

In order to exploit the second idea (of finding an operational solution for a choice expression) that was sketched in the beginning of this subsection, we start with an embedding (Sect. 5.2)

funct *f* = (**m** *x*) **n**:
f'(*x*, E) **where**

funct *f'* = (**m** *x*, **n** *z*) **n**:
some n *y*: Q(*x*, *y*, *z*)

for which

Q(*x*, *y*, E) ≡ **true** ⊢ R(*x*, *y*) ≡ **true**, and
(∃ **n** *y*: R(*x*, *y*)) ≡ **true** ⊢ (∃ **n** *y*: Q(*x*, *y*, E)) ≡ **true**

have to be ensured.

A development of *f'*, analogous to the one above, then straightforwardly leads to the rule

- <u>*Operationalization of a choice III*</u>

funct f = (**m** x) **n**:
  some n y: $R(x, y)$

$$\Big\downarrow \quad \left[\begin{array}{l} Q(x, y, E) \equiv \mathbf{true} \vdash R(x, y) \equiv \mathbf{true}, \\ B(x, z) \equiv \mathbf{true} \vdash Q(x, H(x, z), z) \equiv \mathbf{true}, \\ B(x, z) \equiv \mathbf{false} \vdash Q(x, y, z) \equiv Q(x, y, K(x, z)), \\ \mathsf{DEF}[f(x)] \Leftrightarrow \mathsf{DEF}[f'(x, E)] \end{array}\right.$$

funct f = (**m** x) **n**:
  $f'(x, E)$ **where**
  funct f' = (**m** x, **n** z) **n**:
    if $B(x, z)$ **then** $H(x, z)$ **else** $f'(x, K(x, z))$ **fi**.

In this rule, the second condition for the embedding (as postulated above) is captured by the condition on the definedness.

If we use an embedding that introduces an invariant assertion for the auxiliary function f' (Sect. 5.2), we get the variant

- **funct** f = (**m** x) **n**:
  some n y: $R(x, y)$

$$\Big\downarrow \quad \left[\begin{array}{l} P(x, E) \equiv \mathbf{true}, \\ (P(x, z) \,\Delta\, \neg B(x, z)) \equiv \mathbf{true} \vdash P(x, K(x, z)) \equiv \mathbf{true}, \\ (P(x, z) \,\Delta\, B(x, z)) \equiv \mathbf{true} \vdash R(x, H(x, z)) \equiv \mathbf{true}, \\ \mathsf{DEF}[f(x)] \Leftrightarrow \mathsf{DEF}[f'(x, E)] \end{array}\right.$$

funct f = (**m** x) **n**:
  $f'(x, E)$ **where**
  funct f' = (**m** x, **n** z: $P(x, z)$) **n**:
    if $B(x, z)$ **then** $H(x, z)$ **else** $f'(x, K(x, z))$ **fi**.

Note here that the required definedness condition covers the conditions necessary for the embedding, so that the conditions

$P(x, E) \equiv$ **true**, and
$(P(x, z) \,\Delta\, \neg B(x, z)) \equiv$ **true** $\vdash P(x, K(x, z)) \equiv$ **true**

such that the formulation of the rule could be shortened accordingly. The redundant version of the rule, however, has the advantage that it provides more guidance for finding the new parts that are introduced within the rule. Therefore we prefer to use this redundant version.

The use of this latter transformation can be demonstrated with the following example:

Given a non-empty sequence s of natural numbers, find the index of some minimal element in s.

A descriptive specification of this problem is straightforward:

funct *minindex* = (**natsequ** s: $s \neq$ <>) **nat**:
  some nat i: $1 \le i \le |s| \,\Delta\, (\forall$ (**nat** j: $1 \le j \le |s|$): $s[j] \ge s[i])$.

Obviously, for

$$\mathrm{P}(s, i, j) =_{\mathrm{def}} (s \neq \langle\rangle \;\Delta\; 1 \le i \le j \le |s| \;\Delta\; (\forall\, (\mathbf{nat}\ k\colon 1 \le k \le j)\colon s[k] \ge s[i]))$$

we have for all sequences s with $s \neq \langle\rangle$

- $\mathrm{P}(s, 1, 1) \equiv \mathbf{true}$;
- $(\mathrm{P}(s, i, j) \;\Delta\; j = |s|) \equiv \mathbf{true} \vdash (1 \le i \le |s| \;\Delta\; \forall\, (\mathbf{nat}\ k\colon 1 \le k \le |s|)\colon s[k] \ge s[i]) \equiv \mathbf{true}$;
- $(\mathrm{P}(s, i, j) \;\Delta\; j \neq |s|) \equiv \mathbf{true} \vdash \mathrm{P}(new(s, i, j)) \equiv \mathbf{true}$, where
  $new(s, i, j) =_{\mathrm{def}}$ **if** $s[j] \ge s[i]$ **then** $(s, i, j+1)$ [] $s[j] \le s[i]$ **then** $(s, j, j+1)$ **fi**.

Hence, the above rule can be applied (where proving the definedness condition is straightforward) and yields

```
funct minindex = (natsequ s: s ≠ <>) nat:
   mini(s, 1, 1) where

   funct mini= (natsequ s, nat i, nat j:
                     (s ≠<> Δ 1≤i≤j≤|s| Δ ∀ (nat k: 1≤k≤j): s[k] ≥ s[i])) nat:
      if j = |s| then i else  if s[j] ≥ s[i] then mini(s, i, j+1)
                              [] s[j] ≤ s[i] then mini(s, j, j+1) fi fi.
```

Of course, both ways of finding an operational solution for a choice can be combined. The resulting rules, however, are fairly complicated with a lot of applicability conditions.

5.3.2.2 Operationalization of Quantifiers

Similarly to choices, existential quantifiers in descriptive specifications can be dealt with. Assuming a descriptive specification of the form

```
funct p = (m x) bool:
   ∃ n y: R(x, y)
```

again, the two principle ways of finding an answer as illustrated in the beginning of Sect. 5.3.2.1 can be followed.

In order to find a solution by exploring the domain **m** similar reasoning leads to rules such as

- <u>*Operationalization of an existential quantifier I*</u>

```
E where
funct p = (m x) bool:
   ∃ n y: R(x, y)
        |        ┌ T(x) ≡ true  ⊢  (∃ n y: R(x, y)) ⊒ H(x),
   ─────┼────────┤ T(x) ≡ false ⊢  R(x, y) ≡ R(K(x), y),
        ▼        └ DEF[p(x)]  ⇔  DEF[p'(x)]
E[p' for p] where
funct p' = (m x) bool:
   (T(x) Δ H(x)) ∇ (¬T(x) Δ p'(K(x)))
```

(where $\sqsupseteq$ denotes the descendance relation of Sect. 4.2.2) or

- <u>*Operationalization of an existential quantifier II*</u>

  E **where**
  funct p = (**m** x) **bool**:
  $\exists$ **n** y: R(x, y)

  $\left[\begin{array}{l} T(x) \equiv \textbf{true} \vdash (\exists\, \mathbf{n}\, y: R(x, y)) \supseteq H(x), \\ T(x) \equiv \textbf{false} \vdash \\ (\exists\, \mathbf{n}\, y: R(x, y)) \equiv c'(x, \exists\, \mathbf{n}\, z: R(d_2(x), z)), \\ \mathsf{DEF}[p(x)] \Leftrightarrow \mathsf{DEF}[p'(x)] \end{array}\right.$

  E[p' **for** p] **where**
  funct p' = (**m** x) **bool**:
  $(T(x) \,\Delta\, H(x)) \,\nabla\, (\neg T(x) \,\Delta\, c'(x, p'(d_2(x))))$.

  Again, this latter rule comprises lots of variants, such as

- E **where**
  funct p = (**m** x) **bool**:
  $\exists$ **n** y: R(x, y)

  $\left[\begin{array}{l} T(x) \equiv \textbf{true} \vdash (\exists\, \mathbf{n}\, y: R(x, y)) \supseteq H(x), \\ T(x) \equiv \textbf{false} \vdash \\ \quad (\exists\, \mathbf{n}\, y: R(x, y)) \equiv (\exists_{i=1..n} B_i(x) \,\Delta \exists\, \mathbf{n}\, y: R(K_i(x), y)), \\ \mathsf{DEF}[p(x)] \Leftrightarrow \mathsf{DEF}[p'(x)] \end{array}\right.$

  E[p' **for** p] **where**
  funct p' = (**m** x) **bool**:
  $(T(x) \,\Delta\, H(x)) \,\nabla\, (\neg T(x) \,\Delta\, \exists_{i=1..n} B_i(x) \,\Delta\, p'(K_i(x)))$.

  As an example of how to use these rules, consider the problem

  Test, whether some natural number x occurs in a sequence of natural numbers.

A descriptive specification of this problem is straightforward:

funct *isin* = (**nat** x, **natsequ** s) **bool**:
$\exists$ **nat** i: $1 \le i \le |s| \,\Delta\, s[i] = x$.

Obviously, we have

- $(s = \langle\rangle \,\nabla\, \textbf{first}\, s = x) \equiv \textbf{true} \vdash (\exists\, \textbf{nat}\, i: 1 \le i \le |s| \,\Delta\, s[i] = x) \equiv (s \ne \langle\rangle)$;
- $(s = \langle\rangle \,\nabla\, \textbf{first}\, s = x) \equiv \textbf{false} \vdash$
  $(\exists\, \textbf{nat}\, i: 1 \le i \le |s| \,\Delta\, s[i] = x) \equiv (\exists\, \textbf{nat}\, i: 1 \le i \le |\textbf{rest}\, s| \,\Delta\, (\textbf{rest}\, s)[i] = x)$.

Hence, the rule *operationalization of an existential quantifier I* is applicable (definedness is obvious) and yields immediately

funct *isin'* = (**nat** x, **natsequ** s) **bool**:
$((s = \langle\rangle \,\nabla\, \textbf{first}\, s = x) \,\Delta\, s \ne \langle\rangle) \,\nabla\, (s \ne \langle\rangle \,\Delta\, \textbf{first}\, s \ne x \,\Delta\, isin'(x, \textbf{rest}\, s))$

which, using the definitional transformations for the sequential boolean operators (Sect. 4.4.1), can be further transformed into

funct *isin'* = (**nat** x, **natsequ** s) **bool**:
if $s = \langle\rangle$ **then false**
elsf first$s = x$ **then true else** *isin'*(x, **rest**s) **fi**.

As in the previous subsection, a solution can also be found by "approximating" the result starting from some distinguished element in **n**. Analogously to the reasoning in case of a choice, this leads to rules such as,

- *Operationalization of an existential quantifier III*

$\textbf{funct}\ p = (\textbf{m}\ x)\ \textbf{bool}:$
$\quad \exists\, \textbf{n}\ y\text{: } \mathrm{R}(x, y)$

$$\left[\begin{array}{l} \mathrm{P}(x, \mathrm{E}) \equiv \textbf{true}, \\ (\mathrm{P}(x, z)\ \Delta\ \neg\mathrm{T}(x, z)) \equiv \textbf{true} \vdash \mathrm{P}(x, \mathrm{K}(x, z)) \equiv \textbf{true}, \\ (\mathrm{P}(x, z)\ \Delta\ \mathrm{T}(x, z)) \equiv \textbf{true} \vdash (\exists\, \textbf{n}\ y\text{: } \mathrm{R}(x, y)) \sqsupseteq \mathrm{H}(x, z), \\ \mathsf{DEF}[p(x)] \Leftrightarrow \mathsf{DEF}[p'(x, \mathrm{E})] \end{array}\right.$$

$\textbf{funct}\ p = (\textbf{m}\ x)\ \textbf{bool}:$
$\quad p'(x, \mathrm{E})\ \textbf{where}$
$\quad \textbf{funct}\ p' = (\textbf{m}\ x, \textbf{n}\ z\text{: } \mathrm{P}(x, z))\ \textbf{bool}:$
$\qquad (\mathrm{T}(x, z)\ \Delta\ \mathrm{H}(x, z))\ \nabla\ (\neg\mathrm{T}(x, z)\ \Delta\ p'(x, \mathrm{K}(x, z))).$

In order to demonstrate the use of this last rule, we consider the problem

Test, whether some non-empty sequence of natural numbers contains a certain element which is smaller than a given natural number x.

Again, a descriptive specification of this problem is straightforward:

$\textbf{funct}\ \mathit{isless} = (\textbf{nat}\ x, \textbf{natsequ}\ s\text{: } s \neq \langle\rangle)\ \textbf{bool}:$
$\quad \exists\, \textbf{nat}\ i\text{: } 1 \leq i \leq |s|\ \Delta\ s[i] < x.$

Obviously, for any sequence s with $s \neq \langle\rangle$ and

$$\mathrm{P}(x, s, i) =_{\mathrm{def}} s \neq \langle\rangle\ \Delta\ \forall\, (\textbf{nat}\ k\text{: } 1 \leq k < i)\text{: } s[k] \geq x$$

we have

- $\mathrm{P}(x, s, 1) \equiv \textbf{true}$;
- $(\mathrm{P}(x, s, i)\ \Delta\ (i > |s|\ \nabla\ s[i] < x)) \equiv \textbf{true} \vdash$
  $(\exists\, (\textbf{nat}\ k\text{: } 1 \leq k \leq |s|)\text{: } s[k] < x) \equiv (i \leq |s|)$;
- $(\mathrm{P}(x, s, i)\ \Delta\ i \leq |s|\ \Delta\ s[i] \geq x) \equiv \textbf{true} \vdash \mathrm{P}(x, s, i+1) \equiv \textbf{true}.$

Hence, the rule *operationalization of an existential quantifier III* is applicable (definedness is obvious) and yields

$\textbf{funct}\ \mathit{isless} = (\textbf{nat}\ x, \textbf{natsequ}\ s\text{: } s \neq \langle\rangle)\ \textbf{bool}:$
$\quad \mathit{isless}'(x, s, 1)\ \textbf{where}$

$\quad \textbf{funct}\ \mathit{isless}' = (\textbf{nat}\ x, \textbf{natsequ}\ s, \textbf{nat}\ i\text{:}$
$\qquad\qquad s \neq \langle\rangle\ \Delta\ (\forall\, (\textbf{nat}\ k\text{: } 1 \leq k < i)\text{: } s[k] \geq x))\ \textbf{bool}:$
$\quad ((i > |s|\ \nabla\ s[i] < x)\ \Delta\ i \leq |s|)\ \nabla\ (i \leq |s|\ \Delta\ s[i] \geq x\ \Delta\ \mathit{isless}'(x, s, i+1))$

which, again, using the definitional transformations for the sequential boolean operators, can be transformed further into

$\textbf{funct}\ \mathit{isless}' = (\textbf{nat}\ x, \textbf{natsequ}\ s, \textbf{nat}\ i\text{:}$
$\qquad\qquad s \neq \langle\rangle\ \Delta\ (\forall\, (\textbf{nat}\ k\text{: } 1 \leq k < i)\text{: } s[k] \geq x))\ \textbf{bool}:$
$\quad \textbf{if}\ i > |s|\ \textbf{then}\ \textbf{false}\ \textbf{elsf}\ s[i] < x\ \textbf{then}\ \textbf{true}\ \textbf{else}\ \mathit{isless}'(x, s, i+1)\ \textbf{fi}.$

Both possibilities discussed above involve a search, either on **m** or **n**, based on a suitable ordering. Sometimes, however, such an ordering is difficult to find or does not even exist. In such a case, the only way of finding a solution to the specified problem is by an exhaustive search. In this case we can use the rule

- *Operationalization of an existential quantifier by exhaustion*

funct p = (**m** x) **bool**:
  ∃ **n** y: R(x, y)

⟶ [DEF[R(x, y)]; **n** finite]

funct p = (**m** x) **bool**:
  p'({**n** y: **true**}) **where**
  funct p' = (**nset** N) **bool**:
    $N \neq \varnothing$ Δ (R(x, y) ∇ $p'(N - y)$ **where n** $y = arb(N)$)
  Syntactic constraints:
    DECL[**nset**] = **mode nset** = SET(**n**, =)

where

funct arb = (**mset** M: $M \neq \varnothing$) **m**: **some m** m: $m \in M$.

Exhaustion is also a general way of making a universal quantifier operational. A respective rule is immediately obtained from the above rule, elementary rules about sequential boolean operators, and the relation between existential and universal quantification (Sect. 4.4.2):

- *Operationalization of a universal quantifier by exhaustion*

funct p = (**m** x) **bool**:
  ∀ **n** y: R(x, y)

⟶ [DEF[R(x, y)]; **n** finite]

funct p = (**m** x) **bool**:
  p'({**n** y: **true**}) **where**
  funct p' = (**nset** N) **bool**:
    $N = \varnothing$ ∇ (R(x, y) Δ $p'(N - y)$ **where n** $y = arb(N)$)
  Syntactic constraints:
    DECL[**nset**] = **mode nset** = SET(**n**, =).

5.3.3 Compact Rules for Particular Data Types

Apart from being used in the development of concrete algorithms, the fundamental rules *case introduction* and *recomposition* (from Sect. 5.3.1) may also be profitably used in deriving new rules, as has been demonstrated in the previous section. Along the same lines, we will derive some rules for particular data types in this section. Concrete rules will be given for (finite) sets which will also play an important role in some of the later developments. Analogous rules for other basic data types such as sequences, bags, trees, or maps can be derived by similar reasoning and are left to the interested reader.

5.3.3.1 Computing Qualifiers for Finite Sets

A large class of problems for (finite) sets requires the computation of a qualifier, such as ∀, ∃, **some**, **that**, or {_}. Formally, this class is defined by

mode mset = ESET(**m**, =);
funct *test-qu*$_Q$ = (**mset** *M*) $\mathbf{r}_Q$:
  Q **n** *x*: P(*M*, *x*)

where

- P is the "qualifying predicate" for which DEF[P(*M*, *x*)] is assumed (for all **mset** *M*, **n** *x*),
- Q stands for some qualifier such as ∀, ∃, **some**, **that**, {_}, and
- $\mathbf{r}_Q$ denotes the "range" of the qualifier, i.e.
  - **bool** for ∀ and ∃,
  - **n** for **some** and **that**, and
  - **nset** for {_}, where **mode nset** = ESET(**n**, =).

Note that in case of Q standing for a set comprehension:

funct *test-qu*$_Q$ = (**mset** *M*) **nset**:
  {**n** *x*: P(*M*, *x*)},

context-correctness requires that

{**n** *x*: P(*M*, *x*)}

has to be of kind **mset**, which in turn means that, according to the definition of SET,

|{**n** *x*: P(*M*, *x*)}| < ∞

has to hold.

For this class of rules we have the transformation rule

- <u>*Computing qualifiers for a finite set*</u>

funct *test-qu*$_Q$ = (**mset** *M*) $\mathbf{r}_Q$:
  Q **n** *x*: P(*M*, *x*)

↓ [$(n \geq 2 \wedge \bigcup_{i=1..n} M_i = M \wedge \forall_{i=1..n} |M_i| < |M|) \equiv$ **true** ⊢
  Q**n** *x*: $P(\bigcup_{i=1..n} M_i, x) \supseteq c'(test\text{-}qu_Q(M_1), ..., test\text{-}qu_Q(M_n))$

funct *test-qu*$_Q$ = (**mset** *M*) $\mathbf{r}_Q$:
  if *M* = ∅ **then** Q **n** *x*: P(∅, *x*)
  elsf |*M*| = 1 **then** Q **n** *x*: P(*M*, *x*)
    else $c'(test\text{-}qu_Q(M_1), ..., test\text{-}qu_Q(M_n))$ **where**
      (**mset** M_1, ..., **mset** M_n) = **some** (**mset** M_1', ..., **mset** M_n'):
        $\bigcup_{i=1..n} M_i' = M \wedge \forall_{i=1..n} |M_i'| < |M|$ **fi**

<u>**Syntactic constraints:**</u>
KIND[*c'*] = **funct** $(\mathbf{r}_Q{}^n)$ $\mathbf{r}_Q$,
NOTOCCURS[*test-qu*$_Q$ **in** *c'*],
DECL[**mset**] = **mode mset** = ESET(**m**, =).

Note, again, that in case of a set comprehension, the general assumption about context-correctness implies finiteness of the sets involved, as **mset** is the mode of finite sets.

Obviously, a similar rule for, say, sequences (instead of sets) can be proved, where simply set union has to be substituted by sequence concatenation.

The above rule scheme comprises a large number of practically useful instances that result from specializing the qualifier, the predicate, or the decomposition of M. Typical examples, where the particular output schemes and syntactic constraints result from simplifying the general case, are:

- **funct** *test-ex* = (**mset** M) **bool**:
  $\exists$ **m** x: $(x \in M \Delta \mathrm{P}(x))$

  ↓

  funct *test-ex* = (**mset** M) **bool**:
  if $M = \varnothing$ **then false else** $\mathrm{P}(m) \vee$ *test-ex*$(M - m)$ **where m** m = *arb*(M) **fi**,

  Syntactic constraints:
  DECL[**mset**] = **mode mset** = SET(**m**, =),

- **funct** *gen* = (**mset** M) **nset**:
  $\{$**n** y: $\exists$ **m** x: $x \in M \Delta \mathrm{Q}(x, y)\}$

  ↓

  funct *gen* = (**mset** M) **nset**:
  if $M = \varnothing$ **then** $\varnothing$ **else** $\{$**n** y: $\mathrm{Q}(m, y)\} \cup$ *gen*$(M - m)$ **where m** m = *arb*(M) **fi**

  Syntactic constraints:
  DECL[**mset**] = **mode mset** = SET(**m**, =),
  DECL[**nset**] = **mode nset** = ESET(**n**, =),

but also

- **funct** *gen* = (**mset** M) **nset**:
  some nset S: $S = \{$**n** y: $\exists$ **m** x: $x \in M \Delta \mathrm{Q}(x, y)\}$

  ↓

  funct *gen* = (**mset** M) **nset**:
  if $M = \varnothing$ **then** $\varnothing$
  elsf $|M| = 1$ **then** $\{$**n** y: $\mathrm{Q}(m, y)\}$ **where m** m = *arb*(M)
  else *gen*$(M_1) \cup$ *gen*(M_2) **where**
  mset M_1, **mset** M_2 = **some mset** M_1', **mset** M_2':
  $M_1' \cup M_2' = M \wedge |M_1'| < |M| \wedge |M_2'| < |M|$ **fi**

  Syntactic constraints:
  DECL[**mset**] = **mode mset** = ESET(**m**, =),
  DECL[**nset**] = **mode nset** = ESET(**n**, =).

Note that the output schemes of the first two rules could be further improved (tail recursion rather than linear recursion) by appropriate embeddings (Sect. 5.2).

5.3.3.2 Computing Closures of Finite Sets

In connection with sets, many problems require computing the closure of a given set with respect to some operation on its elements.

Formally, for

mode mset = ESET(**m**, =),

and an operation f of kind **funct (mset) mset**, computing the closure (with respect to f) can be defined by

> **funct** *cl* = (**mset** M) **mset**:
> **some mset** R: $R = (M \cup f(R))$.

By an *embedding* (Sect. 5.2), this can be transformed into

> **funct** *cl* = (**mset** M) **mset**:
> *close*(∅, M) **where**
>
> **funct** *close* = (**mset** N, **mset** M) **mset**:
> $N \cup$ **some mset** R: $R = (M \cup (f(R) \setminus N))$.

(Note that the function *close* always yields a defined value if f is defined and **m** is finite or a finite submode of some (non-finite) mode, see also [Berghammer 84].)

Then we can use the transformation rule

- <u>*Closure of a finite set*</u>

> **funct** *close* = (**mset** N, **mset** M) **mset**:
> $N \cup$ **some mset** R: $R = (M \cup (f(R) \setminus N))$
>
> ↓ [$N \supseteq f(\varnothing)$, **m** finite
>
> **funct** *close* = (**mset** N, **mset** M) **mset**:
> **if** $M = \varnothing$ **then** N **else** *close*($N \cup M$, $f(M) \setminus (N \cup M)$) **fi**
>
> <u>**Syntactic constraints:**</u>
> KIND[f] = **funct (mset) mset**,
> DECL[**mset**] = **mode mset** = ESET(**m**, =).

By our above considerations on the definedness of *close*, it is obvious that *close* computes the least set with the desired property – which usually is the set one is interested in. For finite **m** an analogous algorithm for computing the greatest set could be derived by starting with the set of all elements of **m** and iterating downwards.

As an example of the use of this transformation, we consider the "reachability problem" in finite, directed graphs. Let a (finite) directed graph G be defined as in Sect. 3.3.5. Then for a given graph G, the set of nodes that are reachable from a given subset $M \subseteq N(G)$ is defined by

> **funct** *reachables* = (**graph** G, **nodeset** M: $M \subseteq N(G)$) **nodeset**:
> **some nodeset** R: $R = M \cup succs(R)$ **where**
>
> **funct** *succs* = (**nodeset** M: $M \subseteq N(G)$) **nodeset**:
> {**node** y: ∃ **node** x: $x \in M \wedge e(x, y) \in E(G)$}.

Using an *embedding* as in our general considerations, we get

funct *reachables* = (**graph** G, **nodeset** M: $M \subseteq N(G)$) **nodeset**:
  rea($\varnothing$, M) **where**

  funct *rea* = (**nodeset** N, **nodeset** M: $M \subseteq N(G)$) **nodeset**:
    $N \cup$ **some nodeset** R: $R = M \cup (succs(R) \setminus N)$.

Hence, by applying our last transformation, we get

funct *rea* = (**nodeset** N, **nodeset** M: $M \subseteq N(G)$) **nodeset**:
  if $M = \varnothing$ **then** N **else** $rea(N \cup M, succs(M) \setminus (N \cup M))$ **fi**

or, simplified using the definition of *succs*,

funct *rea* = (**nodeset** N, **nodeset** M: $M \subseteq N(G)$) **nodeset**:
  if $M = \varnothing$ **then** N
    else $rea(N \cup M$, {**node** y: $y \notin N \cup M \,\Delta$
      $\exists$ **node** x: $x \in M \,\Delta\, e(x, y) \in E(G)$}) **fi**

which can be further developed into one of the well-known efficient algorithms (see again [Berghammer 84] or [Reif, Scherlis 82] for respective transformational developments).

Of course, variants of the rule above hold also for operations f with different functionalities, for example,

KIND[f] = **funct (m) mset** or KIND[f] = **funct (m) m**,

but also for arbitrary tuples of sets:

- **funct** *close* = (**mset** N_1, **mset** M_1, ..., **mset** N_n, **mset** M_n) (**mset**, ..., **mset**):
  some (**mset** R_1, ..., **mset** R_n):
    $\forall_{i=1..n}\, R_i = (M_i \cup (\{f_i(x): x \in \bigcup_{j=1..n} R_j\} \setminus N_i))$

  ↓ [**m** finite

  funct *close* = (**mset** N_1, **mset** M_1, ..., **mset** N_n, **mset** M_n) (**mset**, ..., **mset**):
  if $(M_1, \ldots M_n) = (\varnothing, \ldots, \varnothing)$
    then $(N_1, \ldots, N_n)$
    else $close(N_1 \cup M_1, \{f_1(x): x \in \bigcup_{j=1..n} M_j\} \setminus (N_1 \cup M_1), \ldots$
      $N_n \cup M_n, \{f_n(x): x \in \bigcup_{j=1..n} M_j\} \setminus (N_n \cup M_n))$ **fi**

  Syntactic constraints:
  KIND[f_i] = **funct (m) m** ($1 \le i \le n$),
  DECL[**mset**] = **mode mset** = ESET(**m**, =).

In the considerations above, the restriction on finite **m** was only needed to guarantee the termination of *close*. Hence, the requirement for finite **m** could be weakened to the existence of a finite solution R to
  $R = (M \cup (f(R) \setminus N)$.

5.3.4 Developing Partial Functions from their Domain Restriction

Given an arbitrary specification of a partial function

funct f = (**m** x: P(x)) **n**:
  some n y: Q(x, y),

where

$P(x) \equiv$ **true** $\vdash$ ($\exists$ **n** y: $Q(x, y)) \equiv$ **true**

is assumed, it is sometimes necessary (e.g., with respect to reliability) to totalize this function to **m** by introducing a **dummy** element (as an additional constant of the range of f, as in the introduction to Chap. 5):

funct f = (**m** x) (**n** | **dummy**):
  if P(x) **then some n** y: Q(x, y) **else dummy fi**.

Note, however, that this transition is not a (correct) transformation, but rather an (informal) step in the development of a formal specification.

A typical example for such a problem is

Given a non-empty sequence s of natural numbers and a natural number x, one is requested to give some index of x in s, provided x occurs in s

which can be formalized as

mode natsequ = EESEQU(**nat**, =);

funct *ind* = (**nat** x, **natsequ** s: $s \neq$ <>) (**nat** | **dummy**):
  if $\exists$ **nat** i: $1 \le i \le |s| \,\Delta\, s[i] = x$ **then some nat** i: $1 \le i \le |s| \,\Delta\, s[i] = x$
    else dummy fi.

For the general case suppose, furthermore, that a recursive solution for P is already available, say,

funct p = (**m** x) **bool**:
  $T(x) \,\nabla\, \exists_{i=1..n}(B_i(x) \,\Delta\, p(K_i(x)))$.

The goal is now to develop an operational solution for f from the definition of p under the additional restriction that

DEF[$p(x)$]

holds for all **m** x.

The basic strategy for this development is as follows: first, we extend p to have an additional parameter y of sort **n** that is related to x in such a way that upon termination of p (with **true**), Q is established. In a second step, we use the (totalized) definition of f and the (extended) version of p to achieve an operational solution for f by delivering the actual value of y on termination (with **true**).

For our above example, we proceed as follows:
The condition

$\exists$ **nat** i: $1 \le i \le |s| \,\Delta\, s[i] = x$

within *ind* is computed by (compare *isin* in Sect. 5.3.2.2)

funct *occurs* = (**nat** x, **natsequ** s: $s \neq <>$) **bool**:
  first$s = x \nabla$ (**rest**$s \neq <> \Delta$ *occurs*(x, **rest**s)).

By an *embedding with assertion* we get

funct *occurs* = (**nat** x, **natsequ** s: $s \neq <>$) **bool**:
  occ(s, *1*) **where**

  funct *occ* = (**natsequ** t, **nat** i: $t \neq <> \Delta$
      $\exists$ **natsequ** t': $|t'| = i-1 \Delta t'+t = s \Delta x \notin t'$) **bool**:
    first$t = x \nabla$ (**rest**$t \neq <> \Delta$ *occurs*(x, **rest**t)).

Unfolding the original definition of *occurs* in *occ* leads to

first$t = x \nabla$
  (**rest**$t \neq <> \Delta$ (**first rest**$t = x \nabla$ (**rest rest**$t \neq <> \Delta$ *occurs*(x, **rest rest**t)))).

Now, obviously, for **first**$t \neq x$

(($t \neq <> \Delta \exists$ **natsequ** t': $|t'| = i-1 \Delta t'+t = s \Delta x \notin t'$) $\wedge$ **rest**$t \neq <>$) $\equiv$ **true** $\vdash$
  (**rest**$t \neq <> \Delta$ ($\exists$ **natsequ** t'': $|t''| = i \Delta t''+$**rest**$t = s \Delta x \notin t''$)) $\equiv$ **true**

holds, such that by *folding with assertion* we get

funct *occ* = (**natsequ** t, **nat** i: $t \neq <> \Delta$
    $\exists$ **natsequ** t': $|t'| = i-1 \Delta t'+t = s \Delta x \notin t'$) **bool**:
  first$t = x \nabla$ (**rest**$t \neq <> \Delta$ *occ*(**rest**t, i+1)).

For the general case, we proceed analogously:
By *embedding with assertion* we transform p into

funct p = (**m** x) **bool**:
  $p'(x, \mathrm{E})$ **where**

  funct p' = (**m** z, **n** y: $\mathrm{Q}'(x, z, y)$) **bool**:
    $\mathrm{T}(z) \nabla \exists_{i=1..n}(\mathrm{B}_i(z) \Delta p(\mathrm{K}_i(z)))$

where the correctness of the embedding requires

$\mathrm{Q}'(x, x, \mathrm{E}) \equiv$ **true**.

Unfolding the original definition of p in p' leads to

$\mathrm{T}(z) \nabla \exists_{i=1..n}(\mathrm{B}_i(z) \Delta (\mathrm{T}(\mathrm{K}_i(z)) \nabla \exists_{i=1..n}(\mathrm{B}_i(\mathrm{K}_i(z)) \Delta p(\mathrm{K}_i(\mathrm{K}_i(z))))))$.

Now, if (for all $i \in \{1, ..., n\}$) there exist

funct r_i = (**m** z, **n** y) **n**,

such that

$(\mathrm{Q}'(x, z, y) \Delta \neg\mathrm{T}(z) \Delta \mathrm{B}_i(z)) \equiv$ **true** $\vdash$ $\mathrm{Q}'(x, \mathrm{K}_i(z), r_i(z, y)) \equiv$ **true**

holds, then folding is possible (since, obviously, p' terminates if p does) and finally yields

funct p' = (**m** z, **n** y: $\mathrm{Q}'(x, z, y)$) **bool**:
  $\mathrm{T}(z) \nabla \exists_{i=1..n}(\mathrm{B}_i(z) \Delta p'(\mathrm{K}_i(z), r_i(z, y)))$.

Furthermore, if Q' (in the definition of p') is chosen in such a way that

$$(Q'(x, z, y) \,\Delta\, T(z)) \equiv \textbf{true} \;\vdash\; Q(x, y) \equiv \textbf{true}$$

holds, then also the assertion (where ⇨ denotes sequential implication, Sect. 4.4.1)

$$T(z) \Rightarrow Q(x, y)$$

holds, which means that on termination of p' with **true**, the actual value of y fulfils the predicate Q for the initial argument x.

Thus, p' can be transformed into

$$\begin{array}{l}\textbf{funct}\; p' = (\textbf{m}\; z, \textbf{n}\; y\text{: } T(z) \Rightarrow Q(x, y))\; \textbf{bool}\text{:}\\ \quad T(z) \,\nabla\, \exists_{i=1..n}(B_i(z) \,\Delta\, p'(K_i(z), r_i(z, y))).\end{array}$$

For our example above we have

$$\begin{array}{l}((t \neq \langle\rangle \,\Delta\, \exists\; \textbf{natsequ}\; t'\text{: } |t'| = i-1 \,\Delta\, t'+t = s \,\Delta\, x \not\in t') \,\Delta\, \textbf{first}t = x) \equiv \textbf{true} \;\vdash\\ (t \neq \langle\rangle \,\Delta\, s[i] = x) \equiv \textbf{true},\end{array}$$

and hence

$$((t \neq \langle\rangle \,\Delta\, \textbf{first}t = x) \Rightarrow (s[i] = x)) \equiv \textbf{true}$$

holds, such that the definition of occ can be further transformed into

$$\begin{array}{l}\textbf{funct}\; occ = (\textbf{natsequ}\; t, \textbf{nat}\; i\text{: } (t \neq \langle\rangle \,\Delta\, \textbf{first}t = x) \Rightarrow (s[i] = x)))\; \textbf{bool}\text{:}\\ \quad \textbf{first}t = x \,\nabla\, (\textbf{rest}t \neq \langle\rangle \,\Delta\, occ(\textbf{rest}t, i+1)).\end{array}$$

For particular forms of p this strategy can be made into a rule, in our particular case into

- <u>*Predicate extension I*</u>

$$\begin{array}{l}\textbf{funct}\; p = (\textbf{m}\; x)\; \textbf{bool}\text{:}\\ \quad T(x) \,\nabla\, \exists_{i=1..n}(B_i(x) \,\Delta\, p(K_i(x)))\end{array}$$

$$\Updownarrow \quad \left[\begin{array}{l}Q'(x, x, E) \equiv \textbf{true},\\ (Q'(x, z, y) \,\Delta\, \neg T(z) \,\Delta\, B_i(z)) \equiv \textbf{true} \;\vdash\\ \qquad Q'(x, K_i(z), r_i(z, y)) \equiv \textbf{true} \quad (1 \le i \le n),\\ (Q'(x, z, y) \,\Delta\, T(z)) \equiv \textbf{true} \;\vdash\; Q(x, y) \equiv \textbf{true},\\ \mathsf{DEF}[p(x)] \Leftrightarrow \mathsf{DEF}[p'(x, E)]\end{array}\right.$$

$$\begin{array}{l}\textbf{funct}\; p = (\textbf{m}\; x)\; \textbf{bool}\text{:}\\ \quad p'(x, E)\; \textbf{where}\\ \quad \textbf{funct}\; p' = (\textbf{m}\; z, \textbf{n}\; y\text{: } T(z) \Rightarrow Q(x, y))\; \textbf{bool}\text{:}\\ \qquad T(z) \,\nabla\, \exists_{i=1..n}(B_i(z) \,\Delta\, p'(K_i(z), r_i(z, y))).\end{array}$$

Note that this rule indeed establishes equivalence, since due to the applicability conditions p and p' are both defined and the assertion in p' is redundant.

If p itself already has an assertion, for example

$$\textbf{funct}\; p = (\textbf{m}\; x\text{: } R(x))\; \textbf{bool},$$

then this assertion is simply "added" in p', i.e. the transformation rule results in

$$\textbf{funct}\; p' = (\textbf{m}\; z, \textbf{n}\; y\text{: } R(x) \,\Delta\, (T(z) \Rightarrow Q(x, y)))\; \textbf{bool}.$$

It also can be proved that the above rule holds if n is dependent on the argument x:

- <u>*Predicate extension II*</u>

funct p = (**m** x) **bool**:
  $\mathrm{T}(x) \nabla \exists_{i=1..n(x)}(\mathrm{B}(i, x) \Delta p(\mathrm{K}(i, x)))$

⇕ [$\mathrm{Q}'(x, x, \mathrm{E}) \equiv$ **true**,
  $(1 \leq i \leq n(x) \Delta \mathrm{Q}'(x, z, y) \Delta \neg\mathrm{T}(z) \Delta \mathrm{B}(i, z)) \equiv$ **true** $\vdash$
    $\mathrm{Q}'(x, \mathrm{K}(i, z), r(i, z, y)) \equiv$ **true**,
  $(\mathrm{Q}'(x, z, y) \Delta \mathrm{T}(z)) \equiv$ **true** $\vdash$ $\mathrm{Q}(x, y) \equiv$ **true**,
  DEF[$p(x)$] $\Leftrightarrow$ DEF[$p'(x, \mathrm{E})$]]

funct p = (**m** x) **bool**:
  $p'(x, \mathrm{E})$ **where**
    funct p' = (**m** z, **n** y: $\mathrm{T}(z) \Rightarrow \mathrm{Q}(x, y)$) **bool**:
      $\mathrm{T}(z) \nabla \exists_{i=1..n(x)}(\mathrm{B}(i, z) \Delta p'(\mathrm{K}(i, z), r(i, z, y)))$.

The relationship between this rule and the rule *invariant introduction* is obvious: whereas the latter adds an (invariant) assertion to an embedded function, here the *embedding* and the introduction of the respective assertion are done simultaneously. Again, the application of the rule requires an explicit definition of the auxiliary predicate Q' in order to fulfil the applicability conditions which only (implicitly) characterize this predicate by the respective properties. However, finding Q' is additionally eased by the goal to finally establish the predicate Q as used in the function f introduced in the beginning of this subsection. Therefore, usually Q' will be a 'generalization' of Q (to be found by some *embedding*, Sect. 5.2) combined with the assertion of p.

The second step remains to be dealt with, i.e. given p' as just derived and f as defined earlier in order to derive an operational solution for f.

First, by an embedding, we transform the original definition

funct f = (**m** x) (**n** | **dummy**):
  if $p(x)$ **then some n** y: $\mathrm{Q}(x, y)$ **else dummy fi**

into

funct f = (**m** x) (**n** | **dummy**):
  $f'(x, \mathrm{E})$ **where**

  funct f' = (**m** z, **n** y: $\mathrm{T}(z) \Rightarrow \mathrm{Q}(x, y)$) (**n** | **dummy**):
    if $p'(z, y)$ **then some n** y': $\mathrm{Q}(x, y')$ **else dummy fi**.

Then we can use the rule

- <u>*Argument on termination I*</u>

funct f = (**m** x) **n**:
  $f'(x, \mathrm{E})$ **where**
  funct f' = (**m** z, **n** y: $\mathrm{T}(z) \Rightarrow \mathrm{Q}(x, y)$) (**n** | **dummy**):
    if $p'(z, y)$ **then some n** y': $\mathrm{Q}(x, y')$ **else dummy fi**

↓ [DEF[$p'(z, y)$],
  $\mathrm{B}_i(x) \equiv$ **true** $\vdash$ $\mathrm{B}_j(x) \equiv$ **false** $(1 \leq i,j \leq n,\ i \neq j)$]

funct f = (**m** x) **n**:
  $f'(x, \mathrm{E})$ **where**

```
funct f' = (m z, n y: T(z) ⇨ Q(x, y)) (n | dummy):
   if T(z) then y
   elsf B1(z) then f'(K1(z), r1(z, y))
    :
   elsf Bn(z) then f'(Kn(z), rn(z, y)) else dummy fi
```

Syntactic constraints:

```
DECL[p'] = (m z, n y: T(z) ⇨ Q(x, y)) bool:
                T(z) ∇ ∃i=1..n(Bi(z) Δ p'(Ki(z), ri(z, y))).
```

The example *ind*, given above, can be embedded into

```
funct ind = (nat x, natsequ s: s ≠<>) (nat | dummy):
   ind'(s, 1) where

   funct ind' = (natsequ t, nat i:  t ≠<> Δ
                    (first t = x ⇨ s[i] = x)) (nat | dummy):
      if occ(t, i) then some nat i: 1 ≤ i ≤ |s| Δ s[i] = x else dummy fi
```

in order to meet the input scheme of the rule. The applicability conditions of the rule are trivially fulfilled and application of the rule yields

```
funct ind = (nat x, natsequ s: s ≠<>) (nat | dummy):
   ind'(s, 1) where

   funct ind' = (natsequ t, nat i:  t ≠<> Δ
                    (first t = x ⇨ s[i] = x)) (nat | dummy):
      if first t = x then i
      elsf rest t ≠<> then ind'(rest t, i+1) else dummy fi
```

If the second applicability condition of the above rule does not hold for p', rules for yielding the "argument on termination" can still be given that incorporate rules for eliminating the existential quantifier in p' (Sect. 5.4). An example is

• *Argument on termination II*

```
funct f = (m x) n:
   f'(x, E) where
   funct f' = (m z, n y: T(z) ⇨ Q(x, y)) (n | dummy):
      if p'(z, y) then some n y': Q(x, y') else dummy fi
   |
 ——+——[ DEF[p'(z, y)]
   ↓
funct f = (m x) n:
   f'(x, E) where
   funct f' = (m z, n y: T(z) ⇨ Q(x, y)) (n | dummy):
      if T(z) then y else f''(1, z, y) fi,
   funct f'' = (nat i, m z, n y) (n | dummy):
      if i > n(x) then dummy
                  else if B(i, z) then (n | dummy) y'' = f'(K(i, z), r(i, z, y));
                                   if ¬(y'' is dummy) then y'' else f''(i+1, z, y) fi
                                   else f''(i+1, z, y) fi fi
```

Syntactic constraints:

DECL[p'] = (**m** z, **n** y: T(z) ⇨ Q(x, y)) **bool**:
T(z) ∇ $\exists_{i=1..n(x)}$(B(i, z) Δ p'(K(i, z), r(i, z, y))).

How to use this latter rule is illustrated with the following simple example:

Given a binary tree b of which the leaves are characters, and given a character y, determine a selector path leading to y, provided that y is a leaf of b.

Using

mode bintree = *leaf*(**char** *c*) | *comp*(**bintree** *left*, **bintree** *right*);
mode dir = L | R;
mode pos = SEQU(**dir**);
funct .=. = (**bintree** *a*, **bintree** *b*) **bool**:
((*a* **is** *leaf* ∧ *b* **is** *leaf*) Δ *c*(*a*) = *c*(*b*)) ∨
((*a* **is** *comp* ∧ *b* **is** *comp*) Δ (*left*(*a*) = *left*(*b*) ∧ *right*(*a*) = *right*(*b*)),

the problem can be formally specified by

funct *path* = (**char** *y*, **bintree** *b*) (**pos** | **dummy**):
if *isin*(*b*) **then some pos** *s*: *sel*(*b*, *s*) **is** *leaf* Δ *c*(*sel*(*b*, *s*)) = *y*
else dummy fi where

where *sel* is supposed to be a partial operation

funct *sel* = (**bintree** *b*, **pos** *p*: *b* **is** *leaf* ⇒ *p* =<>) **bintree**,

characterized by

sel(*b*, <>) ≡ *b*;
sel(*comp*(*b1*, *b2*), L+*s*) ≡ *sel*(*b1*, *s*);
sel(*comp*(*b1*, *b2*), R+*s*) ≡ *sel*(*b2*, *s*),

that selects a subtree according to a given access path and where *isin* is already available:

funct *isin* = (**bintree** *b*) **bool**:
(*b* **is** *leaf* Δ *c*(*b*) = *y*) ∇
((*b* **is** *comp* Δ *isin*(*left*(*b*))) ∨ (*b* **is** *comp* Δ *isin*(*right*(*b*)))).

Here, **m** *x* (from the schema *predicate extension*) corresponds to **bintree** *b*, T to

b **is** *leaf* Δ *c*(*b*) = *y*

and Q to

c(*sel*(*b*, *s*)) = *y*.

Now, with **m** *z* corresponding to **bintree** *t* and Q' to

sel(*b*, *s*) = *t* ,

we have obviously

(1) (*sel*(*b*, <>) = *b*) ≡ **true**, i.e., Q'(*b*, *b*, <>) ≡ **true**
(2) (*sel*(*b*, *s*) = *t* Δ (*t* **is** *leaf* Δ *c*(*t*) = *y*)) ≡ **true** ⊢ (*c*(*sel*(*b*, *s*)) = *y*) ≡ **true**
(3) (*sel*(*b*, *s*) = *t* Δ *t* **is** *comp*) ≡ **true** ⊢ (*sel*(*b*, *s*+L) = *left*(*t*)) ≡ **true**
(*sel*(*b*, *s*) = *t* Δ *t* **is** *comp*) ≡ **true** ⊢ (*sel*(*b*, *s*+R) = *right*(t)) ≡ **true**.

Since the definedness of *path* can also be shown, the rule *predicate extension* is applicable and leads to

```
funct isin = (bintree b) bool:
  isin'(b, <>) where

  funct isin' = (bintree t, pos s: (t is leaf Δ c(t) = y) ⇨ c(sel(b,s)) = y) bool:
    (t is leaf Δ c(t) = y) ∇
    ((t is comp Δ isin'(left(t), s+L)) ∨ (t is comp Δ isin'(right(t), s+R))).
```

Accordingly the definition of *path* can be transformed into

```
funct path = (char y, bintree b) pos:
  path'(b, <>) where

  funct path' = (bintree t, pos s:
                 (t is leaf Δ c(t) = y) ⇨ c(sel(b, s)) = y) (pos | dummy):
    if isin'(t, s)  then some pos s: sel(b, s) is leaf Δ c(sel(b, s)) = y
                    else dummy fi.
```

Since the applicability condition for the (appropriate variant of the) rule *argument on termination II* is also fulfilled, we get:

```
funct path = (char y, bintree b) pos:
  path'(b, <>) where

  funct path' = (bintree t, pos s:
                 (t is leaf Δ c(t) = y) ⇨ c(sel(b, s)) = y) (pos | dummy):
    if t is leaf Δ c(t) = y then s else path"(1, t, s) fi,

  funct path" = (nat i, bintree t, pos s) (pos | dummy):
    if i > 2 then dummy
          else if t is comp
                 then (pos | dummy) s' =
                        path'(if i=1 then (left(t), s+L) else (right(t), s+R) fi);
                        if ¬(s' is dummy) then s' else path"(i+1, t, s) fi
                 else path"(i+1, t, s) fi fi
```

and by repeated unfoldings of calls of *p"* and subsequent simplifications

```
funct path = (char y, bintree b) pos:
  path'(b, <>) where

  funct path' = (bintree t, pos s:
                 (t is leaf Δ c(t) = y) ⇨ c(sel(b,s)) = y) (pos | dummy):
    if t is leaf Δ c(t) = y
      then s
      else if t is comp
             then (pos | dummy) s' = path'(left(t), s+L);
                   if ¬(s' is dummy) then s' else path'(right(t), s+R) fi
             else dummy fi fi
```

Although we used a particular recursive form of p for demonstration purposes, other forms of recursion can be dealt with as well along the following

Strategy

Given

funct f = (**m** x) (**n** | **dummy**):
  if $p(x)$ **then some n** y: Q(x, y) **else dummy fi**

and an operational definition for p:

- Embed p into p' using suitable additional parameters and a suitable assertion A that establishes Q upon termination of p (with **true**);
- Develop p' into a function that is independent of p (where particular care has to be taken for maintaining the assertion A);
- Embed f into f' that has the same additional parameters (and also the same assertion A) as p';
- Apply one of the rules *argument on termination* to f'.

Since the rule *argument on termination I* leads to more efficient programs, it is furthermore advisable to transform p' into p'' that has disjoint conditions (as required in the rule *argument on termination I*) and use p'' for the subsequent embedding.

This strategy for extending a predicate by additional parameters is also the basis for a global development strategy termed 'specification by parts' [Merritt 82]. The basic idea of the strategy is as follows.
Given some initial problem description by some predicate P(x), then

- break P into parts $P_1, ..., P_n$ such that $P(x) \equiv P_1(x) \wedge ... \wedge P_n(x)$,
- find ("guess" in [Merritt 82]) an algorithm for some P_i,
- repeatedly "adjust" this algorithm to satisfy P_j ($i \neq j$) too.

In principle, we agree to this strategy since it helps to master complexity. Within our framework, however, we propose three major changes:

- use applicative rather than procedural constructs as in [Merritt 82] (which considerably eases reasoning),
- "develop" a solution for P_i, rather than "guessing" it,
- concentrate on the proper domain for some P_i first and then extend it to the (possibly larger) domain for some P_j by using the tactics just introduced.

5.4 Elimination of Descriptive Constructs in Applicative Programs

Using the rules and strategies given so far, any descriptive specification can be transformed into an operational one. However, it may also happen that developments end in a specification that is not fully operational and still contains descriptive constructs. Alternatively, in the case of predicates, it may still contain existential quantifiers. Since predicates play an important role in many applications as well as for the development of partial functions (Sect. 5.3.4), it seems worthwhile to investigate transformations for eliminating these existential quantifiers.

5.4.1 Use of Sets

The existential quantifiers we want to deal with all reflect *bounded non-determinism*, i.e. they quantify over a finite domain.

A wide class of problems deals with functions of the form (see also Sect. 5.3.2.2)

funct p = (**m** x) **bool**:
  $\mathrm{T}(x) \triangledown \exists_{i=1..n}(\mathrm{B_i}(x) \vartriangle p(\mathrm{K_i}(x)))$.

In an operational view, programs of this form build up a 'computational tree' ('ramification') of the form given in Fig. 5.1.

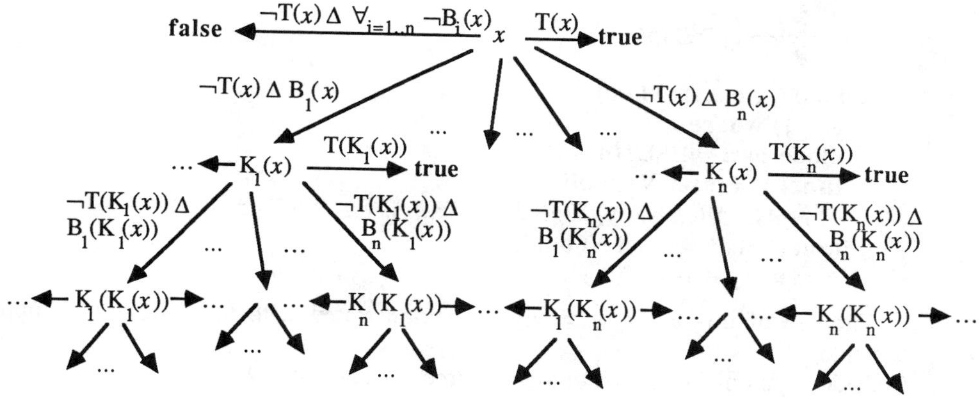

Figure 5.1. 'computational tree'

Obviously, it is possible to eliminate existential quantification by considering the set of all possible new arguments $\mathrm{K_i}(x)$ for which $\mathrm{B_i}(x)$ holds ('exhaustive non-determinism'). In an operational view, this step introduces an explicit 'breadth-first evaluation' in the computational tree spanned by p.

The introduction of breadth-first evaluation is codified by the transformation rule

• <u>∃-elimination by sets</u>

funct p = (**m** x) **bool**:
  $\mathrm{T}(x) \triangledown \exists_{i=1..n}(\mathrm{B_i}(x) \vartriangle p(\mathrm{K_i}(x)))$

$\updownarrow$ [DEF[$p(x)$]

funct p = (**m** x) **bool**:
  $g(\{x\})$ **where**
  mode mset = ESET(**m**, =);
  funct g = (**mset** M) **bool**:
    $M \neq \varnothing \vartriangle (check(M) \triangledown g(\bigcup_{i=1..n}\{\mathrm{K_i}(x)\colon x \in M \vartriangle \mathrm{B_i}(x)\}))$,

funct *check* = (**mset** *M*) **bool**:
  $\exists$ **m** x: $x \in M \,\Delta\, \mathrm{T}(x)$.

Here the auxiliary function *check* simply checks whether there are "terminating" arguments in *M*. An operational realization for *check* can be immediately obtained by using an appropriate instance of the rule *computing qualifiers for finite sets*.

If we omit the condition on the definedness of *p*, the downwards direction of the above rule still holds. It leads to a (more defined) descendant that yields **true** whenever there exists at least one path in the computational tree spanned by *p* that terminates with **true**.

As with most of the rules before, there are special cases and variants of the above rule. This is exemplified below where part of the argument of *p* is not changed during the (recursive) computation:

- **funct** *p* = (**m** *z*, **n** *y*) **bool**:
  $\mathrm{T}(z, y) \,\nabla\, \exists_{i=1..n}(\mathrm{B}_i(z, y) \,\Delta\, p(z, \mathrm{K}_i(y)))$

  ⇕ DEF[$p(x, y)$]

  funct *p* = (**m** *z*, **n** *y*) **bool**:
    $g(\{y\})$ **where**
    mode nset = ESET(**n**, =);
    funct *g* = (**nset** *N*) **bool**:
      $N \neq \varnothing \,\Delta\, (check(N) \,\nabla\, g(\bigcup_{i=1..n}\{\mathrm{K}_i(y): y \in N \,\Delta\, \mathrm{B}_i(z, y)\}))$,
    funct *check* = (**nset** *N*) **bool**:
      $\exists$ **n** y: $y \in N \,\Delta\, \mathrm{T}(z, y)$.

The use of this latter rule may be demonstrated with the following simple example:
Consider again the definition of a binary tree as in Sect. 5.3.4,

mode bintree = *leaf*(**char** *c*) | *comp*(**bintree** *left*, **bintree** *right*),

and the problem

whether a given character x is a leaf in a given binary tree b.

For the definition of *isin* (Sect. 5.3.4),

funct *isin* = (**char** *x*, **bintree** *b*) **bool**:
  (*b* **is** *leaf* Δ $c(b) = x$) ∇
  ((*b* **is** *comp* Δ *isin*(*x*, *left*(*b*))) $\vee$ (*b* **is** *comp* Δ *isin*(*x*, *right*(*b*)))),

obviously the condition on the definedness of *isin*(*x*, *b*) is fulfilled and the application of the (variant of the) rule yields

funct *isin* = (**char** *x*, **bintree** *b*) **bool**:
  isin'($\{b\}$) **where**

  mode bintreeset = ESET(**bintree**, =);

  funct *isin'* = (**bintreeset** *M*) **bool**:
    $M \neq \varnothing \,\Delta\,$ (*check*(*M*) ∇
      isin'($\{left(t): t \in M \,\Delta\, t$ **is** $comp\} \cup \{right(t): t \in M \,\Delta\, t$ **is** $comp\}$)),

funct *check* = (**bintreeset** M) **bool**:
  $\exists$ **bintree** t: ($t \in M \,\Delta\, t$ **is** *leaf* $\Delta\, c(t) = x$).

This could be further improved by an appropriate data type representation to exploit the fact that all trees in M are subtrees of the "original" tree b (Chap. 8).

For the above transformation rule we had two essential restrictions, one to functions yielding boolean results, and the other to a particular form of recursion – both motivated by many applications.

Of course, the basic idea of the above rule is also applicable to predicates containing universal quantifiers and functions with non-boolean ranges, where such rules as

- **funct** p = (**m** x) **bool**:
  $T(x) \,\nabla\, \forall_{i=1..n}(B_i(x) \,\Delta\, p(K_i(x)))$

  $\updownarrow$ [DEF[$p(x)$]

  funct p = (**m** x) **bool**:
    $g(\{x\})$ **where**
    mode mset = ESET(**m**, =);
    funct g = (**mset** M) **bool**:
      $M = \emptyset \,\nabla\, (check(M) \,\nabla\, g(\bigcup_{i=1..n}\{K_i(x): x \in M \,\Delta\, \neg T(x) \,\Delta\, B_i(x)\}))$,
    funct *check* = (**mset** M) **bool**:
      $\forall$ **m** x: $x \notin M \,\nabla\, T(x)$

or

- **funct** f = (**m** x) (**n** | **dummy**):
    if $T(x)$ **then** $H(x)$
    elsf $[]_{i=1..n}$ $B_i(x)$ **then** $f(K_i(x))$ **else dummy fi**

  $\downarrow$ [DEF[$f(x)$]

  funct f = (**m** x) (**n** | **dummy**):
    $g(\{x\})$ **where**
    mode mset = ESET(**m**, =);
    funct g = (**mset** M) (**n** | **dummy**):
      if $M = \emptyset$ **then dummy**
      elsf $check(M)$ **then** $H(y)$ **where m** y = **some m** x: $x \in M \,\Delta\, T(x)$
          else $g(\bigcup_{i=1..n}\{K_i(x): x \in M \,\Delta\, B_i(x)\})$ **fi**,
    funct *check* = (**mset** M) **bool**:
      $\exists$ **m** x: $x \in M \,\Delta\, T(x)$.

can be proved.

The particular form of recursion which we have chosen for demonstration purposes, is not a restriction, since (sometimes with additional effort) any recursive function can be transformed into this form [Pepper, Partsch 86]. Of course, analogous remarks apply to the techniques discussed below.

If **m** is a finite sort, the programs of the form

funct p = (**m** x) **bool**:
$\quad T(x) \,\nabla\, \exists_{i=1..n}(B_i(x) \,\Delta\, p(K_i(x)))$

describe non-deterministic finite state automata (where T characterizes final states and the K_i give the respective state transitions). In this case our transformation corresponds to the well-known powerset construction for transforming a non-deterministic finite state automaton into a deterministic one where the new states are a subset of the powerset of **m** and the new state transition function is given by

funct s = (**mset** r: $r \neq \varnothing \,\Delta\, \neg\exists$ **m** x: $(x \in r \,\Delta\, T(x))$) **mset**:
$\quad \bigcup_{i=1..n}\{K_i(x)\colon x \in r \wedge B_i(x)\}$.

This, as a finite mapping, can be pre-computed (Sect. 6.4.2) and represented by a (transition-)table.

Hence, for arbitrary **m**, programs as defined by the above scheme may be considered as non-deterministic (possibly infinite) state automata and the transition given above describes a transition from a non-deterministic infinite state automaton to a deterministic one.

Another rule for eliminating existential quantifiers by using sets can be given for functions with at least a pair of arguments, for example, for functions of the form

funct p = (**m** x, **n** y) **bool**:
$\quad T(x, y) \,\nabla\, \exists_{i=1..n}(B_i(x) \,\Delta\, p(K_i(x), y))$.

For functions of this form we have the rule

- <u>$\exists$*-elimination by computing the codomain of the relation*</u>

funct p = (**m** x, **n** y) **bool**:
$\quad T(x, y) \,\nabla\, \exists_{i=1..n}(B_i(x) \,\Delta\, p(K_i(x), y))$

$\updownarrow$ $\quad$ DEF[$p(x, y)$], $\;$ $|\{$**n** $y\colon p(x, y)\}| < \infty$

funct p = (**m** x, **n** y) **bool**:
$\quad y \in f'(\varnothing, \{x\}, \varnothing)$ **where**
$\quad$ **mode mset** = ESET(**m**, =);
$\quad$ **mode nset** = ESET(**n**, =);
$\quad$ **funct** f' = (**nset** N, **mset** M, **mset** Q) **nset**:
$\quad\quad$ **if** $M = \varnothing$ **then** N
$\quad\quad\quad$ **else** $f'(N \cup \{$**n** $z\colon x \in M \,\Delta\, T(x, z)\}$,
$\quad\quad\quad\quad \bigcup_{i=1..n}\{K_i(x)\colon x \in M \,\Delta\, \neg T(x, y) \,\Delta\, B_i(x)\} \setminus (Q \cup M), Q \cup M)$ **fi**.

An example of an application of this rule is again provided by an appropriate variant of the "path problem" in finite directed graphs as discussed in Sect. 5.3.1.4.

5.4.2 Classical Backtracking

Another classical technique for (operationally) eliminating existential quantifiers is 'backtracking' which, in contrast to the rule $\exists$*-elimination by sets*, introduces explicit depth-first processing. A corresponding rule reads:

• <u>∃-*elimination by backtracking I*</u>

funct p = (**m** x) **bool**:
  $T(x) \nabla \exists_{i=1..n}(B_i(x) \Delta p(K_i(x)))$

⇕ [DEF[$p(x)$]

funct p = (**m** x) **bool**:
  $T(x) \nabla g(\bigcup_{i=1..n}\{K_i(x): B_i(x)\})$ **where**
  mode mset = ESET(**m**, =);
  funct g = (**mset** M) **bool**:
    $M \neq \varnothing \Delta (p(m) \nabla g(M-m)$ **where m** $m = arb(M)$).

Like for the rule ∃-*elimination by sets*, the condition on the definedness of p could be omitted. Again the rule then would establish descendance.

In the above rule an arbitrary choice is made for the depth-first search. Of course, we may also use a 'sequential choice', i.e. trying B_1 first, then B_2, etc. This is codified by the transformation rule:

• <u>∃-*elimination by backtracking II*</u>

funct p = (**m** x) **bool**:
  $T(x) \nabla \exists_{i=1..n}(B(i, x) \Delta p(K(i, x)))$

⇕ [DEF[$p(x)$]

funct p = (**m** x) **bool**:
  $T(x) \nabla h(1, x)$ **where**
  funct h = (**nat** i, **m** x) **bool**:
    if i>n **then false else** $(B(i, x) \Delta p(K(i, x))) \nabla h(i+1, x)$ **fi**.

Obvious examples of use of these rules are given in all examples dealt with in the previous subsections. The second one has been used in the "queens problem" (Sect. 1.6) and is to be used in the proof of the rule *argument on termination II* (Ex. 5.3-4). Further examples are given in Sect. 5.5.

5.4.3 Finite Look-Ahead

The techniques given in the previous subsections have the advantage of being widely applicable. However, they have the disadvantage of sometimes leading to very inefficient algorithms. In this section, another technique is considered that leads to more efficient algorithms – however, at the cost of a loss in generality and additional applicability conditions.

Again we will concentrate on functions of the form

funct p = (**m** x) **bool**:
  $T(x) \nabla \exists_{i=1..n}(B_i(x) \Delta p(K_i(x)))$.

For such a function the tree-like recursion could be eliminated by trivial sequentialization provided that all B_i are disjoint for arbitrary arguments x.

Now, if the conditions are not disjoint a priori, it is a straightforward idea to replace them by "stronger" conditions C_i in order to enforce disjointedness (compare also [Sintzoff 76]). This is captured by the rule

- *Strengthening of conditions I*

funct p = (**m** x) **bool**:
  $T(x) \nabla \exists_{i=1..n}(B_i(x) \Delta p(K_i(x)))$

$\Big\downarrow$ $\left[\begin{array}{l} C_i(x) \equiv \textbf{true} \vdash B_i(x) \equiv \textbf{true} \;\; (1 \le i \le n), \\ (C_i(x) \wedge C_j(x)) \equiv \textbf{false} \;\; (1 \le i,j \le n,\ i \ne j), \\ (\neg C_i(x) \wedge B_i(x)) \equiv \textbf{true} \vdash p(K_i(x)) \equiv \textbf{false} \;\; (1 \le i \le n) \end{array}\right.$

funct p = (**m** x) **bool**:
  $p'(x)$ **where**
  funct p' = (**m** x) **bool**:
    if $T(x)$ **then true**
    elsf $C_1(x)$ **then** $p'(K_1(x))$
      ⋮
    elsf $C_n(x)$ **then** $p'(K_n(x))$ **else false fi.**

If disjointedness does not hold, we still have the transformation rule

- *Strengthening of conditions II*

funct p = (**m** x) **bool**:
  $T(x) \nabla \exists_{i=1..n}(B_i(x) \Delta p(K_i(x)))$

$\Big\downarrow$ $\left[\begin{array}{l} C_i(x) \equiv \textbf{true} \vdash B_i(x) \equiv \textbf{true} \;\; (1 \le i \le n), \\ (\neg C_i(x) \wedge B_i(x)) \equiv \textbf{true} \vdash p(K_i(x)) \equiv \textbf{false} \;\; (1 \le i \le n) \end{array}\right.$

funct p = (**m** x) **bool**:
  $p'(x)$ **where**
  funct p' = (**m** x) **bool**:
    $T(x) \nabla \exists_{i=1..n}(C_i(x) \Delta p'(K_i(x)))$

which yields a "more deterministic" program where possibly some of the blind alleys are cut off, since C_j is stronger than B_j ($j = 1, ..., n$).

Sufficient criteria for characterizing arbitrary stronger conditions can be found in [Sintzoff 83], however, without giving a way of how to construct them. Constructively, such conditions may be found using the following inductive definition

$$B_{i,0}(x) =_{def} \neg T(x) \Delta B_i(x)$$
$$B_{i,k+1}(x) =_{def} \neg T(x) \Delta B_i(x) \Delta (T(K_i(x)) \nabla \exists_{j=1..n} B_{j,k}(K_i(x))).$$

Intuitively, the idea with this definition is as follows: in order to strengthen some condition B_i we "look ahead" in the computational tree and unite B_i with possible future conditions (a similar idea can be found in [Sintzoff 78]).

A comprehensive example of how to use this construction is given in [Partsch 86]. Other examples are provided by all kinds of games where a (possibly unique) decision can be made by looking a number of tentative moves ahead.

Obviously, if

$(T(x) \wedge B_i(x)) \equiv$ **false** (for all **m** x, $i \in \{1, ..., n\}$), the $B_{i,r}(x)$ (for arbitrary $r \in \mathbb{N}$) fulfil the conditions of the rule *strengthening of conditions II*. Thus a variant of this rule is simply obtained by substituting $B_{i,r}(x)$ for $C_i(x)$. However, it also can be proved that (for all **m** x, i, j $\in$ {1, ..., n})

$$(B_i(x) \wedge B_j(x)) \equiv \textbf{false} \vdash (\forall\ r(i) \in \mathbb{N}: B_{i,r(i)}(x) \wedge B_j(x)) \equiv \textbf{false}$$

holds. This means that disjointedness of two conditions is not destroyed if one (or both) of them is substituted by the respective $B_{i,r(i)}$. Also, the $B_{i,k}$ may be constructed in any order and for each B_i individually.

Hence, we get as a further variant of the above rule

- <u>*Finite look-ahead*</u>

funct p = (**m** x) **bool**:
  $T(x) \nabla \exists_{i=1..n}(B_i(x) \Delta p(K_i(x)))$

funct p = (**m** x) **bool**:
  $T(x) \nabla \exists_{i=1..n}(B_{i,r(i)}(x) \Delta p(K_i(x)))$

<u>**Syntactic constraints:**</u>
  $B_{i,0}(x) =_{def} \neg T(x) \Delta B_i(x)$,
  $B_{i,k+1}(x) =_{def} \neg T(x) \Delta B_i(x) \Delta (T(K_i(x)) \nabla \exists_{j=1..n} B_{j,k}(K_i(x)))$,
  $r(i) \in \mathbb{N}$ $(1 \le i \le n)$.

Consequently, if there exists a (fixed) $r \in \mathbb{N}$ such that (for all **m** x, i, j $\in$ {1, ..., n}, $i \neq j$)

$$(B_{i,r}(x) \wedge B_{j,r}(x)) \equiv \textbf{false},$$

the $B_{i,r}$ even fulfil the conditions for the C_i in the rule *strengthening of conditions I*.

The interesting remaining question is whether given

funct p = (**m** x) **bool**:
  $T(x) \nabla \exists_{i=1..n}(B_i(x) \Delta p(K_i(x)))$

our above inductive definition always leads to (new) conditions that fulfil the conditions in the rule *strengthening of conditions I*. In [Partsch 86] it is proved that this is not the case since the existence of such conditions is not decidable.

5.5 Examples

As in the previous chapter, we demonstrate the use of the strategies and transformations introduced in the previous sections by some examples. For the respective problems and comments on their formalizations, if not stated here, we refer to Sect. 3.6. It also should be mentioned that some of the derivations could be substantially shortened by using the compact rules from Sect. 5.3.1.

5.5.1 Sorting

As a starter, we deal again with the sorting problem as given in Sects. 3.4.3 and 5.3.1.2:

funct *sort* = (**natsequ** *s*) **natsequ**:
  some natsequ x: $issorted(x) \wedge isperm(x, s)$.

Other treatments of the sorting problem, also illustrating the idea of a "family tree" of related algorithms, can be found in [Broy 78], [Clark, Darlington 80], [Darlington 78], [Green, Barstow 78], or [Smith 85b].

<u>Main development</u>

Focus: body of function *sort*
Goal: applicative program for *sort*
Strategy: generalized unfold/fold
Transformations:

step 1: case introduction ($s = \langle\rangle \vee s \neq \langle\rangle$)

if $s = \langle\rangle$ **then some natsequ** x: $issorted(x) \wedge isperm(x, s)$
  else some natsequ x: $issorted(x) \wedge isperm(x, s)$ **fi**

step 2: apply properties:

- $(s = \langle\rangle \wedge isperm(x, s)) \equiv (x = \langle\rangle)$;
- $issorted(\langle\rangle) \equiv$ **true**;
- $(s \neq \langle\rangle \, \Delta \, (x = e+x' \wedge isperm(e+x', s) \wedge issorted(e+x'))) \equiv$ **true** $\vdash$
  $(s \neq \langle\rangle \, \Delta \, (isperm(x, s) \wedge issorted(x))) \equiv$ **true**

if $s = \langle\rangle$ **then** $\langle\rangle$
  else some natsequ x: $x = e'+x''$ **where**
    (**nat** e', **natsequ** x'') = **some** (**nat** e, **natsequ** x'):
    $issorted(e+x') \wedge isperm(e+x', s)$ **fi**

step 3: apply property:
$(issorted(e+x') \wedge isperm(e+x', s)) \equiv (e = min(s) \wedge issorted(x') \wedge isperm(e+x', s)) \equiv$
$(e = min(s) \wedge issorted(x') \wedge isperm(x', delete(s, min(s))))$

if $s = \langle\rangle$ **then** $\langle\rangle$
  else some natsequ x: $x = e'+x''$ **where**
    (**nat** e', **natsequ** x'') = **some** (**nat** e, **natsequ** x'):
    $e = min(s) \wedge issorted(x') \wedge isperm(x', delete(s, min(s)))$ **fi**

step 4: sequentialization of declarations; **some**-simplification

if $s = \langle\rangle$ **then** $\langle\rangle$
  else $min(s)+$**some natsequ** x':
    $issorted(x') \wedge isperm(x', delete(s, min(s)))$ **fi**

step 5: folding

funct *sort* = (**natsequ** *s*) **natsequ**:
  if $s = \langle\rangle$ **then** $\langle\rangle$
    else $min(s)+sort(delete(s, min(s)))$ **fi**.

Here, compared to Sect. 5.3.1.2, we have used different transformations and thus ended in a different program. However, it should be mentioned that the above program also may be obtained by using more or less the same transformations as in Sect. 5.3.1.2. The actual performance of this alternative derivation is left to the interested reader.

5.5.2 Recognition of Context-Free Grammars

When dealing with this problem, we will mainly demonstrate the "generalized unfold/fold strategy" for deriving a particular recognition algorithm. Transformational derivations of other recognition algorithms can be found in [Merritt 82], [Partsch 86], [Scherlis 80]. Furthermore, this example is also used to illustrate the techniques for eliminating quantifiers in applicative programs (Sect. 5.4).

In contrast to other developments in this section, in this subsection particular emphasis is put on illustrating the activities within the three parts of the "generalized unfold/fold strategy":

- decomposition and detailing,
- simplification and rearrangement, and
- composition.

For this reason some obvious steps are delayed or given explicitly.

The development starts from the specification from Sect. 3.6.6:

funct *rp* = (**cfg** *G*, **termstring** *w*: *isterm*(*w*, *G*)) **bool**:
  w ∈ *L*(*G*) **where**

  funct *L* = (**cfg** *G*) **termstrings**:
    {**termstrings** *t*: *S*(*G*) →* *t*}

Main development

Focus: function *rp*
Goal: applicative program for *rp*
Strategy: generalized unfold/fold
Transformations:

step 1: unfold *L*

  funct *rp* = (**cfg** *G*, **termstring** *w*: *isterm*(*w*, *G*)) **bool**:
    w ∈ {**termstring** *t*: *S*(*G*) →* *t*}

step 2: ∈-simplification

  funct *rp* = (**cfg** *G*, **termstring** *w*: *isterm*(*w*, *G*)) **bool**:
    S(*G*) →* *w*

step 3: embedding (of the data types, cf. Sect. 5.2)

  funct *rp* = (**cfg** *G*, **termstring** *w*: *isterm*(*w*, *G*)) **bool**:
    td(*S*(*G*), *w*) **where**

funct td = (**string** u, **termstring** v: $isterm(v, G) \wedge isstr(u, G)$) **bool**:
$u \rightarrow^* v$,

funct $isstr$ = (**string** u, **cfg** G) **bool**:
$u = <> \,\nabla\, (\mathbf{first}u \in (N(G) \cup T(G)) \wedge isstr(\mathbf{rest}u, G))$

Subdevelopment 1

Focus: function *td*
Goal: applicative program for *td*
Strategy: generalized unfold/fold
Transformations:

step 1.1: derivation of an applicative program for *td*

Subdevelopment 1.1

Goal: decomposition and detailing
Transformations:

step 1.1.1: case introduction ($u = <> \,\nabla\, u \neq <>$)

$$(u = <> \,\Delta\, u \rightarrow^* v) \,\nabla\, (u \neq <> \,\Delta\, u \rightarrow^* v)$$

step 1.1.2: apply property $((u \rightarrow^* v) \equiv (u = v \,\nabla\, (\exists\, \mathbf{string}\ z: u \rightarrow z \wedge z \rightarrow^* v)))$

$$(u = <> \,\Delta\, (u = v \,\nabla\, (\exists\, \mathbf{string}\ z: u \rightarrow z \wedge z \rightarrow^* v))) \,\nabla$$
$$(u \neq <> \,\Delta\, u \rightarrow^* v)$$

step 1.1.3: data type property $((u \neq <>) \equiv \mathbf{true} \vdash u \equiv (\mathbf{first}u + \mathbf{rest}u))$

$$(u = <> \,\Delta\, (u = v \,\nabla\, (\exists\, \mathbf{string}\ z: u \rightarrow z \wedge z \rightarrow^* v))) \,\nabla$$
$$(u \neq <> \,\Delta\, \mathbf{first}u + \mathbf{rest}u \rightarrow^* v)$$

step 1.1.4: apply property
$((u = u_1 + \ldots + u_n) \equiv \mathbf{true} \vdash$
$(u \rightarrow^* v) \equiv (\exists\, \mathbf{termstring}\ v_1, \ldots, v_n: v_1 + \ldots + v_n = v \wedge \forall_{i=1..n}: u_i \rightarrow^* v_i))$

$$(u = <> \,\Delta\, (u = v \,\nabla\, (\exists\, \mathbf{string}\ z: u \rightarrow z \wedge z \rightarrow^* v))) \,\nabla$$
$$(u \neq <> \,\Delta\, (\exists\, \mathbf{termstring}\ v_1, v_2: v_1 + v_2 = v \wedge \mathbf{first}u \rightarrow^* v_1 \wedge \mathbf{rest}u \rightarrow^* v_2))$$

step 1.1.5: apply property $((u \rightarrow^* v) \equiv (u = v \,\nabla\, (\exists\, \mathbf{string}\ z: u \rightarrow z \wedge z \rightarrow^* v)))$

$$(u = <> \,\Delta\, (u = v \,\nabla\, (\exists\, \mathbf{string}\ z: u \rightarrow z \wedge z \rightarrow^* v))) \,\nabla$$
$$(u \neq <> \,\Delta\, (\exists\, \mathbf{termstring}\ v_1, v_2: v_1 + v_2 = v \wedge$$
$$(\mathbf{first}u = v_1 \,\nabla\, (\exists\, \mathbf{string}\ z: \mathbf{first}u \rightarrow z \wedge z \rightarrow^* v_1)) \wedge (\mathbf{rest}u \rightarrow^* v_2)))$$

Subdevelopment 1.2

Goal: simplification and rearrangement
Transformations:

step 1.2.1: apply properties:
- $(u = <>) \equiv \mathbf{true} \vdash (\exists\, \mathbf{string}\ z: u \rightarrow z \wedge z \rightarrow^* v) \equiv \mathbf{false}$;
- =-substitution;

$$(u = <> \,\Delta\, v = <>) \,\nabla$$
$$(u \neq <> \,\Delta\, (\exists\, \mathbf{termstring}\ v_1, v_2: v_1 + v_2 = v \wedge$$
$$(\mathbf{first}u = v_1 \,\nabla\, (\exists\, \mathbf{string}\ z: \mathbf{first}u \rightarrow z \wedge z \rightarrow^* v_1)) \wedge (\mathbf{rest}u \rightarrow^* v_2)))$$

step 1.2.2: rearrangement; splitting of an existential quantifier

$(u =<> \Delta\ v =<>)\ \nabla$
$(u \neq<> \Delta$
$((\exists\ \mathbf{termstring}\ v_1, v_2\text{: } v_1+v_2 = v \wedge \mathbf{first}u = v_1 \wedge \mathbf{rest}u\ \rightarrow^*\ v_2)\ \nabla$
$(\exists\ \mathbf{termstring}\ v_1, v_2\text{: } v_1+v_2 = v \wedge$
$(\exists\ \mathbf{string}\ z\text{: } \mathbf{first}u\ \rightarrow z \wedge z\ \rightarrow^*\ v_1) \wedge \mathbf{rest}u\ \rightarrow^*\ v_2)))$

step 1.2.3: quantifier rearrangement; apply property

$(u \neq<>) \equiv \mathbf{true} \vdash$
$(\exists\ \mathbf{termstring}\ v_1, v_2\text{: } v_1+v_2 = v \wedge \mathbf{first}u = v_1 \wedge \mathbf{rest}u\ \rightarrow^*\ v_2) \equiv$
$(v \neq<> \Delta\ (\mathbf{first}u = \mathbf{first}v \wedge \mathbf{rest}u\ \rightarrow^*\ \mathbf{rest}v)))$

$(u =<> \Delta\ v =<>)\ \nabla$
$(u \neq<> \Delta$
$((v \neq<> \Delta\ (\mathbf{first}u = \mathbf{first}v \wedge \mathbf{rest}u\ \rightarrow^*\ \mathbf{rest}v))\ \nabla$
$(\exists\ \mathbf{string}\ z\text{: } \mathbf{first}u\ \rightarrow z \wedge$
$(\exists\ \mathbf{termstring}\ v_1, v_2\text{: } v_1+v_2 = v \wedge z\ \rightarrow^*\ v_1 \wedge \mathbf{rest}u\ \rightarrow^*\ v_2))))$

step 1.2.4: apply property $((\exists\ \mathbf{string}\ z\text{: } \mathbf{first}u\ \rightarrow z) \equiv (pr(\mathbf{first}u, z) \in P(G)))$

$(u =<> \Delta\ v =<>)\ \nabla$
$(u \neq<> \Delta$
$((v \neq<> \Delta\ (\mathbf{first}u = \mathbf{first}v \wedge \mathbf{rest}u\ \rightarrow^*\ \mathbf{rest}v))\ \nabla$
$(\exists\ \mathbf{string}\ z\text{: } pr(\mathbf{first}u, z) \in P(G) \wedge$
$(\exists\ \mathbf{termstring}\ v_1, v_2\text{: } v_1+v_2 = v \wedge z\ \rightarrow^*\ v_1 \wedge \mathbf{rest}u\ \rightarrow^*\ v_2))))$

<u>**Subdevelopment 1.3**</u>

Goal: composition
Transformations:

step 1.3.1: apply property

$((u = u_1+...+u_n) \equiv \mathbf{true} \vdash$
$u\ \rightarrow^*\ v \equiv (\exists\ \mathbf{termstring}\ v_1,...,v_n\text{: } v_1+...+v_n = v \wedge \forall_{i=1..n}\text{: } u_i \rightarrow^*\ v_i))$

$(u =<> \Delta\ v =<>)\ \nabla$
$(u \neq<> \Delta\ ((v \neq<> \Delta\ (\mathbf{first}u = \mathbf{first}v \wedge \mathbf{rest}u\ \rightarrow^*\ \mathbf{rest}v))\ \nabla$
$(\exists\ \mathbf{string}\ z\text{: } pr(\mathbf{first}u, z) \in P(G) \wedge z + \mathbf{rest}u\ \rightarrow^*\ v)))$

step 1.3.2: folding

$\mathbf{funct}\ td = (\mathbf{string}\ u, \mathbf{termstring}\ v\text{: } isterm(v, G) \wedge isstr(u, G))\ \mathbf{bool}\text{:}$
$(u =<> \Delta\ v =<>)\ \nabla$
$(u \neq<> \Delta\ ((v \neq<> \Delta\ (\mathbf{first}u = \mathbf{first}v \wedge td(\mathbf{rest}u, \mathbf{rest}v)))\ \nabla$
$(\exists\ \mathbf{string}\ z\text{: } pr(\mathbf{first}u, z) \in P(G) \wedge td(z + \mathbf{rest}u, v))))$

<u>**Main development continued**</u>

step 4: invariant introduction

$\mathbf{funct}\ rp = (\mathbf{cfg}\ G, \mathbf{termstring}\ w\text{: } isterm(w, G))\ \mathbf{bool}\text{:}$
$td(S(G), w)\ \mathbf{where}$

$\mathbf{funct}\ td = (\mathbf{string}\ u, \mathbf{termstring}\ v\text{: } \exists\ \mathbf{termstring}\ s\text{:}$
$S(G) \rightarrow^* s+u \wedge s+v = w)\ \mathbf{bool}\text{:}$
$(u =<> \Delta\ v =<>)\ \nabla$

$(u \neq \langle\rangle \ \Delta\ ((v \neq \langle\rangle \ \Delta\ (\mathbf{first}u = \mathbf{first}v \wedge td(\mathbf{rest}u, \mathbf{rest}v)))\ \nabla$
$(\exists\ \mathbf{string}\ z: pr(\mathbf{first}u, z) \in P(G) \wedge td(z + \mathbf{rest}u, v))))$.

Obviously, the invariant introduced in the last step implies the assertion we had before. In fact, for the embedding in step 3 we could have used this latter assertion already.

This program (which actually is a scheme for "top-down recognition", [Partsch 86]) is only correct, if the correctness of *folding* in step 1.3.2 is guaranteed. A sufficient condition is, as mentioned earlier, a termination proof for the resulting program. Dealing with this termination proof straightforwardly leads to requiring the absence of left recursion in the production rules as a sufficient condition for termination.

Furthermore, the program still contains an existential quantifier. In order to eliminate this quantifier, we will apply the various techniques discussed in Sect. 5.4.

With

```
mode pstr = mp(string u, termstring v:
                    ∃ termstring s: S(G) →* s+u ∧ s+v = w);
mode pstrset = ESET(pstr, =)
```

the rule ∃-*elimination by sets* straightforwardly yields (after trivial simplifications and using the definitions of the sequential logical connectives)

```
funct rp = (cfg G, termstring w: isterm(w, G)) bool:
   tde({mp(S(G), w)}) where

   funct tde = (pstrset M) bool:
      if M = ∅ then false
      elsf mp(<>, <>) ∈ M then true
         else tde({mp(u, v): ∃ term t: mp(t+u, t+v) ∈ M} ∪
                  {mp(z+u, v): ∃ string y: mp(y+u, v) ∈ M ∧ pr(y, z) ∈ P}) fi.
```

Obviously, *tde* can be simplified substantially, if its argument *M* contains at most one element. Looking for criteria to guarantee this straightforwardly leads to the idea of LL-recognition (details are given in [Partsch 86]).

Using the same mode definitions, the application of ∃-*elimination by backtracking I* to the last version of *td* yields (again with conditional expressions for the sequential logical connectives)

```
funct rp = (cfg G, termstring w: isterm(w, G)) bool:
   tdb(S(G), w) where

   funct tdb = (string u, termstring v:
                    ∃ termstring s: S(G)→*s+u ∧ s+v = w) bool:
      if u =<> Δ v =<> then true
         else g({mp(u', v'): ∃ term t: t+u' = u  ∧ t+v' = v} ∪
                  {mp(z+u', v): ∃ string y: y+u' = u  ∧ pr(y, z) ∈ P}) fi;

   funct g = (pstrset M) bool:
      if M = ∅ then false
      elsf tdb(u, v) then true
                  else g(M\{mp(u, v)}) where mp(u, v) = arb(M) fi,
```

which can be further transformed (by unfoldings and trivial simplifications) into

```
funct rp = (cfg G, termstring w: isterm(w, G)) bool:
   g({mp(z, w): pr(S(G), z) ∈ P}) where

   funct g = (pstrset M) bool:
      if M = ∅ then false
                 else (string u, termstring v) =
                           some (string u', termstring v'): mp(u', v') = arb(M);
                     if u =<> Δ v =<> then true
                     elsf g({mp(u', v'): ∃ term t: t+u' = u ∧ t+v' = v} ∪
                              {mp(z+u', v): ∃ string y:
                                             y+u' = u ∧ pr(y, z) ∈ P}) then true
                                         else g(M\{mp(u, v)}) fi fi.
```

The application of the rule ∃-*elimination by backtracking II* to the last version of *td* requires an explicit enumeration of the production rules of the grammar G. If we assume n productions ($n \in \mathbb{N}$), each of the form (A_i, x_i) for **nont** A_i and **string** x_i $(1 \le i \le n)$, which are furthermore assumed to be represented by two sequences A and x of length n, the result of the above main development also can be written as

```
funct rp = (cfg G, termstring w: isterm(w, G)) bool:
   td'(S(G), w) where

   funct td' = (string u, termstring v:
                    ∃ termstring s: S(G)→*s+u ∧ s+v = w) bool:
      (u =<> Δ v =<>) ∇
      (u ≠<> Δ v ≠<> Δ (firstu = firstv ∧ td'(restu, restv))) ∇
      (u ≠<> Δ (∃i=1..n firstu = A[i] ∧ td'(x[i]+restu, v))).
```

If, as before, we further assume the absence of left recursion in the productions in order to ensure definedness, the rule ∃-*elimination by backtracking II* is applicable and yields

```
funct rp = (cfg G, termstring w: isterm(w, G)) bool:
   td'(S(G), w) where

   funct td' = (string u, termstring v:
                    ∃ termstring s: S(G)→*s+u ∧ s+v = w) bool:
      (u =<> Δ v =<>) ∇ h(1, u, v)

   funct h = (nat i, string u, termstring v) bool:
      if i>n then false
             else (u ≠<> Δ v ≠<> Δ (firstu = firstv ∧ td'(restu, restv))) ∇
                    (u ≠<> Δ (firstu = A[i] ∧ td'(x[i]+restu, v))) ∇ h(i+1, u, v) fi.
```

As above, this can be developed into a version that does not use *td'* any longer.

In order to demonstrate the use of the *finite look-ahead* transformation, more information about the concrete conditions is necessary, for being able to do simplifications. Therefore, for demonstration purposes, we use the concrete grammar (for simple arithmetic expressions)

$G = (\{E, T, F, E', T'\}, \{\oplus, \otimes, [,], a\}, E, P)$

with

$P = \{(E, TE'), (E', \oplus TE'), (E', \langle\rangle), (T, FT'), (T', \otimes FT'), (T', \langle\rangle),$
$(F, [E]), (F, a)\}.$

Instantiation of the last version of *td'* above with this concrete grammar reads

```
funct rp = (termstring w: isterm(w, G)) bool:
   td'(E, w) where

   funct td' = (string u, termstring v:
                    ∃ termstring s: E→*s+u ∧ s+v = w) bool:
      (u =<> Δ v =<>) ∇
      (u ≠<> Δ v ≠<> Δ (firstu = firstv ∧ td'(restu, restv))) ∇
      (u ≠<> Δ (firstu = E ∧ td'(TE'+restu, v))) ∇
      (u ≠<> Δ (firstu = E' ∧ td'(⊕TE'+restu, v))) ∇          (•)
      (u ≠<> Δ (firstu = E' ∧ td'(restu, v))) ∇                 (•)
      (u ≠<> Δ (firstu = T ∧ td'(FT'+restu, v))) ∇
      (u ≠<> Δ (firstu = T' ∧ td'(⊗FT'+restu, v))) ∇          (•)
      (u ≠<> Δ (firstu = T' ∧ td'(restu, v))) ∇                 (•)
      (u ≠<> Δ (firstu = F ∧ td'([E]+restu, v))) ∇              (•)
      (u ≠<> Δ (firstu = F ∧ td'(a+restu, v))).                 (•)
```

Obviously, the conditions in the branches marked by (•) are not disjoint. Therefore, we use the transformation rule *finite look-ahead* in order to construct stronger conditions. This results (after obvious simplifications) in

```
funct rp = (termstring w: isterm(w, G)) bool:
   td'(E, w) where

   funct td' = (string u, termstring v:
                    ∃ termstring s: E→*s+u ∧ s+v = w) bool:
      if u =<> Δ v =<> then true
      elsf u ≠<> Δ v ≠<> Δ firstu = firstv then td'(restu, restv))
      elsf u ≠<> then
         if firstu = E then td'(TE'+restu, v))
         elsf firstu = E' ∧ (v ≠<> Δ firstv = ⊕) then td'(⊕TE'+restu, v)
         elsf firstu = E' ∧ ((restu =<> ∧ v =<>) ∇
               (restu ≠<> Δ v ≠<> Δ first restu = ]) then td'(restu, v)
         elsf firstu = T then td'(FT'+restu, v)
         elsf firstu = T' ∧ (v ≠<> Δ firstv = ⊗) then td'(⊗FT'+restu, v)
         elsf firstu = T' ∧ (restu ≠<> Δ first restu = E') then td'(restu, v)
         elsf firstu = F ∧ (v ≠<> Δ firstv = [) then td'([E]+restu, v)
         elsf firstu = F ∧ (v ≠<> Δ firstv = a)  then td'(a+restu, v)
                                                 else false fi
                  else false fi,
```

where, of course, further simplifications are possible which are left to the reader.

5.5.3 Coding Problem

The "coding problem" was introduced in Sect. 3.6.8. It is formally specified by

funct *encodings* = (**clear** *N*, **rule** *P*) **codes**:
  $\bigcup_{a \in deco(N)}$ *encode*(*a*) **where**

  funct *deco* = (**clear** *N*) **cleartexts**:
    {**cleartext** *a*: *flat*(*a*) = *N* ∧ ∀ (**nat** *i*: $1 \le i \le |a|$): *a*[*i*] ∈ *lhs*(*P*)},

  funct *encode* = (**cleartext** *a*) **codes**:
    {**code** *c*: ∃ **codesequ** *b*: *flat*(*b*) = *c* ∧ |*b*| = |*a*| Δ
      ∀ (**nat** *i*: $1 \le i \le |a|$): *b*[*i*] ∈ *im*(*a*[*i*], *P*)}

Main development

Focus: function *encodings*
Goal: applicative program for *encodings*
Strategy: generalized unfold/fold
Transformations:

step 1: case introduction (*N* =<> ∨ *N* ≠<>)

  if *N* =<> **then** $\bigcup_{a \in deco(N)}$ *encode*(*a*)
    else $\bigcup_{a \in deco(N)}$ *encode*(*a*) **fi**

step 2: simplification

Subdevelopment 1

Focus: function *deco*
Goal: applicative program for *deco* (to be used for simplification)
Strategy: unfold/fold
Transformations:

step 1.1: case introduction (*N* =<> ∨ *N* ≠<>)

  if *N* =<> **then** {**cleartext** *a*: *flat*(*a*) = *N* ∧ ∀ (**nat** *i*: $1 \le i \le |a|$): *a*[*i*] ∈ *lhs*(*P*)}
    else {**cleartext** *a*: *flat*(*a*) = *N* ∧ ∀ (**nat** *i*: $1 \le i \le |a|$): *a*[*i*] ∈ *lhs*(*P*)} **fi**

step 1.2: simplification (under premise *N* =<>):
  {**cleartext** *a*: *flat*(*a*) = *N* ∧ ∀ (**nat** *i*: $1 \le i \le |a|$): *a*[*i*] ∈ *lhs*(*P*)} ≡ {<>}

  if *N* =<> **then** {<>}
    else {**cleartext** *a*: *flat*(*a*)=*N* ∧ ∀ (**nat** *i*: $1 \le i \le |a|$): *a*[*i*] ∈ *lhs*(*P*)} **fi**

step 1.3: simplification (under premise *N* ≠<>):
  {**cleartext** *a*: *flat*(*a*) = *N* ∧ ∀ (**nat** *i*: $1 \le i \le |a|$): *a*[*i*] ∈ *lhs*(*P*)} ≡
  $\bigcup_{l \in llp(N)}$ *l* ⊕ {**cleartext** *a*: *flat*(*a*) = *subtr*(*N*, *l*) ∧ ∀ (**nat** *i*: $1 \le i \le |a|$): *a*[*i*] ∈ *lhs*(*P*)}
  where
    funct *llp* = (**clear** *N*) **clears**:
      {**clear** *l*: *lp*(*l*, *N*) ∧ *l* ∈ *lhs*(*P*)},
    funct *lp* = (**clear** *l*, **clear** *N*) **bool**:
      ∃ **clear** *r*: *l*+*r* = *N*,
    funct *subtr* = (**clear** *N*, **clear** *l*: *lp*(*l*, *N*)) **clear**:
      that clear *r*: *l*+*r* = *N*;
    co for the definition of ⊕, the concatenation of a sequence with all elements of a set of sequences, cf. Sect. 3.6.8 **co**

if N =<> **then** {<>}
else $\bigcup_{l \in llp(N)}$ $l \oplus$ {**cleartext** a: $flat(a) = subtr(N, l) \wedge$ $\forall$ (**nat** i: $1 \le i \le |a|$): $a[i] \in lhs(P)$} **fi**

step 1.4: folding

funct *deco* = (**clear** N) **cleartexts**:
if N =<> **then** {<>}
else $\bigcup_{l \in llp(N)}$ $l \oplus deco(subtr(N, l))$ **fi where**

funct *llp* = (**clear** N) **clears**:
{**clear** l: $lp(l, N) \wedge l \in lhs(P)$},

funct *lp* = (**clear** l, **clear** N) **bool**:
$\exists$ **clear** r: $l+r = N$,

funct *subtr* = (**clear** N, **clear** l: $lp(l, N)$) **clear**:
that clear r: $l+r = N$;

__Subdevelopment 2__

Focus: **then**-branch of *encodings*
Goal: simplification (under premise N=<>)
Strategy: basic rules and properties

$\bigcup_{a \in deco(N)}$ $encode(a)$
≡ [=-substitution]
$\bigcup_{a \in deco(<>)}$ $encode(a)$
≡ [instantiation of *deco*]
$\bigcup_{a \in \{<>\}}$ $encode(a)$
≡ [=-substitution]
encode(<>)
≡ [instantiation of *encode*]
{**code** c: $\exists$ **codesequ** b: $flat(b) = c \wedge |b| = 0 \,\Delta$
$\forall$ (**nat** i: $1 \le i \le 0$): $b[i] \in im(a[i], P)$}
≡ [($\forall$ (**nat** i: $1 \le i \le 0$): $b[i] \in im(a[i], P)$) ≡ **true**]
{**code** c: $\exists$ **codesequ** b: $flat(b) = c \wedge |b| = 0 \,\Delta$ **true**}
≡ [($|b| = 0$) ≡ (b =<>); $flat(b)$ ≡<>; simplifications]
{<>}

__Subdevelopment 3__

Focus: **else**-branch of *encodings*
Goal: simplification (under premise N≠<>)
Strategy: basic rules and properties

$\bigcup_{a \in deco(N)}$ $encode(a)$
≡ [instantiation of *deco*]
$\bigcup_{a \in \bigcup_{l \in llp(N)} l \oplus deco(subtr(N, l))}$ $encode(a)$
≡ [∪–flattening]
$\bigcup_{l \in llp(N)}$ $\bigcup_{a \in l \oplus deco(subtr(N, l))}$ $encode(a)$
≡ [property of sets of sequences]

$\bigcup_{l\in llp(N)} \bigcup_{x\in deco(subtr(N,\, l))} encode(l+x)$

≡ [instantiation of *encode(l+x)*]

$\bigcup_{l\in llp(N)} \bigcup_{x\in deco(subtr(N,\, l))} \bigcup_{b\in im(l)} b \oplus encode(x)$

≡ [commutativity of ∪]

$\bigcup_{l\in llp(N)} \bigcup_{b\in im(l)} b \oplus \bigcup_{x\in deco(subtr(N,\, l))} encode(x)$

Main development continued

if *N* =<>
  then {<>}
  else $\bigcup_{l\in llp(N)} \bigcup_{b\in im(l)} b \oplus \bigcup_{x\in deco(subtr(N,\, l))} encode(x)$ **fi**

step 3: folding

funct *encodings* = (**clear** *N*, **rule** *P*) **codes**:
  if *N* =<> **then** {<>}
    else $\bigcup_{l\in llp(N)} \bigcup_{b\in im(l)} b \oplus encodings(subtr(N, l)), P)$ **fi where**

funct *llp* = (**clear** *N*) **clears**:
  {**clear** *l*: *lp*(*l*, *N*) ∧ *l* ∈ *lhs*(*P*)},

funct *lp* = (**clear** *l*, **clear** *N*) **bool**:
  ∃ **clear** *r*: *l*+*r* = *N*,

funct *subtr* = (**clear** *N*, **clear** *l*: *lp*(*l*, *N*)) **clear**:
  that clear *r*: *l*+*r* = *N*.

Although the above result is not yet operational due to the existential quantification and the unions, we stop the development here and leave the remaining steps of this development to the interested reader.

5.5.4 Cycles in a Graph

The "cycle problem" was introduced in Sect. 3.6.7. As in other subsections, the result of the derivation below is to be used as a starting point for further "optimizing" transformations to be discussed in the next chapter.

funct *hascycle* = (**graph** *g*) **bool**:
  ∃ **nodesequ** *s*: *iscycle*(*s*) **where**

funct *iscycle* = (**nodesequ** *s*) **bool**:
  s ≠<> Δ ∀ (**nat** *i*: 1≤*i* ≤|*s*|): *isarc*(*g*, *s*[*i*], *s*[(*i* **mod** |*s*|)+1])

Main development

Focus: function *hascycle*
Goal: applicative program for *hascycle*
Strategy: generalized unfold/fold
Transformations:

step 1: embedding
  (**idea**: existence of a cycle composed of nodes from a certain set of nodes)

```
funct hascycle = (graph g) bool:
   hc(nodes(g)) where

   funct hc = (nodeset c) bool:
      ∃ nodesequ s: iscyc(s, c),

   funct iscyc = (nodesequ s, nodeset c) bool:
      nset(s) ⊆ c ∧ iscycle(s),

   funct nset = (nodesequ s) nodeset:
      if s =<> then ∅ else nset(rest s) + first s fi
```

<u>Subdevelopment 1</u>

Focus: body of function *hc*
Goal: applicative program for *hc*
Strategy: generalized unfold/fold
Transformations:

step 1.1: case introduction ($sources(c) = \varnothing \vee sources(c) \neq \varnothing$)
(**idea**: nodes without predecessors cannot be on a cycle)

```
if sources(c) = ∅
   then ∃ nodesequ s: iscyc(s, c)
   else ∃ nodesequ s: iscyc(s, c) fi where

funct sources = (nodeset c) nodeset:
   {node x: x ∈ c ∧ preds(x, c) = ∅},

funct preds = (node x, nodeset c) nodeset:
   {node y: y ∈ c ∧ isarc(g, y, x)}
```

step 1.2: simplifications

- $(sources(c) = \varnothing) \equiv$ **true** $\vdash$ ($\exists$ **nodesequ** s: $iscyc(s, c)) \equiv (c \neq \varnothing)$;
- $(sources(c) \neq \varnothing) \equiv$ **true** $\vdash$ $iscyc(s, c) \equiv iscyc(s, c\backslash sources(c))$)

```
if sources(c) = ∅ then c ≠ ∅ else ∃ nodesequ s: iscyc(s, c\sources(c)) fi
```

step 1.3: folding

```
funct hc = (nodeset c) bool:
   if sources(c) = ∅ then c ≠ ∅ else hc(c\sources(c)) fi
```

<u>Main development continued</u>

```
funct hascycle = (graph g) bool:
   hc(nodes(g)) where
   funct hc = (nodeset c) bool:
      if sources(c) = ∅ then c ≠ ∅ else hc(c\sources(c)) fi,

   funct sources = (nodeset c) nodeset:
      {node x: x ∈ c ∧ preds(x, c) = ∅},

   funct preds = (node x, nodeset c) nodeset:
      {node y: y ∈ c ∧ isarc(g, y, x)}.
```

5.5.5 Hamming's Problem

Hamming's problem (Sect. 3.6.4) not only serves as another example for transformational programming, but also illustrates the use of embeddings with assertions.

We start from the descriptive specification

funct *hamming* = (**nat** *N*) **natsequ**:
  some natsequ *s*: $|s| = N \wedge s \preccurlyeq sort(settosequ\{\textbf{nat}\ x: H(x)\})$.

<u>**Main development**</u>

Focus: function *hamming*
Goal: applicative program for *hamming*
Strategy: generalized unfold/fold
Transformations:

step 1: case introduction $(N = 0 \vee N > 0)$

if $N = 0$ **then some natsequ** *s*: $|s| = N \wedge s \preccurlyeq sort(settosequ\{\textbf{nat}\ x: H(x)\})$
  else some natsequ *s*: $|s| = N \wedge s \preccurlyeq sort(settosequ\{\textbf{nat}\ x: H(x)\})$ **fi**

step 2: simplification of **then**- and **else**-branch

if $N = 0$ **then** <>
  else <1> + **some natsequ** *s*:
    $|s| = N-1 \wedge s \preccurlyeq sort(settosequ\{\textbf{nat}\ x: x > 1 \wedge H(x)\})$ **fi**

step 3: embedding (with assertion)

funct *hamming* = (**nat** *N*) **natsequ**:
  if $N = 0$ **then** <> **else** *ham*(<1>, $N-1$) **fi where**

  funct *ham* = (**natsequ** *t*, **nat** *n*: *isham*(*t*)) **natsequ**:
    t + **some natsequ** *s*: $|s| = n \wedge ish(s, \textbf{last}\ t)$,

  funct *ish* = (**natsequ** *s*, **nat** *m*) **bool**:
    $s \preccurlyeq sort(settosequ\{\textbf{nat}\ x: x > m \wedge H(x)\})$,

  funct *isham* = (**natsequ** *t*) **bool**:
    $<1> \preccurlyeq t \preccurlyeq sort(settosequ\{\textbf{nat}\ x: H(x)\})$

<u>**Subdevelopment 1**</u>

Focus: function *ham*
Goal: applicative program for *ham*
Strategy: generalized unfold/fold
Transformations:

step 1.1: case introduction $(n = 0 \vee n > 0)$

if $n = 0$ **then** t + **some natsequ** *s*: $|s| = n \wedge ish(s, \textbf{last}\ t)$
  else t + **some natsequ** *s*: $|s| = n \wedge ish(s, \textbf{last}\ t)$ **fi**

step 1.2: simplification in **then**-branch;
  simplification in **else**-branch (under premise $n > 0$):
  $(n > 0) \equiv \textbf{true} \vdash$
    some natsequ *s*: $|s| = n \wedge ish(s, \textbf{last}\ t) \equiv$

nextham(**last***t*) + **some natsequ** *s*: $|s| = n{-}1 \wedge$ *ish*(*s*, *nextham*(**last***t*)) **where**
funct *nextham* = (**nat** *m*) **nat**:
that nat m': $m < m' \wedge H(m') \wedge \forall$ **nat** z: $m < z < m' \Rightarrow \neg H(z)$

if $n = 0$ **then** t
else t + *nextham*(**last***t*) + **some natsequ** *s*: $|s| = n{-}1 \wedge$
ish(*s*, *nextham*(**last***t*)) **fi**

step 1.3: folding (with assertion)

if $n = 0$ **then** t **else** *ham*(*t*+*nextham*(**last***t*), $n{-}1$) **fi**

<u>**Main development continued**</u>

funct *hamming* = (**nat** N) **natsequ**:
if $N = 0$ **then** $<>$ **else** *ham*($<1>$, $N{-}1$) **fi** **where**

funct *ham* = (**natsequ** *t*, **nat** *n*: *isham*(*t*)) **natsequ**:
if $n = 0$ **then** t **else** *ham*(*t*+*nextham*(**last***t*), $n{-}1$) **fi**,

funct *isham* = (**natsequ** *t*) **bool**:
$<1> \preccurlyeq t \preccurlyeq$ *sort*(*settosequ*{**nat** x: $H(x)$}),

funct *nextham* = (**nat** *m*) **nat**:
that nat m': $m < m' \wedge H(m') \wedge \forall$ **nat** z: $m < z < m' \Rightarrow \neg H(z)$.

It remains to derive an operational specification for *nextham*. A simple way of doing so is by 'linear search':

funct *nextham* = (**nat** *m*) **nat**:
if $H(m)$ **then** m **else** *nextham*(m+1) **fi**.

A more efficient way of computing *nextham* will be derived in Chap. 6.

5.5.6 Unification of Terms

The "unification problem" (Sect. 3.6.9) is used to demonstrate the strategy for developing a partial function from its domain restriction (Sect. 5.3.4). In addition, as in Sect. 5.5.2, we will also clearly indicate the subphases in the 'generalized unfold/fold strategy'.

funct *unify* = (**term** t_1, **term** t_2) (**subst** | **dummy**):
if *unifiable*(t_1, t_2) **then some subst** *s*: $t_1 \diamond s =_t t_2 \diamond s$ **else dummy fi where**

funct *unifiable* = (**term** t_1, **term** t_2) **bool**:
$\exists$ **subst** *s*: $t_1 \diamond s =_t t_2 \diamond s$

<u>**Main development**</u>
Focus: function *unify*
Goal: applicative program for *unify*
Strategy: development of a partial function from its domain restriction
Transformations:

step 1: embedding of the domain of *unifiable*

$$\begin{array}{l}\textbf{funct } unify = (\textbf{term } t_1, \textbf{term } t_2)\ (\textbf{subst} \mid \textbf{dummy}):\\ \quad \textbf{if } s\text{-}unifiable(\langle t_1\rangle, \langle t_2\rangle) \textbf{ then some subst } s: \langle t_1\rangle \blacklozenge s =_{ts} \langle t_2\rangle \blacklozenge s\\ \qquad\qquad \textbf{else dummy fi where}\end{array}$$

$$\begin{array}{l}\textbf{funct } s\text{-}unifiable = (\textbf{termsequ } st_1, \textbf{termsequ } st_2)\ \textbf{bool}:\\ \quad \exists\, \textbf{subst } s: st_1 \blacklozenge s =_{ts} st_2 \blacklozenge s\end{array}$$

step 2: development of an applicative solution for *s-unifiable*

<u>**Subdevelopment 1**</u>

Focus: function *s-unifiable*
Goal: applicative program for *s-unifiable*
Strategy: generalized unfold/fold
Transformations:

step 1.1: development of a first applicative solution for *s-unifiable*

<u>**Subdevelopment 1.1**</u>

Goal: decomposition and detailing
Transformations:

step 1.1.1: case introduction w.r.t. the definition of **termsequ**; =-substitution

$$\begin{array}{l}((st_1 = \langle\rangle \wedge st_2 = \langle\rangle)\ \Delta\ \exists\, \textbf{subst } s: \langle\rangle \blacklozenge s =_{ts} \langle\rangle \blacklozenge s) \vee\\ ((st_1 = \langle\rangle \wedge st_2 \neq \langle\rangle)\ \Delta\ \exists\, \textbf{subst } s: \langle\rangle \blacklozenge s =_{ts} st_2 \blacklozenge s) \vee\\ ((st_1 \neq \langle\rangle \wedge st_2 = \langle\rangle)\ \Delta\ \exists\, \textbf{subst } s: st_1 \blacklozenge s =_{ts} \langle\rangle \blacklozenge s) \vee\\ ((st_1 \neq \langle\rangle \wedge st_2 \neq \langle\rangle)\ \Delta\ \exists\, \textbf{subst } s: st_1 \blacklozenge s =_{ts} st_2 \blacklozenge s)\end{array}$$

step 1.1.2: simplification $((st \blacklozenge s = \langle\rangle) \equiv (st = \langle\rangle))$; unfolding the definition of $\blacklozenge$

$$\begin{array}{l}(st_1 = \langle\rangle \wedge st_2 = \langle\rangle) \vee\\ ((st_1 \neq \langle\rangle \wedge st_2 \neq \langle\rangle)\ \Delta\\ \quad \exists\, \textbf{subst } s: (\textbf{first}st_1 \lozenge s + \textbf{rest}st_1 \blacklozenge s) =_{ts} (\textbf{first}st_2 \lozenge s + \textbf{rest}st_2 \blacklozenge s))\end{array}$$

step 1.1.3: instantiation of $=_{ts}$

$$\begin{array}{l}(st_1 = \langle\rangle \wedge st_2 = \langle\rangle) \vee\\ ((st_1 \neq \langle\rangle \wedge st_2 \neq \langle\rangle)\ \Delta\\ (\exists\, \textbf{subst } s: (\textbf{first}st_1 \lozenge s =_t \textbf{first}st_2 \lozenge s) \wedge (\textbf{rest}st_1 \blacklozenge s =_{ts} \textbf{rest}st_2 \blacklozenge s)))\end{array}$$

step 1.1.4: abstraction; case introduction w.r.t. the definition of **term**

$$\begin{array}{l}(st_1 = \langle\rangle \wedge st_2 = \langle\rangle) \vee\\ ((st_1 \neq \langle\rangle \wedge st_2 \neq \langle\rangle)\ \Delta\\ (\textbf{term } t_1 = \textbf{first}st_1; \textbf{term } t_2 = \textbf{first}st_2;\\ \ \textbf{termsequ } tt_1 = \textbf{rest}st_1; \textbf{termsequ } tt_2 = \textbf{rest}st_2;\\ \ \exists\, \textbf{subst } s: ((t_1 \textbf{ is } op \wedge t_2 \textbf{ is } op)\ \Delta\ t_1 \lozenge s =_t t_2 \lozenge s) \vee\\ \qquad ((t_1 \textbf{ is } var \wedge t_2 \textbf{ is } op)\ \Delta\ t_1 \lozenge s =_t t_2 \lozenge s) \vee\\ \qquad ((t_1 \textbf{ is } op \wedge t_2 \textbf{ is } var)\ \Delta\ t_1 \lozenge s =_t t_2 \lozenge s) \vee\\ \qquad ((t_1 \textbf{ is } var \wedge t_2 \textbf{ is } var)\ \Delta\ t_1 \lozenge s =_t t_2 \lozenge s))\ \Delta\ (tt_1 \blacklozenge s =_{ts} tt_2 \blacklozenge s)))\end{array}$$

Subdevelopment 1.2

Goal: simplification and rearrangement
Focus: existentially quantified subexpression
Transformations:

step 1.2.1: distributivity of Δ and $\vee$;
quantifier rearrangement

$$((t_1 \textbf{ is } op \wedge t_2 \textbf{ is } op)\ \Delta\ \exists\ \textbf{subst } s\text{: } (t_1 \Diamond s =_t t_2 \Diamond s\ \Delta\ tt_1 \blacklozenge s =_{ts} tt_2 \blacklozenge s)) \vee$$
$$((t_1 \textbf{ is } var \wedge t_2 \textbf{ is } op)\ \Delta\ \exists\ \textbf{subst } s\text{: } (t_1 \Diamond s =_t t_2 \Diamond s\ \Delta\ tt_1 \blacklozenge s =_{ts} tt_2 \blacklozenge s)) \vee$$
$$((t_1 \textbf{ is } op \wedge t_2 \textbf{ is } var)\ \Delta\ \exists\ \textbf{subst } s\text{: } (t_1 \Diamond s =_t t_2 \Diamond s\ \Delta\ tt_1 \blacklozenge s =_{ts} tt_2 \blacklozenge s)) \vee$$
$$((t_1 \textbf{ is } var \wedge t_2 \textbf{ is } var)\ \Delta\ \exists\ \textbf{subst } s\text{: } (t_1 \Diamond s =_t t_2 \Diamond s\ \Delta\ tt_1 \blacklozenge s =_{ts} tt_2 \blacklozenge s))$$

step 1.2.2: simplifications (for the proofs, see [Partsch 86])

- $(t_1 \textbf{ is } op \wedge t_2 \textbf{ is } op) \equiv \textbf{true} \vdash$
  $(\exists\ \textbf{subst } s\text{: } (t_1 \Diamond s =_t t_2 \Diamond s)\ \Delta\ (tt_1 \blacklozenge s =_{ts} tt_2 \blacklozenge s)) \equiv$
  $((opsym(t_1) = opsym(t_2))\ \Delta$
  $\exists\ \textbf{subst } s\text{: } ((args(t_1) \blacklozenge s =_{ts} args(t_2) \blacklozenge s)\ \Delta\ (tt_1 \blacklozenge s =_{ts} tt_2 \blacklozenge s)));$
- $(t_1 \textbf{ is } var \wedge t_2 \textbf{ is } op) \equiv \textbf{true} \vdash$
  $(v(t_1) \notin vars(t_2))\ \Delta$
  $\exists\ \textbf{subst } s\text{: } (tt_1 \blacklozenge (v(t_1), t_2)) \blacklozenge s =_{ts} (tt_2 \blacklozenge (v(t_1), t_2)) \blacklozenge s \subseteq$
  $\exists\ \textbf{subst } s\text{: } (t_1 \Diamond s =_t t_2 \Diamond s\ \Delta\ tt_1 \blacklozenge s =_{ts} tt_2 \blacklozenge s);$
- $((t_1 \textbf{ is } var \wedge t_2 \textbf{ is } op)\ \Delta\ (v(t_1) \in vars(t_2))) \equiv \textbf{true} \vdash$
  $(\exists\ \textbf{subst } s\text{: } t_1 \Diamond s =_t t_2 \Diamond s) \equiv \textbf{false};$
- $((t_1 \textbf{ is } var \wedge t_2 \textbf{ is } var)\ \Delta\ (v(t_1) = v(t_2))) \equiv \textbf{true} \vdash$
  $(\exists\ \textbf{subst } s\text{: } tt_1 \blacklozenge s =_{ts} tt_2 \blacklozenge s) \equiv$
  $(\exists\ \textbf{subst } s\text{: } t_1 \Diamond s =_t t_2 \Diamond s\ \Delta\ tt_1 \blacklozenge s =_{ts} tt_2 \blacklozenge s);$
- $((t_1 \textbf{ is } var \wedge t_2 \textbf{ is } var)\ \Delta\ (v(t_1) \neq v(t_2))) \equiv \textbf{true} \vdash$
  $\exists\ \textbf{subst } s\text{: } (tt_1 \blacklozenge (v(t_1), t_2)) \blacklozenge s =_{ts} (tt_2 \blacklozenge (v(t_1), t_2)) \blacklozenge s \subseteq$
  $\exists\ \textbf{subst } s\text{: } (t_1 \Diamond s =_t t_2 \Diamond s\ \Delta\ tt_1 \blacklozenge s =_{ts} tt_2 \blacklozenge s);$
- symmetric case for t_1 **is** $op \wedge t_2$ **is** var

$$((t_1 \textbf{ is } op \wedge t_2 \textbf{ is } op)\ \Delta\ (opsym(t_1) = opsym(t_2))\ \Delta$$
$$\exists\ \textbf{subst } s\text{: } ((args(t_1) \blacklozenge s =_{ts} args(t_2) \blacklozenge s)\ \Delta\ (tt_1 \blacklozenge s =_{ts} tt_2 \blacklozenge s))) \vee$$
$$((t_1 \textbf{ is } var \wedge t_2 \textbf{ is } op)\ \Delta\ (v(t_1) \notin vars(t_2))\ \Delta$$
$$\exists\ \textbf{subst } s\text{: } (tt_1 \blacklozenge (v(t_1), t_2)) \blacklozenge s =_{ts} (tt_2 \blacklozenge (v(t_1), t_2)) \blacklozenge s) \vee$$
$$((t_1 \textbf{ is } op \wedge t_2 \textbf{ is } var)\ \Delta\ (v(t_2) \notin vars(t_1))\ \Delta$$
$$\exists\ \textbf{subst } s\text{: } (tt_1 \blacklozenge (v(t_2), t_1)) \blacklozenge s =_{ts} (tt_2 \blacklozenge (v(t_2), t_1)) \blacklozenge s) \vee$$
$$((t_1 \textbf{ is } var \wedge t_2 \textbf{ is } var)\ \Delta\ (v(t_1) = v(t_2))\ \Delta\ \exists\ \textbf{subst } s\text{: } tt_1 \blacklozenge s =_{ts} tt_2 \blacklozenge s) \vee$$
$$((t_1 \textbf{ is } var \wedge t_2 \textbf{ is } var)\ \Delta\ (v(t_1) \neq v(t_2))\ \Delta$$
$$\exists\ \textbf{subst } s\text{: } (tt_1 \blacklozenge (v(t_1), t_2)) \blacklozenge s =_{ts} (tt_2 \blacklozenge (v(t_1), t_2)) \blacklozenge s)$$

Subdevelopment 1.3

Goal: composition
Transformations:

step 1.3.1: use of properties

- $(st_1 =_{ts} st_2 \wedge st_1' =_{ts} st_2') \equiv \textbf{true} \vdash (st_1 + st_1' =_{ts} st_2 + st_2') \equiv \textbf{true};$
- $(st_1 \blacklozenge s) + (st_2 \blacklozenge s) \equiv (st_1 + st_2) \blacklozenge s$

$$((t_1 \textbf{ is } op \wedge t_2 \textbf{ is } op)\ \Delta\ (opsym(t_1) = opsym(t_2))\ \Delta$$
$$\exists\ \textbf{subst } s\text{: } (args(t_1) + tt_1) \blacklozenge s =_{ts} (args(t_2) + tt_2) \blacklozenge s) \vee$$
$$((t_1 \textbf{ is } var \wedge t_2 \textbf{ is } op)\ \Delta\ (v(t_1) \notin vars(t_2))\ \Delta$$
$$\exists\ \textbf{subst } s\text{: } (tt_1 \blacklozenge (v(t_1), t_2)) \blacklozenge s =_{ts} (tt_2 \blacklozenge (v(t_1), t_2)) \blacklozenge s) \vee$$
$$((t_1 \textbf{ is } op \wedge t_2 \textbf{ is } var)\ \Delta\ (v(t_2) \notin vars(t_1))\ \Delta$$

$\exists$ **subst** s: $(tt_1 \blacklozenge (v(t_2), t_1)) \blacklozenge s =_{ts} (tt_2 \blacklozenge (v(t_2), t_1)) \blacklozenge s) \vee$
$((t_1$ **is** $var \wedge t_2$ **is** $var)\ \Delta\ (v(t_1) = v(t_2))\ \Delta\ \exists$ **subst** s: $tt_1 \blacklozenge s =_{ts} tt_2 \blacklozenge s) \vee$
$((t_1$ **is** $var \wedge t_2$ **is** $var)\ \Delta\ (v(t_1) \neq v(t_2))\ \Delta$
$\exists$ **subst** s: $(tt_1 \blacklozenge (v(t_1), t_2)) \blacklozenge s =_{ts} (tt_2 \blacklozenge (v(t_1), t_2)) \blacklozenge s)$

New focus: function *s-unifiable*
step 1.3.2: folding with *s-unifiable*

funct *s-unifiable* = (**termsequ** st_1, **termsequ** st_2) **bool**:
$(st_1 = \langle\rangle \wedge st_2 = \langle\rangle) \vee$
$((st_1 \neq \langle\rangle \wedge st_2 \neq \langle\rangle)\ \Delta$
(**term** t_1 = **first**st_1; **term** t_2 = **first**st_2;
termsequ tt_1 = **rest**st_1; **termsequ** tt_2 = **rest**st_2;
$((t_1$ **is** $op \wedge t_2$ **is** $op)\ \Delta\ (opsym(t_1)=opsym(t_2))\ \Delta$
$s\text{-}unifiable(args(t_1)+tt_1, args(t_2)+tt_2)) \vee$
$((t_1$ **is** $var \wedge t_2$ **is** $op)\ \Delta\ (v(t_1) \notin vars(t_2))\ \Delta$
$s\text{-}unifiable(tt_1 \blacklozenge (v(t_1), t_2), tt_2 \blacklozenge (v(t_1), t_2))) \vee$
$((t_1$ **is** $op \wedge t_2$ **is** $var)\ \Delta\ (v(t_2) \notin vars(t_1))\ \Delta$
$s\text{-}unifiable(tt_1 \blacklozenge (v(t_2), t_1), tt_2 \blacklozenge (v(t_2), t_1))) \vee$
$((t_1$ **is** $var \wedge t_2$ **is** $var)\ \Delta\ (v(t_1) = v(t_2))\ \Delta\ s\text{-}unifiable(tt_1, tt_2)) \vee$
$((t_1$ **is** $var \wedge t_2$ **is** $var)\ \Delta\ (v(t_1) \neq v(t_2))\ \Delta$
$s\text{-}unifiable(tt_1 \blacklozenge (v(t_1), t_2), tt_2 \blacklozenge (v(t_1), t_2)))))$

Subdevelopment 1 continued

step 1.2: predicate extension

funct *s-unifiable* = (**termsequ** st_1, **termsequ** st_2) **bool**:
$s\text{-}unifiable(\langle t_1\rangle, \langle t_2\rangle, [\,])$ **where**

funct *s-unifiable'* = (**termsequ** st_1, **termsequ** st_2, **subst** s:
$(st_1 = \langle\rangle \wedge st_2 = \langle\rangle) \Rightarrow (\langle t_1\rangle \blacklozenge s =_{ts} \langle t_2\rangle \blacklozenge s))$ **bool**:
$(st_1 = \langle\rangle \wedge st_2 = \langle\rangle) \vee ((st_1 \neq \langle\rangle \wedge st_2 \neq \langle\rangle)\ \Delta$
(**term** t_1 = **first**st_1; **term** t_2 = **first**st_2;
termsequ tt_1 = **rest**st_1; **termsequ** tt_2 = **rest**st_2;
$((t_1$ **is** $op \wedge t_2$ **is** $op)\ \Delta\ (opsym(t_1)=opsym(t_2))\ \Delta$
$s\text{-}unifiable(args(t_1)+tt_1, args(t_2)+tt_2, s)) \vee$
$((t_1$ **is** $var \wedge t_2$ **is** $op)\ \Delta\ (v(t_1) \notin vars(t_2))\ \Delta$
$s\text{-}unifiable(tt_1 \blacklozenge (v(t_1), t_2), tt_2 \blacklozenge (v(t_1), t_2), s[v(t_1)] \leftarrow t_2)) \vee$
$((t_1$ **is** $op \wedge t_2$ **is** $var)\ \Delta\ (v(t_2) \notin vars(t_1))\ \Delta$
$s\text{-}unifiable(tt_1 \blacklozenge (v(t_2), t_1), tt_2 \blacklozenge (v(t_2), t_1), s[v(t_2)] \leftarrow t_1)) \vee$
$((t_1$ **is** $var \wedge t_2$ **is** $var)\ \Delta\ (v(t_1) = v(t_2))\ \Delta\ s\text{-}unifiable(tt_1, tt_2, s)) \vee$
$((t_1$ **is** $var \wedge t_2$ **is** $var)\ \Delta\ (v(t_1) \neq v(t_2))\ \Delta$
$s\text{-}unifiable(tt_1 \blacklozenge (v(t_1), t_2), tt_2 \blacklozenge (v(t_1), t_2), s[v(t_1)] \leftarrow t_2))))$

Main development continued

step 1.3: unfold of *s-unifiable* in *unify*; argument on termination I; trivial rearrangements

funct *unify* = (**term** t_1, **term** t_2) (**subst** | **dummy**):
$s\text{-}unify(\langle t_1\rangle, \langle t_2\rangle, [\,])$ **where**

funct $s\text{-}unify = (\textbf{termsequ}\ st_1, \textbf{termsequ}\ st_2, \textbf{subst}\ s)\ (\textbf{subst} \mid \textbf{dummy})$:
  if $st_1 =\langle\rangle \wedge st_2 =\langle\rangle$ **then** s
  elsf $st_1 \neq\langle\rangle \wedge st_2 \neq\langle\rangle$ **then**
    term $t_1 = \textbf{first}st_1$; **term** $t_2 = \textbf{first}st_2$;
    termsequ $tt_1 = \textbf{rest}st_1$; **termsequ** $tt_2 = \textbf{rest}st_2$;
    if $(t_1\ \textbf{is}\ op \wedge t_2\ \textbf{is}\ op)\ \Delta\ (opsym(t_1)=opsym(t_2))$ **then**
      $s\text{-}unify(args(t_1)+tt_1, args(t_2)+tt_2, s)$
    [] $(t_1\ \textbf{is}\ var \wedge t_2\ \textbf{is}\ op)\ \Delta\ (v(t_1) \notin vars(t_2))$ **then**
      $s\text{-}unify(tt_1 \blacklozenge (v(t_1), t_2), tt_2 \blacklozenge (v(t_1), t_2), s[v(t_1)] \leftarrow t_2)$
    [] $(t_1\ \textbf{is}\ op \wedge t_2\ \textbf{is}\ var)\ \Delta\ (v(t_2) \notin vars(t_1))$ **then**
      $s\text{-}unify(tt_1 \blacklozenge (v(t_2), t_1), tt_2 \blacklozenge (v(t_2), t_1), s[v(t_2)] \leftarrow t_1)$
    [] $(t_1\ \textbf{is}\ var \wedge t_2\ \textbf{is}\ var)\ \Delta\ (v(t_1) = v(t_2))$ **then** $s\text{-}unify(tt_1, tt_2, s)$
    [] $(t_1\ \textbf{is}\ var \wedge t_2\ \textbf{is}\ var)\ \Delta\ (v(t_1) \neq v(t_2))$ **then**
      $s\text{-}unify(tt_1 \blacklozenge (v(t_1), t_2), tt_2 \blacklozenge (v(t_1), t_2), s[v(t_1)] \leftarrow t_2)$
    else dummy fi
  else dummy fi

5.5.7 The "Pack Problem"

The "pack problem" was introduced in Sect. 3.6.10. It is formally specified by

funct $findpack = (\textbf{blockset}\ K, \textbf{boxsequ}\ B)\ (\textbf{corr} \mid \textbf{dummy})$:
  if $pack(K, B)$ **then some corr** A: $legal(A, K, B)$ **else dummy fi where**

  funct $pack = (\textbf{blockset}\ K, \textbf{boxsequ}\ B)\ \textbf{bool}$:
    $\exists\ \textbf{corr}\ A: legal(A, K, B)$,

  funct $legal = (\textbf{corr}\ A, \textbf{blockset}\ K, \textbf{boxsequ}\ B)\ \textbf{bool}$:
    $dom(A) = K \wedge ran(A) \subseteq B \wedge$
      $\forall\ (\textbf{nat}\ i: 1 \leq i \leq |B|): (\sum_{k \in blocks(A, B[i])} |k|) \leq |B[i]|$

Main development
  Focus: function *findpack*
  Goal: applicative program for *findpack*
  Strategy: development of a partial function from its domain restriction (cf. Sect. 5.3.4)
  Transformations:

  step 1: derivation of an applicative program for *pack*

Subdevelopment 1
  Focus: function *pack*
  Goal: applicative program for *pack*
  Strategy: generalized unfold/fold
  Transformations:

  step 1.1: case introduction $(K = \varnothing\ \nabla\ K \neq \varnothing)$

  $(K = \varnothing\ \Delta\ \exists\ \textbf{corr}\ A: legal(A, K, B))\ \nabla\ (K \neq \varnothing\ \Delta\ \exists\ \textbf{corr}\ A: legal(A, K, B))$

step 1.2: simplifications

- =-substitution;
- $(K \neq \varnothing) \equiv$ **true** $\vdash K \equiv ((K\text{–}k) + k$ **where block** $k = arb(K)]$

$(K = \varnothing \,\Delta\, \exists$ **corr** A: $legal(A, \varnothing, B)) \,\nabla$
$(K \neq \varnothing \,\Delta\, (\exists$ **corr** A: $legal(A, (K\text{–}k) + k, B)$ **where block** $k = arb(K)))$

step 1.3: further simplification

Subdevelopment 1.1

Focus: first disjunct of the expression derived in step 1.2
Goal: simplified expression
Strategy: unfold and algebraic properties

$K = \varnothing \,\Delta\, \exists$ **corr** A: $legal(A, \varnothing, B)$
  ≡ [unfold *legal*]
$K = \varnothing \,\Delta\, (\exists$ **corr** A: $dom(A) = \varnothing \wedge ran(A) \subseteq B \wedge$
  $\forall$ (**nat** i: $1 \le i \le |B|$): $(\Sigma_{k \in blocks(A, B[i])} |k|) \le |B[i]|)$
  ≡ [$(dom(A) = \varnothing) \equiv (A = [])$; =–substitution]
$K = \varnothing \,\Delta\, (\exists$ **corr** A: $A = [] \wedge ran([]) \subseteq B \wedge$
  $\forall$ (**nat** i: $1 \le i \le |B|$): $(\Sigma_{k \in blocks([], B[i])} |k|) \le |B[i]|)$
  ≡ [$ran([]) = \varnothing$; $blocks([], B[i]) = \varnothing$]
$K = \varnothing \,\Delta\, (\exists$ **corr** A: $A = [] \wedge \varnothing \subseteq B \wedge$
  $\forall$ (**nat** i: $1 \le i \le |B|$): $(\Sigma_{k \in \varnothing} |k|) \le |B[i]|)$
  ≡ [$(\varnothing \subseteq B) \equiv$ **true**; $(\Sigma_{k \in \varnothing} |k|) \equiv 0$; $(0 \le |B[i]|) \equiv$ **true**]
$K = \varnothing \,\Delta\, (\exists$ **corr** A: $A = [] \wedge$ **true** $\wedge \forall$ (**nat** i: $1 \le i \le |B|$): **true**)
  ≡ [trivial simplifications]
$K = \varnothing$

Subdevelopment 1.2

Focus: second disjunct of the expression derived in step 1.2
Goal: simplified expression
Strategy: algebraic properties

$K \neq \varnothing \,\Delta\, (\exists$ **corr** A: $legal(A, (K\text{–}k) + k, B)$
  ≡ [case introduction; right-distributivity of Δ]
$K \neq \varnothing \,\Delta$
  $((\exists$ (**nat** i: $1 \le i \le |B|$): $|B[i]| \ge |k| \;\Delta\, (\exists$ **corr** A: $legal(A, (K\text{–}k) + k, B)) \vee$
  $(\neg\exists$ (**nat** i: $1 \le i \le |B|$): $|B[i]| \ge |k| \;\Delta\, (\exists$ **corr** A: $legal(A, (K\text{–}k) + k, B)))$
  ≡ [$(\neg\exists$ (**nat** i: $1 \le i \le |B|$): $|B[i]| \ge |k|) \equiv$ **true** $\vdash (\exists$ **corr** A: $legal(A, (K\text{-}k)+k, B) \equiv$ **false**;
   ∨-simplification]
$K \neq \varnothing \,\Delta\, \exists$ (**nat** i: $1 \le i \le |B|$): $|B[i]| \ge |k| \;\Delta\; (\exists$ **corr** A: $legal(A, (K\text{–}k) + k, B))$
  ≡ [$(\exists$ (**nat** i: $1 \le i \le |B|$): $|B[i]| \ge |k|) \equiv$ **true** $\vdash$
   $(\exists$ **corr** A: $legal(A, (K\text{–}k) + k, B)) \equiv (\exists$ **corr** A: $legal(A, K\text{–}k, B[i \Theta k]))$;
   co $B[i \Theta k]$ is short for updating B such that the size of its i-th component is decreased by k **co**]
$K \neq \varnothing \,\Delta\, \exists$ (**nat** i: $1 \le i \le |B|$): $|B[i]| \ge |k| \;\Delta\; (\exists$ **corr** A: $legal(A, K\text{–}k, B[i \Theta k]))$

Subdevelopment 1 continued

```
K = ∅ ∇
(K ≠ ∅ Δ ∃ (nat i: 1≤i≤|B|): |B[i]| ≥ |k| Δ
   (∃ corr A: legal(A, K–k, B[iΘk]) where block k = arb(K))
```

step 1.4: simplification

```
K = ∅ ∇ (∃ (nat i: 1≤i≤|B|): |B[i]| ≥ |k| Δ (∃ corr A: legal(A, K–k, B[iΘk])
where block k = arb(K)))
```

step 1.5: folding *pack*

```
funct pack = (blockset K, boxsequ B) bool:
   K = ∅ ∇ (∃ (nat i: 1≤i≤|B|): |B[i]| ≥ |k|  Δ pack(K–k, B[iΘk])
   where block k = arb(K))
```

step 1.6: predicate extension II

```
funct pack = (blockset K, boxsequ B) bool:
   pack'(K, B, [])  where

   funct pack' =  (blockset K, boxsequ B, corr A:
                    K = ∅ ⇨ legal(K, B, A)) bool:
      K = ∅ ∇ (∃ (nat i: 1≤i≤|B|): |B[i]| ≥ |k|  Δ pack(K–k, B[iΘk], A[k]←i)
                  where block k = arb(K))
```

Main development continued

step 2: embedding (of *findpack*)

```
funct findpack = (blockset K, boxsequ B) (corr | dummy):
   findpack'(K, B, []) where

   funct findpack' = (blockset K, boxsequ B, corr A:
                        K = ∅ ⇨ legal(K, B, A)) (corr | dummy):
      if pack'(K, B, A) then some corr A: legal(A, K, B)
                          else dummy fi;
```

step 3: argument on termination II

```
funct findpack = (blockset K, boxsequ B) (corr | dummy):
   findpack'(K, B, []) where

   funct findpack' = (blockset K, boxsequ B, corr A:
                        K = ∅ ⇨ legal(K, B, A)) (corr | dummy):
      if K = ∅ then A  else h(K, B, A, 1) fi,

   funct h = (blockset K, boxsequ B, corr A, nat i) (corr | dummy):
      if i > |B| then dummy
        else if |B[i]| ≥ k
          then (corr | dummy) A' = findpack'(K–k, B[iΘk], A[k]←i);
                 if ¬(A' is dummy) then A' else h(K, B, A, i+1) fi
          else h(K, B, A, i+1) fi
        where block k = arb(K)  fi,
```

funct *legal* = (**corr** A, **blockset** K, **boxsequ** B) **bool**:
$dom(A) = K \wedge ran(A) \subseteq B \wedge$
$\forall$ (**nat** i: $1 \le i \le |B|$): $(\Sigma_{k \in blocks(A, B[i])} |k|) \le |B[i]|$.

5.6 Exercises

Exercise 5.1-1

The problem of the "truncated dual logarithm" (Sect. 5.1) may also be specified by

that nat a: $a \geq 1 \, \Delta$ ($\exists$ **nat** r: $n = 2^a + r \wedge r < 2^a$).

Prove the equivalence of all four specifications.

Exercise 5.2-1

Given the formal specification (with **div** denoting integer division)

funct *average* = (**natsequ** s: $s \neq$<>) **nat**:
sum(s) **div** *num*(s) **where**
funct *sum* = (**natsequ** s) **nat**: **if** s =<> **then** 0 **else** **first**s + *sum*(**rest**s) **fi**,
funct *num* = (**natsequ** s) **nat**: **if** s =<> **then** 0 **else** 1+ *num*(**rest**s) **fi**,

derive, starting with a suitable embedding, a recursive version of *average* that is independent of *sum* and *num*.

Exercise 5.2-2

Starting with suitable embeddings, transform the descriptive specifications

a) **funct** *split* = (**natsequ** s) (**natsequ**, **natsequ**):
some (**natsequ** a, **natsequ** b): $s = a+b \wedge ||a| - |b|| \le 1$;
b) **funct** *perfect* = (**nat** n) **bool**: $n = \Sigma_{0 \le d < n \wedge d|n} d$
(where "|" denotes divisibility)

into operational ones.

Exercise 5.3-1

Prove, by applying suitable transformations, the correctness of the rule *case introduction* (Sect. 5.3.1).

Exercise 5.3-2

Transform the following descriptive specifications into operational ones (where "|" denotes divisibility):

a) **funct** *all* = (**bitsequ** a) **bool**:
$\forall$ (**nat** i: $1 \le i \le |a|$): $a[i] = 1$,
b) **funct** *prop;* = (**nat** n) **bool**:
$\exists$ **nat** i: $n = 2^i - 1$;
c) **funct** *convert* = (**nat** n) **bitstring**:
some bitstring a: $n = \Sigma_{i=1..|a|} a[i] \times 2^{|a|-i}$;
d) **funct** *mod* = (**nat** a, **nat** b: $b>0$) **nat**:
that nat r: $\exists$ **nat** q: $a = q \times b + r \wedge 0 \le r < b$;

e) **funct** lcm = (**nat** a, **nat** b: $a \geq b$) **nat**:
   some nat k: $(a \mid k) \wedge (b \mid k) \wedge \forall$ **nat** k': $((a \mid k') \wedge (b \mid k')) \Rightarrow k < k'$;

f) **funct** ld = (**nat** n: $n > 0$) **nat**:
   that nat a: $a \geq 1 \;\Delta\; (2^{a-1} \leq n \;\wedge n < 2^a)$.

Exercise 5.3-3

Let the following formal specification be given:

funct $ndiv$ = (**nat** n: $n \neq 0$) **nat**:
  $nd(1)$ **where**
  funct nd = (**nat** k: $k \leq n$) **nat**:
    if $k{=}n$ **then** 0
    [] $k{\neq}n \wedge (k \mid n)$ **then** $1 + nd(k{+}1)$
    [] $k{\neq}n \wedge \neg(k \mid n)$ **then** $nd(k{+}1)$ **fi**.

where "|" denotes divisibility.

a) Starting from the formal specification

   funct $sdiv$ = (**nat** n: $n \neq 0$) **nat**:
     $sd(1)$ **where**
     funct sd = (**nat** k: $k \leq n$) **nat**:
       $\Sigma_{(\textbf{nat}\ i:\ (i|n)\ \wedge\ i \geq k\ \wedge\ i<n)}\, i$,

   derive, by suitable transformations, an operational version of sd;

b) Starting from the formal specification

   funct $nsdiv$ = (**nat** n: $n \neq 0$) (**nat**, **nat**):
     $nsd(1)$ **where**
     funct nsd = (**nat** k: $k \leq n$) (**nat**, **nat**):
       $(nd(k), sd(k))$,

   derive, by using the unfold/fold strategy, a recursive solution for nsd which is independent of nd and sd;

c) By starting with a suitable embedding, derive a function nd' which is equivalent to nd and tail-recursive.

Exercise 5.3-4

Prove, by applying suitable rules, the correctness of the rule *argument on termination II*.

Exercise 5.3-5

Assume the formal specification (Ex. 3.4-5a)

mode sequ = EESEQU(**m**, =);
funct $diff$ = (**sequ** s) **bool**:
  $\forall$ (**nat** i, j: $1 \leq i, j \leq |s|$): $i \neq j \Rightarrow s[i] \neq s[j]$.

a) Prove (for arbitrary **m** x, **sequ** s):
   $x \notin s \equiv \forall$ (**nat** k: $1 \leq k \leq |s|$): $x \neq s[k]$;

b) Prove (for arbitrary **sequ** s):
   $\forall$ (**nat** i, j: $1 \leq i, j \leq |s|$): $i \neq j \Rightarrow s[i] \neq s[j] \equiv$
   $\forall$ (**nat** i, j: $1 \leq i < j \leq |s|$): $s[i] \neq s[j]$;

c) Derive, by transformations, an operational solution for $diff$.

Exercise 5.3-6

For sequences defined by

mode sequ = EESEQU(**m**, =)

derive, by transformations, operational specifications from the following descriptive ones (Ex. 3.4.6):

a) **funct** *del* = (**sequ** *l*, **sequ** *s*: $l \preccurlyeq s$) **sequ**:
    that sequ *r*: $l + r = s$,
b) **funct** *lmcontext* = (**sequ** *s*, **sequ** *p*: $p \subseteq s$) (**sequ**, **sequ**):
    that (**sequ** *l*, **sequ** *r*): $l + p + r = s \wedge$
        $\forall$ (**sequ** *l'*, **sequ** *r'*): $l' + p + r' = s \Rightarrow l \preccurlyeq l'$.

Exercise 5.3-7

a) Given the formal specifications (Sect. 3.6.3)

mode acnr = (**nat** *n*: $1.000.000 \le n \le 9.999.999$);
mode bal = *mb*(**acnr** *acc*, **int** *amount*);
mode afile = EESEQU(**bal**, =);
mode acfile = (**afile** *af*: *isacfile*(*af*));
funct *isacfile* = (**afile** *af*) **bool**:
    $|\{$**acnr** *a*: $\exists$ **int** *b*: $mb(a, b) \in af\}| = |af|$
funct *legalacc* = (**anr** *a*, **acfile** *af*) **bool**:
    $\exists$ **bal** *b*: $b \in af \wedge acc(b) = a$,

derive, by program transformations, operational solutions for *isacfile* and *legalacc*;

b) Given the declarations as in (a) and the additional specifications

mode gtr = *mgt*(**acnr** *acc*, **ttype** *kind*, **int** *amount*);
mode gtfile = ESEQU(**gtr**);
funct *cbal* = (**acfile** *a*, **gtfile** *t*, **acnr** *anr*) (**int** | **error**):
    if *legalacc*(*anr*, *a*) **then** *selacc*(*anr*, *iupdate*(*a*, *t*, *anr*)) **else error fi**;
funct *selacc* = (**acnr** *anr*, **acfile** *a*: *legalacc*(*anr*, *a*)) **int**:
    that bal *b*: $acc(b) = anr \wedge b \in a$;
funct *iupdate* = (**acfile** *a*, **gtfile** *t*, **acnr** *anr*: *legalacc*(*anr*, *a*)) **acfile**:
    if *a* =<> **then** <>
    elsf *acc*(**first***a*) = *anr* **then** *mb*(*anr*, *newgbal*(**first***a*, *t*)) + **rest***a*
        else first*a* + *iupdate*(**rest***a*, *t*, *anr*) **fi**,

derive, by using the technique from Sect. 5.3.4, an operational specification for *cbal*.

Exercise 5.3-8

Given the descriptive specification

mode sequ = ESEQU(**m**);
mode bintree = *et* | *mt*(**bintree** *l*, **m** *n*, **bintree** *r*);
funct *conv* = (**sequ** *s*) **bintree**:
    some bintree *b*: *inord*(*b*) = *s* **where**

```
funct inord = (bintree b) sequ:
    if b is et then <> else inord(l(b)) + n(b) + inord(r(b)) fi,
```

derive, by transformations, an operational specification for *conv*.

Exercise 5.3-9

Simplify the formal specification (Sect. 5.3.4)

```
funct path = (char y, bintree b) pos:
   path'(b, <>) where
   funct path' = (bintree t, pos s:
                    (t is leaf Δ c(t) = y) ⇨ c(sel(b, s)) = y) (pos | dummy):
      if t is leaf Δ c(t) = y then s else path"(1, t, s) fi,
   funct path" = (nat i, bintree t, pos s) (pos | dummy):
      if i > 2 then dummy
      elsf t is comp
         then (pos | dummy) s' = path'(if i=1 then (left(t), s+L)
                                            else (right(t), s+R) fi);
              if ¬(s' is dummy) then s' else path"(i+1, t, s) fi
              else path"(i+1, t, s) fi fi.
```

Exercise 5.3-10

Prove the termination of *s-unify* from Sect. 5.5.6.

6. Modification of Applicative Programs

Applicative programs, irrespective of whether given as an initial operational problem specification or derived using the transformations and tactics dealt with so far, can often be further manipulated. In particular, modifications can be carried out that aim at increasing efficiency by speeding up the performance of certain computations, avoiding duplicated evaluations of expressions, and so on. Most of these manipulations could also be done later in the development, say on a procedural level. However, experience (see for example [Burstall, Darlington 77] and [Pepper, Partsch 80]) has shown that it is advisable to do these manipulations on the applicative level as far as possible, thus profiting from the obvious advantages (such as 'referential transparency' [Quine 60]) of this level of formulation. Thus, for example, all techniques that in a procedural environment are referred to as 'loop fusion' are covered in an applicative scenario by the much more general techniques for merging of computations (see below).

Typical manipulations to be dealt with in the sequel are

- merging of different computations (that have been kept apart in some development for the sake of clear structuring) by
  - function composition (Sect. 6.1.1)
  - function combination (Sect. 6.1.2)
  - "free merging" (Sect. 6.1.3)
- inversion of the flow of computation (Sect. 6.2)
- storing of computed values instead of recomputation by
  - memo-ization (Sect. 6.3.1)
  - tabulation (Sect. 6.3.2)
- "precomputation" of values by
  - evaluation of expressions in advance (Sects. 6.4.1, 6.4.2)
  - partial evaluation (Sect. 6.4.3)
  - finite differencing (Sect. 6.4.4)
- simplification of recursive functions which are not tail-recursive (Sect. 6.5).

There are further techniques for improving applicative programs that require manipulations of the data types involved. These will be discussed in Chap. 8.

Like in the previous sections, the (combined) use of all these techniques will be demonstrated with representative examples (Sect. 6.6).

6.1 Merging of Computations

For the sake of structuring, auxiliary operations are often introduced in problem specifications. These auxiliary operations may introduce "computational overhead", e.g., if certain similar expressions are computed in different auxiliary operations which are independent of each other. A general idea for removing these inefficiencies is to "merge" different computations into a single one, thus ensuring that similar expressions are evaluated at most once. Techniques that follow this general idea will be introduced in the following subsections.

6.1.1 Function Composition

A typical situation where it is appropriate to look for improvements with respect to efficiency is given when a function call $g(x)$ appears as an argument of another function f, i.e. a situation such as $f(g(x))$.

If g appears in a particular expression rather than a call, we may install this situation by a suitable abstraction. In this sense, our considerations will capture the 'specialization technique' of [Scherlis 80, 81] which has only the technical advantage that the functionality of the composed expression is fixed with the folding step. Hence, the 'specialization technique' combines function composition with embedding.

Examples of how to deal with such a situation have already come up in Sects. 4.3, 4.5.1, and 4.5.2. There, although not explicitly mentioned, we followed the

<u>**Strategy**</u>

Given $f(g(x))$ with KIND[f] = **funct** (**n**) **p** and KIND[g] = **funct** (**m**) **n**,

- Define **funct** h = (**m** x) **p**: $f(g(x))$ (if not already given);
- Unfold g in the definition of h;
  Apply transformations (e.g. *distributivity of function call over conditional*, cf. Sect. 4.4.1) and laws of the respective data types such that all calls of f are of the form $f(g(...))$;
- Fold with the original definition of h.

As another simple example of how to use this strategy, consider the frequently encountered generate-and-test problem, where, as in Sect. 5.3.3.1, finiteness of the sets involved is assumed:

funct *gen-and-test* = (**mset** M) **bool**:
  test-ex(*gen*(M)) **where**

  funct *test-ex* = (**mset** M) **bool**:
    if $M = \varnothing$ **then false**
      else P(m) $\vee$ *test-ex*(M–m) **where m** m = *arb*(M) **fi**,

  funct *gen* = (**mset** M) **mset**:
    if $M = \varnothing$ **then** $\varnothing$
      else {**m** y: $y = m \wedge$ Q(y)} $\cup$ *gen*(M–m) **where m** m = *arb*(M) **fi**.

Applying the first two steps of the above strategy yields the following intermediate version

funct *gen-and-test* = (**mset** *M*) **bool**:
  if $M = \varnothing$
    then *test-ex*($\varnothing$)
    else *test-ex* ({**m** y: $y = m \wedge Q(y)$} $\cup$ *gen*($M-m$)) **where m** m = *arb*(M) **fi**.

Then, using the straightforward properties

test-ex($\varnothing$) $\equiv$ **false**,
test-ex($A \cup B$) $\equiv$ *test-ex*(A) $\vee$ *test-ex*(B), and
test-ex ({**m** y: $y = m \wedge Q(y)$}) $\equiv$ ($Q(m)\ \Delta\ P(m)$),

folding is possible and results finally in

funct *gen-and-test* = (**mset** *M*) **bool**:
  if $M = \varnothing$
    then false
    else ($Q(m)\ \Delta\ P(m)$) $\vee$ *gen-and-test*($M-m$) **where m** m = *arb* (M) **fi**.

Obviously, termination for *gen-and-test* is guaranteed. Further improvements, such as the use of ∇ rather than $\vee$ in order to speed up computation, are also obvious.

The same strategy is also applicable to other operational versions of *gen* (by using the transformations in Sect. 5.3.3.1) which in the very end determine the performance of *gen-and-test*, since the composed function inherits the recursion structure of the respective "inner" function. Thus, the possibility of using different operational versions of *gen* corresponds to the idea of different 'subspace-generators' for generate-and-test algorithms as studied in [Smith 86].

As in Chap. 5, the above strategy can be used to prove (under additional applicability conditions) compact rules for function composition.

In [Berghammer 84, 85] such compact rules (for determinate expressions) can be found as (rewritten in our notation)

- **funct** f = (**m** x) **n**: E;
  K

  $\Updownarrow$ [e(E[h **for** f, u **for** x]) $\equiv$ E'[$e \circ h$ **for** g, u **for** x]

  funct f = (**m** x) **n**: E;
  funct g = (**m** x) **p**: E';
  K[g **for** $e \circ f$]

(where $e \circ f$ denotes the function composition of e and f that appears in some expression K) or

- **funct** f = (**m** x) **n**: E;
  K

  $\Updownarrow$ [$e^{-1}(e(x)) \equiv x$

  funct f = (**m** x) **n**: E;
  funct g = (**p** x) **n**: E[$g \circ e$ **for** f, $e^{-1}(x)$ **for** x];
  K[g **for** $f \circ e^{-1}$].

Corresponding rules for non-determinate expressions are given in [Berghammer, Ehler 89].

These compact rules require us to find new entities that satisfy the respective applicability conditions. Of course, part of the information contained in these entities is also needed in the third step of the above strategy. However, for simple cases such as when g is tail-recursive, simple rules such as *distributivity of function call over conditional* are sufficient to perform the modifications aimed at (though obviously this does not hold if we first unfold f instead of g and then try to modify the resulting expressions). And even for linear recursive g, the properties that are needed in the second step of the strategy also have to be proved for the above-mentioned compact rules, in order to finally allow simplification. Therefore using the strategy rather than the corresponding compact rule (which is to cover the most general case) is often simpler and more straightforward.

A particular, but practically important instance of the above strategy occurs, if within a recursive call of a function f a (recursive) auxiliary function h is used to compute the new argument. For such a situation we have the transformation rule

- Local fusion

funct f = (**m** x) **n**:
  if $[]_{i = 1..j-1}$ $B_i(x)$ **then** $E_i(f, x)$
  [] $B_j(x)$ **then** $E_j(f(E(h(x), x)))$
  $[]_{i = j+1..n}$ $B_i(x)$ **then** $E_i(f, x)$ **fi where**
  funct h = (**m** x) **r**:
    if $C(x)$ **then** $H(x)$ **else** $h(K(x))$ **fi**

$(B_j(x) \wedge B_i(x)) \equiv$ **false** $(1 \le i \le n, i \ne j)$,
$(B_j(x)\ \Delta\ \neg C(x)) \equiv$ **true** $\vdash$ $B_j(K(x)) \equiv$ **true**

funct f = (**m** x) **n**:
  if $[]_{i = 1..j-1}$ $B_i(x)$ **then** $E_i(f, x)$
  [] $B_j(x)\ \Delta\ C(x)$ **then** $E_j(f(E[H(x)$ **for** $h(x)]))$
  [] $B_j(x)\ \Delta\ \neg C(x)$ **then** $f(K(x))$
  $[]_{i = j+1..n}$ $B_i(x)$ **then** $E_i(f, x)$ **fi**
  Syntactic constraints:
    NOTOCCURS[h **in** E_i] $(1 \le i \le n, i \ne j)$.

The application of this rule can be demonstrated with rather simple examples. Consider, for instance, the well-known definition for the "greatest common divisor"

funct gcd = (**nat** a, **nat** b) **nat**:
  if $b = 0$ **then** a
  [] $b \ne 0$ **then** $gcd(b, mod(a, b))$ **fi where**

  funct mod = (**nat** a, **nat** b: $b > 0$) **nat**:
    if $a < b$ **then** a **else** $mod(a-b, b)$ **fi**.

The applicability conditions for the rule *local fusion* are obviously fulfilled, and its application yields

funct gcd = (**nat** a, **nat** b) **nat**:
  if $b = 0$ **then** a
  [] $b \ne 0\ \Delta\ a < b$ **then** $gcd(b, a)$
  [] $b \ne 0\ \Delta\ a \ge b$ **then** $gcd(a-b, b)$ **fi**.

Since the above rule states an equivalence, it may be used in the upward direction, too. In this way it primarily provides a means for "introducing structure" (that could be used in the subphase 'decomposition and detailing' of the generalized unfold/fold strategy). Sometimes efficiency can also be improved. This is in particular the case, if a given function

funct f = (**m** x, **n** y) **r**: E,

is known to be used in contexts where additional information on one of the arguments, say x, is available, or the second argument y is the same in all calls of f. Then it is reasonable to look for a pair of functions,

funct f_1 = (**m** x) **p**: E_1,
funct f_2 = (**p** x, **n** y) **r**: E_2,

defined by

$f(x, y) = f_2(f_1(x), y)$ for all **m** x, **n** y,

with the intention of minimizing the work to be done by f_2 by "shifting" as much of the computation as possible to f_1.

The general idea is extensively discussed in [Jørring, Scherlis 86]. We will deal with a particular way of handling such a situation in Sect. 6.4.2.

6.1.2 Function Combination

If a problem requires computing both $f(x)$ and $g(x)$ for some functions f and g, and if the definitions of f and g are "similar", then efficiency can often be improved by defining a function h that computes f and g simultaneously.

An example of this kind is given by the function *gesub* (Ex. 4.5-4). Another typical example of this kind is the following (see also [Bauer, Wössner 82]):
Given two functions

funct *div* = (**nat** a, **nat** b: $b > 0$) **nat**:
  if $a < b$ **then** 0 **else** $1 + div(a-b, b)$ **fi**,

funct *mod* = (**nat** a, **nat** b: $b > 0$) **nat**:
  if $a < b$ **then** a **else** $mod(a-b, b)$ **fi**

that compute (integer) quotient and remainder, it is requested to compute both of them at once:

funct *divmod* = (**nat** a, **nat** b: $b > 0$) (**nat**, **nat**):
  $(div(a, b), mod(a, b))$.

Unfolding *div* and using *distributivity of tuple construction over conditional* yields

funct *divmod* = (**nat** a, **nat** b: $b > 0$) (**nat**, **nat**):
  if $a < b$ **then** $(0, a)$ **else** $(1 + div(a-b, b), mod(a-b, b))$ **fi**.

Since $mod(a-b, b) \equiv 0 + mod(a-b, b)$ holds, the **else**-branch can be rewritten into

$(1, 0) \oplus (div(a-b, b), mod(a-b, b))$

where $\oplus$ denotes elementwise addition of pairs. Folding then results in

funct *divmod* = (**nat** *a*, **nat** *b*: $b > 0$) (**nat**, **nat**):
  if $a < b$ **then** (0, *a*) **else** (1, 0) ⊕ *divmod*(*a*–*b*, *b*) **fi**.

In this particular example *div* and *mod* had the same control structure such that similarity was obvious. For the general case the notion of similarity has to be made more precise. To this end we first introduce the notion of projectability.

For an expression E of kind $\mathbf{m} = (\mathbf{m_1}, ..., \mathbf{m_n})$, $(\mathbf{m_1}\, y_1, ..., \mathbf{m_n}\, y_n) = \mathrm{E}$, and N being a non-empty subsequence of <1, ..., n> we define

$$\mathrm{E}|_\mathrm{N} =_{\mathrm{def}} (y_\mathrm{i})_{\mathrm{i} \in \mathrm{N}},$$

i.e., $\mathrm{E}|_\mathrm{N}$ is the (ordered) tuple consisting of those components of the value of E that are determined by N. In particular, we have for a tuple *x* of identifiers (of kind **m**)

$$x|_\mathrm{N} =_{\mathrm{def}} (x_\mathrm{i})_{\mathrm{i} \in \mathrm{N}}.$$

Now assume $\mathbf{m} = (\mathbf{m_1}, ..., \mathbf{m_n})$, $\mathbf{r} = (\mathbf{r_1}, ..., \mathbf{r_m})$, and N, M being non-empty subsequences of <1, ..., n> and <1, ..., m>, respectively. We call a function

funct *f* = (**m** *x*) **r**:
  if $[]_{\mathrm{j}=1..\mathrm{k}} \mathrm{B_j}(x)$
  then $\mathrm{E_j}(x, f(\mathrm{K_{j,1,1}}(x), ..., \mathrm{K_{j,1,n}}(x)), ..., f(\mathrm{K_{j,lj,1}}(x), ..., \mathrm{K_{j,lj,n}}(x)))$ **fi**,

(where $\mathrm{lj} \geq 0$, for all $1 \leq \mathrm{j} \leq \mathrm{k}$) **projectable w.r.t. (N, M)** iff there exist, for all $1 \leq \mathrm{j} \leq \mathrm{k}$,

- $\mathrm{B_j}'$ such that $\mathrm{B_j}(x) \equiv \mathrm{B_j}'(x|_\mathrm{N})$;
- $\mathrm{K'_{j,l,i}}$ such that $\mathrm{K_{j,l,i}}(x) \equiv \mathrm{K'_{j,l,i}}(x|_\mathrm{N})$, for all $1 \leq \mathrm{i} \leq \mathrm{n}$ and $1 \leq \mathrm{l} \leq \mathrm{lj}$;
- $\mathrm{E_j}'$ such that $(\mathrm{E_j}(x, f(\mathrm{K_{j,1,1}}(x),...,\mathrm{K_{j,1,n}}(x)), ..., f(\mathrm{K_{j,lj,1}}(x),...,\mathrm{K_{j,lj,n}}(x))))|_\mathrm{M} \equiv \mathrm{E_j}'(x|_\mathrm{N}, (f(\mathrm{K_{j,1,1}}(x),...,\mathrm{K_{j,1,n}}(x)))|_\mathrm{M}, ..., (f(\mathrm{K_{j,lj,1}}(x),...,\mathrm{K_{j,lj,n}}(x)))|_\mathrm{M})$.

If *f* is projectable w.r.t. (N, M) then $f|_{(\mathrm{N, M})}$ defined by

funct $f|_{(\mathrm{N, M})} = ((\mathbf{m_i}\, x_\mathrm{i})_{\mathrm{i} \in \mathrm{N}})\ (\mathbf{r_m})_{\mathrm{m} \in \mathrm{M}}$:
  if $[]_{\mathrm{j}=1..\mathrm{k}} \mathrm{B_j}'(x|_\mathrm{N})$
  then $\mathrm{E_j}'(x|_\mathrm{N}, f|_{(\mathrm{N, M})}((\mathrm{K'_{j,1,i}}(x|_\mathrm{N}))_{\mathrm{i} \in \mathrm{N}}), ..., f|_{(\mathrm{N,M})}((\mathrm{K'_{j,lj,i}}(x|_\mathrm{N})_{\mathrm{i} \in \mathrm{N}})))$ **fi**

is called a **projection** of *f* **w.r.t. (N, M)**.

According to these definitions, we have (for *f*, as defined above, being projectable to (N, K))

$$(f(x))|_\mathrm{M} \equiv f|_{(\mathrm{N, M})}((x_\mathrm{i})_{\mathrm{i} \in \mathrm{N}}),$$

for all **m** *x*.

Obviously, there are trivial projections. Any function *f*, as defined above, is projectable with respect to (<1,...,n>, <1,...,m>) with $f|_{(<1,...,n>,\ <1,...,m>)} \equiv f$. Likewise, for any selector operation s_i of kind **funct** (**r**) $\mathbf{r_i}$ ($1 \leq \mathrm{i} \leq \mathrm{m}$), *f* is trivially projectable with respect to (<1,...,n>, <i>) and $f|_{(<1,...,n>,\ <i>)} \equiv s_\mathrm{i} \circ f$.

In the example *divmod* above, *div* and *mod* are trivial projections of the latter kind. As another example to illustrate the notions above, we consider

funct *f* = (**nat** *a*, **nat** *b*, **nat** *c*: $c \geq a$) (**nat**, **nat**):
  if $a = 0$ **then** (*b*, *c*) **else** *f*(*a*–1, *b*+1, *c*–1) **fi**.

According to the definitions above, *f* is projectable with respect to (<1, 2>, <1>), with projection

funct *add* = (**nat** *a*, **nat** *b*) **nat**:
  if $a = 0$ **then** *b* **else** *add*($a-1$, $b+1$) **fi**,

denoting addition on ℕ, as well as w.r.t. (<1, 3>, <2>), with projection

funct *sub* = (**nat** *a*, **nat** *c*: $c \geq a$) **nat**:
  if $a = 0$ **then** *c* **else** *sub*($a-1$, $c-1$) **fi**,

denoting subtraction on ℕ. According to the above definitions, these are also the only non-trivial projections of *f*.

Now, we can make precise what is meant by similar functions:

Two functions *f* and *g*, with KIND[*f*] = **funct (m) r**, and KIND[*g*] = **funct (n) p**, are **similar** iff there exists a function *h* having *f* and *g* as projections.

Using the syntactic predicate CONT[N **in** <1,...,n>], to denote that N is a non-empty subsequence of <1,...,n>, and the semantic predicate PROJ[*h*, (N, M), *f*] to denote the fact that *h* is projectable with respect to (N, M) and $h|_{(N, M)}(x) \equiv f(x)$ holds for all *x*, the following transformation rule can be proved:

- *Function combination*

  $rm(f(x), g(y))$

  ↕ PROJ[*h*, (M, R), *f*],
  PROJ[*h*, (N, P), *g*],
  $dm(x|_M, x|_N) \equiv x$,
  $rm(y|_R, y|_P) \equiv y$

  $h(dm(x, y))$

  Syntactic constraints:
  KIND[*h*] = **funct** ($\mathbf{m_1}$, ..., $\mathbf{m_n}$) ($\mathbf{r_1}$, ..., $\mathbf{r_k}$),
  CONT[M, N **in** <1,...,n>],
  CONT[R, P **in** <1,...,k>].

From a strategic point of view, the purpose of this rule again is twofold: In the downwards direction it provides a means for avoiding duplicated evaluation of similar expressions; in this case, *rm* simply may be taken as the pair constructor on the ranges of *f* and *g*. In the upwards direction it may be considered as a specialization of the *recomposition* transformation (Sect. 5.3.1.2).

How to apply this rule to the simple problem above is obvious, and hence left to the interested reader. In general, however, using this rule requires a good deal of intuition in order to find suitable definitions for the new operations that are introduced. One might think of using for *dm* and *rm* simply the (associative) tuple constructor. This will in general lead to a duplication of arguments in *h* such that further means are needed – in the most general case flow analysis – to eliminate these identical arguments afterwards.

If the rule is to be used in the downward direction one may use the following

Strategy

Given *f* and *g* that are defined similarly:

- transform *f* and *g* such that there exists a function *h* having *f* and *g* as projections;
- apply the rule *function combination*.

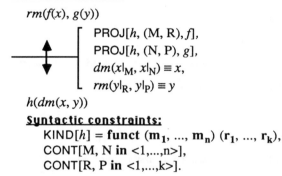

The central question still is how to find h.

For certain particular cases the answer is very simple. Using the abbreviation

$(f, g)(x) =_{\text{def}} (f(x), g(x))$

and given for example

funct f = (**m** x) **r**: **if** T(x) **then** H(x) **else** E(x, f) **fi**

and

funct g = (**m** x) **p**: **if** T(x) **then** G(x) **else** E'(x, g) **fi**,

where E and E' have the same structure, then

funct h = (**m** x) (**r**, **p**): **if** T(x) **then** (H(x), G(x)) **else** E"(x, (f, g))[h **for** (f, g)] **fi**

will do, where E"(x, (f, g)) can be obtained from E and E' by extending the basic operations to corresponding basic operations on pairs.

If such a situation is not given right from the beginning, one can try to establish it by adding parameters and splitting cases using the rules for guarded expressions (Sect. 4.4.5.4).

Consider the following example:

Let (labeled) binary trees be defined by

mode bintree = *leaf*(**char** *c*) | *comp*(**bintree** *left*, **char** *root*, **bintree** *right*).

The number of nodes in a labelled binary tree can be computed by

funct *nnodes* = (**bintree** *b*) **nat**:
  if *b* **is** *leaf* **then** 1
  [] *b* **is** *comp* **then** *nnodes*(*left*(*b*)) + 1 + *nnodes*(*right*(*b*)) **fi**,

and the number of occurrences of a given character x among the nodes of **bintree** b by

funct *occs* = (**char** *x*, **bintree** *b*) **nat**:
  if *b* **is** *leaf* Δ *c*(*b*)=*x* **then** 1
  [] *b* **is** *leaf* Δ *c*(*b*)≠*x* **then** 0
  [] *b* **is** *comp* Δ *root*(*b*)=*x* **then** *occs*(*x*, *left*(*b*)) + 1 + *occs*(*x*, *right*(*b*))
  [] *b* **is** *comp* Δ *root*(*b*)≠*x* **then** *occs*(*x*, *left*(*b*)) + *occs*(*x*, *right*(*b*)) **fi**.

Suppose, furthermore, that it is required to compute the tuple

(*nnodes*(*B*), *occs*(*X*, *B*))

for a given **bintree** *B* and a given **char** *X*.

The last branch in *occs* trivially can be changed into

... **then** *occs*(*x*, *left*(*b*)) + 0 + *occs*(*x*, *right*(*b*)).

In *nnodes* we can introduce an additional (constant) parameter (by *embedding* and the unfold/fold strategy):

funct *nnodes* = (**char** *x*, **bintree** *b*) **nat**:
  if *b* **is** *leaf* **then** 1
  [] *b* **is** *comp* **then** *nnodes*(*x*, *left*(*b*)) + 1 + *nnodes*(*x*, *right*(*b*)) **fi**.

Applying the rule *refinement of branches* then yields

funct *nnodes* = (**char** *x*, **bintree** *b*) **nat**:
  if *b* **is** *leaf* Δ *c*(*b*)=*x* **then** 1
  [] *b* **is** *leaf* Δ *c*(*b*)≠*x* **then** 1
  [] *b* **is** *comp* Δ *root*(*b*)=*x* **then** *nnodes*(*x*, *left*(*b*)) + 1 + *nnodes*(*x*, *right*(*b*))
  [] *b* **is** *comp* Δ *root*(*b*)≠*x* **then** *nnodes*(*x*, *left*(*b*)) + 1 + *nnodes*(*x*, *right*(*b*)) **fi**.

Now, obviously, the functions *nnodes* and *occs* can be obtained by projection from

funct *nnoccs* = (**char** *x*, **bintree** *b*) (**nat**, **nat**):
  if *b* **is** *leaf* Δ *c*(*b*)=*x* **then** (1, 1)
  [] *b* **is** *leaf* Δ *c*(*b*)≠*x* **then** (1, 0)
  [] *b* **is** *comp* Δ *root*(*b*)=*x*
    then *nnoccs*(*x*, *left*(*b*)) ⊕ (1, 1) ⊕ *nnoccs*(*x*, *right*(*b*))
  [] *b* **is** *comp* Δ *root*(*b*)≠*x*
    then *nnoccs*(*x*, *left*(*b*)) ⊕ (1, 0) ⊕ *nnoccs*(*x*, *right*(*b*)) **fi**

(with ⊕ again denoting elementwise addition on pairs). The rule *function combination* then ensures that

(*nnodes*(*B*), *occs*(*X*, *B*))

is equivalent to

nnoccs(*X*, *B*).

Of course, in practice one also may be confronted with situations that allow both *function composition* and *function combination* as, say in

$f(g_1(x), g_2(y))$.

For such a situation it is advisable to use the

Strategy

Given $f(g_1(x), g_2(y))$:

- Develop $g(x, y) =_{def} (g_1(x), g_2(y))$ using the *function combination* strategy;
- Apply the *function composition* strategy to $f(g(x, y))$.

A more comprehensive example of the combined strategy is the following one [Goldberg 86], where for a given non-empty sequence of natural numbers, the statistical mean and its variance are computed:

funct *meanvar* = (**natsequ** *s*: *s* ≠<>) (**real**, **real**):
  (*mean*(*s*), *var*(*s*)) **where**

  funct *mean* = (**natsequ** *s*: *s* ≠<>) **real**:
    sum(*s*)/*size*(*s*),

  funct *sum* = (**natsequ** *s*) **nat**:
    if *s* =<> **then** 0 **else** **first***s* + *sum*(**rest***s*) **fi**,

  funct *size* = (**natsequ** *s*) **nat**:
    if *s* =<> **then** 0 **else** 1 + *size*(**rest***s*) **fi**,

funct *var* = (**natsequ** *s*: $s \neq$<>) **real**:
  ($sumsquares(s) - (sum(s))^2)/(size(s))^2$,

funct *sumsquares* = (**natsequ** *s*) **nat**:
  sum(*squares*(*s*)),

funct *squares* = (**natsequ** *s*) **natsequ**:
  if *s* =<> **then** <> **else** (**first***s*)^2 + *squares*(**rest***s*) **fi**.

In the derivation in [Goldberg 86] *sum*, *size*, *squares*, and *sumsquares* are first transformed into corresponding loops and then subjected to transformations called 'horizontal loop jamming' and 'vertical loop jamming' in order to remove the inefficiencies caused by multiple traversals of the initial sequence. The same result, in an even more straightforward way, can be obtained by using the strategy introduced above.

In the first step we *unfold* the definitions of *mean* and *var* in the definition of *meanvar* and introduce, by *abstraction*, an auxiliary operation *h*:

funct *meanvar* = (**natsequ** *s*: $s \neq$<>) (**real**, **real**):
  (**nat** *su*, **nat** *si*, **nat** *ssq*) = *h*(*s*);
  (su/si, $(ssq - su^2)/si^2$) **where**

  funct *h* = (**natsequ** *s*) (**nat**, **nat**, **nat**):
    (*sum*(*s*), *size*(*s*), *sumsquares*(s)).

Our next efforts concentrate on the auxiliary function *h*. By *unfolding* first *sumsquares* and then *squares* we get

(*sum*(*s*), *size*(*s*), *sum*(**if** *s* =<> **then** <> **else** (**first***s*)^2 + *squares*(**rest***s*) **fi**)).

Using *distributivity of function call over conditional* and thereafter *distributivity of tuple construction over conditional* results in

if *s* =<> **then** (*sum*(*s*), *size*(*s*), *sum*(<>))
  else (*sum*(*s*), *size*(*s*), *sum*((**first***s*)^2 + *squares*(**rest***s*))) **fi**.

This can be simplified, by *instantiations*, to

if *s* =<>
  then (0, 0, 0)
  else (**first***s* + *sum*(**rest***s*), 1 + *size*(**rest***s*), (**first***s*)^2 + *sum*(*squares*(**rest***s*))) **fi**.

Next we introduce an operator ⊕ for the elementwise addition of triples of natural numbers

if *s* =<>
  then (0, 0, 0)
  else (**first***s*, 1, (**first***s*)^2) ⊕ (*sum*(**rest***s*), *size*(**rest***s*), *sum*(*squares*(**rest***s*))) **fi**,

such that first folding *sumsquares* and then folding *h* yields our final result

funct *meanvar* = (**natsequ** *s*: $s \neq$<>) (**real**, **real**):
  (**nat** *su*, **nat** *si*, **nat** *ssq*) = *h*(*s*);
  (su/si, $(ssq - su^2)/si^2$) **where**

funct h = (**natsequ** s) (**nat, nat, nat**):
  if s =<> **then** (0, 0, 0) **else** (**first**s, 1, (**first**s)^2) $\oplus$ h(**rest**s)) **fi**,

which can be straightforwardly further transformed into an imperative form using the techniques introduced in the next sections.

Occasionally, *function composition* and *function combination* can be profitably used for simplifying non-linear recursions. For details we refer to Sect. 6.5. A more comprehensive example of the combined strategy can be found in [Partsch 83].

6.1.3 "Free Merging"

Another kind of merging is possible, if we have two function definitions, such as

funct f_1 = (**m** x) **n**:
  if $[]_{i=1..n}$ B_i **then** $E_{1,i}$ **fi**,

funct f_2 = (**m** x) **n**:
  if $[]_{k=1..m}$ C_k **then** $E_{2,k}$ **fi**,

which do not refer to each other and which are furthermore known to be equivalent, so that

$f_1(x) \equiv f_2(x)$

holds, for all **m** x.

Such a situation might appear if a certain descriptive specification is developed into two different algorithms.

Now, defining

funct f = (**m** x) **n**: $f_1(x)$,

and further assuming

$(\exists_{i=1..n} B_i \vee \exists_{k=1..m} C_k) \equiv$ **true**,

case introduction in f leads to

funct f = (**m** x) **n**:
  if $[]_{i=1..n}$ B_i **then** $f_1(x)$
  $[]_{k=1..m}$ C_k **then** $f_1(x)$ **fi**.

The branches guarded by B_i can be instantiated to $E_{1,i}$. In the branches guarded by C_k we first use $f_1(x) \equiv f_2(x)$, then instantiate the calls of f_2 to $E_{2,k}$, and thereafter use again $f_2(x) \equiv f_1(x)$. Thus we get

funct f = (**m** x) **n**:
  if $[]_{i=1..n}$ B_i **then** $E_{1,i}$
  $[]_{k=1..m}$ $C_k[f_1$ **for** $f_2]$ **then** $E_{2,k}[f_1$ **for** $f_2]$ **fi**,

and by folding with the original definition of f,

funct f = (**m** x) **n**:
  if $[]_{i=1..n}$ $B_i[f$ **for** $f_1]$ **then** $E_{1,i}[f$ **for** $f_1]$
  $[]_{k=1..m}$ $C_k[f$ **for** $f_2]$ **then** $E_{2,k}[f$ **for** $f_2]$ **fi**.

Altogether, we have established the transformation rule

- E **where**
  funct f_1 = (**m** x) **n**:
    if $[]_{i=1..n}$ B_i **then** $E_{1,i}$ **fi**

  $\Updownarrow$ $\left[\begin{array}{l} f_1(x) \equiv f_2(x), \\ (\exists_{i=1..n} B_i \vee \exists_{k=1..m} C_k) \equiv \textbf{true}, \\ \mathsf{DEF}[f] \Leftrightarrow \mathsf{DEF}[f_1] \end{array}\right.$

  E[f **for** f_1] **where**
  funct f = (**m** x) **n**:
    if $[]_{i=1..n}$ $B_i[f$ **for** $f_1]$ **then** $E_{1,i}[f$ **for** $f_1]$
    $[]_{k=1..m}$ $C_k[f$ **for** $f_2]$ **then** $E_{2,k}[f$ **for** $f_2]$ **fi**

  Syntactic constraints:
    DECL[f_2] = (**funct** f_2 = (**m** x) **n**: **if** $[]_{k=1..m}$ C_k **then** $E_{2,k}$ **fi**),
    NOTOCCURS[f, f_1 **in** f_2; f, f_2 **in** f_1].

Of course, there is also an obvious generalization to an arbitrary number of functions f_i. Likewise, there is a generalization where the condition on equivalence of f_1 and f_2 is weakened to the existence of a function f of which f_1 and f_2 are descendants.

As an example of how to use this rule, consider again part (6) of the "simple bank account system" of Sect. 3.6.3. There we had the equivalent specifications

funct *updatef1* = (**acfile** *a*, **gtfile** *t*) **acfile**:
  if *a* =<> **then** <>
    else *mb*(*acc*(**first***a*), *newgbal*(**first***a*, *t*)) + *updatef1*(**rest***a*, *t*) **fi**

and

funct *updatef2* = (**acfile** *a*, **gtfile** *t*) **acfile**:
  if *t* =<> **then** *a*
    else *updatef2*(*upd*(*a*, **first***t*), **rest***t*) **fi**.

By first transforming the conditionals into guarded expressions, the applicability conditions of the above rule are obviously fulfilled, and application of the rule yields immediately

funct *updatef* = (**acfile** *a*, **gtfile** *t*) **acfile**:
  if *t* =<> **then** *a*
  [] *a* =<> **then** <>
  [] *a* ≠<> **then** *mb*(*acc*(**first***a*), *newgbal*(**first***a*, *t*)) + *updatef*(**rest***a*, *t*)
  [] *t* ≠<> **then** *updatef*(*upd*(*a*, **first***t*), **rest***t*) **fi**.

In this particular example, using the rule above does not really improve efficiency, but rather produces a truly non-deterministic, more "symmetric" solution. In other examples a real gain in efficiency might result from subsequent simplifications of the resulting non-deterministic version. In either case, it should be kept in mind that non-deterministic programs are a possible starting point for developing parallel algorithms [Broy 80], and hence, application of the above rule can be considered as a preparatory step towards developing parallel algorithms.

6.2 Inverting the Flow of Computation

'Inversion techniques' cause some computation to be performed in reverse order. They comprise a whole class of techniques which play an important role at nearly all levels of transformational program development. On the level of problem specification and the transition to an operational solution, they are usually used 'implicitly' via equalities or logical connectives. For eliminating non-determinism and/or recursion, they are useful techniques for establishing the applicability of other rules. They are even used in connection with data structures, mainly to prepare subsequent steps that allow to improve efficiency. In the sequel, we will consider a few typical representatives of this class of techniques. For a more elaborate technical treatment of inversion techniques, see [Boiten 89].

As a starter, we will consider the well-known example of computing the factorial of N:

> *fac*(*N*) **where**
> **funct** *fac* = (**nat** *n*) **nat**:
>   **if** n=0 **then** 1 **else** $n \times fac(n-1)$ **fi**.

Here, in the course of evaluating *fac*(*N*), a sequence of (actual) arguments

$$n_0=N,\ n_1=N-1,\ \ldots,\ n_N=0$$

is built up with $n_{i+1} = n_i - 1$. Further characteristics are

- the termination criterion is simply a test for equality with a constant;
- the primitive operation $\times$ is commutative; and
- the operation "–" is invertible;

Obviously, the factorial of N can also be computed by:

> *fac'*(0) **where**
> **funct** *fac'* = (**nat** *n*) **nat**:
>   **if** n=N **then** 1 **else** $(n+1) \times fac'(n+1)$ **fi**.

Here, the evaluation of *fac'*(0) yields the sequence of arguments

$$n'_0=0,\ n'_1=1,\ \ldots,\ n'_N=N$$

where now $n'_{i+1} = n'_i+1$, i.e., the operation for constructing a new n' is just the inverse of the operation for constructing a new n above.

For tail-recursive functions, a transformation rule that reflects the principle used in the factorial example above is obvious and hence left to the interested reader. For linear recursive functions we have the rule (where CONST is the semantic predicate introduced in Sect. 5.3.1.3 that ensures definedness, determinacy, and the absence of free variables)

- *Computational inversion I*

$f(X)$ **where**
funct $f = (\mathbf{m}\ x)\ \mathbf{n}$:
  if $x{=}Y$ **then** $\mathrm{H}(x)$ **else** $p(\mathrm{E}(x), f(\mathrm{K}(x)))$ **fi**

$$\Updownarrow \left[\begin{array}{l} \mathsf{DEF}[\mathrm{K}(x)] \ \vdash\ (\mathrm{K}^{-1}(\mathrm{K}(x)) = x) \equiv \mathbf{true}, \\ \mathsf{CONST}[X, Y], \\ \mathrm{ASSOC}(\mathbf{n}, p) \end{array}\right.$$

$f(Y)$ **where**
funct $f = (\mathbf{m}\ x)\ \mathbf{n}$:
  if $x{=}X$ **then** $\mathrm{H}(x_0)$ **else** $p(\mathrm{E}(\mathrm{K}^{-1}(x)), f(\mathrm{K}^{-1}(x)))$ **fi**

Syntactic constraints:
  $\mathsf{KIND}[p]$ = **funct** (**n**, **n**) **n**.

One of the particularities of this rule is the fact that each actual argument of f has exactly one "successor". In general, however, there may be several successors, or a set of them. In such a case we may use the rule

- *Local inversion on sets*

$f(\{X\})$ **where**
funct f = (**mset** M) **bool**:
  $M \neq \varnothing \mathbin{\Delta} (Y \in M \mathbin{\nabla} f(\bigcup_{x\in M} g(x)))$

$$\Updownarrow \left[\begin{array}{l} \mathsf{CONST}[X, Y], \\ (x \in g(y) \ \Leftrightarrow\ y \in g^{-1}(x)) \equiv \mathbf{true} \end{array}\right.$$

$h(\{Y\})$ **where**
funct h = (**mset** M) **bool**:
  $M \neq \varnothing \mathbin{\Delta} (X \in M \mathbin{\nabla} h(\bigcup_{x\in M} g^{-1}(x)))$

Syntactic constraints:
  $\mathsf{KIND}[g, g^{-1}]$ = **funct** (**m**) **mset**,
  DECL[**mset**] = **mode mset** = ESET(**m**, =).

Intuitively, the idea of this rule is as follows: Given an element X and a function g to compute immediate "neighboring" elements, the problem of determining whether another distinguished element Y is "reachable" from X w.r.t. g can also be solved by starting from Y using g^{-1}, the inverse of g, and determining whether X is "reachable" from Y w.r.t. g^{-1}. Of course, the rule is also correct, if the arguments of the respective recursive calls (in f and h) are $(\bigcup_{x\in M} g(x))\backslash M$ and $(\bigcup_{x\in M} g^{-1}(x))\backslash M$, respectively.

The rule above allows global inversion based on a local invertibility property. Applications of related techniques can be found in [Berry 76], [Dijkstra 78] and [Scherlis 80]. Although the rule is defined for a very specific context, it can be profitably used for a much wider class of problems within the following

Strategy

In order to invert the flow of computation in a given function:

- Transform the given function into an equivalent one having sets as parameters;
- Apply the rule *local inversion on sets*;
- Transform the resulting algorithm to have its original kind of parameters.

For an example of how to use the above rule within this strategy, we consider the following problem:

Compute the sequence of discs to be moved to solve the 'Tower of Hanoi' puzzle with N discs.

As is known from the literature [Gardner 72], the problem is solved by

toh(*N*) **where**

mode pnat= (**nat** *x*: $x > 0$);
mode natsequ = EESEQU(**nat**, =);

funct *toh* = (**pnat** *n*) **natsequ**:
  if n=1 **then** 1 **else** *toh*(n–1)+n+*toh*(n–1) **fi**.

Following the above strategy, we first establish the input scheme for the rule *local inversion on sets*. We define by an embedding

toh'(*N*) **where**

funct *toh'* = (**pnat** *n*) **natsequ**:
  some natsequ *y*: *h*(*n*, *y*) **where**

  funct *h* = (**pnat** *n*, **natsequ** *y*) **bool**:
    y = *toh*(*n*).

Now *h* can be developed into a function that is independent of *toh*:

$y = toh(n)$
  ≡ [unfold *toh*]
$y =$ **if** n=1 **then** 1 **else** $toh(n-1)+n+toh(n-1)$ **fi**
  ≡ [distributivity of conditional over =; sequential connectives for conditional]
$(n=1 \,\Delta\, y=1) \,\nabla\, (n>1 \,\Delta\, y = toh(n-1)+n+toh(n-1))$
  ≡ [abstraction]
$(n=1 \,\Delta\, y=1) \,\nabla\, (n>1 \,\Delta\, \exists$ **natsequ** y': $(y = y'+n+y' \,\Delta\, y'=toh(n-1)))$
  ≡ [folding]
$(n=1 \,\Delta\, y=1) \,\nabla\, (n>1 \,\Delta\, \exists$ **natsequ** y': $(y = y'+n+y' \,\Delta\, h(n-1, y')))$.

Thus, we get the intermediate result

funct *toh'* = (**pnat** *n*) **natsequ**:
  some natsequ *y*: *h*(*n*, *y*) **where**

  funct *h* = (**pnat** *n*, **natsequ** *y*) **bool**:
    $(n=1 \,\Delta\, y=1) \,\nabla\, (n>1 \,\Delta\, \exists$ **natsequ** y': $(y = y'+n+y' \,\Delta\, h(n-1, y')))$.

Next we introduce a new auxiliary operation *h'* with sets of pairs as arguments which results in

funct *h* = (**pnat** *n*, **natsequ** *y*) **bool**:
  h'({*mp*(*n*, *y*)}) **where**

  mode tpair = *mp*(**pnat** *m*, **natsequ** *z*);
  mode tpairset = SET(**tpair**, =);

funct $h' = $ (**tpairset** M) **bool**:
$M \neq \varnothing \,\Delta\, (mp(1, 1) \in M \,\nabla$
$h'(\{$**tpair** $mp(m-1, z'): mp(m, z) \in M \,\Delta\, z = z'+m+z'\}))$.

Now we can apply the rule *local inversion on sets* to the body of h, which yields

funct $h = $ (**pnat** n, **natsequ** y) **bool**:
$h''(\{mp(1, 1)\})$ **where**

funct $h'' = $ (**set tpair** M) **bool**:
$M \neq \varnothing \,\Delta\, (mp(n, y) \in M \,\nabla$
$h''(\{$**tpair** $mp(m+1, z'): mp(m, z) \in M \,\Delta\, z' = z+(m+1)+z\}))$.

Here, the sets involved are all singletons (simple proof by induction), and, thus, we can use elementary objects instead of sets

funct $h = $ (**pnat** n, **natsequ** y) **bool**:
$h^+(1, 1)$ **where**

funct $h^+ = $ (**pnat** m, **natsequ** z) **bool**:
$((m, z) = (n, y)) \,\nabla\, h^+(m+1, z+(m+1)+z)$.

Finally *unfolding* and the appropriate variant of the rule *argument on termination* yield:

funct $toh = $ (**pnat** n) **natsequ**:
$h^*(1, 1)$ **where**

funct $h^* = $ (**pnat** m, **natsequ** y) **natsequ**:
if $m=n$ **then** y **else** $h^*(m+1, y+(m+1)+y)$ **fi**.

As an interesting variant of the rule *local inversion on sets*, we have

- $f(\{X\})$ **where**
  funct $f = $ (**mset** M) **bool**:
  $M \neq \varnothing \,\Delta\, (Y \in M \,\nabla\, f(\bigcup_{x \in M} g(x)))$

  ⇕ [CONST[X, Y],
  $(x \in g(y) \;\Leftrightarrow\; y \in g^{-1}(x)) \equiv$ **true**

  $k(\{X\}, \{Y\})$ **where**
  funct $k = $ (**mset** M, **mset** N) **bool**:
  $(M \neq \varnothing \wedge N \neq \varnothing)\,\Delta$
  $(((M \cap N \neq \varnothing) \vee (G(M) \cap N \neq \varnothing) \vee (M \cap G^{-1}(N) \neq \varnothing)) \,\nabla\, k(G(M), G^{-1}(N)))$

  <u>**Syntactic constraints:**</u>
  KIND[g, g^{-1}] = **funct (m) mset**,
  DECL[G] = **funct** (**mset** M) **mset**: $\bigcup_{x \in M} g(x)$,
  DECL[G^{-1}] = **funct** (**mset** M) **mset**: $\bigcup_{x \in M} g^{-1}(x)$,
  DECL[**mset**] = ESET(**m**, =).

Compared to the previous rule, this variant starts from X and Y simultaneously and finds out whether the elements reachable from X and those reachable from Y have a common intersection. Whereas this variant works "symmetrically", there are further variants working from both sides in an asymmetric fashion. However, these require a much more complicated synchronization.

A similar, but slightly different kind of inversion technique is described by the following rule, the basic principle of which again is local invertibility (here, based on duality of basic operations).

- <u>*Computational inversion II*</u>

funct f = (**n** w, **m** x, **m** y, **nat** i) **bool**:
$(i{=}0 \;\Delta\; \mathrm{P}(x, y)) \;\nabla\; (\exists\, \mathbf{r}\; z\text{: } \mathrm{Q}(w, z) \wedge \mathrm{P}(x, g(z)) \wedge f(\mathrm{K}(w), h(z), y, i-1))$

$\updownarrow$

funct f = (**n** w, **m** x, **m** y, **nat** i) **bool**:
$(i{=}0 \;\Delta\; \mathrm{P}(x, y)) \;\nabla\; (\exists\, \mathbf{r}\; z\text{: } \mathrm{Q}(w, z) \wedge \mathrm{P}(h(z), y) \wedge f(\mathrm{K}(w), x, g(z), i-1))$
<u>**Syntactic constraints:**</u>
KIND[g, h] = **funct** (**r**) **m**.

In order to demonstrate the use of this rule, we consider the following variant of the "reachability problem":

In contrast to Sect. 3.3.4, let finite directed graphs (without isolated nodes) be defined by

mode edge = *me*(**node** *in*, **node** *out*);
mode graph = SET(**edge**, =).

The problem

whether for a given graph G and nodes x, y with x, y occuring in G there exists a path of length n leading from x to y

can be solved by (where x **in** G abbreviates $\exists$ **edge** e: $e \in G \wedge in(e) = x \vee out(e) = x$)

funct *path* = (**graph** G, **node** x, **node** y, **nat** n: x **in** $G \wedge y$ **in** G) **bool**:
$(n = 0 \;\Delta\; x = y) \;\nabla\; (\exists$ **edge** z: z **in** $G \wedge x = in(z) \wedge path(G, out(z), y, n-1))$.

Obviously, the above rule is applicable and yields

funct *path* = (**graph** G, **node** x, **node** y, **nat** n: x **in** $G \wedge y$ **in** G) **bool**:
$(n = 0 \;\Delta\; x = y) \;\nabla\; (\exists$ **edge** z: z **in** $G \wedge out(z) = y \wedge path(G, x, in(z), n-1))$.

Without further restrictions, there seems to be no gain in using this rule. If, however, the graph is known to constitute a tree (i.e., each node is reachable from one distinguished node, the root, through directed edges, and there are no cycles), then the resulting program can be improved substantially, exploiting the fact that the existential quantifier then quantifies over a domain which is at most a singleton:

funct *path* = (**graph** G, **node** x, **node** y, **nat** n: x **in** $G \wedge y$ **in** $G \wedge istree(G)$) **bool**:
$(n = 0 \;\Delta\; x = y) \;\nabla\; (haspred(y, G) \;\Delta\; path(G, x, pred(y, G), n-1))$ **where**

funct *haspred* = (**node** y, **graph** G: y **in** G) **bool**:
$\exists$ **edge** z: z **in** $G \wedge out(z) = y$,

funct *pred* = (**node** y, **graph** G: $haspred(y, G)$) **node**:
that node w: $\exists$ **edge** z: z **in** $G \wedge out(z) = y \wedge w = in(z)$.

6.3 Storing of Values Instead of Recomputation

When dealing with efficiency, there is usually a trade-off between time and space: memory space can be saved at the expense of additional computation time and computation time can be saved at the expense of additional memory space. The techniques to be discussed in the following subsections deal with this latter transition.

6.3.1 Memo-ization

In many recursive routines, in particular in routines having nested or cascade-like recursion structures, inefficiencies are caused by multiple evaluations of identical calls.

Typical examples are found with all kinds of recurrences such as the well-known Fibonacci function

funct *fib* = (**nat** *n*) **nat**:
  if $n \le 1$ **then** 1 **else** $fib(n-1) + fib(n-2)$ **fi**

or the well-known recursive definition for computing the binomial coefficient

funct *bin* = (**nat** *i*, **nat** *j*: $0 \le j \le i$) **nat**:
  if $j=0 \vee j=i$ **then** 1 **else** $bin(i-1, j-1) + bin(i-1, j)$ **fi**.

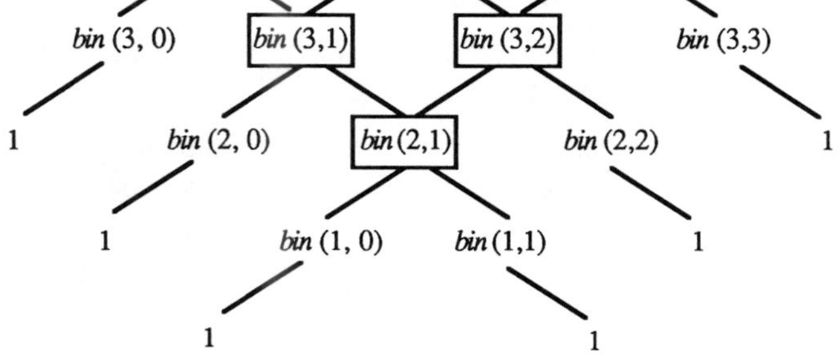

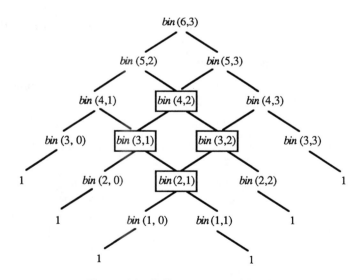

Figure 6.1. Calling structure of *bin*(6, 3)

The inefficiency becomes obvious, if we analyze the evaluation of a concrete call. For example, evaluating the call *bin*(6, 3) yields the calling structure given in Fig. 6.1 where, strictly following the above definition, the calls marked by boxes are actually evaluated several times (e.g., *bin*(4, 2) twice, and *bin*(2, 1) even six times).

However, rather than evaluating a call more than once, it is obviously more efficient to remember (memorize) that a call with a particular argument already has been computed and to look up the respective value, (say in a table) as one would do in a hand computation.

This idea (in [Turner 81] called 'memo-ization', in [Bird 80] called 'exact tabulation') is captured by the rule (where the assertion in the output scheme is to allow later simplifications)

• *Memo-ization*

f(E) **where**
funct f = (**m** x) **n**:
  if B(x) **then** H(x) **else** E'(x, f(K_1(x)), f(K_2(x))) **fi**

↓ [CONST[E]

f'(E, [])[E] **where**
mode map = MAP(**m**, **n**, =);
funct f' = (**m** x, **map** a: *isdef*(a, x) ⇨ $a[x] = f(x)$) **map**:
  if *isdef*(a, x) **then** a
  elsf B(x) **then** $a[x]$ ← H(x)
        else map $y_1 = f'(K_1(x), a)$; **map** $y_2 = f'(K_2(x), y_1)$;
          $y_2[x]$ ← E'(x, $y_2[K_1(x)]$, $y_2[K_2(x)]$) **fi.**

Note that for **m** denoting a tuple an appropriate variant of the type MAP (such as PMAP from Sect. 3.3.2.) can be used instead.

In the current form of the output scheme, the gain in applying this rule seems to be very little, as the savings in computational effort has to be compensated by an additional (complex) argument. In a procedural version, however, this additional argument usually can be made into a global variable, and all changes to it can be realized by selective updating (Chap. 8).

Applying this rule to the Fibonacci function (with an initial call *fib*(N)) yields immediately

fib'(N, [])[N] **where**
mode fibmap = MAP(**nat**, **nat**, =);

funct *fib'* = (**nat** n, **fibmap** a: *isdef*(a, n) ⇨ $a[n] = fib(n)$) **fibmap**:
  if *isdef*(a, n) **then** a
  elsf $n \le 1$ **then** $a[n] \leftarrow 1$
        else fibmap $y_1 = fib'(n-1, a)$; **fibmap** $y_2 = fib'(n-2, y_1)$;
          $y_2[n] \leftarrow (y_2[n-1] + y_2[n-2])$ **fi.**

Obviously, in this particular case it can be proved (for **fibmap** y_1) that

($y_1 = fib'(n-1, a)$) ≡ **true** ⊢ (∀(**nat** k: $k < n$): *isdef*(y_1, k) Δ $y_1[k] = fib(k)$) ≡ **true**

holds. Thus, *fib'* can be further simplified to

funct *fib'* = (**nat** n, **fibmap** a: *isdef*(a, n) ⇨ $a[n] = fib(n)$) **fibmap**:
  if *isdef*(a, n) **then** a
  elsf $n \le 1$ **then** $a[n] \leftarrow 1$
        else fibmap $y_1 = fib'(n-1, a)$; $y_1[n] \leftarrow (y_1[n-1] + y_1[n-2])$ **fi**,

In a similar way, application of *memo-ization* to the binomial coefficient function (with initial call *bin(I, J)*) yields

```
bin'(I, J, []) [I, J] where
mode binmap = PMAP(nat, nat, =);

funct bin' = (nat i, nat j, binmap a:
              0 ≤ j ≤ i ∧ (isdef(a, i, j) ⇨ a[i, j] = bin(i, j))) binmap:
   if isdef(a, i, j) then a
   elsf j=0 ∨ j=i  then a[i, j] ← 1
                   else binmap y1 = bin'(i−1, j−1, a);
                        binmap y2 = bin'(i−1, j, y1);
                        y2[i, j] ← (y2[i−1, j−1] + y2[i−1, j]) fi.
```

How to extend the above rule in order to cover more than two recursive calls in a cascade-like recursion or nested forms of recursion is straightforward and left to the interested reader.

6.3.2 Tabulation

On closer inspection of the final version of *fib'* from Sect. 6.3.1,

```
fib'(N, [])[N] where

funct fib' = (nat n, fibmap a: isdef(a, n) ⇨ a[n] = fib(n)) fibmap:
   if isdef(a, n) then a
   elsf n ≤ 1 then a[n] ← 1
              else fibmap y1 = fib'(n−1, a); y1[n] ← (y1[n−1] + y1[n−2]) fi,
```

we realize that by an appropriate variant of the rule *computational inversion I* (Sect. 6.2) and further simplifications we can obtain

```
fib'(0, [])[N] where

funct fib' = (nat n, fibmap a: isdef(a, n) ⇨ a[n] = fib(n)) fibmap:
   if n > N then a
   elsf n ≤ 1 then fib'(n+1, a[n] ← 1)
              else fib'(n+1, a[n] ← (a[n−1] + a[n−2])) fi.
```

This might suggest to think of a general combination of *memo-ization* and *computational inversion*. The problem, however, is that *computational inversion* requires rather strong applicability conditions and hence is not applicable in quite a number of cases, as already can be seen with the *bin'* example above. Nevertheless, such a combination, which is called **tabulation** (sometimes also 'dynamic programming') is an interesting technique, since as a kind of by-product it also allows simplification of non-linear recursions (see below and also Sect. 6.5).

The effect we are aiming at is achieved by the rule

- *Tabulation*

E **where**
funct f = (**m** x) **n**:
  if T(x) **then** H(x) **else** E(f, x) **fi**

⟶ [LNSORD(**m**, <, c),
 $next(x) \equiv$ (**that m** y: $x < y \wedge (\forall$ **m** z: $x < z \Rightarrow y \leq z)$),
 DEF[$f(next(x))$] ⊢ DEF[$f(x)$]]

E[f' **for** f] **where**
funct f' = (**m** x) **n**:
  tabf(c, [])[x] **where**
  mode tabmap = MAP(**m**, **n**, =);
  funct *tabf* = (**m** y, **tabmap** a: $y \leq next(x) \wedge$
      $\forall$ **m** z: $c \leq z < y$ ⇨ $a[z] = f(z)$) **tabmap**:
   if $y = next(x)$ **then** a
   elsf T(y) **then** *tabf*($next(y)$, $a[y] \leftarrow$ H(y))
      else *tabf*($next(y)$, $a[y] \leftarrow$ E(f, y)) **fi**.

In this rule E(f, x) denotes an arbitrary expression that may contain (an arbitrary number of) recursive calls of f, and LNSORD(**m**, <, c) states that < is a linear Noetherian strict ordering (Sect. 3.3.1.4) on **m** with least element c. As in the *memo-ization* rule, variants of MAP can be used, if appropriate.

The similarity of this rule with *memo-ization* is obvious. The essential difference, however, is the fact that *tabulation* usually causes a change of the recursion structure whereas *memo-ization* leaves it as it is.

Improvement in efficiency while using this rule is by no means guaranteed, since it depends on the concrete form of the function at hand. This can immediately be seen with the simple example

funct f = (**nat** x: $x \leq x_0$) **nat**: **if** $x \geq x_0$ **then** H(x) **else** $f(x+2)$ **fi**.

Here, obviously, *tabulation* can be applied, but the result will be less efficient than the original form, since, in general, a lot of useless values will be computed and tabulated.

Frequently, however, improvement can be achieved, if the rule *tabulation* is used within the

Strategy

In order to improve a non-linear, recursive function

- Apply the rule *tabulation*;
- Simplify, e.g. by using the generated assertion.

To illustrate this strategy, we apply the rule *tabulation* to *fib* as defined in Sect. 6.3.1 and obtain

funct *fib'* = (**nat** n) **nat**:
  tabfib(0, [])[n] **where**
  mode fibmap = MAP(**nat**, **nat**, =);

```
funct tabfib = (nat y, fibmap a: y ≤ n+1 ∧
                ∀ nat z: 0≤z<y ⇨ a[z] = fib(z)) fibmap:
   if y = n+1  then a
   elsf y ≤ 1  then tabfib(y+1, a[y] ← 1)
               else tabfib(y+1, a[y] ← (fib(y–1) + fib(y–2))) fi.
```

Now the assertion of *tabfib* can be used to simplify its body, thus resulting in

```
funct tabfib = (nat y, fibmap a: y ≤ n+1 ∧
                ∀ nat z: 0≤z<y ⇨ a[z] = fib(z)) fibmap:
   if y = n+1  then a
   elsf y ≤ 1  then tabfib(y+1, a[y] ← 1)
               else tabfib(y+1, a[y] ← (a[y–1] + a[y–2])) fi.
```

This could be generalized. If, for a function *f* as defined above, the actual arguments of all recursive calls within E(*f*, *x*) are less with respect to the ordering "<" then *tabulation* and simplification using the assertion could be combined into a new rule.

Another example that can be found in several papers on programming methodology (such as [Dijkstra 76b], [Gnatz, Pepper 77], [Bauer, Wössner 82], [Pettorossi 84]) is

```
funct fusc = (nat n: n>0) nat:
   if n = 1 then 1
          else if ¬odd n then fusc(n/2)
               [] odd n then fusc((n–1)/2) + fusc((n+1)/2) fi fi.
```

Again, *tabulation* is applicable and yields

```
funct fusc' = (nat n: n>0) nat:
   tabfusc(1, [])[n] where

   mode fuscmap = MAP((nat n: n>0), nat, =);

   funct tabfusc = (nat y, fuscmap a: y≤n+1 ∧
                    ∀ nat z: 1≤z<y ⇨ a[z] = fusc(z)) fuscmap:
      if y = n+1 then a
      elsf y = 1 then tabfusc(y+1, a[y] ← 1)
      else tabfusc(y+1, a[y] ← if ¬odd y then fusc(y/2)
                               [] odd y then fusc((y–1)/2)+fusc((y+1)/2) fi) fi.
```

Next, we use the *distributivity of function call over guarded expression* and the generated assertion for simplification which finally result in

```
funct tabfusc = (nat y, fuscmap a: y≤n+1 ∧
                 ∀ nat z: 1≤z<y ⇨ a[z] = fusc(z)) fuscmap:
   if y = n+1 then a
   elsf y = 1 then tabfusc(y+1, a[y] ← 1)
      else if ¬odd y then tabfusc(y+1, a[y] ← a[y/2])
           [] odd y then tabfusc(y+1, a[y] ← (a[(y–1)/2] + a[(y+1)/2])) fi fi.
```

In both examples above, the ordering "<" and the operation *next* that are introduced by the rule caused no difficulties, because they were obvious from the original definition. In general, however, finding appropriate definitions of *next* and

"<" is less straightforward than before. This can be seen when applying the rule *tabulation* to the function *bin* (as defined in the beginning of Sect. 6.3.1).
Here, **m** (from the rule) corresponds to (**nat** i, **nat** j: $0 \le j \le i$). As an ordering "<" on (**nat** i, **nat** j: $0 \le j \le i$), we introduce (recursively)

$$(i, j) < (k, l) =_{\text{def}} (next(i, j) = (k, l) \vee next(i, j) < (k, l))$$

where

```
funct next = (nat i, nat j: 0 ≤ j ≤ i) (nat, nat):
   if j < i then (i, j+1) else (i+1, 0) fi.
```

Furthermore, (0, 0) obviously provides a least element with respect to this ordering.
Now we apply *tabulation*, which results in

```
funct bin' = (nat i, nat j: 0 ≤ j ≤ i) nat:
   tabbin(0, 0, [])[i, j] where
   mode binmap = PMAP(nat, nat, =);
   funct tabbin = (nat k, nat l, binmap a: (k, l) ≤ next(i, j) ∧ 0 ≤ l ≤ k ∧
                  ∀ nat z, z': (0, 0)≤(z, z')<(k, l) ⇨ a[z, z'] = bin(z, z')) binmap:
     if (k, l) = next(i, j) then a
     elsf l=0 ∨ l=k then tabbin(next(k, l), a[k, l] ← 1)
        else tabbin(next(k, l), a[k, l] ← (bin(k–1, l–1) + bin(k–1, l))) fi.
```

By definition of "<" and the assertion $(k, l) \le next(i, j)$, the condition $(k, l) = next(i, j)$ is equivalent to $(j < i \wedge k = i \wedge l = j+1) \vee (j = i \wedge k = i+1 \wedge l = 0)$. The **elsf**-branch can be split up and simplified (by instantiating the calls of *next*) to

```
elsf l=k then tabbin(k+1, 0, a[k, l] ← 1)
elsf l=0 then tabbin(k, 1, a[k, l] ← 1).
```

Moreover, by unfolding the definition of *next*, using the *distributivity of function call over conditional*, and using the assertion for simplification, we finally get

```
funct tabbin =(nat k, nat l, binmap a: (k≤i ∨ (k=i ∧ l≤j)∨(j<i ∧ k=i ∧ l=j+1)∨
                 (j=i ∧ k=i+1 ∧ l=0)) ∧ 0 ≤ l ≤ k ∧
                 ∀ nat z, z': (0, 0)≤(z, z')<(k, l) ⇨ a[z, z'] = bin(z, z')) binmap:
  if (k = i ∧ l = j+1) ∨ (k = i+1 ∧ l = 0) then a
  elsf l=k then tabbin(k+1, 0, a[k, l] ← 1)
  elsf l=0 then tabbin(k, 1, a[k, l] ← 1)
            else tabbin(k, l+1, a[k, l] ← (a[k–1, l–1] + a[k–1, l])) fi.
```

If we compare this version with the one obtained in Sect. 6.3.1, we realize that *memo-ization* usually leads to more "economical" programs, since only those function values are tabulated that are actually needed, whereas *tabulation* may compute table entries which are irrelevant for the result. On the other hand, however, simplification of recursion is usually trivial after having applied *tabulation*, whereas it might be rather complicated after an application of *memo-ization*. Furthermore, there are specialized variants of the *tabulation* rule with weaker conditions on the ordering involved. These variants lead to further improvements, since only those values are tabulated which are actually needed (for details, see [Boiten 89]).

Finding an appropriate ordering is the inventive part in applying the rule *tabulation*. Sometimes, finding that ordering will be eased by first transforming the domain of the given function. To illustrate this, consider the following recursive definition which can be regarded as a generalization of the recursive definition of "polynomial interpolation" (algorithm of Aitken and Neville, [Stoer 72]):

$f(X, Y)$ **where**

funct f = (**nat** x, **nat** y: $0 \le x \le y$) **m**:
  if $x{=}y$ **then** $\mathrm{T}(x, y)$ **else** $\mathrm{r}(f(x{+}1, y), f(x, y{-}1), \mathrm{S}(x, y))$ **fi**.

Here, an ordering that satisfies the applicability conditions of the *tabulation* rule is by no means obvious. Therefore, we transform the above expression (by an embedding) into

$f'(Y, Y{-}X)$ **where**

funct f' = (**nat** x, **nat** y: $0 \le y \le x$) **m**:
  $f(x{-}y, x)$.

Unfolding the definition of f in f' yields

$f'(Y, Y{-}X)$ **where**

funct f' = (**nat** x, **nat** y: $0 \le y \le x$) **m**:
  if $x{-}y = x$ **then** $\mathrm{T}(x{-}y, x)$ **else** $\mathrm{r}(f(x{-}y{+}1, x), f(x{-}y, x{-}1), \mathrm{S}(x{-}y, x))$ **fi**.

Now we apply the properties

$f(x{-}y{+}1, x) \equiv f(x{-}(y{-}1), x)$ and
$f(x{-}y, x{-}1) \equiv f((x{-}1){-}(y{-}1), x{-}1)$,

after which folding results in

$f'(Y, Y{-}X)$ **where**

funct f' = (**nat** x, **nat** y: $0 \le y \le x$) **m**:
  if $x{-}y = x$ **then** $\mathrm{T}(x{-}y, x)$ **else** $\mathrm{r}(f'(x, y{-}1), f'(x{-}1, y{-}1), \mathrm{S}(x{-}y, x))$ **fi**.

Furthermore, $x{-}y = x$ can be simplified to $y = 0$, and accordingly, $\mathrm{T}(x{-}y, x)$ to $\mathrm{T}(x, x)$. Hence, our final version reads

$f'(Y, Y{-}X)$ **where**

funct f' = (**nat** x, **nat** y: $0 \le y \le x$) **m**:
  if $y = 0$ **then** $\mathrm{T}(x, x)$ **else** $\mathrm{r}(f'(x, y{-}1), f'(x{-}1, y{-}1), \mathrm{S}(x{-}y, x))$ **fi**.

Finding an ordering (to apply *tabulation*), perhaps similar to the one for *bin*, is straightforward and left as an exercise to the interested reader.

6.4 Computation in Advance

The techniques considered in the previous section build up tables of values according to a given function definition to save computational effort, as evaluations of function calls can be substituted by (generally "cheaper") table look-ups. In some sense, in particular in connection with the *tabulation* technique, this entails a computation of function values in advance, prior to their use.

Below we will consider some other techniques (sometimes also called 'precomputation techniques', [Jørring, Scherlis 86]) all of which are based on the common underlying idea of computation in advance.

6.4.1 Relocation

The catchword "relocation" summarizes the idea of moving a certain subexpression within some expression to a different location such that the encompassing expression can be simplified afterwards.

One of the most well-known and also most frequently used techniques for improving the performance of (applicative) algorithms by relocation, is the identification of common subexpressions, their solitary evaluation by means of an object declaration, and their substitution in every occurrence by the respective identifier. We have already used this techniques in several of the examples dealt with so far, since it simply means an application of the *abstraction* rule (Sect. 4.3).

A further example of evaluating common subexpressions only once (Sect. 5.3.1.1) is

```
funct minel = (natsequ s: s ≠<>) nat:
   if rest s =<> then first s
   [] rest s ≠<> then if first s ≤ minel(rest s) then first s else minel(rest s) fi fi,
```

which can be transformed into the improved form

```
funct minel = (natsequ s: s ≠<>) nat:
   if rest s =<> then first s
   [] rest s ≠<> then  nat m = minel(rest s);
                       if first s ≤ m then first s else m fi fi.
```

Sometimes, similar effects already can be achieved by the basic rule of *unfolding*. For example, a technique known in a procedural environment as 'flattening of loops' or 'unrolling of loops' [Broy, Pepper 81], corresponds, within an applicative scenario, simply to *unfolding* and subsequent simplification.

Another instance of the relocation idea appears in connection with the *tabulation* technique from Sect. 6.3.2. When analyzing the result of the *tabulation* rule,

```
funct f' = (m x) n:
   tabf(c, [])[x] where

   mode tabmap = MAP(m, n, =);

   funct tabf = (m y, tabmap a: y ≤ next(x) ∧
                      ∀ m z: c≤z<y ⇒ a[z] = f(z)) tabmap:
     if y = next(x) then a  elsf T(y)  then tabf(next(y), a[y] ← H(y))
                                       else tabf(next(y), a[y] ← E(f, y)) fi,
```

one will find out that it still can be improved. Rather than computing the "values on termination" within *tabf*, they can already be supplied for the initial call within *f'*, provided T(*c*) holds. Furthermore, in order to be able to skip the computation of arguments already tabulated, we also need a new function *next'*:

funct f' = (**m** x) **n**:
  tabf(*next'*(c), m)[x] **where**

  mode tabmap = MAP(**m**, **n**, =);
  tabmap m = **that tabmap** m':
    ∀ **m** z: (c≤z≤x Δ T(z)) ⇨ (*isdef*(m', z) Δ m'[z] = H(z));

  funct *tabf* = (**m** y, **tabmap** a:
    ∀ **m** z: $y \le$ *next*(x) Δ c≤z<y ⇨ a[z] = f(z)) **tabmap**:
   if y = *next*(x) **then** a **else** *tabf*(*next'*(*next*(y)), a[y] ← E(f, y)) **fi**,

  funct *next'* = (**m** y) **m**:
   if T(y) ∧ $y \le x$ **then** *next'*(*next*(y)) **else** y **fi**.

It is reasonable to combine *tabulation* with this improvement into a variant of the *tabulation* rule:

- E **where**
  funct f = (**m** x) **n**:
   if T(x) **then** H(x) **else** E(f, x) **fi**

  ⎡ LNSORD(**m**, <, c),
  ⎢ *next*(x) ≡ (**that m** y: $x < y$ ∧ (∀ **m** z: $x < z \Rightarrow y \le z$)),
  ⎢ DEF[f(*next*(x))] ⊢ DEF[f(x)],
  ⎣ T(c) ≡ **true**

  E[f' **for** f] **where**
  funct f' = (**m** x) **n**:
   tabf(c, m)[x] **where**
   mode tabmap = MAP(**m**, **n**, =);
   tabmap m = **that tabmap** m':
     ∀ **m** z: (c≤z≤x ∧ T(z)) ⇒ (*isdef*(m', z) Δ m'[z] = H(z));
   funct *tabf* = (**m** y, **tabmap** a:
     ∀ **m** z: $y \le$ *next*(x) Δ c≤z<y ⇨ a[z] = f(z)) **tabmap**:
    if y = *next*(x) **then** a **else** *tabf*(*next'*(*next*(y)), a[y] ← E(f, y)) **fi**,
   funct *next'* = (**m** y) **m**:
    if T(y) ∧ $y \le x$ **then** *next'*(*next*(y)) **else** y **fi**.

6.4.2 Precomputation

The word 'precomputation' characterizes an idea that essentially exploits the fact that functions on finite domains can be represented by (finite) maps. Rather than evaluating the respective function for particular actual arguments on request, a table of values of the function is created in advance and all function calls are simply substituted by table look-ups.

This idea is codified in the transformation rule

- *Precomputation*

```
E' where
funct f = (m x) n: E
```

⟶ [**m** finite

```
mode mmap = MAP(m, n, =);
mmap m = that mmap m': ∀ m x: isdef(m', x) Δ m'[x] = f(x);
E'[m[E"] for f(E")]
```

Syntactic constraints:
NOTOCCURS[*m* **in** E'].

Of course, using this rule only leads to an improvement, if the computation of the map *m* is "cheaper" than the evaluation of all calls of *f* in E'.

Note that requiring finiteness of **m** is not too restrictive, if an appropriate (finite) submode in *f* is chosen. Note also, that, although not immediately applicable, the rule can often be used after applying the *decomposition* technique mentioned at the end of Sect. 5.1.1.

In order to demonstrate the use of this rule, we consider the problem

Determine some character that occurs in a given (non-empty) character string most often.

A formalization of this problem is fairly obvious:

```
mode char = «some finite character set»;
mode string = EESEQU(char, =);

funct maxocc = (string s: s ≠<>) char:
   some char c: c ∈ s Δ ∀ (char c': c' ∈ s): noccs(c, s) ≥ noccs(c', s) where

   funct noccs = (char c, string s) nat:
      if s =<> then 0
      elsf first s = c then 1 + noccs(c, rest s) else noccs(c, rest s) fi.
```

Using the techniques from Chap. 5 we can derive an operational solution for *maxocc*:

```
funct maxocc = (string s: s ≠<>) char:
   maxocc'(first s, rest s) where

   funct maxocc' = (char c, string t) char:
      if t =<> then c
      elsf noccs(c, t) ≥ noccs(first t, t)  then maxocc'(c, rest t)
                                            else maxocc'(first t, rest t) fi,

   funct noccs = (char c, string s) nat:
      if s =<> then 0
      elsf first s = c then 1 + noccs(c, rest s) else noccs(c, rest s) fi.
```

Here, due to the finiteness of **char**, *precomputation* can be applied to the function *noccs* and yields

```
funct maxocc = (string s: s ≠<>) char:
   maxocc'(first s, rest s) where

   mode frequ = MAP(char, nat, =);
   frequ m = that frequ m': ∀ char x: isdef(m', x) Δ m'[x] = noccs(x, s);

   funct maxocc' = (char c, string t) char:
      if t =<> then c
      elsf m[c] ≥ m[first t]  then maxocc'(c, rest t)
                              else maxocc'(first t, rest t) fi.
```

The gain in efficiency (for a reasonable ratio between the size of the character set and the length of the string *s*) is obvious.

6.4.3 Partial evaluation

Another technique that is also based on the basic idea of doing certain computations in advance, is the paradigm of 'partial evaluation' [Beckman et al. 76], [Wegbreit 76], also called 'partial application' [Ershov 78] or 'mixed computation' [Ershov 82], [Ershov, Ostrovski 86].

These catchwords embody the following idea: given a definition of a function and additionally knowing that one of the arguments of the respective function will take on only very few actual values, derive a system of specialized functions, one for each actual value.

As a simple example, consider

```
funct rpow = (nat a, nat b: b ≤ 4) nat:
   pow(a, b) where

   funct pow = (nat a, nat b) nat:
      if b=0 then 1 elsf b=1 then a else a × pow(a, b–1) fi.
```

Here, by unfolding *pow* in *rpow*, we get

```
funct rpow = (nat a, nat b: b ≤ 4) nat:
   if b=0 then 1
   elsf b=1 then a  else a × pow(a, b–1) fi.
```

In the **else**-branch we have $b \geq 2$, and, hence

$$a \times pow(a, b-1) \equiv a \times a \times pow(a, b-2).$$

Two more unfoldings of *pow*, trivial simplifications (exploiting the assertion on *b*), and abstraction then lead to

```
funct rpow = (nat a, nat b: b ≤ 4) nat:
   if b=0 then 1
   elsf b=1 then a
   else nat c = a × a;
      if b=2 then c elsf b=3 then c × a else c × c fi fi.
```

A somewhat more advanced example of the same kind is the treatment of 'Ackermann's function' in [Bauer, Wössner 82]. There it is shown how by using the partial evaluation technique the general recursive definition can be simplified for particular arguments, thus leading to successor, addition, and multiplication.

Even more advanced examples can be found in connection with the parsing of grammars. Here, general parsers (having the grammar as an argument) can be specialized into parsers for concrete grammars or parsers for grammars with particular properties (such as LL and LR). Details are given in [Ershov, Ostrovski 86].

Applying the partial evaluation paradigm is not only profitable, if the values for one of the arguments are known (as in the example above), but also, if for one of the arguments it is known that certain values occur more often than other ones. Thus, for the above example without the restriction $b \le 4$, it still might be advantageous to have specialized functions, say for computing squares or cubes. In particular, in connection with highly time-consuming numerical computations this technique may lead to substantial increases in efficiency [Goad 82].

Using mainly unfoldings and simplifications to achieve improvements by the partial evaluation strategy requires knowledge about concrete values. But even in cases where only additional information about arguments is available, say in the form of assertions, the same basic idea can be applied, using the technique of currying.

Currying is a technique from logic [Curry, Feys 58]. It allows one to make multi-argument functions into single-argument ones having functions as results and vice versa. It can be described by the transformation rule

• <u>Currying</u>

> *f*(E', E") **where**
> **funct** *f* = (**m** *x*, **m'** *y*) **n**: E
>
> ⇕
>
> *f*'(E')(E") **where**
> **funct** *f*' = (**m** *x*) (**funct** (**m'**) **n**): ((**m'** *y*) **n**: E[*f*'(A)(B) **for** *f*(A, B))] .

In connection with the partial evaluation strategy, *currying* is used to split the computation, finally aiming at finding efficient realizations for the respective parts (in particular for *f*'(*x*), called the 'residual function' in [Ershov 82]). Currying also may be used as a preparatory step for achieving tabulation by *memo-ization* and *function inversion* [Broy, Pepper 81], [Berghammer 86].

Relocation and partial evaluation are especially advantageous, if within a given context the respective functions are multiply used (such that part of their computation can be done once for all occurrences). In such a situation, however, other rules can be used, too. A typical example is the rule ∈*-elimination* (Sect. 4.4.3) which (in the upward direction) transforms a predicate P(*x*) into *x* ∈ {**m** *y*: P(*y*)}. Here, computing the whole set {**m** *y*: P(*y*)} (say in the form of a table) is profitable not only if P has to be computed for several different arguments, but also if the computation of P for a single argument can be improved by *memo-ization* or *tabulation*.

6.4.4 Differencing

The general idea underlying the 'difference technique' is again the computation of values in advance. Its specific idea is as follows: if in the course of evaluating a recursive definition, a new argument n is computed from an old argument o, then frequently, in particular in connection with complex, structured objects, only a certain part δ of o actually has to be computed anew, whereas the remainder of o remains unaffected, i.e., o and n can be represented as

$o = o_0 + \delta$, and
$n = o_0 + \delta'$ (where δ and δ' indicate "differences").

If it is, furthermore, possible to compute δ' from δ, then a lot of computational effort can be saved. However, a computation has to take place in advance to compute o_0 from the original argument o.

This idea is rather old. In the area of optimizing compilers it has been known under the name 'strength reduction' for quite a while [Earley 76]. In transformational programming it has gained new popularity under the names 'finite differencing' or 'formal differentiation' [Paige, Koenig 82], [Sharir 82]. Since then, it has been rediscovered in data base research as 'Δ-optimization' [Bayer 85].

In order to illustrate the basic idea, we consider the problem

Compute the integer square root of a given natural number.

Obviously, this problem can be formalized as

funct sqr = (**nat** n) **nat**:
  that nat k: $k^2 \le n \wedge (k+1)^2 > n$.

Using an embedding, this can be transformed to

funct sqr = (**nat** n) **nat**:
  $h(0, n)$ **where**
  funct h = (**nat** x, **nat** n: $x^2 \le n$) **nat**:
    that nat k: $x \le k \wedge k^2 \le n \wedge (k+1)^2 > n$.

Now, using the techniques from Chap. 5, we can develop a recursive formulation for h. We have

that nat k: $x \le k \wedge k^2 \le n \wedge (k+1)^2 > n$ ≡
that nat k: $(x = k \wedge k^2 \le n \wedge (k+1)^2 > n) \vee (x < k \wedge k^2 \le n \wedge (k+1)^2 > n)$ ≡
that nat k: $(x = k \wedge k^2 \le n \wedge (x+1)^2 > n) \vee (x < k \wedge k^2 \le n \wedge (k+1)^2 > n)$ ≡
if $(x+1)^2 > n$ **then that nat** k: $(x = k \wedge k^2 \le n \wedge (x+1)^2 > n)$
  else that nat k: $(x < k \wedge k^2 \le n \wedge (k+1)^2 > n)$ **fi**.

The **then**-part simplifies to x, for the **else**-part we have

that nat k: $(x < k \wedge k^2 \le n \wedge (k+1)^2 > n)$ ≡
that nat k: $(x+1 \le k \wedge k^2 \le n \wedge (k+1)^2 > n)$,

such that folding (with assertion) yields

funct sqr = (**nat** n) **nat**:
  $h(0, n)$ **where**

  funct h = (**nat** x, **nat** n: $x^2 \le n$) **nat**:
    if $(x+1)^2 > n$ **then** x **else** $h(x+1, n)$ **fi**.

Next, we apply another embedding resulting in

funct sqr = (**nat** n) **nat**:
  $h1(0, 1, n)$ **where**

  funct $h1$ = (**nat** x, **nat** y, **nat** n: $x^2 \le n \wedge y = (x+1)^2$) **nat**:
    $h(x, n)$.

Unfolding h in $h1$ yields

if $(x+1)^2 > n$ **then** x **else** $h(x+1, n)$ **fi**,

which can be simplified (using the assertion in $h1$) to

if $y > n$ **then** x **else** $h(x+1, n)$ **fi**,

and by folding (with assertion) we get

if $y > n$ **then** x **else** $h1(x+1, (x+2)^2, n)$ **fi**.

For the recursive call in the **else**-branch we have furthermore

$h1(x+1, (x+2)^2, n) \equiv h1(x+1, (x^2+2x+1)+2x+3, n) \equiv h1(x+1, y+2x+3, n)$,

such that our next version reads

funct sqr = (**nat** n) **nat**:
  $h1(0, 1, n)$ **where**

  funct $h1$ = (**nat** x, **nat** y, **nat** n: $x^2 \le n \wedge y = (x+1)^2$) **nat**:
    if $y > n$ **then** x **else** $h1(x+1, y+2x+3, n)$ **fi**.

Now we use a further embedding leading to

funct sqr = (**nat** n) **nat**:
  $h2(0, 1, 3, n)$ **where**

  funct $h2$ = (**nat** x, **nat** y, **nat** z, **nat** n: $x^2 \le n \wedge y = (x+1)^2 \wedge z = 2x+3$) **nat**:
    $h1(x, y, n)$.

Again, unfolding of $h1$ in the body of $h2$ leads to

if $y > n$ **then** x **else** $h1(x+1, y+2x+3, n)$ **fi**,

simplification (using the assertion in $h2$) to

if $y > n$ **then** x **else** $h1(x+1, y+z, n)$ **fi**,

folding (with assertion) to

if $y > n$ **then** x **else** $h2(x+1, y+z, 2(x+1)+3, n)$ **fi**,

and simplification, once more using the assertion in $h2$, finally results in

if $y > n$ **then** x **else** $h2(x+1, y+z, z+2, n)$ **fi**.

Hence, as a final result we get

funct *sqr* = (**nat** *n*) **nat**:
  h2(0, 1, 3, *n*) **where**

  funct *h2* = (**nat** *x*, **nat** *y*, **nat** *z*, **nat** *n*: $x^2 \le n \wedge y = (x+1)^2 \wedge z = 2x+3$) **nat**:
    if $y > n$ **then** *x* **else** *h2*(*x*+1, *y*+*z*, *z*+2, *n*) **fi**

where only simple additions are used.

In the above example we have used the

> **<u>Strategy</u>**
>
> Given a definition of a function *f*;
>
> – Define by a suitable embedding (of the domain) a function *f'* (with an appropriate assertion);
> – Derive a recursive version of *f'* which is independent of *f* using the generalized unfold/fold strategy;
> – Repeat the first two steps, if appropriate.

The essential step in this strategy is the embedding and the assertion generated with that embedding which is necessary for the generalized unfold/fold strategy to be successful.

Of course, the first two steps of the above strategy also can be cast into transformation rules, viz.

• *<u>Finite differencing I</u>*

funct *f* = (**m** *x*) **r**:
  if T(*x*) **then** H(*x*) **else** *p*(*x*, *a*(*x*), *f*(K(*x*))) **fi**

⇕ [T(*x*) ≡ **true** ⊢ DEF[*a*(*x*)], *d*(*x*, *a*(*x*)) ≡ *a*(K(*x*))

funct *f* = (**m** *x*) **r**:
  f'(*x*, *a*(*x*)) **where**
  funct *f'* = (**m** *x*, **n** *y*: *y* = *a*(*x*)) **r**:
    if T(*x*) **then** H(*x*) **else** *p*(*x*, *y*, *f'*(K(*x*), *d*(*x*, *y*))) **fi**

and

• *<u>Finite differencing II</u>*

funct *f* = (**m** *x*) **r**:
  if T(*x*) **then** H(*x*) **else** *p*(*x*, *f*(K(*x*))) **fi**

⇕ [T(*x*) ≡ **true** ⊢ DEF[K'(*x*)], *d*(*x*, K'(*x*)) ≡ (K(*x*), K'(K(*x*)))

funct *f* = (**m** *x*) **r**:
  f'(*x*, K'(*x*)) **where**
  funct *f'* = (**m** *x*, **n** *y*: *y* = K'(*x*)) **r**:
    if T(*x*) **then** H(*x*) **else** *p*(*x*, *f'*(*d*(*x*, *y*))) **fi**.

The difference between these two rules is in the position of the "expensive" operation to be substituted by a "cheaper" incremental one. In the rule *finite differencing I* the expensive operation appears outside the recursive call, in *finite differencing II* on argument position. Obviously, the latter rule comprises tail-recursive functions as a special case.

The crucial step in applying these rules is finding suitable new operations (d and K', resp.) such that a gain in efficiency is indeed achieved. To illustrate the use of these rules, we consider another problem:

Compute the sum of all squares from 0 up to some given $n \in \mathbb{N}$,

which formalized may read

funct *sqsum* = (**nat** *n*) **nat**: $\Sigma_{i=0..n}\, i^2$.

Using the techniques from Chap. 5, this can straightforwardly be transformed into the recursive function

funct *sqsum* = (**nat** *n*) **nat**:
  if n=0 **then** 0 **else** $n^2 + sqsum(n-1)$ **fi**.

Now, by associating

$a(n)$ with n^2,
K(n) with $n-1$, and
$d(n, nsq)$ with $nsq - 2n + 1$,

obviously *finite differencing I* is applicable, leading to

funct *sqsum* = (**nat** *n*) **nat**:
  $sqsum'(n, n^2)$ **where**

  funct *sqsum'* = (**nat** *n*, **nat** *nsq*: $nsq = n^2$) **nat**:
    if n=0 **then** 0 **else** $nsq + sqsum'(n-1, nsq-2n+1)$ **fi**.

Furthermore, by associating

K'(n, nsq) with $2n$,
K(n, nsq) with $(n-1, nsq-2n+1)$ and
$d(n, nsq, dbln)$ with $(n-1, nsq-dbln, dbln-2)$,

also *finite differencing II* is applicable to *sqsum'*, thus finally yielding

funct *sqsum* = (**nat** *n*) **nat**:
  $sqsum''(n, n^2, 2n)$ **where**

  funct *sqsum"* = (**nat** *n*, **nat** *nsq*, **nat** *dbln*: $nsq = n^2 \wedge dbln = 2n$) **nat**:
    if n=0 **then** 0 **else** $nsq + sqsum''(n-1, nsq-dbln+1, dbln-2)$ **fi**.

As with the previous example, the gain in efficiency is obvious. But note that efficiency could be further improved by inverting the computation.

The first applicability conditions of the above rules are necessary to guarantee definedness of the arguments of the initial call of the embedded function. If they cannot be established, they can be circumvented by using the following variant of the rule *finite differencing I*,

- **funct** *f* = (**m** *x*) **r**:
  if T(*x*) **then** H(*x*) **else** *p*(*x*, *a*(*x*), *f*(K(*x*))) **fi**

  $\updownarrow$ [*d*(*x*, *a*(*x*)) ≡ *a*(K(*x*))

  funct *f* = (**m** *x*) **r**:
  if T(*x*) **then** H(*x*) **else** *f*'(*x*, *a*(*x*)) **fi** **where**
  funct *f*' = (**m** *x*, **n** *y*: ¬T(*x*) Δ *y* = *a*(*x*)) **r**:
  if T(K(*x*)) **then** *p*(*x*, *y*, H(K(*x*))) **else** *p*(*x*, *y*, *f*'(K(*x*), *d*(*x*, *y*))) **fi**,

or an analogous variant for the rule *finite differencing II*,

- **funct** *f* = (**m** *x*) **r**:
  if T(*x*) **then** H(*x*) **else** *p*(*x*, *f*(K(*x*))) **fi**

  $\updownarrow$ [*d*(*x*, K'(*x*)) ≡ (K(*x*), K'(K(*x*)))

  funct *f* = (**m** *x*) **r**:
  if T(*x*) **then** H(*x*) **else** *f*'(*x*, K'(*x*)) **fi** **where**
  funct *f*' = (**m** *x*, **n** *y*: ¬T(*x*) Δ *y* = K'(*x*)) **r**:
  if T(K(*x*)) **then** *p*(*x*, H(K(*x*))) **else** *f*'(*d*(*x*, *y*)) **fi**.

Using this latter variant instead of *finite differencing II* we obtain for the example above:

funct *sqsum* = (**nat** *n*) **nat**:
if *n*=0 **then** 0 **else** *sqsum*''(*n*, n^2, 2*n*–1) **fi** **where**

funct *sqsum*'' = (**nat** *n*, **nat** *nsq*, **nat** *dbln*: *nsq* = n^2 ∧ *dbln* = 2*n*–1) **nat**:
if *n*=0 **then** 0 **else** *nsq* + *sqsum*''(*n*–1, *nsq*–*dbln*, *dbln*–2) **fi**.

Whether one prefers to use the finite differencing paradigm in the form of a strategy or in the form of a compact rule is more or less a matter of taste. The strategy may have the slight advantage that finding "cheaper" operations is a little more straightforward, however, at the expense of a larger number of transformation steps.

One also could think of having particular instances of the above rules for particular data types, as this would allow using a ready-made collection of 'differencing rules' that result from the respective instantiations of the essential applicability condition

d(*x*, *a*(*x*)) ≡ *a*(K(*x*)) (for all **m** *x*)

for particular operations *a* and K. For **m** (from the rule) being finite sets, this has been extensively studied within the SETL project [Paige 79], [Paige, Koenig 82], [Sharir 81], [Sharir 82].

6.5 Simplification of Recursion

Some of the techniques discussed in the previous sections lead to tail-recursive programs which can immediately be transformed into iteration (Chap. 7). If the resulting program exhibits a more complicated recursion structure, then it is an important step to first transform this recursion structure into tail recursion before performing the transition to iteration.

Recursion removal (or recursion simplification) was the focus of interest in the early days of transformational programming. Hence a vast amount of literature already exists on this specific topic and we may confine ourselves to only a few representative techniques and rules. For a more comprehensive treatment see for example [Bauer, Wössner 82] or [Pepper, Partsch 86].

Before going into technical details, we first make precise what we mean by 'tail-recursive'.

An expression E(*f*, *x*) in *f* and *x* is said to be

- **non-recursive (in *f*)**, iff *f* does not occur in E;
- **tail-recursive (in *f*)**, iff *f* occurs in E(*f*, *x*), and E(*f*, *x*) is of one of the following forms:
  - *f*(K(*x*));
  - **if** C(*x*) **then** $E_1(f, x)$ **else** $E_2(f, x)$ **fi**, where the $E_i(f, x)$ (i = 1, 2) are non-recursive or tail-recursive (in *f*);
  - **if** $[]_{i=1..n}$ $C_i(x)$ **then** $E_i(f, x)$ **fi**, where the $E_i(f, x)$ are non-recursive or tail-recursive (in *f*).

(Note, that by our conventions introduced in Sect. 4.2.1, K(*x*), C(*x*), and the $C_i(x)$ are non-recursive.)

A single function

funct *f* = (**m** *x*) **r**: E

is said to be **tail-recursive;** iff E is tail-recursive (in *f*).

Accordingly, a system of functions (f_1, ..., f_n) is **tail-recursive** iff all bodies E_i ($1 \leq i \leq n$) are tail-recursive (in f_j, $1 \leq j \leq n$).

6.5.1 From Linear Recursion to Tail Recursion

A linear recursive function has the typical form

funct *f* = (**m** *x*) **n**: **if** B(*x*) **then** H(*x*) **else** *p*(E(*x*), *f*(K(*x*))) **fi**.

The standard example for linear recursion is the function computing the factorial

funct *fac* = (**nat** *n*) **nat**: **if** n=0 **then** 1 **else** $n \times fac(n-1)$ **fi**.

In order to simplify the recursion, i.e., to transform the linear recursion to tail recursion, we define by an *embedding*

funct *fact* = (**nat** *m*, **nat** *n*) **nat**: $m \times fac(n)$ **fi**.

Obviously, $fac(N) \equiv fact(1, N)$ holds, for all $N \in \mathbb{N}$.

Unfolding fac in *fact* yields

$m \times$ **if** n=0 **then** 1 **else** $n \times fac(n-1)$ **fi**;

Distributivity of primitive operations over conditional then leads to

if n=0 **then** $m \times 1$ **else** $m \times n \times fac(n$-$1)$ **fi**,

such that using the property $m \times 1 \equiv m$ and subsequent *folding* result in

funct *fact* = (**nat** *m*, **nat** *n*) **nat**:
  if *n*=0 **then** *m* **else** *fact*(*m* × *n*, *n*–1) **fi**.

Hence we can redefine the original definition of *fac* to

funct *fac* = (**nat** *n*) **nat**:
  fact(1, *n*) **where**

  funct *fact* = (**nat** *m*, **nat** *n*) **nat**:
    if *n*=0 **then** *m* **else** *fact*(*m* × *n*, *n*–1) **fi**.

In this derivation we have used the

<u>**Strategy**</u>:

Given a linear recursive function

funct *f* = (**m** *x*) **m**: **if** B(*x*) **then** H(*x*) **else** *p*(E(*x*), *f*(K(*x*))) **fi**,

- Define, by embedding,
  funct *f'* = (**m** *y*, **m** *x*) **m**: *p*(*y*, *f*(*x*)) such that there exists **m** E with
  f'(E, *X*) ≡ *f*(*X*) for all **m** *X*;
- Derive, by using the unfold/fold strategy, a recursive version of *f'* that is independent of *f*;
- Redefine *f* into **funct** *f* = (**m** *x*) **m**: *f'*(E, *X*).

Of course, this strategy, sometimes called 'accumulation strategy' [Bird 84], also can be made into a compact rule [Bauer, Wössner 82]:

- <u>*Simplification of linear recursion I*</u>

funct *f* = (**m** *x*) **m**:
  if B(*x*) **then** H(*x*) **else** *p*(K(*x*), *f*(K'(*x*))) **fi**

⇕ [ASSOC(**m**, *p*),
  NEUTRAL(**m**, *p*, E)

funct *f* = (**m** *x*) **m**:
  f'(E, *x*) **where**
  funct *f'* = (**m** *y*, **m** *x*) **m**:
    if B(*x*) **then** *p*(*y*, H(*x*)) **else** *f'*(*p*(*y*, K(*x*)), K'(*x*)) **fi**.

The applicability conditions of this rule require associativity of the operation *p* as well as the neutrality of E with respect to *p*. These conditions are obviously fulfilled for all kinds of numerical problems, due to the well-known algebraic properties of the basic operations on various kinds of numbers. As an example for other kinds of data structures, we consider the algorithm for sorting a given sequence (as obtained in Sect. 5.5.1)

funct *sort* = (**natsequ** *s*) **natsequ**:
  if *s* =<> **then** <> **else** *min*(*s*)+*sort*(*delete*(*s*, *min*(*s*))) **fi**.

Here, due to associativity of concatenation and the fact that <> is a neutral element with respect to concatenation, the above rule is applicable and results (after trivial simplifications) in

```
funct sort = (natsequ s) natsequ:
   sort'(<>, s) where

   funct sort' = (natsequ r, natsequ s) natsequ:
      if s =<> then r else sort'(r+min(s), delete(s, min(s))) fi.
```

As another example we consider the definition

```
funct meanvar = (natsequ s: s ≠<>) (real, real):
   (nat su, nat si, nat ssq) = h(s);
   (su/si, (ssq – su^2)/si^2) where

   funct h = (natsequ s) (nat, nat, nat):
      if s =<> then (0, 0, 0) else (firsts, 1, (firsts)^2) ⊕ h(rests)) fi,
```

from Sect. 6.1.2. Here, obviously ⊕ is associative with neutral element (0, 0, 0), such that the application of (an appropriate variant of) *simplification of linear recursion I* and *unfolding* of the definition of ⊕ yield immediately

```
funct meanvar = (natsequ s: s ≠<>) (real, real):
   (nat su, nat si, nat ssq) = h(s, 0, 0, 0);
   (su/si, (ssq – su^2)/si^2) where

   funct h = (natsequ s, nat a, nat b, nat c) (nat, nat, nat):
      if s =<> then (a, b, c) else h(rests, a+firsts, b+1, c+(firsts)^2) fi.
```

There are plenty of variants of the above rule taking care of the cases where

- *p* has a functionality other than **funct (m, m) m**;
- a (left-)neutral element does not exist; or
- *p* has the property of right-commutativity
  (i.e., $p(p(x, y), z) \equiv p(p(x, z), y)$ for all x, y, z) instead of associativity.

For details on all these variants see [Bauer, Wössner 82].

A conceptually different kind of technique is applicable, if the primitive operation K (in the definition of a linear recursive function *f*) is known to be invertible, i.e., if there exists an expression K^{-1} such that

$$K^{-1}(K(x)) = x$$

holds for all **m** x. In such a case we have the rule

- <u>*Recursion simplification II*</u>

```
funct f = (m x) n:
   if B(x) then H(x) else p(f(K(x)), E(x)) fi
```

⇕ [DEF[K(x)] ⊢ $(K^{-1}(K(x)) = x) \equiv$ **true**

```
funct f = (m x) n:
   f''(x, x0, H(x0)) where
   m x0 = f'(x);
   funct f' = (m x) m:
      if B(x) then x else f'(K(x)) fi,
   funct f'' = (m x, m y, n z) n:
      if y=x then z else f''(x, K^-1(y), p(z, E(K^-1(y)))) fi.
```

If x_0, the argument on termination in *f*, is known, this rule can be substantially simplified to

- **funct** *f* = (**m** *x*) **n**:
  if *x*=E **then** H(*x*) **else** *p*(*f*(K(*x*)), E'(*x*)) **fi**

  ⇕ [CONST[E],
  DEF[K(*x*)] ⊢ $(K^{-1}(K(x)) = x) \equiv$ **true**

  funct *f* = (**m** *x*) **n**:
  g(*x*, E, H(E)) **where**
  funct *g* = (**m** *x*, **m** *y*, **n** *z*) **n**:
  if *y*=*x* **then** *z* **else** *g*(*x*, $K^{-1}(y)$, *p*(*z*, E'($K^{-1}(y)$))) **fi**.

Obviously, this variant is applicable to the factorial example above and yields

funct *fac'* = (**nat** *n*) **nat**:
fact(*n*, 0, 1) **fi where**

funct *fact* = (**nat** *n*, **nat** *k*, **nat** *m*) **nat**:
if *k*=*n* **then** *m* **else** *fact*(*n*, *k*+1, (*k*+1)×*m*) **fi**.

As a special variant of the rule above we have

- **funct** *f* = (**m** *x*) **n**:
  if *x*=E **then** H(*x*) **else n** *z* = *f*(K(*x*)); *p*(*z*, E'(*x*)) **fi**

  ⇕ [CONST[E],
  DEF[K(*x*)] ⊢ $(K^{-1}(K(x)) = x) \equiv$ **true**

  funct *f* = (**m** *x*) **n**:
  f'(E, H(E)) **where**
  funct *f'* = (**m** *y*, **n** *z*) **n**:
  if *y*=*x* **then** *z* **else** *f'*($K^{-1}(y)$, *p*(*z*, E'($K^{-1}(y)$))) **fi**.

The idea of inversion can be used also for arbitrary forms of recursion which fit the input scheme of the following rule

- <u>*Partial inversion*</u>

  f(*X*, *Y*) **where**
  funct *f* = (**m** *x*, **n** *y*: P(*x*, *y*)) **r**:
  if T(*x*) **then** H(*x*, *y*) **else** E(*f*, K(*x*), *y*) **fi**

  ⇓ [CONST[*X*, *Y*],
  DEF[K(*x*)] ⊢ $(K^{-1}(K(x)) = x) \equiv$ **true**

  f'(*init*(*X*))[*Y*] **where**
  mode nmap = MAP(**n**, **r**, =);
  if *z* = *X* **then** *a* **else** *f'*($K^{-1}(z)$, **some nmap** *b*: *isfmap*(*b*, $K^{-1}(z)$)) **fi**,
  funct *isfmap* = (**nmap** *a*, **m** *x*) **bool**:
  ∀ (**n** *y*: P(*x*, *y*)): *isdef*(*a*, *y*) Δ *a*[*y*] = *f*(*x*, *y*),
  funct *init* = (**m** *x*) (**m**, **nmap**):
  if T(*x*) **then** (*x*, **some nmap** *b*: *isfmap*(*b*, *x*)) **else** *init*(*K*(*x*)) **fi**

  <u>**Syntactic constraints:**</u>
  FIRSTARG[*f* **in** E] = K(*x*).

According to our notational conventions, the expression E(*f*, K(x), y) covers arbitrary forms of recursion, even tree-like ones. The syntactic constraint FIRSTARG[*f* **in** E] = K(x) ensures that any recursive call of *f* in E has the same first argument K(x).

Before going on, a few remarks seem appropriate:

- As in many other rules, the generated assertions are important here, since they usually allow further simplifications in a subsequent step.
- The applicability condition in the rule quantifies over all **m** x. In fact, it could be weakened to (**m** x: $\neg$T(x) ∇ $\exists$ **n** y: P(x, y)).
- Obviously, for particular termination conditions T, the definition of *init* can be simplified. For example, for T(x) $\equiv$ ($x = x_0$), *init*(X) simplifies to (x_0, **some nmap** *b*: *isfmap*(*b*, x_0)).

Note that the rule *recursion simplification II* is just a particular instance of this rule. A given linear recursive function

funct g = (**m** x) **n**:
  if B(x) **then** H(x) **else** p(g(K(x)), E(x)) **fi**

can be transformed (by *embedding*) into

funct g = (**m** x) **n**:
  f(x, x) **where**

  funct *f* = (**m** x, **m** y: $x = y$) **n**:
    if B(x) **then** H(x) **else** p(*f*(K(x), K(y)), E(y)) **fi**

Now, assuming invertibility of K, the rule *partial inversion* can be applied to *f* and results in

f'(*init*(X))[Y] **where**

mode mmap = MAP(**m**, **m**, =);

funct *f'* = (**m** z, **mmap** *a*: *isfmap*(*a*, z)) **mmap**:
  if $z = X$ **then** *a* **else** *f'*($K^{-1}(z)$, **some mmap** *b*: *isfmap*(*b*, $K^{-1}(z)$)) **fi**,

funct *isfmap* = (**mmap** *a*, **m** x) **bool**:
  $\forall$ (**m** y: $x = y$): *isdef*(*a*, y) Δ *a*[y] = *f*(x, y),

funct *init* = (**m** x) (**m**, **mmap**):
  if B(x) **then** (x, **some mmap** *b*: *isfmap*(*b*, x)) **else** *init*(*K*(x)) **fi**.

Here, due to the definition of *isfmap*, in *init* and *f* a singleton map is a possible choice. Therefore, a simple object *a* (of kind **m**) can be used in place of such a (singleton) map, and *isfmap*(*a*, x) may be simplified to $a = f(x, x) = g(x)$. In turn, using the respective instantiations, *init* simplifies to

funct *init* = (**m** x) (**m**, **n**):
  if B(x) **then** (x, H(x)) **else** *init*(*K*(x)) **fi**.

Likewise *f'* simplifies first to

funct *f'* = (**m** z, **n** *a*: $a = g(z)$) **n**:
  if $z = X$ **then** *a* **else** *f'*($K^{-1}(z)$, $g(K^{-1}(z))$) **fi**,

further to

funct f' = (**m** z, **n** a: $a = g(z)$) **n**:
  if $z = X$ **then** a **else** $f'(\mathrm{K}^{-1}(z), p(g(\mathrm{K}(\mathrm{K}^{-1}(z))), \mathrm{E}(\mathrm{K}^{-1}(z)))$ **fi**,

and finally, using the assertion, to

funct f' = (**m** z, **n** a) **n**:
  if $z = X$ **then** a **else** $f'(\mathrm{K}^{-1}(z), p(a, \mathrm{E}(\mathrm{K}^{-1}(z)))$ **fi**.

Hence, together, we have the rule *recursion simplification II* as a special case of the rule *partial inversion.*

For demonstrating the use of the rule *partial inversion*, we reconsider the problem of the binomial coefficient from Sect. 6.3.1:

bin(I, J) **where**

funct *bin* = (**nat** i, **nat** j: $0 \le j \le i$) **nat**:
  if j=0 ∨ j=i **then** 1 **else** *bin*(i–1, j–1) + *bin*(i–1, j) **fi**.

By *case introduction* (on i) and simplification according to the assertion we get

funct *bin* = (**nat** i, **nat** j: $0 \le j \le i$) **nat**:
  if i=0 **then** 1 **else if** j=0 ∨ j=i **then** 1 **else** *bin*(i–1, j–1) + *bin*(i–1, j) **fi fi**.

Straightforward application of the above rule then leads to

bin'(*init*(I))[J] **where**

mode natmap = MAP(**nat**, **nat**, =);

funct *bin'* = (**nat** x, **natmap** a: *isbinmap*(a, x)) **natmap**:
  if $x = I$ **then** a **else** *bin'*(x+1, **some natmap** b: *isbinmap*(b, x+1)) **fi**,

funct *isbinmap* = (**natmap** a, **nat** x) **bool**:
  ∀ (**nat** y: $0 \le y \le x$): *isdef*(a, y) Δ $a[y]$ = *bin*(x, y),

funct *init* = (**nat** x) (**nat**, **natmap**):
  if x = 0 **then** (x, **some natmap** b: *isbinmap*(b, x)) **else** *init*(x–1) **fi**.

Now we aim at simplification. According to the remark immediately after the rule *partial inversion*, the auxiliary operation *init* here obviously simplifies to (0, [][0] ← 1).

For the second argument of the recursive call in *bin'* we have

some natmap b: *isbinmap*(b, x+1) ≡
some natmap b: ∀ (**nat** y: $0 \le y \le x+1$): *isdef*(b, y) Δ $b[y]$ = *bin*(x+1, y) ≡
some natmap b: ∀ (**nat** y: $1 \le y \le x$):
  (*isdef*(b, y) Δ $b[y]$ = *bin*(x, y–1)+*bin*(x, y)) ∧
  (*isdef*(b, x+1) Δ $b[x+1]$ = 1) ∧ (*isdef*(b, 0) Δ $b[0]$ = 1) ≡
some natmap b: ∀ (**nat** y: $1 \le y \le x$): (*isdef*(b, y) Δ $b[y]$ = $a[y-1]$+$a[y]$) ∧
  (*isdef*(b, x+1) Δ $b[x+1]$ = 1) ∧ (*isdef*(b, 0) Δ $b[0]$ = $a[0]$) ≡

upd(a, x) **where**

funct *upd* = (**natmap** *a*, **nat** *x*) **natmap**:
 some natmap *b*: ∀ (**nat** *y*: $1 \le y \le x$): (*isdef*(*b*, *y*) Δ *b*[*y*] = *a*[*y*–1]+*a*[*y*]) ∧
 (*isdef*(*b*, *x*+1) Δ *b*[*x*+1] = 1) ∧ (*isdef*(*b*, 0) Δ *b*[0] = *a*[0]).

Altogether we have

bin'(0, [][0] ← 1)[*I*] **where**

mode natmap = MAP(**nat**, **nat**, =);

funct *bin'* = (**nat** *x*, **natmap** *a*:
 ∀ (**nat** *y*: $0 \le y \le x$): *isdef*(*a*, *y*) Δ *a*[*y*] = *bin*(*x*, *y*)) **natmap**:
 if *x* = *I* **then** *a* **else** *bin'*(*x*+1, *upd*(*a*, *x*)) **fi**,

funct *upd* = (**natmap** *a*, **nat** *x*) **natmap**:
 some natmap *b*: ∀ (**nat** *y*: $1 \le y \le x$): (*isdef*(*b*, *y*) Δ *b*[*y*] = *a*[*y*–1]+*a*[*y*]) ∧
 (*isdef*(*b*, *x*+1) Δ *b*[*x*+1] = 1) ∧ (*isdef*(*b*, 0) Δ *b*[0] = *a*[0])

which is obviously more efficient than the result obtained in Sect. 6.3.2, since less storage is required.

The idea of recursion simplification by function inversion also gives a general technique for recursion simplification by introducing stacks. The basic idea is as follows:

By an *embedding*, the linear recursive definition

funct *f* = (**m** *x*) **n**:
 if B(*x*) **then** H(*x*) **else** *p*(*f*(K(*x*)), E(*x*)) **fi**,

can be transformed into

funct *f* = (**m** *x*) **n**:
 f'(*x*, <>) **where**

 funct *f'* = (**m** *x*, **mstack** *s*) **n**:
 if B(*x*) **then** H(*x*) **else** *p*(*f'*(K(*x*), *s*+*x*), E(*x*)) **fi**.

Now

$K'(x, s) =_{def} (K(x), s+x)$

is (left-)invertible (for $s \ne$ <>) with

$K'^{-1}(x, s) \equiv$ (**last** *s*, **lead** *s*)

and hence the above transformation rule is applicable. In the same way even more complicated, non-linear recursions can be dealt with. For a more detailed treatment, see again [Bauer, Wössner 82] or [Pepper, Partsch 86].

6.5.2 From Non-Linear Recursion to Tail Recursion

One of the techniques to transform arbitrary, non-linear recursions into tail-recursive form is the *tabulation* technique discussed in Sect. 6.3.2. Another one is the *partial inversion* technique discussed above. These techniques, however, are not always applicable, so we now discuss some other techniques (without aiming at completeness or full generality).

For certain cases of tree-like recursions the technique of embedding in a linear combination will help. As an example consider again the Fibonacci function:

funct *fib* = (**nat** *n*) **nat**:
  if $n \leq 1$ **then** 1 **else** $fib(n-1) + fib(n-2)$ **fi**.

Now we define

funct *f* = (**nat** *n*, **nat** *a*, **nat** b) **nat**:
  $a \times fib(n) + b \times fib(n+1)$,

such that, obviously, $fib(N) \equiv f(N, 1, 0)$ for all $N \in \mathbb{N}$.

By *unfolding* the second call of *fib* in *f* we get

$a \times fib(n) + b \times$ **if** $n+1 \leq 1$ **then** 1 **else** $fib(n) + fib(n-1)$ **fi**,

using *distributivity of primitive operations with conditional* yields

if $n+1 \leq 1$ **then** $a \times fib(n) + b \times 1$ **else** $a \times fib(n) + b \times (fib(n) + fib(n-1))$ **fi**,

which, by trivial simplifications, transforms to

if $n=0$ **then** $a+b$ **else** $b \times fib(n-1) + (a+b) \times fib(n)$ **fi**,

such that *folding* finally results in

if $n=0$ **then** $a+b$ **else** $f(n-1, b, a+b)$ **fi**.

Thus *fib*, as defined above, can be redefined into

funct *fib* = (**nat** *n*) **nat**:
  $f(n, 1, 0)$ **where**

  funct *f* = (**nat** *n*, **nat** *a*, **nat** b) **nat**:
    if $n=0$ **then** $a+b$ **else** $f(n-1, b, a+b)$ **fi**.

The example *fusc* of Sect. 6.3.2 can be treated in essentially the same way.

A technique that sometimes helps in connection with nested recursion is the introduction of an additional argument that carries control information. In order to demonstrate the basic idea, consider the following simple example [Manna, McCarthy 69]:

funct *zer* = (**int** *n*) **int**:
  if $n>0$ **then** $n-1$ **else** $zer(zer(n+2))$ **fi**.

By an *embedding* we define

funct *zer'* = (**int** *n*) **int**:
  n_0 **where**
  (**int** n_0, **nat** c_0) = $zer''(n, 1)$ **where**

  funct *zer''* = (**int** *n*, **nat** *c*: $c \geq 1$) (**int**, **nat**):
    if $n>0$ **then** $(n-1, c-1)$
      else (**int** n_1, **nat** c_1) = $zer''(n+2, c+1)$; $zer''(n_1, c_1)$ **fi**,

such that $zer(n) \equiv zer'(n)$ for all $n \in \mathbb{Z}$.

Now it can be proved (by an inductive argument on *n*) that

$((n', c') \equiv zer''(n, c)) \vdash (c'=c-1) \equiv$ **true**

holds; as a consequence, we obtain

$(c_0=0) \equiv$ **true** (in *zer'*).

Whenever one of the recursive calls of *zer''* terminates, there are two possibilities:

- the entire computation is completed, or
- further (suspended) calls of *zer''* have to be dealt with.

Which of these cases applies can be seen from the respective value of *c*. It can be proved that

- if *c*=0 then the entire computation is completed, and
- if *c*>0 then further calls of *zer''* have to be evaluated.

Thus *zer''* can be shown to be equivalent to

```
funct zer'= (int n) int:
   n0 where
   (int n0, nat c0) = zer*(n, 1) where
   funct zer*= (int n, nat c: c≥1) (int, nat):
      if n>0 then aux(n–1, c–1) else zer*(n+2, c+1) fi,
   funct aux = (int n, nat c) (int, nat):
      if c=0 then (n, c) else zer*(n, c) fi.
```

Furthermore, the respective second results in *zer** and *aux* are superfluous, and (the thus modified version of) *aux* can be unfolded in *zer** so that we get as a final result

```
funct zer' = (int n) int:
   zer*(n, 1) where
   funct zer*= (int n, nat c: c≥1) int:
      if n>0 then if c=1 then n–1 else zer*(n–1, c–1) fi else zer*(n+2, c+1) fi.
```

This example had the particular property that the outer recursive call did not depend on the original argument. However, the technique demonstrated with this example is also applicable for nested recursions of the form

$f(f(\mathrm{K}(x), \mathrm{E}_1(x)), \mathrm{E}_2(x))$,

provided K is invertible (which always can be achieved by using stacks, Sect. 6.5.1).

As an example we consider the problem of *traversing a binary tree in preorder*. Let binary trees be defined by

mode bintree = *et* | *cons*(**bintree** *l*, **node** *n*, **bintree** *r*).

Furthermore, we assume the (obvious) specification for "preorder tree traversal"

```
mode nodesequ = SEQU(node);
funct preord = (bintree b) nodesequ:
   if b is et then <> else n(b)+preord(l(b))+preord(r(b)) fi.
```

Since "+" is associative, this specification can be transformed to nested recursion by means of an embedding

```
funct preord = (bintree b) nodesequ:
   preord'(<>, b) where
   funct preord' = (nodesequ s, bintree b) nodesequ:
      if b is et then s else preord'(preord'(s+n(b), l(b)), r(b)) fi.
```

Next, analogously to *zer* above, we introduce an additional argument to keep track of control. Here, differently to *zer*, this additional argument not only has to count the "incarnations" of *preord'*, but also has to keep track of whether the left or right subtree has to be considered next. Therefore multiplication (or integer division) by 2 is used in modifying the additional argument, rather than just incrementing (or decrementing) by 1 as in the example *zer*. Then a reasoning similar to the one above leads to

```
funct preord = (bintree b) nodesequ:
   preord"(<>, b, 1) where
   funct preord" = (nodesequ s, bintree b, nat c) nodesequ:
      if b is et then aux(s, b, c) else preord"(s+n(b), l(b), 2×c) fi,
   funct aux = (nodesequ s, bintree b, nat c) nodesequ:
      if c=1 then s
      elsf odd c then aux(s, f(b), c div 2) else preord"(s, r(f(b)), c+1) fi
```

where *f* ("father") is the inverse of *l* and *r*, resp.

In the above examples, an extra argument had to be introduced. For many other examples this is not necessary, since often it is already available as a function in the other arguments.

As may also be seen from the last example, it is sometimes advisable to transform tree-like recursion into nested recursion for further treatment (compare the technique of 'disentanglement' in [Bauer, Wössner 82]).

6.5.3 From Systems of Recursive Functions to Single Recursive Functions

Up to now we did not distinguish between single recursive functions and systems of (mutually recursive) functions. The reason for not doing so is simple: any system of recursive functions can be made into a single recursive function.

Frequently, a system of tail-recursive functions can be made into a single (tail-recursive) function simply by successive unfoldings. A simple example of this kind is the system (from [Bauer, Wössner 82])

```
even(N) where
funct even = (nat n) bool:
   if n = 0 then true else odd(n – 1) fi,
funct odd = (nat n) bool:
   if n = 0 then false else even(n – 1) fi,
```

that checks whether a given natural number $N \in \mathbb{N}$ is an even number.

Here, by unfolding *odd* in *even* we get immediately

```
even(N) where

funct even = (nat n) bool:
   if n = 0 then true elsf n - 1 = 0 then false else even(n - 2) fi.
```

More advanced examples of the same kind are given by systems describing finite state automata [Bauer, Wössner 82] or the following system that specifies the behaviour of the following Markov algorithm (Ex. 3.4-5)

```
s|  → |s
|m| → ms
m   →
s   → |
```

which determines the maximum of two natural numbers x, y, if applied to the string $|^x m |^y$.

Using an appropriate definition of *lmrepl* for replacing the left-most occurrence of a pattern in a string (Ex. 3.4-6a), this definition can be straightforwardly rewritten in our notation as

```
mode stroke = |;
mode strokes = SEQU(stroke);
mode string = EESEQU((char | stroke), =);

funct max = (strokes x, strokes y) string:
   r1(x + m + y) where

   funct r1 = (string x) string:
      if s| ⊆ x then r1(lmrepl(x, s|, |s)) else r2(x) fi,

   funct r2 = (string x) string:
      if |m| ⊆ x then r1(lmrepl(x, |m|, ms)) else r3(x) fi,

   funct r3 = (string x) string:
      if m ⊆ x then r1(lmrepl(x, m, <>)) else r4(x) fi,

   funct r4 = (string x) string:
      if s ⊆ x then r1(lmrepl(x, s, |)) else x fi.
```

Here, again, by successive unfoldings we get immediately

```
funct max = (strokes x, strokes y) string:
   r1(x + m + y) where

   funct r1 = (string x) string:
      if s| ⊆ x then r1(lmrepl(x, s|, |s))
      elsf |m| ⊆ x then r1(lmrepl(x, |m|, ms))
      elsf m ⊆ x then r1(lmrepl(x, m, <>))
      elsf s ⊆ x then r1(lmrepl(x, s, |)) else x fi.
```

For the general case, assume an arbitrary system $(f_1, \ldots, f_n)$ of recursive functions, each of the form

$\textbf{funct}\ f_i = (\textbf{m}\ x)\ \textbf{n}\textbf{:}\ \textbf{if}\ [\!]_{k=1..mi} B_{i,k}(x)\ \textbf{then}\ E_{i,k}\ \textbf{fi}.$

First, we define a (new) function f

$\textbf{funct}\ f = (\textbf{nat}\ i,\ \textbf{m}\ x)\ \textbf{n}\textbf{:}\ f_i(x).$

By case introduction (on i) we get

$\textbf{funct}\ f = (\textbf{nat}\ i,\ \textbf{m}\ x)\ \textbf{n}\textbf{:}$
$\quad \textbf{if}\ [\!]_{j=1..n}\ i = j\ \textbf{then}\ f_j(x)\ \textbf{fi}.$

Unfolding of the definitions of the f_i leads to

$\textbf{funct}\ f = (\textbf{nat}\ i,\ \textbf{m}\ x)\ \textbf{n}\textbf{:}$
$\quad \textbf{if}\ [\!]_{j=1..n}\ i = j\ \textbf{then}\ \textbf{if}\ [\!]_{k=1..mj} B_{j,k}(x)\ \textbf{then}\ E_{j,k}\ \textbf{fi}\ \textbf{fi},$

which, by the definition of the sequential boolean operator Δ, can be further transformed into

$\textbf{funct}\ f = (\textbf{nat}\ i,\ \textbf{m}\ x)\ \textbf{n}\textbf{:}$
$\quad \textbf{if}\ [\!]_{j=1..n,k=1..mj}\ i = j\ \Delta\ B_{j,k}(x)\ \textbf{then}\ E_{j,k}\ \textbf{fi}.$

Now, the f_i within the $E_{i,k}$ can be folded with the original definition of f (which is correct, since f terminates whenever the f_i terminate), thus leading to

$\textbf{funct}\ f = (\textbf{nat}\ i,\ \textbf{m}\ x)\ \textbf{n}\textbf{:}$
$\quad \textbf{if}\ [\!]_{j=1..n,k=1..mj}\ i = j\ \Delta\ B_{j,k}(x)\ \textbf{then}\ E_{j,k}[f(l, E')\ \textbf{for}\ f_l(E')]\ \textbf{fi}.$

Furthermore, any (initial) call $f_i(X)$ to the original system has to be replaced by $f(i, X)$.

Altogether we have derived the transformation rule

- $f_i(E)\ \textbf{where}$
  $\textbf{funct}\ f_1 = (\textbf{m}\ x)\ \textbf{n}\textbf{:}\ \textbf{if}\ [\!]_{k=1..m1} B_{1,k}(x)\ \textbf{then}\ E_{1,k}\ \textbf{fi},$
  $\vdots$
  $\textbf{funct}\ f_n = (\textbf{m}\ x)\ \textbf{n}\textbf{:}\ \textbf{if}\ [\!]_{k=1..mn} B_{n,k}(x)\ \textbf{then}\ E_{n,k}\ \textbf{fi}$

  ↕ [DET[E]

  $f(i, E)\ \textbf{where}$
  $\textbf{funct}\ f = (\textbf{nat}\ i,\ \textbf{m}\ x)\ \textbf{n}\textbf{:}$
  $\quad \textbf{if}\ [\!]_{j=1..n,k=1..mj}\ i = j\ \Delta\ B_{j,k}(x)\ \textbf{then}\ E_{j,k}[f(l, E')\ \textbf{for}\ f_l(E')]\ \textbf{fi}$

  Syntactic constraints:

  NOTOCCURS[f **in** $f_1, \ldots, f_n$].

Of course, it is assumed that this rule is used within the

> **Strategy**
>
> Given a system of recursive functions
>
> – convert the system into a single function;
> – simplify the resulting single function.

In order to demonstrate the use of the rule and the strategy, we consider again the problem of the greatest common divisor (compare Sect. 6.1.1):

$gcd(A, B)$ **where**

funct gcd = (**nat** a, **nat** b) **nat**:
  if $b = 0$ **then** a
  [] $b \neq 0$ **then** $gcd(b, mod(a, b))$ **fi**,

funct mod = (**nat** a, **nat** b: $b > 0$) **nat**:
  if $a < b$ **then** a
  [] $a \geq b$ **then** $mod(a-b, b)$ **fi**.

The application of the rules yields

$g(1, A, B)$ **where**

funct g = (**nat** i, **nat** a, **nat** b) **nat**:
  if $i = 1 \Delta b = 0$ **then** a
  [] $i = 1 \Delta b \neq 0$ **then** $g(1, b, g(2, a, b))$ **fi**
  [] $i = 2 \Delta a < b$ **then** a
  [] $i = 2 \Delta a \geq b$ **then** $g(2, a-b, b)$ **fi**

which can be further simplified (using the rules from 4.4.5.4) to

$g(1, A, B)$ **where**

funct g = (**nat** i, **nat** a, **nat** b) **nat**:
  if $(i = 1 \Delta b = 0) \vee (i = 2 \Delta a < b)$ **then** a
  [] $i = 1 \Delta b \neq 0$ **then** $g(1, b, g(2, a, b))$
  [] $i = 2 \Delta a \geq b$ **then** $g(2, a-b, b)$ **fi**.

In this particular example we had no truly mutual recursion, as *mod* did not call *gcd*. Of course, the rule is also applicable to truly mutual recursive functions. As an example we consider again the problem of preorder tree traversal from Sect. 6.5.2:

funct *preord* = (**bintree** b) **nodesequ**:
  preord"(<>, b, 1) **where**

  funct *preord*" = (**nodesequ** s, **bintree** b, **nat** c) **nodesequ**:
    if b **is** *et* **then** $aux(s, b, c)$ **else** *preord*"($s+n(b)$, $l(b)$, $2\times c$) **fi**,

  funct *aux* = (**nodesequ** s, **bintree** b, **nat** c) **nodesequ**:
    if c=1 **then** s
    elsf odd c **then** $aux(s, f(b), c$ **div** 2) **else** *preord*"(s, $r(f(b))$, c+1) **fi**.

In order to match the input scheme of the above rule, we first convert the conditionals into guarded expressions

funct *preord* = (**bintree** b) **nodesequ**:
  preord"(<>, b, 1) **where**

  funct *preord*" = (**nodesequ** s, **bintree** b, **nat** c) **nodesequ**:
    if b **is** *et* **then** $aux(s, b, c)$
    [] $\neg$(b **is** *et*) **then** *preord*"($s+n(b)$, $l(b)$, $2\times c$) **fi**,

  funct *aux* = (**nodesequ** s, **bintree** b, **nat** c) **nodesequ**:
    if c=1 **then** s

[] *c* ≠ 1 Δ **odd***c* **then** *aux*(*s*, *f*(*b*), *c***div**2)
[] *c* ≠ 1 Δ **even***c* **then** *preord''*(*s*, *r*(*f*(*b*)), *c*+1) **fi**.

Now the rule above is applicable and yields immediately

funct *preord* = (**bintree** *b*) **nodesequ**:
p(1, <>, *b*, 1) **where**

funct *p* = (**nat** *i*, **nodesequ** *s*, **bintree** *b*, **nat** *c*) **nodesequ**:
if *i* = 1 Δ *b* **is** *et* **then** *p*(2, *s*, *b*, *c*)
[] *i* = 1 Δ ¬(*b* **is** *et*) **then** *p*(1, *s*+*n*(*b*), *l*(*b*), 2×*c*)
[] *i* = 2 Δ *c*=1 **then** *s*
[] *i* = 2 Δ *c* ≠ 1 Δ **odd***c* **then** *p*(2, *s*, *f*(*b*), *c***div**2)
[] *i* = 2 Δ *c* ≠ 1 Δ **even***c* **then** *p*(1, *s*, *r*(*f*(*b*)), *c*+1) **fi**.

6.6 Examples

As in the previous chapters, we consider a few examples in order to demonstrate the combined use of the rules and techniques discussed in the current chapter.

6.6.1 Bottom-up Recognition of Context-Free Grammars

Left-to-right bottom-up recognition of context-free grammars can be formally derived from right-to-left top-down recognition by mainly using the technique of *inverting the flow of computation*. The development starts from the version

funct *rp* = (**cfg** *G*, **termstring** *w*: *isterm*(*w*, *G*)) **bool**:
tdr(*S*(*G*), *w*, <>) **where**

funct *tdr* = (**string** *u*, **termstring** *v*, **termstring** *s*:
S(*G*)→**u*+*s* ∧ *v*+*s* = *w*) **bool**:
(*u* =<> Δ *v* =<> Δ *s* = *w*) ∇
(*u* ≠<> Δ *v* ≠<> Δ **last***u* = **last***v* Δ *tdr*(**lead***u*, **lead***v*, **last***v*+*s*)) ∇
(*u* ≠<> Δ ∃ **string** *z*: *pr*(**last***u*, *z*) ∈ *P*(*G*) Δ *tdr*(**lead***u*+*z*, *v*, *s*)).

This version can be obtained by starting from the embedding

funct *rp* = (**cfg** *G*, **termstring** *w*: *isterm*(*w*, *G*)) **bool**:
tdr(*S*(*G*), *w*, <>) **where**

funct *tdr* = (**string** *u*, **termstring** *v*, **termstring** *s*:
S(*G*)→**u*+*s* ∧ *v*+*s* = *w*) **bool**:
u+*s* →* *v*+*s*

and then using essentially the same steps as in Sect. 5.5.2. The only difference is in step 1.1.3. where now the decomposition (*u* ≠<>) ≡ **true** ⊢ *u* ≡ (**lead***u*+**last***u*) – ultimately leading to right-to-left processing – is used.

The development proceeds as follows:

Main development

Focus: function *rp*
Goal: applicative program for bottom-up recognition
Strategy: inverting the flow of computation
Transformations:

step 1: *∃-elimination by sets* (variant with constant arguments) in function *tdr*

```
tdrs({tr(u, v, s)}) where
mode tset = ESET(triple, =);
mode triple = tr(string u, termstring v, termstring s:
                 S(G)→*u+s ∧ v+s = w);
funct tdrs = (tset M) bool:
  M ≠ ∅ Δ
  ((∃ triple t: t ∈ M Δ u(t) =<> Δ v(t) =<> Δ s(t) = w) ∇
  tdrs({tr(leadu, leadv, lastv+s):
              tr(u, v, s) ∈ M Δ u ≠<> Δ v ≠<> Δ lastu = lastv} ∪
       {tr(leadu+z, v, s): tr(u, v, s) ∈ M Δ
              ∃ string z: pr(lastu, z) ∈ P(G)}));
```

step 2: *unfolding tdr* in *rp*; simplification of *tdrs*

```
funct rp = (cfg G, termstring w: isterm(w, G)) bool:
  tdrs({tr(S(G), w, <>)}) where
  funct tdrs = (tset M) bool:
    M ≠ ∅ Δ
    (tr(<>, <>, w) ∈ M ∇
    tdrs({tr(leadu, leadv, lastv+s):
                tr(u, v, s) ∈ M Δ u ≠<> Δ v ≠<> Δ lastu = lastv} ∪
         {tr(leadu+z, v, s): tr(u, v, s) ∈ M Δ
                ∃ string z: pr(lastu, z) ∈ P(G)}))
```

step 3: *local inversion on sets*

```
funct rp = (cfg G, termstring w: isterm(w, G)) bool:
  bus({tr(<>, <>, w)}) where
  funct bus = (tset M) bool:
    M ≠ ∅ Δ
    (tr(S(G), w, <>) ∈ M ∇
    bus({tr(u+firsts, v+firsts, rests): tr(u, v, s) ∈ M Δ s ≠<>} ∪
        {tr(l+A, v, s): tr(u, v, s) ∈ M Δ
           ∃ nont A, string l, string z: pr(A, z) ∈ P(G) Δ u = l+z}))
```

step 4: apply property
(*tr*(*S*(*G*), *w*, <>) ∈ *M*) ≡ (∃ **triple** *t*: *t* ∈ *M* Δ *u*(*t*) = *S*(*G*) Δ *v*(*t*) = *w* Δ *s*(*t*) =<>);
∃-elimination by sets (applied backwards, see below)

```
funct rp = (cfg G, termstring w: isterm(w, G)) bool:
  bu(<>, <>, w) where
```

```
funct bu = (string u, termstring v, termstring s:
                u→*v ∧ v+s = w) bool:
    (u = S(G) ∧ v = w ∧ s =<>) ∇
    ((s ≠<> Δ bu(u+firsts, v+firsts, rests)) ∨
    (∃ nont A, string l, string z:  pr(A, z) ∈ P(G) ∧ u = l+z  ∧
                                    bu(l+A, v, s)))
```

step 5: simplification (using the assertion)

```
funct rp = (cfg G, termstring w: isterm(w, G)) bool:
   bu(<>, w) where

   funct bu = (string u, termstring s:
                 ∃ termstring v: u→*v ∧ v+s = w) bool:
      (u = S(G) ∧ s =<>) ∇
      ((s ≠<> Δ bu(u+firsts, rests)) ∨
      (∃ string l, nont A: pr(A, y) ∈ P(G) ∧ u = l+y ∧ bu(l+A, s))).
```

In the above derivation, **step 4** was the critical one, since, for being correct (Sect. 5.4), it requires definedness of *bu*. Therefore, for this derivation to be correct, we have to add constraints on the grammar *G*, that guarantee termination of *bu*. A possible (sufficient) condition to ensure termination is the absence of <>-productions and the absence of cycles in the production system:

¬ ∃ **nont** *A*: *A* ∈ *N*(*G*) ∧ *pr*(*A*, <>) ∈ *P*(*G*) and
∀ **nont** *A*: *A* ∈ *N*(*G*) ⇒ ¬(*A*→⁺*A*).

6.6.2 The Algorithm by Cocke, Kasami, and Younger

A context-free grammar G = (N, T, S, P) is said to be in **Chomsky Normal Form** iff every production in P is of one of the forms

- (A, BC), A, B, C ∈ N
- (A, a), A ∈ N, a ∈ T
- (S, <>), provided S does not occur in the right-hand side of any other production.

Cocke, Kasami, and Younger developed, independent of each other, essentially the same algorithm for recognizing context-free grammars in Chomsky Normal Form. This algorithm works in $O(n^3)$ time for arbitrary grammars (even ambiguous ones) where n is the length of the input string to be recognized. We will derive this particular algorithm mainly to demonstrate the tabulation technique.

As in the other examples dealing with context-free recognition (Sects. 5.5.2 and 6.6.1), we will start from an embedding

```
funct rp = (cfg G, termstring w: isterm(w, G) ∧ cnf(G)) bool:
   (w =<> ∧ pr(S(G), <>) ∈ P(G)) ∇ cky(S(G), 1, |w|) where

   funct cky = (nont u, nat i, nat j: 1≤i≤j≤|w|) bool:
      u →* w[i:j],
```

where *cnf* is an auxiliary predicate (with a straightforward formalization) that guarantees that the respective grammar is in Chomsky Normal Form.

The development proceeds as follows:

Main development

Focus: function *cky* (Note: all subsequent steps assume $cnf(G)\ \Delta\ 1 \le i \le j \le |w|$)
Goal: applicative program for *cky*
Strategy: generalized unfold/fold
Transformations:

step 1: apply property $((u \rightarrow^* v)\ \equiv\ (u = v\ \nabla\ (\exists\ \textbf{string}\ z\colon u \rightarrow z \wedge z \rightarrow^* v)))$;
unfolding the definition of $\rightarrow$

$$u = w[i{:}j]\ \ \nabla\ (\exists\ \textbf{string}\ z\colon pr(u, z) \in P(G) \wedge z\ \rightarrow^* w[i{:}j]\ )$$

step 2: simplification
$((u\ \textbf{is nont} \wedge\ w[i{:}j]\ \textbf{is termstring}) \equiv \textbf{true} \vdash\ (u = w[i{:}j]) \equiv \textbf{false})$;
case introduction using the assertion $cnf(G)$ and subsequent simplification

$$pr(u, w[i{:}j]) \in P(G)\ \ \nabla\ \exists\ \textbf{nont}\ x, y\colon pr(u, x{+}y) \in P(G) \wedge x{+}y\ \ \rightarrow^* w[i{:}j]$$

step 3: apply properties
- $(cnf(G) \wedge pr(u, w[i{:}j]) \in P(G)) \equiv \textbf{true} \vdash\ (i = j\ \Delta\ pr(u, w[i]) \in P(G)) \equiv \textbf{true}$
- $(x{+}y\ \ \rightarrow^* w[i{:}j]) \equiv (\exists\ \textbf{nat}\ p\colon i{\le}p{<}j\ \Delta\ (x\ \rightarrow^* w[i{:}p] \wedge y\ \rightarrow^* w[p{+}1{:}j]))$

$$\begin{array}{l}(i = j\ \Delta\ pr(u, w[i]) \in P(G))\ \ \nabla \\ \quad \exists\ \textbf{nont}\ x, y, \textbf{nat}\ p\colon i{\le}p{<}j\ \Delta \\ \quad (pr(u, x{+}y) \in P(G)\ \wedge x\ \ \rightarrow^* w[i{:}p] \wedge y\ \ \rightarrow^* w[p{+}1{:}j])\end{array}$$

step 4: folding

```
funct cky = (nont u, nat i, nat j: 1≤i≤j≤|w|) bool:
    (i = j Δ pr(u, w[i]) ∈ P(G))  ∇
    ∃ nont x, y, nat p: i≤p<j Δ
    (pr(u, x+y) ∈ P(G) ∧  cky(x, i, p) ∧ cky(y, p+1, j))
```

step 5: parameter translation for *cky*

Subdevelopment 1

Focus: function *rp*
Goal: parameter translation (as a preparatory step for tabulation)
Transformations:

step 1.1: embedding

```
funct rp = (cfg G, termstring w: isterm(w, G) ∧ cnf(G)) bool:
    (w =<> ∧ pr(S(G), <>) ∈ P(G)) ∇ cky'(S(G), 1, |w|) where

    funct cky' = (nont u, nat i, nat j: 1≤i≤|w|+1–j ∧ 1≤j≤|w|) bool:
        cky(u, i, j+i–1);
```

New focus: function *cky'*
step 1.2: unfold *cky* in *cky'*

$$\begin{array}{l}(i = j{+}i{-}1\ \Delta\ pr(u, w[i]) \in P(G))\ \ \nabla \\ \exists\ \textbf{nont}\ x, y, \textbf{nat}\ p\colon i{\le}p{<}\ j{+}i{-}1\ \Delta \\ \quad (pr(u, x{+}y) \in P(G) \wedge cky(x, i, p) \wedge cky(y, p{+}1, j{+}i{-}1))\end{array}$$

step 1.3: unfolding the definitions of Δ and ∇; simplifications

```
if j = 1  then pr(u, w[i]) ∈ P(G))
          else ∃ nont x, y, nat p: 1≤p<j ∧ pr(u, x+y) ∈ P(G) Δ
                 (cky(x, i, p+i–1) ∧ cky(y, p+i, j–p+(p+i)–1)) fi
```

step 1.4: folding

```
funct cky' = (nont u, nat i, nat j: 1≤i≤|w|+1–j ∧ 1≤j≤|w|) bool:
   if j = 1  then pr(u, w[i]) ∈ P(G))
             else ∃ nont x, y, nat p: 1≤p<j ∧ pr(u, x+y) ∈ P(G) Δ
                    (cky'(x, i, p) ∧ cky'(y, p+i, j–p)) fi
```

<u>**Main development continued**</u>

step 6: ∈-elimination (applied backwards); abstraction

```
funct rp = (cfg G, termstring w: isterm(w, G) ∧ cnf(G)) bool:
   (w =<> ∧ pr(S(G), <>) ∈ P(G)) ∇ S(G) ∈ cky"(1, |w|) where

   mode ntset = SET(nont, =);

   funct cky" = (nat i, nat j: 1≤i≤|w|+1–j ∧ 1≤j≤|w|) ntset:
      {nont u: cky'(u, i, j) = true}
```

step 7: recursive formulation of *cky"*

<u>**Subdevelopment 2**</u>

Focus: function *cky"*
Goal: recursive formulation independent of *cky'*
Strategy: generalized unfold/fold
Transformations:

step 2.1: unfolding *cky'* in *cky"*;
distributivity of set comprehension and alternative

```
if j = 1 then {nont u: pr(u, w[i]) ∈ P(G)}
         else {nont u: ∃ nont x, y, nat p: 1≤p<j Δ
                 (pr(u, x+y) ∈ P(G) ∧ cky'(x, i, p) ∧ cky'(y, p+i, j–p))} fi
```

step 2.2: ∈-elimination (applied backwards)

```
if j = 1 then {nont u: pr(u, w[i]) ∈ P(G)}
         else {nont u: ∃ nont x, y, nat p: 1≤p<j Δ
                 (pr(u, x+y) ∈ P(G) ∧ x ∈ {nont u: cky'(u, i, p) = true} ∧
                  y ∈ {nont u: cky'(u, p+i, j–p) = true})} fi
```

step 2.3: folding

```
funct cky" = (nat i, nat j: 1≤i≤|w|+1–j ∧ 1≤j≤|w|) ntset:
   if j = 1 then {nont u: pr(u, w[i]) ∈ P(G)}
            else {nont u: ∃ nont x, y, nat p: 1≤p<j Δ
                    (pr(u, x+y) ∈ P(G) ∧ x ∈ cky"(i, p) ∧ y ∈ cky"(p+i, j–p))} fi
```

<u>**Main development continued**</u>

step 8: variant of tabulation (Sect. 6.4.1)

```
funct rp = (cfg G, termstring w: isterm(w, G) ∧ cnf(G)) bool:
  (w =<> ∧ pr(S(G), <>) ∈ P(G)) ∇
  S(G) ∈ tabcky(next'(1, 1), a)[1, |w|] where

   mode ntset = SET(nont, =);
   mode ckymap = PMAP(nat, ntset, =);
   ckymap a = that ckymap a': ∀ nat k, l: ((1,1) ≤ (k,l) ≤ (1,|w|) Δ l=1) ⇒
                    (isdef(a', k, l) Δ a'[k, l] = {nont u: pr(u, w[k]) ∈ P(G))};

   funct tabcky = (nat k, nat l, ckymap a:  (1, 1) ≤ (k, l) ≤ next(1, |w|) Δ
                   ∀ nat m, nat n: (1, 1)≤(m, n)<(k, l) ⇒
                                              a[m, n] = cky"(m, n)) ckymap:
      if (k, l) = next(1, |w|) then a
         else tabcky(next'(next(k, l)),
                     a[k, l] ← {nont u: ∃ nont x, y, nat p: 1≤p<l Δ
                                 (pr(u, x+y) ∈ P(G) ∧ x ∈ cky"(k, p) ∧
                                 y ∈ cky"(p+k, l–p))}) fi,

   funct next' = (nat a, nat b: 1≤a≤|w|+1–b ∧ 1≤b≤|w|) (nat, nat):
      if b = 1 then next'(next(a, b)) else (a, b) fi,

   funct next = (nat a, nat b: 1≤a≤|w|+1–b ∧ 1≤b≤|w|) (nat, nat):
      if a < |w|+1–b then (a+1, b) else (1, b+1) fi
```

step 9: simplifications:

- instantiation of *next'*(1, 1) in *rp*;
- =-substitution in the definition of *a*;
- (1≤*k*≤|*w*|+1–*l* ∧ 1<*l*≤|*w*|) ≡ **true** ⊢ *next'*(*next*(*k*, *l*)) ≡ *next*(*k*, *l*);
- instantiation of *next*(1, |*w*|) and subsequent simplification;
- abstraction;

```
funct rp = (cfg G, termstring w: isterm(w, G) ∧ cnf(G)) bool:
  (w =<> ∧ pr(S(G), <>) ∈ P(G)) ∇ S(G) ∈ tabcky(1, 2, a)[1, |w|] where
  ...
  ckymap a = that ckymap a': ∀ nat k: 1 ≤ k ≤ |w| ⇒
                    isdef(a', k, 1) Δ a'[k, 1] = {nont u:pr(u,w[k]) ∈ P(G)};

  funct tabcky = (nat k, nat l, ckymap a:  (1≤k≤|w|+1–l ∧ 1<l≤|w|+1) Δ
                  ∀ nat m, nat n: (1, 1)≤(m, n)<(k, l) ⇒
                                             a[m, n] = cky"(m, n)) ckymap:
     if l = |w|+1 then a
        else ckymap b = a[k, l] ← {nont u: ∃ nont x, y, nat p: 1≤p<l Δ
                                    (pr(u, x+y) ∈ P(G) ∧ x ∈ cky"(k, p)  ∧
                                    y ∈ cky"(p+k, l–p))};
             tabcky(next(k, l), b) fi
```

step 10: use of assertion in *tabcky*;
unfold definition of *next* and subsequent simplification

```
funct rp = (cfg G, termstring w: isterm(w, G) ∧ cnf(G)) bool:
  (w =<> ∧ pr(S(G), <>) ∈ P(G)) ∇ S(G) ∈ tabcky(1, 2, a)[1, |w|] where
```

mode ntset = SET(**nont**, =);
mode ckymap = PMAP(**nat**, **ntset**, =);
ckymap a = **that ckymap** a': $\forall$ **nat** k: $1 \le k \le |w| \Rightarrow$
$isdef(a', k, 1) \,\Delta\, a'[k, 1] = \{$**nont** u: $pr(u, w[k]) \in P(G)\}$;

funct $tabcky$ = (**nat** k, **nat** l, **ckymap** a: $(1 \le k \le |w|+1-l \wedge 1 < l \le |w|+1) \,\Delta$
$\forall$ **nat** m, **nat** n: $(1, 1) \le (m, n) < (k, l) \Rightarrow$
$a[m, n] = cky''(m, n)$) **ckymap**:
if $l = |w|+1$ **then** a
else ckymap $b = a[k, l] \leftarrow \{$**nont** u: $\exists$ **nont** x, y, **nat** p:
$1 \le p < l \,\Delta\, (pr(u, x+y) \in P(G) \wedge$
$x \in a[k, p] \wedge y \in a[p+k, l-p])\}$;
if $k < |w|+1-l$ **then** $tabcky(k+1, l, b)$ **else** $tabcky(1, l+1, b)$ **fi fi**

6.6.3 Cycles in a Graph

In this section we continue the development of the 'cycle problem' for finite directed graphs. We start from the version that was obtained in Sect. 5.5.4,

funct *hascycle* = (**graph** g) **bool**:
$hc(nodes(g))$ **where**

funct *hc* ;= (**nodeset** c) **bool**:
if $sources(c) = \varnothing$ **then** $c \ne \varnothing$ **else** $hc(c \setminus sources(c))$ **fi**,

funct *sources* = (**nodeset** c) **nodeset**:
$\{$**node** x: $x \in c \wedge preds(x, c) = \varnothing\}$,

funct *preds* = (**node** x, **nodeset** c) **nodeset**:
$\{$**node** y: $y \in c \wedge isarc(g, y, x)\}$.

<u>Main development</u>
Focus: function *hascycle*
Goal: operational improvement avoiding repeated computation of *sources*
Strategy: finite differencing
Transformations:

step 1: embedding (of *hc*)

funct *hascycle* = (**graph** g) **bool**:
$hcs(nodes(g), sources(nodes(g)))$ **where**

funct *hcs*= (**nodeset** c, **nodeset** d: $d = sources(c)$) **bool**:
$hc(c)$

step 2: applicative program for *hcs*

<u>Subdevelopment 1</u>
Focus: body of function *hcs*
Goal: applicative program for *hcs* (independent of *hc*)
Strategy: unfold/fold
Transformations:

step 1.1: unfold *hc*

if $sources(c) = \emptyset$ **then** $c \neq \emptyset$ **else** $hc(c \backslash sources(c))$ **fi**

step 1.2: use assertion of *hcs*

if $d = \emptyset$ **then** $c \neq \emptyset$ **else** $hc(c \backslash d)$ **fi**

step 1.3: fold with assertion

if $d = \emptyset$ **then** $c \neq \emptyset$ **else** $hcs(c \backslash d, sources(c \backslash d))$ **fi**

step 1.4: simplification

Subdevelopment 1.1

Focus: expression $sources(c \backslash d)$ in function *hcs*
Goal: operational simplification under premise $d \neq \emptyset \wedge d = sources(c)$
Transformations:

$sources(c \backslash d)$
≡ [unfold *sources*]
{**node** x: $x \in c \backslash d \wedge preds(x, c \backslash d) = \emptyset$}
≡ [use of premise]
{**node** x: $x \in c \backslash sources(c) \wedge preds(x, c \backslash d) = \emptyset$}
≡ [definition of \ ]
{**node** x: $x \in c \wedge x \notin sources(c) \wedge preds(x, c \backslash d) = \emptyset$}
≡ [unfold *sources* and simplification]
{**node** x: $x \in c \wedge preds(x, c) \neq \emptyset \wedge preds(x, c \backslash d) = \emptyset$}
≡ [$(e \subseteq c) \equiv$ **true** $\vdash$ $(preds(x, c) \equiv preds(x, e) \cup preds(x, c \backslash e))$]
{**node** x: $x \in c \wedge preds(x, c) \neq \emptyset \wedge preds(x, c) = preds(x, d) \cup preds(x, c \backslash d)$
$\wedge\ preds(x, c \backslash d) = \emptyset$}
≡ [=-substitution; simplification]
{**node** x: $x \in c \wedge preds(x, c) \neq \emptyset \wedge preds(x, c) = preds(x, d)$}
≡ [$preds(x, d) \subseteq d$]
{**node** x: $x \in c \wedge preds(x, c) \neq \emptyset \wedge preds(x, c) \subseteq d$}

Main development continued

```
funct hascycle = (graph g) bool:
  hcs(nodes(g), sources(nodes(g))) where

  funct hcs = (nodeset c, nodeset d: d = sources(c)) bool:
    if d = ∅ then c ≠ ∅
       else nodeset e = {node x: x ∈ c ∧preds(x, c) ≠∅ ∧ preds(x, c)⊆ d};
            hcs(c\d, e) fi
```

Focus: function *hascycle*
Goal: operational improvement avoiding repeated computation of *preds*
Strategy: finite differencing
Transformations:

step 3: embedding

```
funct hascycle = (graph g) bool:
  hca(nodes(g), sources(nodes(g)), m) where
```

```
      nodemap m = some nodemap m':
                          ∀ node x: x ∈ nodes(g) ⇨ m'[x] = preds(x, c));

      funct hca = (nodeset c, nodeset d, nodemap m: d = sources(c) ∧
                        (∀ node x: x ∈ c ⇨ m[x] = preds(x, c))) bool:
         hcs(c, d)
```

step 4: derivation of an applicative program for *hca*

<u>Subdevelopment 2</u>

Focus: body of function *hca*
Goal: applicative program for *hca*
Strategy: unfold/fold
Transformations:

step 2.1: unfold *hcs*

```
if d = ∅  then c ≠ ∅
   else nodeset e = {node x: x ∈ c ∧ preds(x, c) ≠ ∅ ∧ preds(x, c)} ⊆ d};
        hcs(c\d, e) fi
```

step 2.2: use of assertion of *hca*

```
if d = ∅  then c ≠ ∅
   else  nodeset e = {node x: x ∈ c ∧ m[x] ≠ ∅ ∧ m[x] ⊆ d};
         hcs(c\d, e) fi
```

step 2.3: fold with assertions

```
if d = ∅  then c ≠ ∅
         else nodeset e = {node x: x ∈ c ∧ m[x] ≠ ∅ ∧ m[x] ⊆ d};
              nodemap n = some nodemap n': ∀ node x:
                    (x ∈ c ⇨ n'[x] = m[x]\d) ∧ (x ∉ c ⇨ n'[x] = m[x]);
              hca(c\d, e, n) fi
```

<u>Main development continued</u>

```
funct hascycle = (graph g) bool:
   hca(nodes(g), sources(nodes(g)), m) where

   nodemap m = that nodemap m':
                 ∀ node x: x ∈ nodes(g) ⇨ (m'[x] = preds(x, c));

   funct hca = (nodeset c, nodeset d, nodemap m: d = sources(c, g) ∧
                  (∀ node x: x ∈ c ⇨ m[x] = preds(x, c))) bool:
      if d = ∅ then c ≠ ∅
              else nodeset e = {node x: x ∈ c ∧ m[x] ≠ ∅ ∧ m[x] ⊆ d};
                   nodemap n = some nodemap n': ∀ node x:
                        (x ∈ c ⇨ n'[x] = m[x]\d) ∧ (x ∉ c ⇨ n'[x] = m[x]);
                   hca(c\d, e, n) fi,

   funct sources = (nodeset c) nodeset:
      {node x: x ∈ c ∧ preds(x, c) = ∅},
```

funct *preds* = (**node** *x*, **nodeset** *c*) **nodeset**:
  {**node** *y*: $y \in c \wedge isarc(g, y, x)$}

Of course, rather than using the finite differencing idea in the form of the respective strategy, we also could have used the rules given in Sect. 6.4.4. This alternative development is left as an exercise for the interested reader.

6.6.4 Hamming's Problem

We start from the specification obtained in Sect. 5.5.5:

funct *hamming* = (**nat** *N*) **natsequ**:
  if $N = 0$ **then** <> **else** *ham*(<1>, $N-1$) **fi** **where**

  funct *ham* = (**natsequ** *t*, **nat** *n*: *isham*(*t*)) **natsequ**:
    if $n = 0$ **then** *t* **else** *ham*(*t*+*nextham*(**last***t*), $n-1$) **fi**,

  funct *isham* = (**natsequ** *t*) **bool**:
    <1> $\preccurlyeq t \preccurlyeq$ *sort*(*settosequ*{**nat** *x*: $H(x)$}),

  funct *nextham* = (**nat** *l*) **nat**:
    that nat *m*: $l < m \wedge H(m) \wedge \forall$ **nat** *z*: $l < z < m \Rightarrow \neg H(z)$.

In Sect. 5.5.5 we gave an operational specification for *nextham* that used the last element of *t* as a starting point to compute, by a linear search, the next element to be added to the output sequence. In particular, we did not take into account that any member in the output sequence (except for the very first) can also be uniquely characterized as a multiple of 2, 3, or 5 of some element already in the output sequence constructed so far:

($|t|>1 \wedge isham(t)) \equiv$ **true** $\vdash$
($\exists$ **nat** *i2*, *i3*, *i5*: ($1 \le i2, i3, i5 < |t|$) Δ **last***t* = *nexth*(*t*, *i2*, *i3*, *i5*)) $\equiv$ **true**

where

funct *nexth*= (**natsequ** *t*, **nat** *i2*, **nat** *i3*, **nat** *i5*:
      ($1 \le i2, i3, i5 \le |t|$) $\wedge$ *isham*(*t*)) **nat**:
  min{$2 \cdot t[i2]$, $3 \cdot t[i3]$, $5 \cdot t[i5]$};

Based on this observation, we use the finite differencing technique to derive a more efficient operational specification for *nextham*.

<u>Main development</u>
Focus: function *hamming*
Goal: operational improvement
Strategy: finite differencing
Transformations:

step 1: embedding (of *ham*)

funct *hamming* = (**nat** *N*) **natsequ**:
  if $N = 0$ **then** <> **elsf** $N = 1$ **then** <1> **else** *ham'*(<1, 2>, $N-2$, 1, 1, 1) **fi**

where

funct *ham'* = (**natsequ** *t*, **nat** *n*, **nat** *i2*, **nat** *i3*, **nat** *i5*: $((1 \le i2, i3, i5 < |t|) \wedge$
isham(*t*)) Δ **last***t* = *nexth*(*t*, *i2*, *i3*, *i5*)) **natsequ**:
ham(*t*, *n*)

step 2: unfolding *ham* in *ham'*

if $n = 0$ **then** *t* **else** *ham*(*t*+*nextham*(**last***t*), *n*–1) **fi**

step 3: abstraction

if $n = 0$ **then** *t*
else (**nat** *m*, **nat** *i2'*, **nat** *i3'*, **nat** *i5'*) = *nextargs*(*t*, *i2*, *i3*, *i5*);
ham(*t*+*m*, *n*–1) **fi where**

funct *nextargs* = (**natsequ** *t*, **nat** *i2*, **nat** *i3*, **nat** *i5*:
$((1 \le i2, i3, i5 < |t|) \wedge$ *isham*(*t*)) Δ
last*t* = *nexth*(*t*, *i2*, *i3*, *i5*)) (**nat**, **nat**, **nat**, **nat**):
that (**nat** *m*, **nat** *i2'*, **nat** *i3'*, **nat** *i5'*): *m* = *nextham*(**last***t*) $\wedge$
$(1 \le i2', i3', i5' < |t+m|) \wedge$ *isham*(*t*+*m*) Δ *m* = *nexth*(*t*+*m*, *i2'*, *i3'*, *i5'*)

step 4: folding (with assertion)

funct *ham'* = (**natsequ** *t*, **nat** *n*, **nat** *i2*, **nat** *i3*, **nat** *i5*:
$((1 \le i2, i3, i5 < |t|) \wedge$ *isham*(*t*)) Δ
last*t* = *nexth*(*t*, *i2*, *i3*, *i5*)) **natsequ**:
if $n = 0$ **then** *t*
else (**nat** *m*, **nat** *i2'*, **nat** *i3'*, **nat** *i5'*) = *nextargs*(*t*, *i2*, *i3*, *i5*);
ham'(*t*+*m*, *n*–1, *i2'*, *i3'*, *i5'*) **fi**

It remains to derive an operational specification for the auxiliary function *nextargs*. We have

isham(*t*) ≡ **true** ⊢ (∀ (**nat** *i*, *j*: $1 \le i < j \le |t|$): $t[i] < t[j]$) ≡ **true**,
m ≡ *nextham*(**last***t*) ⊢ (**last***t* < *m* ∧ ∀ **nat** *z*: **last***t* < *z* < *m* ⇒ ¬*H*(*z*)) ≡ **true**.

Thus, for (*i2'*, *i3'*, *i5'*) satisfying the specification of *nextargs*,

$((i2, i3, i5) < (i2', i3', i5') \le (i2+1, i3+1, i5+1)) \equiv$ **true**

holds. In turn, under the assertion of *nextargs*, we can prove that

last*t* ≡ **min**$\{2 \cdot t[i2], 3 \cdot t[i3], 5 \cdot t[i5]\}$ ⊢
nextham(**last***t*) ≡ **min**$\{2 \cdot t[i2'], 3 \cdot t[i3'], 5 \cdot t[i5']\}$

holds where

(**nat** *i2'*, **nat** *i3'*, **nat** *i5'*) = *next*(*t*, *i2*, *i3*, *i5*) **where**

funct *next* = (**natsequ** *t*, **nat** *i2*, **nat** *i3*, **nat** *i5*: $((1 \le i2, i3, i5 < |t|) \wedge$ *isham*(*t*)) Δ
last*t* = *nexth*(*t*, *i2*, *i3*, *i5*)) (**nat**, **nat**, **nat**):
(**if last***t* = $2 \cdot t[i2]$ **then** *i2*+1 **else** *i2* **fi**,
if last*t* = $3 \cdot t[i3]$ **then** *i3*+1 **else** *i3* **fi**,
if last*t* = $5 \cdot t[i5]$ **then** *i5*+1 **else** *i5* **fi**).

Furthermore, obviously,

$(1 \leq nexth(t, i2, i3, i5) \leq |t| < |t{+}nextham(\mathbf{last}\,t)|) \equiv \mathbf{true}$ and
$(isham(t) \wedge m = nextham(\mathbf{last}\,t)) \equiv \mathbf{true} \;\vdash\; isham(t{+}nextham(t)) \equiv \mathbf{true}$

hold, too. Consequently, it follows that

$(nexth(t, next(t, i2, i3, i5)), next(t, i2, i3, i5))$

satisfies the specification of *nextargs*.
Obviously, *nexth* can be further developed into

```
funct nexth = (natsequ t, nat i2, nat i3, nat i5:
                  (1 ≤ i2, i3, i5 ≤ |t|) ∧ isham(t)) nat:
   begin (nat a2, nat a3, nat a5) = (2·t[i2], 3·t[i3], 5·t[i5]);
   if a2 ≤ a3 ∧ a2 ≤ a5 then a2
   [] a3 ≤ a2 ∧ a3 ≤ a5 then a3
   [] a5 ≤ a3 ∧ a5 ≤ a2 then a5 fi  end.
```

Altogether, after eliminating the auxiliary function *nextargs* by unfolding, we have derived the operational specification

```
funct hamming = (nat N) natsequ:
   if N = 0 then <> elsf N = 1 then <1> else ham'(<1, 2>, N–2, 1, 1, 1) fi
   where

   funct ham' = (natsequ t, nat n, nat i2, nat i3, nat i5: ((1 ≤ i2, i3, i5 < |t|) ∧
                  isham(t)) Δ last t = nexth(t, i2, i3, i5)) natsequ:
      if n = 0 then t
         else ham'(t+nexth(t, next(t, i2, i3, i5)), n–1, next(t, i2, i3, i5)) fi,

   funct isham = (natsequ t) bool:
         <1> ≼ t ≼ sort(settosequ{nat x: H(x)}),

   funct nexth = (natsequ t, nat i2, nat i3, nat i5:
                  (1 ≤ i2, i3, i5 ≤ |t|) ∧ isham(t)) nat:
      begin (nat a2, nat a3, nat a5) = (2·t[i2], 3·t[i3], 5·t[i5]);
      if a2 ≤ a3 ∧ a2 ≤ a5 then a2
      [] a3 ≤ a2 ∧ a3 ≤ a5 then a3
      [] a5 ≤ a3 ∧ a5 ≤ a2 then a5 fi  end,

   funct next = (natsequ t, nat i2, nat i3, nat i5:  ((1 ≤ i2, i3, i5 < |t|) ∧
                  isham(t)) Δ last t = nexth(t, i2, i3, i5)) (nat, nat, nat):
      (if last t = 2·t[i2] then i2+1 else i2 fi,
       if last t = 3·t[i3] then i3+1 else i3 fi,
       if last t = 5·t[i5] then i5+1 else i5 fi).
```

6.7 Exercises

Exercise 6.1-1

The functions

```
funct pol = (realsequ a, real x: a ≠<>) real:
   if |a| = 1 then firsta else firsta + x × pol(resta, x) fi,
funct der = (realsequ a, real x: a ≠<>) real:
   if |a| = 1 then 0 else pol(resta, x) + x × der(resta, x) fi;
```

allow the computation of the value of a given polynomial $p(X) = \Sigma_{i=1..|a|} a_i X^{i-1}$ and the value of its (first) derivative for a given argument. Apply the technique of *function combination* to achieve an improvement in efficiency.

Exercise 6.1-2

Given the specification

```
funct TP = (nat n: n ≥ 1) (nat, nat):
   (T(n), P(n)) where
   funct T = (nat n: n ≥ 1) nat:
      if n=1 then 1 else n + T(n–1) fi,
   funct P = (nat n: n ≥ 1) nat:
      if n=1 then 1 else T(n) + P(n–1) fi,
```

derive, by transformations, a definition of *TP* which is independent of *T* and *P*.

Exercise 6.1-3

Given the formal specification (for enumerating pairs of natural numbers)

```
funct ik = (nat n) (nat, nat):
   (i(n), k(n)) where
funct i = (nat n) nat:
   if n = 0 then 0
             else if i(n–1) = k(n–1) then k(n–1) + 1
                  [] i(n–1) ≠ k(n–1) then k(n–1) fi fi,
funct k = (nat n) nat:
   if n = 0 then 0
             else if i(n–1) = k(n–1) then 0
                  [] i(n–1) > k(n–1) then i(n–1)
                  [] i(n–1) < k(n–1) then i(n–1) + 1 fi fi,
```

derive a more efficient solution for *ik*.

Exercise 6.1-4

The problem

whether a character x occurs in a given string s

can be solved by either of the (equivalent) specifications

```
funct occ1 = (char x, string s) bool:
   if s =<> then false
   [] s ≠<> then x = firsts ∨ occ1(x, rests) fi;
```

funct $occ2$ = (**char** x, **string** s) **bool**:
  if s =<> **then false**
  [] s ≠<> **then** x = **last**s ∨ $occ2(x$, **lead**$s)$ **fi**;

funct $occ3$ = (**char** x, **string** s) **bool**:
  if s =<> **then false**
  [] s ≠<> **then** $x=y \lor occ3(x, s_1) \lor occ3(x, s_2)$ **where**
  (**string** s_1, **char** y, **string** s_2) =
    some (**string** s_1', **char** y', **string** s_2'): $s = s_1'+y'+s_2'$ **fi**.

Transform these specifications into a single one.

Exercise 6.3-1

Improve the algorithm (for the 'Stirling numbers')

funct s = (**nat** n, **nat** m: $1 \le m \le n$) **nat**:
  if $n=m \lor m=1$ **then** 1 **else** $s(n-1, m-1) + n \times s(n-1, m)$ **fi**

by applying the *tabulation* technique.

Exercise 6.3-2

Apply the *tabulation* technique to the specification (Sect. 6.3.2)

$f'(Y, Y-X)$ **where**
funct f' = (**nat** x, **nat** y: $0 \le y \le x$) **m**:
  if $y = 0$ **then** $T(x, x)$ **else** $r(f'(x, y-1), f'(x-1, y-1), S(x-y, x))$ **fi**.

Exercise 6.3-3

Given the formal specification (for 'Hermite polynomials')

funct H = (**nat** n, **real** x) **real**:
  if $n = 0$ **then** 1
  [] $n = 1$ **then** $2 \times x$
  [] $n > 1$ **then** $2 \times x \times H(n-1, x) - 2 \times n \times H(n-2, x)$ **fi**,

apply the technique of *tabulation* in order to improve efficiency.

Exercise 6.3-4

Given the formal specification (a variant of the 'trinomial coefficients')

funct T = (**nat** i, **nat** j: $j \le 2i$) **nat**:
  if $j = 0 \lor j = 2i$ **then** 0
  elsf $j = 1 \lor j = 2i-1$ **then** 1
  else $T(i-1, j-2) + T(i-1, j-1) + T(i-1, j)$ **fi**,

apply the *tabulation* technique in order to improve efficiency.

Exercise 6.3-5

Let an $n \times n$ matrix be covered by a word of length $2n-1$ in such a way that the successor of each letter (in the word) appears in the respective next row and column entry of the matrix. As an example consider for n=4

P R O B
R O B L
O B L E
B L E M.

The number of paths along which the given word can be found in the matrix is computed by

funct *words* = (**nat** *n*) **nat**:
  w(*n*, *n*) **where**
  funct *w* = (**nat** *i*, **nat** *k*: $1 \le i, k \le n$) **nat**:
    if *i*=1 **then** 1 **elsf** *i*>*k* **then** *w*(*k*, *i*) **else** *w*(*i*–1, *k*) + *w*(*i*, *k*–1) **fi**.

Improve computational efficiency by applying the *tabulation* technique.

Exercise 6.3-6

Improve the algorithm

funct *lhd* = (**nat** *i*, **nat** *j*: $1 \le j \le i$) (**nat**, **nat**):
  if $i=j \vee j=1$ **then** (1, *i*) **else** *lhd*(*i*–1, *j*–1) ® *lhd*(*i*, *j*–1) **fi** **where**
  (a, b) ® (c, d) $=_{def}$ $(a \times d - b \times c, b \times d)$

by applying the *tabulation* technique.

Exercise 6.4-1

Transform the descriptive specification (Sect. 6.4.2)

funct *genmap* = **mmap**:
  that mmap *m'*: ∀ **m** *x*: *isdef*(*m'*, *x*) Δ *m'*[*x*] = *f*(*x*),

where **m** is known to be finite, into an operational one.

Exercise 6.4-2

Given the formal specification (Sect. 6.4.2)

mode char = «some finite character set»;
mode string = EESEQU(**char**, =);
funct *maxocc* = (**string** *s*: *s* ≠<>) **char**:
  some char *c*: *c* ∈ *s* Δ ∀ (**char** *c'*: *c'* ∈ *s*): *noccs*(*c*, *s*) ≥ *noccs*(*c'*, *s*)
  where
  funct *noccs* = (**char** *c*, **string** *s*) **nat**:
    if *s* =<> **then** 0
    elsf first*s* = *c* **then** 1 + *noccs*(*c*, **rest***s*) **else** *noccs*(*c*, **rest***s*) **fi**,

derive, by transformations, an operational specification for *maxocc*.

Exercise 6.4-3

For the *finite differencing* rules (Sect. 6.4.4) prove

a) correctness (through application of elementary transformation);
b) DEF[*f*] ⇔ DEF[*f'*].

Exercise 6.5-1

Given the formal specification (Ex. 5.2-1)

funct *average* = (**natsequ** *s*: *s* ≠<>) **nat**:
  u **div** *v* **where**
  funct *av* = (**natsequ** *s*) (**nat**, **nat**):
    if *s* =<> **then** (0, 0)
      else (**first***s* + *u*, 1 + *v*) **where** (**nat** *u*, **nat** *v*) = *av*(**rest***s*) **fi**;
  (**nat** *u*, **nat** *v*) = *av*(*s*),

derive, by transformations, a tail recursive definition of *average*.

Exercise 6.5-2

Given the formal specification (Ex. 6.1-2)

funct *ik* = (**nat** *n*) (**nat**, **nat**):
  if $n = 0$ **then** (0, 0)
        else(**nat** *a*, **nat** *b*) = *ik*(n–1);
          if $a = b$ **then** (b + 1, 0)
          [] $a > b$ **then** (b, a)
          [] $a < b$ **then** (b, a+1) **fi fi**,

derive, by transformations, a tail recursive definition of *ik*.

Exercise 6.5-3

Given the formal specification (Ex. 6.1-1)

funct *derpol* = (**realsequ** *a*, **real** *x*: $a \neq$<>) (**real**, **real**):
  if $|a| = 1$ **then** (0, **first**a)
        else (**real** *d*, **real** *p*) = *derpol*(**rest**a, x); (p+$x \times d$, **first**a+$x \times p$) **fi**,

derive, by transformations, a tail recursive definition of *derpol*.

Exercise 6.5-4

The system of functions [Bauer, Wössner 82]

funct *divisible* = (**bitsequ** *y*) **bool**:
  rest0(y) **where**
  funct *rest0* = (**bitsequ** *x*) **bool**:
    if x =<> **then true**
    [] $x \neq$<> **then if last**x = 0 **then** *rest0*(**lead**x) **else** *rest1*(**lead**x) **fi fi**,
  funct *rest1* = (**bitsequ** *x*) **bool**:
    if x =<> **then false**
    [] $x \neq$<> **then if last**x = 0 **then** *rest2*(**lead**x) **else** *rest0*(**lead**x) **fi fi**,
  funct *rest2* = (**bitsequ** *x*) **bool**:
    if x =<> **then false**
    [] $x \neq$<> **then if last**x = 0 **then** *rest1*(**lead**x) **else** *rest2*(**lead**x) **fi fi**,

corresponds to a finite automaton that checks whether a natural number (in binary representation) is divisible by 3. Transform this system of functions into a single function.

7. Transformation of Procedural Programs

In the previous chapters, it has been mentioned several times that the major part of any program development by transformations can be done at the level of applicative formulations. Nevertheless, when aiming at the efficient running of programs on conventional von Neumann machines, a few more transformations have to be available for introducing variables (the key concept of the von Neumann machine) together with related constructs such as assignment, iteration, and loops. In contrast to the transformations dealt with in earlier sections, these rules are of a much more mechanical nature. One can thus imagine that they might be performed automatically, for example by a suitable optimizing compiler. Since the whole subject, sometimes called 'optimizing transformations', is extensively treated in standard textbooks on compiler construction and also in [Bauer, Wössner 82] or [Illsley 88], our treatment here will be a little sketchy and by no means comprehensive. Still, it suffices to give at least a rough impression of what these rules are about.

In this chapter we will concentrate on aspects of control structures. An analogous treatment of data structures requires a more elaborate discussion of the fundamentals of data structure development and is deferred to the next chapter.

7.1 From Tail Recursion to Iteration

In the previous chapter, tail recursion was claimed to be the ultimate goal of modifying applicative programs, since tail recursion allows a simple transition to imperative programs. This transition has to introduce new concepts for the imperative level of formulation. Such constructs are variables and statements, such as assignments, conditional statements, and loops.

In CIP-L, statements may only occur within a segment. A **segment** is an expression consisting of a sequence of declarations and statements followed by an expression. In order to maintain the property of referential transparency [Quine 60], segments with "side-effects" are not allowed, i.e., segments in which the value of a non-local variable is changed. The value of a segment is the value of its final expression after execution of its statements. The semantics of variables and statements is specified by axiomatic transformation rules that allow the reduction of every segment to an expression of the applicative language introduced in Chap. 3.

Variables can be viewed as reusable identifiers and therefore their meaning is defined in terms of object declarations by the transformation rules [Bauer et al. 85]:

- **var m** $x := \mathrm{E}_1; \mathrm{E}_2$

  $\updownarrow$

  m $x = \mathrm{E}_1; \mathrm{E}_2$,

and

- $x := \mathrm{E}_1; \mathrm{E}_2$

  $\updownarrow$

  m $y = \mathrm{E}_1; \mathrm{E}_2[y$ **for** $x]$

  Syntactic constraints:

  KIND[x] = **var m**,

  NOTOCCURS[y **in** $\mathrm{E}_1, \mathrm{E}_2$],

  $x \notin$ ABUSED[E_2] .

Here, ABUSED[E] denotes the set of all free identifiers occurring within abstractions in the expression E. The condition $x \notin$ ABUSED[E_2] guarantees that the bottom-up direction of the rule does not produce an abstraction with non-local variable identifiers. Note that, according to our conventions, **m** x stands for an arbitrary tuple. Hence, the rules above deal with single as well as with multiple declarations and assignments, i.e. assignments of a tuple of values to a tuple of variables. Note also that, according to the above definitions, the variables introduced in the left-hand side of a declaration cannot occur on the right-hand side.

As for variables and assignments, axiomatic rules can be given for other kinds of statements, such as

- **if** B **then** PP_1 **else** PP_2 **fi** (*conditional statement*),
- **begin** PP **end** (*block*),
- **begin** PP_1 [] ... [] PP_n **end** (*finite choice*),
- **if** B_1 **then** PP_1 [] ... [] B_n **then** PP_n **else** PP_{n+1} **fi** (*guarded statement*),
- **while** B **do** PP **od** (**while** *loop*),
- **goto** L (*jump*),
- L: S (*labeled statement*),
- **proc** p = (**var m** x, **n** y): **begin** PP **end** (*procedure*)

(where PP stands for a sequence of declarations and statements, B denotes a boolean expression, L is a label identifier, and S denotes a statement). The axiomatic rules mentioned above allow the reduction of a segment containing either of these statements to a corresponding (equivalent) expression of the applicative language.

However, we are only interested in imperative programs as results of transformational developments starting from descriptive or applicative specifications. Therefore, we will only deal with those transformations needed to achieve a final transition from an applicative program to an imperative one. For a complete semantic definition of all imperative constructs (by means of axiomatic transformation rules), the reader is referred to [Bauer et al. 85].

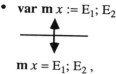

7.1.1 while Loops

Any single tail-recursive function *f* (Sect. 6.5) can be transformed into the form

(*) **funct** *f* = (**m** *x*) **r**:
  if B(*x*) **then** H(*x*) **else** *f*(K(*x*)) **fi**

by means of the elementary transformation rules given in Chap. 4. In turn, any tail-recursive function *f* of the form (*) can be converted into iteration using **while** loops according to the rule

- *Tail recursion to iteration*

  funct *f* = (**m** *x*) **r**:
    if B(*x*) **then** H(*x*) **else** *f*(K(*x*)) **fi**

  $\Updownarrow$

  funct *f* = (**m** *x*) **r**:
    begin var m *vx* := *x*; **while** ¬B(*vx*) **do** *vx* := K(*vx*) **od**; H(*vx*) **end**

  Syntactic constraints:
    NOTOCCURS[*vx* **in** B, H, K].

Note that, if **m** denotes a proper tuple, this rule introduces multiple declarations and assignments. The transformation of these into single declarations and assignments is dealt with in Sect. 7.2.1.

Rather than first transforming a given tail-recursive function *f* into the form (*) and then applying the rule *tail recursion to iteration*, for practical purposes it is convenient to have compact rules that combine these two steps into one.

Assume, for instance, the definition

funct *f* = (**m** *x*) **r**:
  if B(*x*) **then** H(*x*) **else if** C(*x*) **then** $f(K_1(x))$ **else** $f(K_2(x))$ **fi fi**.

Using the rule *distributivity of function call over conditional*, the body of *f* can be transformed into

if B(*x*) **then** H(*x*) **else** *f*(**if** C(*x*) **then** $K_1(x)$ **else** $K_2(x)$ **fi**) **fi**.

Now, we can apply the rule *tail recursion to iteration* and obtain

begin var m *vx* := *x*;
  while ¬B(*vx*) **do** *vx* := **if** C(*vx*) **then** $K_1(vx)$ **else** $K_2(vx)$ **fi od**;
  H(*vx*) **end**.

Finally, using the rule *distributivity of assignment over conditional* (Sect. 7.2.3), we get

begin var m *vx* := *x*;
  while ¬B(*vx*) **do if** C(*vx*) **then** *vx* := $K_1(vx)$ **else** *vx* := $K_2(vx)$ **fi od**;
  H(*vx*) **end**.

Altogether, we have derived the following variant of the rule *tail recursion to iteration*:

- ```
  funct f = (m x) r:
     if B(x) then H(x) else if C(x) then f(K1(x)) else f(K2(x)) fi fi
  ```

  $\Updownarrow$

  ```
  funct f = (m x) r:
     begin var m vx := x;
        while ¬B(vx) do if C(vx) then vx := K1(vx)
                                 else vx := K2(vx) fi od;
        H(vx) end
  ```

  <u>**Syntactic constraints:**</u>

  NOTOCCURS[vx **in** B, C, H, K_1, K_2].

Similarly, we can derive other variants e.g.

- ```
  funct f = (m x) r:
     if B(x) then H(x) else if []i=1..n Ci(x) then f(Ki(x)) fi fi
  ```

  $\Updownarrow$

  ```
  funct f = (m x) r:
     begin var m vx := x;
        while ¬B(vx) do if []i=1..n Ci(vx) then vx := Ki(vx)) fi od; H(vx) end
  ```

  <u>**Syntactic constraints:**</u>

  NOTOCCURS[vx **in** B, H, C_i, K_i] ($1 \le i \le n$)

or

- ```
  funct f = (m x) r:
     if B(x) then H(x)
     elsf C(x) then G(x) else f(K(x)) fi
  ```

  $\Updownarrow$

  ```
  funct f = (m x) r:
     begin var m vx := x;
        while ¬(B(vx) Δ C(vx) do vx := K(vx) od;
        if B(vx) then H(vx) else G(vx) fi end
  ```

  <u>**Syntactic constraints:**</u>

  NOTOCCURS[vx **in** B, C, H, G, K].

These transformation rules can immediately be applied to almost all applicative programs that resulted from optimizations as discussed in the previous chapter. For example, application to

```
funct fact = (nat m, nat n) nat:
   if n = 0 then m else fact(m × n, n–1) fi
```

from Sect. 6.5.1 results in

```
funct fact = (nat m, nat n) nat:
   begin (var nat vm, var nat vn) := (m, n);
      while vn ≠ 0 do (vm, vn) := (vm × vn, vn–1) od; vm end.
```
```

Likewise, application to

```
funct gcd = (nat a, nat b) nat:
   if b = 0  then a
            else if a < b then gcd(b, a)
                  [] a ≥ b then gcd(b, a–b) fi fi
```

(Sect. 6.1.1) and

```
funct h2 = (nat x, nat y, nat z, nat n: x² ≤ n ∧ y = (x+1)² ∧ z = 2x+3) nat:
   if y > n then x else h2(x+1, y+z, z+2, n) fi
```

(Sect. 6.4.4) yields

```
funct gcd = (nat a, nat b) nat:
   begin (var nat va, var nat vb) := (a, b);
      while vb ≠ 0 do if va < vb then (va, vb) := (vb, va)
                       [] va ≥ vb then (va, vb) := (vb, va–vb) fi od; va end
```

and

```
funct h2 = (nat x, nat y, nat z, nat n: x² ≤ n ∧ y = (x+1)² ∧ z = 2x+3) nat:
   begin (var nat vx, var nat vy, var nat vz, var nat vn) := (x, y, z, n);
      while vy ≤ vn do (vx, vy, vz, vn) := (vx+1, vy+vz, vz+2, vn) od;
      vx end.
```

In order to apply one of the above rules to *zer** (Sect. 6.5.2) in

```
funct zer' = (int n) int:
   zer*(n, 1) where

   funct zer*= (int n, nat c: c≥1) int:
      if n>0 then if c=1 then n–1 else zer*(n–1, c–1) fi else zer*(n+2, c+1) fi,
```

we first transform *zer** into

```
funct zer*= (int n, nat c: c≥1) int:
   if n>0 Δ c=1 then n–1 else if n>0 then zer*(n–1, c–1) else zer*(n+2, c+1) fi fi,
```

and then get (by applying the appropriate variant)

```
funct zer' = (int n) int:
   zer*(n, 1) where

   funct zer*= (int n, nat c: c≥1) int:
      begin (var int vn, var nat vc) := (n, c);
         while vn=0 ∇ vc>1 do
            if vn>0 then (vn, vc) := (vn–1, vc–1)
                    else (vn, vc) := (vn+2, vc+1) fi od;
         vn–1 end.
```

Now, by a simple unfolding, the embedding can be undone, yielding

```
funct zer' = (int n) int:
   begin (var int vn, var nat vc) := (n, 1);
      while vn=0 ∇ vc>1 do
```

```
        if vn>0 then (vn, vc) := (vn-1, vc-1) else (vn, vc) := (vn+2, vc+1) fi od;
    vn-1 end.
```

Of course, this, too, gives rise to further variants of the above general rules, such as

- *Embedded tail recursion to iteration*

```
funct f = (m x) r:
   f'(x, E) where
   funct f' = (m x, n y) r:
      if B(x, y) then H(x, y) else f'(K(x, y)) fi

funct f = (m x) r:
   begin (var m vx, var n vy) := (x, E);
      while ¬B(vx, vy) do (vx, vy) := K(vx, vy) od; H(vx, vy) end
```

Syntactic constraints:
NOTOCCUR[vx, vy **in** f'].

Application of this variant to

```
funct sqr = (nat n) nat:
   h2(0, 1, 3, n) where

   funct h2 = (nat x, nat y, nat z, nat n: x^2 ≤ n ∧ y = (x+1)^2 ∧ z = 2x+3) nat:
      if y > n then x else h2(x+1, y+z, z+2, n) fi,
```

then yields

```
funct sqr = (nat n) nat:
   begin (var nat vx, var nat vy, var nat vz, var nat vn) := (0, 1, 3, n);
      while vy ≤vn do (vx, vy, vz, vn) := (vx+1, vy+vz, vz+2, vn) od; vx end.
```

Likewise, we obtain for

```
funct meanvar = (natsequ s: s ≠<>) (real, real):
   (nat su, nat si, nat ssq) = h(s, 0, 0, 0);
   (su/si, (ssq – su^2)/si^2) where

   funct h = (natsequ s, nat a, nat b, nat c) (nat, nat, nat):
      if s =<> then (a, b, c) else h(rest s, a+first s, b+1, c+(first s)^2) fi
```

from Sect. 6.5.1

```
funct meanvar = (natsequ s: s ≠<>) (real, real):
   begin (var natsequ vs, var nat su, var nat si, var nat ssq) := (s, 0, 0, 0);
      while vs ≠<>
         do (vs, su, si, ssq) := (rest vs, su+first vs, si+1, ssq+(first vs)^2) od;
      (su/si, (ssq – su^2)/si^2) end,
```

which is essentially the imperative program given in [Goldberg 86].

7.1.2 Jumps and Labels

The rule *while loop and jumps* from Sect. 4.4.1 relates iteration (as introduced in the previous subsection) with jumps and labels. Using this relationship leads to further variants such as

- <u>*Tail recursion to jumps*</u>

  funct *f* = (**m** *x*) **r**:
  if B(*x*) **then** H(*x*) **else** *f*(K(*x*)) **fi**

  $\Updownarrow$

  funct *f* = (**m** *x*) **r**:
  begin var m *vx* := *x*;
  M: **if** ¬B(*vx*) **then** *vx* := K(*vx*); **goto** *M* **else skip fi**; H(*vx*) **end**

  <u>**Syntactic constraints:**</u>
  NOTOCCUR[*M*, *vx* **in** B, H, K].

Note that jumps introduced in this disciplined way are not at all 'harmful' (see also [Knuth 74]), since they are just another notation for particular loops.

A practically useful variant (in particular, for the case of several terminating branches in a recursive definition) of the latter rule is the following one where a result variable is introduced:

- **funct** *f* = (**m** *x*) **r**:
  if B(*x*) **then** H(*x*) **elsf** C(*x*) **then** G(*x*) **else** *f*(K(*x*)) **fi**

  $\Updownarrow$

  funct *f* = (**m** *x*) **r**:
  begin var m *vx* := *x*; **var r** *r*;
  M: **if** B(*vx*) **then** *r* := H(*vx*)
  elsf C(*vx*) **then** *r* := G(*vx*) **else** *vx* := K(*vx*); **goto** *M* **fi**; *r* **end**

  <u>**Syntactic constraints:**</u>
  NOTOCCURS[*M*, *vx*, *r* **in** B, C, H, G, K].

The generalization of this rule to the case of more than two terminating branches is obvious.

For single tail-recursive functions, the transition to both, **while** loops and jumps, is possible, and a preference for either of the two is simply a matter of taste. For systems of mutually tail-recursive functions, however, only a transition to jumps is possible. For these we have rules such as

- *Mutual tail recursion to jumps*

```
funct f = (m x) r:
   g(x) where
   funct g = (m x) r:
      if B1(x) then H1(x) elsf C(x) then g(K1(x)) else h(K2(x)) fi,
   funct h = (m x) r:
      if B2(x) then H2(x) elsf D(x) then h(K3(x)) else g(K4(x)) fi
```

$\Updownarrow$

```
funct f = (m x) r:
   begin var m vx := x; var r r;
      G: if ¬B1(vx) then
               if C(vx) then vx := K1(vx); goto G else vx := K2(vx); goto H fi
                        else r := H1(vx); goto E fi;
      H: if ¬B2(vx) then
               if D(vx) then vx := K3(vx); goto H else vx := K4(vx); goto G fi
                        else r := H2(vx); goto E fi;
      E: r  end
```

Syntactic constraints:

NOTOCCUR[G, H, E, vx, r **in** g, h].

The generalization of this rule to arbitrary systems of mutual recursive functions, as well as the integration of other forms of tail-recursive expressions (analogous to the discussion on **while** loops above) is obvious, and again left to the interested reader.

As an example of how to use this rule we consider the problem [Bauer, Wössner 82]:

Let a sequence s consisting of signs "+" and "–" be given. Decide whether s can be reduced to "+" by means of the usual rules on signs, known from arithmetic.

This problem is solved by the system of functions

```
mode sign = (+, –);
mode signsequ = ESEQU(sign);

funct posneg = (signsequ x) bool:
   pos(x) where

   funct pos = (signsequ x) bool:
      if x =<> then true elsf first x = + then pos(rest x) else neg(rest x) fi,

   funct neg = (signsequ x) bool:
      if x =<> then false elsf first x = + then neg(rest x) else pos(rest x) fi.
```

Using the rule *mutual tail recursion to jumps* this specification can be transformed into

```
funct posneg = (signsequ x) bool:
   begin var signsequ vx := x; var bool r;
      G: if vx ≠<>
```

```
            then if firstvx = + then vx := restvx; goto G
                                else vx := restvx; goto H fi
            else r := true; goto E fi;
      H: if vx ≠<>
            then if firstvx = + then vx := restvx; goto H
                                else vx := restvx; goto G fi
            else r := false; goto E fi;
      E: r  end.
```

In this particular example, further simplifications (Sect. 7.2.3) are possible which lead to

```
funct posneg = (signsequ x) bool:
   begin var signsequ vx := x; var sign vs; var bool r;
      G: if vx ≠<>
            then vs := firstvx; vx := restvx;
                 if vs = + then goto G else goto H fi
            else r := true; goto E fi;
      H: if vx ≠<>
            then vs := firstvx; vx := restvx;
                 if vs = + then goto H else goto G fi
            else r := false; goto E fi;
      E: r  end.
```

In Sect. 6.5.3 we introduced a transformation rule for transforming a system of recursive functions into a single recursive function. Hence, rather than using the rule *mutual tail recursion to jumps*, we can first convert such a system into a single tail-recursive function and then apply one of the rules for single tail-recursive functions.

Application of the rule from Sect. 6.5.3 to the above example yields (after trivial simplifications)

```
funct posneg = (signsequ x) bool:
   posneg'(1, x) where

   funct posneg' = (nat i, signsequ x) bool:
      if x =<> then i = 1
      elsf firstx = + then posneg'(i, restx)
                      else posneg'((i mod 2) + 1, restx) fi.
```

Now we can apply the rule *embedded tail recursion to iteration* and obtain

```
funct posneg = (signsequ x) bool:
   begin (var nat vi, var signsequ vx) := (1, x);
      while vx ≠<> do
         if firstvx = + then (vi, vx) := (vi, restvx)
                        else (vi, vx) := ((vi mod 2) + 1, restvx) fi od; vi = 1 end.
```

Of course, these two transformation steps can also be applied to arbitrary systems of mutually tail-recursive functions. In general, however, this will result in programs that are less efficient than the corresponding ones obtained by the rule *mutual tail recursion to jumps*.

7.1.3 Further Loop Constructs

In addition to **while** loops and jumps, further forms of repetition are provided by conventional programming languages. All these additional constructs can be integrated into our language by appropriate (axiomatic) transformation rules. As an example we give rules that define **for** loops (similar to those known from Algol or Pascal) as notational variants of particular **while** loops:

- <u>*Upward-***for***-loop*</u>

  begin var n *vx* := E;
  for *vk* **from** F **by** *succ* **upto** G **do** *vx* := E' **od**; H(*vx*) **end**

  ⇕ [SLINORD(**m**, <, =, *succ*)

  begin (**var m** *vk*, **var n** *vx*) := (F, E);
  while *vk* < G ∨ *vk* = G **do** (*vk*, *vx*) := (*succ*(*vk*), E') **od**; H(*vx*) **end**

  <u>Syntactic constraints:</u>
  NOTOCCUR[*vk*, *vx* **in** F, G],

- <u>*Downward-***for***-loop*</u>

  begin var n *vx* := E;
  for *vk* **from** F **by** *pred* **downto** G **do** *vx* := E' **od**; H(*vx*) **end**

  ⇕ [SLINORD(**m**, >, =, *pred*)

  begin (**var m** *vk*, **var n** *vx*) := (F, E);
  while *vk* > G ∨ *vk* = G **do** (*vk*, *vx*) := (*pred*(*vk*), E') **od**; H(*vx*) **end**

  <u>Syntactic constraints:</u>
  NOTOCCUR[*vk*, *vx* **in** F, G].

In these rules, SLINORD(**m**, <, =, *succ*) (Ex. 3.3-5c) states that "<" and "=" define a total ordering on **m**, and *succ* is an operation of kind **funct(m)m** which yields for any object of kind **m** its successor with respect to "<".

A simple example of how to use these rules is given with the factorial function (Sect. 7.1.1)

funct *fact* = (**nat** *m*, **nat** *n*) **nat**:
  begin (**var nat** *vm*, **var nat** *vn*) := (*m*, *n*);
    while *vn* ≠ 0 **do** (*vm*, *vn*) := (*vm* × *vn*, *vn*–1) **od**; *vm* **end**,

which immediately transforms into

funct *fact* = (**nat** *m*, **nat** *n*) **nat**:
  begin var nat *vm* := *m*;
    for *vn* **from** *n* **by** –1 **downto** 0 **do** *vm* := *vm* × *vn* **od**; *vm* **end**

(where "–1" is an abbreviation for "(**nat** *m*) **nat**: *m* – 1").

Further rules that allow a direct transition from various other forms of tail recursion to **for** loops, for example embedded tail recursion, can be obtained by simply composing the respective transformation rules given so far.

For similar transformations dealing with other forms of repetition we refer to [Bauer, Wössner 82].

7.2 Simplification of Imperative Programs

Although all substantial transformations aiming at improvements should have been done before switching to the imperative level, still a few, though fairly simple rules are needed for final polishing of an imperative program. In order to be able to formulate these rules concisely, we use, according to the conventions in Sect. 4.2.2, S ≡ S' to denote the equivalence of an arbitrary segment containing a statement S with the same segment where S is replaced by another statement S'. Analogously, we also use the abbreviation S ⊆ S'.

7.2.1 Sequentialization

Most of the programs resulting from applying the rules given in the previous section contain multiple declarations or assignments which are usually not available at the level of the classical, strongly sequential von Neumann machine. Therefore, we introduce below a few rules for dealing with sequentialization.

In fact, no rules are necessary for the sequentialization of declarations, since, according to the definition of the language, the variables introduced by the left-hand side of a declaration cannot occur in the right-hand side. Therefore, multiple declarations may be sequentialized in an arbitrary order, in particular from left to right. Thus, for the example of the function *sqr* (Sect. 7.1.1) we could write

funct *sqr* = (**nat** *n*) **nat**:
  begin var nat *vx* := 0; **var nat** *vy* := 1; **var nat** *vz* := 3; **var nat** *vn* := *n*;
    while *vy* ≤ *vn* **do** (*vx*, *vy*, *vz*, *vn*) := (*vx*+1, *vy*+*vz*, *vz*+2, *vn*) **od**; *vx* **end**.

In this example, the multiple assignment could also be sequentialized, say left to right, leading to

funct *sqr* = (**nat** *n*) **nat**:
  begin var nat *vx* := 0; **var nat** *vy* := 1; **var nat** *vz* := 3; **var nat** *vn* := *n*;
    while *vy* ≤ *vn* **do** *vx* := *vx*+1; *vy* := *vy*+*vz*; *vz* := *vz*+2; *vn* := *vn* **od**; *vx* **end**.

Obviously, a sequentialization such as

vx := *vx*+1; *vy* := *vy*+*vz*; *vn* := *vn*; *vz* := *vz*+2

would be correct as well. However

vx := *vx*+1; *vz* := *vz*+2; *vy* := *vy*+*vz*; *vn* := *vn*

would be incorrect.

In general, some care has to be taken in sequentializing multiple assignments. For an arbitrary multiple assignment of the form

$(x_1, ..., x_k) := (E_1, ..., E_k);$

a left-to-right sequentialization is possible, if none of the E_i contains a variable x_j with $j<i$. If this situation is not given a priori, it often can be established by a suitable permutation of the constituents of the multiple assignment. This is captured by the rule

- $(x_1, ..., x_k) := (E_1, ..., E_k)$

↓

$x_i := E_i;\ (x_1, ..., x_{i-1}, x_{i+1}, ..., x_k) := (E_1, ..., E_{i-1}, E_{i+1}, ..., E_k)$

Syntactic constraints:

NOTOCCURS[x_j **in** E_i] $(1 \le j \le k \wedge j \ne i \wedge k > 1)$.

But there may still be cases where a permutation of the constituents does not exist, as can be seen from the well-known example of interchanging values as in

$(x, y) := (y, x);$

Here, it is necessary to introduce an auxiliary variable to memorize either the value of a variable from the left-hand side of the assignment,

var m $h := x;\ x := y;\ y := h,$

or the value of the corresponding right-hand side expression,

var m $h := y;\ y := x;\ x := h.$

Both possibilities can be cast into corresponding rules, such as

- $(x_1, ..., x_k) := (E_1, ..., E_k)$

↓

begin var m $y := x_i$;
 $(x_1, ..., x_k) := (E_1[y$ **for** $x_i], ..., E_k[y$ **for** $x_i])$ **end**

Syntactic constraints:

NOTOCCURS[y **in** E_i] $(1 \le i \le k)$,
KIND[x_i] = **var m**.

Finding a sequentialization which is optimal with respect to the number of auxiliary variables is non-trivial, in particular, if also procedures and subscripted variables are involved [Belady 66].

7.2.2 Elimination of Superfluous Assignments and Variables

Due to the rather general way of transforming recursion into iteration, it may happen that – after sequentialization – trivial assignments of the form

$x := x$

are generated. These can be trivially eliminated by the rule

- $x := x$

↕ [DEF[x]

skip

where the empty statement **skip** itself also can be eliminated using the rule *definition of the empty statement* (Sect. 4.4.1).

Another example of a rule for eliminating superfluous assignments is

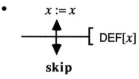

- $x := E_1$; $x := E_2$

  ⇕

  $x := E_2$

  <u>Syntactic constraints:</u>
  NOTOCCURS[x **in** E_2];

If, after using these rules (or similar ones), there remains a block with a declaration

var m *vx* := E

and without any further assignment to *vx* in the block, then the variable declaration may be changed into a constant declaration (according to the rules given at the beginning of Sect. 7.1).

m *vx* = E.

This, in turn, may be unfolded, provided E is determinate.

If the variable *vx* is not even used within the block, the respective declaration may simply be omitted:

- **begin var m** *vx* := E; PP **end**

  ⇓

  begin PP **end**

  <u>Syntactic constraints:</u>
  NOTOCCURS[*vx* **in** PP]

(where PP stands for an arbitrary sequence of declarations and statements).

In the previous section we have derived the function

funct *sqr* = (**nat** *n*) **nat**:
  begin var nat *vx* := 0; **var nat** *vy* := 1; **var nat** *vz* := 1; **var nat** *vn* := *n*;
    while *vy* ≤ *vn* **do** *vx* := *vx*+1; *vz* := *vz*+2; *vy* := *vy*+*vz*; *vn* := *vn* **od**; *vx* **end**.

Here, *vn* := *vn* is obviously a superfluous assignment, and hence can be omitted. Since this is the only assignment to *vn* and *n* is determinate, *vn* can be substituted by its value upon declaration. This yields our final version of *sqr*:

funct *sqr* = (**nat** *n*) **nat**:
  begin var nat *vx* := 0; **var nat** *vy* := 1; **var nat** *vz* := 1;
    while *vy* ≤ *n* **do** *vx* := *vx*+1; *vz* := *vz*+2; *vy* := *vy*+*vz*; **od**; *vx* **end**.

Similar to assignments, other superfluous constructs that have been introduced by rule application can be eliminated. A typical example is

- **for** *i* **from** F **by** *incr* **to** G **do** S **od**

  ⇕ [(S; S) ≡ S

  S.

Further examples are obvious.

7.2.3 Rearrangement of Statements

Although an optimal ordering in which individual statements appear in an imperative program should be achieved mainly by appropriate transformations on the applicative level and a careful sequentialization, it still may happen – e.g. due to simplifications of the kind discussed in the previous subsection – that further improvements are possible by suitable rearrangements of statements. Therefore we will also discuss this topic briefly.

One of the rules of this kind already has been used in Sect. 7.1.1:

- *Distributivity of assignment over conditional*

vx := **if** B **then** E_1 **else** E_2 **fi**

⇕

if B **then** *vx* := E_1 **else** *vx* := E_2 **fi**.

Other distributivity rules include

- *Distributivity of* **for** *loop over conditional*

for *i* **from** F **by** *incr* **to** G **do if** B **then** S_1 **else** S_2 **fi od**

⇕

if B **then for** *i* **from** F **by** *incr* **to** G **do** S_1 **od**
else for *i* **from** F **by** *incr* **to** G **do** S_2 **od fi**

Syntactic constraints:
NOTOCCURS[*i* **in** B]

or

- *Distributivity of assignment over block*

vx := **begin var m** *vy* := E; S; *vy* **end**

⇕

vx := E; S[*vx* **for** *vy*]

Syntactic constraints:
NOTOCCURS[*vx* **in** S].

Further rules of a similar kind include

- *Unrolling of loops*

while B **do** S **od**

⇕

if B **then** S; **while** B **do** S **od else skip fi**

which corresponds to an unfolding on the applicative level (Sect. 6.4.1),

- *Constant propagation*

  while B **do** $(vx, vy) := (E_1, E_2)$ **od**

  $\updownarrow$

  if B **then** $(vx, vy) := (E_1, E_2)$; **while** B **do** $vy := E_2$ **od else skip fi**

  Syntactic constraints:

  NOTOCCUR[vx, vy **in** E_1],

- *Exchange of statements*

  $S_1; S_2$

  $\updownarrow$

  $S_2; S_1$

  Syntactic constraints:

  NOTOCCUR[USEDVARS[S_1] **in** ASSIGNEDVARS[S_2]],
  NOTOCCUR[USEDVARS[S_2] **in** ASSIGNEDVARS[S_1]]

(where USEDVARS[S] gives the set of all variable identifiers occurring in S, and ASSIGNEDVARS[S] yields the set of all variable identifiers to which an assignment occurs in S)

- *Propagation of common statements*

  if B(x) **then** S_1; S_2 **else** S_1; S_3 **fi**

  $\updownarrow$

  S_1; **if** B(x) **then** S_2 **else** S_3 **fi**

  Syntactic constraints:

  NOTOCCURS[x **in** S_1].

Further examples are transitions to jumps and labels (as a preparatory step towards a more machine-oriented level of formulation) as in

- *Conditional statement to jumps*

  if B **then** S_1 **else** S_2 **fi**; S

  $\updownarrow$

  if $\neg$B **then goto** L **else skip fi**;
  S_1; **goto** E; L: S_2; E: S

  Syntactic constraints:

  NOTOCCUR[E, L **in** B, S_1, S_2, S],

or suppression and elimination of parameters in procedures (see below).

Although any kind of merging of computations should have been done already at the level of applicative formulation (Sect. 6.1), it may happen, for example in case of a too early sequentialization, that possibilities for merging computations are only detected at the imperative level. From a methodological point of view, in such a case one should backtrack in the development, perform the respective merging at the applicative level, and then rework the subsequent development steps. In practice, however, it is sometimes convenient to simply continue a derivation without backtracking. This requires corresponding rules, such as

- **for** *i* **from** F **by** *incr* **upto** G **do** S_1 **od**;
  for *i* **from** F **by** *incr* **upto** G **do** S_2 **od**

  ⇕ [$(S_1; S_2) \equiv (S_2; S_1)$

  for *i* **from** F **by** *incr* **upto** G **do** S_1; S_2 **od**,

which are condensed schematic redevelopments that can be derived by means of the elementary rules given so far.

7.2.4 Procedures

On the applicative level of formulation, functions have been introduced for structuring expressions by means of abstraction. As an analogous construct for structuring (sequences of) statements by abstraction, we now introduce procedures.

We start by illustrating the relationship between functions and procedures with an example. In Sect. 6.5.1 we derived

```
funct sort = (natsequ s) natsequ:
   sort'(<>, s) where

   funct sort' = (natsequ r, natsequ s) natsequ:
      if s =<> then r else sort'(r+min(s), delete(s, min(s))) fi
```

where we have assumed that the function *delete* is defined elsewhere. Of course, we can also give an explicit definition for *delete*, such as

```
funct delete = (natsequ s, nat x) natsequ:
   delete'(<>, s, x) where

   funct delete' = (natsequ r, natsequ s, nat x) natsequ:
      if s =<> then r
               elsf firsts = x then r+rests else delete'(r+firsts, rests, x) fi.
```

If we apply the appropriate variant of rule *tail recursion to iteration* (Sect. 7.1.1), *sort* can be transformed into

```
funct sort = (natsequ s) natsequ:
   begin (var natsequ vr, var natsequ vs) := (<>, s);
      while vs ≠<> do (vr, vs) := (vr+min(vs), delete(vs, min(vs))) od; vr end.
```

By *sequentialization* this can be further transformed into

```
funct sort = (natsequ s) natsequ:
   begin var natsequ vr := <>; var natsequ vs := s;
      while vs ≠<> do vr := vr+min(vs); vs := delete(vs, min(vs)) od; vr end.
```

Next, we focus on the assignment

vs := *delete*(*vs*, *min*(*vs*)).

The function *delete* is tail-recursive itself, and hence could be transformed into the corresponding iterative form. However, rather than doing so, we exploit the fact that *delete* appears in the special context where its result is assigned to one of its arguments. In such a context, functions can be transformed into procedures. The introduction of procedures is captured by the rule

- <u>*Introduction of procedures*</u>

  vx := *f*(*vx*)

  $\Updownarrow$

  p(*vx*)

  <u>**Syntactic constraints:**</u>
  NOTOCCURS[*vx* **in** *f*],
  DECL[*f*] = **funct** (**m** *x*) **m**: E,
  DECL[*p*] = **proc** (**var m** *vx*): **begin** *vx* := *f*(*vx*) **end**.

Having applied this rule, the body of *p* can be further developed using the unfold/fold strategy, into a form where *f* no longer appears. In this way, variants of the above rule for specific definitions of *f* can be derived. An example is

- *vx* := *f*(*vx*)

  $\Updownarrow$

  p(*vx*)

  <u>**Syntactic constraints:**</u>
  NOTOCCURS[*vx* **in** *f*],
  DECL[*f*] = **funct** (**m** *x*) **m**: **if** B(*x*) **then** H(*x*) **else** *f*(K(*x*)) **fi**,
  DECL[*p*] = **proc** (**var m** *vx*):
  begin while ¬B(*vx*) **do** *vx* := K(*vx*) **od**; *vx* := H(*vx*) **end**.

Of course, there are again variants, for example if one of the arguments of *f* is constant or if *f* is embedded in *f'*, and *f'* has another form of tail recursion:

- *vx* := *f*(*vx*, *y*)

  $\Updownarrow$

  p(*vx*, *y*)

  <u>**Syntactic constraints:**</u>
  NOTOCCURS[*vx* **in** *f*],
  DECL[*f*] = **funct** (**m** *x*, **n** *c*) **m**: *f'*(E, *x*, *c*) **where**
  funct *f'* = (**p** *y*, **m** *x*, **n** *c*) **r**:
  if B(*x*, *y*) **then** H(*x*, *y*)
  elsf C(*x*, *y*, *c*) **then** G(*x*, *y*, *c*) **else** *f'*(K(*x*, *y*), *c*) **fi**,
  DECL[*p*] = **proc** (**var m** *vx*):
  begin var p *vy* := E;

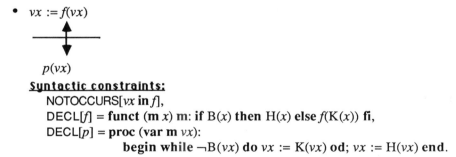

while ¬B(*vx*, *vy*) Δ ¬C(*vx*, *vy*, *c*) **do**
    (*vx*, *vy*) := K(*vx*, *vy*) **od**;
if B(*vx*, *vy*) **then** *vx* := H(*vx*, *vy*)
                    else *vx* := G(*vx*, *vy*, *c*) **fi end**.

Applying this latter variant to the assignment *vs* := *delete*(*vs*, *min*(*vs*)) within the definition of *delete* above leads to introducing the declaration

proc *del* = (**var natsequ** *vs*, **nat** *x*):
  begin var natsequ *vr* := <>;
    while *vs* ≠<> Δ **first***vs* ≠ *x* **do** (*vr*, *vs*) := (*vr*+**first***vs*, **rest***vs*) **od**;
      if *vs* =<> **then** *vs* := *vr* **else** *vs* := *vr*+**rest***vs* **fi end**

such that the definition of *sort* can be transformed into

funct *sort* = (**natsequ** *s*) **natsequ**:
  begin var natsequ *vr* := <>; **var natsequ** *vs* := *s*;
    while *vs* ≠<> **do** *vr* := *vr*+*min*(*vs*); *del*(*vs*, *min*(*vs*)) **od**; *vr* **end**.

If the particular context that allows transforming a function into a procedure is not given a priori (say for some outermost call), procedures can still be introduced by first using the transformation rule

- *f*(*x*)

  $\updownarrow$

  begin var m *vy* := *f*(*x*); *vy* **end**

  Syntactic constraints:
    KIND[*f*] = **funct** (**m**) **m**,

which introduces a form that allows to proceed as above.

Like functions, procedures can be unfolded using the rule [Bauer et al. 85]

- *p*(*vx*, E)

  $\downarrow$

  begin n *c* = E; S[*vx* **for** *x*] **end**

  Syntactic constraints:
    DECL[*p*] = **proc** (**var m** *x*, **n** *c*): S.

As in the previous subsections, further variants of the above rules are obvious and therefore left to the interested reader.

7.3 Examples

As in the previous chapters, the use of the transformation rules introduced in the previous subsections will be demonstrated by a few examples which have already been used in previous sections.

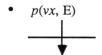

7.3.1 Hamming's Problem

In Sect. 6.6.4 we derived the applicative program

```
funct hamming = (nat N) natsequ:
   if N = 0 then <> elsf N = 1 then <1> else ham'(<1, 2>, N–2, 1, 1, 1) fi
   where

   funct ham' = (natsequ t, nat n, nat i2, nat i3, nat i5: ((1 ≤ i2, i3, i5 < |t|) ∧
                       isham(t)) Δ last t = nexth(t, i2, i3, i5)) natsequ:
      if n = 0 then t
         else ham'(t+nexth(t, next(t, i2, i3, i5)), n–1, next(t, i2, i3, i5)) fi,

   funct isham = (natsequ t) bool:
      <1> ≼ t ≼ sort(settosequ{nat x: H(x)});

   funct nexth = (natsequ t, nat i2, nat i3, nat i5:
                       (1 ≤ i2, i3, i5 ≤ |t|) ∧ isham(t)) nat:
      begin (nat a2, nat a3, nat a5) = (2t[i2], 3t[i3], 5t[i5]);
         if a2 ≤ a3 ∧ a2 ≤ a5 then a2
         [] a3 ≤ a2 ∧ a3 ≤ a5 then a3
         [] a5 ≤ a3 ∧ a5 ≤ a2 then a5 fi  end;

   funct next = (natsequ t, nat i2, nat i3, nat i5:  ((1 ≤ i2, i3, i5 < |t|) ∧
                    isham(t)) Δ last t = nexth(t, i2, i3, i5)) (nat, nat, nat):
      (if last t = 2t[i2] then i2+1 else i2 fi,
      if last t = 3t[i3] then i3+1 else i3 fi,
      if last t = 5t[i5] then i5+1 else i5 fi).
```

which can be further transformed into an imperative program as follows:

<u>Main development</u>

Focus: function *hamming*
Goal: imperative program
Transformations:

step 1: embedded tail recursion to iteration

```
if N = 0 then <>
elsf N = 1 then <1>
   else begin
         (var natsequ vt, var nat vi2, var nat vi3, var nat vi5, var nat vn) :=
              (<1, 2>, 1, 1, 1, N–2);
         while vn ≠ 0 do
              (vt, vi2, vi3, vi5, vn) :=
                 (vt+nexth(vt, next(vt, vi2, vi3, vi5)),
                    next(vt, vi2, vi3, vi5, vm), vn–1))) od;
         vt end fi
```

new focus: inner segment
step 2: (partial) sequentialization

```
begin var natsequ vt := <1, 2>;
   var nat vi2 := 1; var nat vi3 := 1;  var nat vi5 := 1; var nat vn := N–2;
   while vn ≠ 0 do
      (vi2, vi3, vi5) := next(vt, vi2, vi3, vi5);
      vt := vt + nexth(vt, vi2, vi3, vi5);
      vn := vn – 1 od;
   vt end
```

step 3: unfold *next* and *nexth;* sequentialization

```
funct hamming = (nat N) natsequ:
   if N = 0 then <>
   elsf N = 1 then <1>
      else begin var natsequ vt := <1, 2>;
            var nat vi2 := 1; var nat vi3 := 1; var nat vi5 := 1; var nat vn := N–2;
            while vn ≠ 0 do
               vi2 := if lastvt = 2vt[vi2] then vi2+1 else vi2 fi;
               vi3 := if lastvt = 3vt[vi3] then vi3+1 else vi3 fi;
               vi5 := if lastvt = 5vt[vi5] then vi5+1 else vi5 fi;
               (nat a2, nat a3, nat a5) = (2vt[vi2], 3vt[vi3], 5vt[vi5]);
               if a2 ≤ a3 ∧ a2 ≤ a5 then vt := vt + a2
               [] a3 ≤ a2 ∧ a3 ≤ a5 then vt := vt + a3
               [] a5 ≤ a3 ∧ a5 ≤ a2 then vt := vt + a5 fi od;
               vn := vn – 1; vt end fi.
```

This program is essentially the one that can be found in [Dijkstra 76a].

7.3.2 Cycles in a Graph

In Sect. 6.6.3 we derived the following applicative program:

```
funct hascycle = (graph g) bool:
   hca(nodes(g), sources(nodes(g)), m) where

   funct hca = (nodeset c, nodeset d, nodemap m: d = sources(c, g) ∧
                (∀ node x: x ∈ c ⇨ m[x] = preds(x, c))) bool:
      if d = ∅  then c ≠ ∅
                else nodeset e = {node x: x ∈ c ∧ m[x] ≠ ∅ ∧ m[x] ⊆ d};
                     nodemap n = some nodemap n':
                                    ∀ node x: (x ∈ c ⇨ n'[x] = m[x]\d) ∧
                                    (x ∉ c ⇨ n'[x] = m[x]);
                     hca(c\d, e, n)   fi;

   nodemap m = that nodemap m':
                  ∀ node x: x ∈ nodes(g) ⇨ (m'[x] = preds(x, c));

   funct sources = (nodeset c) nodeset:
      {node x: x ∈ c ∧ preds(x, c) = ∅};

   funct preds = (node x, nodeset c) nodeset:
      {node y: y ∈ c ∧ isarc(g, y, x)}.
```

<u>Main development</u>

Focus: function *hascycle*
Goal: imperative program
Transformations:

step 1: embedded tail recursion to iteration

```
begin (var nodeset vc, var nodeset vd, var nodemap vm) :=
                                   (nodes(g), sources(nodes(g)), m);
   while vd ≠ ∅ do
      nodeset e = {node x: x ∈ vc ∧ vm[x] ≠ ∅ ∧ vm[x] ⊆ vd};
      nodemap n = some nodemap n': ∀ node x:
               (x ∈ vc ⇨ n'[x] = vm[x]\vd) ∧ (x ∉ vc ⇨ n'[x] = vm[x]);
      (vc, vd, vm) := (vc\vd, e, n) od; vc ≠ ∅ end
```

step 2: sequentialization

```
begin
   var nodeset vc := nodes(g);
   var nodeset vd := sources(vc);
   var nodemap vm := m;
   while vd ≠ ∅ do
      nodeset e = {node x: x ∈ vc ∧ vm[x] ≠ ∅ ∧ vm[x] ⊆ vd};
      nodemap n = some nodemap n': ∀ node x:
               (x ∈ vc ⇨ n'[x] = vm[x]\vd) ∧ (x ∉ vc ⇨ n'[x] = vm[x]);
      vm := n;
      vc := vc\vd;
      vd := e od;
   vc ≠ ∅ end
```

step 3: unfold *sources*, *m*, *n*

```
begin
   var nodeset vc := nodes(g);
   var nodeset vd := {node x: x ∈ vc ∧ preds(x, vc) = ∅};
   var nodemap vm := that nodemap m':
                        ∀ node x: x ∈ vc ⇨ (m'[x] = preds(x, vc));
   while vd ≠ ∅ do
      nodeset e = {node x: x ∈ vc ∧ vm[x] ≠ ∅ ∧ vm[x] ⊆ vd};
      vm := some nodemap n: ∀ node x:
               (x ∈ vc ⇨ n[x] = vm[x]\vd) ∧ (x ∉ vc ⇨ n[x] = vm[x]);
      vc := vc\vd;
      vd := e od;
   vc ≠ ∅ end.
```

A further development requires transformations of data structures. These transformations will be dealt with in the next chapter where we also resume the above development.

7.4 Exercises

Exercise 7-1

Transform the following functions into imperative form:

a) *divmod* (Sect. 6.1.2),
b) *toh* (Sect. 6.2),
c) *tabbin* (Sect. 6.3.2),
d) *fib* (Sect. 6.5.2).

Simplify the respective results, if possible.

Exercise 7-2

Derive further variants of the transformation rules:

a) *tail recursion to iteration,*
b) *tail recursion to jumps,*
c) *mutual recursion to jumps.*

Exercise 7-3

Give another rule for the sequentialization of a multiple assignment by introducing auxiliary variables.

Exercise 7-4

Given the function (Ex. 5.3-5)

funct *ndiv* = (**nat** *n*: $n \neq 0$) **nat**:
  nd(1) **where**
  funct *nd* = (**nat** *k*: $k \leq n$) **nat**:
    if $k=n$ **then** 0
    [] $k \neq n \wedge divides(k, n)$ **then** $1 + nd(k+1)$
    [] $k \neq n \wedge \neg divides(k, n)$ **then** $nd(k+1)$ **fi**,

derive, by suitable transformations, an imperative version of *ndiv*. Simplify this imperative version as much as possible.

Exercise 7-5

Transform the function

funct *ord* = (**nat** *a*, **nat** *b*, **nat** *c*, **nat** *d*) (**nat**, **nat**, **nat**, **nat**):
  if $a \leq b \wedge b \leq c \wedge c \leq d$ **then** (a, b, c, d)
    else **if** $a > b$ **then** $ord(b, a, c, d)$
      [] $b > c$ **then** $ord(a, c, b, d)$
      [] $c > d$ **then** $ord(a, b, d, c)$ **fi fi**

into imperative form. Simplify the resulting imperative version as much as possible.

Exercise 7-6

Transform the function (Ex. 6.5-2)

funct *ik* = (**nat** *n*) (**nat**, **nat**):
  ik'(0, 0, 0) **where**

```
funct ik' = (nat m, nat a, nat b) (nat, nat):
   if m = n  then (a, b)
             else if a = b then ik'(m+1, b+1, 0)
                  [] a > b then ik'(m+1, b, a)
                  [] a < b then ik'(m+1, b, a+1) fi fi
```

into imperative form. Simplify, if possible.

Exercise 7-7

Transform the function (Ex. 6.5-1)

```
funct derpol = (realsequ a, real x: a ≠<>) (real, real):
   derpol'(leada, 0, lasta) where
   funct derpol' = (realsequ a, real d, real p) (real, real):
      if |a| = 0 then (d, p) else derpol'(leada, p + x × d, lasta + x × p) fi,
```

into imperative form. Simplify, if possible.

Exercise 7-8

Transform the function

```
funct TP = (nat n: n ≥ 1) (nat, nat):
   if n=1 then (1, 1) else (nat a, nat b) = TP(n–1); (n + a, n + a + b) fi
```

into imperative form using

a) a **while** loop,
b) a **for** loop,
c) jumps and labels.

Exercise 7-9

Transform the following functions into imperative form:

a) *preord* (Sect. 6.5.2),
b) *unify* (Sect. 5.5.6).

Exercise 7-10

By composition of the respective rules derive new transformation rules for the (direct) transition

a) from embedded tail recursion to jumps,
b) from various forms of tail recursion to **for** loops,
c) from embedded tail recursion to **for** loops.

Exercise 7-11

Give definitional transformations for the introduction of

a) **until** loops,
b) **do - od** loops with **exit** statement.

8. Transformation of Data Structures

A program development typically starts with a formal specification (of an abstract program) based on some suitably defined abstract type (or a hierarchy of types). In the course of developing a program by transforming the control constructs (using the techniques introduced in the previous chapters) a situation will be reached where a further successful development is subject to an appropriate change of the data structures involved.

Similar to the different hierarchical levels on the control structure side, there are different (hierarchical) levels on the data structure side. In a formal program development data structures may appear in quite different formalizations:

- descriptive-axiomatic: abstract types (Sect. 3.3)
- descriptive/operational-applicative: computation structures (Sect. 3.4.5)
- operational-procedural: modules (Sect. 8.2.4)
- operational-state-oriented: devices (Sect. 8.2.4).

Accordingly, there is a variety of transitions on and between these levels (see for example [Bauer, Wössner 82], [Partsch, Broy 79]). Examples are given by transformations of one algebraic type definition into another, transformations of a type definition into a concrete structure, transformations of computation structures, and even transformations in order to improve efficiency, for example by switching from functions to procedures.

From a more abstract viewpoint the different kinds of transitions need not be viewed as separate kinds of activities, but rather may be considered uniformly as transformations of one abstract type into another, since even the available programming environment can be specified by suitable abstract types (such that the environment is a model of these types). For this reason, in the following we will mainly deal with transformations of one abstract type into another. This is usually called an implementation.

As for transformations of the control structure, correctness is also the central issue for type transformations.

In general, correctness of a type transformation means that an arbitrary (abstract) program must retain its (observable) behavior when its underlying type is replaced by an (arbitrary) correct implementation of this type.

Particular situations arise, when a type T is part of a system of types or when it is known to occur only in a specific context, e.g., within an expression C.

In the former case there are modifications of the system of types that are not generally covered by the notion of a correct implementation and thus need particular attention.

In the latter case, as in the previous chapters, a transition from T to T' is a correct transformation, if one of the semantic relations introduced in Chap. 4 holds between C and the expression that results from substituting T by T' in C.

All these kinds of transformations will be dealt with in the sequel:

The first three sections deal with the implementation of abstract types. In Sect. 8.1 the theoretical foundations and a technique for proving the correctness of an implementation will be given. Section 8.2 deals with the problem of implementing a type in terms of specific types that characterize particular programming environments. Section 8.3 introduces the idea of a library of implementations for basic data types and raises the issue of how to select a suitable implementation with respect to efficiency.

Whereas individual types are the subject of the first three sections, Sect. 8.4 deals with whole systems of types and how to transform these, by means of a representative technique, in the course of a program development.

Section 8.5 raises the issue of joint development and introduces several techniques where data types and control constructs are transformed simultaneously.

Finally, Sects. 8.6 and 8.7, as in the previous chapters, give more comprehensive examples and exercises.

For certain complex rules in the previous chapters a representation in the form of a strategy was preferred to a schematic representation. We will see that the notational vehicle of strategies is also more appropriate for describing data type transformations.

8.1 Implementation of Types in Terms of Other Types

A general strategy for the implementation of a type in terms of another one is provided by the algebraic constructions "enrich; forget; identify" [Ehrig et al. 80].

Assume that a type T is to be implemented in terms of a type T'. Then

- *Enrich* means defining new functions in T' that are to implement the abstract operations of T.
- *Forget* means restricting the operations and object sets of the (enriched) type T' to the operations of T and the objects that are reachable by these operations.
- *Identify* finally refers to the fact that certain abstract objects (in T) may have several representations in T' which are identified with respect to the axioms of T (using suitable congruence relations).

In this section and the following ones we will deal with the problem of constructing an implementation along this strategic guideline. As a running example we will use *priority queues* (see [Pepper et al. 82] and also Sect. 3.6.11). This data structure defines an object set **pqueue** of priority queues, the elements of which belong to a linearly ordered object set **m**, and typical operations such as *emptyq* (the empty priority queue), *add* (addition of an element), *min* (yielding the minimal element), or *remove* (deletion of the minimal element). The necessary restriction of these last two functions to non-empty priority queues is achieved by a predicate *isempty* (the test for emptiness).

A formal specification of priority queues by an abstract type can be given as follows (where LINORD(**m**, ≤), cf. Ex. 3.3-5b, defines "≤" to be a linear ordering on **m**):

type PQUEUE = (**sort m**, **funct** (**m**, **m**) **bool** .≤.: LINORD(**m**, ≤))
pqueue, *emptyq*, *isempty*, *add*, *min*, *remove*:
based on BOOL,
sort pqueue,
pqueue *emptyq*,
funct (**pqueue**) **bool** *isempty*,
funct (**pqueue**, **m**) **pqueue** *add*,
funct (**pqueue** q: $\neg isempty(q)$) **m** *min*,
funct (**pqueue** q: $\neg isempty(q)$) **pqueue** *remove*,
laws pqueue q, **m** x:
$isempty(emptyq) \equiv$ **true**,
$isempty(add(q, x)) \equiv$ **false**,
$min(add(q, x)) \equiv$ **if** $isempty(q)$ **then** x
elsf $x \leq min(q)$ **then** x **else** $min(q)$ **fi**,
$remove(add(q, x)) \equiv$ **if** $isempty(q)$ **then** $emptyq$
elsf $x \leq min(q)$ **then** q **else** $add(remove(q), x)$ **fi**
endoftype.

8.1.1 Theoretical Foundations

The basic concept of our considerations is the notion of a hierarchical abstract type T = (Σ, E, P) as introduced in Sect. 3.3.1.2 (with Σ, E, P being the signature, a collection of first-order axioms, and the primitive type, respectively).

In order to make the intuitive notions of input/output behavior and correct implementation (that were used in the introduction) more precise, we follow [Broy et al. 86]. Since we are interested in dealing with the transformation of types independently of their use within certain expressions, our notion of correctness from Sect. 4.1 is not applicable. Therefore, we first have to introduce an appropriate notion of correctness.

First we define an **abstract program** over a hierarchical type T to be a function of the form

funct p = ($\mathbf{m}_1$ x_1, ..., $\mathbf{m}_k$ x_k) **m**: P,

where $\mathbf{m}_1$, ..., $\mathbf{m}_k$, **m** are primitive sorts of T and P is an expression built from the operations of T and the language constructs introduced in the previous chapters.

The restriction to functions with primitive objects as input and output is justified by the fact that we are only interested in the 'observable behavior' of programs with respect to these primitive objects.

Domain and range of an abstract program are described by a **precondition** I and a **postcondition** O, respectively. These conditions are boolean-valued terms over the operations of T and free variables x_1, ..., x_k, i.e., $I \in W(\Sigma \cup \{x_1, \ldots, x_k\})$ and $O \in W(\Sigma \cup \{p\} \cup \{x_1, ..., x_k\})$ (with W denoting the term algebra, Sect. 3.3.1.1). Different from other approaches, it is also required that I is **total** over T, i.e., its interpretations are totally defined for all models of T.

An abstract program p is called

- **partially correct** over T with respect to I and O, if T is consistent and in all models of T the following property holds:

  $\forall\ \mathbf{m_1}\ x_1, ..., \mathbf{m_k}\ x_k\colon\ \mathrm{I} \equiv \mathbf{true} \Rightarrow (\mathrm{O} \equiv \mathbf{true} \vee \neg\ \mathbf{defined}(p(x_1, ..., x_k))$

- **strongly correct** over T with respect to I and O, if T is consistent and in all models of T the following property holds:

  $\forall\ \mathbf{m_1}\ x_1, ..., \mathbf{m_k}\ x_k\colon\ \mathrm{I} \equiv \mathbf{true} \Rightarrow (\mathrm{O} \equiv \mathbf{true} \wedge\ \mathbf{defined}(p(x_1, ..., x_k)).$

This induces corresponding notions for implementations of types:

Let T and T' be hierarchical types over the same primitive type. T' is called a **partially/strongly correct implementation** of T, if for every abstract program p over T and for every pair (I, O) of input and output conditions, p is partially/strongly correct with respect to I and O over T', if it is so over T.

Note that this definition implies that:

- the operations of T must also occur in T', and
- T' is consistent, if T is consistent.

Although perfect from a theoretical point of view, for use in practice the above definition of correctness of an implementation of a type T by a type T' has the disadvantage that it refers to all abstract programs over T. Therefore, in the following we will introduce particular relations between T and T' that guarantee that T' is a (strongly) correct implementation of T (without referring to all possible abstract programs over T).

In order to define these relations, a few additional notions for Σ-algebras (which define the semantics of types as in Sect. 3.3.1) are needed:

Let Σ = (S, C, F), where S, C, F are families of carrier sets, constants, and partial operations, respectively. And let Σ' = (S', C', F') where $\Sigma' \subseteq \Sigma$, i.e., $S' \subseteq S$, $C' \subseteq C$, and $F' \subseteq F$.

The **Σ'-reduct** A' of a Σ-algebra A is the Σ'-algebra defined by $s^{A'} = s^A$ for all $s \in S'$, $c^{A'} = c^A$ for all $c \in C'$, and $f^{A'} = f^A$ for all $f \in F'$ (where f^A denotes the interpretation of f in A, etc.).

According to this definition, any model of the primitive type P = (Σ_P, E_P) of a persistent hierarchical type T = (Σ, E, P) is a Σ_P-reduct of a model of T. For example, for any Σ_{NAT}-algebra, where NAT is defined as in Sect. 3.3.1.2, any Σ_{BOOL}-algebra is a Σ_{BOOL}-reduct.

A Σ-algebra A' is called a **subalgebra** of a Σ-algebra A, if $s^{A'} \subseteq s^A$ for all $s \in S$, $c^{A'} = c^A$ for all $c \in C$, and $f^{A'} = f^A|_{A'}$ for all $f \in F$ (where $f^A|_{A'}$ denotes the restriction of f^A to A'), and if A' is closed under the operations in Σ.

A Σ'-algebra A' is called a **Σ'-subalgebra** of a Σ-algebra A, if it is a subalgebra of a Σ'-reduct of A.

Obviously, any Σ-algebra is its own Σ-subalgebra. A simple example of a proper Σ'-subalgebra is provided by the natural numbers (together with the successor operation) which form a NAT-subalgebra of the integral numbers (together with predecessor and successor operation).

Informally, the difference between reduct and subalgebra may be explained as follows: A reduct is formed by selecting a subfamily of carrier sets, constants, and functions, whereas a subalgebra is formed from subsets of all carrier sets and appropriate restrictions of the functions to these subsets.

Following [Broy et al. 86] a whole hierarchy of more and more liberal relations between types can be defined. Each of these relations is transitive and guarantees a strongly correct implementation.

Let Σ = (S, C, F) and Σ' = (S', C', F') be signatures, and let T = (Σ, E, P) and T' = (Σ', E', P) be hierarchical types (over the same primitive type). Finally, as in Sect. 3.3.1.1, let GEN(T) denote the class of all term-generated models of T.

According to the semantic definition of a type,

- T and T' are **equivalent**, if $\Sigma = \Sigma'$ and GEN(T) = GEN(T').

Further, more general relations between T and T' can be obtained by weakening the relationship between Σ and Σ' and the relationship between the models of T and T', respectively. For all these relations we require $\Sigma \subseteq \Sigma'$ and $\varnothing \neq$ GEN(T'). We define:

- T' is an **axiomatic enrichment** of T, if $\Sigma = \Sigma'$ and GEN(T') $\subseteq$ GEN(T).
- T' is an **enrichment** of T, if for every algebra A' in GEN(T') the Σ-reduct of A' is in GEN(T).
- T' is an **extension** of T, if every algebra A' from GEN(T') comprises a Σ-subalgebra B from GEN(T).
- T' is an **weak** (resp. **strong**) **representant** of T, if for every algebra A' from GEN(T') there exists a surjective weak (resp. strong) Σ-homomorphism from the Σ-reduct A of A' to some algebra B from GEN(T).
- T' is an **algebraic implementation** of T, if for every algebra A' from GEN(T') with its term-generated Σ-subalgebra A there exists a surjective weak Σ-homomorphism from A to an algebra B from GEN(T).

In order to illustrate these notions we consider a simple definition of finite sets [Broy et al. 86]:

type SSET = (**sort elem**, **funct** (**elem**, **elem**) **bool** .=.: EQUIV(**elem**, =))
    set, ∅, .+., .∈ .:
  based on BOOL,
  sort set,
  set ∅,
  funct (**set**, **elem**) **set** .+.,
  funct (**elem**, **set**) **bool** .∈ .,
  laws set *s*, **elem** *x*, *y*:
    $x \in \varnothing \equiv$ **false**,
    $y \in (s + x) \equiv (x = y) \vee (y \in s)$
endoftype.

An axiomatic enrichment is obtained, if we add an axiom to SSET that does not lead to an inconsistency, for example the axiom that states the commutativity of +:

type COMMSET = (**sort elem**, **funct** (**elem**, **elem**) **bool** .=.:
    EQUIV(**elem**, =))
    set, ∅, .+., .∈ .:
  :

$(s + x) + y \equiv (s + y) + x,$

⋮

endoftype.

An enrichment is obtained by adding additional operations and corresponding axioms which define these new operations in terms of the existing ones. For example, we could enrich SSET to

type ESSET = (**sort elem**, **funct** (**elem**, **elem**) **bool** .=.: EQUIV(**elem**, =))
set, $\emptyset$, .+., .$\in$., .–.:

⋮

funct (**set**, **elem**) **set** .–.,

⋮

$\emptyset - x \equiv \emptyset,$
$(s + x) - y \equiv$ **if** $x = y$ **then** s **else** $(s - y) + x$ **fi**,
$(x \in s) \equiv$ **true** $\Rightarrow s + x \equiv s$
endoftype.

Another example for an enrichment is an implementation of SSET in terms of SEQU (Sect. 3.3.1.3):

type SSETOVERSEQU = (**sort elem**, **funct** (**elem**, **elem**) **bool** .=.:
EQUIV(**elem**, =))
set, $\emptyset$, .+., .$\in$.:
include SEQU(**elem**) **as** (**set**, , , , , *add*),
set $\emptyset$,
funct (**set**, **elem**) **set** .+.,
funct (**elem**, **set**) **bool** .$\in$.,
laws set s, **elem** x:
$\emptyset \equiv <>,$
$s + x \equiv add(s, x),$
$x \in s \equiv$ **if** $s =<>$ **then false else** (**first**$s = x$) $\vee$ ($x \in$ **rest**s) **fi**
endoftype.

SSETOVERSEQU is not an enrichment of COMMSET, since commutativity of "+" does not hold in SSETOVERSEQU. However, it is a strong representant of COMMSET, since there is an obvious congruence relation that identifies sequences which are permutations of each other.

An implementation of ESSET in terms of SEQU is provided by

type ESSETOVERSEQU = (**sort elem**, **funct** (**elem**, **elem**) **bool** .=.:
EQUIV(**elem**, =))
set, $\emptyset$, .+., .$\in$., *delete*:
include SEQU(**elem**) **as** (**set**, , , , , *add*),
set $\emptyset$,
funct (**set**, **elem**) **set** .+.,
funct (**elem**, **set**) **elem** .$\in$.,
funct (**set**, **elem**) **set** *delete*,
laws set s, **elem** x:
$\emptyset \equiv <>,$
$s + x \equiv$ **if** $x \in s$ **then** s **else** $add(s, x)$ **fi**,

$x \in s \equiv$ **if** s =<> **then false else** (**first**$s = x$) $\vee$ ($x \in$ **rest**s) **fi**,
delete$(s, x) \equiv$
if s =<> **then** s
elsf first$s = x$ **then rest**s **else** *add*(*delete*(**rest**s, x), **first**s) **fi**
endoftype.

In this latter type the operation *delete* only fulfils the laws of ESSET if we consider only sequences without multiple occurrences of elements. But it is just these sequences that are generated if we restrict ourselves to the visible constituents as given above. Therefore, ESSETOVERSEQU is an extension of ESSET and thus a correct implementation. Furthermore, obviously, ESSETOVERSEQU is an algebraic implementation of COMMSET.

The various relationships illustrated by the above examples may be graphically sketched as in Fig. 8.1.

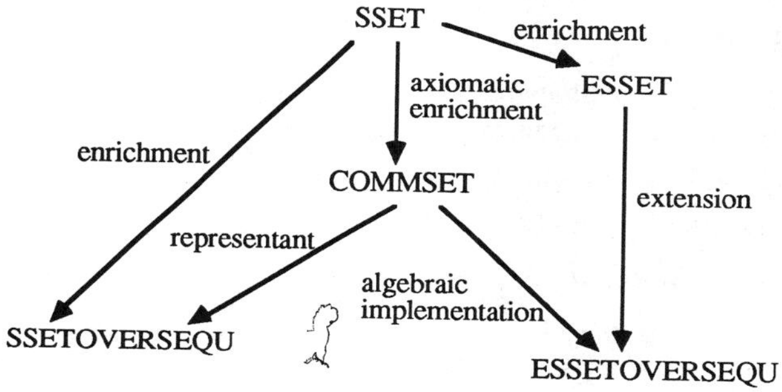

Figure 8.1. Different implementations of SSET

The relations enrichment, extension, and representant formalize the intuitive notions 'enrich', 'forget', 'identify' that were introduced at the beginning of this subsection. The notion of an algebraic implementation is a combination of all these relations. In a simplified view, to say that T' is an algebraic implementation of T, is to say that every model of T' contains a Σ-subalgebra that is equivalent (with respect to its externally observable behavior) to some model of T.

8.1.2 Proving the Correctness of an Algebraic Implementation

In the previous subsection we have introduced relations between types that guarantee the correctness of an implementation. We have illustrated these relations by examples, but without giving an explicit proof. This subsection deals with the problem of how to perform such a proof.

Correctness of an (algebraic) implementation T' = (Σ', E', P) of T = (Σ, E, P) may be proved as follows [Broy 84a]:

First, specify

- a signature morphism $\sigma: \Sigma \rightarrow \Sigma'$;
- a predicate REP to characterize those terms of T' that are used to represent the objects of T; and
- a predicate EQ specifying whether two terms of T' (satisfying REP) represent the same abstract object.

Then T' is a (strongly) correct implementation of T, iff

- the axioms of T can be verified in T', if "$\equiv$" is substituted by EQ, the operations are substituted by their σ-images, and the quantification is restricted to elements y for which REP(y) holds; and
- for every model M' of T' a model M of T exists such that there are two families of mappings
  - the *abstraction functions* $(\text{ABS}_s)_{s \in S}$

    $$\text{ABS}_s\text{: } \sigma(\mathbf{s})^{M'} \rightarrow \mathbf{s}^M$$

    that are partial, surjective and Σ-homomorphic, and
  - the *implementation mappings* $(\text{IMP}_s)_{s \in S}$

    $$\text{IMP}_s\text{: } \mathbf{s}^M \rightarrow \mathcal{P}(\sigma(\mathbf{s})^{M'})$$

    that are total and one-to-many,

  which, for $\mathbf{s} \in S$, fulfil the following properties:

  $\forall\, x \in \mathbf{s}^M, y, y_1, y_2 \in \sigma(\mathbf{s})^{M'}$:

  (1) $(y \in \text{IMP}(x)) \equiv \textbf{true} \Rightarrow \text{ABS}(y) \equiv x$

  (2) $\text{REP}(y) \equiv \textbf{true} \Rightarrow (y \in \text{IMP}(\text{ABS}(y))) \equiv \textbf{true}$

  (3) $(\text{REP}(y_1) \equiv \textbf{true} \wedge \text{REP}(y_2) \equiv \textbf{true} \wedge \text{ABS}(y_1) \equiv \text{ABS}(y_2)) \Rightarrow$
  $\text{EQ}(y_1, y_2) \equiv \textbf{true}$

  (4) $\textbf{defined}(\text{ABS}(y)) \Rightarrow \text{REP}(y) \equiv \textbf{true}.$

Obviously, the proof requires a lot of intuition and enormous effort in the general case. However, the effort can be significantly reduced for particular situations:

- If the implementation mappings are one-to-one, then conditions (1) and (2) trivially simplify to

  $\forall\, x \in \mathbf{s}^M, y \in \sigma(\mathbf{s})^{M'}$:

  (1') $\text{ABS}(\text{IMP}(x)) \equiv x$,

  (2') $\text{REP}(y) \equiv \textbf{true} \Rightarrow y \equiv \text{IMP}(\text{ABS}(y))$;

- If IMP is one-to-one, injective, and Σ-homomorphic, and REP identically **true** on the image of IMP, then the above formulas (1) – (4) are obviously fulfilled for ABS = IMP^{-1} and for EQ being the original equality in T'. Hence it remains to verify the axioms of T in T', i.e. for the respective σ-images.

The proof method given above may be viewed constructively and gives rise to the following

Strategy:

For proving the correctness of an implementation of T in terms of T'

- Enrich T' to T^+ by operations suited for implementing those of T, and define an appropriate signature morphism $\sigma: \Sigma \to \Sigma'$;
- Forget in T^+ those operations that are not needed for the representation, i.e., restrict T^+ to an appropriate subsignature (e.g., by hiding the remaining operations) and characterize by an appropriate predicate REP those terms over T^+ that are used to represent the objects of T;
- Identify, by means of a suitable equality predicate EQ, those terms over T^+ that represent the same object of T;
- Define ABS and IMP and prove that T' is a correct implementation.

We will illustrate this strategy by considering an implementation of priority queues in terms of sequences.

First we have to fix the homomorphism σ. Trivially we can define

$\sigma(\mathbf{pqueue}) = \mathbf{sequ}$,
$\sigma(emptyq) = \langle\rangle$,
$\sigma(isempty) = =\langle\rangle$.

In order to find representations for the remaining functions of PQUEUE we have several possibilities.

An obvious possibility is to define

$\sigma(add) = +$,

enrich SEQU by

funct (**sequ** s: $\neg(s =\langle\rangle)$) **m** m,
funct (**sequ** s: $\neg(s =\langle\rangle)$) **sequ** r,

(which still have to be defined), and choose

$\sigma(min) = m$,
$\sigma(remove) = r$.

Now we have to give appropriate axioms for m and r. Guided by the axioms of PQUEUE we define (for s different from $\langle\rangle$)

$m(x + \langle\rangle) \equiv x$,
$m(x + s) \equiv$ **if** $x \le m(s)$ **then** x **else** $m(s)$ **fi**,

and, similarly,

$r(x + \langle\rangle) \equiv \langle\rangle$,
$r(x + s) \equiv$ **if** $x \le m(s)$ **then** s **else** $x + r(s)$ **fi**.

Then with

$\text{REP}(s) =_{def}$ **true**,

$\text{EQ}(x, y) =_{def} (x =\langle\rangle \wedge y =\langle\rangle) \vee$
$((x \ne\langle\rangle \wedge y \ne\langle\rangle) \,\Delta\, (m(x) = m(y) \wedge \text{EQ}(r(x), r(y))))$,

ABS: $\text{ABS}(\langle\rangle) =_{def} emptyq$,
$\text{ABS}(x + s) =_{def} add(\text{ABS}(s), x)$,

and

IMP: $\text{IMP}(emptyq) =_{\text{def}} \{<>\}$,
$\text{IMP}(add(q, x)) =_{\text{def}} \{x + \text{IMP}(q)\}$,

the proof that the chosen implementation is correct is straightforward (and hence left to the reader).

A different possibility is to aim at an implementation in terms of ordered sequences. To this end we enrich SEQU by

funct (sequ, m) sequ *insert*

(which is still to be defined) and choose

$\sigma(add) = insert$.

This still leaves some freedom for design decisions. Since we have ordered sequences in mind, for *min* we may choose

$\sigma(min) = \textbf{first}$

which in turn means

$\sigma(remove) = \textbf{rest}$.

Now, again, we have to specify *insert* by appropriate axioms. Having again the axioms of PQUEUE in mind, we define (for s different from $<>$)

$insert(<>, x) \equiv x + <>$,
$insert(s, x) \equiv$ **if** $x \leq \textbf{first}s$ **then** $x + s$ **else** $\textbf{first}s + insert(\textbf{rest}s, x)$ **fi**.

Now IMP defined by

$\text{IMP}(emptyq) =_{\text{def}} <>$,
$\text{IMP}(add(q, x)) =_{\text{def}} \{insert(\text{IMP}(q), x)\}$

is one-to-one, injective, and Σ-homomorphic, and

$\text{REP}(s) =_{\text{def}} s =<> \triangledown \textbf{rest}s =<> \triangledown (\textbf{first}s \leq \textbf{first}(\textbf{rest}s) \wedge \text{REP}(\textbf{rest}s))$,

is identically **true** on the image of IMP. Thus, according to the above remark on particular situations, the correctness of our implementation is proved by verifying the axioms of PQUEUE for their σ-images. This, however, is straightforward and left as an exercise to the reader.

In exactly the same way – though technically somewhat more cumbersome – we could deal with implementations of priority queues in terms of other types, say various forms of trees such as heaps, selection trees [Partsch 83], or different forms of balanced trees [Pepper 81].

As indicated above, there are a lot of choices to be made when constructing an implementation according to the strategy above. Depending on the choices the respective implementations will have different characteristics. For example, in the first implementation of priority queues above, addition of elements to the queue is "cheap" and access to the queue is "expensive", whereas in the second implementation it is just the other way around. This raises the obvious question which implementation to choose, which will be dealt with in Sect. 8.3.2.

8.2 Implementation of Types for Specific Environments

So far we considered the problem of implementing a type in terms of another type. Practically, however, any implementation activity will be directed towards implementations in terms of types that characterize an available programming environment. Therefore, in this subsection we will deal with implementations of types in terms of particular types. As examples we will use implementations in terms of computation structures, implementations in terms of modes, implementations in terms of pointers and arrays, and procedural implementations.

8.2.1 Implementations by Computation Structures

According to Sect. 3.3.6, a computation structure consists of mode declarations, object declarations, and explicit function declarations. Since many existing programming languages provide these constructs, computation structures may be viewed as characterizations of particular programming environments.

Any hierarchical computation structure CS (with signature (S, C, F) and primitive type P) where all constituents are determinate can be associated with an algebra as follows [Bauer et al. 87], [Ehler 87]:

For D being a model of P, the **algebra** A(D) **associated** with CS (w.r.t. D) is defined by

$A(D) =_{def} (S^{A(D)}, C^{A(D)}, F^{A(D)})$

where (for all $s \in S$, $f \in F$, $c \in C$, DOM and B defined as in Sect. 4.1)

$\mathbf{s}^{A(D)} =_{def} \mathsf{DOM}_D[\![\mathbf{s}]\!]$;
$f^{A(D)} =_{def}$ h' where $B_D[\![f]\!] = \{h\}$ and $h'(x)$ is undefined, if $h(x) = \bot$ and $h'(x) = h(x)$, otherwise;
$c^{A(D)} =_{def}$ undefined, if $B_D[\![c]\!] = \bot$ and, otherwise, u, if $B_D[\![c]\!] = \{u\}$, $u \neq \bot$;

CS as defined above thus provides a **correct implementation** of a type T = ((S, C, F), E, P), iff for any D a congruence "$\approx$" exists such that the quotient $A(D)/\approx$ is a model of T.

For example, the type SEQU (Sect. 3.3.1) can be equivalently defined (Sect. 3.3.5) by

mode sequ = <> | *add*(**m** *first*, **sequ** *rest*).

Hence, a computation structure that correctly implements SSET (Sect. 8.1.1) is immediately obtained from SSETOVERSEQU:

structure SSETOVERSEQU = (**sort elem**, **funct** (**elem**, **elem**) **bool** .=.:
EQUIV(**elem**, =))
set, ∅, .+., .∈.:
based on BOOL,
mode set = ∅ | *add*(**m** *first*, **sequ** *rest*),
funct .+. = (**set** *s*, **elem** *x*) **set**:
add(*s*, *x*),

```
    funct .∈ . = (elem x, set s) bool:
        if s is ∅ then false else first(s) = x ∨ x ∈ rest(s) fi
  endofstructure.
```

Although by definition the operations in a model of an algebraic type have to be determinate, computation structures with non-determinate operations correspond quite naturally to types where the behavior of certain operations is not completely specified. Of course, this requires us to generalize the notion of a correct implementation: a non-determinate computation structure CS, i.e., a computation structure with non-determinate operations, is a **correct implementation** of some type T, if all determinate descendants of CS, i.e., computation structures which result from CS by substituting determinate descendants for all non-determinate operations, are correct implementations of T.

According to this definition, for example,

```
  structure CSETOVERSEQU = (sort elem, funct (elem, elem) bool .=.:
                             EQUIV(elem, =))
                             set, ∅, .+., .∈ ., .=∅, arb:
    based on BOOL,
    mode set = ∅ | add(m first, sequ rest),
    funct .+. = (set s, elem x) set:
        add(s, x),
    funct .∈ . = (elem x, set s) bool:
        if s =∅ then false else first(s) = x ∨ x ∈ rest(s) fi,
    funct .=∅ = (set s) bool:
        s is ∅,
    funct arb = (set s: ¬(s =∅)) m:
        some m s: x ∈ s
  endofstructure,
```

can be proved to be a correct implementation of

```
  type CSET = (sort elem, funct (elem, elem) bool .=.: EQUIV(elem, =))
               set, ∅, .+., .∈ ., .=∅, arb:
    based on BOOL,
    sort set,
    set ∅,
    funct (set, elem) set .+.,
    funct (elem, set) bool .∈ .,
    funct (elem, set) bool .=∅,
    funct (set s: ¬(s =∅)) m arb,
    laws set s, elem x, y:
        x ∈ ∅ ≡ false,
        y ∈ (s + x) ≡ (x = y) ∨ (y ∈ s),
        ∅ =∅ ≡ true,
        (s + x) =∅ ≡ false,
        arb(s) ∈ s ≡ true provided ¬(s =∅)
  endoftype.
```

For certain restricted algebraic types even transformation rules leading to implementations in terms of computation structures can be given. For details, which go beyond the scope of this treatment, see [Bauer et al. 87], [Ehler 87].

Once a type has been implemented in terms of a computation structure, further development is obvious: for the respective constituents of the computation structure the techniques introduced in the previous chapters can be used.

8.2.2 Implementations in Terms of Modes

So far, we have simply assumed the availability of our implementing type, without bothering where it came from. In the following we will discuss a technique where the implementing type is constructed from the one to be implemented. We will illustrate this technique with our running example PQUEUE and only give hints for the general case.

Our considerations are to be seen within the following

<u>Strategy</u>:
Given some consistent type T,

- Derive a type T' that consists of mode declarations "extracted" from T;
- Construct an implementation of T in terms of T'.

8.2.2.1 Construction of an Implementing Type in Terms of Modes

For dealing with the first part of this strategy we need the notion of a "minimal constructor set" of a type.

Let T = ((S, C, F) $\cup$ Σ_P, E, P) be a hierarchical type, where Σ_P denotes the primitive signature and (S, C, F) the non-primitive signature Σ. A set $C_c \cup F_c$ (where $C_c \subseteq C$, $F_c \subseteq F$) of constants and operations is called a **constructor set** of T, if the constants and operations from $C_c \cup F_c$ suffice to denote all terms from T, that is, if the following property holds:

$$\forall\, t \in W(\Sigma)\colon \exists\, t' \in W((S, C_c, F_c))\colon E \vdash t \equiv t'.$$

The terms from W((S, C_c, F_c)) (i.e., the term algebra over (S, C_c, F_c) as in Sect. 3.3.1.1) are called **constructor terms**.

A constructor set $C_c \cup F_c$ is called **minimal**, if for each constructor set $C_c' \cup F_c'$ with $C_c' \subseteq C_c$, $F_c' \subseteq F_c$ we have $C_c' = C_c$ and $F_c' = F_c$.

A constructor set $C_c \cup F_c$ is furthermore called **free**, if no identities of constructor terms can be deduced from the axioms of the type, i.e., if the following property holds:

$$\neg \exists\, t, t' \in W((S, C_c, F_c))\colon t \neq t' \wedge E \vdash t \equiv t'.$$

Obviously, any free constructor set is also minimal.

For our example PQUEUE, it is obvious that

{*emptyq*, *add*}

is a unique, minimal constructor set that is even free.

The construction of an implementing type PQUEUE' proceeds as follows:

First, we define a new sort

sort pqueue',

and new constructors

pqueue' *emptyq'*,
funct (pqueue', m) pqueue' *add'*

(where renaming is simply to avoid confusion).

Then we introduce for each of the new constructors "identification functions"

funct (pqueue') bool *ise*, and
funct (pqueue') bool *isa*,

characterized by

$ise(emptyq') \equiv$ **true**,	$ise(add'(p, x)) \equiv$ **false**,
$isa(emptyq') \equiv$ **false**,	$isa(add'(p, x)) \equiv$ **true**.

Furthermore, we introduce (partial) "decomposition operations" for each non-constant constructor, for accessing the components of constructor terms. In our case we introduce

funct (pqueue' *p*: *isa*(*p*)) **pqueue'** *da1*, and
funct (pqueue' *p*: *isa*(*p*)) **m** *da2*.

These operations are defined by

$da1(add'(p, x)) \equiv p$, and
$da2(add'(p, x)) \equiv x$.

Altogether we get for our example

```
type PQUEUE' = (sort m, funct (m, m) bool .≤.: LINORD(m, ≤))
               pqueue', emptyq', add', ise, isa, da1, da2:
   based on BOOL,
   sort pqueue',
   pqueue' emptyq',
   funct (pqueue', m) pqueue' add',
   funct (pqueue') bool ise,
   funct (pqueue') bool isa,
   funct (pqueue' p: isa(p)) pqueue' da1,
   funct (pqueue' p: isa(p)) m da2,
   laws pqueue' p, m x:
      ise(emptyq') ≡ true,
      ise(add'(p, x)) ≡ false,
      isa(emptyq') ≡ false,
      isa(add'(p, x)) ≡ true,
      da1(add'(p, x)) ≡ p,
      da2(add'(p, x)) ≡ x
endoftype,
```

which, according to Sect. 3.3.5, can be abbreviated to

mode pqueue' = *emptyq'* | *add'*(**pqueue'** *da1*, **m** *da2*).

Due to the particular form of PQUEUE' we have the obvious additional properties:

(1) $\forall$ **pqueue'** p: $(isa(p) \vee ise(p)) \equiv$ **true**,
(2) $\forall$ **pqueue'** p: $isa(p) \equiv$ **true** $\Rightarrow p \equiv add'(da1(p), da2(p))$,
(3) $\forall$ **pqueue'** p: $ise(p) \equiv$ **true** $\Rightarrow p \equiv emptyq'$.

Furthermore, PQUEUE', as an instance of a direct sum, is monomorphic (by definition, Sect. 3.3.5) and "≡" coincides with the syntactical equality on terms.

Of course, these steps can also be performed in general:
Given a (hierarchical) type $T = ((S, C, F) \cup \Sigma_P, E, P)$ with a minimal constructor set $C_c \cup F_c$, we build up a new (monomorphic) type T' (over the same primitive type P) as follows:

$$T' =_{def} ((S', C_c', F_c' \cup I \cup D) \cup \Sigma_P, E_I \cup E_D, P)$$

where the primes simply indicate an (arbitrary, consistent) renaming,

$$I =_{def} \{\textbf{funct}\ (s')\ \textbf{bool}\ i_c\colon c \in C_c' \cup F_c' \wedge s' \in S'\}$$

is a set of unique 'identification functions' (one for each constructor) defined by the axioms

$$E_I =_{def} \{i_c(c(x_1, ..., x_{nc})) \equiv \textbf{true}\colon\ c \in C_c' \cup F_c'\} \cup$$
$$\{i_c(c'(x_1, ..., x_{nc'})) \equiv \textbf{false}\colon\ c, c' \in C_c' \cup F_c' \wedge c \neq c'\},$$

(where nc, nc' ≥ 1 denote the number of arguments of c and c', resp.), and

$$D =_{def} \{\textbf{funct}\ (s'\ t\colon\ i_c(t))\ \mathbf{m}_{c,i}\ d_{c,i}\colon c \in F_c' \wedge 1 \leq i \leq nc \wedge s' \in S\}$$

a set of (partial) 'decomposition functions' that allow us to regain the respective constituents of a constructor term, and which are defined by

$$E_D =_{def} \{d_{c,i}(c(x_1, ..., x_{nc})) \equiv x_i\colon\ c \in F_c' \wedge 1 \leq i \leq nc\}$$

with $\mathbf{m}_{c,i}$ denoting the kind of the i-th component of the domain of c.

8.2.2.2 Derivation of an Enrichment for Particular Cases

According to the above strategy we now aim at implementing T in terms of T'. Thus, we have to enrich T' by (operational) definitions of new functions that will correspond to those functions of T not yet considered. However, rather than simply giving a definition and then proving the correctness of the implementation, as we did in the previous section, we want to derive the new definitions from the respective old ones, such that the implementation is correct by construction. In addition, we aim at definitions where the new functions are specified for arbitrary arguments (rather than constructor terms), since this allows, in a next step, an immediate transition to computation structures.

According to the remark in Sect. 8.1.2, in order to prove T' a correct implementation of T it suffices to verify the axioms of T for the σ-images in T', provided IMP is one-to-one, Σ-homomorphic, and injective, and REP identically **true** on the image of IMP. Hence we now concentrate on finding suitable IMP and REP and construct the additional axioms in T' from the respective axioms in T such that the axioms of T hold for the σ-images in T' by construction.

For our particular example we define σ simply by adding primes to the respective constituents from PQUEUE. Next we define a one-to-one, Σ-homomorphic, injective implementation function IMP by

$$\text{IMP}(\mathit{emptyq}) =_{\text{def}} \langle\rangle,$$
$$\text{IMP}(\mathit{add}(q, x)) =_{\text{def}} \mathit{add}'(\text{IMP}(q), x),$$

and

$$\text{REP} =_{\text{def}} \mathbf{true}.$$

Determined by σ, the functionalities of *isempty'*, *min'*, and *remove'* are

funct (**pqueue'**) **bool** *isempty'*,
funct (**pqueue'** q: $\neg$*isempty'*(q)) **m** *min'*,
funct (**pqueue'** q: $\neg$*isempty'*(q)) **pqueue'** *remove'*.

For our implementation to be correct, *isempty'* has to be defined in such a way that

$$\mathit{isempty}'(\mathit{emptyq}') \equiv \mathbf{true}, \text{ and}$$
$$\mathit{isempty}'(\mathit{add}'(q, x)) \equiv \mathbf{false}$$

hold. Thus, using the properties (1) - (3) given in the previous subsection, we can derive a definition of *isempty'* as follows:

$\mathit{isempty}'(q)$
  $\equiv$ [property (1)]
$(\mathit{ise}(q) \vee \mathit{isa}(q)) \,\Delta\, \mathit{isempty}'(q)$
  $\equiv$ [distributivity]
$(\mathit{ise}(q) \,\Delta\, \mathit{isempty}'(q)) \vee (\mathit{isa}(q) \,\Delta\, \mathit{isempty}'(q))$
  $\equiv$ [properties (2) and (3)]
$(\mathit{ise}(q) \,\Delta\, \mathit{isempty}'(\mathit{emptyq}')) \vee (\mathit{isa}(q) \,\Delta\, \mathit{isempty}'(\mathit{add}'(\mathit{da1}(q), \mathit{da2}(q))))$
  $\equiv$ [intended properties of *isempty'*]
$(\mathit{ise}(q) \,\Delta\, \mathbf{true}) \vee (\mathit{isa}(q) \,\Delta\, \mathbf{false})$
  $\equiv$ [simplification]
$\mathit{ise}(q)$.

Now, obviously, *isempty'*, defined by

$$\mathit{isempty}'(q) \equiv \mathit{ise}(q),$$

has the desired property.

In order to derive a definition for *min'* we proceed analogously. The property we want to establish for *min'* is

$$\mathit{min}(\mathit{add}(q, x)) \equiv \mathbf{if}\ \mathit{isempty}(q)\ \mathbf{then}\ x\ \mathbf{elsf}\ x \le \mathit{min}(q)\ \mathbf{then}\ x\ \mathbf{else}\ \mathit{min}(q)\ \mathbf{fi}.$$

This allows us to derive a definition of *min'* as follows:

$\neg\, \mathit{isempty}'(q)$
  $\equiv$ [definition of *isempty'*]
$\neg\, \mathit{ise}(q)$
  $\equiv \mathit{isa}(q)$ [property (1)]

and

$isa(q) \equiv \mathbf{true} \Rightarrow$
$\quad min'(q)$
$\qquad \equiv$ [property (2)]
$\quad min'(add'(da1(q), da2(q))$
$\qquad \equiv$ [intended property of *min*]
$\quad$ **if** $isempty'(da1(q))$ **then** $da2(q)$
$\quad$ **elsf** $da2(q) \leq min'(da1(q))$ **then** $da2(q)$ **else** $min'(da1(q))$ **fi.**

Again, *min'*, defined by

$\neg\, isempty'(q) \equiv \mathbf{true} \Rightarrow$
$\quad min'(q) \equiv$ **if** $isempty'(da1(q))$ **then** $da2(q)$
$\qquad\qquad$ **elsf** $da2(q) \leq min'(da1(q))$ **then** $da2(q)$ **else** $min'(da1(q))$ **fi,**

has the desired property.

In an analogous way, we can derive an axiom for *remove'*:

$\neg\, isempty'(q) \equiv \mathbf{true} \Rightarrow$
$\quad remove'(q) \equiv$
$\qquad$ **if** $isempty'(da1(q))$ **then** $emptyq'$
$\qquad$ **elsf** $da2(q) \leq min(da1(q))$ **then** $da1(q)$ **else** $add(remove(da1(q)), da2(q))$ **fi.**

Altogether, we have constructed an extension of PQUEUE', namely the type

type PQUEUE" = (**sort m**, **funct** (**m**, **m**) **bool** .≤.: LINORD(**m**, ≤))
$\qquad\qquad\qquad$ **pqueue**, *emptyq'*, *isempty'*, *add'*, *min'*, *remove'*,
$\qquad\qquad\qquad$ *ise*, *isa*, *da1*, *da2*:
$\quad$ **include** PQUEUE',
$\quad$ **funct** (**pqueue'**) **bool** *isempty'*,
$\quad$ **funct** (**pqueue'** q: $\neg isempty'(q)$) **m** *min'*,
$\quad$ **funct** (**pqueue'** q: $\neg isempty'(q)$) **pqueue'** *remove'*,
$\quad$ **laws pqueue'** q, **m** x:
$\quad isempty'(q) \equiv ise(q)$,
$\quad \neg\, isempty'(q) \equiv \mathbf{true} \Rightarrow$
$\qquad min'(q) \equiv$
$\qquad\quad$ **if** $ise(da1(q))$ **then** $da2(q)$
$\qquad\quad$ **elsf** $da2(q) \leq min'(da1(q))$ **then** $da2(q)$ **else** $min'(da1(q))$ **fi,**
$\quad \neg\, isempty'(q) \equiv \mathbf{true} \Rightarrow$
$\qquad remove'(q) \equiv$
$\qquad\quad$ **if** $ise(da1(q))$ **then** $emptyq'$
$\qquad\quad$ **elsf** $da2(q) \leq min'(da1(q))$ **then** $da1(q)$
$\qquad\qquad$ **else** $add'(remove'(da1(q)), da2(q))$ **fi**
endoftype,

which, by construction, is a correct implementation of PQUEUE.

After unfolding the **include** clause, renaming, and forgetting *ise*, *isa*, *da1*, *da2*, this latter type definition can be straightforwardly transformed into the computation structure

structure PQUEUE = (**sort m**, **funct** (**m**, **m**) **bool** .≤.: LINORD(**m**, ≤))
$\qquad\qquad\qquad$ **pqueue**, *emptyq*, *isempty*, *add*, *min*, *remove*:
$\quad$ **based on** BOOL,
$\quad$ **mode pqueue** = *emptyq* | *add*(**pqueue** *da1*, **m** *da2*),

funct *isempty* = (**pqueue** *q*) **bool**:
q **is** *emptyq*,
funct *min* = (**pqueue** *q*: ¬*isempty*(*q*)) **m**:
if *isempty*(*da1*(*q*)) **then** *da2*(*q*)
elsf *da2*(*q*) ≤ *min*(*da1*(*q*)) **then** *da2*(*q*) **else** *min*(*da1*(*q*)) **fi**,
funct *remove* = (**pqueue** *q*: ¬*isempty*(*q*)) **pqueue**:
if *isempty*(*da1*(*q*)) **then** *emptyq*
elsf *da2*(*q*) ≤ *min*(*da1*(*q*)) **then** *da1*(*q*)
else *add*(*remove*(*da1*(*q*)), *da2*(*q*)) **fi**
endofstructure.

With this particular example we were lucky in two respects. The particular form of the axioms of PQUEUE allowed us to derive the definitions of the non-constructor operations and we had a free constructor set. Both aspects will be further discussed in the sequel.

8.2.2.3 Finding an Enrichment in General

The non-constructor operations in PQUEUE possessed the nice property of being essentially homomorphisms on the term structure, which, in turn, allowed us to derive the respective new axioms from the old ones. However, even if this is not the case, the methodical line illustrated in the example PQUEUE can be followed to find appropriate new axioms for the non-constructor operations. As an example we will deal with the type CLIST from Sect. 3.3.4.3:

type CLIST = (**sort m**) **clist**, *empty*, *isempty*, *insert*, *lmove*, *rmove*, *delete*, *read*:
based on BOOL,
sort clist,
clist *empty*,
funct (**clist**) **bool** *isempty*,
funct (**clist**, **m**) **clist** *insert*,
funct (**clist**) **clist** *lmove*,
funct (**clist**) **clist** *rmove*,
funct (**clist** *c*: ¬*isempty*(*c*)) **clist** *delete*,
funct (**clist** *c*: ¬*isempty*(*c*)) **m** *read*,
laws clist *c*, **m** *x*, *y*:
isempty(*empty*) ≡ **true**,
isempty(*insert*(*c*, *x*)) ≡ **false**,
lmove(*empty*) ≡ *empty*,
lmove(*insert*(*empty*, *x*)) ≡ *insert*(*empty*, *x*),
lmove(*insert*(*insert*(*c*, *x*), *y*)) ≡ *insert*(*lmove*(*insert*(*c*, *y*)), *x*),
rmove(*lmove*(*c*)) ≡ *c*,
delete(*insert*(*c*, *x*)) ≡ *c*,
read(*insert*(*c*, *x*)) ≡ *x*
endoftype.

Obviously,

{*empty*, *insert*}

is a free constructor set for CLIST, and we can use

type CLIST' = (**sort m**) **clist'**, *empty'*, *insert'*, *ise*, *isi*, *l*, *e*:
based on BOOL,
sort clist',
clist' *empty'*,
funct (**clist'**, **m**) **clist'** *insert'*,
funct (**clist'**) **bool** *ise*,
funct (**clist'**) **bool** *isi*,
funct (**clist'** *c*: *isi*(*c*)) **clist'** *l*,
funct (**clist'** *c*: *isi*(*c*)) **m** *e*,
laws clist' *c*, **m** *x*:
$ise(empty') \equiv$ **true**,
$ise(insert'(c, x)) \equiv$ **false**,
$isi(empty') \equiv$ **false**,
$isi(insert'(c, x)) \equiv$ **true**,
$l(insert'(c, x)) \equiv c$,
$e(insert'(c, x)) \equiv x$
endoftype

as a basis for our implementation, which, furthermore, can be abbreviated to

mode clist' = *empty'* | *insert'*(**clist'** *l*, **m** *e*).

Now, derivation of axioms for *isempty'*, *delete'*, and *read'* is trivial. We get (for arbitrary **clist'** *c*)

$isempty'(c) \equiv ise(c)$,
$\neg isempty'(c) \equiv$ **true** $\Rightarrow delete'(c) \equiv l(c)$,
$\neg isempty'(c) \equiv$ **true** $\Rightarrow read'(c) \equiv e(c)$,

With respect to *lmove'* we proceed as in the example PQUEUE:

lmove'(*c*)
≡ [case introduction; simplification]
if *isempty'*(*c*) **then** *lmove'*(*empty'*)
elsf *isempty'*(*l*(*c*)) **then** *lmove'*(*insert'*(*empty'*, *e*(*c*)))
else *lmove'*(*insert'*(*insert'*(*l*(*l*(*c*)), *e*(*l*(*c*)), *e*(*c*))) **fi**
≡ [intended property of *lmove'*; simplification]
if *isempty'*(*c*) **then** *empty'*
elsf *isempty'*(*l*(*c*)) **then** *c*
else *insert'*(*lmove'*(*insert'*(*l*(*l*(*c*)), *e*(*c*))), *e*(*l*(*c*))) **fi**.

However, this does not work as smoothly for *rmove*, since *rmove* is defined implicitly via *lmove* and not as a homomorphism. Therefore, we now have to use the axioms for *lmove* from right to left, in order to get terms of the form *rmove'*(*lmove'*(...)) to which the (intended) axiom for *rmove'*,

$rmove'(lmove'(c)) \equiv c$,

applies:

rmove'(*c*)
≡ [case introduction as in *lmove'*]

if $isempty'(c)$ **then** $rmove'(empty')$
elsf $isempty'(l(c))$ **then** $rmove'(insert'(empty', e(c)))$
  else $rmove'(insert'(l(c), e(c)))$ **fi**
    $\equiv$ [axioms of *lmove'*]
if $isempty'(c)$ **then** $rmove'(lmove'(empty'))$
elsf $isempty'(l(c))$ **then** $rmove'(lmove'(insert'(empty', e(c))))$
  else $rmove'(insert'(l(c), e(c)))$ **fi**
    $\equiv$ [intended property of *rmove'*]
if $isempty'(c)$ **then** $empty'$
elsf $isempty'(l(c))$ **then** c
  else $rmove'(insert'(l(c), e(c)))$ **fi.**

In order to modify the **else** branch, the term *insert'*(...) has to be converted into the form *lmove'*(...) – which is always possible according to the axioms of *lmove'*. To this end we assume new operations

funct (**clist'** c: $\neg isempty'(c)$) **clist'** $r1$,
funct (**clist'** c: $\neg isempty'(c)$) **m** $r2$,

which are (implicitly) specified by

(*) $\neg isempty'(c) \equiv$ **true** $\Rightarrow c \equiv lmove'(insert'(r1(c), r2(c)))$.

Then we can proceed in the **else** branch as follows:

...**else** $rmove'(insert'(l(c), e(c)))$ **fi**
    $\equiv$ [(*)]
...**else** $rmove'(insert'(lmove'(insert'(r1(l(c)), r2(l(c)))), e(c)))$ **fi**
    $\equiv$ [axioms of *lmove'*]
...**else** $rmove'(lmove'(insert'(insert'(r1(l(c)), e(c)), r2(l(c)))))$ **fi**
    $\equiv$ [intended property of *rmove'*]
...**else** $insert'(insert'(r1(l(c)), e(c)), r2(l(c)))$ **fi.**

To find definitions of $r1$, $r2$ we use (*) and again the axioms of *lmove'*. We get eventually:

$r1(c) \equiv$ **if** $isempty'(l(c))$ **then** $empty'$ **else** $insert'(r1(l(c)), e(c))$ **fi**,
$r2(c) \equiv$ **if** $isempty'(l(c))$ **then** $e(c)$ **else** $r2(l(c))$ **fi.**

Thus, finding an appropriate axiom for *rmove'* could be reduced to finding appropriate definitions for $r1$, $r2$ which were already characterized by (*). Proving that $r1$ and $r2$ indeed satisfy (*) is straightforward and left to the reader.

Hence, altogether, we have (after renaming and minor improvements) the following implementation of CLIST:

structure CLIST = (**sort m**) **clist**, *empty*, *isempty*, *insert*, *lmove*, *rmove*,
        delete, *read*:
  based on BOOL,
  mode clist = *empty* | *insert*(**clist** *delete*, **m** *read*),
  funct *isempty* = (**clist** c) **bool**:
    c **is** *empty*,
  funct *lmove* = (**clist** c) **clist**:
    if $isempty(c) \triangledown isempty(delete(c))$ **then** c
      else $insert(lmove(insert(delete(delete(c)), read(c))), read(delete(c)))$ **fi**,

funct *rmove* = (**clist** *c*) **clist**:
  if *isempty*(*c*) ∇ *isempty*(*delete*(*c*)) **then** *c*
    else *insert*(*insert*(*r1*(*delete*(*c*)), *read*(*c*)), *r2*(*delete*(*c*)) **fi fi**,
funct *r1* = (**clist** *c*: ¬*isempty*(*c*)) **clist**:
  if *isempty*(*delete*(*c*)) **then** *empty* **else** *insert*(*r1*(*delete*(*c*)), *read*(*c*)) **fi**,
funct *r2* = (**clist** *c*: ¬*isempty*(*c*)) **clist**:
  if *isempty*(*delete*(*c*)) **then** *read*(*c*) **else** *r2*(*delete*(*c*)) **fi**
endofstructure.

8.2.2.4 Enrichment in Case of an Unfree Minimal Constructor Set

Since PQUEUE had a free constructor set, finding a one-to-one, Σ-homomorphic injective implementation function IMP and a predicate REP which is identically **true** on the image of IMP was particularly simple. For types T which do not have a free constructor set basically the same approach can be used:

- In a first step we construct our implementing type T' as before.
- Identities between constructor terms intuitively mean that (syntactically) different terms represent the same abstract object. Hence, when looking for an appropriate extension of T', we first have to define new constructors for T' that fulfil those axioms in T which identify constructor terms, in order to be able to give an injective, Σ-homomorphic implementation function.
- Having introduced these new constructors, those (non-constructor) operations of T that are not yet considered can be treated as before, but using the new constructors instead of the old ones.

In order to demonstrate these ideas with an example, we assume a definition of PQUEUE that has the additional axiom

$add(add(q, x), x) \equiv add(q, x)$.

First, we define PQUEUE' as before. Then we define

$\mathrm{IMP}(emptyq) =_{\mathrm{def}} \langle\rangle$,
$\mathrm{IMP}(add(q, x)) =_{\mathrm{def}} add''(\mathrm{IMP}(q), x)$,

and

$\mathrm{REP} =_{\mathrm{def}}$ **true**,

where *add''* is to fulfil the property

(*) $add''(add''(q, x), x) \equiv add''(q, x)$.

By intuition we may come up with

(**) $add''(q, x) \equiv$ **if** $isin(x, q)$ **then** q **else** $add'(q, x)$ **fi**

where

funct (m, pqueue) bool *isin*

is defined by

$isin(x, emptyq') \equiv$ **false**,
$isin(x, add'(q, y)) \equiv (x = y) \vee isin(x, q)$.

Proving that *add''* as defined by (**) fulfils the property (*) is straightforward and left to the interested reader.

As before, we now have to derive definitions for the functions implementing *min* and *delete*, respectively. This can be done as before and leads (after renaming) to the computation structure

structure PQUEUE = (**sort m**, **funct** (**m**, **m**) **bool** .≤.: LINORD(**m**, ≤))
pqueue, *emptyq*, *isempty*, *add'*, *min*, *remove*:
  based on BOOL,
  mode pqueue = *emptyq* | *add*(**pqueue** *da1*, **m** *da2*),
  funct *add'* = (**pqueue** *q*, **m** *x*) **pqueue**:
    if *isin*(*x*, *q*) **then** *q* **else** *add*(*q*, *x*) **fi**,
  funct *isempty* = (**pqueue** *q*) **bool**:
    q **is** *emptyq*,
  funct *min* = (**pqueue** *q*: ¬*isempty*(*q*)) **m**:
    if *isempty*(*da1*(*q*)) **then** *da2*(*q*)
    elsf *da2*(*q*) ≤ *min*(*da1*(*q*)) **then** *da2*(*q*) **else** *min*(*da1*(*q*)) **fi**,
  funct *remove* = (**pqueue** *q*: ¬*isempty*(*q*)) **pqueue**:
    if *isempty*(*da1*(*q*)) **then** *emptyq*
    elsf *da2*(*q*) ≤ *min*(*da1*(*q*)) **then** *da1*(*q*)
    else *add*(*remove*(*da1*(*q*)), *da2*(*q*)) **fi**
endofstructure.

8.2.3 Implementations in Terms of Pointers and Arrays

Frequently, available programming environments allow efficient implementations of data structures in terms of pointers and arrays.

Pointers are names used for identifying objects. However, in contrast to identifiers in a program text, they may be manipulated by the program; in particular, they may be compared. The association of pointers with objects is recorded in a 'plexus' similar to the collection of pointers in PASCAL. Intuitively, a plexus is a finite mapping. But in contrast with the type MAP (Sect. 3.3.2), the index set of a plexus is anonymous and not freely accessible. Therefore, pointers and plexuses are defined simultaneously by the following type scheme [Bauer et al. 85]:

type PLEX = (**sort m**) **pt**, **plex**, *nil*, .≡., *emptyplex*, *new*, *updatable*, *pt*, *isdef*, *deref*, *update*:
  based on BOOL,
  sort pt, **sort plex**,
  pt *nil*,
  funct (**pt**, **pt**) **bool** .≡.,
  plex *emptyplex*,
  funct (**plex**) **plex** *new*,
  funct (**pt**, **plex**) **bool** *updatable*,
  funct (**plex**) **pt** *pt*,
  funct (**pt**, **plex**) **bool** *isdef*,
  funct (**pt** *p*, **plex** *q*: *isdef*(*p*, *q*)) **m** *deref*,

```
    funct (pt p, m x, plex q: updatable(p, q)) plex update,
    laws pt p, p', plex q, q', m x:
      nil ≅ nil ≡ true,
      nil ≅ pt(new(q)) ≡ false,
      pt(new(q)) ≅ nil ≡ false,
      pt(new(q)) ≅ pt(new(q')) ≡ pt(q) ≅ pt(q'),
      pt(emptyplex) ≡ nil,
      pt(update(p, x, q)) ≡ pt(q) provided updatable(p, q),
      isdef(p, emptyplex) ≡ false,
      isdef(p, new(q)) ≡ isdef(p, q),
      isdef(p, update(p', x, q)) ≡ (p ≅ p' ∇ isdef(p, q)) provided updatable(p', q),
      updatable(p, emptyplex) ≡ false,
      updatable(nil, q) ≡ false,
      updatable(p, new(q)) ≡ updatable(p, q) ∨ p ≅ pt(new(q)),
      updatable(p, update(p',x, q)) ≡ updatable(p, q) provided updatable(p', q),
      deref(p, new(q)) ≡ deref(p, q),
      deref(p, update(p', x, q)) ≡ if p ≅ p' then x else deref(p, q) fi
         provided updatable(p', q)
  endoftype.
```

The intuition behind the operations is as follows:

- .≅. is the equality test for pointers;
- *nil* is a "pseudo-pointer" which may never be associated with an object;
- *emptyplex* is a plexus containing only *nil*;
- *new* (applied to a plexus) generates a new pointer;
- *pt* allows retrieval of a pointer generated by *new*;
- *updatable* asks whether a pointer has already been generated (and thus can be associated with an object);
- *update* is used for associating a pointer with an object;
- *isdef* allows asking whether a pointer is associated with an object;
- for a pointer associated with an object, *deref* gives the corresponding object;

As an example for the use of PLEX, we consider an implementation of SEQU by a one-way linked list:

```
  structure ONE-WAY-LINKED-LIST = (sort m)
                                   sequ, <>, .=<>, .≠<>, first., rest., .+.:
    based on BOOL,
    mode sequel = c(m info, ptsequ next),
    include PLEX(sequel) as (ptsequ, sequplex, ...),
    mode sequ = p(sequplex list, ptsequ top),
    sequ <> = p(emptyplex, nil),
    funct .=<> = (sequ s) bool:
      top(s) ≅ nil,
    funct .≠<> = (sequ s) bool:
      ¬(s =<>),
    funct first. = (sequ s: s ≠<>) m:
      info(deref(top(s), list(s))),
```

funct rest. = (**sequ** *s*: $s \neq$<>) **sequ**:
  p(*list*(*s*), *next*(*deref*(*top*(*s*), *list*(*s*))),
funct .+. = (**m** *x*, **sequ** *s*) **sequ**:
  begin sequel *sx* = *c*(*x*, *top*(*s*));
    sequplex *sp* = *new*(*list*(*s*));
    ptsequ *ps* = *pt*(*sp*);
    p(*update*(*ps*, *sx*, *sp*), *ps*) **end**
endofstructure.

In a similar way, of course, other well-known pointer implementations of sequences, for example by means of doubly linked lists (Ex. 8-8), can be given.

For proving the correctness of an implementation in terms of pointers the techniques introduced in Sect. 8.1 have to be used.

Implementations in terms of pointers are particularly suited for types that result from using the technique from Sect. 8.2.2, that is, types defined in terms of (recursive) modes.

Methodically, the transition from a recursive mode declaration to an implementation in terms of pointers proceeds as follows:

For simplicity, assume a mode declaration such as

mode m = $c \mid c_1(\mathbf{m}_1\ s_1) \mid c_2(\mathbf{m}\ s_{21}, \mathbf{m}_2\ s_{22})$

where c is a constant and $\mathbf{m}_1$ and $\mathbf{m}_2$ are primitive kinds. Then within an implementation by means of pointers simply use

mode mel = $c_1'(\mathbf{m}_1\ s_1') \mid c_2'(\mathbf{ptm}\ s_{21}', \mathbf{m}_2\ s_{22}')$;
include PLEX(**mel**) **as** (**ptm**, **mplex**, ...);
mode m = *p*(**mplex** *pl*, **ptm** *obj*);
m *c* = (*emptyplex*, *nil*);
funct s_1 = (**m** *m*: $\neg$(*obj*(*m*) $\equiv$ *nil*) Δ *deref*(*obj*(*m*), *pl*(*m*)) **is** c_1') $\mathbf{m}_1$:
  s_1'(*deref*(*obj*(*m*), *pl*(*m*))),
funct s_{21} = (**m** *m*: $\neg$(*obj*(*m*) $\equiv$ *nil*) Δ *deref*(*obj*(*m*), *pl*(*m*)) **is** c_2') **m**:
  s_{21}'(*deref*(*obj*(*m*), *pl*(*m*))),
funct s_{22} = (**m** *m*: $\neg$(*obj*(*m*) $\equiv$ *nil*) Δ *deref*(*obj*(*m*), *pl*(*m*)) **is** c_2') $\mathbf{m}_2$:
  s_{22}'(*deref*(*obj*(*m*), *pl*(*m*))),
funct c_1 = ($\mathbf{m}_1$ *x*) **m**:
  begin mplex *mp* = *new*(*emptyplex*);
    ptm *pm* = *pt*(*mp*);
    p(*update*(*pm*, c_1'(*x*), *mp*), *pm*) **end**,
funct c_2 = (**m** *m*, $\mathbf{m}_2$ *x*) **m**:
  begin mel *mx* = c_2'(*obj*(*m*), *x*);
    mplex *mp* = *new*(*obj*(*m*));
    ptm *pm* = *pt*(*mp*);
    p(*update*(*pm*, *mx*, *mp*), *pm*) **end**.

Typical examples are an implementation of priority queues by means of one-way linked lists or an implementation of circular lists by doubly linked lists.

Like pointers, also arrays as known from existing programming languages can be defined by corresponding type schemes [Bauer et al. 85]:

```
type ARRAY = (sort m) array, vac, put, get, hib, lob, isacc:
   based on BOOL, INT,
   sort array,
   funct (nat, nat) array vac,
   funct (array a, nat i, m x: lob(a) ≤ i ≤ hib(a)) array put,
   funct (array a, nat i: lob(a) ≤ i ≤ hib(a)) bool isacc,
   funct (array a, nat i: isacc(a, i)) m get,
   funct (array) nat lob,
   funct (array) nat hib,
   laws array a, nat i, j, m, n, m x: lob(a) ≤ i ≤ hib(a):
      lob(vac(m, n)) ≡ m,
      hib(vac(m, n)) ≡ n,
      lob(put(a, i, x)) ≡ lob(a),
      hib(put(a, i, x)) ≡ hib(a),
      isacc(put(a, i, x), j) ≡ if j ≡ i then true else isacc(a, j) fi,
      isacc(vac(m, n), i) ≡ false,
      get(put(a, i, x), j) ≡ if j ≡ i  then x
                                       else get(a, j) fi provided isacc(put(a, i, x), j)
endoftype.
```

Arrays can be used for an implementation of bounded stacks in the following way:

```
structure BOUNDED-STACK = (sort m, nat max)
                                   stack, <>, isempty, isfull, top., pop., .push.:
   based on BOOL, NAT,
   include ARRAY(m) as (stackrep, ...),
   mode stack = p(stackrep a, nat top: lob(a)–1 ≤ a ≤ hib(a)),
   stack <> = p(vac(1, max), 0),
   funct isempty = (stack s) bool:
      top(s) = 0,
   funct isfull = (stack s) bool:
      top(s) = max,
   funct top. = (stack s: ¬isempty(s)) m:
      get(a(s), top(s)),
   funct pop. = (stack s: ¬isempty(s)) stack:
      p(a(s), top(s) – 1),
   funct .+. = (stack s, m x: ¬isfull(s)) stack:
      p(put(a(s), top(s) + 1, x), top(s) + 1)
endofstructure.
```

Again, correctness has to be proved using the techniques introduced in Sect. 8.1.

8.2.4 Procedural Implementations

In the previous subsection we introduced algebraic types that characterize pointers and arrays. However, we have not yet taken into account that these concepts usually are used in many existing programming languages, within an imperative style of programming that allows assignments, selective updating and the like. In Sect. 7.2.4

we introduced procedures as a concept of the procedural level that corresponds to functions. Allowing procedures within implementations of algebraic types straightforwardly leads to the concepts of module and device.

Modules are similar to computation structures except that they may also export procedures, whereas the visible constituents of computation structures must be purely applicative. Thus modules provide a step on the way from applicative to procedural formulations [Laut 80].

The declaration of a module takes the form

module M = («parameters») «constituents»:
  $D_1, \ldots, D_k$
endofmodule,

where the D_i denote

- declarations of modes, constants, functions, and procedures, or
- instantiations of types, structures, modules, and devices.

Suppressed variable parameters are not allowed for the functions and procedures of a module. Thus, modules are still referentially transparent.

In analogy to computation structures, instantiation and constituent renaming of a (parametrized) module M are written as

module («constituents») = M(«arguments»).

Like procedures (Sect. 7.2.4), modules do not have an independent semantics. Rather, a module instantiation is equivalent to unfolding the body with appropriate parameter substitution and renaming. Then the definitional transformation rules for procedures (Sect. 7.2.4) take over.

An example for a module for arrays is

module MARRAY = (**sort m**) **array**, *vac*, .[.]:=., .[.], *hib*, *lob*, *isacc*:
  based on BOOL, INT,
  based on (**array**, *vac*, *put*, .[.], *hib*, *lob*, *isacc*) = ARRAY(**m**),
  proc .[.]:=. = (**var array** *a*, **nat** *i*, **m** *x*: $lob(a) \le i \le hib(a)$):
    $a := put(a, i, x)$
endofmodule.

Devices couple the concepts of modules and variables. Their declaration takes the form

device D = («parameters») «constituents»:
  $SD_1; \ldots; SD_k$
endofdevice

where each of the SD_i is

- a collection of declarations of modes, constants, functions, or procedures, separated by commas,
- an initialized variable declaration,
- a statement, or
- an instantiation of a type, structure, module, or device.

Thus, besides the constituents of a module, devices may additionally contain variable declarations as well as statements that are global for the entire device.

However, the variables are hidden, i.e, they may not occur in the list of constituents. In this way they can only be accessed using the functions and procedures of the module and cannot be manipulated wildly. The statement part (if any) provides an initialization for the hidden variables.

Devices may contain instantiations of types, structures, modules, and other devices; however, they may not be based on each other cyclically. The instantiation of a (parametrized) device D may occur at any place where a statement may occur. It is denoted by

device («constituents») = D(«arguments»)

and is again explained by textual substitution of the body of D (after appropriate renaming) for the instantiation. In particular, the statement part is executed upon instantiation. The context condition for the instantiation requires that the phrases which result from the unfolding are context-correct again.

An example for a device for pointers and plexuses [Bauer et al. 85] is:

device PT = (**sort m**) **pt**, *nil*, .≡., *pnew*, *pupdatable*, *pisdef*, *pderef*, *pupdate*:
  based on PLEX(**m**);
  var plex *q* := *emptyplex*;
  proc *pnew* = (**var pt** *p*):
    begin *q* := *new*(*q*); *p* := *pt*(*q*) **end**,
  funct *pisdef* = (**pt** *p*) **bool**:
    isdef(*p*, *q*),
  funct *pderef* = (**pt** *p*, **plex** *q*: *pisdef*(*p*)) **m**:
    deref(*p*, *q*),
  funct *pupdatable* = (**pt** *p*) **bool**:
    updatable(*p*, *q*),
  proc *pupdate* = (**pt** *p*, **m** *x*: *pupdatable*(*p*)):
    q := *update*(*p*, *x*, *q*)
endofdevice.

Note that PT hides the sort **plex** as well as its variable *q*. Upon instantiation of PT the initializing assignment *q* := *emptyplex* is performed. Afterwards the hidden plex *q* can only be changed by the procedures *pnew* and *pupdate*. Thus, PT obviously models the operations on pointers as they are available in, say, PASCAL.

8.3 Libraries of Implementations

Rather than always starting from scratch with respect to the development of data structures, it seems reasonable to have available libraries of implementations – at least for the basic data types such as sets, sequences, bags, maps, and trees. As a running example in the sequel we will use (finite) sets. Our considerations will be restricted to implementations in terms of other types. Further implementations, for example by computation structures, modules, or devices, can be obtained using the techniques introduced in the previous section.

8.3.1 "Ready-Made" Implementations

As an example of a whole collection of different implementations for a particular type, we consider, in the sequel, a variety of (correct) implementations for sets in terms of other data types. The correctness of these implementations can be proved using the technique from Sect. 8.1.1.

If the parameter sort of SET is known to be finite (and not too big), an implementation by bitvectors is straightforward. Bitvectors over a (finite) object set **m** can be simply defined by

type BITVECTOR = (**sort m**, **funct** (**m**, **m**) **bool** .=.: **include** EQUIV(**m**, =))
bitvector, *init*, *put*, *get*:
based on BOOL,
include TMAP(**m**, **bool**, =) **as** (**bitvector**, *init*, *put*, *get*)
endoftype,

that is, by finite mappings where each index is initially associated with a particular value (Sect. 3.3.2).

An implementation for SET is then immediately obtained by enrichment:

type SETOVERBV = (**sort m**, **funct** (**m**, **m**) **bool** .=.: **include** EQUIV(**m**, =))
set, ∅, .+., .∈ ., .∉ ., .−.:
include BITVECTOR(**m**) **as** (**set**, ...),
set ∅,
funct (**set**, **m**) **set** .+.,
funct (**m**, **set**) **bool** .∈ .,
funct (**m**, **set**) **bool** .∉ .,
funct (**set**, **m**) **set** .−.,
laws set *s*, **m** *x*:
$\varnothing \equiv init(\mathbf{false})$,
$s + x \equiv put(s, x, \mathbf{true})$,
$x \in s \equiv get(s, x)$,
$x \notin s \equiv \neg get(s, x)$,
$s - x \equiv put(s, x, \mathbf{false})$
endoftype.

A corresponding procedural implementation for SET using a module for bitvectors is obvious and left as an exercise to the interested reader.

If the argument type of SET is not finite, a straightforward implementation for SET is provided by sequences (Sect. 8.1.1.1). To allow for a broader variety of implementations, rather than just using the type SET from Sect. 3.3.2, we will deal with the following extension (which is different from the one in Sect. 3.3.3):

type ESET' = (**sort m**, **funct** (**m**, **m**) **bool** .=., **funct** (**m**, **m**) **bool** .≤.:
include EQUIV(**m**, =) ∧ **include** LINORD(**m**, ≤))
set, ∅, .+., .∈ ., .∉ ., .−., .=∅, ≠∅, .∪., .∩., *min*, *max*:
based on SET(**m**),
funct (**set**) **bool** .=∅,
funct (**set**) **bool** .≠∅,
funct (**set**, **set**) **set** .∪.,

funct (**set**, **set**) **set** $.\cap.$,
funct (**set** s: $s \neq\emptyset$) **m** min,
funct (**set** s: $s \neq\emptyset$) **m** max,
laws set s, t, **m** x:
$\emptyset =\emptyset \equiv$ **true**,
$(s + x) =\emptyset \equiv$ **false**,
$s \neq\emptyset \equiv \neg(s =\emptyset)$,
$s \cup \emptyset \equiv s$,
$s \cup (t + x) \equiv (s + x) \cup t$,
$s \cap \emptyset \equiv \emptyset$,
$s \cap (t + x) \equiv$ **if** $x \in s$ **then** $(s \cap t) + x$ **else** $s \cap t$ **fi**,
$min(\emptyset + x) \equiv x$,
$max(\emptyset + x) \equiv x$,
$min(s + x) \equiv$ **if** $x \leq min(s)$ **then** x **else** $min(s)$ **fi** **provided** $s \neq\emptyset$,
$max(s + x) \equiv$ **if** $x \geq max(s)$ **then** x **else** $max(s)$ **fi** **provided** $s \neq\emptyset$
endoftype.

The operations defined by the extension are

- $.=\emptyset$, $.\neq\emptyset$, comparison with the empty set;
- $.\cup.$, set union;
- $.\cap.$, set intersection;
- *min* (*max*), the minimum (maximum) of a non-empty set.

Along the lines indicated in Sect. 8.1.1.3, a straightforward implementation of ESET' in terms of ESEQU is provided by

type SETOVERSEQU =
(**sort m**, **funct** (**m**, **m**) **bool** $.=.$, **funct** (**m**, **m**) **bool** $.\leq.$:
include EQUIV(**m**, =) $\wedge$ **include** LINORD(**m**, $\leq$))
set, $\emptyset$, $.+.$, $.\in.$, $.\notin.$, $.-.$, $.=\emptyset$, $\neq\emptyset$, $.\cup.$, $.\cap.$, min, max:
include ESEQU(**m**) **as** (**set**, , , , , , *add*, , , , *conc*, , ,),
set $\emptyset$,
funct (**set**, **m**) **set** $.+.$,
funct (**m**, **set**) **bool** $.\in.$,
funct (**m**, **set**) **bool** $.\notin.$,
funct (**set**, **m**) **set** $.-.$,
funct (**set**) **bool** $.=\emptyset$,
funct (**set**) **bool** $.\neq\emptyset$,
funct (**set**, **set**) **set** $.\cup.$,
funct (**set**, **set**) **set** $.\cap.$,
funct (**set** s: $s \neq\emptyset$) **m** min,
funct (**set** s: $s \neq\emptyset$) **m** max,
laws set s, t, **m** x:
$\emptyset \equiv$ <>,
$s + x \equiv add(x, s)$,
$x \in s \equiv$ **if** $s =$<> **then false else first**$s = x \vee x \in$ **rest**s **fi**,
$x \notin s \equiv \neg\, x \in s$,
$s - x \equiv$ **if** $s =$<> **then** s
elsf first$s \neq x$ **then** $add($**first**s, **rest**$s - x)$ **else rest**$s - x$ **fi**,

```
    s =∅ ≡ s =<>,
    s ≠∅ ≡ s ≠<>,
    s ∪ t ≡ conc(s, t),
    s ∩ t ≡ if t =<> then ∅
              elsf firstt ∈ s then add(firstt, s ∩ restt) else s ∩ restt fi,
    min(∅ + x) ≡ x,
    max(∅ + x) ≡ x,
    min(s + x) ≡ if x ≤ min(s) then x else min(s) fi  provided s ≠∅,
    max(s + x) ≡ if x ≥ max(s) then x else max(s) fi  provided s ≠∅
endoftype.
```

A slightly different implementation results by using sequences without multiple occurrences of elements (where the parts indicated by dots are the same as in SETOVERSEQU):

```
type SETOVERSSEQU =
            (sort m, funct (m, m) bool .=., funct (m, m) bool .≤.:
            include EQUIV(m, =) ∧ include LINORD(m, ≤))
            set, ∅, .+., .∈ ., .∉ ., .−., .=∅, ≠∅, .∪., .∩., min, max:
  include SEQU(m) as (set, , , , , , add),
      ⋮
    s + x ≡ if x ∉ s then add(x, s) else s fi,
      ⋮
    s − x ≡ if s =<> then s
              elsf firsts ≠ x then add(firsts, rests − x) else rests fi,
      ⋮
    s ∪ t ≡ if t =<> then s
              elsf firstt ∈ s then s ∪ restt else add(firstt, s) ∪ restt fi,
      ⋮
endoftype.
```

Yet another implementation is obtained if ordered sequences (without multiple occurrences of elements) are used (where again the parts indicated by dots are the same as in SETOVERSEQU):

```
type SETOVEROSEQU =
            (sort m, funct (m, m) bool .=., funct (m, m) bool .≤.:
            include EQUIV(m, =) ∧ include LINORD(m, ≤))
            set, ∅, .+., .∈ ., .∉ ., .−., .=∅, ≠∅, .∪., .∩., min, max:
  include SEQU(m) as (set, , , , , , add),
      ⋮
  funct (set, m) set insert,
  laws set s, t, m x:
      ⋮
    s + x ≡ if x ∉ s then insert(s, x) else s fi,
    insert(s, x) ≡ if s =<> ∇ firsts ≥ x then add(x, s)
                      else add(firsts, insert(rests, x)) fi,
      ⋮
    s − x ≡ if s =<> then s
              elsf firsts < x then add(firsts, rests − x) else rests fi,
```

$\vdots$

$s \cup t \equiv$ **if** $t = <>$ **then** s
elsf first$t \in s$ **then** $s \cup$ **rest**t **else** add(**first**t, s) $\cup$ **rest**t **fi**,

$\vdots$

$min(s) \equiv$ **first**s **provided** $s \neq \emptyset$,
$max(s) \equiv$ **last**s **provided** $s \neq \emptyset$
endoftype.

We have given above several implementations for finite sets in terms of abstract types. Of course, the underlying idea of having libraries of ready-made implementations is not restricted to types, but applies equally well to computation structures, or even modules and devices. One even could imagine coexisting implementations of a type on different levels of formulation.

8.3.2 Complexity and Efficiency

In the previous subsection we introduced libraries of implementations as a way of providing a variety of ready-made implementations for particular basic data types to the average user. Of course, for practical use it is important not only to have such libraries, but also to know when one implementation is preferable to another, since, as with the development of control structures, the development of data structures not only aims at finding an arbitrary implementation, but usually focuses on finding an efficient one. Being a little more precise with respect to efficiency, however, requires some discussion on complexity.

As an example we consider the function (Sect. 6.5.1)

funct $sort$ = (**natsequ** s) **natsequ**:
$sort'(<>, s)$ **where**

funct $sort'$ = (**natsequ** r, **natsequ** s) **natsequ**:
if $s = <>$ **then** r **else** $sort'(r+min(s), s - min(s))$ **fi**.

If we assume the basic operations

$r + min(s)$ and $s - min(s)$

to be of constant complexity, then the (relative) complexity of $sort'$ is obviously linear in the length of s. In order to deal with the total complexity, however, we also have to take into consideration the complexities of the respective basic operations.

If we assume some of the standard implementations of sequences (as discussed in the previous sections) both the operations min and "–" will turn out to be of linear complexity themselves, such that the total complexity of $sort'$ is quadratic in the length of s.

Thinking about possible improvements on this result, we will realize that, without changing the algorithm, the relative complexity cannot be improved (as each element of the sequence has to be inspected at least once). Thus improvement in the overall complexity can be achieved only, if we find a more efficient implementation of sequences – more efficient in the sense that min and "–" have a complexity less than linear in this specific implementation.

In fact, it is known that there exists such an implementation, namely the implementation of a sequence by means of a heap. A **heap** is a balanced binary tree where the value of the root is the minimum of all values in the corresponding subtrees. For example, the sequence

$<5, 3, 1, 4, 7, 2, 9>$

might be represented (not uniquely!) by the heap

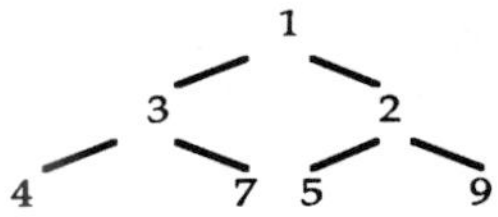

A heap, in turn, can be implemented by indexed sequences (or arrays) where

- the root of the heap is selected by index 1 and
- the direct successors of a node with index i are selected by the indexes $2i$ and $2i+1$, respectively.

Thus, our sample sequence from above would be represented by the indexed sequence

$<1, 3, 2, 4, 7, 5, 9>$.

Both, construction of a heap from the original sequence s and modification (selection and deletion of the minimum element such that the result is again a heap) can be done with logarithmic complexity in the length of s [Aho et al. 75] such that the total complexity of *sort'* now reduces to $O(n \log n)$ with $n = |s|$.

In the example *sort'* above, we found the particular case that an implementation of sequences by heaps reduced the complexities of both, *min* and "–". In general, however, there will be conflicting interests. This becomes obvious in Fig. 8.2 where we consider various possibilities for implementing finite sets over a given set S (where $m = |M|$, $n = |N|$, $s = |S|$) and the respective complexities of some of the basic operations for finite sets.

	M=∅	x∈M	M+x	M−x	M∪N	M∩N	*min* M	*max* M
bitvector	O(s)	const	const	const	O(s)	O(s)	O(s)	O(s)
sequence	const	>O(m)	const	>O(n)	const	>O(m∗n)	>O(n)	>O(n)
sequence without duplication	const	O(m)	O(m)	O(m)	O(m∗n)	O(m∗n)	O(m)	O(m)
ordered sequence	const	O(m)	O(m)	O(m)	O(m+n)	O(m+n)	const	const
heap	const	O(logm)	O(logm)	O(logm)	O(nlogm)	O(nlogm)	const	O(logm)

Figure 8.2. Various possibilities for implementing finite sets

Here, as in many other cases, there is an obvious trade-off between construction and access operations: if construction of a complex object is cheap, then usually access to its constituents is expensive, and vice versa. This phenomenon already appeared in Sect. 8.1.2 where we gave two different implementations for priority queues, which clearly illustrated this trade-off.

Of course, for any implementation in a library of implementations, efficiency information as above can be given. But even if this information is available, it is still a problem to make a good choice of an appropriate implementation, since the usage of a data type and its operations within an algorithm have to be analyzed. In order to find a good implementation, one has to

- analyze the relative frequencies of the basic operations; and
- choose that implementation which minimizes the complexity, depending on the relative frequencies of the occurring basic operations.

Even this strategy may not be able to find the implementation tailored to a certain situation. One could, for example, have fast responses if one is prepared to spend extra time on initialization.

There are a few ideas for extraction of efficiency information for data structure selection from a given algorithm by formal means [Wegbreit 75], [Kant 77], [Schonberg et al. 81], [Zimmermann 88]. These approaches aim at support in making a decision in favour of a particular implementation. In general, this certainly non-trivial task is still a topic of current research.

8.4 Transformation of Type Systems

In connection with the development or the tuning of a formal specification that involves algebraic types there are certain modifications which in general do not fit the requirements of a correct transformation (neither in the sense of Chap. 4 nor in the extended sense as introduced in the beginning of this chapter). Yet these modifications are interesting, in particular since under further assumptions they may be considered correct transformations.

In most cases these modifications do not consider a single type, but rather a whole system of types or at least part of such a system. This situation is comparable to the situation on the control structure side where we also had transformations concerning an individual function as well as transformations concerning a whole system of functions.

Simple examples of this class of modifications are

- restructuring of a type system by decomposition,
- change of the parametrization of operations from certain types of a system,
- partial instantiation of (primitive) types,
- addition/deletion of operations.

As a representative of this class of modifications we will deal with the technique of tuning algebraic types by *type merging* [Laut, Partsch 82]. This modification in general results in a type that admits more models – remember that an algebraic implementation will have less models than the original type – and thus is not a correct transformation. However, it is an interesting technique for the development of specifications where maximal generality is a desirable criterion in order to leave as much freedom as possible for later implementations. In addition, under certain (technical) restrictions type merging will even be a correct transformation.

Hierarchical types as introduced in Chap. 3 allow a comprehensible and well-structured specification even of relatively large, complex problems. In such a specification it frequently happens that a type T is hierarchically based on another type P which is only introduced for the sake of a more transparent specification. Such a situation will in particular occur if predefined type schemes are used for constructing new types adapted to specific requirements.

This particular situation with respect to data types is comparable with a problem specification (using the constructs from Sect. 3.4) that introduces auxiliary operations which are to be removed during the development process.

As an example consider a situation where a computation structure is involved that may be informally characterized as "an array of priority queues". Such a structure for instance seems appropriate for all kinds of problems where a finite number of (ordered) streams has to be merged. In this structure one is not directly interested in the array nor the priority queues themselves, but only in the observable behavior of the whole structure (considered as a 'black box'). This means, in particular, that neither the operations for arrays nor the operations for priority queues are needed in full generality. For example, instead of having access to a whole priority queue associated with a particular index, it is sufficient to have access to the minimum of the respective queue.

A typical specification for such an array of priority queues could be:

type PQARRAY = (**sort m**, **funct (m, m) bool** .≤.: LINORD(**m**, ≤))
  array, *init*, *put*, *get*, *hib*, *lob*:
  based on PQUEUE(**m**, ≤), NAT,
  sort array,
  funct (pqueue, nat, nat) array *init*,
  funct (array a, **nat** i, **pqueue** q: $lob(a) \le i \le hib(a)$) **array** *put*,
  funct (array a, **nat** i: $lob(a) \le i \le hib(a)$) **pqueue** *get*,
  funct (array) nat *lob*,
  funct (array) nat *hib*,
  laws array a, **nat** i, j, m, n, **pqueue** q: $lob(a) \le i, j \le hib(a)$:
    $get(init(q, m, n), i) \equiv q$ **provided** $m \le i \le n$,
    $get(put(a, i, q), i) \equiv q$,
    $get(put(a, i, q), j) \equiv get(a, j)$ **provided** $i \neq j$,
    $lob(init(q, m, n)) \equiv m$,
    $hib(init(q, m, n)) \equiv n$,
    $lob(put(a, i, q)) \equiv lob(a)$,
    $hib(put(a, i, q)) \equiv hib(a)$
endoftype.

Although this specification is quite acceptable with respect to understandability, it is certainly not a good starting point for finding an efficient implementation, since both types (PQARRAY and PQUEUE) have to be implemented in full, whereas according to the original intention, only a structure with restricted operations is aimed at. Hence, to be able to get an efficient implementation, the definition of PQARRAY should be transformed into a definition where a distinction is no longer made between arrays and priority queues, before developing PQARRAY by appropriate data type transformations towards an implementation.

The technique we use for achieving such a new type definition is a transformation called type merging [Laut, Partsch 82]. The basic idea of this technique is similar to the technique of function composition (Sect. 6.1.1). In a more abstract sense this transformation too can be built on the basic algebraic constructions 'enrich, forget, identify' of Sect. 8.1.

Given a type T and a primitive type P (that defines a sort **s**) in a situation as the one illustrated above, a new type definition, where T and P are merged, can be derived formally according to the following

<u>**Strategy**</u>:
- unfold P in T with the result denoted by T◊P;
- Enrich T◊P by new operations that are defined as particular compositions of the old operations;
- Hide the primitive sort **s** and all operations of T that are used in the compositions.

Furthermore, if possible (see below)
- Derive, for the new operations, new axioms that do not use the old operations;
- Forget the primitive sort **s** and all operations that are used in the compositions.

T◊P, the result of unfolding P in T, is enriched with three sets of new operations that are defined by compositions according to one of the following patterns:

$f \circ f'$ where
- f is an operation from T with one parameter of sort **s**, and
- f' is an 'input operation' from P, i.e., an operation with result sort **s** but no parameters of sort **s**.

For our example, **s** corresponds to **pqueue**, the operations in ARRAY having a parameter of kind **pqueue** are {*init*, *put*}, and *emptyq* is the only input operation of PQUEUE. Thus we get as new operations of the form $f \circ f'$:

funct (nat, nat) array *initemptyq*
initemptyq(*m*, *n*) ≡ *init*(*emptyq*, *m*, *n*),

funct (array *a*, **nat** *i*: *lob*(*a*) ≤ *i* ≤ *hib*(*a*)) **array** *putemptyq*
putemptyq(*a*, *i*) ≡ *put*(*a*, *i*, *emptyq*) **provided** *lob*(*a*) ≤ *i* ≤ *hib*(*a*).

$f' \circ f$ where
- f is an 'output operation' from T, i.e. an operation having **s** as result sort, and
- f' is an output operation from P, i.e., an operation with an argument of sort **s** and a result sort different from **s**.

For the example, *get* is the only output operation of PQARRAY with result sort **pqueue**, and {*isempty*, *min*} are the output operations of PQUEUE. Thus we get

funct (**array** a, **nat** i: $lob(a) \le i \le hib(a) \wedge \neg isemptyget(a, i)$) **m** *minget*,
$minget(a, i) \equiv min(get(a, i))$
provided $lob(a) \le i \le hib(a) \wedge \neg isemptyget(a, i)$,

funct (**array** a, **nat** i: $lob(a) \le i \le hib(a)$) **bool** *isemptyget*,
$isemptyget(a, i) \equiv isempty(get(a, i))$ **provided** $lob(a) \le i \le hib(a)$.

$up(f) \circ h \circ f$ where
- h is a 'transput operation' of P, i.e., an operation with **s** as parameter and result sort,
- f is an output operation of T with result sort **s** and
- $up(f)$ is a (unique) transput operation of T that "updates" f, i.e., an operation that changes exactly that component that is selected by f.

For the example, {*add*, *remove*} are the transput operations of PQUEUE and *put* updates *get* which is the only output operation of PQARRAY with result sort **pqueue**. Thus we get

funct (**array** a, **nat** i, **m** x: $lob(a) \le i \le hib(a)$) **array** *putaddget*,
$putaddget(a, i, x) \equiv put(a, i, add(get(a, i), x))$
provided $lob(a) \le i \le hib(a)$,

funct (**array** a, **nat** i: $lob(a) \le i \le hib(a) \wedge$
$\neg isemptyget(a, i)$) **array** *putremoveget*,
$putremoveget(a, i) \equiv put(a, i, remove(get(a, i)))$
provided $lob(a) \le i \le hib(a) \wedge \neg isemptyget(a, i)$.

Next, according to the strategy above, the sort **s** and the operations involved in the merging can be hidden (and only the new ones and those untouched by the merging – such as *hib*, *lob* – remain visible). This results in the type

type PQARRAY = (**sort m**, **funct** (**m**, **m**) **bool** .≤.: LINORD(**m**, ≤))
array, *initemptyq*, *putemptyq*, *minget*, *isemptyget*,
putaddget, *putremoveget*, *hib*, *lob*:
based on NAT,
include PQUEUE(**m**, ≤),
sort array,
funct (**nat**, **nat**) **array** *initemptyq*,
funct (**array** a, **nat** i: $lob(a) \le i \le hib(a)$) **array** *putemptyq*,
funct (**array** a, **nat** i: $lob(a) \le i \le hib(a) \wedge \neg isemptyget(a, i)$) **m** *minget*,
funct (**array** a, **nat** i: $lob(a) \le i \le hib(a)$) **bool** *isemptyget*,
funct (**array** a, **nat** i, **m** x: $lob(a) \le i \le hib(a)$) **array** *putaddget*,
funct (**array** a, **nat** i: $lob(a) \le i \le hib(a) \wedge$
$\neg isemptyget(a, i)$) **array** *putremoveget*,
funct (**pqueue**, **nat**, **nat**) **array** *init*,
funct (**array** a, **nat** i, **pqueue** q: $lob(a) \le i \le hib(a)$) **array** *put*,
funct (**array** a, **nat** i: $lob(a) \le i \le hib(a)$) **pqueue** *get*,
funct (**array**) **nat** *lob*,
funct (**array**) **nat** *hib*,
laws array a, **nat** i, j, m, n, **pqueue** q: $lob(a) \le i, j \le hib(a)$:
$initemptyq(m, n) \equiv init(emptyq, m, n)$,
$putemptyq(a, i) \equiv put(a, i, emptyq)$ **provided** $lob(a) \le i \le hib(a)$,

minget(*a*, *i*) ≡ *min*(*get*(*a*, *i*))
    provided *lob*(*a*) ≤ *i* ≤ *hib*(*a*) Δ ¬*isemptyget*(*a*, *i*),
isemptyget(*a*, *i*) ≡ *isempty*(*get*(*a*, *i*)) **provided** *lob*(*a*) ≤ *i* ≤ *hib*(*a*),
putaddget(*a*, *i*, *x*) ≡ *put*(*a*, *i*, *add*(*get*(*a*, *i*), *x*)) **provided** *lob*(*a*) ≤ *i* ≤ *hib*(*a*),
lob(*a*) ≤ *i* ≤ *hib*(*a*) Δ ¬*isemptyget*(*a*, *i*)
get(*init*(*q*, *m*, *n*), *i*) ≡ *q* **provided** *m* ≤ *i* ≤ *n*,
get(*put*(*a*, *i*, *q*), *i*) ≡ *q*,
get(*put*(*a*, *i*, *q*), *j*) ≡ *get*(*a*, *j*) **provided** *i*≠*j*,
lob(*init*(*q*, *m*, *n*)) ≡ *m*,
hib(*init*(*q*, *m*, *n*)) ≡ *n*,
lob(*put*(*a*, *i*, *q*)) ≡ *lob*(*a*),
hib(*put*(*a*, *i*, *q*)) ≡ *hib*(*a*)

endoftype.

For our particular example, a further transition can be performed. Up to now the new operations are defined in terms of the hidden ones. Under particular circumstances (for details see [Laut, Partsch 82]) we can derive a new independent axiom set for the new operations. The left-hand sides of the new axioms are formed according to the theorem from [Guttag, Horning 78] (Sect. 3.3.1.2). The corresponding right-hand sides can be derived using the old axioms and the defining axioms of the new operations.

As an example, consider for (*lob*(*a*) ≤ *i*, *j* ≤ *hib*(*a*) ∧ *i*≠*j*) ≡ **true** the left-hand side

minget(*putaddget*(*a*, *i*, *q*), *j*) ≡ ... .

Then the corresponding right-hand side can be computed by the available axioms:

minget(*putaddget*(*a*, *i*, *x*), *j*) ≡
min(*get*(*putaddget*(*a*, *i*, *x*), *j*)) ≡
min(*get*(*put*(*a*, *i*, *add*(*get*(*a*, *i*), *x*)), *j*)) ≡
min(*get*(*a*, *j*)) ≡
minget(*a*, *j*) **provided** *lob*(*a*) ≤ *i*, *j* ≤ *hib*(*a*) ∧ *i*≠*j*.

Similarly, we can derive new axioms for all the other newly introduced operations.

Altogether we obtain the new type definition

type PQARRAY = (**sort m**, **funct** (**m**, **m**) **bool** .≤.: LINORD(**m**, ≤))
    array, *initemptyq*, *putemptyq*, *minget*, *isemptyget*,
    putaddget, *putremoveget*, *hib*, *lob*:
  based on NAT,
  sort array,
  funct (**nat**, **nat**) **array** *initemptyq*,
  funct (**array** *a*, **nat** *i*: *lob*(*a*) ≤ *i* ≤ *hib*(*a*)) **array** *putemptyq*,
  funct (**array** *a*, **nat** *i*: *lob*(*a*) ≤ *i* ≤ *hib*(*a*) Δ ¬*isemptyget*(*a*, *i*)) **m** *minget*,
  funct (**array** *a*, **nat** *i*: *lob*(*a*) ≤ *i* ≤ *hib*(*a*)) **bool** *isemptyget*,
  funct (**array** *a*, **nat** *i*, **m** *x*: *lob*(*a*) ≤ *i* ≤ *hib*(*a*)) **array** *putaddget*,
  funct (**array** *a*, **nat** *i*: *lob*(*a*) ≤ *i* ≤ *hib*(*a*) Δ
    ¬*isemptyget*(*a*, *i*)) **array** *putremoveget*,
  funct (**array**) **nat** *hib*,
  funct (**array**) **nat** *lob*,

laws array a, **nat** i, j, m, n, **m** x: $lob(a) \le i, j \le hib(a)$:
$lob(initemptyq(m, n)) \equiv m$,
$lob(putemptyq(a, i)) \equiv lob(a)$,
$lob(putaddget(a, i, x)) \equiv lob(a)$,
$hib(initemptyq(m, n)) \equiv n$,
$hib(putemptyq(a, i)) \equiv hib(a)$,
$hib(putaddget(a, i, x)) \equiv hib(a)$,
$isemptyget(initemptyq(m, n), i) \equiv$ **true**,
$isemptyget(putemptyq(a, i), j) \equiv (i=j) \vee isemptyget(a, j)$,
$minget(putemptyq(a, i), j) \equiv minget(a, j)$ **provided** $\neg isemptyget(a, i) \wedge i \neq j$,
$minget(putaddget(a, i, x), j) \equiv$
if $i \neq j$ **then** $minget(a, j)$ **elsf** $x \le minget(a, i)$ **then** x **else** $minget(a, i)$ **fi**
provided $\neg isemptyget(a, i) \wedge \neg isemptyget(a, j)$,
$putremoveget(putaddget(a, i, x), j) \equiv$
if $i \neq j$ **then** $putremoveget(a, j)$
elsf $x \le minget(a, i)$ **then** a **else** $putaddget(putremoveget(a, j), i, x)$ **fi**
provided $\neg isemptyget(a, i) \wedge \neg isemptyget(a, j)$
endoftype.

It should be added that type merging is horizontally and vertically associative, which is rather important, since this means that the order in which different mergings are performed is irrelevant.

As already mentioned, in general the type obtained by deriving a new axiom set will have more models than the one immediately obtained by the merging. However, under rather weak (more or less technical) restrictions [Laut, Partsch 82], these types can be shown to be equivalent with respect to their observable behavior. In turn, this means that it does not matter which one is taken for a specification that does not rely on internal properties of the type.

8.5 Joint Development

Usually a program development does not treat control structure and data type in separate ways, but tries to benefit from their mutual influences. Although in this process of joint development certain aspects of data type development and control structure development are independent of each other (and thus can be done in either order, even in parallel) there are certain steps on the one side that have essential influence on the further development of the other side. A typical example is given by recursion simplification where a clever technique can be applied provided the underlying data types have nice properties (such as allowing function inversion). Likewise, the use of a data type within a particular environment gives valuable hints on finding a suitable implementation (Sect. 8.3.2).

Therefore, in contrast to the type transformations dealt with in the previous sections, we are now interested in type transformations that take into account that some type is only used in a particular context, say, in the context of an expression. This implies that control structure and data structure have to be considered jointly. Additionally, there are two major consequences: transformation rules can be given in a schematic way and for their correctness the (simple) definition from Chap. 4 can be used (see also the remarks in the introduction to Chap. 8).

In the considerations of the previous sections we aimed at type transformations where some data structure be represented everywhere by another. Mainly due to the lack of appropriate linguistic means, this general form of data type transformations could be given in the form of a strategy only. In this subsection, however, where a particular data structure is assumed to be fixed within a certain context, type transformations in principle also can be given in the form of a schematic rule. Nevertheless the strategic form will occasionally be preferred here, too.

For a number of different transformational techniques, assertions play an important role (Sects. 5.3.1.3, 5.3.2, 6.3, 6.4.4). Assertions also provide a way of dealing with (context dependent) data structure transformations, as illustrated by the techniques discussed below.

8.5.1 Changing the Arguments of Functions

In this subsection, we will deal with the problem of transforming data structures in the particular context of function declarations, which means that certain arguments of a function are to be replaced by other arguments (possibly of other kinds). In some sense, the differencing technique (Sect. 6.4.4) may be considered as a particular instance of this kind of transformation, since there a (complex) argument might be replaced by simpler ones.

The key for the differencing technique is the use of assertions, which will also be the major idea in our subsequent consideration of data type transformations in a wider sense. To illustrate the basic idea we reconsider the problem of finding the minimal element of a sequence from Sect. 5.3.2.1:

mode natsequ = EESEQU(**nat**, =);

funct *minel* = (**natsequ** *s*: *s* ≠<>) **nat**:
  minel"(**first***s*, **rest***s*) **where**

  funct *minel"* = (**nat** *z*, **natsequ** *s*) **nat**:
    if *s* =<> **then** *z* **else** *minel"*(*min*(*z*, **first***s*), **rest***s*) **fi**.

By an embedding we define

funct *minel* = (**natsequ** *s*: *s* ≠<>) **nat**:
  *minel**(**first***s*, **rest***s*, 2) **where**

  funct *minel** = (**nat** *z*, **natsequ** *t*, **nat** *i*: $1 \le i \le |s|+1 \wedge t = s[i : |s|]$) **nat**:
    minel"(*z*, *t*).

Unfolding *minel"* then leads to

funct *minel** = (**nat** *z*, **natsequ** *t*, **nat** *i*: $1 \le i \le |s|+1 \wedge t = s[i : |s|]$) **nat**:
  if *t* =<> **then** *z* **else** *minel"*(*min*(*z*, **first***t*), **rest***t*) **fi**.

Now we can use the assertion in the body of *minel**. From

$(1 \le i \le |s|+1 \wedge t = s[i : |s|]) \equiv$ **true**

it follows that

$(t = \langle\rangle) \equiv (i = |s|+1)$,

and (under the assumption $t \neq \langle\rangle$)

$((\mathbf{first}\, t \equiv s[i]) \wedge (\mathbf{rest}\, t \equiv s[i+1 : |s|])) \equiv \mathbf{true}$

hold, and thus we get

funct *minel** = (**nat** *z*, **natsequ** *t*, **nat** *i*: $1 \leq i \leq |s|+1 \wedge t = s[i : |s|]$) **nat**:
  if $i = |s|+1$ **then** *z* **else** *minel''*(*min*(*z*, *s*[*i*]), *s*[*i*+1 : |*s*|]) **fi**,

which, by folding (with assertion) leads to

funct *minel** = (**nat** *z*, **natsequ** *t*, **nat** *i*: $1 \leq i \leq |s|+1 \wedge t = s[i : |s|]$) **nat**:
  if $i = |s|+1$ **then** *z* **else** *minel**(*min*(*z*, *s*[*i*]), *s*[*i*+1 : |*s*|], *i*+1) **fi**.

Now we realize that the argument *t* is not used within *minel** and may be omitted. As a consequence, the assertion in *minel** can be simplified. This leads to our final solution

funct *minel* = (**natsequ** *s*: $s \neq \langle\rangle$) **nat**:
  *minel**(*z*, 2) **where**
  funct *minel** = (**nat** *z*, **nat** *i*: $1 \leq i \leq |s|+1$) **nat**:
    if $i = |s|+1$ **then** *z* **else** *minel**(*min*(*z*, *s*[*i*]), *i*+1) **fi**,

which could be further developed into imperative form.

The gain in efficiency of this simple data type transformation (from sequences to indexed sequences) is obvious here. Rather than manipulating a complex data structure, viz. a sequence, *minel** now operates on a simple data structure, viz. natural numbers. Also obvious is the fact that this change of the argument type could be done only simultaneously with a change of the respective context.

The reasoning above can be generalized and made into the following

Strategy:

Given a situation such as

mode tm = T(**m**);
funct *f* = (**tm** *x*) **r**: E;
E'

- Define by an embedding (with some fixed *Y* for which $P(Y) \wedge E = E'(Y)$ holds)
  mode tm' = T'(**m**);
  funct *f'* = (**tm** *x*, **tm'** *y*: $P(y) \wedge x = E''(y)$) **r**: *f*(*x*);
  funct *f* = (**tm** *x*) **r**: E;
  E'[*f'*(*x*, *Y*) **for** *f*(*x*)];
- Develop, using the unfold-fold strategy, a version of *f'* which is independent of *f* and where all occurrences of *x* are substituted by expressions in *y* according to the assertion in *f'*;
- Eliminate the now superfluous argument *x*.

Of course, in particular, this strategy can be used to derive the following compact transformation rule

- <u>*Data structure representation*</u>

  f(E) **where**
  funct *f* = (**m** *x*: ∃ **n** *y*: P(*x*, *y*)) **r**:
  F(*f*, *x*)

  $\Big\downarrow$ $\left[\begin{array}{l}\text{CONST[E, E']},\\ \text{P(E, E')} \equiv \textbf{true},\\ \text{P}(x, y) \equiv \textbf{true} \;\vdash\; \text{F}(f, x) \equiv \text{F}'(f', y)\end{array}\right.$

  f'(E') **where**
  funct *f'* = (**n** *y*) **r**:
  F'(*f'*, *y*).

The correctness of this rule is essentially guaranteed by the third applicability condition which requires finding an appropriate expression F'(*f'*, *y*). If more information on **m**, **n**, and F is available, however, F' can often be "constructed" from F using the assertion.

Assume, for instance, an expression such as

f(*X*) **where**
funct *f* = (**sequ** *s*: ∃ (**nat** *i*, *j*: $1 \le i \le j+1 \le |X|+1$): $s = X[i : j]$) **r**: E.

Here, from the assertion we can derive "facts" such as

first *s* ≡ $X[i]$,
last *s* ≡ $X[j]$,
rest *s* ≡ $X[i+1 : j]$,
lead *s* ≡ $X[i : j-1]$,
$|s| \equiv j-i+1$,

but also

lead rest *s* ≡ $X[i+1, j-1]$, or
∃ **sequ** s_1, s_2: $s_1+s_2 = s \wedge$ E'(s_1, s_2) ≡ ∃ **nat** *k*: $i-1 \le k \le j$: E'$(X[i : k], X[k+1, j])$.

Thus, a new expression F' can be obtained from F by simply replacing occurrences of the left-hand sides of those facts by the corresponding right-hand sides. In this way, we obtain a representation of a sequence by a pair of indices.

Obviously, similar facts can be derived in all cases where a certain data structure is not modified but just selectively inspected. In these cases improvement always can be achieved by representing the selected parts by the original argument and some "selector" (which is usually of a simpler kind). Of course, the same idea also works in cases with several arguments. Likewise, similar rules (based on the same idea) for other data structures are obvious.

As an application of the above technique, we consider again the palindrome example from Sect. 4.5.2:

pal(*S*) **where**
funct *pal* = (**sequ** *s*) **bool**:
  if $|s| \le 1$ **then true**
  elsf first *s* ≠ **last** *s* **then false else** *pal*(**lead rest** *s*) **fi**.

Using the rule *invariant introduction* (Sect. 5.3.1.3) we get (in our specific context)

funct pal = (**sequ** s: $\exists$ (**nat** i, j: $1 \le i \le j+1 \le |S|+1$): $s = S[i : j]$) **bool**:
  if $|s| \le 1$ **then true**
  elsf first$s \ne$ **last**s **then false else** pal(**lead rest** s) **fi**.

Matching with the input scheme of the rule *data type representation* yields the instance

pal	for f,
S	for E,
(**nat** i, j: $1 \le i \le j+1 \le |S|+1$)	for **n**, and
$s = S[i : j]$	for P.

If, furthermore, we use the "facts" (derivable from the assertion)

$(|s| \le 1) \equiv (j \le i)$,
(**first**$s \ne$ **last**s) $\equiv$ $(S[i] \ne S[j])$,
(**lead rest** s) $\equiv X[i+1, j-1]$,

then application of the rule *data type representation* yields

$pal'(1, |S|)$ **where**
funct pal' = (**nat** i, **nat** j: $1 \le i \le j+1 \le |S|+1$) **bool**:
  if $j \le i$ **then true**
  elsf $S[i] \ne S[j]$ **then false else** $pal'(i+1, j-1)$ **fi**.

The idea expressed in the above strategy or the rule *data type representation* is not restricted to the special case where certain arguments of a function are substituted by a global argument of the same type and additional arguments of "simpler" types. In fact it may be used to achieve (in the context of some expression) an arbitrary change in the representation of a data structure.

As an example we consider a representation of bags by total maps (Sect. 3.3.2). Given the definitions

mode bag = BAG(**m**, eq);
funct f = (**bag** b) **r**: E(f, b),

we can first apply the rule *invariant introduction* and get

mode tmap = TMAP(**m**, **nat**, eq);
mode bag = BAG(**m**, eq);
funct f = (**bag** b: $\exists$ **tmap** m: $\forall$ **m** x: $m[x] = \#occs(x, b)$) **r**: E(f, b).

From the assertion, we can derive correspondences between bags and total maps such as

$init(0)$	corresponds to	$\varnothing$,
$m[x] \leftarrow (m[x]+1)$	corresponds to	$b+x$,
$m[x] \leftarrow (m[x]-1)$	corresponds to	$b-x$,

or facts such as

$m[x]>0 \equiv x \in b$,
$m[x]=0 \equiv x \notin b$,
$m[x] \equiv \#occs(x, b)$.

This information then can be used to derive a new expression E' that is equivalent to E and uses total maps instead of bags.

Further examples of the same kind are representations of

- sets of tuples by maps,
- total maps by indexed sequences,
- bags of pairs instead of pairs of bags, or
- ('non-overlapping') maps by a single map.

Finding appropriate assertions, correspondences, and facts (derivable from the assertions) for these changes in representation is straightforward and left to the reader.

8.5.2 "Attribution"

In connection with an implementation of a type by means of mode declarations, the strategy from the previous subsection may also be used for particular improvements which we will refer to as attribution. The basic idea of this kind of improvements is to change dynamic information into static information which simply means that the values of recursively defined functions over the respective type are "frozen" in additional components of the type (similar to the 'attributes' in the well-known 'attributed trees'). Again, we will have transformations that jointly concern data type and control structure.

The formal background is as follows:

Suppose an object kind **m** is defined by some mode definition (possibly obtained as a result of applying the technique from Sect. 8.2.2). Suppose further that o is a function over **m**, and that K is some expression containing objects of kind **m** and occurrences of o. Thus, we assume a situation such as

mode m = c_1 | c_2(**m** s_1, **p** s_2);
funct o = (**m** x: $\neg(x$ **is** $c_1)$) **q**: E(o, x);
K

where

- the particular form of **m** has been chosen for keeping the presentation reasonably short; the subsequent considerations can be straightforwardly applied to other forms of **m** also;
- the kinds **p** and **q** are assumed to be defined elsewhere;
- E(o, x) is a recursively defined expression using primitive operations and the operations of **m**;
- K is some expression that uses o, primitive operations, and the operations of **m**.

An example of such a situation is given within the type PQUEUE' from Sect. 8.2.2.1, where, e.g., *min* corresponds to the operation o above.

Given a situation as above, the definition of **m** can be transformed as follows: First we define a new object kind

mode m* = c_1* | c_2'(**m*** s_1*, **p** s_2*, **q** o*),

and relate it to **m** by a mapping

α: **m** $\rightarrow$ **m***,

which is defined by

$\alpha(c_1) =_{\text{def}} c_1^*$,
$\alpha(c_2(x, y)) =_{\text{def}} c_2^*(\alpha(x), y)$,

where

funct c_2^* = (**m*** z, **p** y) **m***:

is defined by

(*) $c_2^*(\alpha(x), y) \equiv c_2'(\alpha(x), y, o(c_2(x, y)))$.

This mapping is obviously total, homomorphic, and injective.

An operational definition E* (which is independent of o and c_2) of c_2^* can be obtained from (*) and the operational definition of o. This will be demonstrated by an example below.

Now we have

$s_1^*(c_2^*(\alpha(x), y)) \equiv \alpha(x) \equiv \alpha(s_1(c_2(x, y)))$,
$s_2^*(c_2^*(\alpha(x), y)) \equiv y \equiv s_2(c_2(x, y))$,
$o^*(c_2^*(\alpha(x), y)) \equiv o^*(c_2'(\alpha(x), y, o(c_2(x, y)))) \equiv o(c_2(x, y))$,

i.e., the operations of **m** and those of **m*** have the same observable behavior. Thus, the above situation can be transformed into

mode m* = c_1^* | c_2'(**m*** s_1^*, **p** s_2^*, **q** o^*);
funct c_2^* = (**m*** x, **p** y) **m***: E*;
K[**m*** **for m**, c_1^* **for** c_1, c_2^* **for** c_2, s_1^* **for** s_1, s_2^* **for** s_2, o^* **for** o].

The situation we started from and the one we ended with could be characterized by corresponding definitions of types T and T*, respectively. Obviously, α corresponds to IMP from Sect. 8.1.2, and the replacement in K corresponds to a signature morphism. Since α is total, one-to-one, Σ-homomorphic, and injective, it suffices (according to the remark at the beginning of Sect. 8.1.2) to verify the axioms of T in T*, in order to prove T* a correct implementation of T; but this is trivial due to the particular construction of the functions in T*.

In order to demonstrate this technique we consider again the example of priority queues. We start from the situation (Sect. 8.2.4):

mode pqueue = *emptyq* | *add*(**pqueue** *da1*, **m** *da2*);
funct *min* = (**pqueue** *q*: $\neg$ (*q* **is** *emptyq*)) **m**:
  if *da1*(*q*) **is** *emptyq* **then** *da2*(*q*)
  elsf *da2*(*q*) $\leq$ *min*(*da1*(*q*)) **then** *da2*(*q*) **else** *min*(*da1*(*q*)) **fi**;
K,

where K is an arbitrary context in which **pqueue** and *min* are used.

First we define

mode pqueue* = *emptyq** | *add'*(**pqueue****da1**, **m** *da2**, **m** *min**).

Then we define

α: **pqueue** $\rightarrow$ **pqueue***

by

$\alpha(emptyq) \equiv emptyq^*$,
$\alpha(add(q, x)) \equiv add'(\alpha(q), x, min(add(q, x)))$,

and

funct (pqueue*, m) pqueue* *add**,

by

$add^*(\alpha(q), x) \equiv add'(\alpha(q), x, min(add(q, x)))$.

We have obviously

(1) q **is** $emptyq \equiv \alpha(q)$ **is** $emptyq^*$,
(2) $\neg(\alpha(q)$ **is** $emptyq^*) \equiv$ **true** $\Rightarrow min^*(\alpha(q)) \equiv min(q)$.

Now we derive a new definition for *add**:

$add^*(\alpha(q), x)$
  ≡ [definition *add**]
$add'(\alpha(q), x, min(add(q, x)))$
  ≡ [definition *min*]
$add'(\alpha(q), x,$ **if** $da1(add(q, x))$ **is** $emptyq$ **then** $da2(add(q, x))$
    elsf $da2(add(q, x)) \le min(da1(add(q, x)))$ **then** $da2(add(q, x))$
      else $min(da1(add(q, x)))$ **fi**)
  ≡ [definition **pqueue**]
$add'(\alpha(q), x,$ **if** q **is** $emptyq$ **then** x
    elsf $x \le min(q)$ **then** x **else** $min(q)$ **fi**)
  ≡ [distributivity of conditional]
if q **is** $emptyq$ **then** $add'(\alpha(q), x, x)$
elsf $x \le min(q)$ **then** $add'(\alpha(q), x, x)$ **else** $add'(\alpha(q), x, min(q))$ **fi**
  ≡ [properties (1) and (2)]
if $\alpha(q)$ **is** $emptyq^*$ **then** $add'(\alpha(q), x, x)$
elsf $x \le min^*(\alpha(q))$ **then** $add'(\alpha(q), x, x)$ **else** $add'(\alpha(q), x, min^*(\alpha(q)))$ **fi**.

Thus, the situation we started from can be transformed into

mode pqueue* = *emptyq** | *add'*(**pqueue***$da1^*$, **m** $da2^*$, **m** min^*);
funct *add** = (**pqueue*** q, **m** x) **pqueue***:
  if q **is** $emptyq^*$ ∇ $x \le min^*(q)$ **then** $add'(q, x, x)$ **else** $add'(q, x, min^*(q))$ **fi**;
K[**pqueue* for pqueue**, *empty** **for** *empty*, *add** **for** *add*,
  *da1** **for** *da1*, *da2** **for** *da2*, *min** **for** *min*].

Of course, the above transformation also can be used to derive an implementation of PQUEUE, namely the type

type PQUEUE = (**sort m**, **funct (m, m) bool** .≤.: LINORD(**m**, ≤))
    pqueue, *emptyq*, *isempty*, *add*, *min*, *remove*:
  based on BOOL,
  mode pqueue = *emptyq* | *add'*(**pqueue** *da1*, **m** *da2*, **m** *min*),
  funct (pqueue) bool *isempty*,
  funct (pqueue q: $\neg isempty(q)$**) pqueue** *remove*,
  funct (pqueue, m) pqueue *add*,
  laws pqueue q, **m** x:
    $isempty(emptyq) \equiv$ **true**,

isempty(*add*(*q*, *x*)) ≡ **false**,
add(*q*, *x*) ≡ **if** *isempty*(*q*) ∇ $x \leq min(q)$ **then** *add*'(*q*, *x*, *x*)
else *add*'(*q*, *x*, *min*(*q*)) **fi**,
¬*isempty*(*q*) ≡ **true** ⇒
remove(*q*) ≡ **if** *da2*(*q*) ≡ *min*(*q*) **then** *da1*(*q*)
else *add*(*remove*(*da1*(*q*)), *da2*(*q*)) **fi**

endoftype.

In this latter type, *min* is now an operation that can be performed in constant time (however at the cost of extra space), whereas *remove* is still an operation that requires time proportional to the length of the priority queue. Therefore, one might think of applying the technique from above also to *remove*. Doing so, however, would not only need additional space (as for *min*), but also change the complexity of *add* from constant to linear. Hence, in general, this latter step will not lead to an improvement.

8.5.3 Compositions

A particular context for the joint development of data type and control structure is provided when particular kinds of function compositions are given.

Consider for instance the task of developing a particular algorithm for the problem of computing certain objects of a sort **r** from arbitrary objects of a sort **p**, that is, a mapping

a: **p** → **r**.

A common method to facilitate the specification process for a wide class of problems is to introduce an auxiliary internal structure, that is, some abstract type **t**, and split a into mappings

a_1: **p** → **t**,
a_2: **t** → **r**,

which are characterized by

$a(x) \equiv a_2(a_1(x))$ (for arbitrary **p** x).

However, in contrast to the easy specifiability of a_1 and a_2, it may be the case that the performance of the final algorithm will be not satisfactory – even if a_1 and a_2 are merged (using the technique of function composition from Sect. 6.1.1).

The basic idea now is to move in a situation as above from the intermediate type **t** to a related type **t**' that is connected to **t** either by a mapping

α: **t**' → **t**

or by a mapping

β: **t** → **t**'

such that the diagrams given in Fig. 8.3 are commutative.

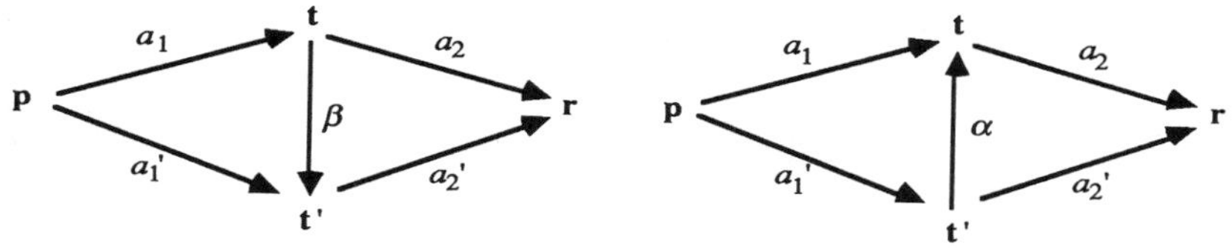

Figure 8.3. Diagrams for functional composition

Obviously, for given α or β, a_1' or a_2' may be derived from a_1 and a_2 using the commutativity properties of the above diagrams, using

$$a_2'(a_1'(x)) \equiv a_2'(\beta(a_1(x))) \equiv a_2(a_1(x)), \text{ or}$$
$$a_2'(a_1'(x)) \equiv a_2(\alpha(a_1'(x))) \equiv a_2(a_1(x)).$$

Thus, each of the mappings α or β gives rise to a representation of **t** in terms of **t'**. This representation does not change the semantics of the mapping a: **p** $\rightarrow$ **r**, and hence is a correct transformation.

A generalization of the reasoning above to cases with more than one auxiliary internal structure is straightforward.

A detailed example for a program development based on this technique can be found in [Partsch 83] where a particular sorting algorithm (sorting by replacement selection) is first based on multisets (as auxiliary structure) and then transformed into an equivalent one based on a tree-like structure.

8.5.4 Transition to Procedural Constructs for Particular Data Types

Certain data types, such as maps or sets, play a distinguished role in programming, since respective procedural counterparts are frequently ready-made available in certain programming environments. Therefore, it seems reasonable to consider for such data types joint transformations that combine the transition to a procedural implementation with an immediate transition from an applicative, maybe even descriptive, level of formulation to an imperative style. A few representative examples of this kind will be considered in the sequel.

Maps play an important role, since, under certain further restrictions, they correspond to arrays known from programming languages. As with arrays, we can introduce a module for maps by

```
module MMAP = (sort m, sort n, funct (m, m) bool eq:
              include EQUIV(m, eq))
              map, [], .[.]←., .[.]:=., .[.], isdef:
   based on BOOL, INT,
   based on MAP(m, n, eq),
   proc .[.]:=. = (var map a, nat i, m x):
      a := (a[i] ← x)
endofmodule.
```

This definition will be used in some of the transformations given below.

Some of our sample developments still contain descriptive constructs, for example of the form

some map *m*: ∀ (**m** *i*: $b \le i \le e$): *isdef*(*m*, *i*) Δ *m*[*i*] = E,

or

{**m** *x*: $x \in s$ Δ P}.

Of course, these constructs can be transformed into an imperative style by first transforming them into an operational form, then improving this operational form, and finally converting this improved form into an imperative style. Instead of this, however, we can also derive, for specific data types, particular transformation rules that achieve this transition in one step. A typical example of such a rule is

• Elementwise construction of maps

some map *m*: ∀ (**m** *i*: $b \le i \le e$): *isdef*(*m*, *i*) Δ *m*[*i*] = E

⟶ ↓ [SLINORD(**m**, <, =, *succ*)

begin var map *vm* := [];
  for *vi* **from** *b* **by** *succ* **upto** *e* **do** *vm*[*vi*] := E **od**; *vm* **end**

Syntactic constraints:
  NOTOCCUR[*m*, *vm* **in** E];
  DECL[**map**] = (**mode map** = MMAP(**m**, **n**, =)),

which, for a map with a totally ordered index domain, allows an elementwise construction using a **for** loop (see also Sect. 7.1.3).

A variant of this rule can be derived for the case where E depends on some other map *m'*:

some map *m*: ∀ (**m** *i*: $b \le i \le e$): *isdef*(*m*, *i*) Δ *m*[*i*] = E(*m'*, *i*)

⟶ ↓ [SLINORD(**m**, <, =, *succ*),
  ORIENTED[E, <, =]

begin var map *vm* := *m'*;
  for *vi* **from** *b* **by** *succ* **upto** *e* **do** *vm*[*vi*] := E[*vm* **for** *m'*] **od**; *vm* **end**

Syntactic constraints:
  NOTOCCUR[*m*, *vm* **in** E];
  KIND[*m'*] = **map**;
  DECL[**map**] = (**mode map** = MMAP(**m**, **n**, =)).

Informally, the applicability condition ORIENTED[E, <, =] means that E(*m'*, *i*) contains only values *m'*[*j*] with $j \ge i$. Formally it is defined [Möller 89] by:

ORIENTED[E, <, =] $=_{def}$
  ∀ **map** *m*, *m'*, (**m** *i*, *j*: $b \le i \le j \le e$):
  (*isdef*(*m*, *i*) ∧ *isdef*(*m'*, *i*)) Δ (*m*[*j*] = *m*[*j*] ⇒ E(*m*, *i*) = E(*m'*, *i*)).

Of course, there are further straightforward variants of these rules that lead to a 'downward **for** loop' instead of the 'upward **for** loop' as above. These variants can be used for example in the further development of the algorithm for computing the binomial coefficient. In Sect. 6.5.1 we derived the program

bin'(0, [][0] ← 1)[*J*] **where**
mode natmap = MMAP(**nat**, **nat**, =);

funct *bin'* = (**nat** *x*, **natmap** *a*:
∀ (**nat** *y*: $0 \le y \le x$): *isdef*(*a*, *y*) Δ *a*[*y*] = *bin*(*x*, *y*)) **natmap**:
if *x* = *I* **then** *a* **else** *bin'*(*x*+1, *upd*(*a*, *x*)) **fi**;

funct *upd* = (**natmap** *a*, **nat** *x*) **natmap**:
some natmap *b*: ∀ (**nat** *y*: $1 \le y \le x$): (*isdef*(*b*, *y*) Δ *b*[*y*] = *a*[*y*–1]+*a*[*y*]) ∧
(*isdef*(*b*, *x*+1) Δ *b*[*x*+1] = 1) ∧ (*isdef*(*b*, 0) Δ *b*[0] = *a*[0]),

where the type instantiation has already been substituted by the corresponding module instantiation.

Obviously, *embedded tail recursion to iteration* yields

begin (**var nat** *vx*, **var natmap** *va*) := (0, [][0] ← 1);
while *vx* < *I* **do** (*vx*, *va*) := (*vx*+1, *upd*(*va*, *vx*)) **od**; *va*[*J*] **end**,

and by *sequentialization* we get further

begin var nat *vx* := 0; **var natmap** *va* := []; *va*[0] := 1;
while *vx* < *I* **do** *va* := *upd*(*va*, *vx*); *vx* := *vx*+1 **od**; *va*[*J*] **end**.

Furthermore, the body of *upd* can be rewritten into the equivalent form

natmap *h* = **some natmap** *b*: ∀ (**nat** *y*: $1 \le y \le x$):
(*isdef*(*b*, *y*) Δ *b*[*y*] = *a*[*y*–1]+*a*[*y*] Δ *b*[0] = *a*[0]);
h[*x*+1] ← 1.

Now, the above-mentioned variant (with a downward **for** loop) can be applied, which leads to

natmap *h* =
begin var natmap *vb* := *a*;
for *y* **from** *x* **by** –1 **downto** 1 **do** *vb*[*y*] := *vb*[*y*–1]+*vb*[*y*] **od**; *vb* **end**;
((*h*[*x*+1]) ← 1)[0] ← 1,

and further to

funct *upd* = (**natmap** *a*, **nat** *x*) **natmap**:
begin var natmap *vb* := *a*;
for *y* **from** *x* **by** –1 **downto** 1 **do** *vb*[*y*] := *vb*[*y*–1]+*vb*[*y*] **od**;
vb[*x*+1] := 1; *vb* **end**.

As a last step we unfold *upd* in the program above, apply the *distributivity of assignment over block* and get as our final version

begin var nat *vx* := 0; **var natmap** *va* := []; *va*[0] := 1;
while *vx* < *I* **do**
for *y* **from** *vx* **by** –1 **downto** 1 **do** *va*[*y*] := *va*[*y*–1]+*va*[*y*] **od**;
va[*x*+1] := 1; *vx* := *vx*+1 **od**;
va[*J*] **end**.

The rules above assumed a totally ordered index domain of the respective map, which allowed a transition to a **for** loop. For the case where the domain of the map is a finite set instead of an interval of an ordered domain further rules can be given, such as

- **some map** *m*: ∀ (**m** *i*: *i* ∈ *s*): *isdef*(*m*, *i*) Δ *m*[*i*] = E

  ↓ [EQUIV(**m**, =),
  m finite]

  begin var map *vm* := [];
  forall *i* ∈ *s* **do** *vm*[*i*] := E **od**; *vm* **end**

  Syntactic constraints:
  NOTOCCUR[*m*, *vm*, **in** E];
  KIND[*s*] = **mset**;
  DECL[**mset**] = (**mode mset** = MSET(**m**, =));
  DECL[**map**] = (**mode map** = MMAP(**m**, **n**, =)),

where the **forall** construct is a particular 'iterator' to be supplied by an appropriate procedural implementation MSET of SET.

Similar to maps, also finite sets can be constructed elementwise by using the rule

- *Elementwise construction of finite sets*

  {**m** *i*: *i* ∈ *s* Δ P}

  ↓ [EQUIV(**m**, =),
  m finite]

  begin var mset *vs* := ∅;
  forall *i* ∈ *s* **do if** P **then** *vs* := *vs* + *i* **else skip fi od**; *vs* **end**

  Syntactic constraints:
  NOTOCCURS[*vs* **in** P];
  KIND[*s*] = **mset**;
  DECL[**mset**] = (**mode mset** = MSET(**m**, =)).

Due to the (trivial) equivalence

$\{\mathbf{m}\ x: x \in s \,\Delta\, P\} \equiv \bigcup_{x \in s} \{\mathbf{m}\ x: P\}$

this rule not only captures set comprehension, but also iterated set union.

Further similar rules for other basic data types, such as sequences or bags, are obvious.

8.6 An Example: Cycles in a Graph

In the preceding sections a lot of examples have already been given to illustrate the various rules and strategies that have been introduced. Therefore, in this section only one more example, the cycle problem, will be dealt with, mainly in order to finish this particular development.

The algorithm for the cycle problem from Sect. 7.3.2:

funct *hascycle* = (**graph** *g*) **bool**:
begin
var nodeset *vc* := *nodes*(*g*);
var nodeset *vd* := {**node** *x*: *x* ∈ *vc* ∧ *preds*(*x*, *vc*) = ∅};

```
        var nodemap vm := some nodemap m':
                    ∀ node x: x ∈ vc ⇒ (m'[x] = preds(x, vc));
        while vd ≠ ∅ do
           nodeset e = {node x: x ∈ vc ∧ vm[x] ≠ ∅ ∧ vm[x] ⊆ vd};
           vm := some nodemap n: ∀ node x:
                       (x ∈ vc ⇒ n[x] = vm[x]\vd) ∧ (x ∉ vc ⇒ n[x] = vm[x]);
           vc := vc\vd;
           vd := e od;
        vc ≠ ∅
     end
```

can be further developed as follows:

Main development

Focus: function *hascycle*

Goal: low level improvements

Transformations:

step 1: simple transformation of the universally quantified expressions (to enable the elementwise construction of maps and sets)

```
  begin
     var nodeset vc := nodes(g);
     var nodeset vd := {node x: x ∈ vc ∧ preds(x, vc) = ∅};
     var nodemap vm := some nodemap m':
                                     ∀ (node x: x ∈ vc): m'[x] = preds(x, vc);
     while vd ≠ ∅ do
        var nodeset ve := {node x: x ∈ vc ∧ vm[x] ≠ ∅ ∧ vm[x] ⊆ vd};
        vm := some nodemap n: ∀ (node x: x ∈ {node y: true}):
              isdef(n, x) Δ if x ∈ vc then n[x] = vm[x]\vd else n[x] = vm[x] fi;
        vc := vc\vd;
        vd := ve od;
     vc ≠ ∅
  end
```

step 2: elementwise constructions

```
  begin
     var nodeset vc := nodes(g);
     var nodeset vd :=
        begin var nodeset vd' := ∅;
        forall x ∈ vc do
           if preds(x, vc) = ∅ then vd' := vd' + x  else skip fi od;
        vd' end;
     var nodemap vm :=
        begin var nodemap vm' := [];
        forall x ∈ vc do vm'[x] := preds(x, vc) od;
        vm' end;
     while vd ≠ ∅ do
        var nodeset ve :=
           begin var nodeset ve' := ∅;
           forall x ∈ vc do
```

```
                if vm[x] ≠ ∅ ∧ vm[x] ⊆ vd   then ve' := ve' + x
                                            else skip fi od;
             ve' end;
          vm :=
             begin var nodemap vn := vm;
             forall x ∈ {node y: true} do
                if x ∈ vc then vn[x] := vn[x]\vd else vn[x] := vn[x] fi od;
             vn end;
          vc := vc\vd;
          vd := ve od;
       vc ≠ ∅
    end
```

step 3: distributivity of assignment over block; simplifications

```
    begin
       var nodeset vc := nodes(g);
       var nodeset vd := ∅;
       forall x ∈ vc do if preds(x, vc) = ∅ then vd := vd + x else skip fi od;
       var nodemap vm := [];
       forall x ∈ vc do vm[x] := preds(x, vc) od;
       while vd ≠ ∅ do
          var nodeset ve := ∅;
          forall x ∈ vc do
             if vm[x] ≠ ∅ ∧ vm[x] ⊆ vd then ve := ve + x else skip fi od;
          forall x ∈ vc do vm[x] := vm[x]\vd od;
          vc := vc\vd;
          vd := ve od;
       vc ≠ ∅
    end
```

step 4: rearrangement of statements

```
funct hascycle = (graph g) bool:
    begin
       var nodeset vc := nodes(g);
       var nodeset vd := ∅;
       var nodemap vm := [];
       forall x ∈ vc do
          vm[x] := preds(x, vc);
          if vm[x] = ∅ then vd := vd + x else skip fi od;
       while vd ≠ ∅ do
          var nodeset ve := ∅;
          forall x ∈ vc do
             if vm[x] ≠ ∅ ∧ vm[x] ⊆ vd then ve := ve + x else skip fi;
             vm[x] := vm[x]\vd od;
          vc := vc\vd;
          vd := ve od;
       vc ≠ ∅
    end
```

Now we could implement the sets, the size of which is restricted by the number of nodes in the given graph, for example by appropriate modules for bitmaps (Sect. 8.3.1). Likewise, the maps involved could obviously be implemented by appropriate modules for arrays. This, however, is straightforward and left as an exercise for the reader.

8.7 Exercises

Exercise 8-1

Using the technique from Sect. 8.1.2, give implementations of sets (Sect. 3.3.2) in terms of

a) (unrestricted) sequences,
b) ordered sequences (without multiple occurrences of elements),
c) BMAP where, using the type MAP, BMAP is defined as follows:

type BMAP = (**sort index**, **funct** (**index**, **index**) **bool** *eq*:
　　include EQUIV(**index**, *eq*))
　　bmap, [], *settrue*, *setfalse*, *istrue*, *isfalse*:
　based on BOOL;
　include MAP(**index**, **bool**, *eq*) **as** (**bmap**, ...),
　funct (**bmap**, **index**) **bmap** *settrue*,
　funct (**bmap**, **index**) **bmap** *setfalse*,
　funct (**bmap**, **index**) **bool** *istrue*,
　funct (**bmap**, **index**) **bool** *isfalse*;
　laws index *i*, **bmap** *m*, **bool** *x*:
　　settrue(*m*, *i*) ≡ *m*[*i*]← **true**,
　　setfalse(*m*, *i*) ≡ *m*[*i*]← **false**,
　　istrue(*m*, *i*) ≡ *isdef*(*m*, *i*) Δ *m*[*i*] = **true**,
　　isfalse(*m*, *i*) ≡ ¬*isdef*(*m*,*i*) ∨ (*isdef*(*m*, *i*) Δ *m*[*i*] = **false**)
endoftype.

Exercise 8-2

Give an implementation of bags in terms of TMAP (Sect. 3.3.2).

Exercise 8-3

Complete the correctness proofs given in Sect. 8.1.2 for the implementation of priority queues in terms of sequences and ordered sequences.

Exercise 8-4

Using

mode sequ = <> | *add*(**m** *first*, **sequ** *rest*)

(Sect. 8.2.1), give implementations by computation structures for

a) ESEQU (Sect. 3.3.3),
b) EESEQU (Sect. 3.3.3).

Exercise 8-5

Using the technique from Sect. 8.2.2, give implementations in terms of modes for (Sect. 3.3.4.2)

a) BREL,
b) PORD,
b) EREL_1.

Exercise 8-6

Prove that the functions *r1* and *r2* from Sect. 8.2.2.3 satisfy the postulated properties.

Exercise 8-7

Using the definition of *isin* from Sect. 8.2.2.4, prove that the function

funct (pqueue, m) pqueue *add''* ,

defined by

$add''(q, x) \equiv$ **if** $isin(x, q)$ **then** q **else** $add'(q, x)$ **fi**,

fulfils the property

(*) $add''(add''(q, x), x) \equiv add''(q, x)$.

Exercise 8-8

Give pointer implementations for

a) sequences (allowing access on both sides) by doubly linked lists,
b) CLIST (Sect. 3.3.4.3).

Exercise 8-9

Give implementations in terms of arrays (Sect. 8.2.3) for

a) EREL_1 (Sect. 3.3.4.2),
b) EREL_2 (Sect. 3.3.4.2),
c) DGRAPH_2 (Sect. 3.3.4.3),
d) DAG (Sect. 3.3.4.3).

Exercise 8-10

Give a device for implementing priority queues.

Exercise 8-11

Specify

a) triples as pairs (Sect. 3.3.4.1) consisting of a pair and an element,
b) 'bitmatrices' as vectors of bitvectors (Sect. 8.3.1),
c) 'double-stacks' as pairs of stacks,
d) 'symbol tables' (to be used in the compilation of languages with block structure) as stacks of maps.

Apply the technique of type merging (Sect. 8.4) to either of these specifications.

Exercise 8-12

Find suitable assertions, correspondences, and facts for representations of

a) sets of tuples by maps,
b) total maps by indexed sequences,
c) bags of pairs by pairs of bags,
d) (non-overlapping) maps by a single map.

Exercise 8-13

Complete the development in Sect. 8.6 by giving appropriate procedural implementations for **nodeset** and **nodemap**.

9. Complete Examples

In the previous chapters a lot of examples have been given to illustrate various transformation rules and strategies. The emphasis there was on demonstrating different (individual) techniques in the overall software development process, for example the transition from descriptive to operational specifications or improvement of applicative programs. Certain problems have been considered in various stages scattered over different chapters. Except for the queens problem of Sect. 1.6, however, there were no complete treatments of problems leading from an informal problem statement to an efficient procedural program. Therefore, in this chapter, a couple of further examples will be considered in a more complete way.

In contrast with the treatment of examples in the previous chapters, where the emphasis was on the technical side of the individual transformation steps, the emphasis now is on the essential ideas to be used in a complete derivation. Therefore, instead of the semi-formalism for describing derivations that was introduced in Sect. 4.2.3, we will use a more informal way of describing the development process. Particular emphasis will be on motivating design decisions and on giving hints for alternative development steps.

Furthermore, the examples in the following subsections also aim at stressing, once more, different important aspects of our approach to software development by formal specification and transformational programming.

The treatment of Warshall's algorithm in Sect. 9.1 will demonstrate again how to bridge the huge gap between a descriptive problem specification and an efficient imperative program for solving the problem.

Dealing with the 'majority problem' in Sect. 9.2 will contribute to the ongoing discussion on reusability. With this example it can be seen how the availability of a transformational development for a particular problem can be reused to solve a related, here more general, problem. An exisiting derivation is "adapted" to a modified specification and advantage is taken of the new particular context within certain simplifications.

The derivation of Boyer and Moore's fast pattern matching algorithm in Sect. 9.3 will exemplify once more how to suitably combine transformational and assertional reasoning in order to come up with a tricky but highly efficient program.

Finally, in the development of the text editor in Sect. 9.4 the emphasis will mainly be on the formalization process. In particular, we show how a formal specification for a realistic problem can be obtained in a systematic way. Some of the advantages of formal methods over conventional software development are highlighted.

9.1 Warshall's Algorithm

Warshall's algorithm is a well-known algorithm for efficiently deciding the existence of a path between two nodes of a finite directed graph by computing the transitive closure of the graph using boolean matrix multiplication.

Informally the problem may be stated as follows:

Is there a path from node X to node Y in a given finite directed graph G with N nodes (denoted by natural numbers from 1 to N)?

The problem and the algorithm that efficiently solves the problem can be found in lots of introductory textbooks on programming. A transformational treatment of the problem may be found in [Broy, Pepper 81].

9.1.1 Formal Problem Specification

Using the respective type definitions from Sect. 3.3 a descriptive formal specification of the problem is straightforward. The problem domain can be simply formalized by

mode node = (**nat** n: $1 \le n \le N$);
mode graph = DGRAPH$_3$(**node**, =);
mode nodesequ = ESEQU(**node**).

On this basis, the problem proper can be formalized by

path(X, Y, G) **where**

funct *path* = (**node** x, **node** y, **graph** g) **bool**:
  $\exists$ **nodesequ** p: *ispath*($x + p + y$) **where**

  funct *ispath* = (**nodesequ** p) **bool**:
    $\forall$ (**nat** k: $1 \le k < |p|$): *isarc*(g, $p[k]$, $p[k+1]$).

Our derivation proceeds along the global strategy outlined in the previous chapters: derivation of an operational specification; improvement of the operational specification; transformation of the operational specification into an efficient imperative program.

9.1.2 Derivation of an Operational Specification

The existential quantifier in *path* ranges over an unrestricted domain. Therefore, in order to eliminate it we have to look for an appropriate restriction of its domain. To this end the essential idea is the following: if there is a path, then there is also a minimal one which does not contain the same node twice and where all nodes are smaller than an appropriate upper bound. This idea suggests an *embedding* that uses the fact that nodes are natural numbers smaller than N+1:

funct *path* = (**node** x, **node** y, **graph** g) **bool**:
  pa(N+1, x, y) **where**

funct pa = (**nat** i, **node** x, **node** y: $1 \le i \le N+1$) **bool**:
  ∃ **nodesequ** p: $ispath(x + p + y) \wedge min(p, i)$,

funct $ispath$ = (**nodesequ** p) **bool**:
  ∀ (**nat** k: $1 \le k < |p|$): $isarc(g, p[k], p[k+1])$,

funct min = (**nodesequ** p, **nat** i) **bool**:
  ∀ (**nat** j, k: $1 \le j, k \le |p|$): $(j \ne k \Rightarrow p[j] \ne p[k]) \wedge (p[k] < i)$.

Obviously, the following properties hold:

$ispath(x + p_1 + (i-1) + p_2 + y) \equiv$
  $ispath(x + p_1 + (i-1)) \wedge ispath((i-1) + p_1 + y)$ (2.1)
$min(p, 1) \equiv p = \langle\rangle$ (2.2)
$(min(p, i) \wedge (i-1) \notin p) \equiv min(p, i-1)$ (2.3)
$min(p_1 + (i-1) + p_2, i) \equiv \textbf{true} \vdash (min(p_1, i-1) \wedge min(p_2, i-1)) \equiv \textbf{true}$ (2.4)

Our next efforts concentrate on pa. We calculate as follows:

∃ **nodesequ** p: $ispath(x + p + y) \wedge min(p, i)$
  ≡ [*case introduction* on i ($i = 1 \vee i > 1$); (2.2); simplification]
if $i = 1$ **then** $isarc(g, x, y)$ **else** ∃ **nodesequ** p: $ispath(x + p + y) \wedge min(p, i)$ **fi**
  ≡ [*case introduction* ($(i-1) \notin p \vee (i-1) \in p$) in **else** branch; (2.3)]
if $i = 1$ **then** $isarc(g, x, y)$
    else (∃ **nodesequ** p: $ispath(x + p + y) \wedge min(p, i-1) \vee$
      (∃ **nodesequ** p: $ispath(x + p + y) \wedge min(p, i) \wedge (i-1) \in p$) **fi**. (2.5)

For transforming (2.5) we use the (obvious) property of sequences

∃ **nodesequ** p: $E(p) \wedge (i-1) \in p$ ≡ ∃ **nodesequ** p_1, p_2: $E(p_1 + (i-1) + p_2)$ (2.6)

(where E is an arbitrary expression):

∃ **nodesequ** p: $ispath(x + p + y) \wedge min(p, i) \wedge (i-1) \in p$
  ≡ [(2.6)]
∃ **nodesequ** p_1, p_2: $ispath(x + p_1 + (i-1) + p_2 + y) \wedge min(p_1 + (i-1) + p_2, i)$
  ≡ [(2.1); (2.4)]
∃ **nodesequ** p_1, p_2: $ispath(x + p_1 + (i-1)) \wedge ispath((i-1) + p_2 + y) \wedge$
      $min(p_1, i-1) \wedge min(p_2, i-1)$
  ≡ [rearrangement]
(∃ **nodesequ** p_1: $ispath(x + p_1 + (i-1)) \wedge min(p_1, i-1)) \wedge$
  (∃ **nodesequ** p_2: $ispath((i-1) + p_2 + y) \wedge min(p_2, i-1)$).

Thus, altogether we have

if $i = 1$ **then** $isarc(g, x, y)$
    else (∃ **nodesequ** p: $ispath(x + p + y) \wedge min(p, i-1)) \vee$
      ((∃ **nodesequ** p_1: $ispath(x + p_1 + (i-1)) \wedge min(p_1, i-1)) \wedge$
      (∃ **nodesequ** p_2: $ispath((i-1) + p_2 + y) \wedge min(p_2, i-1)$)) **fi**.

Folding (with assertion) with the original definition of pa then results in

funct pa = (**nat** i, **node** x, **node** y: $1 \le i \le N+1$) **bool**:
  if $i = 1$ **then** $isarc(g, x, y)$
    else $pa(i-1, x, y) \vee (pa(i-1, x, i-1) \wedge pa(i-1, i-1, y))$ **fi**

and *unfolding* the definition of **node** (in order to have uniformly natural numbers) yields

funct pa = (**nat** i, **nat** x, **nat** y: $1 \le i \le N{+}1 \wedge 1 \le x, y \le N$) **bool**:
  if $i = 1$ **then** $isarc(g, x, y)$
    else $pa(i{-}1, x, y) \vee (pa(i{-}1, x, i{-}1) \wedge pa(i{-}1, i{-}1, y))$ **fi**.

9.1.3 Operational Improvements

In order to transform our last version of *pa* into tail recursion we apply the rule *partial inversion* (Sect. 6.5.1) to $pa(N{+}1, x, y)$ and yield

$pa'(init(N{+}1))[X, Y]$ **where**

mode nodemap = PMAP(**nat**, **bool**, =);

funct pa' = (**nat** i, **nodemap** a: $ispamap(a, i)$) **nodemap**:
  if $i = N{+}1$ **then** a **else** $pa'(i{+}1$, **some nodemap** b: $ispamap(b, i{+}1))$ **fi**,

funct $ispamap$ = (**nodemap** a, **nat** i) **bool**:
  $\forall$ (**nat** x, y: $1 \le x, y \le N$): $isdef(a, x, y) \,\Delta\, a[x, y] = pa(i, x, y)$,

funct $init$ = (**nat** x) (**nat**, **nodemap**):
  if $x = 1$ **then** (x, **some nodemap** b: $ispamap(b, x)$) **else** $init(x{-}1)$ **fi**.

In our particular context the expressions $init(N{+}1)$ and **some nodemap** b: $ispamap(b, i{+}1)$ can be further simplified as follows:

$init(N{+}1)$
  ≡ [*simplification*]
(1, **some nodemap** b: $ispamap(b, 1)$)
  ≡ [unfold *ispamap*]
(1, **some nodemap** b:
  $\forall$ (**nat** x, y: $1 \le x, y \le N$): $isdef(b, x, y) \,\Delta\, b[x, y] = pa(1, x, y)$)
  ≡ [*instantiate* $pa(1, x, y)$]
(1, **some nodemap** b:
  $\forall$ (**nat** x, y: $1 \le x, y \le N$): $isdef(b, x, y) \,\Delta\, b[x, y] = isarc(g, x, y)$)
  ≡ [*abstraction*]
(1, *initialize*) **where**
funct *initialize* = **nodemap**:
  some nodemap b: $\forall$ (**nat** x, y: $1 \le x, y \le N$):
    $isdef(b, x, y) \,\Delta\, b[x, y] = isarc(g, x, y)$.

some nodemap b: $ispamap(b, i{+}1)$
  ≡ [unfold *ispamap*]
some nodemap b: $\forall$ (**nat** x, y: $1 \le x, y \le N$):
    $isdef(b, x, y) \,\Delta\, b[x, y] = pa(i{+}1, x, y)$
  ≡ [*instantiate* $pa(i{+}1, x, y)$]
some nodemap b: $\forall$ (**nat** x, y: $1 \le x, y \le N$): $isdef(b, x, y) \,\Delta$
    $b[x, y] = (pa(i, x, y) \vee (pa(i, x, i) \wedge pa(i, i, y)))$
  ≡ [assertion $ispamap(a, i)$]

```
some nodemap b:  ∀ (nat x, y: 1 ≤ x, y ≤ N): isdef(b, x, y) Δ
                        b[x, y] = (a[x, y] ∨ (a[x, i] ∧ a[i, y]))
   ≡ [ abstraction ]
upd(a, i) where
funct upd = (nodemap a, nat i) nodemap:
   some nodemap b:  ∀ (nat x, y: 1 ≤ x, y ≤ N): isdef(b, x, y) Δ
                           b[x, y] = a[x, y] ∨ (a[x, i] ∧ a[i, y]);
```

Thus, we have so far

```
funct path = (node x, node y, graph g) bool:
   pa'(1, initialize)[x, y] where

   mode nodemap = PMAP(nat, bool, =);

   funct pa' = (nat i, nodemap a: ∀ (nat x, y: 1 ≤ x, y ≤ N):
                  isdef(a, x, y) Δ a[x, y] = pa(i, x, y)) nodemap:
      if i = N+1 then a else pa'(i+1, upd(a, i)) fi,

   funct upd = (nodemap a, nat i) nodemap:
      some nodemap b:  ∀ (nat x, y: 1 ≤ x, y ≤ N): isdef(b, x, y) Δ
                              b[x, y] = a[x, y] ∨ (a[x, i] ∧ a[i, y]),

   funct initialize = nodemap:
      some nodemap b: ∀ (nat x, y: 1 ≤ x, y ≤ N):
                              isdef(b, x, y) Δ b[x, y] = isarc(g, x, y).
```

9.1.4 Transition to an Imperative Program

Application of the rule *embedded tail recursion to iteration* to *path* yields

```
funct path = (node x, node y, graph g) bool:
   begin (var nat vi, var nodemap va) := (1, initialize);
      while vi < N ∨ vi = N do (vi, va) := (vi+1, upd(va, vi)) od;
      va end,
```

which can be further transformed into a **for** loop (Sect. 7.1.3):

```
funct path = (node x, node y, graph g) bool:
   begin var nodemap va := initialize;
      for vi from 1 by +1 upto N do va := upd(va, vi) od;
      va end.
```

For the functions *initialize* and *upd*, we use the respective rules (for the elementwise construction of maps) from Sect. 8.1.2.3. Thus we get

```
funct initialize = nodemap:
   begin var nodemap vb := [];
      for vx from 1 by +1 upto N do
         for vy from 1 by +1 upto N do vb[vx, vy] := isarc(g, vx, vy) od od;
      vb end,
```

respectively,

```
funct upd = (nodemap a, nat i) nodemap:
   begin var nodemap vb := a;
      for vx from 1 by +1 upto N do
         for vy from 1 by +1 upto N do
         vb[vx, vy] := vb[vx, vy] ∨ (vb[vx, i] ∧ vb[i, vy]); od od;
     vb end.
```

In transforming *upd* we have used the fact that (for each fixed *i*)

$$vb[i, vy] \equiv a[i, vy] \vee (a[i, i] \wedge a[i, vy]) \equiv a[i, vy]$$

and

$$vb[vx, i] \equiv a[vx, i] \vee (a[vx, i] \wedge a[i, i]) \equiv a[vx, i]$$

hold.

Within *upd*, sequential evaluation of the logical connectives in the right-hand side of the assignment yields

```
vb[vx, vy] := if vb[vx, i]  then if vb[i, vy] then true else vb[vx, vy] fi
                            else vb[vx, vy] fi;
```

which can be further transformed into

```
if vb[vx, i]
   then if vb[i, vy] then vb[vx, vy] := true else vb[vx, vy] := vb[vx, vy] fi
   else vb[vx, vy] := vb[vx, vy] fi;
```

and into

```
if vb[vx, i] then if vb[i, vy] then vb[vx, vy] := true else skip fi
             else skip fi.
```

Finally, the inner **for** loop in *upd* can be distributed over the conditional assignment (Sect. 7.2.3), such that the final version of *upd* reads

```
funct upd = (nodemap a, nat i) nodemap:
   begin var nodemap vb := a;
      for vx from 1 by +1 upto N do
         if vb[vx, i]
            then for vy from 1 by +1 upto N do
               if vb[i, vy] then vb[vx, vy] := true else skip fi od
            else skip fi  od;
     vb end.
```

By unfolding *initialize* and *upd* in *path* and additionally using the rule *distributivity of assignment over block* (Sect. 7.2.3), we get our final version

```
path(X, Y, G) where

funct path = (node x, node y, graph g) bool:
   begin var nodemap a := [];
      for vx from 1 by +1 upto N do
         for vy from 1 by +1 upto N do vb[vx, vy] := isarc(g, vx, vy) od od;
     for vi from 1 upto N do
        for vx from 1 by +1 upto N do
```

```
        if vb[vx, vi]
           then for vy from 1 by +1 upto N do
              if vb[vi, vy] then vb[vx, vy] := true else skip fi od
           else skip fi  od;
   a[x, y] end
```

where by another unfolding the definition of *path* could also be eliminated.

9.2 The Majority Problem

In this section we consider two (related) problems which, in essence, are also dealt with in [Misra, Gries 82]. The simpler of the two problems is ascribed to Boyer and Moore (see the remark in [Misra, Gries 82]) and may be worded as follows:

> *Given a bag b of size n, find an element in b which occurs more than n* ***div*** *2 times.*

The second problem is a generalization of the first one and reads:

> *Given a bag b of size n and a natural number k with 2 ≤ k ≤ n, find elements in b which occur more than n* ***div*** *k times.*

The problems in [Misra, Gries 82] are formulated for arrays rather than bags. Arrays are one possibility of implementing bags. Hence, any solution for bags also provides a solution for arrays, and therefore we will use bags from the beginning.

It will turn out that a solution to the simpler problem can be derived straightforwardly using our generalized unfold/fold strategy from Sect. 5.3. Additionally, we will see that a solution to the second problem can be obtained by generalizing and reusing the first derivation in an obvious way.

9.2.1 Formal Specification

Using the definition of (simple) bags from Sect. 3.3.2 we define an extension by

type EBAG = (**sort m**, **funct (m, m) bool** *eq*: **include** EQUIV(**m**, *eq*))
    bag, ∅, .+., .∈ ., .∉ ., .−., *#occs*,
    |.|, .=∅, .≠∅, .∪., .∩., .\., .⊆ .:
  based on BOOL, NAT,
  include BAG(**m**, *eq*),
  funct (bag) nat |.|,
  funct (bag) bool .=∅,
  funct (bag) bool .≠∅,
  funct (bag, bag) bag .∪.,
  funct (bag, bag) bag .∩.,
  funct (bag, bag) bag .\.,
  funct (bag, bag) bool .⊆ .,
  laws m *x*, **bag** *a*, *b*:

$|\varnothing| \equiv 0,$
$|a + x| \equiv |a| + 1,$
$\varnothing = \varnothing \equiv$ **true**,
$(a + x) = \varnothing \equiv$ **false**,
$a \neq \varnothing \equiv \neg(a = \varnothing),$
$a \cup \varnothing \equiv a,$
$a \cup (b + x) \equiv (a + x) \cup b,$
$a \cap \varnothing \equiv \varnothing,$
$a \cap (b + x) \equiv$ **if** $x \in a$ **then** $(a \cap b) + x$ **else** $a \cap$ b **fi**,
$a \setminus \varnothing \equiv a,$
$a \setminus (b + x) \equiv (a - x) \setminus b,$
$\varnothing \subseteq a \equiv$ **true**,
$(b + x) \subseteq a \equiv x \in a \ \Delta\ b \subseteq (a - x)$
endoftype.

Let us, furthermore, introduce the abbreviation

funct *arb* = (**bag** b: $b \neq \varnothing$) **m**:
  some m x: $x \in b$.

Now formal specifications of the problems stated above are straightforward. For the simple problem we have

funct *absolute-majority* = (**bag** b) (**m** | **bool**):
  if *has-maj*(b) **then** *arb-maj*(b) **else false fi where**

  funct *has-maj* = (**bag** b) **bool**:
    $\exists$ **m** x: $x \in b \wedge$ *is-maj*(x, b),

  funct *arb-maj* = (**bag** b: *has-maj*(b)) **m**:
    some m x: $x \in b \wedge$ *is-maj*(x, b),

  funct *is-maj* = (**m** x, **bag** b) **bool**:
    #occs(x, b) > ($|b|$ **div** 2).

For the generalized problem we have, analogously,

funct *k-majority* = (**bag** b, **nat** k: $2 \leq k \leq |b|$) (**bag** | **bool**):
  if *has-k-maj*(b, k) **then** *arb-k-maj*(b, k) **else false fi where**

  funct *has-k-maj* = (**bag** b, **nat** k: $2 \leq k \leq |b|$) **bool**:
    $\exists$ **bag** c: $c \neq \varnothing \wedge c \subseteq b \wedge$ *is-k-maj*(c, b, k),

  funct *arb-k-maj* = (**bag** b, **nat** k: $2 \leq k \leq |b| \wedge$ *has-k-maj*(b, k)) **bag**:
    some bag c: $c \neq \varnothing \wedge c \subseteq b \wedge$ *is-k-maj*(c, b, k),

  funct *is-k-maj* = (**bag** c, **bag** b, **nat** k: $2 \leq k \leq |b|$) **bool**:
    ($\forall$ **m** x: $x \in c$): *#occs*(x, b) > ($|b|$ **div** k).

9.2.2 Development of an Algorithm for the Simple Problem

The problem as formalized above involves a search for a particular element within a given complex data structure. A common and well-known strategy for such kinds of problems is first to prune the data structure, in order to restrict the search space. To this end we use the following straightforward transformation rule for pruning bags:

- <u>*bag pruning 1*</u>

  $(x \in M \wedge P(x, M))$

  $\Updownarrow$

  $(x \in prune(M, P) \wedge P(x, M))$ **where**
  funct *prune* = (**bag** *M*, **funct** (**m**, **bag**) **bool** *P*) **bag**:
  some bag M': $M' \subseteq M \wedge \forall$ **m** y: $y \in M \wedge y \notin M' \Rightarrow \neg P(y, M)$.

In our derivation below, we will just deal with the existence problem, since any constructive solution to the existence problem can be extended to a solution to the full problem using the techniques given in Sect. 5.3.4. Hence, the starting point and current focus of our considerations is

funct *has-maj* = (**bag** *b*) **bool**:
$\exists$ **m** x: $x \in b \wedge$ *is-maj*(x, b).

By *case introduction* (on *b*, following the axiomatic definition of bags), trivial *simplifications*, and *embedding* we have immediately

has-maj$(\varnothing) \equiv$ **false**; (2.1)
has-maj$(b+y)$ (2.2)
  $\equiv$ [unfold]
$\exists$ **m** x: $x \in (b+y) \wedge$ *is-maj*$(x, b+y)$
  $\equiv$ [laws of EBAG]
$\exists$ **m** x: $x \in \{y\} \cup b \wedge$ *is-maj*$(x, b+y)$
  $\equiv$ [*bag pruning 1*]
$\exists$ **m** x: $x \in$ *prune*$(\{y\} \cup b$, *is-maj*$) \wedge$ *is-maj*$(x, b+y)$
  $\equiv$ [embedding]
$\exists$ **m** x: $x \in$ *cands*$(\{y\}, b) \wedge$ *is-maj*$(x, b+y)$ **where**
  funct *cands* = (**bag** *a*, **bag** *b*: *diversity*$(a) \le 1$)) **bag**:
    prune$(a \cup b$, *is-maj*$)$ **where**
    mode mset = SET(**m**, =);
    funct *diversity* = (**bag** *a*) **nat**:
      |**that mset** *s*: $\forall$ **m** x: $x \in s \Leftrightarrow x \in a$|.

The assertion in *cands* is inspired by the observation that, if *has-maj* yields **true**, there is at most one element *x* in *b* which has the desired property:

$(|\{$**m** x: $x \in b \wedge$ *is-maj*$(x, b)\}| \le 1) \equiv$ **true**. (2.3)

In fact, *cands* formalizes the intuitive idea of looking for a possible majority candidate.

Our next efforts concentrate on *cands*. By suitable *case introductions* and *simplifications* (exploiting the assertion in *cands*) we aim at deriving a recursive definition in line with the generalized unfold/fold strategy. Particular care in folding is necessary with respect to the assertion in *cands*. We have

cands$(a, \varnothing) \equiv$ *prune*$(a$, *is-maj*$) \supseteq a$ (2.4) (which says a is a possible choice for $cands(a, \emptyset)$) and, by unfolding the definition of *cands*,

$$cands(a, (b+x)) \equiv prune(a \cup (b+x), is\text{-}maj).$$

In order to proceed in our derivation we need another *case introduction*. If $diversity(a) < 1$ holds, then we can calculate:

$$\begin{aligned}
&prune(a \cup (b+x), is\text{-}maj)\\
&\quad \equiv [\ diversity(a) < 1 \Leftrightarrow a = \emptyset\ ]\\
&prune(b+x, is\text{-}maj)\\
&\quad \equiv [\ \text{laws of EBAG}\ ]\\
&prune(\{x\} \cup b, is\text{-}maj)\\
&\quad \equiv [\ diversity(\{x\}) \le 1;\ \text{folding}\ ]\\
&cands(\{x\}, b).
\end{aligned} \tag{2.5}$$

In case $diversity(a) = 1$ holds, yet another *case introduction* is needed. If $x \in a$ holds, we can calculate:

$$\begin{aligned}
&prune(a \cup (b+x), is\text{-}maj)\\
&\quad \equiv [\ \text{laws of EBAG}\ ]\\
&prune((a+x) \cup b, is\text{-}maj)\\
&\quad \equiv [\ (diversity(a) \le 1 \wedge x \in a) \Rightarrow diversity(a+x) \le 1;\ \text{folding}\ ]\\
&cands(a+x, b).
\end{aligned} \tag{2.6}$$

If $diversity(a) = 1$ and $x \notin a$ holds, then for **m** $z = arb(a)$ our calculation is as follows:

$$\begin{aligned}
&prune(a \cup (b+x), is\text{-}maj)\\
&\quad \supseteq [\ \text{refinement, see below}\ ]\\
&prune((a-z) \cup b, is\text{-}maj)\\
&\quad \equiv [\ diversity(a) \le 1 \Rightarrow diversity(a-z) \le 1;\ \text{folding}\ ]\\
&cands(a-z, b).
\end{aligned} \tag{2.7}$$

It remains to justify the application of the rule *refinement* (Sect. 5.2) in the calculation above. The second applicability condition is obviously fulfilled. As to the first condition, we reason as follows:

Under the premise $diversity(a)=1 \wedge x \notin a$, we have for $a = a'+z$ and arbitrary **m** y:

$$\begin{aligned}
&(\#occs(y, a' \cup b) \le (|a' \cup b|\ \mathbf{div}\ 2)) \equiv \mathbf{true} \vdash\\
&(\#occs(y, (a \cup (b+x)) \le \#occs(y, a' \cup b)+1 \le (|a' \cup b|\ \mathbf{div}\ 2)+1 =\\
&\quad (|a \cup (b+x)|\ \mathbf{div}\ 2)) \equiv \mathbf{true}
\end{aligned} \tag{2.8}$$

and hence

$$\begin{aligned}
&(M' \sqsubseteq (a' \cup b) \wedge \forall\ \mathbf{m}\ y: y \in (a' \cup b) \wedge y \notin M' \Rightarrow \neg is\text{-}maj(y, a' \cup b)) \equiv \mathbf{true} \vdash\\
&(M' \sqsubseteq (a \cup (b+x)) \wedge\\
&\quad \forall\ \mathbf{m}\ y: y \in (a \cup (b+x)) \wedge y \notin M' \Rightarrow \neg is\text{-}maj(y, a \cup (b+x))) \equiv \mathbf{true}.
\end{aligned} \tag{2.9}$$

By just collecting the results (2.1) to (2.7) obtained so far we have

funct *has-maj* = (**bag** *b*) **bool**:
  if $b = \emptyset$ **then false**
    else m $y = arb(b)$; $\exists$ **m** x: $x \in cands'(\{y\}, b-y) \wedge is\text{-}maj(x, b)$ **fi**
where

```
funct cands = (bag a, bag b: diversity(a) ≤ 1) bag:
   if b =∅ then a
      else m x = arb(b);
           if diversity(a) < 1 then cands({x}, b–x)
           [] diversity(a) = 1 ∧ x∈a then cands(a+x, b–x)
           [] diversity(a) = 1 ∧ x∉a then cands(a–z, b–x)
                                 where m z = arb(a) fi fi.
```

The termination of *cands*, and hence the correctness of the folding steps above, is straightforward. Furthermore, obviously, the result of *cands* also fulfils the assertion on *a*:

$$(diversity(cands(a, b)) \le 1) \equiv \mathbf{true}. \tag{2.10}$$

Bags *a* having the property *diversity*(*a*) ≤ 1 can be replaced using a simple data type transformation (Sect. 8.2.1) by a pair consisting of an element *c* of kind **m** and a natural number *d* (denoting the number of occurrences of *c* in *a*). Using this rule results in

```
funct has-maj = (bag b) bool:
   if b =∅ then false
          else m y = arb(b); (m x, nat d) = cands'({y}, 1, b–y);
               d ≠ 0 ∧ is-maj(x, b) fi where
funct cands' = (m c, nat d, bag b) (m, nat):
   if b =∅ then (c, d)
          else m x = arb(b);
               if d = 0 then cands'(x, d+1, b–x)
               [] d ≠ 0 ∧ x = c then cands'(c, d+1, b–x)
               [] d ≠ 0 ∧ x ≠ c then cands'(c, d–1, b–x) fi fi
```

which is the essence of the original algorithm by Boyer and Moore. The further development, i.e. extension of this algorithm to the problem of *finding* an element with the desired property, operational definition of *has-maj*, and transition to an imperative program, is obvious and left as an exercise to the interested reader.

9.2.3 Development of an Algorithm for the Generalized Problem

We now aim at deriving a solution for the generalized problem. The strategic idea is to reuse the derivation from the previous section and adapt it to the new problem by appropriate generalizations.

As in the previous development, we concentrate on deriving a constructive solution to the existence problem. Hence, we start from

```
funct has-k-maj = (bag b, nat k: 2 ≤ k ≤ |b|) bool:
   ∃ bag c: c ≠∅ ∧ c⊆b ∧ is-k-maj(c, b, k).
```

By comparison of *has-maj* with *has-k-maj*, we realize that the latter is a generalization of the former in two different respects:

(a) it asks for the existence of a bag of elements, instead of just an element; and
(b) it is dependent on an additional parameter k.

In Sect. 5.2 these aspects of generalization are dealt with by embedding of the data type and embedding of the domain, respectively. Below, both aspects will be dealt with in succession. We first generalize the previous derivation in such a way that it still solves the old problem for bags instead of elements. Then we generalize once more in order to also cover aspect (b) above.

Dealing with aspect (a) is the crucial activity in generalization, since generalization of a data type usually entails also appropriate generalization of the operations used. Therefore, we change the respective specifications of Sect. 9.2.1 into

funct *has-maj'* = (**bag** b) **bool**:
  $\exists$ **bag** c: $c \neq \varnothing \wedge c \subseteq b \wedge$ *is-maj'*(c, b);

funct *is-maj'* = (**bag** c, **bag** b) **bool**:
  ($\forall$ **m** x: $x \in c$): *#occs*$(x, b) > (|b|$ **div** 2).

The generalization of the data type also affects the transformation rule for pruning bags which has to be generalized, too:

- <u>*bag pruning 2*</u>

  $(c \subseteq M \wedge (\forall$ **m** $x: x \in c): P(x, M))$

  $\Updownarrow$

  $(c \subseteq prune(M, P) \wedge (\forall$ **m** $x: x \in c): P(x, M))$ **where**
  funct *prune* = (**bag** M, **funct** (**m**, **bag**) **bool** P) **bag**:
    some bag M': $M' \subseteq M \wedge \forall$ **m** y: $y \in M \wedge y \notin M' \Rightarrow \neg P(y, M)$.

Now, using *bag pruning 2* instead of *bag pruning 1*, the steps (2.1) and (2.2) of the derivation in Sect. 9.2.2 can be reused (without further change) and we get immediately

has-maj'$(\varnothing) \equiv$ **false**; (3.1)
has-maj'$(b+y) \equiv \exists$ **bag** c: $c \neq \varnothing \wedge c \subseteq$ *cands*$(\{y\}, b) \wedge$ *is-maj'*$(c, b+y)$. (3.2)

Next, as in the previous section, we concentrate on the development of *cands*. Here, only the calculation of (2.7) has to be generalized to removing a (singleton) bag from a instead of an element:

prune$(a \cup (b+x)$, *is-maj*)
  $\supseteq$ [if $x \notin a$ and **bag** c = **some bag** c': $c' \subseteq a \wedge$ *diversity*$(c') = 1 \wedge |c'| = 1$; refinement]
prune$((a \setminus c) \cup b$, *is-maj*)
  $\equiv$ [*diversity*$(a \setminus c) \leq 1$; folding]
cands$(a \setminus c, b)$. (3.7)

The justification of applying the rule *refinement* in this calculation is now as follows:

Under the premise *diversity*$(a) = 1 \wedge x \notin a$ we have for arbitrary **m** y and $a = a' \cup c$ where **bag** c = **some bag** c': $c' \subseteq a \wedge$ *diversity*$(c') = 1 \wedge |c'| = 1$:

(*#occs*$(y, a' \cup b) \leq (|a' \cup b|$ **div** 2)) $\equiv$ **true** $\vdash$

$(\#occs(y, (a \cup (b+x)) \leq \#occs(y, a' \cup b)+1 \leq (|a' \cup b| \textbf{ div } 2)+1 =$
$(|a \cup (b+x)| \textbf{ div } 2)) \equiv \textbf{true}$ (3.8)

and hence

$(M' \subseteq (a' \cup b) \wedge \forall \textbf{ m } y: y \in (a' \cup b) \wedge y \notin M' \Rightarrow \neg is\text{-}maj'(y, a' \cup b)) \equiv \textbf{true} \vdash$
$(M' \subseteq (a \cup (b+x)) \wedge$
$\forall \textbf{ m } y: y \in (a \cup (b+x)) \wedge y \notin M' \Rightarrow \neg is\text{-}maj'(y, a \cup (b+x))) \equiv \textbf{true}.$ (3.9)

So far, by reuse, we have derived the following algorithm:

```
funct has-maj' = (bag b) bool:
   if b =∅ then false
      else m y = arb(b); ∃ bag c: c ≠∅ ∧ c⊆ cands({y}, b–y) ∧ is-maj'(c, b) fi
   where

   funct cands = (bag a, bag b: diversity(a) ≤ 1) bag:
      if b =∅ then a
         else  m x = arb(b);
               if diversity(a) < 1 then cands(a+x, b–x)
               [] diversity(a) = 1 ∧ x∈ a then cands(a+x, b–x)
               [] diversity(a) = 1 ∧ x∉ a then cands(a \ c, b–x) where
                  bag c = some bag c': c'⊆ a ∧ diversity(c') = 1 ∧ |c'| = 1 fi fi.
```

After these preparatory steps, dealing with aspect (b) from above is much simpler. Following the idea of finding generalizations by creating constants and making them into parameters (Sect. 5.2), we first substitute all occurrences of "1" in the functions above by "2–1". Then we simply add k as an additional parameter (as in the specification in Sect. 9.2.1) and generalize all occurrences of "2" into k. Thus, in particular, the assertion in *cands* is changed into $diversity(a) \leq k-1$ which, again, coincides with the (obvious) property

$(|\{\textbf{m } x: x \in b \wedge is\text{-}k\text{-}maj(\{x\}, b, k)\}| \leq k) \equiv \textbf{true}.$ (3.3)

Summarizing the results gained so far, we have the algorithm

```
funct has-k-maj = (bag b, nat k: 2 ≤ k ≤ |b|) bool:
   if b =∅ then false
      else m y = arb(b);
           ∃ bag c: c ≠∅ ∧ c⊆ cands({y}, b–y) ∧ is-k-maj(c, b, k) fi where

   funct cands = (bag a, bag b: diversity(a) ≤ k–1) bag:
      if b =∅ then a
         else  m x = arb(b);
               if diversity(a) < k–1 then cands(a+x, b–x)
               [] diversity(a) = k–1 ∧ x∈ a then cands(a+x, b–x)
               [] diversity(a) = k–1 ∧ x∉ a then cands(a \ c, b–x) where
                  bag c = some bag c':
                          c'⊆ a ∧ diversity(c') = k–1 ∧ |c'| = k–1 fi fi.
```

As in the previous section, it remains to find a suitable implementation for the auxiliary bag a. However, the last step in the development there cannot be reused, since particular properties of a are exploited in the implementation step. Therefore, in the following, we concentrate on finding another implementation of a bag a with the property $diversity(a) \le k{-}1$.

In order to get rid of the auxiliary predicate *diversity*, we use the *differencing technique* (Sect. 6.4.4). Formally, we define by an *embedding*

```
funct cands' = (bag a, nat d, bag b:
                (diversity(a) ≤ k–1) ∧ d = diversity(a)) bag:
   cands(a, b)
```

and change the call of *cands* in *has-k-maj* into *cands'*$(\{y\}, 1, b{-}y)$. Next we develop a definition of *cands'* (independent of *cands*), using the unfold/fold strategy and the assertion on d. This leads to

```
funct cands' = (bag a, nat d, bag b: d ≤ k–1) bag:
   if b =∅ then a
      else m x = arb(b);
            if x∈a then cands'(a+x, d, b–x)
            [] d < k–1 ∧ x∉a then cands'(a+x, d+1, b–x)
            [] d = k–1 ∧ x∉a then cands'(a \ c, diversity(a \ c), b–x) where
               bag c = some bag c': c'⊆a ∧ diversity(c') = k–1 ∧ |c'| = k–1 fi fi.
```

Finally, by *abstraction*, we introduce a new auxiliary operation:

```
funct cands' = (bag a, nat d, bag b: d ≤ k–1) bag:
   if b =∅ then a
      else m x = arb(b);
            if x∈a then cands'(a+x, d, b–x)
            [] d < k–1 ∧ x∉a then cands'(a+x, d+1, b–x)
            [] d = k–1 ∧ x∉a then cands'(k-reduce(a), b–x) fi fi where

   funct k-reduce = (bag a: diversity(a) = k–1) (bag, nat):
      (a \ c, diversity(a \ c)) where
      bag c = some bag c': c'⊆a ∧ diversity(c') = k–1 ∧ |c'| = k–1.
```

Essentially, this is the "second algorithm" in [Misra, Gries 82], where also the remaining steps, namely implementing **bag** by AVL-trees and giving an appropriate operational definition for *k-reduce*, can be found.

9.3 Fast Pattern Matching According to Boyer and Moore

In general, highly efficient algorithms are difficult to understand and hard to prove correct. This is a consequence of clarity and modularity being sacrificed in favor of efficiency, and of a number of essential design decisions being hidden in the final code. The pattern matching algorithm in [Boyer, Moore 77] is a representative example of this phenomenon.

Given a string s and a pattern p, a naive approach to pattern matching is the following: first check whether an occurrence of p can be found as a prefix of s. If such an occurrence is found, then we are done. Otherwise, we repeat the above process with respect to p and the string s' obtained from s by removing its first element. This process can be thought of as repeatedly shifting our attention one position to the right in s until an occurrence of p has been found. In the worst case this algorithm has complexity $O(n*m)$ where n and m are the lengths of p and s, respectively. Boyer and Moore's algorithm is more sophisticated. In their algorithm, under certain conditions, attention can be shifted more than one position to the right, and thus superfluous comparisons of characters can be avoided. Another improvement of the naive algorithm is the elimination of multiple evaluations of identical function calls. Both improvements lead to an algorithm where in the average case not all characters of the string have to be inspected.

9.3.1 Formal Specification

An informal description of the pattern matching problem is as follows [Boyer, Moore 77]:

*Given two sequences of characters, p (a pattern) and s (a string), find the starting position of the first occurrence of p in s, provided such a position exists. If such a position does not exist, then yield **false**.*

For the sake of brevity, we will assume a non-empty pattern p. An extension to empty patterns is straightforward. Thus, assuming a (predefined) character set **char** with an equality predicate "=", a formal specification of the pattern matching problem is straightforward:

mode res = (**nat** | **bool**);
mode string = EESEQU(**char**, =);

funct *find* = (**string** *p*, **string** *s*: $p \neq$<>) **res**:
  if *occurs*(*p*, *s*) **then** *first-occ*(*p*, *s*) **else false fi where**

  funct *occurs* = (**string** *p*, **string** *s*) **bool**:
    $\exists$ **string** l, r: $s = l+p+r$,

  funct *first-occ* = (**string** *p*, **string** *s*) **nat**:
    min {**nat** i: $\exists$ **string** l, r: $s = l+p+r \wedge i = |l|+1$]}.

Here, for a non-empty set S of natural numbers, **min** S yields the minimum element of S.

We next aim at finding an operational solution of the formal specification given above. This is the subject of the following four subsections.

9.3.2 Development of the Function *occurs*

The function *find* belongs to the class of problems dealt with in Sect. 5.3.4. Therefore, in the sequel we first concentrate on

funct *occurs* = (**string** *p*, **string** *s*) **bool**:
  $\exists$ **string** l, r: $s = l+p+r$.

Introduction of Indices

In general, concatenation of strings and indexed access to strings are related by the following obvious properties:

$\exists$ **string** a: $c = a+b \equiv \exists$ **nat** i: $0 \le i \le |c| \wedge c[i+1 : |c|] = b$ (2.1)

$\exists$ **string** b: $c = a+b \equiv \exists$ **nat** i: $0 \le i \le |c| \wedge c[1 : i] = a$ (2.2)

Hence, a definition of *occurs* using indexed access to strings can be calculated as follows:

$\exists$ **string** l, r: $s = l+p+r$
  $\equiv$ [(2.2)]
$\exists$ **string** l, **nat** j: $0 \le j \le |s| \wedge s[1 : j] = l+p$
  $\equiv$ [(2.1)]
$\exists$ **nat** k, **nat** j: $0 \le j \le |s| \wedge 0 \le k \le |s[1 : j]| \wedge (s[1 : j])[k+1 : |s[1 : j]|] = p$
  $\equiv$ [simplification]
$\exists$ **nat** k, **nat** j: $0 \le j \le |s| \wedge 0 \le k \le j \wedge s[k+1 : j] = p$
  $\equiv$ [$(p = s[k+1 : j]) \equiv$ **true** $\vdash$ $(j = |p|+k) \equiv$ **true**]
$\exists$ **nat** k: $0 \le |p|+k \le |s| \wedge s[k+1 : |p|+k] = p$
  $\equiv$ [simplification; index translation]
$\exists$ **nat** i: $|p| \le i \le |s| \wedge s[i-|p|+1 : i] = p$
  $\equiv$ [abstraction]
$\exists$ **nat** i: $|p| \le i \le |s| \wedge eq(i)$ **where** (2.3)
  funct eq = (**nat** i) **bool**: $s[i-|p|+1 : i] = p$.

Generalization of the Specification

Specification (2.3) suggests an *embedding* by generalizing one of the bounds in the range of the quantifier and by making it into an additional parameter. We decide on generalizing $|p|$. Since the parameters p and s remain unchanged, they can be suppressed. Thus, we obtain

funct *occurs* = (**string** p, **string** s) **bool**:
  $occ(|p|)$ **where**

  funct *occ* = (**nat** k) **bool**:
    $\exists$ **nat** i: $k \le i \le |s| \wedge eq(i)$.

Looking for a *generalization* is part of the strategy mentioned above, which suggests considering constants as candidates for additional parameters. Finding a suitable candidate, however, is left to the developer's intuition.

By using *case introduction* and simple unfold-fold steps, a recursive definition of *occ* can be derived:

funct *occ* = (**nat** k) **bool**:
  $k \le |s| \wedge (eq(k) \vee occ(k+1))$.

This version of the function *occ* formalizes the naive algorithm described in the introduction, where attention is shifted exactly one position to the right in the string s.

Instead of shifting attention just one position, one could possibly do better and shift more than one position. However, no available information on the additional parameter k allows such an improvement. This is because we used a naive *embedding* where we have not related the new argument of the embedded function to the old ones by an appropriate assertion.

By (2.3) we are inspired to use an *embedding* (with assertion) as follows:

funct *occurs* = (**string** *p*, **string** *s*) **bool**:
  occ(|*p*|) **where**

  funct *occ* = (**nat** *k*: *no-match*(*k*)) **bool**:
    $\exists$ **nat** *i*: $k \le i \le |s| \;\Delta\; eq(i)$. (2.4)

The assertion *no-match*(*k*) is defined by

funct *no-match* = (**nat** *k*) **bool**:
  $\forall$ **nat** *k'*: $(|p| \le k' < k \wedge k' \le |s|) \Rightarrow \neg eq(k')$. (2.5)

It ensures that no occurrence of the string *p* in the string *s* ending at a position less than *k* can be found. In the sequel we can profit from this assertion, since it will allow certain simplifications within the function *occ*. Furthermore, we will use the obvious property (for all **nat** *i*)

$no\text{-}match(i) \equiv$ **true** $\vdash$ ($\forall$ **nat** *j*: $j \le i \Rightarrow no\text{-}match(j)) \equiv$ **true**. (2.6)

Intuitively, one can shift the attention by an arbitrary number of positions less than or equal to the length of the pattern, provided a possible matching is not missed. Therefore, we define

funct δ_1 = (**nat** *k*) **nat**:
  some nat *i*: $1 \le i \le |p| \;\Delta\; no\text{-}match(k+i)$. (2.7)

The function δ_1 is defined non-deterministically on purpose. Non-determinism here allows us to postpone the decision how much to shift to the right, until further and more detailed information for finding an efficient operational definition is available.

Development of the Function occ

Now we concentrate on the body of the function *occ*, defined by (2.4). According to the semantics of our language, from the assertion *no-match*(*k*) defined in (2.5) and definition (2.7), it follows that in the body of *occ*

$\forall$ **nat** *i*: $k \le i < k+\delta_1(k) \le |s| \Rightarrow eq(i) \equiv$ **false** (2.8)

holds.

Thus, by a *case introduction* with three cases, where *i* satisfies (for **nat** $d = \delta_1(k)$)

$i = k \le |s|,\quad k < i < k+d \le |s|,\quad$ or $k+d \le i \le |s|$,

and trivial *simplifications*, we get that (2.4) is equivalent to

$k \le |s| \;\Delta\; (eq(k) \;\nabla\; (\exists$ **nat** *i*: $k+\delta_1(k) \le i \le |s| \;\Delta\; eq(i))$.

By *folding with assertion* (where termination is guaranteed by the definition of δ_1), we obtain

funct *occ* = (**nat** *k*: *no-match*(*k*)) **bool**:
  $k \le |s| \;\Delta\; (eq(k) \;\nabla\; occ(k+\delta_1(k)))$.

Transition to Characterwise Comparisons

Our next intermediate goal is to eliminate the operation *eq* occurring in *occ*. Using the property

$$(\mathrm{a} \mathbin{\Delta} \mathrm{b}) \mathbin{\nabla} \mathrm{c} \equiv (\mathrm{a} \mathbin{\Delta} (\mathrm{b} \mathbin{\nabla} \mathrm{c})) \mathbin{\nabla} (\neg\mathrm{a} \mathbin{\Delta} \mathrm{c}) \tag{2.9}$$

of sequential boolean operators (Ex. 4.4-2), we calculate as follows:

$k \le |s| \mathbin{\Delta} (eq(k) \mathbin{\nabla} occ(k+\delta_1(k)))$
  $\equiv$ [unfold *eq*, definition of =]
$k \le |s| \mathbin{\Delta} ((\forall \textbf{ nat } i\text{: } 1 \le i \le |p| \Rightarrow (s[k-|p|+1 : k])[i] = p[i]) \mathbin{\nabla} occ(k+\delta_1(k)))$
  $\equiv$ [property of strings]
$k \le |s| \mathbin{\Delta} ((\forall \textbf{ nat } i\text{: } 1 \le i \le |p| \Rightarrow s[k-|p|+i] = p[i]) \mathbin{\nabla} occ(k+\delta_1(k)))$
  $\equiv$ [splitting a universal quantification]
$k \le |s| \mathbin{\Delta} ((s[k] = p[|p|] \mathbin{\Delta} (\forall \textbf{ nat } i\text{: } 1 \le i \le |p|-1 \Rightarrow s[k-|p|+i] = p[i])) \mathbin{\nabla}$
    $occ(k+\delta_1(k)))$
  $\equiv$ [(2.9)]
$k \le |s| \mathbin{\Delta}$
  $((s[k] = p[|p|] \mathbin{\Delta} ((\forall \textbf{ nat } i\text{: } 1 \le i \le |p|-1 \Rightarrow s[k-|p|+i] = p[i]) \mathbin{\nabla} occ(k+\delta_1(k)))) \mathbin{\nabla}$
  $(s[k] \ne p[|p|] \mathbin{\Delta} occ(k+\delta_1(k))))$.

Towards a Fully Operational Definition of occ

The final expression for *occ* is almost operational except for δ_1 and the universal quantification in the sub-expression

$$(\forall \textbf{ nat } i\text{: } 1 \le i \le |p|-1 \Rightarrow s[k-|p|+i] = p[i]) \mathbin{\nabla} occ(k+\delta_1(k)). \tag{2.10}$$

In order to make the universal quantification operational we aim at introducing, by *abstraction*, an auxiliary function definition which then in turn can be transformed into a recursive definition. As a preparatory step for the *abstraction* we first *generalize* δ_1 and define

funct δ = (**nat** k, **nat** l) **nat**:
  some nat i: $1 \le i \le |p| \mathbin{\Delta} no\text{-}match(k+|p|-l+i)$. (2.11)

Obviously, we have

$$\delta(k, |p|) \equiv \delta_1(k), \tag{2.12}$$

and $(\forall \textbf{ nat } j\text{: } 1 \le j \le l)$:

$$\delta(k, l) \equiv \delta(k-j, l-j). \tag{2.13}$$

Now we can calculate from (2.10)

$(\forall \textbf{ nat } i\text{: } 1 \le i \le |p|-1 \Rightarrow s[k-|p|+i] = p[i]) \mathbin{\nabla} occ(k+\delta_1(k))$
  $\equiv$ [(2.12)]
$(\forall \textbf{ nat } i\text{: } 1 \le i \le |p|-1 \Rightarrow s[k-|p|+i] = p[i]) \mathbin{\nabla} occ(k+\delta(k, |p|))$
  $\equiv$ [(2.13), arithmetic]
$(\forall \textbf{ nat } i\text{: } 1 \le i \le |p|-1 \Rightarrow s[k-1-(|p|-1)+i] = p[i]) \mathbin{\nabla} occ(k+\delta(k-1, |p|-1))$
  $\equiv$ [abstraction]
try-match(k–1, $|p|$–1) **where**
  funct *try-match* = (**nat** k, **nat** l:
          $no\text{-}match(k+|p|-l) \mathbin{\Delta} partial\text{-}match(k, l)$) **bool**:
    $(\forall \textbf{ nat } i\text{: } 1 \le i \le l \Rightarrow s[k-l+i] = p[i]) \mathbin{\nabla} occ(k+|p|-l+\delta(k, l))$. (2.14)

The assertion *partial-match* is defined by

funct *partial-match* = (**nat** k, **nat** l) **nat**:
$$l \le |p| \,\Delta\, k+|p|-l \le |s| \,\Delta\, s[k+1 : k+|p|-l] = p[l+1 : |p|]. \quad (2.15)$$

Here, as with *embedding* above, we have coupled the *abstraction* with the introduction of an assertion. The assertion *partial-match*(k, l) guarantees that to the right of the k-th position in s the next $|p|-l$ characters of s and the last $|p|-l$ characters of p coincide.

Development of the Function try-match

A recursive definition of the function *try-match* can be calculated from (2.14) as follows:

$(\forall$ **nat** i: $1 \le i \le l \Rightarrow s[k-l+i] = p[i]) \,\nabla\, occ(k+|p|-l+\delta(k, l))$
  ≡ [*case introduction*: $l = 0 \vee l > 0$; simplification]
$l = 0 \,\nabla\, ((\forall$ **nat** i: $1 \le i \le l \Rightarrow s[k-l+i] = p[i]) \,\nabla\, occ(k+|p|-l+\delta(k, l)))$
  ≡ [splitting a universal quantification]
$l = 0 \,\nabla$
$(s[k] = p[l] \,\Delta\, (\forall$ **nat** i: $1 \le i \le l-1 \Rightarrow s[k-l+i] = p[i])) \,\nabla\, occ(k+|p|-l+\delta(k, l))$
  ≡ [(2.9)]
$l = 0 \,\nabla$
$(s[k] = p[l] \,\Delta\, ((\forall$ **nat** i: $1 \le i \le l-1 \Rightarrow s[k-l+i] = p[i]) \,\nabla\, occ(k+|p|-l+\delta(k, l)))) \,\nabla$
$(s[k] \ne p[l] \,\Delta\, occ(k+|p|-l+\delta(k, l)))$
  ≡ [arithmetic; (2.13)]
$l = 0 \,\nabla$
$(s[k] = p[l] \,\Delta\, ((\forall$ **nat** i: $1 \le i \le l-1 \Rightarrow s[k-l+i] = p[i]) \,\nabla$
  $occ(k-1+|p|-(l-1)+\delta(k-1, l-1)))) \,\nabla$
$(s[k] \ne p[l] \,\Delta\, occ(k+|p|-l+\delta(k, l)))$
  ≡ [*folding* (with assertion)]
$l = 0 \,\nabla\, (s[k] = p[l] \,\Delta\, try\text{-}match(k-1, l-1)) \,\nabla$
$(s[k] \ne p[l] \,\Delta\, occ(k+|p|-l+\delta(k, l)))$.

Summary

Summarizing, we have arrived at the following specification:

funct *occurs* = (**string** p, **string** s) **bool**:
  $occ(|p|)$ **where**

  funct *occ* = (**nat** k: *no-match*(k)) **bool**:
    $k \le |s| \,\Delta\, ((s[k] = p[|p|] \,\Delta\, try\text{-}match(k-1, |p|-1)) \,\nabla$
      $(s[k] \ne p[|p|] \,\Delta\, occ(k+\delta(k, |p|))))$;

  funct *try-match* = (**nat** k, **nat** l: *no-match*($k+|p|-l$) Δ *partial-match*(k, l)) **bool**:
    $l = 0 \,\nabla\, (s[k] = p[l] \,\Delta\, try\text{-}match(k-1, l-1)) \,\nabla$
      $(s[k] \ne p[l] \,\Delta\, occ(k+|p|-l+\delta(k, l)))$

where the assertions *no-match* and *partial-match* are defined by (2.5) and (2.15), respectively.

9.3.3 Deriving an Operational Version of δ

It now remains to find an operational definition for δ used in the definitions of *occ* and *try-match*. Since δ is defined non-deterministically, we still have freedom of choice. Aiming at an efficient algorithm, of course, we try to make the best possible choice and aim at a value which is as large as possible within the respective context. To this end we can profit from our assertions, since they convey, in a condensed form, additional information (for maximizing the respective values) about the arguments of δ, which otherwise would have to be deduced from the context by global reasoning.

δ(*k*, *l*) always occurs in a context where

$$(\textit{no-match}(k+|p|-l) \ \Delta \ \textit{partial-match}(k, l) \ \Delta \ l > 0 \ \Delta \ s[k] \neq p[l]) \equiv \textbf{true}$$

holds. Using this information, our goal is to find an operational definition of δ which approximates

$$\textbf{max}\ \{\textbf{nat}\ i\text{: } 1 \leq i \leq |p| \ \Delta \ \textit{no-match}(k+|p|-l+i)\} \qquad (3.1)$$

(where for a non-empty set *S*, **max** *S* yields the maximum element of *S*) as close as possible.

Some General Properties

In order to treat maxima of non-empty and of empty sets in the same way in our calculation for (3.1), we introduce

$$\textbf{max}_0\ \{\textbf{nat}\ i\text{: } \mathrm{P}(i)\} \ =_{\text{def}} \ \textbf{if}\ \exists\ \textbf{nat}\ i\text{: } \mathrm{P}(i)\ \textbf{then}\ \textbf{max}\ \{\textbf{nat}\ i\text{: } \mathrm{P}(i)\}\ \textbf{else}\ 0\ \textbf{fi}.$$

Furthermore, we will use the following obvious properties of maxima and minima (of sets of natural numbers):

$$\textbf{min}\ \{\textbf{nat}\ i\text{: } a \leq i \leq b \ \Delta \ \mathrm{P}(i)\} \ \equiv \ b - \textbf{max}\ \{\textbf{nat}\ i\text{: } 0 \leq i \leq b-a \ \Delta \ \mathrm{P}(b-i)\} \qquad (3.2)$$

$$\exists\ \textbf{nat}\ i\text{: } \mathrm{P}(i) \vee \mathrm{Q}(i) \equiv \textbf{true} \vdash$$
$$\textbf{max}\{\textbf{nat}\ i\text{: } \mathrm{P}(i) \vee \mathrm{Q}(i)\} \ \equiv \ \textbf{max}\{\textbf{max}_0\{\textbf{nat}\ i\text{: } \mathrm{P}(i)\}, \textbf{max}_0\{\textbf{nat}\ i\text{: } \mathrm{Q}(i)\}\} \qquad (3.3)$$

$$\forall\ \textbf{nat}\ i\text{: } \mathrm{P}(i) \Rightarrow \mathrm{Q}(i) \equiv \textbf{true} \vdash$$
$$(\textbf{max}_0\ \{\textbf{nat}\ i\text{: } \mathrm{P}(i)\} \leq \textbf{max}_0\ \{\textbf{nat}\ i\text{: } \mathrm{Q}(i)\}) \equiv \textbf{true} \qquad (3.4)$$

Calculation of δ

With these prerequisites, (3.1) can be transformed as follows:

$$\textbf{max}\ \{\textbf{nat}\ i\text{: } 1 \leq i \leq |p| \ \Delta \ \textit{no-match}(k+|p|-l+i)\}$$
$$\equiv \ [\ (2.6);\ \text{property of } \textbf{nat};\ \text{simplification}\ ]$$
$$\textbf{min}\ \{\textbf{nat}\ i\text{: } 1 \leq i \leq |p| \ \Delta \ \textit{no-match}(k+|p|-l+i) \ \Delta$$
$$(i = |p| \ \nabla \ \neg\textit{no-match}(k+|p|-l+i+1))\}$$
$$\equiv \ [\ (3.2)\ ]$$
$$|p| - \textbf{max}\ \{\textbf{nat}\ i\text{: } 0 \leq i < |p| \ \Delta \ \textit{no-match}(k+|p|-l+|p|-i) \ \Delta$$
$$(|p|-i = |p| \ \nabla \ \neg\textit{no-match}(k+|p|-l+|p|-i+1))\}$$
$$\equiv \ [\ \text{case introduction; simplification}\ ]$$
$$|p| - \textbf{max}\ \{\textbf{nat}\ i\text{: } (0 < i < |p| \ \Delta \ \textit{no-match}(k+|p|-l+|p|-i) \ \Delta$$
$$\neg\textit{no-match}(k+|p|-l+|p|-i+1)) \vee (0 = i \ \Delta \ \textit{no-match}(k+|p|-l+|p|-i))\}$$
$$\equiv \ [\ (3.3)\ ]$$

$$|p| - \textbf{max}\{\textbf{max}_0\{\textbf{nat}\ i\text{: } 0 < i < |p|\ \Delta\ \textit{no-match}(k{+}|p|{-}l{+}|p|{-}i)\ \Delta$$
$$\neg\textit{no-match}(k{+}|p|{-}l{+}|p|{-}i{+}1)\}, \qquad (3.5)$$
$$\textbf{max}_0\{\textbf{nat}\ i\text{: } 0 = i\ \Delta\ \textit{no-match}(k{+}|p|{-}l{+}|p|{-}i)\}\} \qquad (3.6)$$
$\geq$ [individual calculation of the subexpressions (3.5) and (3.6), see below]
$$|p| - \textbf{max}\ \{\ \textbf{max}_0\ \{\textbf{nat}\ i\text{: } (|p|{-}l < i < |p|\ \Delta$$
$$(p[i{-}|p|{+}l{+}1 : i] = p[l{+}1 : |p|] \wedge p[i{-}|p|{+}l] = s[k])) \vee$$
$$(0 < i \leq |p|{-}l\ \Delta\ p[1 : i] = p[|p|{-}i{+}1 : |p|])\},\ \ 0\}$$
$\equiv$ [(3.3); simplification]
$$|p| - \textbf{max}\ \{\textbf{nat}\ i\text{: } (|p|{-}l < i < |p|\ \Delta$$
$$(p[i{-}|p|{+}l{+}1 : i] = p[l{+}1 : |p|] \wedge p[i{-}|p|{+}l] = s[k])) \vee$$
$$(0 \leq i \leq |p|{-}l\ \Delta\ p[1 : i] = p[|p|{-}i{+}1 : |p|])\}.$$

Hence

funct δ = (**nat** k, **nat** l) **nat**:
$$|p| - \textbf{max}\ \{\textbf{nat}\ i\text{: } (|p|{-}l\ < i < |p|\ \Delta$$
$$(p[i{-}|p|{+}l{+}1 : i] = p[l{+}1 : |p|] \wedge p[i{-}|p|{+}l] = s[k])) \vee$$
$$(0 \leq i \leq |p|{-}l\ \Delta\ p[1 : i] = p[|p|{-}i{+}1 : |p|])\}$$

satisfies our initial goal.

The individual calculation of (3.5) is as follows:

$$\textbf{max}_0\ \{\textbf{nat}\ i\text{: } 0 < i < |p|\ \Delta\ \textit{no-match}(k{+}|p|{-}l{+}|p|{-}i)\ \Delta\ \neg\textit{no-match}(k{+}|p|{-}l{+}|p|{-}i{+}1)\}$$
$\equiv$ [definition *no-match*; simplification]
$$\textbf{max}_0\ \{\textbf{nat}\ i\text{: } 0 < i < |p|\ \Delta\ \textit{eq}(k{+}|p|{-}l{+}|p|{-}i)\}$$
$\equiv$ [definition *eq*]
$$\textbf{max}_0\ \{\textbf{nat}\ i\text{: } 0 < i < |p|\ \Delta\ s[k{+}|p|{-}l{-}i{+}1 : k{+}|p|{-}l{+}|p|{-}i] = p\}$$
$\equiv$ [case introduction; simplification]
$$\textbf{max}_0\ \{\textbf{nat}\ i\text{: } (|p|{-}l < i < |p|\ \Delta\ s[k{+}|p|{-}l{-}i{+}1 : k{+}|p|{-}l{+}|p|{-}i] = p) \vee$$
$$(0 < i \leq |p|{-}l\ \Delta\ s[k{+}|p|{-}l{-}i{+}1 : k{+}|p|{-}l{+}|p|{-}i] = p)\}$$
$\equiv$ [splitting s]
$$\textbf{max}_0\ \{\textbf{nat}\ i\text{: } (|p|{-}l < i < |p|\ \Delta$$
$$(s[k{+}|p|{-}l{-}i{+}1 : k{-}1] + s[k] + s[k{+}1 : k{+}|p|{-}l] + s[k{+}|p|{-}l{+}1 : k{+}|p|{-}l{+}|p|{-}i]) = p) \vee$$
$$(0 < i \leq |p|{-}l\ \Delta\ (s[k{+}|p|{-}l{-}i{+}1 : k{+}|p|{-}l] + s[k{+}|p|{-}l{+}1 : k{+}|p|{-}l{+}|p|{-}i]) = p)\}$$
$\equiv$ [assertion: *partial-match*(k, l)]
$$\textbf{max}_0\ \{\textbf{nat}\ i\text{: } (|p|{-}l < i < |p|\ \Delta$$
$$(s[k{+}|p|{-}l{-}i{+}1 : k{-}1] + s[k] + p[l{+}1 : |p|] + s[k{+}|p|{-}l{+}1 : k{+}|p|{-}l{+}|p|{-}i]) =$$
$$(p[1 : l{-}1] + p[l] + p[l{+}1 : |p|])) \vee$$
$$(0 < i \leq |p|{-}l\ \Delta\ (p[|p|{-}i{+}1 : |p|] + s[k{+}|p|{-}l{+}1 : k{+}|p|{-}l{+}|p|{-}i]) =$$
$$(p[1 : i] + p[i{+}1 : |p|]))\}$$
$\leq$ [obvious property of strings; (3.4)]
$$\textbf{max}_0\ \{\textbf{nat}\ i\text{: } (|p|{-}l < i < |p|\ \Delta\ (p[i{-}|p|{+}l{+}1 : i] = p[l{+}1 : |p|] \wedge p[i{-}|p|{+}l] = s[k])) \vee$$
$$(0 < i \leq |p|{-}l\ \Delta\ p[1 : i] = p[|p|{-}i{+}1 : |p|])\}.$$

For (3.6) we have

$$\textbf{max}_0\ \{\textbf{nat}\ i\text{: } 0 = i\ \Delta\ \textit{no-match}(k{+}|p|{-}l{+}|p|{-}i)\}$$
$\equiv$ [definition of $\textbf{max}_0$; simplification]
$$0.$$

Summary

The definition of δ as derived above depends on the character $s[k]$ rather than on k itself. This leads to a redefinition of δ by

$$\begin{aligned}&\textbf{funct } \delta = (\textbf{char } c, \textbf{nat } l)\ \textbf{nat}:\\ &\quad |p| - \textbf{max}\ \{\textbf{nat } i:\ (|p|-l < i < |p|\ \Delta\\ &\qquad\qquad (p[i-|p|+l+1 : i] = p[l+1 : |p|] \wedge p[i-|p|+l] = c)) \vee\\ &\qquad\qquad (0 \le i \le |p|-l\ \Delta\ p[1 : i] = p[|p|-i+1 : |p|])\}\end{aligned}$$

and an according change of k into $s[k]$ in the calls of δ within *occ* and *try-match*.

The intuition behind δ is as follows: Within the contexts in which calls $\delta(s[k], l)$ occur, the last $|p|-l$ characters of $|p|$ have been found to match a sequence, of length $|p|-l$, of characters in s. This information is described by the assertion *partial-match*. As this means that the strings $p[l+1 : |p|]$ and $s[k+1 : k+|p|-l]$ coincide and that $p[l] \neq s[k]$ holds, we could align the substring $s[k+1 : k+|p|-l]$ with a (partial) reoccurrence of $p[l+1 : |p|]$ in p, provided such a reoccurrence exists and is preceeded by $s[k]$. In order not to overlook a possibility of a match, we consider the right-most such reoccurrence. In case, a complete reoccurrence of the string $p[l+1 : |p|]$ in p does not exist, the right-most partial reoccurrence is looked for.

9.3.4 Final Version of the Function *occurs*

Summarizing, we have arrived at the following specification:

$$\begin{aligned}&\textbf{funct } occurs = (\textbf{string } p, \textbf{string } s)\ \textbf{bool}:\\ &\quad occ(|p|)\ \textbf{where}\\ &\quad \textbf{funct } occ = (\textbf{nat } k{:}\ no\text{-}match(k))\ \textbf{bool}:\\ &\qquad k \le |s|\ \Delta\ ((s[k] = p[|p|]\ \Delta\ try\text{-}match(k-1, |p|-1))\ \nabla\\ &\qquad\qquad (s[k] \neq p[|p|]\ \Delta\ occ(k+ \delta(s[k], |p|))));\\ &\quad \textbf{funct } try\text{-}match = (\textbf{nat } k, \textbf{nat } l{:}\\ &\qquad\qquad no\text{-}match(k+|p|-l)\ \Delta\ partial\text{-}match(k, l))\ \textbf{bool}:\\ &\qquad l = 0\ \nabla\ (s[k] = p[l]\ \Delta\ try\text{-}match(k-1, l-1))\ \nabla\\ &\qquad\qquad (s[k] \neq p[l]\ \Delta\ occ(k+|p|-l+ \delta(s[k], l)));\\ &\quad \textbf{funct } \delta = (\textbf{char } c, \textbf{nat } l)\ \textbf{nat}:\\ &\qquad |p| - \textbf{max}\ \{\textbf{nat } i:\ (|p|-l < i < |p|\ \Delta\\ &\qquad\qquad (p[i-|p|+l+1 : i] = p[l+1 : |p|] \wedge p[i-|p|+l] = c)) \vee\\ &\qquad\qquad (0 \le i \le |p|-l\ \Delta\ p[1 : i] = p[|p|-i+1 : |p|])\}.\end{aligned}$$

This is the essence of the pattern matching algorithm in [Boyer, Moore 77].

Our algorithm differs from the one in [Boyer, Moore 77] only in the definition of δ. We require, in case of a complete reoccurrence, $p[i-|p|+l] = s[k]$, whereas Boyer and Moore just require that in this case $p[i-|p|+l] \neq p[l]$ holds, which is implied by our condition. Their definition,

$$\begin{aligned}&\textbf{funct } \delta' = (\textbf{nat } l)\ \textbf{nat}:\\ &\quad |p| - \textbf{max}\ \{\textbf{nat } i:\ (|p|-l < i < |p|\ \Delta\\ &\qquad\qquad (p[i-|p|+l+1 : i] = p[l+1 : |p|] \wedge p[i-|p|+l] \neq \mathrm{p}[l])) \vee\\ &\qquad\qquad (0 \le i \le |p|-l\ \Delta\ p[1 : i] = p[|p|-i+1 : |p|])\},\end{aligned}$$

can be derived by changing the last step in the individual calculation of (3.4) accordingly. From the use of (3.3) in this last step, it is also obvious that the shifting of the pattern described by δ is always at least as large as the one described by δ'.

9.3.5 Remarks on Further Development

The algorithm above captures the essence of Boyer and Moore's algorithm. In order to come closer to their formulation, however, a few more steps are necessary. Since all these steps are straightforward, we will just comment on them and leave the technical details to the interested reader.

The solution of *occurs* presented above leads, in general, to multiple evaluations of identical function calls of δ. To eliminate this inefficiency, we apply the technique of *precomputation* (see Sect. 6.4.2). In fact, rather than just storing the values of δ, it is even more economic to store, in a table d, the values of the respective expressions in which this function occurs. This table is defined (for **char** c, **nat** l: $1 \le l \le |p|$) by

$$d[c, l] =_{\text{def}} |p| - l + \delta(s[k], l).$$

The respective expressions in the program are then substituted by corresponding table look-ups.

As a next step we can eliminate the sequential boolean operators and replace them, according to their definitions (Sect. 4.4.1), by conventional conditional expressions.

The final step concerns the fact that, so far, we have concentrated on the existence problem. According to the strategy from Sect. 5.3.4, we should now aim at extending the solution to the existence problem by an additional parameter that will yield the result upon termination. However, this is trivial here, since obviously

$$(\textit{no-match}(k+|p|-l) \mathbin{\Delta} \textit{partial-match}(k, l) \mathbin{\Delta} l = 0) \Rightarrow (k = \textit{first-occ}(p, s)) \equiv \textbf{true}.$$

Thus it remains to apply the rule *argument of termination I* which then yields our final program

```
funct find = (string p, string s) res:
  find'(|p|, |p|) where

  funct find'= (nat k, nat l) res:
     if k > |s| then false
     elsf s[k] ≠ p[|p|] then find'(k+d[s[k], |p|], |p|) else try-match'(k–1, l–1) fi;

  funct try-match'= (nat k, nat l) res:
     if l = 0 then k+1
     elsf s[k] = p[l] then try-match'(k–1, l–1)
                      else find'(k+d[s[k], l], |p|) fi.
```

9.3.6 Concluding Remarks

The derivation of Boyer and Moore's pattern matching algorithm exemplifies that the transformational programming technique in combination with assertional reasoning is a powerful and well-suited approach for the development of fairly complex algorithms. In fact, using our techniques, we rather straightforwardly came up with an algorithm that compares well with the 'improved version' in [Boyer, Moore 77]. Moreover, in the derivation a clear distinction between mechanical aspects, captured by transformation rules and strategies, and ideas to be supplied by the developer could be made.

Except for the fact that we did not perform a trivial final transformation step that leads to an imperative style of formulation, our final algorithm differs from the one presented in [Boyer, Moore 77] in the definition of the function that is called δ in our treatment. As in [Boyer, Moore 77], in δ we have taken into account the possible reoccurrence of a final substring of the pattern and a preceding character. We require that this preceding character coincides with the one from the string which was mismatched, whereas in [Boyer, Moore 77] only the reoccurrence has to be preceded by a different character. Therefore, the values of our function δ are at least as large as the values of theirs. As a consequence, however, our function δ needs a character as a second argument, and thus needs more storage. Hence, whether our change is an improvement depends on the concrete forms of the string and the pattern.

9.4 A Text Editor

The text editor is one example from a collection of examples intended and successfully used within IFIP working group WG 2.1 as a common basis for discussing various specification and program development techniques. In several discussions, this particular example has turned out to be a real challenge for specification languages and specification methodologies as well as for program development techniques. This is probably due to the difficulty inherent in giving a reasonably high-level treatment of a system with an obviously low-level procedural appearance.

The verbal statement of the problem is literally quoted from [WG 2.1 79]:

EXAMPLE NUMBER 4 – TEXT EDITOR

This problem asks for the implementation of a simple line oriented editor for use in an interactive environment. The specification is actually a subset of an editor which has been implemented on several machines.

The input device is a keyboard/display. Input from the keyboard is obtained one character at a time and is one of the following characters: letters, digits, blank, {cr} (line return), {esc} (escape), {bs} (backspace).

The display device is controlled by outputting single characters from the following set: letters, digits, blank, {cr} (line return), {bs} (backspace), {bel} (sound alarm).

Note that the keyboard and display are completely independent, "echoing" of input characters must be done by the program. The effect of sending a {cr} is to roll the screen up and set the cursor to the start of the next line. {bs} moves the cursor back one (no effect if at start of line). {bel} sounds an alarm, but has no effect on the cursor position.

The current text is a sequence of lines which can be modified by entering edit commands. There is no need to consider the problem of opening files, reading text etc. Assume that the current text is available as a variable (or equivalent).

The editor outputs a prompt character '?' to invite entry of commands. The following commands are available. Note that most commands are not terminated by a {cr}.

b	:	position to start of first line in file and print out the first line.
e	:	position past last line of file, and display <end-of-file>.
m<old>{cr}<new>{cr}	:	search for occurrence of the string <old> in the current line, and replace it by string <new>. Display the modified line.
i	:	enter insert mode. The cursor moves to the start of the next line and text can be entered (one or several lines) which is inserted following the current line. Each new line is terminated by a {cr}. To leave insert mode, {esc} is typed after the last inserted line.
k	:	delete the current line and store it in a stack (see u command). Display the line after the one deleted.
u	:	retrieve the line on top of the delete stack and insert it just before the current line, then display the retrieved line (note: the sequence ku leaves the file as it was).
n+	:	move n (decimal integer) lines forward in the file and type new current line.
n–	:	move n (decimal integer) lines backward in the file and type new current line.
s<key> {cr}	:	search forward from the current position for a line containing the string <key>, and display the line.
a<rep> {cr}	:	alter the <key> just found by the search (s) command to the given replacement <rep>. Display the modified line.
f	:	forget (undo) the effect of the m or a command just entered.
w	:	display window consisting of the nine lines either side of the current line.

The {bel} character is transmitted to the display if any command syntax error is detected or for an unsuccessful search etc. The backspace key may be pressed during entry of any text string, the effect is to erase the previous character and backup the cursor. If the backspace key is used to erase the m or s character which starts a command, then a completely new type of command can be entered.

We use this informal problem description as it stands, since this allows us to mimic some problems of real-life software development that have not been treated with any other example:

- It is a fact of real-world software development that an informal problem description and a formalization of the problem are given by different persons.
- Dealing with a problem stated by someone else forces oneself to solve even nasty problems and thus prevents oneself from cheating by adapting the problem statement to fit a nice and elegant treatment.
- Formalizing an informal problem statement given by someone else entails a lot of design decisions which would never have appeared in a self-made problem statement. These design decisions give us an opportunity to comment on alternatives with respect to the specification.

9.4.1. Formal Specification

In order to formalize the problem stated above, we follow the methodological guideline from Sect. 3.2. Additionally, we will see that for this particular example the top-down approach described in Sect. 3.5 is adequate and profitable.

9.4.1.1 The Overall Behavior of the Editor

In contrast to many other problems, finding a suitable concept for the specification is a critical issue for the editor problem which asks for an interactive system.

A Concept for Specifying Interactive Systems

Interactive systems are communicating systems. Hence it would be straightforward to specify an interactive system using the formalisms developed for describing communicating systems (e.g. CSP [Hoare 78], CCS [Milner 80], or recursive stream equations [Broy 83, 84b]). On the other hand, interactive systems are very specific communicating systems with only two (communicating) processes, the user and the system. In addition, communication between these processes takes place in a restricted, rather disciplined way in the form of a 'dialogue'.

A dialogue in an interactive system can be seen [Kupka, Wilsing 73] as an alternating sequence $i_1\, o_1\, i_2\, o_2 \ldots\, i_k\, o_k$ of inputs i_n and outputs o_m. An i_n usually originates from the user's unconstrained will, but an o_m surely depends on the respective i_m and probably also on the history, i.e., the i_n with $n < m$:

$$\left.\begin{array}{lcl} \text{input } i_1 & \rightarrow & \text{output } o_1 \\ \text{input } i_2 & \rightarrow & \text{output } o_2 \\ \vdots & & \vdots \\ \text{input } i_n & \rightarrow & \text{output } o_n \end{array}\right\} \text{“visible effect”}$$

Thus, in an abstract view, an interactive system can be seen as a function from input sequences to output sequences. Consequently, its behavior can be adequately specified by defining the system's reaction to arbitrary input sequences.

Following these lines, the overall behavior of the editor can be specified by a function

funct *edit* = (**input** *in*) **output**,

where the object kind **input** characterizes sequences of characters,

mode input = EESEQU(**char**, =),

and the object kind **output** characterizes sequences of certain actions to be observed by the user of the editor,

mode output = EESEQU(**action**, =).

Here, **char** and **action** are considered as primitive object kinds for both of which an equality "=" is defined. A further detailing can be found later.

Decomposition into Subtasks

The formalization of the problem now aims at giving a definition for *edit*. Since, due to the complexity of the problem, such a definition is not at all straightforward, we follow the methodological line from Sect. 3.2 and decompose the function *edit* into smaller, more manageable logical units, viz.

- mapping from (concrete) input character sequences to sequences of (abstract) commands;
- effects of commands (or sequences of commands) within the system;
- mapping from (abstract) effects to (concrete) physical output.

This structuring may be illustrated as in Fig. 9.1.

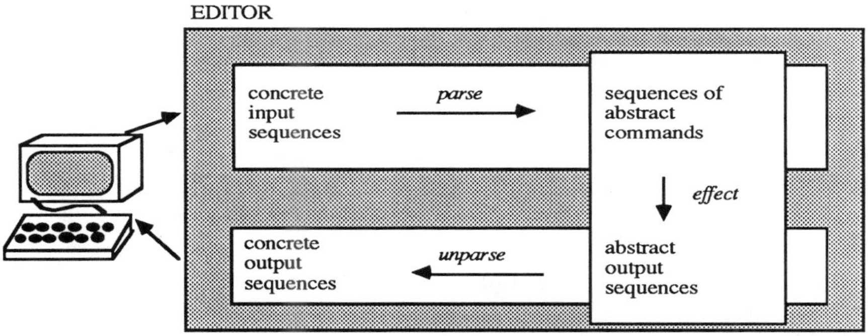

Figure 9.1. Structure of the editor

The objects to be manipulated by sequences of commands are texts, outputs (whatever that means), and an internal stack (see commands k and u). For the current level of refinement, however, we can abstract from these details and combine the objects that are manipulated into the notion of a 'state'. Thus the essential part of the editor will be a mapping

funct *effect* = (**commsequ** *cs*, **state** *s*) **state**,

(where **commsequ** and **state** denote the object kinds characterizing sequences of commands and states) which associates a new state with each sequence of abstract commands and a given state.

We use

funct *parse* = (**input** *in*) **commsequ**

for mapping concrete input to abstract commands,

state *initstate*

for providing an initial state, and

funct *unparse* = (**state** *s*) **output**

for mapping abstract output to a concrete one, such that the overall behavior of the editor can be completely specified by

edit(*in*) ≡ *unparse*(*effect*(*parse*(*in*), *initstate*)).

According to our global development strategy, we now aim at providing definitions for the newly introduced operations *effect*, *parse*, and *unparse*, and for the constant *initstate*. As outlined in Sect. 3.2, this either means considering individual cases or referring to further new operations.

9.4.1.2 Translation between External and Internal Representation

The translation between external and internal representation of sequences of commands is to deal with the operations *parse* and *unparse*. However, we will just concentrate on the function *parse* and not deal with the formal specification of *unparse* mainly for two reasons:

- The informal specification is fairly imprecise about output. Thus, a formalization would require a proper extension of the informal description that goes substantially beyond the original problem description. Our goal, however, is to solve the task as given in [WG 2.1 79].
- If the information about output had been more precise and complete, a formalization of *unparse* would be rather analogous to that of *parse* (as dealt with below) and thus would add no real substance to our considerations.

Definition of the Data Structures Involved

In order to be able to give a formal specification of

funct *parse* = (**input** *in*) **commsequ**,

we first have to define the data structures involved.

For being complete, the definition

mode input = EESEQU(**char**, =)

(as introduced above) requires a further definition of admissible characters. Therefore, according to the informal requirements, we define

mode letter = (a, b, c, ...), and
mode digit = (0, 1, 2, ...).

The set of possible input characters is then characterized by

mode char = **letter** | **digit** | **blank** | {bs} | {esc} | {cr}

(where we have simply adopted the notation for the special characters that was used in the informal description; furthermore we assume an equality "=" on **char**).

For the definition of *parse* we will also need input strings that do not contain the characters {cr} and {esc}. These strings are defined by

mode string = EESEQU((**char** c: $c \notin$ {cr, esc}), =).

Furthermore we need sequences composed of digits and {bs}, defined by

mode dstring = EESEQU((**digit** | {bs}), =).

According to the informal description, commands are either simple, consisting of a single letter (such as b), or are "parametrized", consisting of a command letter and "arguments" (such as m <*old*><*new*>). For the definition of commands we use

mode command = (b | e | k | u | f | w | m | s | a | i | + | – | i' | ec),

where

- b, e, k, u, f, and w are to denote the respective (simple) commands;
- m, s, a, i, +, and – are shorthand notations for the respective parametrized commands. They are supposed to stand for tuples consisting of the respective command letter and the types of the arguments of the command. Thus, m abbreviates (m, **string**, **string**), s is short for (s, **string**), + is short for (+, **nat**), and so on;
- i' and ec are commands produced by *parse* that are not available to the user; ec denotes an additional error command in case of syntactically illegal input and i' is used for the decomposition of an insertion command into linewise insertions (see below).

For sequences of commands we simply use the definition

mode commsequ = EESEQU(**command**, =)

which, again, assumes an equality "=" on **command**.

In the following we use the type EESEQU as defined in Sect. 3.3.3. For reasons of readability, however, we use ε instead of <>.

The Problem of Backspaces

According to the informal description, a {bs} character may erase certain preceding characters. In case of certain parametrized commands it may even be used to erase the respective command letter.

One might be tempted to try a specification where first all {bs} characters are removed from the input string before parsing takes place. However, a closer look at the informal description tells us immediately that the erasing effect of a {bs} character depends on the respective state of the parsing process when the {bs} is detected.

Thus, e.g. an input string of the form

(*) b{bs}k{bs}{bs}c...

has the same effect as

bkc...

provided a new command is currently being recognized. If, however, the string (*) is the beginning of a text to be inserted, i.e.

ib{bs}k{bs}{bs}c...,

then it has the same effect as

ic...

(if we assume that an i command cannot be undone by {bs}, cf. below). And if the string (*) is the beginning of the argument for a search, i.e.

sb{bs}k{bs}{bs}c...,

then even the preceding command letter s is to be erased.

Because of this interrelation between parsing and backspace removal it is appropriate to specify the effect of backspaces jointly with parsing rather than specifying both tasks independent of each other.

For modelling the effect of {bs} we will use the auxiliary operations

funct *mbl* = (**string** *t*) **nstring** ("move backspaces left"),

and

funct *dlb* = (**nstring** *n*) **nbsstring** ("delete leading backspaces"),

where

mode nbsstring = (**string** *s*: {bs} $\notin$ *s*),

defines strings containing no backspaces,

mode bsstring = EESEQU({bs}, =),

defines strings consisting of backspaces only, and

mode nstring = (**string** *s*: $\exists$ **nbsstring** *n*, **bsstring** *b*: $s = b + n$)

defines ('normalized') strings having backspaces only at the beginning.

The operation *mbl* deletes pairs of characters consisting of a character (different from {bs}) and an immediately following {bs} character. Remaining {bs} characters accumulate to the left of the resulting string, as can be seen from the property $mbl(\{bs\}+s) \equiv \{bs\}+mbl(s)$. Formally this operation is defined by

$\forall$ **string** s, s_1, s_2, **char** c: $c \notin \{cr, esc\}$:
$mbl(s) \equiv mbl(s_1+s_2)$ **provided** $s = s_1+c+\{bs\}+s_2$,
$mbl(s) \equiv s$ **provided** $s \neq s_1+c+\{bs\}+s_2$.

The operation *dlb* simply skips all leading {bs} characters (from a string where all backspaces are at the beginning) until a character different from {bs} is encountered. It is defined by

$dlb(\varepsilon) \equiv \varepsilon$,
$dlb(\{bs\}+s) \equiv dlb(s)$,
$dlb(c+s) \equiv c+s$ **provided** $c \neq \{bs\}$.

For both operations, completeness of the definition is obvious.

For the formal specification of parsing, it is convenient to have in addition an auxiliary predicate that checks for a given string whether all backspaces can be removed:

funct *nbs* = (**string** *t*) **bool**:
$mbl(t) = \varepsilon \ \nabla$ **first**$(mbl(t)) \neq \{bs\}$.

Parsing Correct Input

Now we have all we need to give a formal specification of the operation *parse*. We first concentrate on those cases that are obvious from the verbal problem description.

Assuming the general quantification

$\forall$ **input** sc, **char** c, **string** t_1, t_2, **dstring** t_d:

we define *parse* as follows:

Empty input yields an empty command sequence,

$parse(\varepsilon) \equiv \varepsilon$.

A single b, e, k, u, f, w character is recognized as the respective command,

$parse(c{+}sc) \equiv c + parse(sc)$ **provided** $c \in \{\text{b, e, k, u, f, w}\}$.

With respect to the m, s, and a command, we have to differentiate according to the form of their first argument. If all backspaces in this argument can be removed, i.e., if *nbs* holds for this argument, we follow the verbal description and define

$parse(\text{m}{+}t_1{+}\{\text{cr}\}{+}t_2{+}\{\text{cr}\}{+}sc) \equiv (\text{m}, mbl(t_1), dlb(mbl(t_2))){+}parse(sc)$
provided $nbs(t_1)$,
$parse(\text{s}{+}t_1{+}\{\text{cr}\}{+}sc) \equiv (\text{s}, mbl(t_1)){+}parse(sc)$ **provided** $nbs(t_1)$,
$parse(\text{a}{+}t_1{+}\{\text{cr}\}{+}sc) \equiv (\text{a}, mbl(t_1)){+}parse(sc)$ **provided** $nbs(t_1)$.

In case $\neg\, nbs(t_1)$ holds, $mbl(t_1)$ starts with a backspace which erases the preceding command letter. Therefore we specify

$parse(c{+}t_1{+}sc) \equiv parse(\textbf{rest}(mbl(t_1)) + sc)$ **provided** $\neg\, nbs(t_1) \wedge c \in \{\text{m, s, a}\}$.

Note that this axiom implies the axiom

$parse(c{+}\{\text{bs}\}{+}sc) \equiv parse(sc)$ **provided** $c \in \{\text{m, s, a}\}$

which formalizes the informal requirement that the backspace key may be used to erase an m or s character which starts a command.

With respect to the i command, we have to make a decision: obviously, the i command could be specified by analogy with the m, s, or a command above. However, taking into account the particular insertion mode mentioned in the informal description, it also seems reasonable to assume that an i character starting an insertion command cannot be erased by a following {bs}. Deciding in favour of the latter we specify:

$parse(\text{i}{+}t_1{+}\{\text{cr}\}{+}sc) \equiv (\text{i}, dlb(mbl(t_1)){+}\{\text{cr}\}){+}parse(\text{i}{+}sc)$,
$parse(\text{i}{+}t_1{+}\{\text{esc}\}{+}sc) \equiv (\text{i'}, dlb(mbl(t_1)){+}\{\text{cr}\}){+}parse(sc)$.

Here the pseudo-command i' is used to signal that the last line of an insertion command has been recognized.

A correct move command requires a non-empty sequence of digits followed by a "+" or "–" sign. Hence, parsing a move command can be specified by

$parse(t_d{+}sig{+}sc) \equiv (sig, conv(mbl(t_d), 0)){+}parse(sc)$
provided $(mbl(t_d) \neq \varepsilon\ \Delta\ \textbf{first}(mbl(t_d)) \neq \{\text{bs}\}) \wedge sig \in \{+, -\}$.

Here we have used another auxiliary operation, namely

funct $conv$ = (**nbsdstring** d, **nat** n) **nat**

where

$$\textbf{mode nbsdstring} = \text{EESEQU}(\textbf{digit}, =),$$

characterizes strings consisting of digits only. The operation *conv* describes the translation of a sequence of digits into a decimal number. It is formally defined by

$$conv(\varepsilon, in) \equiv in,$$
$$conv(n+sd, in) \equiv conv(sd, in\times 10+n).$$

Parsing Incorrect Input

One of the major benefits of using the algebraic specification technique is the availability of the theoretical notion of sufficient completeness (Sect. 3.3.1.2). This considerably helps in detecting incompletenesses even in a seemingly complete verbal specification such as ours. In our particular example, for instance, we immediately find out that the informal requirements contain no information on how to react to erroneous situations which may come up in connection with syntactically wrong or incomplete input.

Obviously, incomplete input has no effect and yields an empty command sequence:

$$parse(c+t_1) \equiv \varepsilon \ \textbf{provided} \ c \in \{\text{m, a, s, i}\} \wedge nbs(t_1),$$
$$parse(\text{m}+t_1+\{\text{cr}\}+t_2) \equiv \varepsilon \ \textbf{provided} \ nbs(t_1),$$
$$parse(t_\text{d}) \equiv \varepsilon \ \textbf{provided} \ mbl(t_\text{d}) \neq \varepsilon.$$

By contrast, syntax errors result in an "error command" ec. Syntax errors occur whenever, in a situation where a command is expected, a character appears that does not start a legal command:

$$parse(c+sc) \equiv \text{ec}+parse(sc) \ \textbf{provided} \ c \notin (\{\text{b, e, m, i, k, u, s, a, f, w}\} \cup \textbf{digit}).$$

Another erroneous situation is the illegal use of an {esc} character in connection with an m, s, or a command:

$$parse(c+t_1+\{\text{esc}\}+sc) \equiv \text{ec}+parse(sc) \ \textbf{provided} \ nbs(t_1) \wedge c \in \{\text{m, a, s}\},$$
$$parse(\text{m}+t_1+\{\text{cr}\}+t_2+\{\text{esc}\}+sc) \equiv \text{ec}+parse(sc) \ \textbf{provided} \ nbs(t_1).$$

Finally, an error situation occurs, if a sequence of digits is not followed by a "+" or "–" sign:

$$parse(t_\text{d}+c+sc\} \equiv \text{ec}+parse(sc)$$
$$\textbf{provided} \ (mbl(t_\text{d}) \neq \varepsilon \ \Delta \ \textbf{first}(mbl(t_\text{d})) \neq \{\text{bs}\}) \ \wedge \ c \notin (\{+, -\} \cup \textbf{digit}).$$

Here we have specified a very simplistic view of error handling. We simply indicate the presence of an error or ignore incomplete input. Of course, we also could have specified a much better error diagnosis by informing the user on the kind of error that has occurred. With little additional effort, we also could have made a specification in such a way that in the case of an incomplete command, the system attempts to process the available part of the input, and requests the missing part from the user. For reasons of space, however, we have abandoned this possibility.

Above, we have treated leading {bs}, {esc}, or {cr} characters as an erroneous situation. One also could imagine simply ignoring them, but only at the expense of an additional axiom for *parse*.

Summary

To allow easier checking of consistency and formal completeness, we now simply summarize the definition of *parse* (by collecting all axioms given so far, while, for the sake of brevity, deliberately omitting the corresponding type header and the functionalities). As a kind of first step towards an implementation, in this summary we rearrange and rephrase the above axioms in such a way that the left-hand sides of the axioms just differentiate between empty and non-empty input sequences. Furthermore, in the case of non-empty input sequences, axioms concerning the same leading character are grouped together:

$\forall$ **input** *in*, *sc*, **char** *c*, **digit** *d*, **string** t_1, t_2, **dstring** t_d:

$parse(\varepsilon) \equiv \varepsilon$,

$parse(c{+}in) \equiv c + parse(in)$ **provided** $c \in \{\mathrm{b, e, k, u, f, w}\}$,

$parse(c{+}in) \equiv \mathrm{ec}{+}parse(in)$ **provided** $c \notin (\{\mathrm{b, e, m, i, k, u, s, a, f, w}\} \cup \textbf{digit})$,

$parse(\mathrm{m}{+}in) \equiv (\mathrm{m}, mbl(t_1), dlb(mbl(t_2))){+}parse(sc)$
  provided $in = t_1{+}\{\mathrm{cr}\}{+}t_2{+}\{\mathrm{cr}\}{+}sc \wedge nbs(t_1)$,
$parse(\mathrm{m}{+}in) \equiv parse(\mathbf{rest}(mbl(t_1)){+}sc)$ **provided** $in = t_1{+}sc \wedge \neg\, nbs(t_1)$,
$parse(\mathrm{m}{+}in) \equiv \varepsilon$
  provided $(in \in \textbf{string} \,\Delta\, nbs(in)) \vee (in = t_1{+}\{\mathrm{cr}\}{+}t_2 \wedge nbs(t_1))$,
$parse(\mathrm{m}{+}in) \equiv \mathrm{ec}{+}parse(sc)$
  provided $(in = t_1{+}\{\mathrm{cr}\}{+}t_2{+}\{\mathrm{esc}\}{+}sc \wedge nbs(t_1)) \vee$
  $(in = t_1{+}\{\mathrm{esc}\}{+}sc \wedge nbs(t_1))$,

$parse(\mathrm{i}{+}in) \equiv (\mathrm{i}, dlb(mbl(t_1)){+}\{\mathrm{cr}\}){+}parse(\mathrm{i}{+}sc)$ **provided** $in = t_1{+}\{\mathrm{cr}\}{+}sc$,
$parse(\mathrm{i}{+}in) \equiv (\mathrm{i'}, dlb(mbl(t_1)){+}\{\mathrm{cr}\}){+}parse(sc)$ **provided** $in = t_1{+}\{\mathrm{esc}\}{+}sc$,
$parse(\mathrm{i}{+}in) \equiv \varepsilon$ **provided** $in \in \textbf{string}$,

$parse(\mathrm{s}{+}in) \equiv (\mathrm{s}, mbl(t_1)){+}parse(sc)$ **provided** $in = t_1{+}\{\mathrm{cr}\}{+}sc \wedge nbs(t_1)$,
$parse(\mathrm{s}{+}in) \equiv parse(\mathbf{rest}(mbl(t_1)){+}sc)$ **provided** $in = t_1{+}sc \wedge \neg\, nbs(t_1)$,
$parse(\mathrm{s}{+}in) \equiv \varepsilon$ **provided** $in \in \textbf{string} \,\Delta\, nbs(in)$,
$parse(\mathrm{s}{+}in) \equiv \mathrm{ec}{+}parse(sc)$ **provided** $in = t_1{+}\{\mathrm{esc}\}{+}sc \wedge nbs(t_1)$,

$parse(\mathrm{a}{+}in) \equiv (\mathrm{a}, mbl(t_1)){+}parse(sc)$ **provided** $in = t_1{+}\{\mathrm{cr}\}{+}sc \wedge nbs(t_1)$,
$parse(\mathrm{a}{+}in) \equiv parse(\mathbf{rest}(mbl(t_1)){+}sc)$ **provided** $in = t_1{+}sc \wedge \neg\, nbs(t_1)$,
$parse(\mathrm{a}{+}in) \equiv \varepsilon$ **provided** $in \in \textbf{string} \,\Delta\, nbs(in)$,
$parse(\mathrm{a}{+}in) \equiv \mathrm{ec}{+}parse(sc)$ **provided** $in = t_1{+}\{\mathrm{esc}\}{+}sc \wedge nbs(t_1)$,

$parse(d{+}in) \equiv (sig, conv(mbl(t_d), 0)){+}parse(sc)$
  provided $in = t_d{+}sig{+}sc \wedge (mbl(t_d) \neq \varepsilon \,\Delta\, \mathbf{first}(mbl(t_d)) \neq \{\mathrm{bs}\}) \wedge sig \in \{+, -\}$,
$parse(d{+}in) \equiv parse(\mathbf{rest}(mbl(t_1)){+}sc)$ **provided** $in = t_1{+}sc \wedge \neg\, nbs(t_1)$,
$parse(d{+}in) \equiv \varepsilon$ **provided** $in \in \textbf{dstring} \,\Delta\, mbl(d{+}in) \neq \varepsilon$,
$parse(d{+}in) \equiv \mathrm{ec}{+}parse(sc)$
  provided $d{+}in = t_d{+}c{+}sc \wedge (mbl(t_d) \neq \varepsilon \,\Delta$
  $\mathbf{first}(mbl(t_d)) \neq \{\mathrm{bs}\}) \wedge c \notin \{+, -\} \cup \textbf{digit}$.

Now the proofs of sufficient completeness and soundness (i.e. non-overlapping left-hand sides) of the specification are straightforward, although not trivial. These are left as an exercise to the interested reader.

9.4.1.3 The kernel of the editor

The kernel of the editor (or its abstract, internal behavior) is captured by the operation *effect* that maps a sequence of commands and a state to a new state. The state transition resulting from a single command is described by an auxiliary operation *apply*.

The Effect of Sequences of Commands

Either a sequence is empty or it can be decomposed into an individual element and a sequence. Thus, an unreflected formalization would immediately lead to

$effect(\varepsilon, s) \equiv \ldots$
$effect(c + cs, s) \equiv \ldots$

where s denotes an arbitrary state, cs a sequence of commands, and c an individual command.

However, on closer inspection of the verbal requirements for an individual command, we soon find out that there are commands of different quality, namely commands having effects on states, and others (such as a or f), having effects on other commands. In particular, this latter observation suggests that in our formalization below two leading elements of a sequence should always be considered simultaneously.

Using the definitions of **command** and **commsequ** as introduced in the previous subsection, the overall behavior of the editor may be specified, according to the verbal description, by

$\forall$ **command** c, c', **commsequ** cs, **state** s:
(1) $effect(\varepsilon, s) \equiv s$,
(2a) $effect(c+\varepsilon, s) \equiv s$ **provided** $c \in \{\mathrm{a}, \mathrm{f}\}$,
(2b) $effect(c+\varepsilon, s) \equiv apply(c, s)$ **provided** $c \notin \{\mathrm{a}, \mathrm{f}\}$,
(3a) $effect(c+c'+cs, s) \equiv effect(c'+cs, s)$ **provided** $c \in \{\mathrm{a}, \mathrm{f}\}$,
(3b) $effect(c+c'+cs, s) \equiv effect(c'+cs, apply(c, s))$ **provided** $c \notin \{\mathrm{a}, \mathrm{f}\} \wedge c' \notin \{\mathrm{a}, \mathrm{f}\}$,
(3c) $effect(c+\mathrm{f}+cs, s) \equiv effect((\mathrm{s}, key)+cs, s)$ **provided** $c = (\mathrm{m}, key, rep)$,
(3d) $effect(c+c'+cs, s) \equiv effect((\mathrm{m}, key, rep)+cs, apply((\mathrm{s}, key), s))$
provided $c' = (\mathrm{a}, rep) \wedge c = (\mathrm{s}, key)$,
(3e) $effect(c+\mathrm{f}+cs, s) \equiv effect(c+cs, s)$ **provided** $c \notin \{\mathrm{a}, \mathrm{f}, \mathrm{m}\}$,
(3f) $effect(c+\mathrm{a}+cs, s) \equiv effect(c+cs, s)$ **provided** $c \notin \{\mathrm{a}, \mathrm{f}, \mathrm{s}\}$.

Here we have deliberately used shorthand notations such as $c \notin \{\mathrm{a}, \mathrm{f}\}$ for

$\neg \exists$ **string** x: $c = (\mathrm{a}, x) \wedge c \neq \mathrm{f}$.

Of course, we could have combined, say, axioms (2a) and (3a) into one axiom. However, the form used above has the advantage that the formal completeness of this specification, as well as its soundness, are obvious: axiom (1) covers empty command sequences; axioms (2a) and (2b) deal with the case of singleton command sequences; and axioms (3a) - (3f) deal with all possibilities of command sequences containing at least two elements.

As before, the above specification also had to take care of problems not mentioned in the informal requirements, such as

– What is the effect of an f command applied after a command that is not an a or m command ?
– What is the effect of an a command applied to a command different from an s command ?

both of which were simply decided to have no effect.

Definition of State
In order to be able to specify the function *apply* used in the above specification, we first have to define what a 'state' is.

As already outlined, the abstract notion of state served for collectively referring to the internal objects of the editor, i.e., the text file, the delete stack (see commands k and u) and the output sequence. Thus, an obvious definition for state is a triple consisting of these entities:

mode state(=) = TRIPLE(**file**, **stack**, **output**).

Here TRIPLE is an appropriate type defining triples of objects with elementwise equality analogously to pairs with elementwise equality (Sect. 3.3.4.1); the triple constructor is denoted by <.,.,.>.

Consequently, the constant *initstate* denoting the initial state can be defined by

state *initstate* = $<\varepsilon_f, \varepsilon_d, \varepsilon_o+?>$

where ε_f denotes the empty file, ε_d the empty stack, and ε_o the empty output. The '?' in the output sequence reflects the verbal requirement that "the editor outputs a prompt character '?' to invite the entry of commands".

Of course, one also could imagine other definitions of *initstate* such as

state *initstate* = $<init(tf), \varepsilon_d, \varepsilon_o+?>$

where *tf* is a function for retrieving a (non-empty) text from some secondary store and *init* initializes the file for text processing. The specification of the editor itself, however, is not influenced by this decision.

From the informal requirements we know that a text is a sequence of lines. Obviously, a (proper) line is a (possibly empty) string composed of letters, digits, and blanks, terminated by a {cr}:

mode pline = (**input** l: $\exists$ **nbsstring** n: $l = n+\{\text{cr}\}$),

and hence a text can be specified by

mode text = EESEQU(**pline**, =)

(where ε_t is used to denote the empty text).

Phrases like "first line in the file", "next line", "current line", etc. suggest considering the current text file as a triple consisting of some piece of text (that might be empty), an actual line, followed by another piece of (possibly empty) text. However, there is also the case of the empty file, containing nothing at all. In order not to be forced to always distinguish between empty and non-empty files, we introduce a 'pseudo-line' (denoted by ε_l) and extend the above definition of a line to be either a proper line (as defined above) or a pseudo-line:

mode line = (**pline** | ε_l),

then define files uniformly by triples consisting of text, (extended) line, and text, by

mode file(=) = TRIPLE(**text**, **line**, **text**)

(where ε_f denotes the triple $<\varepsilon_t, \varepsilon_l, \varepsilon_t>$ which models the empty file).

Furthermore we assume

mode action = (d(.), p(.), t(.), ...)

(this is a collection of output actions where d(.), p(.), and t(.) are abstract representations for the actions "display", "print", "type", etc., that are used in the informal description).

Application of Single Commands

Based on the above decomposition of **state**, we are now prepared to attempt a formal definition of the function *apply* used above.

Obviously (inherited by the above level of our specification) *apply* only has to deal with commands that are not an a or f command. Therefore it suffices to consider

funct *apply* = (**command'** *c*, **state** *s*) **state**,

where

mode command' = (**command** $x : x \notin \{a, f\}$),

since, according to the axioms (2b), (3b), and (3d), f or a commands may not occur as arguments of *apply*.

For defining the semantics of the individual commands, we have to give appropriate axioms, at least one for each of them. From the aspect of presentation, it seems reasonable to point out similarities between different commands whenever there are any. Thus, obviously all commands (except for the e, i, i', and the u command) display the {bel} if the text file is empty:

$\forall$ **command'** *c*, **stack** *d*, **output** $o : c \notin \{e, i, i', u\}$:
$apply(c, <\varepsilon_f, d, o>) \equiv <\varepsilon_f, d, o+\mathrm{d}(\{\mathrm{bel}\})+?>$.

This means that for all commands (except for e, i, i', and u) a non-empty text file may be assumed. Therefore, for the remaining axioms we assume the general quantification

$\forall$ **text** t_1, t_2, t_3, **pline** l, l_1, **stack** *d*, **output** o: $t_3 \neq \varepsilon_t$:

which will be supplemented by additional restrictions when dealing with the individual commands.

From the informal requirements the specification of the "regular" behavior of the editor (in cases where t_3 denotes a non-empty text and l, l_1 denote proper lines) is straightforward.

(a) The b command

$apply(\mathrm{b}, <<t_1, l, t_2>, d, o>) \equiv$
$<<\varepsilon_t, \mathbf{first}(t_1+l+t_2), \mathbf{rest}(t_1+l+t_2)>, d, o+\mathrm{p}(\mathbf{first}(t_1+l+t_2))+?>$.

The prerequisite for the definedness of the partial operations **first** and **rest** is fulfilled here, as $t_1+l+t_2 \neq \varepsilon_t$ is guaranteed by the definition of **pline**.

(b) The e command

$$apply(\mathrm{e}, <<t_1, l, t_2>, d, o>) \equiv <<t_1{+}l{+}t_2, \varepsilon_l, \varepsilon_t>, d, o{+}\mathrm{d}(\{\mathrm{eof}\}){+}?>,$$
$$apply(\mathrm{e}, <\varepsilon_f, d, o>) \equiv <\varepsilon_f, d, o{+}\mathrm{d}(\{\mathrm{eof}\}){+}?>.$$

(c) The m command

$$\forall\ \mathbf{nbsstring}\ x, y:$$
$$apply((\mathrm{m}, x, y), <<t_1, l, t_2>, d, o>) \equiv$$
$$<<t_1, repl(l, x, y), t_2>, d, o{+}re(l, x, y){+}?>.$$

Here *repl* means the replacement of *x* by *y* in *l*, and *re* means *repl* in case of a successful search and {bel} otherwise. Due to our strict top-down design philosophy *repl* and *re* can be defined on the next level of refinement, e.g. in connection with lines. These definitions then have to deal also with the question which occurrence is to be replaced, if there are several. Note also that according to the definition of **nbsstring** both *x* and *y* may be empty.

(d) The i command

$$apply((\mathrm{i}, l), <\varepsilon_f, d, o>) \equiv <<\varepsilon_t, l, \varepsilon_t>, d, o{+}\mathrm{d}(l)>,$$
$$apply((\mathrm{i}, l), <<t_1, l_1, t_2>, d, o>) \equiv <<t_1{+}l_1, l, t_2>, d, o{+}\mathrm{d}(l)>,$$
$$apply((\mathrm{i}', l), <\varepsilon_f, d, o>) \equiv <<\varepsilon_t, l, \varepsilon_t>, d, o{+}\mathrm{d}(l){+}?>,$$
$$apply((\mathrm{i}', l), <<t_1, l_1, t_2>, d, o>) \equiv <<t_1{+}l_1, l, t_2>, d, o{+}\mathrm{d}(l){+}?>,$$

For the i command we used the fact that the syntactic analysis converts a complex i command (i.e., insertion of several lines of text) into a sequence of insertions of lines. Only after the last line to be inserted (signaled by the pseudo-command i') a prompt has to be output. Note also that by the definition of *parse* the argument *l* of an i command is always guaranteed to be a (proper) line.

(e) The k command

$$apply(\mathrm{k}, <<t_1, l, t_3>, d, o>) \equiv$$
$$<<t_1, \mathbf{first}\,t_3, \mathbf{rest}\,t_3>, d\ \mathbf{push}\ l, o{+}d(\mathbf{first}\,t_3){+}?>.$$

(f) The u command

$$apply(\mathrm{u}, <\varepsilon_f, d\ \mathbf{push}\ l, o>) \equiv <<\varepsilon_t, l, \varepsilon_t>, d, o{+}\mathrm{d}(l){+}?>,$$
$$apply(\mathrm{u}, <<t_1, l, t_2>, d\ \mathbf{push}\ l_1, o>) \equiv <<t_1, l_1, l{+}t_2>, d, o{+}\mathrm{d}(l_1){+}?>.$$

(g) The move commands

$$\forall\ \mathbf{nat}\ i:$$
$$apply((+, 0), <<t_1, l, t_2>, d, o>) \equiv <<t_1, l, t_2>, d, o{+}\mathrm{t}(l){+}?>,$$
$$apply((+, i{+}1), <<t_1, l, t_3>, d, o>) \equiv apply((+, i), <<t_1{+}l, \mathbf{first}\,t_3, \mathbf{rest}\,t_3>, d, o>),$$
$$apply((-, 0), <<t_1, l, t_2>, d, o>) \equiv <<t_1, l, t_2>, d, o{+}\mathrm{t}(l){+}?>,$$
$$apply((-, i{+}1), <<t_3, l, t_2>, d, o>) \equiv apply((-, i), <<\mathbf{lead}\,t_3, \mathbf{last}\,t_3, l{+}t_2>, d, o>).$$

(h) The s command

$$\forall\ \mathbf{nbsstring}\ key:$$
$$apply((\mathrm{s}, key), <<t_1, l, t_2>, d, o>) \equiv$$
$$<<t_1, l, t_2>, d, o{+}\mathrm{d}(l){+}?>\ \mathbf{provided}\ key\ \mathbf{isin}\ l,$$
$$apply((\mathrm{s}, key), <<t_1, l, t_3>, d, o>) \equiv$$
$$apply((\mathrm{s}, key), <<t_1{+}l, \mathbf{first}\,t_3, \mathbf{rest}\,t_3>, d, o>)\ \mathbf{provided}\ \neg(key\ \mathbf{isin}\ l).$$

Here **isin** denotes a predicate checking whether the string *key* occurs in *l* .

(i) The w command

$$apply(\text{w}, \langle\langle t_1, l, t_2\rangle, d, o\rangle) \equiv \langle\langle t_1, l, t_2\rangle, d, o+\text{d}(wind(t_1, l, t_2))+?\rangle.$$

Again, *wind* denotes an auxiliary operation that generates a window of the desired size.

Erroneous Situations

So far we have specified what has been required from the commands in the verbal specification. A simple formal examination, however, will again yield that the specification of *apply* is not complete, since borderline cases (that do not appear in the verbal specification) still have to be dealt with.

Of course, there are several possibilities to get rid of these marginal cases. One way is to use partial functions. However, the use of partial functions does not make sense in our particular example, since it is hard to imagine what 'undefined' should mean (should it mean that the screen bursts, or what ?). Another (simpler) way in our particular example would be to transmit the {bel} character as a kind of 'universal' error message. This would be similar (and, hence, similarly unsatisfactory) to what in error-handling in compilers is known as 'panic mode'. What is really tacitly expected (at least from the customer's side) is friendly behavior – whenever in such a borderline case there is still a chance to do something reasonable, the system should do so. It also seems reasonable to additionally output {bel} in order to signal a warning in these cases.

Aiming at such friendly behavior, we define :

ad (e)

$$apply(\text{k}, \langle\langle t_1, l, \varepsilon_t\rangle, d, o\rangle) \equiv$$
$$\langle\langle t_1, \varepsilon_l, \varepsilon_t\rangle, d \textbf{ push } l, o+\text{d}(\{\text{eof}\})+\text{d}(\{\text{bel}\})+?\rangle.$$

In the verbal specification it is required to display the line after the one deleted. However, if there is none, it cannot be displayed.

ad (f)

$$apply(\text{u}, \langle\langle t_1, l, t_2\rangle, \varepsilon_d, o\rangle) \equiv \langle\langle t_1, l, t_2\rangle, \varepsilon_d, o+\text{d}(\{\text{bel}\})+?\rangle.$$

Here we have assumed that the u command has no effect on the state, if the delete stack is empty – again a case that is not considered in the verbal requirements.

ad (g)

$$apply((+, i+1), \langle\langle t_1, l, \varepsilon_t\rangle, d, o\rangle\rangle) \equiv \langle\langle t_1, l, \varepsilon_t\rangle, d, o+\text{d}(\{\text{bel}\})+?\rangle$$

(and, of course, analogously for $(-, i+1)$).

The informal requirements might suggest that + and – have converse effects, say,

$$(-, \text{m}) + (+, \text{n}) \equiv \begin{cases} (-, (\text{m}-\text{n})) & \text{if m>n} \\ (+, (\text{n}-\text{m})) & \text{if n>m} \\ (+, 0) & \text{if n=m} \end{cases}$$

(and analogously for (+, m) + (–, n)).

If we had specified in this way, we would not only have forgotten that each move command also generates output even if the file is not changed, we also would have prevented any user-friendly solution to the above-mentioned borderline case.

ad (h)

$\forall$ **nbsstring** *key*:
apply((s, *key*), <<t_1, l, ε_t>, d, o>) ≡ <<t_1, l, ε_t>, d, o+d({bel})+?>
provided ¬(*key* **isin** l).

Still two more questions have to be tackled.

First, we have not yet specified what happens if the current line of the file is the pseudo-line ε_l. As we assume that files can only be created using the editor operations, the case <t_1, ε_l, t_2> always implies $t_2 = \varepsilon_t$, since (for a non-empty file) <t_1, ε_l, t_2> can only result from applying an e or k command. Hence, the case <t_1, ε_l, t_2> with $t_2 \neq \varepsilon_t$ does not need to be considered explicitly, and an appropriate invariant assertion can be added to *apply*:

funct *apply* = (**command'** c, **state** s: ∃ **stack** d, **output** o, **text** t_1, t_2:
s = <<t_1, ε_l, t_2>, d, o> ⇒ $t_2 = \varepsilon_t$) **state**.

When the current line is the pseudo-line we have

$\forall$ **command'** $c \notin$ {i, i', u, b, e, –}:
apply(c, <<t_1, ε_l, ε_t>, d, o >) ≡ <<t_1, ε_l, ε_t>, d, o+d({bel})+?>

and

apply((i, l), <<t_1, ε_l, ε_t>, d, o>) ≡ <<t_1, l, ε_t>, d, o+d(l)>,
apply((i', l), <<t_1, ε_l, ε_t>, d, o>) ≡ <<t_1, l, ε_t>, d, o+d(l)+?>,
apply(u, <<t_1, ε_l, ε_t>, d **push** l, o>) ≡ <<t_1, l, ε_t>, d, o+d(l)+?>,
apply(b, <<t_3, ε_l, ε_t>, d, o>) ≡ <<ε_t, **first**t_3, **rest**t_3>, d, o+p(**first**t_3)+?>,
apply(e, <<t_1, ε_l, ε_t>, d, o>) ≡ <<t_1, ε_l, ε_t>, d, o+d({eof})+?>,
apply((–, 0), <<t_1, ε_l, ε_t>, d, o>) ≡ <<t_1, ε_l, ε_t>, d, o+d({bel})+?>,
apply((–, i+1), <<t_3, ε_l, ε_t>, d, o >) ≡ *apply*((–, i), <<**lead**t_3, **last**t_3, ε_t>, d, o>).

Secondly we have to deal with the fact that any syntactically incorrect input is mapped to an (abstract) error command ec. This error command can simply be specified by

$\forall$ **file** f:
apply(ec, <f, d, o>) ≡ <f, d, o+d({bel})+?>.

Summary

As for the function *parse*, we now summarize the axioms of *apply* and rearrange and rephrase them in order to ease the proofs of soundness and formal completeness. Thus we get altogether:

funct *apply* = (**command'** c, **state** s: ∃ **stack** d, **output** o, **text** t_1, t_2:
s = <<t_1, ε_l, t_2>, d, o> ⇒ $t_2 = \varepsilon_t$) **state**,

$\forall$ **file** f, **stack** d, **output** o, **nat** i, **text** t_1, t_2, **pline** l, l_1, **nbsstring** x, y:

apply(b, <ε_f, d, o>) ≡ <ε_f, d, o+d({bel})+?>,

apply(b, <<t_1, l, t_2>, d, o>) ≡
<<ε_t, **first**(t_1+l+t_2), **rest**(t_1+l+t_2)>, d, o+p(**first**(t_1+l+t_2))+?>,
apply(b, <<t_1, ε_l, ε_t>, d, o>) ≡ <<ε_t, **first**t_1, **rest**t_1>, d, o+p(**first**t_1)+?>
provided $t_1 \neq \varepsilon_t$,

$apply(\mathrm{e}, <<t_1, l, t_2>, d, o>) \equiv <<t_1+l+t_2, \varepsilon_l, \varepsilon_t>, d, o+\mathrm{d}(\{\mathrm{eof}\})+?>,$
$apply(\mathrm{e}, <<t_1, \varepsilon_l, \varepsilon_t>, d, o>) \equiv <<t_1, \varepsilon_l, \varepsilon_t>, d, o+\mathrm{d}(\{\mathrm{eof}\})+?>,$

$apply((\mathrm{m}, x, y), <<t_1, l, t_2>, d, o>)$
$\quad \equiv <<t_1, repl(l, x, y), t_2>, d, o+re(l, x, y)+?>,$
$apply((\mathrm{m}, x, y), <<t_1, \varepsilon_l, \varepsilon_t>, d, o>) \equiv <<t_1, \varepsilon_l, \varepsilon_t>, d, o+\mathrm{d}(\{\mathrm{bel}\})+?>,$

$apply((\mathrm{i}, l), <<t_1, l_1, t_2>, d, o>) \equiv <<t_1+l_1, l, t_2>, d, o+\mathrm{d}(l)>,$
$apply((\mathrm{i}, l), <<t_1, \varepsilon_l, \varepsilon_t>, d, o>) \equiv <<t_1, l, \varepsilon_t>, d, o+\mathrm{d}(l)>,$
$apply((\mathrm{i'}, l), <<t_1, l_1, t_2>, d, o>) \equiv <<t_1+l_1, l, t_2>, d, o+\mathrm{d}(l)+?>,$
$apply((\mathrm{i'}, l), <<t_1, \varepsilon_l, \varepsilon_t>, d, o>) \equiv <<t_1, l, \varepsilon_t>, d, o+\mathrm{d}(l)+?>,$

$apply(\mathrm{k}, <<t_1, l, t_2>, d, o>) \equiv <<t_1, \mathbf{first}\, t_2, \mathbf{rest}\, t_2>, d\ \mathbf{push}\ l, o+d(\mathbf{first}\, t_2)+?>$
$\quad \mathbf{provided}\ t_2 \neq \varepsilon_t,$
$apply(\mathrm{k}, <<t_1, l, \varepsilon_t>, d, o>) \equiv <<t_1, \varepsilon_l, \varepsilon_t>, d\ \mathbf{push}\ l, o+\mathrm{d}(\{\mathrm{bel}\})+?>,$
$apply(\mathrm{k}, <<t_1, \varepsilon_l, \varepsilon_t>, d, o>) \equiv <<t_1, \varepsilon_l, \varepsilon_t>, d, o+\mathrm{d}(\{\mathrm{eof}\})+\mathrm{d}(\{\mathrm{bel}\})+?>,$

$apply(\mathrm{u}, <<t_1, l, t_2>, d, o>) \equiv <<t_1, \mathbf{top}\ d, l+t_2>, \mathbf{pop}\ d, o+\mathrm{d}(\mathbf{top}\ d)+?>$
$\quad \mathbf{provided}\ d \neq \varepsilon_d,$
$apply(\mathrm{u}, <f, \varepsilon_d, o>) \equiv <f, \varepsilon_d, o+\mathrm{d}(\{\mathrm{bel}\})+?>,$
$apply(\mathrm{u}, <<t_1, \varepsilon_l, \varepsilon_t>, d, o>) \equiv <<t_1, \mathbf{top}\ d, \varepsilon_t>, \mathbf{pop}\ d, o+\mathrm{d}(\mathbf{top}\ d)+?>$
$\quad \mathbf{provided}\ d \neq \varepsilon_d,$

$apply((+, 0), <<t_1, l, t_2>, d, o>) \equiv <<t_1, l, t_2>, d, o+\mathrm{t}(l)+?>,$
$apply((+, i), <<t_1, \varepsilon_l, \varepsilon_t>, d, o>) \equiv <<t_1, \varepsilon_l, \varepsilon_t>, d, o+\mathrm{d}(\{\mathrm{bel}\})+?>,$
$apply((+, i+1), <<t_1, l, t_2>, d, o>) \equiv apply((+, i), <<t_1+l, \mathbf{first}\, t_2, \mathbf{rest}\, t_2>, d, o>)$
$\quad \mathbf{provided}\ t_2 \neq \varepsilon_t,$
$apply((+, i+1), <<t_1, l, \varepsilon_t>, d, o>) \equiv <<t_1, l, \varepsilon_t>, d, o+\mathrm{d}(\{\mathrm{bel}\})+?>,$

$apply((-, 0), <<t_1, l, t_2>, d, o>) \equiv <<t_1, l, t_2>, d, o+\mathrm{t}(l)+?>,$
$apply((-, 0), <<t_1, \varepsilon_l, \varepsilon_t>, d, o>) \equiv <<t_1, \varepsilon_l, \varepsilon_t>, d, o+\mathrm{d}(\{\mathrm{bel}\})+?>,$
$apply((-, i+1), <<t_1, l, t_2>, d, o>) \equiv apply((-, i), <<\mathbf{lead}\, t_1, \mathbf{last}\, t_1, l+t_2>, d, o>)$
$\quad \mathbf{provided}\ t_1 \neq \varepsilon_t,$
$apply((-, i+1), <<\varepsilon_t, l, t_2>, d, o>) \equiv <<\varepsilon_t, l, t_2>, d, o+\mathrm{d}(\{\mathrm{bel}\})+?>,$
$apply((-, i+1), <<t_1, \varepsilon_l, \varepsilon_t>, d, o>) \equiv apply((-, i), <<\mathbf{lead}\, t_1, \mathbf{last}\, t_1, \varepsilon_t>, d, o>)$
$\quad \mathbf{provided}\ t_1 \neq \varepsilon_t,$
$apply((-, i+1), <\varepsilon_f, d, o>) \equiv <\varepsilon_f, d, o+\mathrm{d}(\{\mathrm{bel}\})+?>,$

$apply((\mathrm{s}, x), <<t_1, l, t_2>, d, o>) \equiv <<t_1, l, t_2>, d, o+\mathrm{d}(l)+?>\ \ \mathbf{provided}\ x\ \mathbf{isin}\ l\,,$
$apply((\mathrm{s}, x), <<t_1, l, t_2>, d, o>) \equiv apply((\mathrm{s}, x), <<t_1+l, \mathbf{first}\, t_2, \mathbf{rest}\, t_2>, d, o>)$
$\quad \mathbf{provided}\ t_2 \neq \varepsilon_t \wedge \neg(x\ \mathbf{isin}\ l),$
$apply((\mathrm{s}, x), <<t_1, l, \varepsilon_t>, d, o>) \equiv <<t_1, l, \varepsilon_t>, d, o+\mathrm{d}(\{\mathrm{bel}\})+?>$
$\quad \mathbf{provided}\ \neg(x\ \mathbf{isin}\ l),$
$apply((\mathrm{s}, x), <<t_1, \varepsilon_l, \varepsilon_t>, d, o>) \equiv <<t_1, \varepsilon_l, \varepsilon_t>, d, o+\mathrm{d}(\{\mathrm{bel}\})+?>,$

$apply(\mathrm{w}, <<t_1, l, t_2>, d, o>) \equiv <<t_1, l, t_2>, d, o+\mathrm{d}(wind(t_1, l, t_2))+?>$
$\quad \mathbf{provided}\ l \neq \varepsilon_l,$
$apply(\mathrm{w}, <<t_1, \varepsilon_l, \varepsilon_t>, d, o>) \equiv <<t_1, \varepsilon_l, \varepsilon_t>, d, o+\mathrm{d}(\{\mathrm{bel}\})+?>,$

$apply(\mathrm{ec}, <f, d, o>) \equiv <f, d, o+\mathrm{d}(\{\mathrm{bel}\})+?>.$

Formal vs. Informal Specification

To make a contribution to the ongoing discussion on formal specification versus informal specification we would like to comment briefly on the remark "note: the sequence ku leaves the file as it was" stated in the informal requirements.

If our formal specification adequately mirrors the informal requirements, we should be able to use our axioms to prove the theorem (note that ku means first applying k and then applying u, and uk means first u then k):

$\forall$ **file** f, **stack** d, **output** o:

(*) $f' \equiv f$ **where** $<f', d', o'> = apply(\text{u}, apply(\text{k}, <f, d, o>))$.

We have (by simple case analysis) :

(i) $f = \varepsilon_f$ and $d = \varepsilon_d$:
$apply(\text{u}, apply(\text{k}, <\varepsilon_f, \varepsilon_d, o>)) \equiv apply(\text{u}, <\varepsilon_f, \varepsilon_d, o\text{+d}(\{\text{eof}\})\text{+d}(\{\text{bel}\})\text{+?}>) \equiv$
$<\varepsilon_f, \varepsilon_d, o\text{+d}(\{\text{eof}\})\text{+d}(\{\text{bel}\})\text{+?+d}(\{\text{bel}\})\text{+?}>$
and thus $f' \equiv f$;

(ii) $f = <\varepsilon_t, l, \varepsilon_t>$:
$apply(\text{u}, apply(\text{k}, <<\varepsilon_t. l, \varepsilon_t>, d, o>)) \equiv apply(\text{u}, <\varepsilon_f, d\ \mathbf{push}\ l, o\text{+d}(\{\text{bel}\})\text{+?}>\equiv$
$<<\varepsilon_t, l, \varepsilon_t>, d, o\text{+d}(\{\text{bel}\})\text{+?+d}(l)\text{+?}>$
and thus $f' \equiv f$;

(iii) $f = <t_1, l, t_3>$:
$apply(\text{u}, apply(\text{k}, <<t_1, l, t_3>, d, o> \equiv$
$apply(\text{u}, <<t_1, \mathbf{first}t_3>, d\ \mathbf{push}\ l, o\text{+d}(\mathbf{first}t_3)\text{+?}> \equiv$
$<<t_1, l, t_3>, d, o\text{+d}(\mathbf{first}t_3)\text{+?+d}(l)\text{+?}>$
and again $f' \equiv f$.

However, we also will find out that (*) does not hold for $f = \varepsilon_f$ and $d \neq \varepsilon_d$.

Provability of (*) for $f = \varepsilon_f$ and $d \neq \varepsilon_d$ would require a modification in one of the axioms concerning u, namely

$apply(\text{u}, <\varepsilon_f, d, o>) \equiv <\varepsilon_f, d, o>$.

But this modification in turn would imply the unprovability of (*) for $f = <\varepsilon_t, l, \varepsilon_t>$.

Summing up, this means that in our particular formalization (in particular with our notion of state) the verbal requirements cannot be fulfilled.

Several conclusions can be drawn from this observation:

- The verbal requirements are inconsistent.
- We should use another definition of state. Actually we have tried other definitions without finding one that does not lead to inconsistencies. It is quite likely that there is no other definition, if friendly behavior is assumed. In particular, we feel that ours is a straightforward formalization of the informal requirements.
- (*) is only supposed to hold for the normal cases, and the borderline cases simply have been forgotten.

No matter which conclusion is drawn, a conflicting situation like the one above can only be resolved by a thorough discussion between the partners in the specification, namely the specifier and his customer.

9.4.2 Transformational Development

The subsequent transformational development will deal with the functions *effect*, *apply*, and *parse*. Its emphasis is on the transition from the respective algebraic specifications to equivalent (tail recursive) applicative programs working in an on-line fashion, that is, processing one unit after the other (without knowing the full history).

The overall strategy we are going to follow is the same as with the examples in the previous sections: first, we transform the algebraic specification into an applicative program; second, we apply suitable transformations to improve this program. The main techniques to be used for this particular example are rephrasing of axioms on the level of algebraic specification, and *abstraction*, *embedding*, *case introduction*, and *unfold/fold* for the operational improvement.

9.4.2.1 Development of an Operational Version of *effect*

The operation *effect*, describing the overall behavior of the editor, was defined on sequences of commands rather than on individual commands to be processed one at a time. In this way, we were able to specify the effects of the commands a and f, which depend on previous commands, in a very elegant way. In the sequel we are going to transform this abstract specification into an equivalent one where commands are individually processed.

Condensing the Specification of Effect

The formulation of the axioms for *effect* in Sect. 9.4.1.3 was primarily guided by the intention to ease a completeness proof. This led to a fairly large number of axioms. Therefore our first development step aims at reducing this number while simultaneously providing somewhat more uniformity for the right-hand sides of the axioms in order to keep the presentation reasonably short.

To this end we introduce

funct *apply'* = (**command** *c*, **state** *s*) **state**:
  if $c \in \{\text{a}, \text{f}\}$ **then** *s* **else** *apply*(*c*, *s*) **fi**

which allows us to combine the three axiom pairs (2a) and (2b), (3a) and (3b) and (3e) and (3f) into three single axioms. Thus we get a new (equivalent) specification for *effect*:

$\forall$ **command** *c*, *c'*, **commsequ** *cs* , **state** *s*:

(1) $effect(\varepsilon, s) \equiv s$,

(2ab) $effect(c+\varepsilon, s) \equiv apply'(c, s)$,

(3ab) $effect(c+c'+cs, s) \equiv effect(c'+cs, apply'(c, s))$
  provided $c \in \{\text{a}, \text{f}\} \vee c' \notin \{\text{a}, \text{f}\}$,

(3c) $effect(c+c'+cs, s) \equiv effect((\text{s}, key)+cs, apply'(c', s))$
  provided $c' = \text{f} \wedge c = (\text{m}, key, rep)$,

(3d) $effect(c+c'+cs, s) \equiv effect((\text{m}, key, rep)+cs, apply'(c, s))$
  provided $c' = (\text{a}, rep) \wedge c = (\text{s}, key)$,

(3ef) $effect(c+c'+cs, s) \equiv effect(c+cs, apply'(c', s))$
  provided $c \notin \{\text{a}, \text{f}\} \wedge ((c' = \text{f} \wedge c \neq \text{m}) \vee (c' = \text{a} \wedge c \neq \text{s}))$.

Introduction of Delimiter Symbols

We still have to differentiate between empty sequences, singleton sequences, and sequences with more than one element. Hence our next efforts aim at making this distinction disappear. Intuitively, we use a technique that is well-known in the areas of compiler construction or string processing. There, strings are frequently supplemented by (unique) delimiter symbols such that recognizing an empty string is reduced to recognizing the respective delimiter symbol. Thus normal and borderline cases can be treated alike.

Formally, we perform a simple data type transformation changing a command sequence into one which is delimited at both ends by the (new) delimiter symbols "#" (acting as dummy commands). To this end we introduce

– sequences consisting of commands and delimiter symbols, defined by

  mode commsequ' = EESEQU(**command**$^{\#}$, =)

  where

  mode command$^{\#}$ = **command** | {#},

– sequences of commands that have a delimiter symbol at their right end,

  mode commsequ$^{\#}$ = (**commsequ'** s': $\exists$ **commsequ** s : $s' = s$ + #), and

– sequences of commands that have delimiter symbols at both ends,

  mode commsequ$^{\#\#}$ = (**commsequ'** s': $\exists$ **commsequ** s : s' = # + s + #).

Next we adjust *apply'* and *effect* to these new data types, i.e. we transform them into functions $apply^{\#}$ and $effect^{\#}$ that work on delimited command sequences, but otherwise are the same. (Note that, by definition, for all objects *cs* of types **commsequ**$^{\#}$ and **commsequ**$^{\#\#}$ respectively, $cs \neq \varepsilon$ holds.)

We get

funct $apply^{\#}$ = (**command**$^{\#}$ c, **state** s) **state**:
  if $c \in$ {a, f, #} **then** s **else** $apply(c, s)$ **fi** ,

and

funct (**commsequ**$^{\#\#}$, **state**) **state** $effect^{\#}$,

defined by

$\forall$ **command**$^{\#}$ c, **command** c', **commsequ**$^{\#}$ cs , **state** s:

(1/2) $effect^{\#}(c+\#, s) \equiv apply^{\#}(c, s)$,

(3ab) $effect^{\#}(c+c'+cs, s) \equiv effect^{\#}(c'+cs, apply^{\#}(c, s))$
  provided $c \in$ {a, f, #} $\vee$ $c' \notin$ {a, f},

(3c) $effect^{\#}(c+c'+cs, s) \equiv effect^{\#}((\text{s}, key)+cs, apply^{\#}(c', s))$
  provided $c' = \text{f} \wedge c = (\text{m}, key, rep)$,

(3d) $effect^{\#}(c+c'+cs, s) \equiv effect^{\#}((\text{m}, key, rep)+cs, apply^{\#}(c, s))$
  provided $c' = (\text{a}, rep) \wedge c = (\text{s}, key)$,

(3ef) $effect^{\#}(c+c'+cs, s) \equiv effect^{\#}(c+cs, apply^{\#}(c', s))$
  provided $c \notin$ {a, f, #} $\wedge$ $((c' = \text{f} \wedge c \neq \text{m}) \vee (c' = \text{a} \wedge c \neq \text{s}))$.

The right-hand sides of (3c) and (3ef) can be further simplified using the respective premises and the definition of $apply^{\#}$. We get

(3c) ... $\equiv$ *effect*$^\#$((s, *key*)+*cs*, *s*) **provided** ... ,
(3ef) ... $\equiv$ *effect*$^\#$(*c*+*cs*, *s*) **provided** ... .

Of course, the definition of *edit* has also to be adapted to these new data types

$$edit(in) \equiv unparse(effect^\#(\# + parse(in) + \#, initstate)),$$

such that the previous transformation step technically amounts to an *embedding*.

Shifting the Focus of the Computation

Due to the fact that commands may have effects on other commands, the definition of *effect* must always take two commands at a time into account. In the previous definition of *effect*, this fact was reflected by looking one command ahead. Of course, the same situation can also be handled by remembering the command considered before.

In order to achieve this shift of the focus of the computation, we add two arguments to *effect* which are to remember the previous command and the previous state. Technically, this is achieved by another *embedding*. We introduce

funct (**commsequ**$^\#$*cs*, **state** *s'*, **command**$^\#$*c*, **state** *s*:
 $s' = apply^\#(c, s)$) **state** *eff*,

defined by

$$eff(cs, apply^\#(c, s), c, s) \equiv effect^\#(c+cs, s),$$

and transform the definition of *edit* into

$$edit(in) \equiv unparse(eff(parse(in) + \#, initstate, \#, initstate)).$$

Obviously, this definition is equivalent to the previous one, as (according to the definition of *apply*$^\#$)

$$apply^\#(\#, initstate) \equiv initstate.$$

The goal now is to derive a definition of *eff* which is independent of *effect*$^\#$.

Using the above definition of *eff*, the axioms for *effect*$^\#$ directly translate to

$\forall$ **command**$^\#$ *c*, **command** *c'*, **commsequ**$^\#$ *cs*, **state** *s*, *s'*: $s' = apply^\#(c, s)$:
(1/2) $eff(\#, s', c, s) \equiv s'$,
(3ab) $eff(c'+cs, s', c, s) \equiv eff(cs, apply^\#(c', s'), c', s')$
 provided $c \in \{a, f, \#\} \vee c' \notin \{a, f\}$,
(3c) $eff(c'+cs, s', c, s) \equiv eff(cs, apply^\#((s, key), s), (s, key), s)$
 provided $c' = f \wedge c = (m, key, rep)$,
(3d) $eff(c'+cs, s', c, s) \equiv eff(cs, apply^\#((m, key, rep), s'), (m, key, rep), s')$
 provided $c' = (a, rep) \wedge c = (s, key)$,
(3ef) $eff(c'+cs, s', c, s) \equiv eff(cs, s', c, s)$
 provided $c \notin \{a, f, \#\} \wedge ((c' = f \wedge c \neq m) \vee (c' = a \wedge c \neq s))$.

Finally, *apply*$^\#$ can be eliminated:
By simple unfolding, the assertion translates to

$$s' = \textbf{if } c \in \{a, f, \#\} \textbf{ then } s \textbf{ else } apply(c, s) \textbf{ fi}$$

which can be further simplified to

$$(c \in \{a, f, \#\} \,\Delta\, s' = s) \,\nabla\, s' = apply(c, s).$$

Unfolding $apply^{\#}$ in the axioms is trivial for (3c) and (3d) and leads to a case distinction for (3ab).

Altogether we get

$\forall$ **command**$^{\#}$ c, **command** c', **commsequ**$^{\#}$ cs, **state** s, s':
$(c \in \{a, f, \#\} \,\Delta\, s' = s) \,\nabla\, s' = apply(c, s)$:
(1/2) $eff(\#, s', c, s) \equiv s'$,
(3a) $eff(c'+cs, s', c, s) \equiv eff(cs, s', c', s')$ **provided** $c \in \{a, f, \#\} \wedge c' \in \{a, f\}$,
(3b) $eff(c'+cs, s', c, s) \equiv eff(cs, apply(c', s'), c', s')$ **provided** $c' \notin \{a, f\}$,
(3c) $eff(c'+cs, s', c, s) \equiv eff(cs, apply((s, key), s), (s, key), s)$
provided $c' = f \wedge c = (m, key, rep)$,
(3d) $eff(c'+cs, s', c, s) \equiv eff(cs, apply((m, key, rep), s'), (m, key, rep), s')$
provided $c' = (a, rep) \wedge c = (s, key)$,
(3ef) $eff(c'+cs, s', c, s) \equiv eff(cs, s', c, s)$
provided $c \notin \{a, f, \#\} \wedge ((c' = f \wedge c \neq m) \vee (c' = a \wedge c \neq s))$.

Note that this version could also have been derived without introducing the auxiliary operations *apply'* and $apply^{\#}$, respectively. However, this would have involved considerably more effort in keeping the number of axioms as small as possible.

An Equivalent Applicative Program

Our last version of *eff* can immediately be converted into the definition of an applicative function

```
funct eff' = (commsequ# cs, state s', command# c, state s:
              (c ∈ {a, f, #} Δ s' = s) ∇ s' = apply(c, s)) state:
   begin command# c' = firstcs;
   if c' = #  then s'
              else commsequ# cs' = restcs;
                   if c ∈ {a, f, #} ∧ c' ∈ {a, f} then eff'(cs', s', c', s')
                   [] c' ∉ {a, f} then eff'(cs', apply(c', s'), c', s')
                   [] c' = f ∧ c = (m, key, rep)
                        then eff'(cs', apply((s, key), s), (s, key), s)
                   [] c' = (a, rep) ∧ c = (s, key)
                        then eff'(cs', apply((m, key, rep), s'), (m, key, rep), s')
                   [] c ∉ {a, f, #} ∧ ((c' = f ∧ c ≠ m) ∨ (c' = a ∧ c ≠ s))
                        then eff'(cs', s', c, s) fi fi end
```

where, by definition, the last branch of the guarded expression simply can be abbreviated to **else**.

9.4.2.2 Introduction of On-line Processing

The previous definition of *eff'* still assumes that the complete input sequence is already parsed into a sequence of commands. Our next intermediate goal is the introduction of on-line behavior, to enable the parsing and processing of single commands one after the other rather than considering (pre-parsed) command sequences as done so far.

Combining Parsing and Processing of Single Commands

Technically, the introduction of on-line behavior is achieved by simple function composition, applied to *eff'* and *parse* in the right-hand side of the definition of *edit*, viz.

$$edit(in) \equiv unparse(eff'(parse(in) + \#, initstate, \#, initstate)).$$

This composition can simply be done by using the unfold/fold strategy. First, we redefine *edit* into

$$edit(in) \equiv unparse(eff''(in, initstate, \#, initstate)),$$

where

funct *eff''* = (**input** *in*, **state** *s'*, **command**# *c*, **state** *s*:
  $(c \in \{a, f, \#\} \Delta s' = s) \nabla s' = apply(c, s))$ **state**:
 eff'(parse(in)+#, s', c, s).

By unfolding (the simplified version of) *eff'*, we get

funct *eff''* = (**input** *in*, **state** *s'*, **command**# *c*, **state** *s*:
  $(c \in \{a, f, \#\} \Delta s' = s) \nabla s' = apply(c, s))$ **state**:
 begin command# *c'* = **first**(*parse*(*in*)+#);
 if *c'* = # **then** *s'*
  else commsequ# *cs'* = **rest**(*parse*(*in*)+#);
   if $c \in \{a, f, \#\} \wedge c' \in \{a, f\}$ **then** *eff'(cs', s', c', s')*
   [] $c' \notin \{a, f\}$ **then** *eff'(cs', apply(c', s'), c', s')*
   [] $c' = f \wedge c = (m, key, rep)$
    then *eff'(cs', apply((s, key), s), (s, key), s)*
   [] $c' = (a, rep) \wedge c = (s, key)$
    then *eff'(cs', apply((m, key, rep), s'), (m, key, rep), s')*
    else *eff'(cs', s', c, s)* **fi fi end**.

This last version still contains sequences of commands that have to be eliminated. We do this in two steps. First, by abstraction, we introduce auxiliary operations

funct *nextcommand* = (**input** *in*) **command**#:
 first(*parse*(*in*)+#)

and

funct *inputrest* = (**input** *in*: $parse(in) \neq \varepsilon$) **input**:
 some input *z*: *parse*(*z*)+# = **rest**(*parse*(*in*)+#).

Obviously, *parse*(*inputrest*(*in*))+# ≡ **rest**(*parse*(*in*)+#), and, hence, our next intermediate version reads

funct *eff''* = (**input** *in*, **state** *s'*, **command**# *c*, **state** *s*:
  $(c \in \{a, f, \#\} \Delta s' = s) \nabla s' = apply(c, s))$ **state**:
 begin command# *c'* = *nextcommand*(*in*);
 if *c'* = # **then** *s'*
  else input *in'* = *inputrest*(*in*); **commsequ**# *cs'* = *parse*(*in'*)+#;
   if $c \in \{a, f, \#\} \wedge c' \in \{a, f\}$ **then** *eff'(cs', s', c', s')*
   [] $c' \notin \{a, f\}$ **then** *eff'(cs', apply(c', s'), c', s')*

$[]\ c' = \mathrm{f} \wedge c = (\mathrm{m}, key, rep)$
then $\mathit{eff}'(cs', apply((\mathrm{s}, key), s), (\mathrm{s}, key), s)$
$[]\ c' = (\mathrm{a}, rep) \wedge c = (\mathrm{s}, key)$
then $\mathit{eff}'(cs', apply((\mathrm{m}, key, rep), s'), (\mathrm{m}, key, rep), s')$
else $\mathit{eff}'(cs', s', c, s)$ **fi fi end**.

Next, by simply unfolding the declaration of cs', we get

funct eff'' = (**input** *in*, **state** s', **command**$^\#$ c, **state** s:
$(c \in \{\mathrm{a}, \mathrm{f}, \#\}\ \Delta\ s' = s)\ \nabla\ s' = apply(c, s))$ **state**:
begin command$^\#$ $c' = nextcommand(in)$;
if $c' = \#$ **then** s'
else input $in' = inputrest(in)$;
if $c \in \{\mathrm{a}, \mathrm{f}, \#\} \wedge c' \in \{\mathrm{a}, \mathrm{f}\}$ **then** $\mathit{eff}'(parse(in')+\#, s', c', s')$
$[]\ c' \notin \{\mathrm{a}, \mathrm{f}\}$ **then** $\mathit{eff}'(parse(in')+\#, apply(c', s'), c', s')$
$[]\ c' = \mathrm{f} \wedge c = (\mathrm{m}, key, rep)$
then $\mathit{eff}'(parse(in')+\#, apply((\mathrm{s}, key), s), (\mathrm{s}, key), s)$
$[]\ c' = (\mathrm{a}, rep) \wedge c = (\mathrm{s}, key)$
then $\mathit{eff}'(parse(in')+\#, apply((\mathrm{m}, key, rep), s'), (\mathrm{m}, key, rep), s')$
else $\mathit{eff}'(parse(in')+\#, s', c, s)$ **fi fi end**.

Now folding (with assertion) of eff'' is possible, and our final result is

funct eff'' = (**input** *in*, **state** s', **command**$^\#$ c, **state** s:
$(c \in \{\mathrm{a}, \mathrm{f}, \#\}\ \Delta\ s' = s)\ \nabla\ s' = apply(c, s))$ **state**:
begin command$^\#$ $c' = nextcommand(in)$;
if $c' = \#$ **then** s'
else input $in' = inputrest(in)$;
if $c \in \{\mathrm{a}, \mathrm{f}, \#\} \wedge c' \in \{\mathrm{a}, \mathrm{f}\}$ **then** $\mathit{eff}''(in', s', c', s')$
$[]\ c' \notin \{\mathrm{a}, \mathrm{f}\}$ **then** $\mathit{eff}''(in', apply(c', s'), c', s')$
$[]\ c' = \mathrm{f} \wedge c = (\mathrm{m}, key, rep)$
then $\mathit{eff}''(in', apply((\mathrm{s}, key), s), (\mathrm{s}, key), s)$
$[]\ c' = (\mathrm{a}, rep) \wedge c = (\mathrm{s}, key)$
then $\mathit{eff}''(in', apply((\mathrm{m}, key, rep), s'), (\mathrm{m}, key, rep), s')$
else $\mathit{eff}''(in', s', c, s)$ **fi fi end**.

In this final version, all commands are recognized (by the function *nextcommand*) and processed one at a time.

A More Detailed Version

Obviously, within the given context,

$$(c' \notin \{\mathrm{a}, \mathrm{f}\}) \equiv$$
$$(c' = \mathrm{ec} \vee c' = \mathrm{b} \vee c' = \mathrm{e} \vee c' = (\mathrm{m}, key, rep) \vee c' = (\mathrm{i}, l) \vee c' = (\mathrm{i}', l) \vee$$
$$c' = \mathrm{k} \vee c' = \mathrm{u} \vee c' = (+, n) \vee c' = (-, n) \vee c' = (\mathrm{s}, key) \vee c' = \mathrm{w}).$$

Hence, the respective branch in the above program can be further detailed. Additionally, we combine the auxiliary operations *nextcommand* and *inputrest* into a single new auxiliary operation

funct *nextcomm* = (**input** *in*) (**command**$^\#$, **input**):
(*nextcommand*(*in*), **if** *parse*(*in*) = ε **then** ε **else** *inputrest*(*in*) **fi**).

This leads to

funct *eff''* = (**input** *in*, **state** *s'*, **command#** *c*, **state** *s*:
$(c \in \{a, f, \#\} \Delta s' = s) \nabla s' = apply(c, s))$ **state**:
begin (**command#** *c'*, **input** *in'*) = *nextcomm*(*in*);
if $c' = \#$ **then** *s'*
else if $c \in \{a, f, \#\} \wedge c' \in \{a, f\}$ **then** *eff''*(*in'*, *s'*, *c'*, *s'*)
[] c' = ec **then** *eff''*(*cs'*, *apply*(ec, *s'*), ec, *s'*)
[] c' = b **then** *eff''*(*cs'*, *apply*(b, *s'*), b, *s'*)
[] c' = e **then** *eff''*(*cs'*, *apply*(e, *s'*), e, *s'*)
[] c' = (m, *key*, *rep*)
then *eff''*(*cs'*, *apply*((m, *key*, *rep*), *s'*), (m,*key*,*rep*), *s'*)
[] c' = (i, *l*) **then** *eff''*(*cs'*, *apply*((i, *l*), *s'*), (i, *l*), *s'*)
[] c' = (i', *l*) **then** *eff''*(*cs'*, *apply*((i', *l*), *s'*), (i', *l*), *s'*)
[] c' = k **then** *eff''*(*cs'*, *apply*(k, *s'*), k, *s'*)
[] c' = u **then** *eff''*(*cs'*, *apply*(u, *s'*), u, *s'*)
[] c' = (+, *n*) **then** *eff''*(*cs'*, *apply*((+, *n*), *s'*), (+, *n*), *s'*)
[] c' = (–, *n*) **then** *eff''*(*cs'*, *apply*((–, *n*), *s'*), (–, *n*), *s'*)
[] c' = (s, *key*) **then** *eff''*(*cs'*, *apply*((s, *key*), *s'*), (s, *key*), *s'*)
[] c' = w **then** *eff''*(*cs'*, *apply*(w, *s'*), w, *s'*)
[] $c' = f \wedge c$ = (m, *key*, *rep*)
then *eff''*(*in'*, *apply*((s, *key*), *s*), (s, *key*), *s*)
[] c' = (a, *rep*) $\wedge$ c = (s, *key*)
then *eff''*(*in'*, *apply*((m, *key*, *rep*), *s'*), (m, *key*, *rep*), *s'*)
else *eff''*(*in'*, *s'*, *c*, *s*) **fi fi end**.

An Explicit, Axiomatic Definition of nextcomm

So far, the auxiliary operation *nextcomm* is defined using the operation *parse*. Our next intermediate goal is to derive a definition of *nextcomm* which is independent of *parse*.

First, by unfolding the respective definitions of *nextcommand* and *inputrest*, we get

funct *nextcomm* = (**input** *in*) (**command#**, **input**):
(**first**(*parse*(*in*)+#),
if *parse*(*in*) = ε **then** ε **else some input** *z*: *parse*(*z*)+# = **rest**(*parse*(*in*)+#) **fi**).

An axiomatic definition of *nextcomm* can be obtained from the axioms of *parse* in a straightforward way (again by using unfold/fold steps and the definition of *nextcomm*):

∀ **input** *in*, *sc*, **char** *c*, **digit** *d*, **string** t_1, t_2, **dstring** t_d:

nextcomm(ε) ≡ (#, ε),

nextcomm (*c*+*in*) ≡ (*c*, *in*) **provided** $c \in \{b, e, k, u, f, w\}$,

nextcomm(*c*+*in*) ≡ (ec, *in*)
provided $c \notin (\{b, e, m, i, i', k, u, s, a, f, w\} \cup$ **digit**),

nextcomm(m+*in*) ≡ ((m, $mbl(t_1)$, $dlb(mbl(t_2))$), *sc*)
provided $in = t_1+\{cr\}+t_2+\{cr\}+sc \wedge nbs(t_1)$,

$nextcomm(\text{m}+in) \equiv nextcomm(\textbf{rest}(mbl(t_1))+sc)$
  provided $in = t_1+sc \;\wedge \neg\, nbs(t_1)$,
$nextcomm(\text{m}+in) \equiv (\#, \varepsilon)$
  provided $(in \in \textbf{string}\;\Delta\; nbs(in)) \vee (in = t_1+\{\text{cr}\}+t_2 \wedge nbs(t_1))$,
$nextcomm(\text{m}+in) \equiv (\text{ec}, sc)$
  provided $(in = t_1+\{\text{cr}\}+t_2+\{\text{esc}\}+sc \wedge nbs(t_1)) \vee (in = t_1+\{\text{esc}\}+sc \wedge nbs(t_1))$,

$nextcomm(\text{i}+in) \equiv ((\text{i}, dlb(mbl(t_1))+\{\text{cr}\}), \text{i}+sc)$ **provided** $in = t_1+\{\text{cr}\}+sc$,
$nextcomm(\text{i}+in) \equiv ((\text{i'}, dlb(mbl(t_1))+\{\text{cr}\}), sc)$ **provided** $in = t_1+\{\text{esc}\}+sc$,
$nextcomm(\text{i}+in) \equiv (\#, \varepsilon)$ **provided** $in \in$ **string**,

$nextcomm(\text{s}+in) \equiv ((\text{s}, mbl(t_1)), sc)$ **provided** $in = t_1+\{\text{cr}\}+sc \;\wedge nbs(t_1)$,
$nextcomm(\text{s}+in) \equiv nextcomm(\textbf{rest}(mbl(t_1))+sc)$ **provided** $in = t_1+sc \;\wedge \neg\, nbs(t_1)$,
$nextcomm(\text{s}+in) \equiv (\#, \varepsilon)$ **provided** $in \in$ **string** $\Delta\; nbs(in)$,
$nextcomm(\text{s}+in) \equiv (\text{ec}, sc)$ **provided** $in = t_1+\{\text{esc}\}+sc \wedge nbs(t_1)$,

$nextcomm(\text{a}+in) \equiv ((\text{a}, mbl(t_1)), sc)$ **provided** $in = t_1+\{\text{cr}\}+sc \;\wedge nbs(t_1)$,
$nextcomm(\text{a}+in) \equiv nextcomm(\textbf{rest}(mbl(t_1))+sc)$ **provided** $in = t_1+sc \;\wedge \neg\, nbs(t_1)$,
$nextcomm(\text{a}+in) \equiv (\#, \varepsilon)$ **provided** $in \in$ **string** $\Delta\; nbs(in)$,
$nextcomm(\text{a}+in) \equiv (\text{ec}, sc)$ **provided** $in = t_1+\{\text{esc}\}+sc \;\wedge nbs(t_1)$,

$nextcomm(d+in) \equiv ((sig, conv(mbl(t_d), 0)), sc)$
  provided $in = t_d+sig+sc \wedge (mbl(t_d) \neq \varepsilon\, \Delta\, \textbf{first}(mbl(t_d)) \neq \{\text{bs}\}) \wedge sig \in \{+, -\}$,
$nextcomm(d+in) \equiv nextcomm(\textbf{rest}(mbl(t_1))+sc)$ **provided** $in = t_1+sc \wedge \neg\, nbs(t_1)$,
$nextcomm(d+in) \equiv (\#, \varepsilon)$ **provided** $in \in$ **dstring** $\Delta\; mbl(d+in) \neq \varepsilon$,
$nextcomm(d+in) \equiv (\text{ec}, sc)$
  provided $d+in = t_d+c+sc \;\wedge\; (mbl(t_d) \neq \varepsilon\; \Delta$
    $\textbf{first}(mbl(t_d)) \neq \{\text{bs}\}) \;\wedge\; c \notin \{+, -\} \cup$ **digit**.

An Operational Definition for nextcomm

It remains to derive operational versions for *nextcomm* starting with the axiomatic definition given above. As an example, we will deal with the s command in detail.

First, we redefine (by abstraction) the respective axioms,

(1) $nextcomm(\text{s}+in) \equiv ((\text{s}, mbl(t_1)), sc)$ **provided** $in = t_1+\{\text{cr}\}+sc \;\wedge nbs(t_1)$,
(2) $nextcomm(\text{s}+in) \equiv nextcomm(\textbf{rest}(mbl(t_1))+sc)$
  provided $in = t_1+sc \;\wedge \neg\, nbs(t_1)$,
(3) $nextcomm(\text{s}+in) \equiv (\#, \varepsilon)$ **provided** $in \in$ **string** $\Delta\; nbs(in)$,
(4) $nextcomm(\text{s}+in) \equiv (\text{ec}, sc)$ **provided** $in = t_1+\{\text{esc}\}+sc \;\wedge nbs(t_1)$,

into

$nextcomm(\text{s}+in) \equiv$
  if $in = \varepsilon$ **then** $(\#, \varepsilon)$
  elsf **first**in = {bs} **then** $nextcomm(\textbf{rest}in)$
    else $ps(\textbf{first}in, \textbf{first}in, \textbf{rest}in)$ **fi**

where the auxiliary operation *ps* parses an s command and is defined by

funct ps = (**nstring** p, **string** o, **input** in:
    $p = mbl(o) \wedge (o \neq \varepsilon\; \Delta\; \textbf{first}o \neq \{\text{bs}\})$) (**command**#, **input**):
  $nextcomm(\text{s}+o+in)$.

Next, we derive axioms for *ps* using its definition, the assertion on the parameters, unfold and folding with assertion. As we specified *nextcomm* in such a way that all axioms are disjoint, no special care with respect to overlapping cases has to be taken. We get

$\forall$ **nstring** p, **string** o, **input** in, **char** c, c':
$c' \notin \{\text{bs}, \text{cr}, \text{esc}\} \wedge c \notin \{\text{bs}, \text{cr}, \text{esc}\}$:
$ps(p, o, \varepsilon) \equiv nextcomm(\text{s}+o+\varepsilon) \equiv (\#, \varepsilon)$
[according to (3)]
$ps(p+c, o, \{\text{bs}\}+in) \equiv nextcomm(\text{s}+o+\{\text{bs}\}+in) \equiv ps(p, o+\{\text{bs}\}, in)$
[by folding, as $(p+c = mbl(o) \wedge (o \neq \varepsilon \,\Delta\, \textbf{first}o \neq \{\text{bs}\})) \equiv \textbf{true} \vdash$
$(p = mbl(o+\{\text{bs}\}) \wedge (o+\{\text{bs}\} \neq \varepsilon \,\Delta\, \textbf{first}(o+\{\text{bs}\}) \neq \{\text{bs}\})) \equiv \textbf{true}$]
$ps(\varepsilon, o, \{\text{bs}\}+in) \equiv nextcomm(\text{s}+o+\{\text{bs}\}+in) \equiv nextcomm(in)$
[according to (2), as $\varepsilon \equiv mbl(o) \vdash mbl(o+\{\text{bs}\}) \equiv \{\text{bs}\} \vdash \neg nbs(o+\{\text{bs}\}) \equiv \textbf{true}$]
$ps(p, o, \{\text{cr}\}+in) \equiv nextcomm(\text{s}+o+\{\text{cr}\}+in) \equiv ((\text{s}, p), in)$
[according to (1), as $(p \in \textbf{nstring} \wedge p = mbl(o) \wedge nbs(o)) \equiv \textbf{true}$]
$ps(p, o, \{\text{esc}\}+in) \equiv nextcomm(\text{s}+o+\{\text{esc}\}+in) \equiv (\text{ec}, in)$
[according to (4), as $(p \in \textbf{nstring} \wedge p = mbl(o) \wedge nbs(o)) \equiv \textbf{true}$]
$ps(p, o, c'+in) \equiv nextcomm(\text{s}+o+c'+in) \equiv ps(p+c', o+c', in)$
[by folding, as $(c' \notin \{\text{bs}, \text{cr}, \text{esc}\} \wedge p = mbl(o) \wedge (o \neq \varepsilon \,\Delta\, \textbf{first}o \neq \{\text{bs}\})) \equiv \textbf{true} \vdash$
$(p+c' = mbl(o+c') \wedge (o+c' \neq \varepsilon \,\Delta\, \textbf{first}(o+\{\text{bs}\}) \neq \{\text{bs}\})) \equiv \textbf{true}$].

This definition of *ps* can be transformed into a recursive function in a straightforward way:

```
funct ps = (nstring p, string o, input in:
            p = mbl(o) ∧ (o ≠ ε Δ firsto ≠ {bs})) (command#, input):
   if in = ε  then (#, ε)
              else if firstin = {bs}
                      then if p = ε  then nextcomm(restin)
                                     else ps(p, o+{bs}, restin) fi
                   [] firstin = {cr} then ((s, p), restin)
                   [] firstin = {esc}then (ec, restin)
                   else ps(p + firsti, o + firsti, restin) fi fi.
```

In an analogous way, also the remaining axioms in *nextcomm* for a, s, m, i, or move commands can be treated to finally obtain a fully operational version of *nextcomm*.

The result obtained so far does not yet exhibit true on-line behavior, since *unparse* (in the definition of *edit*) is applied just to the final state rather than successively to all intermediate states.

Obviously, another function composition (here of *unparse* and *eff''*) is necessary which, although straightforwardly analogous to the treatment of *parse*, cannot be demonstrated in detail due to the absence of a specification of *unparse*.

9.4.2.3 Remarks on Further Development

We have stopped our derivation at the level of applicative programs. We are convinced that the steps towards a conventional programming language which are still missing are fairly obvious. Nevertheless we would like to add a few more comments on these final optimization steps.

First, the definition of *apply* has to be transformed such that there is exactly one axiom for each command. Starting with the definition of *apply* from above this is straightforward and left as an exercise to the reader.

Next, we can get rid of the auxiliary structures **state** and **file** by simply unfolding the respective definitions. Of course, this also requires unfolding of all calls of *apply* in *eff''* (where the recursively defined axioms have to be made into appropriate auxiliary operations). This also leads to a redefinition of *edit* into

$$edit(in) \equiv unparse(eff^*(in, \varepsilon_t, \varepsilon_l, \varepsilon_t, \varepsilon_d, \varepsilon_o, \#, \varepsilon_t, \varepsilon_l, \varepsilon_t, \varepsilon_d, \varepsilon_o))$$

where the explicit definition of

funct eff^* = (**input** in, **text** t_1, **line** l, **text** t_2, **stack** d, **output** o,
command# c, **text** ot_1, **line** ol, **text** ot_2, **stack** od, **output** oo)
(**text**, **line**, **text**, **stack**, **output**),

which is characterized by

$$eff^*(in, t_1, l, t_2, d, o, c, ot_1, ol, ot_2, od, oo) \equiv$$
$$eff''(in, <<t_1, l, t_2>, d, o>, c, <<ot_1, ol, ot_2>, od, oo>),$$

again is straightforward.

The definition of eff^* also allows a possible further optimization according to the general idea of saving storage at the expense of additional computational effort. Rather than keeping the "old state" $<<ot_1, ol, ot_2>, od, oo>$ explicitly, it is perhaps more economic to just have the "current state" $<<t_1, l, t_2>, d, o>$, some information *inf*, and an operation *restore*, that fulfils

$$restore(<<t_1, l, t_2>, d, o>, inf) \equiv <<ot_1, ol, ot_2>, od, oo>,$$

i.e., recomputes the information contained in $<<ot_1, ol, ot_2>, od, oo>$ in case it is needed. Whether this last transformation, which in some sense is a counterpart to the technique of *finite differencing* (Sect. 6.4.4), is really an improvement depends on further facts that go beyond the scope of this treatment.

The function eff^* and its further optimized versions are all tail-recursive. This means that a transition to iteration (including final polish-up transformations for imperative programs) could be added as a final optimization step.

9.4.3 Concluding Remarks

By means of a realistic case study we have demonstrated how the paradigms of algebraic specification and transformational programming can be used to bridge the gap between informally stated requirements and a running program. In particular, we have demonstrated how an abstract view taken in an algebraic specification is to be transformed into a practically reasonable operational version.

A reader inexperienced in using formal techniques in program development might be intimidated by the number of formulas needed for a detailed formal problem description. He may also be discouraged or even bored by the persistence necessary to follow its development. Such a reader should simply be reminded of the fact that writing a program without formal development would require at least the same number of formulas (or statements) and of the well-known difficulty of making sure that the program really does what it should do.

Likewise, the ratio between specification and development, with more effort for the specification than for the development, might appear strange to some readers. We think that this phenomenon is a simple consequence of the fact that formal specifications require a precise and complete statement of the problem. This leaves no room for "hand waving" or hiding aspects of the problem in the development of an algorithm. Thus, program development starting from a formal specification can concentrate exclusively on making constructs operational and efficient without being bothered by aspects of problem analysis. This obviously requires less effort than the traditional approach to software development.

Although more effort has still to be invested to complete this sample derivation, for example to add a suitable treatment of cursor positions (which we have deliberately left out due to the lack of relevant information in the informal requirements), the general way of dealing with such kinds of problems should have become obvious. In particular, the attentive reader with a basic knowledge of algebraic specification and transformational programming should be able to perform similar developments, for example on existing, commercially available editors, himself or herself.

References

[Agresti 86a]
Agresti, W.M. (ed.): New paradigms for software development. Washington, D.C.: IEEE Computer Society Press 1986

[Agresti 86b]
Agresti, W.M.: What are the new paradigms? In: [Agresti 86a], pp. 6–10

[Aho et al. 75]
Aho, A.V., Hopcroft, J.E., Ullman, J.D.: The design and analysis of computer programs. Reading, Mass.: Addison-Wesley 1975

[Aho, Ullman 72]
Aho, A.V., Ullman, J.D.: The theory of parsing, translation, and compiling. Volume I: Parsing. Englewood Cliffs, N.J.: Prentice-Hall 1972

[Alford 77]
Alford, M.W.: A requirements engineering methodology for real-time processing requirements. IEEE Transactions on Software Engineering SE-**3**:1, 60–69 (1977)

[Alford et al. 77]
Alford, M.W., et al.: Software Requirements Engineering Methodology. SREP Final Report, Vol. I. Huntsville, Al.: TRW Defense and Space Systems Group, 1977

[Aubin 75]
Aubin, R.: Some generalization heuristics in proofs by induction. Proc. Int. Symp. on Proving and Improving Programs, Arc-et-Senans, France, 1975, pp. 197–208

[Babb, Tripp 80]
Babb, R., Tripp, L.: Towards tangible realizations of software systems. Proc. 13th Hawaii Int. Conf. on System Sciences, 1980

[Backhouse 86]
Backhouse, R.C.: Program construction and verification. London: Prentice-Hall 1986

[Backus 78]
Backus, J.: Can programming be liberated from the von Neumann style? A functional style and its algebra of programs. Comm. ACM **21**, 613–641 (1978)

[Balzer 81a]
Balzer, R.M.: Transformational implementation: an example. IEEE Transactions on Software Engineering SE-**7**:1, 3–14 (1981)

[Balzer 81b]
Balzer, R.: Final report on GIST. USC/ISI, Marina del Rey, Technical Report 1981

[Balzer, Goldman 79]
Balzer, R., Goldman, N.: Principles of good software specification and their implications for specification languages. Proc. Specifications of Reliable Software, Cambridge, Mass., 1979, pp. 58–67

[Balzer et al. 83]
Balzer, R., Cheatham, T.E.Jr., Green, C.: Software technology in the 1990's: using a new paradigm. IEEE Computer **16**:11, 39–45 (1983)

[Balzert 81]
Balzert, H.: Methoden, Sprachen und Werkzeuge zur Definition, Dokumentation und Analyse von Anforderungen an Software-Produkte. Informatik-Spektrum **4**, 145–163, 246–260 (1981)

[Balzert 82]
Balzert, H.: Die Entwicklung von Software-Systemen. Prinzipien, Methoden, Sprachen, Werkzeuge. Mannheim: Bibliographisches Institut 1982

[Bauer 72]
Bauer, F.L.: Software Engineering. In: Information Processing 71. Amsterdam: North-Holland, 1972, pp. 530–537

[Bauer 76]
Bauer, F.L.: Programming as an evolutionary process. Proc. 2nd Int. Conf. on Software Engineering, San Francisco, Ca., 1976, pp. 223–234

[Bauer 81]
Bauer, F.L.: Programming as fulfillment of a contract. In: Henderson, P. (ed.): System design. Infotech State of the Art Report, Series 9, Number 6, Maidenhead: Pergamon Infotech Ltd. 1981, pp. 165–174

[Bauer 82]
Bauer, F.L.: From specifications to machine code: program construction through formal reasoning. Proc. 6th Int. Conf. on Software Engineering, Tokyo, Japan, 1982, pp. 84–91

[Bauer 85]
Bauer, F.L.: Programs as formal objects. Unpublished manuscript 1985

[Bauer, Wössner 82]
Bauer, F.L., Wössner, H.: Algorithmic language and program development. Berlin: Springer 1982

[Bauer, Wössner 83]
Bauer, F.L., Wössner, H.: Beispiele zur Programmentwicklung: Abgebrochener Dual-Logarithmus. Institut für Informatik der TU München, TUM-I8312, 1983

[Bauer et al. 79]
Bauer, F.L., Broy, M., Partsch, H., Pepper, P., Wössner, H.: Systematics of transformation rules. In: Bauer, F.L., Broy, M. (eds.): Program construction. Lecture Notes in Computer Science **69**, Berlin: Springer 1979, pp. 273–289

[Bauer et al. 81]
Bauer, F.L., Broy, M., Dosch, W., Gnatz, R., Krieg-Brückner, B., Laut, A., Luckmann, M., Matzner, T., Möller, B., Partsch, H., Pepper, P., Samelson, K., Steinbrüggen, R., Wirsing, M., Wössner, H.: Programming in a wide spectrum language: a collection of examples. Science of Computer Programming **1**, 73–114 (1981)

[Bauer et al. 85]
Bauer, F.L., Berghammer, R., Broy, M., Dosch, W., Geiselbrechtinger, F., Gnatz, R., Hangel, E., Hesse, W., Krieg-Brückner, B., Laut, A., Matzner, T., Möller, B., Nickl, F., Partsch, H., Pepper, P., Samelson, K., Wirsing, M., Wössner, H.: The Munich project CIP. Volume I: The wide spectrum language CIP-L. Lecture Notes in Computer Science **183**, Berlin: Springer 1985

[Bauer et al. 87]
Bauer, F.L., Ehler, H., Horsch, A., Möller, B., Partsch, H., Paukner, O., Pepper, P.: The Munich project CIP. Volume II: The transformation system CIP-S. Lecture Notes in Computer Science **292**, Berlin: Springer 1987

[Bauer et al. 89]
Bauer, F.L., Möller, B., Partsch, H., Pepper, P.: Programming by formal reasoning - computer-aided intuition-guided programming. IEEE Transactions on Software Engineering, **15**:2, 165–180 (1989)

[Bayer 85]
Bayer, R.: Data base technology for expert systems. In: Brauer, W., Radig, B. (eds.): Wissensbasierte Systeme. Informatik-Fachberichte **112**, Berlin: Springer 1985, pp. 1–16

[Beckman et al. 76]
Beckman, L., Haraldson, A., Oskarsson, Ö., Sandewall, E.: A partial evaluator, and its use as a programming tool. Artificial Intelligence **7**, 319–357 (1976)

[Belady 66]
Belady, L.A.: A study of replacement algorithms for virtual storage computers. IBM Systems Journal **5**, 78–101 (1966)

[Bell et al. 77]
Bell, T.E., Bixter, D.C., Dyer, M.E.: An extendable approach to computer-aided software requirements engineering. IEEE Transactions on Software Engineering, SE-**3**:1, 49–59 (1977)

[Berghammer 84]
Berghammer, R.: Zur formalen Entwicklung von graphentheoretischen Algorithmen durch Transformation. Fakultät für Mathematik und Informatik der TU München, Dissertation, TUM-I8403, 1984

[Berghammer 85]
Berghammer, R.: On the use of composition in transformational programming. Institut für Informatik der TU München, TUM-I8512, 1985

[Berghammer 86]
Berghammer, R.: A transformational development of several algorithms for testing the existence of cycles in a directed graph. Institut für Informatik der TU München TUM-I8615, 1986

[Berghammer, Ehler 89]
Berghammer, R., Ehler, H.: On the use of elements of functional programming in program development by transformations. In: Broy, M., Wirsing, M. (eds.): Methodik des Programmierens. Fakultät für Mathematik und Informatik, Universität Passau, Report MIP-8915, 1989, pp. 53–76

[Berghammer et al. 87]
Berghammer, R., Ehler, H., Zierer, H.: Development of several reachability algorithms for directed graphs. Institut für Informatik, TU München, Internal Report 1987

[Berry 76]
Berry, G.: Bottom-up computations of recursive programs. R.A.I.R.O. Informatique théorétique **10**:3, 17–82 (1976)

[Biewald et al. 79]
Biewald, J., Göhner, P., Lauber, R., Schelling, H.: EPOS - A specification and design technique for computer controlled real-time automation systems. Proc. 4th. Int. Conf. on Software Engineering, München, Germany, 1979, pp. 245–250

[Bird 80]
Bird, R.S.: Tabulation techniques for recursive programs. ACM Computing Surveys **12**:4, 403–417 (1980)

[Bird 84]
Bird, R.S.: The promotion and accumulation strategies in transformational programming. ACM TOPLAS **6**:4, 487–504 (1984)

[Bird 87]
Bird, R.S.: An introduction to the theory of lists. In: Broy, M. (ed.): Logic of programming and calculi of discrete design. NATO ASI Series, Series F: Computer and System Sciences, vol. 36. Berlin: Springer 1987, pp. 5–42

[Bird, Wadler 88]
Bird, R.S., Wadler, P.L.: Introduction to functional programming. Hemel Hempstead: Prentice Hall International 1988

[Bloch 77]
Bloch, A.: Murphy's Law and other reasons why things go wrong. Los Angeles: Price/Stern/Sloan 1977

[Boehm 75]
Boehm, B.W.: The high cost of software. In: [Horowitz 75], pp. 3–14

[Boehm 76]
Boehm, B.: Software Engineering. IEEE Transaction on Computers C-**25**:12, 1226–1241 (1976)

[Boehm 81]
Boehm, B.: Software Engineering Economics. Englewood Cliffs, N.J.: Prentice-Hall 1981

[Boiten 89]
Boiten, E.: Inverting the flow of computation. Dept. of Informatics, University of Nijmegen, Technical Report No. 89-10, June 1989

[Boyer, Moore 77]
Boyer, R.S., Moore, J.S.: A fast string searching algorithm. Comm. ACM **20**:10, 762–772 (1977)

[Brittan 80]
Brittan, J.N.G.: Design for a changing environment. Computer Journal **23**:1, 13–19 (1980)

[Broy 78]
Broy, M.: A case study in program development: sorting. Institut für Informatik der TU München, TUM-INFO-7831, 1978

[Broy 80]
Broy, M.: Transformational semantics for concurrent programs. Information Processing Letters **11**, 87–91 (1980)

[Broy 83]
Broy, M.: Fixed point theory for communication and concurrency. In: Bjørner, D. (ed.): IFIP TC2 Working Conference on Formal Description of Programming Concepts II, Garmisch-Partenkirchen, Germany, 1982. Amsterdam: North-Holland 1983, pp. 125–148

[Broy 84a]
Broy, M.: Algebraic methods for program construction: the project CIP. In: Pepper, P. (ed.): Program Transformations and Programming Environments. NATO ASI Series, Series F: Computer and System Sciences, vol. 8. Berlin: Springer 1984, pp. 199–222

[Broy 84b]
Broy, M.: Semantics of communicating processes. Information and Control **61**, 202–246 (1984)

[Broy, Pepper 81]
Broy, M., Pepper, P.: Programming as a formal activity. IEEE Transactions on Software Engineering SE-**7**:1, 10–22 (1981)

[Broy, Pepper 82]
Broy, M., Pepper, P.: Combining algebraic and algorithmic reasoning; an approach to the Schorr-Waite-Algorithm. ACM TOPLAS **4**, 362–381 (1982)

[Broy, Pepper 83]
Broy, M., Pepper, P.: On the coherence of programming language and programming methodology. In: Bormann, I. (ed.): Proc. IFIP TC2 Working Conference on Programming Languages and System Design, Dresden, GDR, 1983. Amsterdam: North-Holland, 1983, pp. 41–53

[Broy et al. 79a]
Broy, M., Gnatz, R., Wirsing, M.: Problemspezifikation - eine Grundlage für Programmentwicklung. In: Raulefs, P. (ed.): Workshop on Reliable Software. Applied Computer Science **14**, München: Hanser 1979, pp. 235–246

[Broy et al. 79b]
Broy, M., Gnatz, R., Wirsing, M.: Semantics of nondeterministic and noncontinuous constructs. In: Bauer, F.L., Broy, M. (eds.): Program construction. Lecture Notes in Computer Science **69**. Berlin: Springer 1979, pp. 553–592

[Broy et al. 82]
Broy, M., Pepper, P., Wirsing, M.: On the algebraic definition of programming languages. Institut für Informatik der TU München, TUM-I8204, 1982. Also: ACM TOPLAS **9**, 54–99 (1987)

[Broy et al. 86]
Broy, M., Möller, B., Pepper, P., Wirsing, M.: Algebraic implementations preserve program correctness. Science of Computer Programming **7**, 35–53 (1986)

[Burstall, Darlington 77]
Burstall, R.M., Darlington, J.: A transformation system for developing recursive programs. Journal ACM **24**:1, 44–67 (1977)

[Burstall, Feather 78]
Burstall, R.M., Feather, M.S.: Program development by transformation: an overview. In: Amirchahy, M., Neel, D. (eds.): Les fondements de la programmation. Proc. Toulouse CREST Course on Programming, IRIA-SEFI, Le Chesnay, France, 1978

[Buxton, Randell 69]
Buxton, J.N., Randell, B. (eds.): Software engineering techniques. Report on a conference sponsored by the NATO Science Committee, Rome, Italy, 1969

[Clark, Darlington 80]
Clark, K.L., Darlington, J.: Algorithm classification through synthesis. Computer Journal **23**:1, 61–65 (1980)

[Curry, Feys 58]
Curry, H.B., Feys, R.: Combinatory logic, Vol. I. Amsterdam: North-Holland 1958

[Darlington 75]
Darlington, J.: Applications of program transformation to program synthesis. Proc. Int. Symp. on Proving and Improving Programs, Arc-et-Senans, France, 1975, pp. 133–144

[Darlington 78]
Darlington, J.: A synthesis of several sort programs. Acta Informatica **11**:1, 1–30 (1978)

[Darlington 79]
Darlington, J.: Program transformation: an introduction and survey. Computer Bulletin, Dec. 1979, 22–24

[Darlington 81]
Darlington, J.: The structured description of algorithm derivations. In: de Bakker, J., van Vliet, H. (eds.): Algorithmic languages. Amsterdam: North-Holland 1981, pp. 221–250

[Darlington 87]
Darlington, J.: Software development using functional programming languages. ICL Technical Journal, May 1987, 492–508.

[Darlington, Feather 80]
Darlington, J., Feather, M.S.: A transformational approach to program modification. Department of Computing and Control, Imperial College, London, Technical Report 80/3, 1980

[Darlington et al. 82]
Darlington, J., Henderson, P., Turner, D.A. (eds.): Functional programming and its applications. Cambridge: University Press 1982

[Davis, Vick 77]
Davis, C.G., Vick, C.R.: The software development system. IEEE Transactions on Software Engineering SE-**3**:1, 69–77 (1977)

[Dijkstra 76a]
Dijkstra, E.W.: A discipline of programming. Englewood Cliffs, N.J.: Prentice-Hall 1976

[Dijkstra 76b]
Dijkstra, E.W.: On a gauntlet thrown by David Gries. Acta Informatica **12**, 1–3 (1976)

[Dijkstra 78]
Dijkstra, E.W.: Program inversion. In: Bauer, F.L., Broy, M. (eds.): Program construction. Lecture Notes in Computer Science **69**, Berlin: Springer 1978, pp. 54–57

[Dijkstra, Feijen 85]
Dijkstra, E.W., Feijen, W.H.J.: Methodik des Programmierens. Addison-Wesley Verlag (Deutschland) GmbH 1985

[Dyer 77]
Dyer, M.E.: REVS Users Manual. SREP Final Report, Vol. II. Huntsville, Al.: TRW Defence and Space Systems Group, 1977

[Earley 76]
Earley, J.: High-level iterators and a method for automatically designing data structure representation. Computer Languages **1**, 321–342 (1976)

[Ehler 85]
Ehler, H.: Making formal specifications readable. Institut für Informatik der TU München, TUM-I8527, 1985

[Ehler 87]
Ehler, H.: Ansätze zur transformationellen Implementierung algebraischer Spezifikationen. In: Simon, F. (ed.): Programmspezifikation. Institut für Informatik und Praktische Mathematik der Universität Kiel, Bericht Nr. 8711, 1987

[Ehrig et al. 80]
Ehrig, H., Kreowski, H.-J., Padawitz, P.: Algebraic implementation of abstract data types: concept, syntax, semantics and correctness. Proc. 7th Int. Coll. on Automata, Languages and Programming, Noordwijkerhout, Netherlands, 1980. Lecture Notes in Computer Science **85**, Berlin: Springer 1980, pp. 142–156

[Eriksson 84]
Eriksson, L.-H.: Synthesis of a unification algorithm in a logic programming calculus. Journal of Logic Programming **1**:3, 3–18 (1984)

[Ershov 78]
Ershov, A.P.: On the essence of compilation. In: Neuhold, E.J. (ed.): Proc. TC2 IFIP Working Conference on Formal Description of Programming Concepts, St. Andrews, Canada, 1977. Amsterdam: North-Holland 1978, pp. 391–420

[Ershov 82]
Ershov, A.P.: Mixed computation: potential applications and problems for study. Theoretical Computer Science **18**, 41–67 (1982)

[Ershov, Ostrovski 86]
Ershov, A.P., Ostrovski, B.N.: Controlled mixed computation and its application to systematic development of language oriented parsers. In: Meertens, L.G.L.T. (ed.): Proc. IFIP TC2 Working Conference on Program Specification and Transformation, Bad Tölz, Germany, 1986. Amsterdam: North-Holland 1987, pp. 31–48

[Fairley 85]
Fairley, R.: Software engineering concepts. New York: McGraw-Hill 1985

[Feather 86]
Feather, M.S.: A survey and classification of some program transformation approaches and techniques. In: Meertens, L.G.L.T. (ed.): Proc. IFIP TC2 Working Conference on Program Specification and Transformation, Bad Tölz, Germany, 1986. Amsterdam: North-Holland 1987, pp. 165–196

[Gardner 72]
Gardner, M.: The curious properties of the Gray Code and how it can be used to solve puzzles. Scientific American **227**:2, 106–109 (1972)

[GI 85]
Fachgespräch 1: Requirements Engineering und Projektmanagement. In: Hansen, H.R. (ed.): GI/OCG/ÖGI-Jahrestagung 1985. Informatik-Fachberichte **108**, Berlin: Springer 1986

[Gnatz, Pepper 77]
Gnatz, R., Pepper, P.: fusc: An example in program development. Institut für Informatik der TU München, TUM-INFO-7711, 1977

[Goad 80]
Goad, C.: Computational uses of the manipulation of formal proofs. Comp. Sc. Dept., Stanford University, Report No. STAN-CS-80-819, 1980

[Goad 82]
Goad, C.: Automatic construction of special purpose programs. Comp. Sc. Dept., Stanford University, Report. No. STAN-CS-82-897, 1982

[Goldberg 86]
Goldberg, A.T.: Knowledge-based programming: a survey of program design and construction techniques. IEEE Transactions on Software Engineering SE-**12**:7, 752–768 (1986)

[Gram 86]
Gram, A.: Raisonner pour progammer. Paris: Bordas 1986

[Green, Barstow 78]
Green, C., Barstow, D.: On program synthesis knowledge. Artificial Intelligence **10**, 241–279 (1978)

[Gresse 83]
Gresse, C.: Automatic programming from data types decomposition. Proc. Int. Joint Conf. on Artificial Intelligence, Karlsruhe, Germany, 1983, pp. 37–39

[Gries 81]
Gries, D.: The science of programming. Berlin: Springer 1981

[Guiho 83]
Guiho, G.: Automatic programming using abstract data types. Proc. Int. Joint Conf. on Artificial Intelligence, Karlsruhe, Germany, 1983, pp. 1–9

[Guiho et al. 80]
Guiho, G., Gresse, C., Bidoit, M.: Conception et certification de programmes a partir d'une décomposition par les données. R.A.I.R.O. Informatique/Computer Science **14**:4, 319–351 (1980)

[Guttag, Horning 78]
Guttag, J.V., Horning, J.J.: The algebraic specification of abstract data types. Acta Informatica **10**, 27–52 (1978)

[Hach 83]
Hach, J.-P.: Digitale Elektronik in Verkehrsflugzeugen. Erste Erfahrungen eines Anwenders. In: Test und Verifikation von Software bei digitalen Systemen der Luft- und Raumfahrt. DGLR-Bericht 83-02, 1983

[Harrison 78]
Harrison, M.A.: Introduction to formal language theory. Reading, Mass.: Addison-Wesley 1978

[Hehner et al. 86]
Hehner, E.C.R., Gupta, L.E., Malton, A.J.: Predicative Methodology. Acta Informatica **23**, 487–505 (1986)

[Henderson 80]
Henderson, P.: Functional programming: application and implementation. Englewood Cliffs, N.J.: Prentice-Hall 1980

[Henderson 81]
Henderson, P.: System design: analysis. Infotech State of the Art Report, Series 9, Number 6: System design. Maidenhead: Pergamon Infotech Ltd., pp. 5–163 (1981)

[Heninger 80]
Heninger, K.: Specifying software requirements for complex systems: New techniques and their application. IEEE Transactions on Software Engineering SE-**6**:1, 2–13 (1980)

[Hoare 78]
Hoare, C.A.R.: Communicating sequential processes. Comm. ACM **21**:8, 666–677 (1978)

[Hoare et al. 87]
Hoare, C.A.R., Hayes, I.J., He Jifeng, Morgan, C.C., Roscoe, A.W., Sanders, J.W., Sorensen, I.H., Spivey, J.M., Suffrin, B.A.: Laws of programming. Comm. ACM **30**:8, 672–686 (1987)

[Hopcroft, Ullman 79]
Hopcroft, J., Ullman, J.: Introduction to automata theory, languages, and computation. Reading, Mass.: Addison-Wesley 1979

[Horowitz 75]
Horowitz, E. (ed.): Practical strategies for developing large software systems. Reading, Mass.: Addison-Wesley 1975

[IEEE 77]
Special Collection on Requirement Analysis. IEEE Transactions on Software Engineering SE-**3**:1, 2–84 (1977)

[IEEE 83]
IEEE Standard Glossary of software engineering terminology. IEEE Standard 729, 1983

[Illsley 88]
Illsley, M.: Transforming imperative programs. Ph.D. thesis, University of Edinburgh, 1988

[IRP 80]
Einführung in das Entwurfsunterstützende Prozeß-orientierte Spezifikationssystem EPOS 80. Institut für Regelungstechnik und Prozeßautomatisierung der Universität Stuttgart, 1980

[Jones 80]
Jones, C.B.: The role of formal specifications in software development. In: Wallis, P.J. (ed.): Life-cycle management. Infotech State of the Art Report. Maidenhead: Pergamon Infotech Ltd. 1980

[Jørring, Scherlis 86]
Jørring, U., Scherlis, W.L.: Compilers and staging transformations. 13th ACM Symp. on Principles of Programming Languages, St. Petersburg Beach, Fl., 1986, pp. 86–96

[Kant 77]
Kant, E.: The selection of efficient implementations for a high-level language. SIGPLAN Notices **12**:8, 140–146 (1977)

[Knuth 74]
Knuth, D.E.: Structured programming with **go to** statements. Computing Surveys **6**, 261–301 (1974)

[Kott 78]
Kott, L.: About a transformation system: a theoretical study. In: Robinet, B. (ed.): Program Transformations. 3rd Int. Symp. on Programming, Paris, France, 1978. Paris: Bordas 1978, pp. 232–247

[Kott 82]
Kott, L.: Unfold/fold program transformations. INRIA Centre de Rennes, Rapport de Recherche No 155 (1982)

[Kowalski 79]
Kowalski, R.A.: Algorithm = logic + control. Comm. ACM **22**:7, 424–436 (1979)

[Kowalski 83]
Kowalski, R.A.: Logic programming. Proc. IFIP Congress 83, Paris, France. Amsterdam: North-Holland, 1983, pp. 133–145

[Krämer 87]
Krämer, B.: Segras – a formal and semigraphical language combining Petri Nets and abstract data types for the specification of distributed systems. Proc. 9th Int. Conf. on Software Engineering, Monterey, Ca., 1987, pp. 116–125

[Kühnel et al. 87]
Kühnel, B., Partsch, H., Reinshagen, K.P.: Requirements Engineering - Versuch einer Begriffsklärung. Informatik-Spektrum **10**:6, 334–335 (1987)

[Kupka, Wilsing 73]
Kupka, I., Wilsing, N.: Functions describing interactive programming. In: Günther et al. (eds.): International Computing Symposium 1973, Amsterdam: North-Holland 1974, pp.41–45

[Laut 80]
Laut, A.: Safe procedural implementations of algebraic types. Information Processing Letters **11**, 147–151 (1980)

[Laut, Partsch 82]
Laut, A., Partsch, H.: Tuning algebraic specifications by type merging. 5th International Symposium on Programming, Turin, April 1982. Lecture Notes in Computer Science **137**, Berlin: Springer 1982, pp. 283–304

[Lehman 80]
Lehman, M.M.: Programs, life cycles, and laws of software evolution. Proc. IEEE **68**:9, 1060–1076 (1980)

[London, Feather 82]
London, P., Feather, M.: Implementing specification freedoms. Science of Computer Programming **2**, 91–131 (1982)

[Lucas, Scholl 83]
Lucas, M., Scholl, P.C.: Un exemple de recherche systématique de plusieurs solutions pour la construction d'un programme. Rapport de Recherche, IMAG, Grenoble 1983

[Manna 74]
Manna, Z.: Mathematical theory of computation. New York: McGraw-Hill 1974

[Manna, McCarthy 69]
Manna, Z., McCarthy, J.: Properties of programs and partial function logic. In: Michie, D. (ed.): Machine Intelligence, Vol. 5. Edinburgh University Press 1969, pp. 27–37

[Manna, Waldinger 80]
Manna, Z., Waldinger, R.: A deductive approach to program synthesis. ACM TOPLAS **2**:1, 90–121 (1980)

[Manna, Waldinger 81]
Manna, Z., Waldinger, R.: Deductive synthesis of the unification algorithm. Science of Computer Programming **1**, 5–48 (1981)

[Mehlhorn 84]
Mehlhorn, K.: Data structures and algorithms **1**: sorting and searching. Berlin: Springer 1984

[Meertens 86]
Meertens, L.G.L.T.: Algorithmics – towards programming as a mathematical activity. In: de Bakker, J.W., Hazewinkel, M., Lenstra, J.K. (eds.): Proc. CWI Symposium on Mathematics and Computer Science. CWI-Monographs Vol. 1, 1986, pp. 289–334.

[Merritt 82]
Merritt, S.M.: The role of high level specification in programming by transformations: specification and transformation by parts. Dept. of Comp. Sc., Courant Institute of Math. Sc., New York University, Ph.D. thesis, 1982

[Milner 80]
Milner, R.: A calculus for communicating systems. Lecture Notes in Computer Science **92**, Berlin: Springer, 1980

[Misra, Gries 82]
Misra, J., Gries, D.: Finding repeated elements. Science of Computer Programming **2**, 143–152 (1982)

[Möller 84]
Möller, B. (ed.): A survey of the project CIP: Computer-aided, intuition-guided programming – wide spectrum language and program transformations. Institut für Informatik der TU München, TUM-I8406, 1984

[Möller 87]
Möller, B.: Higher-order algebraic specifications. Habilitation thesis, Fakultät für Mathematik und Informatik, Technische Universität München, 1987

[Möller 89]
Möller, B.: Applicative assertions. In: Van de Snepscheut, J.L.A. (ed.): Mathematics of Program Construction. Lecture Notes in Computer Science **375**, Berlin: Springer 1989, pp. 348–362

[Morgan 86]
Morgan, C.: The specification statement. Oxford University, Programming Research Group, 1986. Also: ACM TOPLAS **10**:3, 403–419 (1988)

[Naur, Randell 68]
Naur, P., Randell, B. (eds.): Software Engineering. Report on a Conference. Garmisch 1968. Brussel: NATO Scientific Affairs Division 1969

[Nilsson 82]
Nilsson, N.J.: Principles of Artificial Intelligence. Berlin: Springer 1982

[Paige 79]
Paige, R.: Expression continuity and formal differentiation of algorithms. Courant Computer Science Report #15, Courant Institute, New York University, 1979. Also: Lab. for Comp. Sc. Research, Rutgers University, New Brunswick, N.J., Report LCSR-TR-9, 1981

[Paige, Koenig 82]
Paige, R., Koenig, S.: Finite differencing of computable expressions. ACM TOPLAS **4**:3, 402–454 (1982)

[Partsch 83]
Partsch, H.: An exercise in the transformational derivation of an efficient program by joint development of control and data structure. Science of Computer Programming **3**:1, 1–35 (1983)

[Partsch 84]
Partsch, H.: Structuring transformational developments: a case study based on Earley's recognizer. Science of Computer Programming **4**:1, 17–44 (1984)

[Partsch 86]
Partsch, H.: Transformational program development in a particular problem domain. Science of Computer Programming **7**:2, 99–241 (1986)

[Partsch, Broy 79]
Partsch, H., Broy, M.: Examples for changes of types and object structures. In: Bauer, F.L., Broy, M. (eds.): Program construction. Lecture Notes in Computer Science **69**, Berlin: Springer 1979, pp. 421–463

[Partsch, Möller 87]
Partsch, H., Möller, B.: Konstruktion korrekter Programme durch Transformation. Informatik-Spektrum **10**:6, 309–323 (1987)

[Partsch, Pepper 83]
Partsch, H., Pepper, P.: Abstract data types as a tool for requirements engineering. In: Hommel, G., Krönig, D. (Hrsg.): Requirements Engineering. Informatik-Fachberichte **74**, Berlin: Springer 1983, pp. 42–55

[Partsch, Steinbrüggen 83]
Partsch, H., Steinbrüggen, R.: Program transformation systems. ACM Computing Surveys **15**, 199–236 (1983).

[Pepper 81]
Pepper, P.: On program transformations for abstract data types and concurrency. Comp. Sc. Dept., Stanford University, Technical Report STAN-CS-81-883, 1981

[Pepper 84]
Pepper, P.: A simple calculus for program transformations (inclusive of induction). Institut für Informatik der TU München, TUM-I8409, 1984. Also: Science of Computer Programming **9**, 221–262 (1987)

[Pepper, Partsch 80]
Pepper, P., Partsch, H.: On the feedback between specifications and implementations: an example. Institut für Informatik der TU München, TUM-I8011, 1980

[Pepper, Partsch 86]
Pepper, P., Partsch, H.: Program transformations expressed by algebraic type manipulations. Technology and Science of Informatics **5**:3, 197–212, 1986

[Pepper et al. 82]
Pepper, P., Broy, M., Bauer, F.L., Partsch, H., Dosch, W., Wirsing, M.: Abstrakte Datentypen: die algebraische Definition von Rechenstrukturen. Informatik-Spektrum **5**:2, 107–119 (1982)

[Peterson 81]
Peterson, J.L.: Petri Net theory and the modelling of systems. Englewood Cliffs, N.J.: Prentice-Hall 1981

[Petri 66]
Petri, C.A.: Communication with automata. Final report, Volume 1 Supplement 1. RADC TR-65-377-vol-1-suppl 1, Applied Data. Research, Princeton, N.J., 1966

[Pettorossi 84]
Pettorossi, A.: A powerful strategy for deriving efficient programs by transformation. Proc. 1984 ACM Symp. on LISP and Functional Programming, Austin, Tex., 1986, pp. 273–281

[Pettorossi 87]
Pettorossi, A.: Program development using lambda abstraction. Proc. 7th Int. Conf. on Foundations of Software Technology and Theoretical Computer Science, Pune, India, 1987. Lecture Notes in Computer Science **287**, Berlin: Springer 1987, pp. 401–434

[Pless, Plünnecke 80]
Pless, E., Plünnecke, H.: A bibliography of net theory. Second Edition. ISF-Report 80.05. GMD Bonn 1980

[Pooch 74]
Pooch, U.: Translation of decision tables. ACM Computing Surveys **6**:2, 125–151 (1974)

[Pritchard 81]
Pritchard, P.: Another look at the "longest ascending subsequence" problem. Acta Informatica **16**, 87–91 (1981)

[Quine 60]
Quine, W.V.: Word and object. Cambridge, Mass.: MIT Press, and New York: Wiley 1960

[Reif, Scherlis 82]
Reif, J.H., Scherlis, W.L.: Deriving efficient graph algorithms. Comp. Sc. Dept., Carnegie-Mellon University, Pittsburgh, Pa., Report CMU-CS-82-155, 1982

[Reisig 85]
Reisig, W.: Petrinetze – eine Einführung. Zweite, überarbeitete und erweiterte Auflage. Berlin: Springer 1985

[Riddle 79]
Riddle, W.: An approach to software system behavior descriptions. Computer Languages **4**:1, 49–66 (1979)

[Roscoe, Hoare 86]
Roscoe, A.W., Hoare, C.A.R.: The laws of occam programming. Oxford University Computing Laboratory, Programming Research Group, Technical Monograph RRG-53, 1986

[Ross 77]
Ross, D.T.: Structured Analysis (SA): A language for communicating ideas. IEEE Transactions on Software Engineering SE-**3**:1, 16–34 (1977)

[Ross 85]
Ross, D.T.: Applications and extensions of SADT. IEEE Computer 18:4, 25–34 (1985)

[Ross, Schoman 77]
Ross, D.T., Schoman, K.E.: Structured Analysis for requirements definition. IEEE Transactions on Software Engineering SE-**3**:1, 6–15 (1977)

[Royce 75]
Royce, W.W.: Software requirements analysis: sizing and costing. In: [Horowitz 75], pp. 15–53

[Rzepka, Ohno 85]
Rzepka, W., Ohno, Y.: Requirements Engineering environments: Software tools for modelling user needs. IEEE Computer, **18**:4, 9–12 (1985)

[Salomaa 73]
Salomaa, A.: Formal languages. New York: Academic Press 1973

[Scherlis 80]
Scherlis, W.L.: Expression procedures and program derivation. Comp. Science Dept., Stanford University, Report STAN-CS-80-818, 1980

[Scherlis 81]
Scherlis, W.L.: Program improvement by internal specialization. Proc. 8th ACM Symp. on Principles of Programming Languages, Williamsburg, Va., 1981, pp. 41–49

[Schmitz 78]
Schmitz, L.: An exercise in program synthesis: algorithms for computing the transitive closure of a relation. Hochschule der Bundeswehr München, Fachbereich Informatik, Bericht 7801, 1978. Also: Science of Computer Programming **1**:3, 235–254 (1982)

[Schonberg et al. 81]
Schonberg, E., Schwartz, J.T., Sharir, M.: An automatic technique for selection of data representations in SETL programs. ACM TOPLAS **3**:2, 126–143 (1981)

[Schwartz 75]
Schwartz, J.: Construction of software: problems and practicalities. In: [Horowitz 75], pp. 57–71

[Scott 70]
Scott, D.C.: Outline of a mathematical theory of computation. Proc. 4th Annual Princeton Conference on Information Sciences and Systems 1970, pp. 169–176. Also: Oxford University Computing Laboratory, Programming Research Group, Technical Monograph PRG-2, 1970

[Sharir 81]
Sharir, M.: Formal integration. A program transformation technique. Computer Languages **6**, 35–46 (1981)

[Sharir 82]
Sharir, M.: Some observations concerning formal differentiation of set theoretic expressions. ACM TOPLAS **4**:2, 196–226 (1982)

[Shaw 78]
Shaw, A.: Software descriptions with flow expressions. IEEE Transactions on Software Engineering SE-**4**:3, 242–254 (1978)

[Shaw 80]
Shaw, A.: Software specification languages based on regular expresions. In: Riddle, W., Fairley, R. (eds.): Software development tools. Berlin: Springer 1980, pp. 148–175

[Siekmann 84]
Siekmann, H.J.: Universal unification. Proc. 7th Int. Conf. on Automated Deduction. Lecture Notes in Computer Science **170**, Berlin: Springer 1984, pp. 1–42

[Sintzoff 76]
Sintzoff, M.: Eliminating blind alleys from backtrack programs. 3rd Int. Coll. on Automata, Languages and Programming. Edinburgh, U.K., 1976, pp. 531–557

[Sintzoff 78]
Sintzoff, M.: Inverting program construction rules. In: Hibbard, P.G., Schuman, S.A. (eds.): Constructing quality software. Amsterdam: North-Holland 1978

[Sintzoff 80]
Sintzoff, M.: Suggestions for composing and specifying program design decisions. In: Robinet, B. (ed.): International Symposium on Programming. Lecture Notes in Computer Science **83**, Berlin: Springer 1980, pp. 311–326

[Sintzoff 83]
Sintzoff, M.: Bounded-horizon goal-oriented specialization of inference programs. Unité d'Informatique, Université Catholique de Louvain, Research Report 83-1, 1983

[Smith 83]
Smith, D.R.: A problem reduction approach to program synthesis. Proc. Int. Joint Conf. on Artificial Intelligence, Karlsruhe, Germany, 1983, pp. 32–36

[Smith 85a]
Smith, D.R.: The design of divide-and-conquer algorithms. Science of Computer Programming **5**, 37–58 (1985)

[Smith 85b]
Smith, D.R.: Top-down synthesis of divide-and-conquer algorithms. Artificial Intelligence **27**:1, 43–96 (1985)

[Smith 86]
Smith, D.R.: On the design of generate-and-test algorithms: subspace generators. In: Meertens, L.G.L.T. (ed.): Proc. IFIP TC2 Working Conference on Program Specification and Transformation, Bad Tölz, Germany, 1986. Amsterdam: North-Holland 1987, pp. 207–220

[Smith 87]
Smith, D.R.: Applications of a strategy for designing divide-and-conquer algorithms. Science of Computer Programming **8**, 213–229 (1987)

[Smith 88]
Smith, D.R.: KIDS: A knowledge-based software development environment.. Proc. Workshop on Automating Software Design, St. Paul, Minn., 1988, pp. 129–136

[Smith, Lowry 89]
Smith, D.R., Lowry, M.: Algorithm theories and design tactics. In: Van de Snepscheut, J.L.A. (ed.): Mathematics of Program Construction. Lecture Notes in Computer Science **375**, Berlin: Springer 1989, pp. 379–398

[Stoer 72]
Stoer, J.: Einführung in die Numerische Mathematik I. Heidelberger Taschenbücher **105**, Berlin: Springer 1972

[Stucky 79]
Present to F.L. Bauer on occasion of the 4th Int. Conf. on Software Engineering, München, Germany, 1979

[Sommerville 89]
Sommerville, I.: Software Engineering. 3rd Edition. Reading, Mass.: Addison-Wesley 1989

[Swartout 82]
Swartout, W.: GIST English generator. Proc. of Amer. Assoc. for Art. Int. 82, Pittsburgh, Pa., 1982, pp. 404–409

[Swartout 83]
Swartout, W.: The GIST behavior explainer. Proc. of the 1983 National Conference on Artificial Intelligence. Washington, D.C.: AAAI 1983, pp. 402–407

[Teichroew, Hershey 77]
Teichroew, D., Hershey, E.A.: PSL/PSA: A computer-aided technique for structured documentation and analysis of information processing systems. IEEE Transactions on Software Engineering SE-**3**:1, 41–48 (1977)

[Turner 81]
Turner, D.A.: The semantic elegance of applicative languages. Proc. ACM Conf. on Functional Programming Languages and Computer Architecture, Portsmouth, N.H., 1981, pp. 83–92

[Vytopil, Abdali 81]
Vytopil, J., Abdali, S.K.: Theorem generalization in program verification. Math. Sc. Dept., Rensselaer Polytechnic Institute, Troy, N.Y., Technical Report CS-8102, 1981

[Wasserman 80]
Wasserman, A.I.: Information system design methodology. Journal of the American Society for Information Science **3**:1, 5–24 (1980)

[Webster 74]
Webster's New World Dictionary. Second College Edition. Cleveland: William Collings + World Publishing 1974

[Wegbreit 75]
Wegbreit, B.: Mechanical program analysis. Journal ACM **18**:9, 528–539 (1975)

[Wegbreit 76]
Wegbreit, B.: Goal-directed program transformation. Proc. 3rd ACM Symp. on Principles of Programming Languages, Atlanta, Ga., 1976, pp. 153–170

[WG 2.1 79]
Working material of the 26th meeting of IFIP Working Group 2.1, Brussels, Belgium, 1979

[WG 2.1 81]
Working material of the 28th meeting of IFIP Working Group 2.1, Nijmegen, The Netherlands, 1981

[Wirsing et al. 83]
Wirsing, M., Pepper, P., Partsch, H., Dosch, W., Broy, M.: On hierarchies of abstract data types. Institut für Informatik der TU München, TUM-I8007. Also: Acta Informatica **20**, 1–33 (1983)

[Wirsing, Broy 81]
Wirsing, M., Broy, M.: An analysis of semantic models for algebraic specifications. In: Broy, M., Schmidt, G. (eds.): Theoretical foundations of programming methodology. Dordrecht: Reidel 1981

[Wirth 71]
Wirth, N.: Program development by step-wise refinement. Comm. ACM **14**, 221–227 (1971)

[Yeh, Zave 80]
Yeh, R.T., Zave, P.: Specifying software requirements. Proc. IEEE Vol. **68**, No. 9, 1980, pp. 1077–1085

[Zave 79]
Zave, P.: A comprehensive approach to requirements problems. Proc. COMPSAC 79, Chicago, Ill., 1979, pp. 117–127

[Zimmerman 88]
Zimmerman, W.: How to mechanize complexity analysis. GMD Forschungsstelle Karlsruhe, Technical Report 1988

Index

(page numbers in italics refer to the first of several pages)

Types, structures and modes

Operations and functions

Transformation rules and applicability conditions

Language symbols and keywords

Texts and Monographs in Computer Science

Suad Alagić
Object-Oriented Database Programming
1989. XV, 320 pages, 84 illus.

Suad Alagić
Relational Database Technology
1986. XI, 259 pages, 114 illus.

Suad Alagić and Michael A. Arbib
The Design of Well-Structured and Corrected Programs
1978. X, 292 pages, 68 illus.

S. Thomas Alexander
Adaptive Signal Processing: Theory and Applications
1986. IX, 179 pages, 42 illus.

Michael A. Arbib, A. J. Kfoury, and Robert N. Moll
A Basis for Theoretical Computer Science
1981. VIII, 220 pages, 49 illus.

Friedrich L. Bauer and Hans Wössner
Algorithmic Language and Program Development
1982. XVI, 497 pages, 109 illus.

Kaare Christian
A Guide to Modula-2
1986. XIX, 436 pages, 46 illus.

Edsger W. Djikstra
Selected Writings on Computing: A Personal Perspective
1982. XVII, 362 pages, 13 illus.

Edsger W. Djikstra and Carel S. Scholten
Predicate Calculus and Program Semantics
1990. XII, 220 pages

Nissim Francez
Fairness
1986. XIII, 295 pages, 147 illus.

R. T. Gregory and E. V. Krishnamurthy
Methods and Applications of Error-Free Computation
1984. XII, 194 pages, 1 illus.

David Gries, Ed.
Programming Methodology: A Collection of Articles by Members of IFIP WG2.3
1978. XIV, 437 pages, 68 illus.

David Gries
The Science of Programming
1981. XV, 366 pages

Micha Hofri
Probabilistic Analysis of Algorithms
1987. XV, 240 pages, 14 illus.

A. J. Kfoury, Robert N. Moll, and Michael A. Arbib
A Programming Approach to Computability
1982. VIII, 251 pages, 36 illus.

E. V. Krishnamurthy
Error-Free Polynomial Matrix Computations
1985. XV, 154 pages

Ernest G. Manes and Michael A. Arbib
Algebraic Approaches to Program Semantics
1986. XIII, 351 pages

Robert N. Moll, Michael A. Arbib, and A. J. Kfoury
An Introduction to Formal Language Theory
1988. X, 203 pages, 61 illus.

Helmut A. Partsch
Specification and Transformation of Programs
1990. XIII, 493 pages, 44 illus.

Franco P. Preparata and Michael Ian Shamos
Computational Geometry: An Introduction
1988. XII, 390 pages, 231 illus.

Brian Randell, Ed.
The Origins of Digital Computers: Selected Papers, 3rd Edition
1982. XVI, 580 pages, 126 illus.

Thomas W. Reps and Tim Teitelbaum
The Synthesizer Generator: A System for Constructing Language-Based Editors
1989. XIII, 317 pages, 75 illus.

Thomas W. Reps and Tim Teitelbaum
The Synthesizer Generator Reference Manual, 3rd Edition
1989. XI, 171 pages, 79 illus.

Arto Salomaa and Matti Soittola
Automata-Theoretic Aspects of Formal Power Series
1978. X, 171 pages

J. T. Schwartz, R. B. K. Dewar, E. Dubinsky, and E. Schonberg
Programming with Sets: An Introduction to SETL
1986. XV, 493 pages, 31 illus.

Alan T. Sherman
VLSI Placement and Routing: The PI Project
1989. XII, 189 pages, 47 illus.

Santosh K. Shrivastava, Ed.
Reliable Computer Systems
1985. XII, 580 pages, 215 illus.

William M. Waite and Gerhard Goos
Compiler Construction
1984. XIV, 446 pages, 196 illus.

Niklaus Wirth
Programming in Modula-2, 4th Edition
1988. II, 182 pages